The Concept of Man

THE CONCEPT OF MAN

A STUDY IN COMPARATIVE PHILOSOPHY

EDITED BY

S. RADHAKRISHNAN

AND

P. T. RAJU

SINCE 1901

MOTILAL BANARSIDASS
PUBLISHING HOUSE

*Reprint: Delhi, **2026***
Second Edition: 1966
First Indian Edition: Delhi, 1992

Also available at:
MOTILAL BANARSIDASS PUBLISHING HOUSE

- 4637/20, F-2, Hari Sadan, First Floor, Ansari Road, Darya Ganj Delhi–110 002 *Tel.*: (+91-11) 4559 7999
- 1st Floor, 1/2 Rathnavilas Road, Basvanagudi, Next to Pai Vista Convention Hall, South End Circle, Bengaluru–560004 (India) *Tel.*: +91-80-41275911

ISBN: 978-93-5760-722-3 (Hardcover)
ISBN: 978-93-5760-688-2 (Paperback)

Printed & Published by
Rajendra P Jain *for*
Motilal Banarsidass Publishing House
A-44, Naraina Industrial Area, Phase I, New Delhi–110 028 (INDIA)
Email: naraina@mlbd.in Website: www.mlbd.in
Tel.: (+91-11) 4751 1592

CONTENTS

PROLOGUE TO THE SECOND EDITION
by P. T. Raju *page* 9

PREFATORY REMARKS
by S. Radhakrishnan 23

PART I

INTRODUCTION
by P. T. Raju, Rajasthan University, Jodhpur, India (now The College of Wooster, Wooster, Ohio, U.S.A.) 29

1. Man's Self-affirmation; 2. The Rise of Comparative Philosophy; 3. Man is the Common Denominator of Comparative Philosophy; 4. Man is Man for all That; 5. General Plan of the Work

I. THE CONCEPT OF MAN IN GREEK THOUGHT
by John Wild, Harvard University, Cambridge, Mass., U.S.A. (now at Yale University, New Haven, Conn.) 56

1. Introduction; 2. The Sophists; 3. Socrates and Plato; 4. Aristotle; 5. The Influence of Greek Thought on Religious Traditions.

II. THE CONCEPT OF MAN IN JEWISH THOUGHT
by A. J. Heschel, Jewish Theological Seminary, New York, U.S.A. 122

1. The Meaning of Existence; 2. A Need of God; 3. The Paradox of Divine Concern; 4. Image and Likeness; 5. Man the Symbol of God; 6. Image and Dust; 7. The Self and the Deed.

III. THE CONCEPT OF MAN IN CHINESE THOUGHT
by W. T. Chan, Dartmouth College, Hanover, N.H., U.S.A. 172

1. Introduction; 2. The Importance of Man in Chinese Thought; 3. Doctrine of Human Nature; 4. Human Nature according to Ancient Classics and Confucius; 5. Mencius' Doctrine of Human Nature; 6. Doctrines of Human Nature in Later Chou and Medieval Times; 7. Neo-Confucian Ideas on Human Nature and on the Emergence of Evil; 8. The Concept of Jen; 9. The Individual; 10. Man and Society; 11. Man, Animals and Things; 12. Man and Nature; 13. Man and God; 14. The Full Realization of Human Nature.

Contents

IV. THE CONCEPT OF MAN IN INDIAN THOUGHT
by P. T. Raju 220

1. Introduction; 2. The Vedic Conception of Man; 3. Man in Jainism and Buddhism; 4. Man in the Epics; 5. Man in the Orthodox Schools and Systems; 6. Conclusion.

V. COMPARISONS AND REFLECTIONS
by P. T. Raju 320

1. Introduction; 2. Aims of Philosophy; 3. The Ideal Man; 4. Man and Nature; 5. Man and Society; 6. Man and the Divine Spirit; 7. Man and Evolution; 8. Nature of the Human Individual; 9. Life's Ideals and Their Attainment; 10. Influence on Religious Traditions; 11. Education as the Development of the Highest in Man; 12. Conceptions of Man Complementary.

VI. THE CONCEPT OF MAN IN CHRISTIAN THOUGHT
by Ernst Benz, University of Marburg, Marburg, West Germany 394

1. The Sources of Christian Anthropology; 2. Man, the Image of God; 3. Man and the Universe; 4. The Lordship of Man over Earth; 5. The Problem of Evil; 6. The Risk of Freedom; 7. The Christian Understanding of God Becoming Man; 8. The Suffering Servant of God; 9. The Secret of the Cross; 10. The Significance of Resurrection; 11. Christ, the New Adam; 12. The Main Schemata of the Christian Concept of Man; 13. The Neighbour as the Christ Present; 14. Community of Believers as the Body of Christ; 15. Christ in the World; Christian Asceticism; 16. Christianity and Secularization.

VII. THE CONCEPT OF MAN IN ISLAMIC THOUGHT
by Ibrahim Madkour, Academy of Arabic Language, Cairo, Egypt (U.A.R.) 452

1. Introduction; 2. Human Values; 3. The Essence of Man; 4. Conclusion.

VIII. THE CONCEPT OF MAN IN MARXIST THOUGHT
by M. B. Mitin, Academy of Sciences in U.S.S.R., Moscow 476

1. Introduction; 2. The Concept of Man in the History of Philosophy; 3. The Pessimistic Conception of Man; 4. Some Recent Attacks on the Marxian Concept; 5. The Humanism of Marx and Engels; 6. Concrete Man as a Social Creature; 7. Private Property and the Self-alienation of Man; 8. Conclusion.

IX. EPILOGUE
by P. T. Raju 536

INDEX 540

Prologue to the Second Edition

P. T. RAJU

IT is a satisfaction to know that the first edition of *The Concept of Man* is exhausted, and the publishers have called on me to prepare the second. This proves how the new subject, comparative philosophy, has begun to attract the minds of educated readers. It is also a sign of the contemporary interest in man and his nature, an interest that has become earnest and anxious in the face of his tremendous achievements, which have become also potent and potential dangers to his very existence. This book is not planned merely to glorify man, who has done too much havoc in the world to deserve undiluted praise. Man is attempting also to overcome the very evil that he has himself created and is creating, to evolve something good out of that very evil, or turn evil into good. It seems that this dialectical process of turning good into evil and evil into good is an aspect of the history of culture and civilization, through which the unending creativity of man is expressed.

But whence does man derive this unending capacity? He appears to be a speck in the cosmic dust. Is he really the tiny creature he appears to be? He seems to have infinite creative power somehow working through a finite physical body. What is the source of this infinite power that manifests itself not as omnipotence, but as an endless evolving capacity to overcome difficulties? If man is merely the mechanical or the organic body he appears to be, how can he be creative of these four or five thousand years of culture and civilization? A creative being is and must be a free being. From where does man derive his freedom, if he is only the physical body? Or is his being rooted in something great and infinite, which is metaphysically too deep to fathom and does not manifest itself in its completeness at any one time?

Now, can we formulate the concept of such a being, the depths of whom are unfathomable, the workings of whom cannot be fixed completely in terms of the determinate laws of cause and effect, and who asserts his freedom and becomes elusive the moment we attempt to determine his nature? Some friends and critics expected the formulation of a new concept of man at the end of the last edition and a definition of the concept. The present is, in many philosophical centres of the world, an age of conceptual analysis. If a new concept of man were formulated, it could perhaps be analysed, be torn to pieces, or bandied about among groups of young philosophers arguing for, against, or in the middle. Several definitions of man have been given in the history of philosophy. There is Aristotle's definition that man is a rational animal and another that he is a political animal. But it is now said that man is not the only animal that is political or rational. Some of the higher animals are said to exhibit these characteristics. According to another definition, man is a moral or ethical animal. But again, some animals show ethical behaviour. It is said that man is the meeting point of the finite and the infinite. But which object does not touch the infinite and is not a meeting point of the finite and the infinite? Another definition is that man is a self-conscious animal. But we get into difficulties, if we are to define 'self-conscious'. We are told by depth-psychologists that man is not fully conscious of himself; and if degrees of self-consciousness are admitted, many animals have it up to a degree. If, as Leibniz said, every monad is an infinite in itself and if, to his conception, we add that nothing in the world is absolutely self-subsistent, what definition can we give of anything, if the definition is to give a complete idea of the nature of that object? How can we give a formula that fully expresses the content of its concept? The above definitions are valuable descriptions and we have to know their implications and presuppositions. We can, indeed, give the definition of an object for a purpose and so of man also, but such a definition cannot reveal the aspects of man not covered by the purpose. In the sciences, e.g., in physics, a complete understanding of an event or object is expected to result in its conceptual formulation, formalization, and symbolization. But when the object to be understood is man, such an expectation seems to be, at least at the present time, an intellectual over-ambition. In this book, we encounter several concepts of man: man is the image of God; man is the image or reflection of the Brahman; man is the image or product of Nirvaṇa or Śūnya; man is a unity of spirit and body; man is a unity of spirit, soul, and body; man is a unity of spirit, reason, mind, life, and body; and so on. These definitions—or descriptions—may be added to those mentioned above. Let the reader formulate, if he likes, a new concept or definition then.

The aim of this book is in fact to discover the content of the concept of man; it is not to give a new definition or to formulate a new concept. It is rather to obtain insight into the full nature of man, to understand his nature in the light of the important traditions of the world, which are influencing our thought and action in almost all spheres of life, to determine the truth of each, and to view it in the light of the others. However, such a task is only one of the aims of the editors. The other aim is to find out a basis for comparative philosophy. What can be the basis for comparing the different philosophical traditions? What should be the common denominator for the comparison? Should we start accepting some religion or some philosophy as the model, as containing the final truth, and examine the others to find out how far they approximate to, or how far they differ from this final truth? First, this book does not wish to be a book on comparative religion. On this subject many works have been written. To accept some religion as having the final truth, unless philosophically and self-reflectively done—if it can be done then at all—hurts the feelings of the men of other religions, who think that their own religion is the true prop of human life. Besides, the ideas of truth and human life lead to philosophy, not merely to religion, except in those cases in which philosophy and religion cannot be separated and are called by the same name. If we wish to avoid such cases, we have to omit the entire philosophies of India and China, and also of Judaism. This book will then be only one on western philosophy. With the idea of not including religions as such, Christianity and Islam were not included in the first edition. But as all scholars accept that the main important centres of philosophical origin in the world are China and India in the East and Palestine and Greece in the West—although Palestine is called a part of the Middle East, its chief philosophical contributions have been absorbed by the West—the first edition was devoted to these four traditions.

The contemporary interest in man—one may call it humanism or philosophical anthropology or whatever other name one likes —and the search for a common denominator for comparing and evaluating the philosophies of the East and the West coincided.

And as the first book in a series on the subject of comparative philosophy, it was thought, a volume on the comparative study of the nature of man as understood in the four philosophical traditions of the world would be appropriate. The other volumes on metaphysics, logic, ethics etc., are to follow. But the greatest stumbling block was the general misunderstanding of Indian philosophy, which is not as simple as the indigenous philosophy of China and to which western philosophers could not give as much time as required and which they wanted to over-simplify. *First*, the misunderstandings are due to the equating of Indian philosophy to the Vedānta, that to the Advaita, and that to the doctrine of Māyā, so that the moment the word 'Indian philosophy' is uttered, the western student thinks of Māyā and the unreality of the world. But there are nearly as many philosophical traditions in India as anywhere else. *Secondly*, one speaks of Indian philosophy as Hindu philosophy, as though Jainism and Buddhism are not Indian. The misunderstanding is intensified by the fact that no distinction is made by the philosophers of these traditions between philosophy and religion or religious thought—a point that has unfortunately to be repeated every now and then. Religion for the people of India is a way of life and philosophy is reflection on the way of life, however argumentative and academical it be. Hinduism, Jainism, and Buddhism are not faiths in the sense in which Christianity and Islam are, whatever be the advantages and disadvantages of not being such faiths. A Hindu is jokingly said to be one who does not mind being called a Hindu. There is no philosophy that has called itself Hindu philosophy. *Thirdly*, it has been usual to regard the philosophies of salvation, particularly the Vedānta philosophies, as the only philosophies of life and religion in India. But the Vedānta philosophies are based only on the last two parts of the Veda, which is the source, directly or indirectly, of all the philosophies of India. The Mīmāmsā philosophy, which is a philosophy of thorough-going active life and which is based on the first two parts of the Veda, is ignored except for saying that it is a philosophy of rituals and sacrifices. But curiously enough, the life of an orthodox Jew is as full of ritual as the life of an orthodox Mīmāmsaka; yet out of the ritualized activity and sacrifice and their relation to God, the whole Jewish ethical thought is derived and is then absorbed into the Christian ethical thought. Similarly, it is in the

Mīmāmsā philosophy that we find supported a life of unending activity. To ignore the importance of the Mīmāmsā philosophy of action, which is based on the first two parts of the Veda, is to ignore half the Veda and to give a one-sided picture of the Indian conception of the life of man. The conceptions of the Mīmāmsā and the Vedānta have been in conflict for hundreds of years and several attempts have been made to reconcile them by some Vedāntins, by some Mīmāmsakas who turned Vedāntic, and particularly by the epics and ethical codes. A complete omission of the epics and the ethical codes in the presentation of the nature of man in Indian thought is not at all justified. All this explains why the chapter on Indian thought appeared comparatively long and complicated to those critics who expected to see a simple picture of man according to what they considered to be the simple 'unworldly Hindu Philosophy'. If we want to understand any foreign philosophy, we should be prepared to be as modest, patient, and persevering as when we study western philosophy. Over-simplification may lead to quick popularization, but not to true mutual understanding.

Not only the desire to remove some misunderstandings and to correct some one-sided interpretations of Indian thought, but also the necessity of including more than three thousand years of its history made the chapter on Indian thought longer than any of the others—to which some critics took objection. In India there has been a continuous development of philosophies from the beginning to about the end of the fifteenth century. Chinese and Jewish thought, although equally hoary and continuous, do not seem to present the same complexity as the Indian. This fact has to be recognized and is too often overlooked. In this book all the modern developments in India from the time of the advent of the British have been completely omitted and only what is considered to be an exposition of the ancient is included, with the aim of avoiding over-simplified and one-sided presentation. The reader, it was thought, should know the facts as such, before he attempted to draw conclusions from them.

In this age, when religion, philosophy, and even human life itself are in danger, it is time for every one of us to reflect upon what we consider to be our own philosophy, not merely to know where our strength lies, but also to locate our weak points, and to bring together the strong points of all traditions. In the last chapter of the first edition, I may have missed some important points here and there, but I did not think that any tradition contained the whole truth that could be said. And I may repeat, even all put together do not contain the whole truth in its detail. The future may bring to clearer focus new truths and new insights, just as the depth-psychologists have compelled the world to accept the reality of the Unconscious, which was only a speculative concept in German philosophy and a spiritual one in the Indian. It may be repeated also that the interest of neither the editors nor the contributors was religious in the sense of propagating one and criticizing others.

The above is my reaction to the comments and criticisms of friends and reviewers of the first edition, many of which were really encouraging. Comparative philosophy is a new subject and my aim is to make it self-conscious and self-reflective. In philosophy, anything new, a new approach—in truth nothing can be absolutely new in the human situation—cannot easily be fitted into an established conceptual framework. But if there is any truth, any value, any usefulness, in the new, it will be absorbed and may even be recognized to be old. It is such absorption and recognition that are wanted for the thinking man.

The idea of the second edition is the result not only of the contemporary interest in man, but also of the demand and suggestion that the work should include the concept of man in Christian, Islamic, and communist philosophies. The book can then be fairly comprehensive and the reader can get a general idea of the concepts of man that are influencing the destinies of the contemporary world; he can reflect on what other cultures are thinking of man and his destiny, and also on what he is thinking about himself; and through such reflection and self-reflection, he can know how man and his destiny ought to be understood. For fear about the length of the book, it has been found advisable to limit the work to the basic ruling philosophies.

The plan for preparing the three new chapters submitted to their authors is the same as before, with of course the same freedom to modify it according to convenience and nature of the material. As before, the views expressed by the authors are theirs, not those of the editors. The authors of these new chapters also are first-rate authorities in their fields and their outstanding representatives. Dr. Ernst Benz is the Director of the Evangelical Theological Faculty at the University of Marburg;

Dr. Ibrahim Madkour is the Secretary General of the Academy of the Arabic Language in Cairo; and Professor M. B. Mitin is a member of the Academy of Sciences of the U.S.S.R. and Professor I. M. Bochenski regards him as 'the most outstanding representative of contemporary dialectical materialism'.[1]

I have not devoted another chapter to comparing the philosophies of the three new concepts with one another and with those of the first edition for several reasons, the chief of which lies in the peculiarity of these traditions each of which maintains more strongly than those of the first edition that it is self-sufficient. And if each of them is requested to examine the others, then space should be found for the answers also. These comments and answers may sometimes lead also to emotional and sentimental reactions for which it is difficult to give place in this book. The last chapter of the first edition gives a general idea of the approach one may make to the comparative understanding and estimate of the different concepts. The same approach may be made to the new chapters also, of course with necessary modifications. If the book is critically studied and taught in the countries in which the different traditions are current, criticisms and counter-criticisms are bound to occur anyway. Examination of others ought and will necessarily lead to self-examination; and in and through this passing from others to self and vice versa, a progressive clarification and enrichment of the concept of man can take place. Comparison of philosophies with one's own as the norm can lead nowhere except to self-glorification. Comparisons for pointing out incidental similarities and differences may become cheap and insignificant, unless it has the higher aim of evolving richer concepts and of leading to deeper understanding. This task in its concrete form and detail, at the present stage of the development of comparative philosophy, may be left to thinkers and teachers of the subject in the different countries. However, without the readiness to give and take, comparative studies become insignificant and truncated, although we may concede that, at the start, the presupposed absolute normative model may not be too different from one's own.

Humanity is at no time more afraid than now of global wars and world-conquerors that may arise in the name of religion or

[1] J. M. Bochenski; *Contemporary European Philosophy*, p.64 (Eng. tr. by D. Nicholl and K. Aschenbrenner, University of California Press, Berkeley, 1965)

ideology; for they may end up only in constructing—in the words of Kant—gigantic cemeteries of mankind, which only some aboriginal cave-dwellers may survive to see. The present concern of man for man is immediate and concrete, not merely religiously or intellectually remote and abstract. All religions, ideologies, and speculative philosophies—in fact all types of philosophy—have now to face the demand to answer several questions about the nature of man. Is man free? What is the nature of his freedom and where does it lie? What are its foundations? Does the individual possess an individuality of his own, a destiny of his own? And what is the nature of his individuality and destiny? What is meant by the dignity of the individual and what is it factually and concretely? What is meant by the spirit of man? Is it an empty word, the name of some activity, or a substantive? What is the nature of man as he exists and how are freedom, individuality and its dignity related to it? What is his essential relation to other human beings and how should he live with them? What should be his orientation to his inner spirit, if it is real? And how is man to be trained and educated for realizing his potentialities and destiny? These are additional questions for guiding the study of the new chapters also. These are questions which every philosophy has to answer, religious or otherwise. All philosophies are interested in defending the reality, freedom, individuality, and dignity of man. The reader may read the chapters with these questions in mind, cull the answers, and see how and in what sense the ideas are defended in the different philosophies; and he may examine the grounds of defence. He can find out what is acceptable, what is unacceptable, the validity or invalidity of the grounds for the views expressed, the applicability of the views, and determine for himself what the philosophy can and ought to be the elements of which are to include every idea that is valuable, acceptable, and applicable, and its grounds. There is and must be a common area of interest for all the philosophies of man—the reader can see it—and it is at least the life and welfare of man, both as an individual and as a member of society and humanity. This area at least can be the point of approach for all philosophies and from this we can raise questions about the implications of the different philosophies, with of course the good of man, of humanity, and of world-peace in view. Even if there is no new chapter on comparisons and evaluations, the reader may reflect on these problems and the answers given by the different traditions. In this age, which is full of hope and yet full of apprehension, we have to reflect.

It may be repeated again that comparative philosophy has come to a consciousness of itself only recently. Indeed, there is no thinking that does not involve in some way, tacitly or overtly, some comparison; but for that reason, every thinking is not called comparative philosophy. Again, Plato compared in his mind the views of Parmenides and Heraclitus; but he did not consider himself a comparative philosopher. Besides, there are comparative disciplines other than comparative philosophy, such as comparative religion, comparative literature, comparative politics, comparative anthropology, comparative culture, and even comparative methodology—some of which are older than comparative philosophy and all of which are now attempting to be self-reflective and self-conscious and are groping for significance and a meaningful method. This search for significance and method is of great promise, for it can go to the roots of the disciplines and ask: What is philosophy? What is anthropology? What is methodology? and so on. Nobody would be interested in the comparison: Ceylon is an island and Cambodia is land-locked, unless there is some purpose in making it. As the purpose is human, geography, which was once a mere description of land and sea, has become a human (social) science. So the view that comparative philosophy is meant only to point out similarities and differences among cultures and find geographical, social, and racial conditions as reasons for the similarities and differences is an outdated one. What, otherwise, will mark out comparative philosophy from comparative culture? Many comparative studies are and can be overlapping but there must be something to distinguish one from another. The interest of the man of comparative philosophy is philosophical and that of the man of comparative culture is cultural; although, if philosophy is the essential self-expression of culture, one may draw cultural conclusions from philosophy and philosophical conclusions from culture.

The comparative philosopher carries out his comparisons and estimates in terms of a model philosophy. But this model is either clear in his mind or a vague ideal for which his rational consciousness is aspiring and groping and to which it is attempting to provide a rational content through comparative study.

In the latter case, he is raising to himself the question: What is an ideal philosophical system or world-view and how much and in what ways do the different philosophical traditions of the world approximate to it? In the former case, he has already accepted a standard, a model, which is his own. His question will be: By how much do the other philosophies fall short of his own? But the philsopher who thinks that his own philosophy is the absolute model does not gain anything from comparative philosophy. He is already self-assured, and his interest can at the most be one of vain curiosity or self-glorification. And to him will be applicable the words of Caliph Omar[1] *mutatis mutandis*: 'If the other philosophies say what mine says, they are unnecessary; if they do not say what mine says, they are false.' But I should add that this remark does not apply to those researchers who are trying to find out whether the governments newly constituted after the pattern of the American, British, or Swiss democracies have come up to their standards. In such cases, the model is already accepted. But in disciplines in which a model is not accepted as the absolute norm, one should appreciate the desirability of avoiding subjectivity and provincialism.

Comparative philosophy is and ought to be purposive. This can be said of all the basic comparative studies, so that they can know what they are, what they ought to be, what they are doing, what they ought to do, and what their limits can be. Otherwise, they may become trivial and insignificant.[2] The primary questions which comparative philosophy—in fact every basic comparative discipline—should ask itself are: What should I compare? When should I compare? Why should I compare? and How should I compare? One may increase the number of questions, depending on the nature of the subject. But of all of them, the What, Why, and How are the most important. These three point to the subject matter, purpose,

[1] It is now believed that it was not the Muslims, but some fanatical Christians that destroyed the library of Alexandria. See H. E. Barnes: *An Intellectual and Cultural History of the World*, Vol. I, pp. 153–4. (Dover Publications, New York, 1965.)

[2] Like the umbrellology humorously propounded by John Somerville, in which the lengths, colours etc., of all the umbrellas used in a certain period in a certain area were statistically given without any purpose. (M. G. Singer and R. R. Ammerman: *Introductory Readings in Philosophy*, pp. 36 fol. Charles Scribner's, New York, 1962.)

and method, and the three determine one another up to a degree. It seems that there are some who are preoccupied with method and want to determine it without reference to subject matter and purpose. But such philosophers may be compared to those men who want to learn the methods of swimming before entering water. Purpose and subject matter determine method, which is to be adequate to them. It is not necessary to explain that every subject matter does not serve every purpose and the method must be in accord with the nature of the subject matter and purpose.

Although philosophers are now wrangling what philosophy is and ought to be, in its history it has covered the whole life of man up to death and even beyond. Unless one accepts that religious ideas are unphilosophical and fall outside the scope of philosophy—which I along with many others do not accept—the question inevitably poses itself about the applicability of philosophy to life, its concern, direct and indirect, for life here and beyond. Whatever be the traditions and the differences among them, the primary concern of philosophy is to throw light on the life of man, not merely on any part of it but on the whole. Incomplete knowledge does not merely remain as such, it may become dangerous by becoming the only guide. If philosophy does not aim at throwing light on the life of man as a whole, we have no other subject to undertake the task. That is why the question of the applicability of philosophy to man's life arises not merely with reference to the life beyond or to some ultimate metaphysical and ontological problems, but also with reference to the life here or to the ethical (including the social and political) and cosmological problems. The study of man's life as a whole, the study of his life here and beyond—including the problem whether there is a beyond—is the study of the meaning of life, the explanation of which belongs to the sphere of philosophy, but not merely to the delimited sciences of life. For this reason also viz., the meaning of man's life has to be elucidated by philosophy, man becomes the common denominator of comparative philosophy. He becomes the common denominator not as a material body, but as the living, acting, purposive, self-conscious material body. The content of the concept of such a being—including all that such a concept implies or presupposes—becomes the centre of philosophy and also of comparative philosophy. If the different philosophical systems, traditions, and outlooks are judged in terms of some ideal philosophy, which is either sub-consciously presupposed or consciously built up, even that ideal has to be judged in terms of its applicability to the whole life of man. And as human knowledge is finite, any concept of man has to be accepted not as one with a fixed content, but as one with a growing content, unless we equate philosophy to conceptual analysis and want to show the sharpness of our intellect. Conceptual analysis and even synthesis are unavoidable in philosophy. But we should recognize that they are not meant merely to sharpen and exercise our intellect. The significance of a philosophy is not due merely to the keenness of the philosopher's intellect, but to the depth, width, and maturity of his mind. Otherwise, the freshmen in our colleges and universities who have mastered the logical calculus and start exploding Plato and Kant will have to be regarded as greater philosophers than Plato and Kant. They cannot understand the philosophers they study, if their aim is only to expose logical fallacies, conceptual confusions. When a mature mind undertakes such a task, it can, if it makes an effort, easily discover in its background norms developed and developing. If such norms are brought to the foreground of consciousness and are interrelated with everything else that is interrelatable, a new philosophy is found as the ideal, model, and norm. The study of this book, it is hoped, will lead to such a philosophy of man.

It gives me great pleasure to acknowledge my thanks to friends and philosophers who have given me encouragement and co-operation in bringing out the second edition. First, my thanks are due to my colleagues in the College of Wooster, who pointed out the desirability of adding the three new chapters. Professor W. C. Smith, who is himself a well-known authority on Islamic thought and who is now the Director of the Center for the Study of World Religions at Harvard, helped me in obtaining Dr Ibrahim Madkour for preparing the chapter on the Islamic concept. I am grateful to Professor Smith for this help. I am thankful also to the authors of the three new chapters, Dr Ernst Benz, Dr Ibrahim Madkour, and Professor M. B. Mitin. It has been the policy of this book to have the ideas presented by representatives of the different traditions themselves. It was a real difficulty to obtain the chapter from a distinguished philosopher of the USSR. My grateful acknowledgments are due to the Embassy of the USSR in Washington D.C. and to Mr Edward Saratov of its Press Department for helping me out of the difficulty. And I am thankful to the Novosti Press Agency of the USSR for requesting Professor Mitin to write the chapter and for sending its English version. My thanks are due to Professor Harold B. Smith and other colleagues of the Department of Religion and to Professor W. I. Schreiber, my colleague in the Department of German, for helping me in preparing the English version of the German manuscript of Professor Ernst Benz. Finally, I am thankful to the College of Wooster and its President, Dr Howard Lowry, for the facilities and opportunities they have given me for my work.

P. T. RAJU

Prefatory Remarks

RADHAKRISHNAN

THE commonwealth of humanity has no written constitution; it is based on community of ideals, freedom and dignity of the individual, rule of law, economic opportunity for all citizens and love of peace.

The basic principle of the dignity and freedom of the individual is common to all religious faiths. Marx even denied God, because he believed in the potential divinity of man. The Jain thinkers hold that man can attain divinity, and God is only the highest, noblest and fullest manifestation of all the powers that lie latent in the soul of man. We have a verse in the *Mahābhārata* which tells us that there is nothing higher than man on earth:—

Guhyam brahma tadidam vo bravīmi
na mānuṣāt śreṣṭhataram hi kiñcit

(I tell you this, the secret of the Brahman: there is nothing higher than man.) Pascal tells us that man is a thinking reed superior to all the unthinking forces that fill the universe. Man is subject, not object. This subjectivity gives him inwardness and freedom. If he loses himself in the objective, he lapses into routine, rigidity, mindlessness. Democracy requires us to respect and develop the free spirit of man, which is responsible for all progress in human history.

Parliamentary democracy, which is based on faith in man and yet recognizes his fallibility, is a political arrangement which helps us to be governed by our chosen leaders. It does not adopt the view: If you do not agree with us, we will hit you. We have to try to persuade others by the force of logic and not by the force of arms.

In non-parliamentary systems, unless they are monarchical, every succession becomes a crisis marked by internal upheavals and frequently by outward disturbances. In non-parliamentary governments, leaders tend to become laws unto themselves and try to impose their will on their people leading to the corruption of minds and degradation of souls. Rightly, the cult of the individual is repudiated by all political systems. It is not the individual, whether he is good or bad, powerful or powerless, but the cult that is repudiated. If we accept the infallibility of any one, persecution becomes justified; men who refuse to flatter are silenced, opponents become criminals. No society can progress if it demands hypocracy, punishes truth and stifles the growing mind. Dictators are critical of overpraise of others, but are pleased with overpraise of themselves. The former does no harm, but the latter may be their ruin.

Parliamentary democracy is likely to be adopted even by countries which do not have it now. With the maturity of leadership political systems may alter. Even Soviet leaders are eager to change their systems; they do not wish to relapse into rigidity.

Democracy is also a method by which we attempt to raise the living standards of the people and to give opportunities to every man to develop his personality. When a country attains political freedom, there is a great release of energy which till then was consumed in the struggle for freedom. Great expectations are roused and people are lifted out of the torpor of centuries and pass through all the pangs of a new birth. Many of the people in Asia and Africa live very little above the starvation level. They have very little energy left to think about life and the higher values. If political democracy is to be sustained, economic development has to be speeded up. We have to crowd the sweat and tears of centuries into a generation, reduce inequalities, shake up social relations which are unjust and free ourselves from hallowed abuses and archaic customs. We have so little time to do so much. In a democratic society the rich have to accept social obligations for the poor and so it is in the world community. The advanced nations have to assist the less advanced.

In the world today we have pledged ourselves to international co-operation and peace. There is no isolation any more, geographical, political, economic or cultural. The spirit of co-operativeness is to be carried beyond the nation to the community of nations. Democracy means respect for the opponent in politics, ethics and religion. If we believe in a certain cause and find that there are nations which do not agree with us, the democratic way requires us to try to persuade them to agree with our point of view. Even as the democratic way forbids in internal problems, direct action, mob rule or resort to violence, in international problems also we have to assume the reasonableness of human beings and adopt the methods of negotiation, discussion, adjustment and agreement.

Unfortunately, as the world happens to be divided at the moment into two groups, we have great fear of the future, fear of the unseen peril which is subject to unlimited exaggeration.

When internal combustion engine, wireless, aviation were devised, they were welcomed by all as creditable achievements of science and technology. The penetration of outer space by Soviet scientists, which is a great attempt to push back the frontiers of the unknown, would, in normal circumstances, have been received with joy and pride, but actually we have fear and foreboding, for in the present cold war atmosphere we look upon these artificial satellites from the military point of view, for from them nuclear missiles can be dispatched to long distances. So the Sputniks have caused confusion and intensified the race of nuclear armaments with its fearful prospects. No people or government wish to bring about the extinction of the human race on earth; yet the unrest in the heavens has caused confusion on earth. Man has begun to distrust himself and his achievements.

All governments which are democratic admit that we should give all the people of the world the opportunity for a full and fruitful life. The American Declaration of Independence states eloquently that all men have a right to life, liberty and the pursuit of happiness. We are imperilling these rights and are darkening the future of the world.

The democratic way requires us to adopt peaceful co-existence and co-operative living. It asks us to strive patiently and persistently for mutual understanding, explore every avenue to reach agreement. We do not ask for submission which is the product of despair, or appeasement which is the result of demoralization. At the same time we should not be governed by fixed ideas. We should admit the fallibility of man as a constant factor in human affairs. In an equitable settlement neither group will win or lose absolutely. There would be a good deal of give and take.

The basic issue is no longer the victory of this or that nation, of this or that group, this or that religion or ideology. It is the survival or suicide of man. It is a time for decision, not despair. The choice is either extinction or human brotherhood. It cannot be left to the vagaries of chance. The test of a nation's right to survive today is measured not by the size of its armaments, but by the extent of its concern for the human community as a whole. We must support the concept of a United Nations with adequate authority under law to prevent aggression, to compel and enforce disarmament, to settle disputes among nations according to principles of justice. If we develop a higher loyalty to the world community, the greatest era of human society will be within our reach. This requires us to understand man, to rediscover the power of the spirit in him and re-define his purpose. Democracy, if it is to survive, must be born again. It must unlearn its national and economic idolatries, cease to be self-seeking and recapture its soul by returning to its inmost ideas.

Historians tell us that destiny hangs over individual lives as well as over states. Herodotus writes: 'As I go forward in my story, I will make notes of cities great and small, for those that were once great, most of them have become small and those that were great in my day were formerly small. Knowing therefore that human prosperity never abides in the same place, I shall write of both alike.' Prosperity leads to arrogance, to what the Greeks call *hubris*, to disaster. Love of power is dangerous. It is not the weak nations of the world that are responsible for the present situation in the world. The political leaders of the big powers threaten to bring the human race to the edge of disaster. They should recast their policies and ask for a suspension of nuclear tests and work on the achievement of disarmament.

Gandhi spelt out the moral principles on which civilizations rest, truth and love, *satya* and *ahimsā*. Civilizations are saved only to the extent to which they respond to these principles and it is for us to work while yet it is day. Evil can be broken only if we respond to it with good. It is no use cursing darkness. We must have faith in the spirit of man, the spirit capable of suffering and compassion, of endurance and sacrifice, the spirit which has inspired human progress all these centuries. If we in the commonwealth of man produce a few leaders of understanding, courage and conviction, the conscience and good will of the many will support them.

If democracy is based on the recognition of the individuality and dignity of man, we have to know what they are in him, and so what man has been understood to be in the great cultural traditions of the world. This volume aims at presenting that understanding.

Introduction

P. T. RAJU

I. MAN'S SELF-AFFIRMATION

IT is not wrong to say that the present age is an age of humanism. Philosophical interest has shifted, rightly or wrongly, from God, matter, and science to man. Radhakrishnan wrote: 'The world has found itself as one body. But physical unity and economic interdependence are not by themselves sufficient to create a universal human community, a sense of personal relationships among men. Though this human consciousness was till recently limited to the members of the political states, there has been a rapid extension of it after the War. The modes and customs of all men are now a part of the consciousness of all men. Man has become the spectator of man. A new humanism is on the horizon. But this time it embraces the whole of mankind.'[1] This was written in the year 1939 in the Preface to his book, *Eastern Religions and Western Thought*, and what was on the horizon at that time has become distinct now. But what kind of humanism is it? We have had several forms of it: the Deweyan form, which is naturalistic; the form given to it by F. C. S. Schiller, which is evolutionary and pragmatistic; the communistic form, given to it by the Marxians, based upon economics and class struggle; another form, given to it by Julian Huxley, which is evolutionary and scientific; some forms, given to it by thinkers like Lamont, which are more or less materialistic; the theological forms, like that of Maritain, based upon Catholic thought; and the existential forms which are of various kinds, ranging from the theological, like that of Mercier, to the atheistic, like that of Sartre. Some of these forms again overlap. In spite of these differences, however, there is a common trend in all: the emphasis on man and his values. Whether as an apology for the classical religions and philoso-

[1] *Eastern Religions and Western Thought*, p. vii (London: Oxford University Press, 1940).

phies and their defence or as a reassertion of man and his values, humanism has come to the forefront again. Man cannot be ignored by any philosophy; he has to be retained at its centre. Towards the end of World War II, when the price of everything rose, the saying was on the lips of almost every man: the value of everything has risen except that of human life. Thinkers began to be repelled by the devaluation of human life, whether in the name of science, culture, religion, or political ideology. Even the claim of absolute value for science is being questioned. Man and his values are primary; their primacy has to be acknowledged by any philosophy.

Philosophy, if it is true to itself, has to be a philosophy of life, not of one part of life but of the whole. This life is the life of man. He wants a theory of life as a guide. Other creatures do not care for any such theory, the drives themselves of their nature are enough for them. The aim of philosophy to be a guide to life is tacitly recognized by thinkers like Russell, who, speaking of logical analysis, says at the end of his book, *A History of Western Philosophy*, that it also is meant to suggest and inspire a way of life. Scientific and analytic thought has helped in dispelling many superstitions; but what we want is that this growing scientific and analytic spirit should not also destroy the values of life which are of lasting importance.

James B. Conant says: 'Can these value judgments that do not now involve scientific concepts be replaced in principle by those that originated in scientific investigations? . . . I doubt its applicability to the wider topic that I am attempting to explore; there is nothing to be gained by asserting that in principle all our common sense ideas about the universe and human behaviour, all our ethical principles, and our moral convictions could be replaced by "concepts growing out of experiment and observation". Even in the restricted area of the physical sciences there are huge spots where empiricism alone is the guide for the conduct of scientists as scientists.'[2] This is an important observation by a leading scientist and educator of one of the most scientifically advanced countries. Science has not said the last word about what even material things are in themselves, much less has it been able to say

[2] *Modern Science and Modern Man*, pp. 97–8 (New York: Columbia University Press, 1953).

about what men are in themselves. Bridgman makes an important observation: 'Finally, I come to what seems to me may well be from the long range point of view the most revolutionary of the insights to be derived from our recent experiences in physics, more revolutionary than the insights afforded by the discoveries of Galileo and Newton, or of Darwin. This is the insight that it is impossible to transcend the human reference point. The new insight comes from a realization that the structure of nature may eventually be such that our processes of thought do not correspond to it sufficiently to permit us to think about it at all. . . . We are now approaching a bound beyond which we are for ever stopped by pushing our enquiries not by the construction of the world, but by the construction of ourselves.'[3] Now, there is the dire necessity of reconstructing ourselves. We have to understand ourselves, understand man behind all his activities, scientific, ethical, spiritual. Science cannot dictate what man is to be; but man must understand what scientific activity is, for it is his activity. Accumulation of scientific evidence suggests and strengthens a policy, not a creed; but a policy is a guide to human action.[4] The difference, even in theory, between pure and applied science is fast disappearing. A true theory is that which works; and work is human activity.

So we come to the old advice of Socrates: 'Know thyself'. Pope said that the noblest study of mankind is man himself. The Upaniṣads also declared: 'Know thy self' (*ātmānam viddhi*). Confucius in China made the same appeal. (All thought, and all theories of human activity, are to be based upon a proper understanding of man). How is man understood in the different philosophical traditions? This is the theme of the present work. He may have been understood differently, from different points of view, according to the different problems posed by the cultural and physical milieu of the countries in which the philosophical traditions started. But now, because the whole world is coming together more intimately and consciously than ever before, the problems of each have become the problems of all. It would be interesting and useful, therefore, to know how man, his nature, his ideals and values were understood by each tradition.

[3] *Ibid*, quoted on pp. 50–1.
[4] *Ibid*, p. 54.

2. THE RISE OF COMPARATIVE PHILOSOPHY

Comparative philosophy, as a systematic study, has begun to acquire a definite shape. In one sense it is very old, almost as old as philosophy itself. When some ancient Indian and Greek philosophers met in Greece or India or in the Persian Empire conquered by Alexander, and discussed and compared their ideas, they were doing comparative philosophy. When the Buddhists entered China, and they on the one side and the Confucianists and Taoists on the other entered into controversies, all of them also were doing comparative philosophy. In fact, the Chinese philosophers developed a method called *Ko Yi*, which is really the first systematic attempt at comparative philosophy.[5] During modern times comparative philosophy started mainly with comparative religion, and continued as such until recently. So long as religion was accepted as the basis of all culture, and so of philosophy, which is culture become self-reflective, interest in comparative religion was strong. But when, later, some important thinkers began to question the absoluteness of the claims of religion, the usefulness of religion itself was being examined in terms of man and society. Radhakrishnan writes: 'Humanism is a legitimate protest against those forms of religion which separate the secular and the sacred, divide time and eternity and break up the unity of soul and flesh. Religion is all or nothing. Every religion should have sufficient respect for the dignity of man and the right of human personality.'[6] 'Humanist revivals occur when religions disintegrate and fail to attract men's attention.'[7] Again, 'but the silence and uncertainty of religious teachers in regard to social problems such as slums and unemployment, their indifference to the common people who are depressed by hunger and weakened by artificial divisions have lowered the prestige of religion.'[8] But in this age of the reassertion of man and human values, comparative religion does not fully satisfy the enquiring spirit.

Whether as a theory of religion or of man and the world, philosophy has always been there. So, when interest in com-

[5] See Chapter XIV, *Radhakrishnan, Comparative Studies in Philosophy Presented in Honour of His Sixtieth Birthday*, edited by P. T. Raju and others (London: Allen & Unwin Ltd., 1951).

[6] *The Recovery of Faith*, p. 49 (London: Allen & Unwin Ltd., 1956).

[7] *Ibid*, p. 44.

[8] *Ibid*, p. 26.

parative religion decreased, interest in comparative philosophy came to the forefront. After the World War II, in which huge masses of humanity were thrown into conflict, people have come to face each other more closely than before. They now wish to understand each other intimately and to avoid conflicts, which, in future will involve the whole of the globe. People realize that they have only two alternatives before them: recognition of the brotherhood of man or annihilation of man and civilization. This necessity to understand each other, each other's point of view, each other's culture, outlook, values and even religion has given comparative philosophy a new seriousness and importance. But the problems are complex; for we find not only different outlooks and cultural traditions but also different systems of philosophy in the same tradition with the same general outlook on life; we find similarities also in different outlooks and cultural traditions; and, in addition, we have conflicts between science and religion, conflicts that are keenly felt by countries in which science and technology are the most advanced, but which accepted revealed religions. Men do not use science in their laboratories only; they develop what is called a scientific attitude towards all problems of life. James B. Conant writes: 'Scientific concepts are so much a part of the equipment of men and women in our culture that they are used both consciously and unconsciously in making decisions that we call ethical or moral.'[9] Contemporary logical positivism, which is an extreme example of scientific attitude in philosophy, is able to say little to justify ethics. Ethical and religious concepts lose their philosophical importance and become emotional ideas. Science has thus come into conflict even with the grand traditions of philosophy. The problems of comparative philosophy are not only those generated by the clash of cultural and philosophical traditions, but also those generated by the conflict of science and scientific thought on the one side and the great philosophical and religious traditions on the other. It is not enough for us in this century to solve the first set of problems without reference to the second, because, even before we solve the old problems, man's life creates new ones. Both old and new have to be solved together and in the light of each other. What are the values for which men have been living and dying in different parts of the globe? What are their relative

[9] *Modern Science and Modern Man*, p. 62.

validity? Answers to these questions can be obtained by a comparative study of the basic philosophical traditions of the world. They give us varying conceptions of man, of his nature and of the values he cherishes. We may not be satisfied with the answer. We may say: These are ancient ideas, partly or wholly mistaken, not of much use for our present life. We like to judge them in the light of the concepts of science and judge the value of the concepts of science in their terms. For even the concepts of science need transvaluation in terms of man and his life's ideals. Only when this has been achieved, only then can the old and the new conflicts be resolved.

The present work does not have so ambitious an aim as to find solutions for all conflicts. It attempts to present the concept of man in the different philosophical traditions in the hope that, as a result, a more comprehensive idea of man can be obtained than is given in any one tradition, and that in the light of this idea a solution of our modern problems can be attempted. Human life is essentially a corporate life. Any solution of the present day problems, which are vast in their scope and significance, must be a co-operative enterprise. And this enterprise may be everlasting so long as humanity continues to inhabit the globe. This work is therefore made a co-operative project.

3. MAN IS THE COMMON DENOMINATOR OF COMPARATIVE PHILOSOPHY

This work, it is hoped, will be useful for comparative philosophy. Comparative philosophy is approached in three different ways. First, it is taken to be a phenomenological study: philosophers of the different traditions are studied in relation to their environments, both natural and cultural, and are treated as functions of these environments. This is a disinterested philosophical discipline. Secondly, comparisons are made of philosophers, schools, and systems belonging to the same tradition. Every philosophy is taken to be a rounded out system of the same universe. But if man and universe are the same, why are there different systems of philosophy? The concepts they use, it is thought, must have different significance and meaning derived from the systems. Thus, comparative philosophy becomes a study of the comparative significance of concepts;

and the significance of the concepts becomes a function of the system. In the third place, comparative philosophy began as a study and evaluation of the different cultural and philosophical traditions, sometimes to show the superiority of the one over the others, sometimes to show only the peculiarities of each, sometimes to determine the values of each, and at other times to effect a synthesis of the best in each. There is a definite human purpose in the last. The first two forms can be made to serve the last. But the work so far done has not been very systematic and comprehensive because of the difficulties of mastering the languages concerned and of understanding sympathetically the significance of the conceptual forms expressed in those languages.

But more important than all these difficulties is the undeveloped nature of comparative philosophy as a discipline. It has not yet formulated its methods and is not definite about its aims. Yet the value of comparative philosophy is increasingly being felt. The world which has become economically one longs to be consciously one. No nation, however great, can now isolate itself and choose to have a life of its own. It wants to know what others are thinking about it and how they are going to act towards it. Brotherhood of nations is considered to be as important as the brotherhood of man in any particular country, in whatever language—political, economic or ideological—the idea is expressed. Rich countries are as much concerned about the poverty of backward countries as about the poverty of their own backward classes and want to know why they are poor. What are their ways of life and thought? Why do they not think and work like we? Do they enjoy values of life which we do not and which make them contented with poverty? Do they have the same problems as we do? If they do not, what are the values of life by the cherishing of which they are able to avoid the problems? Then, in what respects is our culture superior to theirs and in what is theirs superior to ours? Can we give and take in these respects? When these questions are raised, the value of comparative philosophy as a stepping stone to a true, and a more adequate and more comprehensive philosophy of life becomes clear. As a systematic discipline, however, the subject has not yet been adequately developed.

One important requirement for comparative philosophy is a

common denominator. In terms of what are we to determine the value of the philosophies we compare? We may ask: Are they self-consistent? Every philosophy has been shown by its rivals to contain some inconsistency or other. Suppose we build up a thoroughly self-consistent system. In that case, the mathematical logicians tell us, it can only be a system of analytic propositions, saying nothing about the universe and existence; it cannot be a philosophy of life. Rejecting, for argument's sake, this contention of the mathematical logicians, and assuming that we succeed in building up a consistent philosophy, what guarantee do we have that it is true to all the facts of life? As Bosanquet said about 'flatland' and as scientific fiction and novels show, we can have a logically consistent construction of a fictitious world. Our criterion must be: is it applicable to the life of man and to the world in which he lives and acts? Logic alone is not the test: the real test is the life of man. We want a logical construction of man's life and man's world. Man himself, therefore, becomes the centre of our interest. He is the subject of our study and the test and value of that study as well. Philosophy now becomes the reflection of man about himself—a reflection which employs logical principles and avoids illogicalities. But logic by itself cannot tell us what facts are; it can enable us only to separate the spurious from the true.

When one religion takes upon itself the task of criticizing another, the criterion it uses is generally man and his values. We may consider the simple case of the differences in the methods of disposing of the dead. According to some religions, the body is to be cremated; whereas according to some others, it is to be buried. The latter say that the human body, which is highly valued in life, ought not to be reduced to ashes immediately after death. Even this criticism is based upon considerations of human value. When the Christian missions were criticizing Islam and Hinduism for their treatment of women, they were again appealing to human values. Now, when religion itself is criticized, the stand-point is that of man and his values. When communists and western democracies criticize each other, it is again in terms of the value of man. The last but not the least important is the criticism of science by ethical leaders. Science has not strengthened our sense of human values but weakened it. One tendency which scientific attitude and its methods of analysis have inculcated is to reduce the higher to the lower. Max Otto refers to a psychologist who preached that the essential nature of man can be discovered by a study of monkeys: 'the proper study of mankind is monkeys,'[10] because man was a monkey at one time. Instead of understanding man in terms of what he may become, he is to be understood in terms of what he was[11]. Reduce man further into material components, we get a purely materialistic view of him. This method of understanding man may be wrong; yet it is called the scientific method. But why do we call it wrong? Because it has struck at the very roots of human values. Reductionism is wrong, not because of any *a priori* logical principle, but because it cannot do justice to the life of man. Ethics, which distinguishes man from animals, is in danger. The progress of science has turned men into intellectual animals, manufacturing and handling tools. Our intellect has developed fast; but our ethical nature has not made a corresponding progress; and so we are tending to ignore and even forget human values. In this criticism also, man comes up as the critic of science. In all this, man is the common denominator with reference to which religions, philosophies, political and social ideologies and even science are tested. I think therefore that comparative philosophy cannot but accept man as the common denominator.

If comparative philosophy does not work with man as the common denominator, the only result will be finding out whether the philosophies are idealistic, realistic, naturalistic, monistic, pluralistic, materialistic, organistic, etc., and whether they are so consistently. This can be discovered within any single tradition, and merely amounts to classifying philosophies under several headings. Pepper, for instance, in his excellent small book, *World Hypotheses*,[12] has done this for philosophies of the West. One may apply similar classifications to the philosophies of the other traditions also. But the results, though interesting and useful, cannot be the end of comparative philosophy. At the most, we merely place every other tradition in the perspective of the Western tradition and its classifications, but, in doing so, we do not discover what is

[10] *Science and the Moral Life*, p. 27 (New York: New American Library, 1955).
[11] *Ibid*, p. 33.
[12] *University of California Press*, Berkeley, 1948.

lacking in the Western tradition itself. The procedure may result also in forcibly pressing other traditions into the moulds of the West, and into either discarding as unimportant whatever does not fit into those moulds, although it is peculiar to many of its systems, or criticizing it as irrational and untrue. Such procedure, therefore, will be detrimental to the very aim of comparative philosophy, which is to pave the way to a deeper and more comprehensive philosophy of life. One of the main purposes of comparative philosophy is to make available to each tradition the values of the others, so that each can develop by incorporating all that is valuable in the rest. And the value of any tradition can be appreciated only with reference to man.

The reference here is to the whole man, not merely to any one aspect of his nature or form of his activity. He is a material being, whose body acts on the material environment and is acted upon by it. He is also a living being with an internal purpose or immanent teleology, and strives to maintain himself intact in his surroundings. Again, he is a psychological being with a mind of his own, looking backwards into the past and forwards into the future, and with an inwardness that is his own and is private. He is a social and ethical being, with emotions and sentiments developed in the direction of other men, his personality developing and taking shape in a social environment. The ethical situation leads not only to an intensification of his own inwardness but also to a recognition of the same inwardness in others. And man is a religious being, craving and searching for cosmic and divine support for his life and activity, and desiring communion with it. He is, in addition, a rational being, questioning himself, evaluating his thinking and acting, wondering if he is mistaking fancies for truths or truth for falsity, right for wrong and good for evil. He is thus a complex creature, leading an inward and outward life and craving stable support both ways.

A philosophy of life for so complex a being as man cannot be mere epistemology, science, biology, psychology, sociology, ethics, or religion. What satisfies the criteria of one may not satisfy the criteria of the rest. But man's need is for all. Can we then have a system of knowledge embracing all? Can we have a unified knowledge of the world with its innumerable forms? We come here to an old question. The present state of human knowledge does not warrant that we claim such knowledge.

Yet such a unified system has been and must be accepted as the ideal of knowledge. Attempts at building up such knowledge have usually resulted in reducing all else to one form, that is, in different kinds of reductionism. We have the materialistic view of the world. One form at least of logical positivism is physicalism: all philosophical statements are to be reduced to physical statements, which will be the same as reducing, for philosophical purposes, all other forms of being to physical entities. This kind of philosophy cannot do justice to religion, ethics, psychology, and sociology. Sociology, like ethics, has to treat men as persons, as physical beings with minds of their own. However, we have also the biologist's view of the world, the psychologist's view of the world, the ethicist's view of the world, and the religionist's view of the world. But none of these views, not even the religious, as it has been given to us so far, has been found to be self-sufficient and adequate. Radhakrishnan, who certainly advocates a spiritual view of the world, says that humanism is a justified protest against the shortcomings of traditional religions. That there have been such protests shows that traditional religions have shortcomings. A purely religious view of the world tends to ignore values other than the religious and is, therefore, also a form of reductionism. Each view of the world is thus a protest against the others, but in the very act of protesting it becomes itself deepened, enriched and broadened. Yet no view of the world has been found to be all-sufficient. The common practice has been, if the scientific view of the world is accepted, to accept also the thesis that matter is not merely the primary stuff but that it is also the only reality. Correspondingly, to accept the biologist's view is to accept life as the primary reality and the rest of the world as its forms, as something to be explained in its terms. Similarly, to accept the religious view of the world amounts to accepting God or the Absolute as the primary reality and to explain everything else as His or its forms. There is nothing *a priori* wrong in any of these procedures. The only criticism is that none has been successful. The criterion of success here again must be man and his life. If materialism is adequate—assuming for argument's sake that it is—to explain man's body, it has been inadequate to explain his ethical conduct and much more inadequate to explain his spiritual experiences. Nor has any spiritual philosophy been able to give an adequate explanation of man's material nature. Man is the most wonderful of creatures, offering the most obstinate problems to thinkers, because he is an integral unity of matter, life, mind, reason, and spirit. Studies have been started to understand each; and, individually, these studies have made great progress. But the problem of the unity of all, which is given as a fact in man, has made very little progress. It is the common practice of all students of philosophy to criticize Descartes (seventeenth century) for having been unable to solve the body-mind problem and for having given rise to occasionalism and its difficulties. Three centuries have passed; but who has solved the problem? We have manufactured automata to solve intricate mathematical problems; but we have not created a person out of matter. The integrality of man is far deeper than is the relation between mind and matter; otherwise the problem could have been solved.

As the situation now stands, a unified system of knowledge, a kind of mathematical deductive system embracing the totality of man and the world, is very remote, although it may always remain as an ideal against which humanity should test its intellectual achievements. We may say also that our knowledge of man as an integral unity of several distinct forms, like matter and life, will be complete only when the ideal of knowledge is complete; and *vice versa*. The unity of the universe as a system of deductive relationships between matter, life, mind, reason, and spirit is not yet in our possession even as a fact; that is to say, at the macrocosmic level the unity is not given to us as a fact, we only *speak* of it. But at the microcosmic level, that is, at the level of man, we have the unity as a fact, but also as a mystery to be unravelled. Even then, even before we unravel it as a mystery, we have to test our philosophies with that unravelled mystery as the denominator. The more we are able to understand the mystery, the clearer will be our process of testing. Yet we are not able to wait until that understanding is complete; for we are living through that mystery, and life does not wait for the final solution. The denominator which is our criterion may become clearer and richer for future generations; but, however imperfectly understood, it has to be used as our test even now. Impatient philosophers, when they are dissatisfied with religious solutions, may adopt the biological point of view; and when they find this too defective, they may adopt the materialistic position. When they find the latter inadequate, they may swing to the opposite extreme, the religious. Thus they may substitute matter, life, mind, reason or spirit for man. But, unfortunately, man, as he exists, is not simply any one of these; nor can any one of them be the common denominator for testing philosophies of life.

There is much to be said in favour of the contention that each of the disciplines—sciences (both physical and natural), logic, mathematics, psychology, ethics, and philosophy of religion—should be allowed its own autonomy; for their subject matters, as we study them, are not exactly the same. In the present state of knowledge, reduction, either upwards or downwards, is detrimental to the adequacy of philosophy. Conant writes: 'Whether the unifying principle can be a dualism of matter and spirit, mechanism, formism, or some form of idealism, the whole attempt seems to me to be in the wrong direction. My preference would be for more adequate explanation of special limited areas of experience; one of these would include those experiences which can be ordered in terms of a system of spiritual values.'[13] Similarly, Galloway, one of the important writers on religion, says that, though the idea of a completed system of philosophy remains an ideal, we have to claim a great measure of independence for the special philosophical disciplines.[14] In our study each experience has to be given its own autonomy until we are able to attain the ideal of a perfectly unified knowledge; for we are not yet able to understand how the objects of each kind of experience are related to objects of all other kinds. We know only that they can be related and must be related, because they are related in man. Logical empiricism, for instance, is perfectly justified within a limited field of inquiry. But it has no right to say that the facts of ethical and religious experience are not as true as the facts of sense experience. When it says that these facts are emotions or sentiments, it is encroaching upon psychology, which it eschews, and is denying everything of value in ethics and religion. Moral and religious writers may retort by saying that sense experience is not true. In fact, why should man accept sensory objects as ultimately true and make them the basis of philosophical deduction or logical construction? This con-

[13] *Modern Science and Modern Man*, p. 99.

[14] *The Philosophy of Religion*, p. 43 (Edinburgh: T. & T. Clerk, 1951).

troversy only bewilders man, who begins to wonder whether he himself is an existent fact at all. If the existence of man is doubted, there will be an end to all philosophy. Reason and logic should remove superstitions; but they should not destroy facts that are the support of man's life.

For a comparative study of philosophy—in fact, for all philosophy—it is not enough to approach the problems from the point of view of epistemology, or of logic or of metaphysics alone. The approach must be from man. The common denominator and criterion is man—his life, his action, and his values. The more we understand him, the greater will be the content of the denominator, which grows with the growth of knowledge; for the study of man includes the study of everything that pertains to him; epistemology, logic, ethics, religion, and much else besides. As the specific disciplines progress, philosophy of life also progresses. When any important new concept or theory is introduced into the specific sciences, man has to confront himself with the question: How am I to understand the world now? How am I to act in it? If the new idea is of sufficient importance, man's philosophy of life may change and, with it, the unified picture he wants to build of his life—and the world. It may be imperfect; yet he builds it, even knowing that he cannot complete it. The ideal of unified knowledge stands before the mind of every thinking man.

4. MAN IS MAN FOR ALL THAT

But if man is not the same everywhere, how can he be the common denominator for all philosophies? It has been customary to distinguish between 'eastern man' and 'western man,' as if they belong to different species. 'Eastern man' is said to be intuitive and 'western man' intellectual; 'eastern man' lethargic and 'western man' active; 'eastern man' spiritual and 'western man' materialistic; 'eastern man' mystical and 'western man' ethical; 'eastern man' introvert and 'western man' extrovert; 'eastern man' contented and 'western man' always discontented and craving for more; and so on. This kind of differentiation raises a very important question.

The differentiation, of course, is not accepted by all either in the East or the West. For instance, Radhakrishnan believes that man, eastern or western, is the same in spite of all the differences in cultural achievements. Man's basic urges, instincts, aspirations, ideals are the same. Not only is man's basic nature the same everywhere, but also 'when we take a long view of history we will find that there is not an Eastern view which is different from the Western view of life.'[15].

First, when we are comparing the eastern man with the western, are we comparing their cultural achievements or their innate natures? When a psychologist, for instance, compares the I.Q.'s of two boys, he does not compare their Achievement Quotients (A.Q.'s). A graduate student may have a lower I.Q. than a high school student; but the achievements of the former will generally be higher. Similarly, if we are to understand man's essential nature for a philosophy of life, it is not enough to understand the cultural achievements of the East and the West. There is something still deeper and more basic than achievements; and that has to be accepted as common to all men, eastern or western. Without such a faith in the universality of man, comparative philosophy will be of little use. Why should we compare if there is very little in common? Habit and custom, which are the basis of culture and civilization, i.e. of the achievements of man, are only second nature; human nature as such is primary even with respect to them.

Secondly, when a psychologist studies man and formulates general laws about emotion, sensation, thought, etc., he assumes that his laws are applicable to all men. Otherwise works written by western psychologists will be of little use to eastern man, and *vice versa*. Without assuming that the basic nature of man is the same everywhere, works on psychology will have very little scientific value. The very principle of the uniformity of nature, however it be interpreted, will have to be rejected, at least at the level of man, unless man is basically the same everywhere.

In the third place, if man is not the same everywhere, why should western democracies encourage democracies in the East? The so-called psychological differences between the East and the West have to be regarded as not fundamental. We may go further and generalize. The United Nations and the UNESCO, working to make available the values of all cultures to each, have to assume that man everywhere is the same and can

[15] Radhakrishnan: *East and West: Some Reflexions*, p. 13 (London: Allen & Unwin Ltd., 1955).

welcome and utilize these values. If the eastern man were different from the western, neither could utilize the values of the other or assimilate them, and the great world organizations, which are the hope of mankind, would be attempting the impossible. In fact, the very conception of natural law, which animated the Roman jurists and inspired Cicero and Dante and which is traced to the Stoic conception of nature, is based on the conviction that man is the same everywhere. From it is derived the idea of the natural rights of men—rights, which also are considered to be the same everywhere. Cicero said that there were no different laws at Rome and Athens; and this has to be accepted so far as the basic nature of man is concerned.[16]

Fourthly, there is a still more basic question. Behaviourism has made the idea current and fashionable that a thing is its behaviour. The origin of the idea may be traced to scientific procedure. Material objects and organisms like plants and animals are studied only in their behaviour. We do not know what electricity and magnetism are in themselves; we know them only through what they do. So the behaviourists say that mind also is what mind does. Mind is its behaviour, there is nothing there apart from its behaviour. A principle which is originally a principle of method is generalized. So it is said that man is what man does in the East or in the West.

But are we right in generalizing this behaviouristic principle? I may not know what electricity is in itself, because I do not see it and cannot enter it. Similarly, I do not know how a tiger is feeling its pains and pleasures, because I cannot enter its life. So in the case of these objects, I may work with the principle that a thing is what it does. But I know my own pains and pleasures. The pain I am having at the boil on my hand is not the same as the pus it gives out. My toothache is not the same as the decay of my tooth. The thing as such is not exactly the same as its expression, adequate or inadequate. Similarly, the western or the eastern man is not the same as his cultural expression. Ernst Cassirer rightly observes: 'But a consistent and radical behaviourism fails to attain its end. It can warn us against possible methodological errors, but it cannot solve the problems of human psychology. We may criticize or suspect the purely introspective view, we cannot supress or eliminate it.

[16] A. P. d'Entreves: *Natural Law*, p. 21 (London: Hutchison's University Library, 1951).

Without introspection, without an immediate awareness of feelings, emotions, perceptions, thoughts, we could not even define the field of human psychology.'[17] Yet Cassirer says that introspection alone cannot give us a comprehensive view of human nature. Man lives in a world of culture, not merely in the world of physics; and the world of culture consists of language, myth, art, religion, etc., which is the symbolic world. Hence, the study of man is to be based on a study of these symbols. But here also we have to say that symbols are not the same as the things symbolized. In symbols we may get some clues concerning human nature; but no symbol or group of symbols can give an exhaustive account of the thing they stand for. Even here we have to recognize the limits of behaviourism, seeing that behaviourism can only be a help in checking hasty generalizations.

In the fifth place, leaders of humanity like Christ, Buddha, Mohammad, or Gandhi, can change the nature of man to such an extent that, after a few generations, their followers may show different traits of character. The question arises, therefore, whether or not social psychology can be a purely inductive study. Some thinkers feel that the subject cannot be studied properly without studying the ideals and values of the social groups. What holds true of a group in this century—particularly of a progressive group—may not hold true of it two centuries later. I wonder whether the culture of the Americans who entered the country in the *Mayflower* is exactly the same as that of the present-day Americans. Changes occur because man is a creative being. He cannot create himself; but he creates and changes social relationships, ideals, and forms of activity. He changes his attitude towards life and the world. But there is another idea that must be considered. Just as rain is not the same as clouds but is their effect, so language, myth and other cultural achievements, are not the same as man but are the results of his outlook and activity, differing from place to place and from time to time. And as the agent of that activity, man is creative. In this sense, history is not deterministic, but is the result of man's creativity. Creativity implies freedom from the forms created; without freedom, they can neither be created nor changed. However, even confined to the history of culture, the philosophy of man must be a creative

[17] *An Essay on Man*, pp. 1–2 (Yale University Press, New Haven, 1948).

humanism, not a deterministic humanism, as it has to take man as a creative being. But since even this view ignores man's inherent nature, a complete philosophy of man must be more than creative humanism. After all, man also is a creature. Culture is the creation of man, but man himself is a creature. He frames ideals, changes them, and transforms nature according to them. Great leaders of mankind succeed in changing the ideals and cultures and in making man act in new ways. Their success is due to the fact that the nature of man behind his creations is not exhausted in his creations.

In the sixth place, we cannot say with justification that nature is the only factor that stirs man into cultural activity. Ideals of life which may not be present in a group in its primitive state may enter it later from outside and become assimilated. They may themselves get transformed in the process, but not without transforming the original culture. Buddhism entered China and got transformed into Chinese Buddhism, but, at the same time, it did not leave Confucianism and Taoism unchanged. This is true not only of religious ideals but also of social, political, and economic ideals as well. Differing natural environments do not fix the national character once and for all. Nature is only one of the conditioning factors. Others are not only found within a group but also imported from outside. If now and in the future the major conditions of life are going to be the same everywhere, if values of life will be similar everywhere, the differences in national characters are bound to be toned down gradually until man behaves similarly in similar situations in every part of the globe. Because man is the same everywhere, he can adapt himself similarly to the changing conditions of life and to new values that enter his mental horizon. So long as nothing new enters, he may remain the same; but if it does, he changes. Natural conditions do not determine once and for all his culture. Indeed, they do play a role in determining the shape of the houses, the kind of food eaten, the dress worn, etc., which in turn determine to a degree man's aesthetic sense. But it is difficult to believe that they determine the psychological nature of man to the extent of differentiating the eastern man from the western. The differences usually drawn can be found within the West or within the East itself.

We now come to the seventh point. When we are comparing two cultures, are we sure that we are not comparing an advanced with a backward group? Even in the case of important civilizations—the Chinese, the Hindu, and the Western—each advanced in certain respects and remained backward in certain others. Does this mean that each of these cultures cannot advance in those respects in which it remained backward? An affirmative answer has no foundation in fact. If we take the cultures as they are—note that they are not static now—then, indeed, they are advanced in certain respects and backward in certain others. But if we take them as they are, we are ignoring the creative man behind the culture. Confucius did not know modern technology; but many modern Chinese do, and they are changing their culture. Many Indians have been saying that western culture is materialistic and theirs is spiritual. But there are many who add that material backwardness is not the same as spirituality, and material wealth is not the same as lack of spirituality. How are these new ideas able to enter our lives if 'eastern man' is essentially and inherently content with material poverty and spiritual richness? Backwardness in any respect does not exclude the possibility of advancing in that very respect; to advance in it is now felt to be even a necessity. Similarly, if 'western man' is by nature satisfied with material wealth and does not appreciate and care for spiritual depth, why are the western leaders complaining that ethical and spiritual life has not made a progress corresponding to that of science? What is the use of preaching ethics and spirituality to 'western man,' if, by nature, he is not meant to receive them? It is often said that the West has not produced a single religious founder: even Jesus Christ was an Asian. It produced only social and political leaders. But Confucius is the first philosopher of democracy, although this form of government was first established in the West. But democracy has come back to the East now. That men of certain cultures did not accomplish certain things is due to conditions which, so far as human nature goes, are an accident; it is not to be explained as due to man's innate nature. The need may not have been felt acutely by them or may have been met in a wider context and thus lost its conspicuity.

It will perhaps be said that culture is an integral and organic whole and that the backwardness or progress of any of its aspects is inherent to it and necessary for it. This may be true if we take culture as separated from the man behind it. What generally happens is that man slowly changes his culture; and the more educated he becomes, the more rapid can be the change. What is backward may become advanced; and what is advanced may be pushed back, if it is found to be marching in the wrong direction. There is no culture that is necessarily static; it either advances or decays. As Whitehead says, life is a protest against repetitive mechanism. Cultural traditions, if they have life at all, are not mere repetitions but creative transformations, transforming themselves as well as the new entries. But changes in transformation may be spread over a long period of history and may not be sudden and immediately perceptible. Again, when a culture decays, two things may happen: either that culture may be given up slowly or the members belonging to it may diminish in numbers. This is generally true of primitive cultures. The groups either take to new forms of activity or die out when, for some reason, they are not able to adapt themselves to changing conditions. When old forms survive and obtain fresh life from new forms, we say that the culture lives and progresses. But in all this, we should not talk of culture as if it were a fixed entity, just as we should not talk of evolution as if it were an agent controlling nature's processes. The man behind culture is more important and is not to be lost sight of. And he is the same everywhere.

It is the faith that man is the same everywhere, in spite of the different attitudes he has adopted to life, in spite of the differences of his cultural achievements, that is the motif of the editors of this volume. If the attitudes are different, are some of them false? If not false, do they need modification in the light of the differences? If they are beneficial to humanity somewhere, can they be beneficial everywhere? Are the values of life accepted by one philosophical tradition values for the others also? The book is meant to help find answers to such questions as these.

When Professor Northrop[18] pleads for a synthesis of eastern and western cultures at the level of epistemology by synthesizing intellect and intuition, he is assuming that such a synthesis is as useful to the eastern man as to the western. This assumption is justified only by the further assumption—which is also my faith—that man is the same everywhere and that he can be benefited by such a synthesis. Many critics of Professor

[18] *Meeting of East and West* (New York: Macmillan Co., 1947).

Northrop feel that his differentiation between intellect and intuition as representative of the West and the East is an oversimplification of the differences between the East and the West, which are not really so clear-cut. However, his final assumption that man is the same everywhere and his faith that man can assimilate the values of every part of the globe and be benefited by them is most important. But it is disconcerting to read Dr Haas's pessimistic conclusion that the eastern and the western forms of consciousness can never be united. He writes: 'The divergence of Western and Eastern mind and civilization must have evoked serious doubt as to whether, beyond the sphere of pragmatic exchange and understanding, any real communication between them can be possible. The stand-point from which the problem may be evaluated can be found only in the answer to this seemingly paradoxical question—Can two antagonistic forms of consciousness co-exist in one and the same mind, and if so, how? It would appear that conciliation of this antagonism can take place only in a third and higher form of consciousness. This, however, is nowhere to be found, nor can it be imagined in theory.'[19] But it has been imagined and propounded in theory by thinkers like Northrop. I do not mean that everyone should accept Dr Northrop's doctrine as it is given by him. I would rather say that the two forms of consciousness are always together in the life of man, but with varying predominance; they can never be separated except by abstraction for purposes of study. Are the two forms really antagonistic and so antagonistic that they cannot be synthesized? First, let us assume that they are antagonistic. Even then, as Hegel says, the very consciousness which holds them in antagonism is itself their synthesis. To see the merits and defects of each is also to see the way to the synthesis of their respective merits. Time can synthesize and has synthesized many opposites in life. The task may not be performed in one generation; but it may be accomplished, given enough time. Secondly, the so-called antagonism is no antagonism at all; it is only a difference in emphasis on divergent aspects of consciousness. It is wrong to think that the West is evolutionary and the East has a 'state-character' (that is, is static). It is interesting to note that some who held this view, when

[19] William S. Haas: *The Destiny of Mind: East and West*, p. 281 (London: Faber & Faber, 1956).

confronted with the evidence of rapid progress in the East, said that even such progress was a sign of the East's 'state-character', because intermittent steps were very few or none. Such answers convince no one. The truth is otherwise. If, as some logicians like Bradley say, the object is more than all the predicates we can refer to it, man is more than the culture he has created. He finds it more urgent to create certain forms of culture and civilization at one place and others at another. Sometimes he has to introduce changes more rapidly than at other times. But this does not make him different at different places or at different times. Speaking of the Near East, Dr Haas says that West and East alone represent clearly demonstrable forms of consciousness; the Near East does not. Why not? Because it has not overemphasized either aspect of culture, like the West and the East. If man can do so in the Near East and if it is necessary for all to do so, what is there to prevent the western or the eastern man from doing so? That he has not done it in the past—if he had not done—is no reason why he will not do it in the future. If he felt the need, he could have done it in the past also. He now feels the need; there is nothing to prevent him from doing it. History is not completely deterministic.

Besides, if a pragmatic exchange of ideas and forms of religious, social, political, and economic life takes place, will this change have no influence on the mind that receives them? Will it not produce a change in the consciousness in which it takes place? I find it difficult to say, No. Before our eyes vast changes are taking place in the East, sometimes evolutionary, sometimes revolutionary. I wonder whether any serious thinker will say that revolutionary changes are eastern. There have been many revolutions in the West also. We have to remember again that we have to understand not only man through his expressions but also expressions through man. Man can change his expressions to a far greater degree than expressions determine man.

5. GENERAL PLAN OF THE WORK

One who wishes to show that man is the same in the East and the West can collect at least as much evidence as the one who wishes to show that he is not the same. No one can be blind to the differences; and yet no one should miss the similarities. But similarities are more important than differences, because they touch the essence of man and offer hope for the future. Indian thinkers say that communism is a child of the West; but western democracies say that it is of the East. Until communism appeared, Russia was West and communist philosophy was developed in what is still called West. These words, therefore, have lost their meaning. What is communism? It is, as professed in Russia, economic determinism plus self-sufficient humanism plus science and technology plus atheism. What is western democracy? It is capitalism plus humanism plus science and technology plus religion. These descriptions are not exactly true of every communist country any more than they are true of every democratic country. But let us accept them for the sake of argument. Still, we can have permutations and combinations of these descriptions. For instance, capitalism can go with atheism and communism with theism. So, instead of dividing the world arbitrarily into East and West, using terms which have no definite denotation and connotation; we may fruitfully study man if we understand him as he is presented in the four great philosophical traditions; the Greek, the Jewish, the Indian, and the Chinese.

The book, it is hoped, will serve another purpose, namely, that of bringing back philosophy to what Schweitzer[20] would call the elemental stand-point. Philosophy started as an attempt to give man a theory of life as a guide. But it has forgotten its starting point and purpose: the very man for whom its activities are meant. It will be interesting and useful, it is hoped, to undertake a study of man in the four traditions. It is not a study from the side of the great religions; and so Christianity and Islam have not been given separate chapters. For the Jewish, the Indian, and the Chinese philosophies there is no separation between philosophy and religious thought. India and China do not have what are strictly called revealed religions, and philosophy has been identical with religious thought. Judaism may be called revealed religion; the commandments were revealed to Moses; but it has no philosophy apart from religious thought. Hence there is no other course than to include Jewish, Chinese, and Indian philosophies as they exist. Besides, the philosophical thought in Christianity and Islam

[20] *Civilization and Ethics*, p. xiv (London: A. & C. Black, 1949).

is either Platonic, Aristotelian, or Neo-Platonic. However, the book aims to be philosophical, not religious.

The work does not claim to offer final solutions to the problems connected with man's life. Such a work will have to be both narrower and wider in its scope; narrower because it cannot give a connected presentation of the traditions; and wider because it has to bring all the problems and their solutions into co-ordination and system. The present work attempts only to show how the thought currents of the traditions ran and to give clues to the solutions of the problems raised. For what is missed in one tradition may be found in another and what is considered to be of secondary importance in one may be treated as of primary importance in another.

What is found in one tradition and not in another may be considered outlandish by the latter. But in what appears strange may be hidden truths for which search might have been made along wrong paths. Some of the strange approaches to the problems may be the right approaches. Here comparative philosophy broadens our vision and acquaints us with ways of life and thought which really belong to the intricate web of experience, but the reality and importance of which are missed by some traditions for one reason or another.

It is not the intention of the editors and contributors to raise or lower any religion or philosophy. All have the good of mankind in view. As Leon Roth says,[21] it is not only the Romans who constructed roads, other nations did it too; but the Romans developed road-building into a science and an art. Similarly, all religions and philosophies are concerned with almost all problems; but to some they have given more thought than to others. Because the problems are at least latently there in each, each can imbibe and assimilate much from the rest. It is time that every gentleman should hesitate to use words like pagan, kafir, and *mleccha*, and that he should stop fighting for things which he does not understand. We have more important objectives to work and fight for than ideologies, religious or political. The welfare of humanity, a fuller and deeper life for man on earth, is a more urgent problem than is the spread of one's own religion or philosophy and defeat of all others. What is man and what is meant by a fuller and deeper life? This is the question that animated the project of this

[21] *Jewish Thought as a Factor in Civilization*, p. 9 (Paris: UNESCO, 1954).

work. We have indeed old rivalries and conflicts of ideas; but these rivalries and conflicts must become moments of the advancing force of universal ethos that unites East and West into one march of humanity. On this faith does the hope of the future of mankind depend.

In this epoch of the growing unification of world outlook, it is hoped that the book will form a useful study. Already the study of man has come to the forefront and is included in the undergraduate courses of some western universities. This book will form a useful guide and help in such courses and can be used even as a text. Textbooks on a comparative study of man are very few; and teachers are obliged to make the best of whatever material is available. This book may meet the need of such teachers and be useful to students. Being one of the first attempts on the subject, even if its comparisons and conclusions cannot give finally acceptable opinion on the topics, it can at least be a guide to further study and research. Although the concept of man can be found in the arts, in literature, and in other aspects of culture, it is thought that the best, consistent and definitely formulated views can be found only in the philosophies of the different traditions; for a consistent and systematic expression of any culture can be found in its philosophies.

The editors have asked recognized specialists to contribute chapters on the different traditions. The editors wish to express their sincere thanks to them for their labour of love, which will contribute to mutual understanding of cultures and philosophies and thus to a sympathetic 'give and take'. It is also hoped that the book, which is a co-operative enterprise, can be a basic work for comparative philosophy. Each contributor is responsible for the views he expresses and for the interpretations he has given of his tradition. The editors are aware that each tradition was not equally concerned with, and attracted by, all the problems we now associate with the study of man. So it was left to the contributors to rearrange, omit, or add to the topics suggested for inclusion in their contributions. The topics suggested were:

I. Man and His Environment
  1. Man and Nature
  2. Man and Society

3. Man and the Divine Spirit

II. Man and Evolution

III. The Complexity of the Human Individual and its Factors—Matter, Life, Mind and Spirit—Psycho-physical urges and Rational Life.

IV. Man and His Life's Ideals—Ways of Achieving them

V. Influence on Religious Traditions

VI. Education as the Development of the Highest in Man

The contributors are not only authorities on the different traditions but also belong to them. Each chapter may therefore be taken as the utterance of the tradition itself. Many foreign friends who saw my previous publications, which were meant to present Indian thought in the light of the western tradition rather than to be works on comparative philosophy itself, expressed their interest to have works on the subject itself. This is one of the reasons for the present book.

Finally, I express my thanks to many friends, both Indian and foreign, for the co-operation and encouragement I received from them. I cannot be too grateful to His Excellency Dr S. Radhakrishnan, to whom my interest in comparative philosophy is due and to whom comparative philosophy itself owes a great deal for whatever progress it has been able to make. He has helped me in planning the work, co-operated with me in editing it, and contributed the Preface. I am deeply indebted to Dr W. H. Werkmeister, Director of the School of Philosophy, University of Southern California, for carefully revising the manuscript of my chapters and for making valuable and detailed suggestions about ideas and their expression. I am thankful to Professor Max Fisch of the University of Illinois for reading parts of the manuscript and for bringing the book to the notice of American friends. I am thankful also to Professor H. W. Schneider of Columbia University, Dr Charles A. Moore of Hawaii University, Dr Cornelius Kruse of Wesleyan University, Dr Brand Blanshard and Dr W. H. Sheldon of Yale University, Dr E. A. Burtt of Cornell University, and Dr Virgil C. Aldrich of the Kenyon College for the interest they have been taking in, and for the encouragement they have been giving to my work in Comparative Philosophy. Comparative Philosophy is a need of the present; and yet, without the interest and encouragement of many leading thinkers, it can make little progress. My sincere thanks are due also to Professor G. C. Chatterji, Vice-chancellor of the University of Rajasthan, not only for his sympathetic encouragement of my studies in Comparative Philosophy, but also for the financial support he has obtained from the University of Rajasthan and the University Grants Commission, as a subsidy for publishing the present work. The University of Rajasthan and the University Grants Commission have made grants of £125 each towards the subsidy required for publishing the book, and I acknowledge their help with thanks.

CHAPTER I

The Concept of Man in Greek Thought

JOHN WILD

I. INTRODUCTION

MAN is a marvellous and many-sided creature. This much at least is clear. In common with all the beings of nature, he has a physical body composed of the basic elements, which grows, decays, and interacts with other processes. In common with plants, this body is animated by a moving principle that nourishes and reproduces itself. With the other animals, it is capable of locomotion, and is endowed with sensory organs which enable him to direct his acts by an awareness of external things and his own pleasures and pains. In addition to these, he possesses a freedom which makes him the master of his own life by deliberation and choice. Finally he is, as Proclus said, a praying animal, who is able to enter into communion with a being higher than himself.

It is possible to single out each of these phases, and to regard the whole of human nature from this point of view. Thus we have an astronomical view of man which looks at him as a tiny physical process lost in the vast encompassing spaces of the galactic universe. There is the biological view of man which focuses him as a living being and regards him as the last stage of a protracted planetary evolution. There is the animalistic view of man which concentrates upon his awareness of pleasure and pain and his elementary appetites. Sharply set off from these is the libertarian view which focuses his freedom of choice, and sees him as the master of his history. Finally there is the religious view of man which interprets his whole being in terms of a relation to eternal spirit.

In other times and places, these views have been given definitive expression. Most of them were well known to the

Greeks. But their intellectual life was dominated by a very different conception. As Aristotle tersely expressed it: man is the *zoón ekonlogov*, the animal possessing speech. He talks and thinks and deliberates. This is the most essential and distinctive characteristic of man, on the basis of which the rest of his being is most adequately understood. The greatest Hellenic thinkers worked out this view of man to the last detail. This is their distinctive contribution to the history of Western thought and to world anthropology. In this chapter we shall try to explain the structure of this point of view and to trace out the broad outline of its history.

In the earliest pre-Socratic phase of Greek thought the concept of man was not sharply focused. Noteworthy remarks were made about man. But the chief object of speculative interest was the order of nature as a whole. Man was simply a part of the cosmos, and attention was never concentrated on his peculiar nature as an object of special concern. Therefore, owing to limitations of space, we shall have to pass over this formative period, except in so far as it constitutes an essential background and contrast to what comes after. Our treatment of the theme of man in Greek thought will fall into four major divisions: first, the period of fifth-century Sophists with special emphasis on the thought of Protagoras; second, the philosophy of Socrates and his brilliant disciple Plato; third, Aristotle; and finally stoicism and the final period of decline when Greek thought was merged with other alien elements.

In each of these major parts we shall deal with the view of man under seven divisions: 1, man and nature; 2, man and society; 3, man and the Divine Spirit; 4, evolution and human history; 5, the analysis of the individual human person; 6, the moral ideal and the means of realizing it; and finally 7, the process of education. We shall conclude our discussion with an examination of the influence of Greek thought on later religious traditions.

2. THE SOPHISTS

The Greek peninsula and the Aegean islands were invaded by northern tribes who sacked the city of Cnossus and conquered the Cretan Empire about 1400 B.C. This era of bold adventure and conquest is celebrated in the great Homeric epics. These invaders settled down finally in the Cretan cities, and set up communities of their own. The prevailing form of government was monarchic and aristocratic, with rigid class lines, and religious worship was polytheistic in form. The larger cities were independent, each having its own special deities, and distinctive traditions adapted to its peculiar history and circumstances. This mode of life persisted until the seventh and sixth centuries B.C. when a very considerable increase in population brought forth new problems. The poverty of the poorer classes, especially the farmers, generated strong pressures for social change and even revolution. Some cities met the long range problem by colonization. Others, like Athens, went in for commerce and trade. This solution proved successful, and by the beginning of the fifth century B.C., Athens had become strong enough to play a leading role in defeating the Persian invasion under Xerxes.

But these events had led to important changes in social life and moral attitudes. Aristocratic rule was now seriously qualified by democratic trends, especially in commercial and naval cities like Athens. This brought forth a serious questioning of ancient traditions and modes of thought, which was intensified by the first hand knowledge of alien customs resulting from foreign trade. In cities like Athens, the ordinary citizens now met in the assembly, and played an active role in the making of political decisions. Skill in public debate was the road to social success. The rise of the lower classes had resulted in the establishment of people's courts. Each citizen needed to know how to protect his civil rights. If sued, he had to defend himself in court. There were no professional lawyers. This intensified the need for teachers of rhetoric and political theory from whom the ambitious young citizen could gain some knowledge of his literature and cultural history, and some skill in public debate. The fifth-century Sophists were the answer to this basic need.

Let us now consider their views of the nature of man, especially those of the great teacher, writer, and friend of Pericles, Protagoras of Abdera.

(i) *Man and Nature*

As we have already pointed out, the earlier philosophers had devoted themselves to cosmological speculations concerning the whole of nature. But they had arrived at very different results.

Thales had asserted that the world was full of Gods, while the atomists had maintained that spirits were non-existent, and that bodies alone were real. Parmenides and his followers believed that all was immobile, while Heraclitus held that all was in flux. This radical disagreement tended to discredit such speculation. There was also the new interest in political problems brought forth by social unrest. These factors were primarily responsible for the new Sophistic and man-centred philosophy found in Protagoras. He is interested in man rather than the cosmos, in ethics and the theory of knowledge rather than cosmology.

Nevertheless, while it was certainly not the central object of his concern, Protagoras did have a view of the world of nature. His notion of being was very simple. There are no modes or levels of being. A thing either is or it is not. The test of this is my sensation. If I feel cold, then it is cold for me, though it may feel hot to another. If I taste sweet, then it is sweet. If I have a certain opinion, then this is so for me, no matter what others may think. Sensing, opining, fearing, and loving *are* when I have them. When I do not have them they *are not*. Hence it is impossible for me, or for anyone, to think what is false, for even to think nothing is a real thought if I actually have it. Hence you or I, as individual men, are the measure of being, of things that are that they are, and of things that are not that they are not.[1]

Our senses tell us that all is in flux, for no sensation is ever repeated. Hence as Plato says, the hidden roots of Protagoras' philosophy are to be found in the dynamism of Heraclitus. To be is to be in becoming.[2] All that I see or feel or hear, including myself, is in constant transition. Nothing ever stands still. Furthermore, these changes are relative and interdependent. The sugar works on my tongue and brings forth a taste. But this organ is also in transition, and how it tastes will depend also on the state of this transition. At one time the sugar will be sweet; at another sour. My sensations do not occur of themselves, but always in relation to some stimulating process. This in turn is not experienced as it is in itself, but only as it is in relation to me and to my organs of perception.

[1] *Theaetetus*, 152 A. Plato was certainly familiar with Protagoras' works. In this passage he makes it very clear that for the great Sophist, individual sensation, *my* feeling is the test of truth.

[2] *Theaet.*, 152 C. ff.

The universe is, therefore, a great maze of interacting processes in constant transformation. It is futile to speculate about any ultimate source.[3] The events of nature have happened of themselves. They simply are. That is all we can know. Their nature is to change. One set of changes is what we call man, an extraordinary cosmic accident endowed with peculiar capacities. One of these is foresight which has enabled him to invent the arts, and thus to survive amongst the stronger animals and alien forces of nature. Another is a sense of justice and respect towards his fellows which enables him to live together in groups.[4]

Each community must set up its own rules of justice. If not, it will fall into chaos and perish. But these laws of convention are indefinitely variable. Only that city which is unified and strong will survive and rule. Only those acts which lead to this end are really expedient. This is the law of nature, which is sharply opposed to conventional notions of justice and morality. Protagoras often masked this conflict between artificial man-made virtue and natural interest by his use of conventional language in referring to the latter. But it lay implicit in his theory[5] and was clearly and openly expressed by such later Sophists as Thrasymachuss and Callicles.

(ii) *Man and Society*

According to the Promethean myth which Protagoras probably used in his influential treatise on the origin of human culture,[6] the first men lived apart from one another.[7] They banded together only later for the sake of mutual protection. As Glaucon develops this view in the second Book of Plato's *Republic*,[8] social life and the rules of justice it requires are a necessary evil. Each individual would be much better off if he were uninhibited by such prohibitions, and able to satisfy his desires to an unlimited degree. But unfortunately he lacks the

[3] Protagoras wrote a treatise *On the Gods*. *Cf.* Diels, *Vorsokratiker* Fragm. 4, and Plato *Theaet.*, 162 D.

[4] *Cf.* the myth in Plato's *Protagoras*, 320 D ff.

[5] *Theaetetus*, 166 D.

[6] The ideas about primitive man expressed in Plato's myth agree with the views of Democritus which are also attributed to Protagoras by later sources. It is probable, therefore, that they were first expressed in Protagoras' famous treatise on the origin of human culture. *Cf.* Diels, *Vors.*, 74 B, 8b.

[7] Plato, *Protagoras*, 322 A.

[8] *Republic*, 359 E.

necessary power. As Hobbes pithily put the matter later, in the state of nature, life is nasty, brutish and short. So, as a lesser evil, he met with his fellows and agreed to make those sacrifices of natural liberty which are necessary for community life.

Each city makes up laws of its own which determine its way of life. These laws are viewed as technical contrivances, like the art of flute-playing.[9] The only difference is that virtue is an art which all men must learn to some degree in order to live together. Hence all men are teachers of virtue. Every normal adult knows something of courage, justice, and political wisdom. From his earliest youth, the child is 'forced' by reward and punishment into an invented pattern of action. Virtue is a peculiarly important form of technical proficiency. To incur guilt is simply to make a mistake; punishment is technical correction. Moral progress is identified with the increase in technical proficiency from generation to generation. The lowest criminal of an 'advanced' society is 'virtuous' in comparison with a primitive savage.[10] Human history is the record of a constant moral advance.

Some system of law is necessary for co-operation and survival. But the actual systems are very different, having grown up in response to very different circumstances. No one body of law and virtue is truer than any other. Each is simply as it is. Some, however, which lead to survival and growth are better than others which lead to destruction. A wise man is not one who can distinguish the true from the false, for falsity is non-existent. He is rather one like Protagoras, who has the gift of persuasion, an expert in social change who can transform man from destructive habits to those which are better.[11] Like a doctor, he does not deny the evil condition he is asked to cure, but accepts it as it is, and then changes it into something more sound.

(iii) *The Divine*

The Sophists were sceptical about the existence of the gods, and criticized all religious traditions as primitive superstition. Thus in his treatise *On the Gods*, Protagoras disavowed any knowledge 'as to whether they exist or do not exist, since many

[9] *Protag.*, 327 D.
[10] *Op. cit.*, 327 E.
[11] *Theaet.*, 167 A.

obstacles stand in the way, the obscurity of the object and the shortness of human life.'[12] This sceptical treatise, of which a few fragments remain, was finally burned in the market place of Athens.

Some confusion has been caused by the fact that in the myth attributed to Protagoras in Plato's dialogue of that name, man is said to have a divine origin and to have been saved from destruction by the direct intervention of Zeus. The Sophists were in the habit of using such well known stories as their point of departure, but not as something to be taken literally. Thus in his interpretation of the myth, Protagoras makes no mention of divinity nor of any divine influence on human affairs.[13] All events fall into only two classes, those due to chance or nature which happen of themselves, and those due to human contrivance.[14] Plato emphasizes the roles played by the demonic brothers Prometheus (Fore-thought) and Epimetheus (After-thought), and intepretes them as true and false or pragmatic art (flattery or *kolakeia*), the bane of human culture.[15] But Protagoras ignores them completely. Man is a sheer accident of nature who has managed to survive by his technical skill which is always good.

Another expression of this common Sophistic teaching is found in a fragment of the tragedy *Sysiphus*, written by Plato's uncle, Critias, one of the thirty tyrants who ruled Athens after the collapse at the end of the great war (430–401 B.C.). According to this influential doctrine, religious belief is the invention of a wise statesman who wished to restrain men from secret and hidden vices. Hence he devised and cultivated the belief in an allseeing and allhearing observer located high in heaven, who is the source of thunder and lightning as well as of the gentle and fructifying rain.[16]

(iv) *Evolution and Human History*

Protagoras was the author of an influential treatise on the *First Origin of Human Culture*. With the aid of Plato's *Protagoras* and the comments of other later authors, it is now possible to reconstruct the outline of this lost work. As we have

[12] Fragment 4 (Diels, *op. cit.*) *Cf.* Plato, *Theaetetus*, 162 D.
[13] *Protag.*, 322 E ff.
[14] *Op. cit.*, 323 D.
[15] 361 D. *cf. Gorgias*, 464 C ff.
[16] Diels, *Vors.*, 81 B, 25.

seen, the first men were helpless accidents of nature who lived apart without cities in the prehistoric forests. Lacking the speed, armour, tusks, and claws possessed by the other animals, they managed to survive only by their early development of the arts. Democritus, also of Abdera, later developed an imitation theory of the arts. Man learned to build dwellings from the swallow, to spin from the spider, to sing from the birds, etc. It is probable that this idea was first developed in Protagoras' famous treatise. But even with these arts, man was still weak in comparison with the other animals. He would have been destroyed had it not been for his invention of the art of speech and of government which enabled him to live co-operatively in cities. But even these were insufficient to eliminate mutual jealousy and conflict. To meet this threat, the ideas of justice and respect were constructed.[17]

Since this time, man has been able, in spite of wars and other setbacks, to steadily advance by the perfection of these arts, and others which have followed in their train. Most of the Sophists shared this optimistic view, definitely opposed to the traditional theory of a pristine golden age from which later history constitutes a sad decline. Nature is made up of conflicting processes and forces. By nature man is very weak. But by his inventions and constructions he has made himself strong. Human history is the record of a gradual but on the whole continuous advance from a barbaric stage of anti-social helplessness, to later stages of technical proficiency and social strength, towards a golden age which lies in the future. Man is a technical animal. His salvation lies in the cultivation and elaboration of his Promethean foresight.

(v) *The Human Individual*

Very little is known concerning any theory of Protagoras about the nature of the human individual. He was primarily devoted to the teaching of argument and rhetoric. In connection with this, he is reported to have said that textbooks are worthless without practice, and practice without textbooks, which seems to imply a theoretical as well as a practical capacity in man.[18] But theoretical apprehension is reduced to sensation. He asserted that the soul is nothing besides its sensations.[19]

[17] *Protag.*, 322 E.

[18] Diels, *Vors.*, 74 B, 10.

[19] *Ibid.*, 74, A.I., 51.

To know is to sense, which includes seeing, hearing, smelling, touching, the feeling of hot and cold, pleasure, pain, desire, fear, hope, etc. These feelings result from the action of some physical process on a sense organ. Hence the relativistic subjectivism which leads him to assert that each individual is the measure of all things.

The active phase of human life is reduced to sensory desire. No substantial soul is recognized. The individual is a complex of changes interacting with other forces, and seeking to satisfy its desires as long as it endures.[20] But these forces are very weak. The individual by himself is helpless. Hence the social life of man, which brings forth co-operative power. The greatest prize of political life is the mastery of this power which is gained by rhetoric. The trained rhetorician learns how to attack any opposed position no matter how 'true' or how strong it may be, and to defend any position, no matter how false or how weak.[21] All that is said is equally true, for falsity is non-existent. The aim of argument is not truth, but rather victory.

The implicit materialism of this point of view was openly expressed by Critias who said that mind is simply blood around the heart.[22]

(vi) *Human Ideals and Ways of Achieving Them*

The subjectivism of Protagoras' position, if consistently held, would have led him to an unqualified relativism in ethics. What is good for one man is bad for another; what is bad for one community in certain circumstances is good for another. Indeed, there is evidence that he did at certain times express this aspect of his theory. But he did not stick to it consistently, for this would have seriously undermined his claims to be a wise man and a teacher of virtue and political art.[23] The attitudes of one man are as typical as those of another, but they may not be equally good. This of course implies some stable and universal standard of goodness. Protagoras, however, did not clearly identify and defend such a standard. This would have wrecked the relativistic part of his theory. He rather identified goodness loosely with the prevailing moral concep-

[20] Plato, *Theaetetus*, pp. 152 ff.
[21] *Vors.*, 74 A, 21.
[22] Diels, *Vors.*, 81b, 23.
[23] Plato, *Theaetetus*, 166–7.

tions of a given community, leaving it vague and undefined. But on his own view, one such conception is as true and, therefore, as good as another.[24] This difficulty was seen by some of the other Sophists who began to appeal to nature as a fixed and stable norm. Different traditions that prevail in different communities divide them from one another, and force them to do many things which are against nature. An educated man, according to Antiphon, should rather act in accordance with nature, which has made all men alike and akin.[25] He also used the same argument to attack differences of class and social status, including slavery. It is arbitrary custom that sets up class differences. By nature men are equal.

But this view was incompatible with the original differences in power and intelligence which are found in man, and indeed with the whole conception of a chaotic nature which is implicit in the thought of Protagoras. The world is not a coherent order but an accidental array of conflicting forces. In such a world, the law of nature is the rule of might. It was this implication of their basic position which became increasingly prominent among the later Sophists who were active at the end of the great Peloponnesian war.

Thus Polus, the disciple of Gorgias, admires Archelaus, the Macedonian tyrant, who gained power by murdering his close relations and throwing his younger brother into a well.[26] Thrasymachus sneers at conventional justice as mere obedience to the wishes of those in power. The natural end of life is to realize my own individual desires to the maximum degree. Hence the tyrant is the happiest of men.[27] For Callicles, the really superior man is the man with power, and the law of nature is clearly proclaimed as might makes right.[28] One of the chief means of achieving power in a human community is proficiency in rhetoric which comes with 'education' and training in the techniques of debate. These nihilistic views were implicit, but concealed, in the speeches and writings of the earlier Sophists. Now they are removed from their coverings and expressed with naked clarity.

[24] *Ibid.*, 166 B–C.

[25] See Antiphon's treatise *On Truth*, *Oxyrh*. *Pap*, XI and XV, No., 1797. For an earlier view, *cf.* Hippias statement in Plato, *Protag.*, 337 D.

[26] *Gorgias*, 471.

[27] *Rep.*, 343–355 C.

[28] *Gorgias*, 484 B–C.

(vii) *Education*

The earlier Sophists had taught literature, history, grammar, the art of debate, and other arts to the ambitious youth. They dabbled in philosophy, but tended to evade such basic questions as the nature of the good. In spite of their rejection of traditional morality, they claimed also to teach virtue and justice, often finding it convenient to identify these terms with vague popular conceptions and attitudes. Thus Protagoras tells the youthful Hippocrates that he will make him a better man day by day,[29] and claims to be able to shift the attitudes of a whole community into a sounder condition.[30] Gorgias also, while having no careful analysis of these notions to offer, admits, when pressed, that in addition to the art of rhetoric, he also teaches his disciples how to use this power well.[31] Protagoras is even prepared to recognize the crucial importance of traditional education in binding a given community together,[32] though this process may often go astray and require improvement from experts like himself.

But this acceptance of traditional norms was utterly inconsistent with the relativism which lay at the heart of the whole Sophistic trend. Hence it is no wonder that a search began for stable natural norms. But as we have pointed out, the prevailing conception of nature justified no norm of this sort, save that of physical power. Nature is automatic and happens of itself. Hence the natural good of man requires no philosophic study and clarification. We do not have to learn about it. Such supposed education is a waste of time. The natural good is an inborn tendency in every individual to assert himself without limit. This tendency is only diluted and distorted by philosophical ideas.

The task of education is rather to strip all such conventional strappings away, to let this tendency go on of itself, and then to place in its hands the necessary technical means. Hence the later Sophists also taught literature, grammar, rhetoric and other arts, but now as pure instruments of power. Education has no intrinsic value whatsoever. It is well for a young man to know something of the history and literature of his own culture, and something of his own language and the art of

[29] *Protag.*, 318 A.
[30] *Theaet.*, 167 A–C.
[31] *Gorgias*, 460 A.
[32] *Protag.*, 324 ff.

debate, in order to talk persuasively to his contemporaries, and to get on in the world. These subjects of the curriculum have no value of their own. They are sheer instruments of power. Hence as Callicles points out,[33] the time devoted to them should be strictly limited.

It is all right for a child or a youth to train his intelligence by arguing over philosophic problems. But it is disgraceful for a mature man to waste his valuable time over such matters. The real business of life is proceeding on the battle field and in the market place. This is where men gain the real power to satisfy their desires, and where they actually satisfy them too. Education is a subordinate means of power. Hence the later Roman saying which stems from the *Gorgias: Philosophari sed paucis;* let us philosophize yes, but not too much! Here is the Sophistic view of education.

3. SOCRATES AND PLATO

Socrates was held by the general public to be a Sophist, and indeed he had much in common with these fifth-century teachers. But in spite of the fact that he produced no written treatises, he was a most original thinker who radically changed the whole direction of the Sophistic movement, and laid the foundations for a new way of thought which dominated European philosophy for two millennia and still survives in our own day. In his study of past thinkers, particularly Anaxagoras, and in his discourses with great fifth-century teachers like Protagoras, Gorgias, Hippias and Prodicus, and finally in his conversations with young men and citizens in the streets of Athens, he worked out a novel view of man and of the universe which broke sharply with Sophistic opinion.

This view is clearly indicated in the early dialogues of Plato, which were written to keep alive the Socratic spirit, and to some extent in the middle dialogues where Plato begins to introduce new developments of his own. It is, of course, a difficult problem in all the dialogues to separate out what is truly Socratic from what is Platonic. But by using information gained from other sources, particularly Xenophon and Aristotle, it is now possible to do this with some degree of probability. On the whole, the tendency of recent research is to take more

[33] *Gorgias,* 485.

seriously Plato's own statements that he gained the basic insights of his philosophy from his master, and to trust the *essential*, historical accuracy of the picture of Socrates which is presented in the early and even in the middle dialogues. In this section, we shall try to summarize the new Socratic view of man and nature, and to suggest the chief respects in which Plato developed this view.

(i) *Man and Nature*

Aristotle tells us that Socrates made two basic contributions to rational methodology, inductive arguments and universal definition.[34] This is clear to readers of the dialogues who follow Socrates in his constant attempt to focus the essence of some natural object or virtue. After examining one particular instance, he will set up a provisional definition which is then refined and clarified by successive examinations of different instances. The result will be some universal structure of properties which is always present in every instance, and constitutes the essence or *ti esti* (what it is) of the object in question.

Since he was able to focus certain stable structures of this sort, especially in the fields of ethics and mathematics, he was also able to formulate a cogent answer to that flux philosophy which underlay the subjectivism and relativism of Protagoras. In spite of the constant change which pervades the whole of nature, it is possible for the human mind to apprehend and to clearly distinguish certain fixed natures which remain stable in the flux and are present in innumerable examples. The world is something more than the confused transition which is revealed by sense; it has a changeless structure which makes each thing *what it is* irrespective of whether it is known or not. This stable, independent structure is grasped not by sense but by reason, and can be formulated in intelligible universal definitions.

While these natures are independent of human sensation and desire, they are not independent of one another. Thus life on the earth depends upon the sun, and the virtues of courage and temperance depend upon wisdom. This enabled Socrates to see that nature is not an accidental chaos, as the previous Sophists had thought, but is rather an ordered array of interacting agencies which on the whole support one another. Thus

[34] *Metaphysics*, 1078 b, 28.

each part of the human organism serves the others and benefits the whole. Many examples of this are given in the Socratic discourses reported by Xenophon.[35] Thus the light required for seeing is sent by the sun and the moon (*Mem.*, 4, 3, 3). The eyelids do not merely happen to grow before the eyes. They serve as a protection during sleep, the eyelashes while we are awake. The eyebrows intercept the sweat that rolls down from our foreheads.[36] This emphasis upon natural order is borne out by Plato's early dialogues. Thus Socrates in the *Phaedo* speaks of the deep impression made upon him by Anaxagoras' doctrine that the cosmos is governed by mind, and of his conviction that even though our knowledge may not often grasp it, everything really is ordered for the best.[37]

Of all visible beings, man alone possesses this faculty of rational insight, weak though it is. Hence Socrates was led to a new view of the soul, and a radically novel theory of human nature as a whole. Man is not a cosmic accident, but a culminating phase of the whole natural order with a peculiar and important function to perform. He alone can bring nature into the light of understanding, and consciously direct his life and activities into voluntary harmony with this order. This explains the intense passion with which Socrates urged upon himself and his contemporaries, wherever he met them and at every situation, even as an old man at the time of his trial, the supreme importance of not sinking down to the level of dumb creatures, but of tending those precious souls which they alone possess, in order to perform the unique and essential function for which they were brought into existence. Such souls are not found among the other beings of nature. Nevertheless they must have their ground in something outside. Thus Xenophon tells us that Socrates held that just as our bodies are composed of the same matter which is found throughout the universe, so must our human reason be part of a universal cosmic reason.[38]

Plato, the pre-eminent disciple of Socrates, was deeply stirred by these ideas. Immediately after the execution of his master in 399 B.C. he wrote those early dialogues in which he reported the acts and sayings of Socrates as accurately as he

[35] Xenophon, *Memorabilia*, 4, 3, 3.
[36] *Mem.*, 1, 4, 5 ff.
[37] Plato, *Phaedo*, 97 C.
[38] *Mem.*, 1, 4, 8.

could, in order to undo the work of the hemlock so far as this was possible. But afterwards, when more mature, in his middle and late dialogues, he began to expand and develop these Socratic ideas in his own way. Socrates had simply said that the forms were in the individual changing instances which we sense. But Plato began to reflect more seriously on what this relation was, and what this 'in' could mean.

Many possibilities occurred to him, and he experimented with the idea that the forms existed in a separate realm of their own, of which our material world was a copy. He pondered the natural order which Socrates had brought to light, and analysed it into an indeterminate factor (*apeiron*), a limit (*peras*), and an active cause (*aition*) bringing the two together.[39] He focused many further examples of it, especially in the life of man, and worked out its ethical implications in far richer detail. He also considered many problems connected with the origin of this order, and in his *Timaeus* sketched out a semi-mythical account of how the world may have come into being. In the *Philebus*, he developed the Socratic notion that human reason must have its source in an external and independent reason of the whole world. He owed the basic insights which lay at the root of his thought to Socrates. But at the end of his life, he had immeasurably deepened and enriched these insights, and had applied them to many further fields to which we must now turn.

(ii) *Man and Society*

Socrates was radically opposed to the moral and social relativism of Protagoras and the Sophists. Xenophon reports a conversation with Hippias which brings this opposition into a sharp light[40]. Hippias here denies any universal validity to traditional laws, and any value to legal conformity, because of the constant variation of such laws even within a single community. Socrates answers this by referring to the universal value (or utility) of legal conformity, not only for the community as a whole, but for each individual as well. Without such conformity to law and custom, the city would dissolve. His training in logic and induction has enabled him to discern basic similarities underlying the more striking

[39] Plato, *Philebus*, 23 D ff.
[40] *Mem.*, 4, 4, 14 ff.

differences which are found in various instances. Thus the laws of different communities may be strikingly different, and even those of the same community at different times. But whatever the specific content may be, there is always law of some kind, and conformity to law. This is a necessity of nature.

As this passage strongly indicates, he had a profound feeling for the many benefits conferred on man by social life. Hence he differed sharply with the Sophistic view that men once lived dispersed without the bonds of society. This is sheer fantasy, for the human individual is too weak, especially in infancy, to live alone by himself. Family life at least is required for mere survival, and the family is a society, indeed the root of all society. Hence man is social by nature. He needs society not only to survive, but also to satisfy many other basic needs of his nature. Hence Socrates rejects the Sophistic view, expressed by Glaucon in the *Republic*, that social life and the restraints it imposes are a necessary evil. The end of man is not to realize his sensuous appetites to an unlimited degree. In fact, to seek anything without limit is always a sign of ignorance which must lead to distortion and injury. Hence the social restraint of material desires is not evil, but good, since only in this way is it possible to realize the higher and more important needs of human nature for art, knowledge, friendship, and religion. None of these is possible without co-operation.

Socrates fought in several major campaigns of the great War, and in his last years lived through the troubled times of the fall of Athens. We are told in the *Apology* how Critias, the uncle of Plato, and the other thirty tyrants tried to implicate him in their bloody tyranny by the command to apprehend Leon of Salamis.[41] He refused to do this at the risk of his life. With this history in mind, it is not difficult to understand how he became bitterly critical of the increasingly desperate and ruthless policy of the Athenian empire, and laid the foundations for a political philosophy radically opposed to that of Pericles, Protagoras, and the Athenian 'democracy'. To do injustice is far worse than suffering, for this corrupts not the body but the soul, which is the very core of the human person. Hence the tyrant is the most miserable of men, for his soul is full of disease.[42]

[41] *Apology*, 32 C.
[42] *Gorgias*, 479 D–E.

The genuine ruler is a shepherd of the people who knows how to make them happy.[43] He is not guided by his own whims and lusts but rather by his knowledge of the immutable laws of nature which bind him to act for the common good, irrespective of the desires of the people. To fulfil these obligations is an onerous task. Hence cities will never be relieved of their misery until they are ruled by philosophers who have no wish to rule.[44] Ruling is an art which requires knowledge to be exercised effectively. Hence Socrates was sarcastic about the 'democratic' custom of choosing magistrates by lot, and used to ask what would happen if navigators and architects were selected in this way? Some of those who listened to him, like Critias, doubtless interpreted such remarks as a praise of Spartan autocracy. But this was a mistake. The Socratic ideal is not the rule of one man, one class, or the people as a whole, but rather the rule of reason and the law of nature for the common good of all.

Plato took over all these ideas, and in his *Republic* and *Laws* expressed them with clarity, and developed them with a great richness of detail. One result that is made very explicit in the *Republic* is a new view of the human community, which the sophists had regarded as merely a number of people bound together by an instinctive urge for safety, ties of blood, and geographic propinquity. The human community may originate in agglomerations and herds of this kind. But the true community is quite different. Its unity is based upon a rationally articulated constitution (*politeia*) rather than upon blood and soil. The complex nature of the common good to be achieved by co-operative action must be present before the minds of the guardians in charge of the common life. It must be held at least by right opinion in the minds of all the citizens and loved by them. Without such understanding the city must decline into anarchy and tyranny. Hence education in truth and goodness is the very heart of sound community life, and in any soundly organized community, the school will be the central institution on which its major energies are expended.

This new social philosophy was expounded by Plato in the school that he founded, the *Academy*, in his *Republic*, and later in the *Laws*. It is radically opposed both to German

[43] *Mem.*, 3, 2, 4.
[44] *Rep.*, 346 E–347.

totalitarianism and to Anglo-Saxon individualism which have dominated modern political theory. Indeed for modern thought in general, strongly influenced by what Plato once called sophistry, it is a new and strange conception, whose foundations and implications have never been clearly focused. It is to be hoped that it may be revived again in our contemporary world, for it may be able to offer us interesting solutions to problems that now press on us for solution.

(iii) *The Divine*

It is very clear from the evidence of Plato as well as that of Xenophon, that in opposition to sophistic agnosticism and atheism, Socrates was an intensely religious man. Indeed, his new discovery of rational intelligence and natural order led him implacably to a recognition of the Divine. The existence of a cosmic order requires a cosmic ordering agency, certainly higher than man. As the *Phaedo* indicates,[45] he was probably led to see the force of this type of argument from his acquaintance with Anaxagoras and his disciple Archelaus. We have already referred to his inference, reported by Xenophon, that the reasoning agency in man, since it could not have come from nothing, must have an external and similar cause. A third type of argument was based on his own experience of the inner warning voice which he speaks of in the *Apology*[46] as something luminous and divine, and the source of which, according to Xenophon,[47] was the Divinity Himself (*ho theos*).

That Socrates was given to the practice of prayer and meditation is evidenced by the account of a long trance before the battle of Potidaea,[48] confirmed by his description of the ecstasy of love,[49] and of the divine madness in the *Phaedrus*.[50] As A. E. Taylor has argued, there is no reason to believe that these passages are not truly Socratic.[51] God is sometimes referred to in the plural and sometimes in the singular, both in Xenophon and Plato. One passage in the former[52] distinguishes between many intermediate divine agencies or gods, and the

[45] 97 C.
[46] *Apology*, 31 D.
[47] *Mem.*, 4, 8, 6.
[48] *Symposium*, 220 B.
[49] *Ibid.*, 211.
[50] *Phaedrus*, 250.
[51] *Socrates*, pp. 45 ff.
[52] *Mem.*, 4, 3, 13.

one supreme God who orders the whole world and holds it together. This is probably the Socratic view. God Himself is eternal and watches over the affairs of man to the last detail. Like the human soul, God is invisible, but becomes evident in His effects. Rationality and care for men are the chief attributes of the Divinity.[53]

All of these religious ideas are found in Plato, together with further elaborations and developments. Thus in addition to the Socratic inferences, Plato adds his elaborate argument from physical motion to a self-moving cause in the tenth book of the *Laws*. He is rational and watches over the affairs of men.[54] In fact He sustains the whole cosmic order.[55] In the second Book of the *Republic*, it is also argued that He is perfect, the author only of good, changeless, and incapable of deception.[56] He is the model for human action, and we should try to approximate these divine attributes so far as this is possible for a mortal changing being. Hence Plato often summarizes his ethics by the pithy formula-likeness to God (*homoiosis theo*).[57] In conscious opposition to Protagoras and common Sophistic teaching, he roundly asserts in *Laws* 716: 'not man but God is the measure of all things.'

(iv) *Evolution and Human History*

We have no reason for attributing any of the views expressed in Plato's dialogues concerning history to Socrates. Indeed it is likely that his intensely practical and systematic interest in ethics led him away from historical studies and speculations concerning the philosophy of history. Plato, however, certainly did engage in such studies, and his interest in history increased towards the end of his life. He rejected both the traditional theory of an inevitable decline from the time of the golden age, and the Sophistic theory of constant technological advance and progress. The art of life, for which Socrates was seeking, cannot be identified with any subordinate technology, nor with all of them put together. He felt that the development of such a philosophic way of life in ordinary corrupted cities, like the Athens of his own day, was almost

[53] *Mem.*, 1, 4, 17.
[54] *Laws*, 900–901.
[55] *Laws*, 715 E–716.
[56] *Rep.*, 379–383.
[57] *Theaet.*, 176 B 1–2; *Rep.*, 501 A–C; and *Laws*, 716 C.

impossible because of provincial prejudices preserved and intensified by a debased system of education.

But the gods are constantly concerned with the affairs of men. Hence they grant special aid to certain exceptional individuals, like Socrates, who spring up from time to time, and by a certain divine destiny (*theia moira*) may be able to stem the tide of social decay by their luminous and vital influence on others.[58] The reception and development of such influences, however, never happens inevitably. It requires the arduous exercise of rational faculties and sacrificial devotion which are subject to free choice. Hence, God, the orderer of all, is like a helmsman who has to take account of opposing forces, and to steer a narrow and intricate course.[59] In the myth of the *Statesman*, it is asserted that God sometimes turns over this guiding function to lesser Deities.[60] Then *hubris* and lethargy are apt to increase, and things in general fall into disorder until the Supreme Shepherd again takes the helm. In the light of this and other passages, there is no doubt that Plato held a cyclical view of history. Throughout the ages and aeons of past time, periods of order and progress had been followed by those of corruption ending in vast natural cataclysms and floods, after which a cycle of advance would begin once more.

At the end of his life, Plato planned a great world history beginning with the formation of the whole universe (*Timaeus*), an account of the earliest pre-history of man, begun in the *Critias* but never completed, later recorded history summarized in the third Book of the *Laws*, and the description of a sounder and better but still possible human society to be founded in the future, which is presented in the rest of the *Laws*. Whether Plato held that an ultimate cyclic destruction in the future was inevitable, or whether he believed that, with Divine aid, human intelligence and devotion might be capable of setting up a sound and lasting society on the earth is uncertain. But the *Laws* ends on a hopeful note.

(v) *The Human Individual*

The pre-Socratic philosophers had made no sharp distinction between soul and body. Life and consciousness were thought to

[58] *Rep.*, 496 B ff.

[59] *Statesman*, 271 ff.

[60] 271 D.

be active manifestations of physical parts. The atomists held that soul consisted of finer material atoms, and Heraclitus had identified soul with fire. Simmias, as a Pythagorean, argues in the *Phaedo* that it is an equilibrium or harmony of the physical elements in the body, resulting from their arrangement and entirely dependent upon them. Anaxagoras had boldly asserted that mind was something unmixed with matter and capable of independent purposive action. But he failed to sustain this position, and finally identified the causes of human action with 'air and ether and water' leaving no real place for mind.[61]

We have noted how this physicalist view was taken over by Protagoras who stated that soul is nothing besides sensation. For Homer, the soul is a sort of ghost which attends the living body like a shadow. It may survive death, but then lacks all awareness which is located in the body. The soul plays a more important role in the Orphic religion where it is regarded as a superhuman and even super-personal agency which enters the mind in sleep and mystic ecstasy, but is divorced from the real personality of waking life.[62]

Socrates introduced a novel conception of the soul quite distinct from all these preceding theories, which has exercised an important influence on the western view of man ever since. The soul is neither an arrangement of atoms (something pysical) nor a superpersonal agency endowed with super-human knowledge and capacities. It is rather the primary guiding part of the human person, that by which he understands and consciously directs his life. Like God himself, this precious centre of human life is immaterial, invisible, and known only through its effects. This part of man can oppose and govern the body.[63] It retains its identity throughout physical change, and even survives the complete disintegration of the body at death. The corruptions of ignorance and vice, which affect this naturally ruling part of the soul, are far worse than any diseases of the body, for they result in a misdirected life in which every good thing is misused and becomes evil. Hence as Socrates constantly asserted, the chief obligation of every man is first of all to tend his own soul, and then so far as this is possible, to help others in tending theirs.

[61] *Cf. Phaedo*, 98 B ff.
[62] *Cf.* A. E. Taylor, *Socrates*, pp. 143–6.
[63] Xenophon, *Mem.*, 4, 3, 14.

This new view of the human soul gave rise to two results which have played an important role in western thought ever since, one a problem, the other a cultural attitude. The human individual as such is more than an organized body, extended in space. He is a compound of such a body, together with a knowing, planning agency. This agency can unite with the stable forms of things as they really are, and can direct its activities in the light of such knowledge, which no physical thing can do Hence man is a union of physical body with non-physical soul. How can two such diverse elements be united in one single being? This mind-body problem, as it has been called, has played an important role in Western thought ever since the time of Socrates.

Knowledge of things as they really are is the most precious gift of nature to man. Without this, he is the most defenceless of animals, and could not even have survived. All the arts and techniques on which civilization is based, depend upon such knowledge. In fact, it is through knowledge alone that man has any access to other values, for we cannot even strive to a good that we do not know. Hence the greatest force and power is useless to us and becomes harmful if we do not know how to use it. Now the individual human person is physically weak and his life very short. But he alone has a soul. He alone can provide the precious jewels of knowledge which alone guide human life and social effort towards what is really good. This is the source of that respect for the physically insignificant and short-lived individual which has been an important strand in western life down to the present day, when it is once again being threatened by powerful movements of materialistic thought.

If the individual is only a complex set of physico-chemical processes, the organized community of which he is only a part is much larger, stronger, and permanent. Therefore it is far more worthy of respect. The consistent materialist, therefore, must always subordinate the individual person and his acts to the state. What is one stomach to a hundred million stomachs? Hence he must be adjusted to the interests of the whole. His so-called freedom is an insignificant, anarchic factor. But for the follower of Socrates, these opinions are false, because they fail to take any account of the immaterial nature of knowledge—which can be attained by the individual mind alone, with the help of other minds functioning freely and individually. Without freedom, or the ability to follow the argument wherever it may lead, the individual mind cannot function, and the truth cannot be gained.

Plato took over these basic insights from Socrates, but analysed them more deeply and extended them much further. He went beyond Socrates in asserting that the stable forms of natural entities such as man, horse, tree, etc., and of virtues such as temperance and justice, exist apart from changing things in a world of their own where they are eternal and immutable. The soul can know these separated forms, and unite with them in knowing. This, he thought, strengthened the case for immortality. The more we can know, the more immortal we are. In addition to this pure abstract knowledge which the soul achieves by herself alone, she has access to other subordinate modes of knowing by using the bodily organs of sense. By this means she can gain some relative information about concrete changing things.[64] Each mode of knowing determines a distinct mode of desire.

In the fourth book of the *Republic* and in the myth of the *Phaedrus*, Plato distinguishes three such levels of knowledge and desire.[65] First, there is the pure knowledge of the forms as they are in themselves, which guides the loftiest mode of aspiration towards intelligible objects, the love, or *eros*, symbolized by the wings in the myth of the charioteer. Second, there is the spirited element (*thumos*) by which we estimate the long range welfare of the organism and feel anger and shame. This faculty of the soul acts in harmony with reason, when it is functioning properly, to control the urges of immediate desire. This third factor (*epithumia*) includes the manifold objects of sensory apprehension, and the immediate appetites called forth by them. When reason and love fall into lethargy, this insatiable part of the soul assumes a control of the whole of life which it is not fit to exercise, and leads the soul into anarchy and finally into the tyranny of fixed obsessions. In addition to these faculties, Plato also recognizes that of fantasy[66] which paints pictures in the mind, and which can fall under the domination either of reason, or of sense, with fateful consequences for the person.

Plato denied that sensation was knowledge, which he held

[64] *Theaet.*, 159–60.

[65] *Rep.*, 437–441; *Phaedrus*, 246 ff.

[66] *Philebus*, 39.

to be a purely immaterial mode of apprehension entirely independent of the body, though he admitted that sensations might remind the soul of some intelligible object, and thus occasion it to know some pure form. His solution of the mind-body problem, therefore, took a sharply dualistic form. The soul is in the body as a sailor is in a ship. It entered at a certain time. While it is on board, it can act independently and use the body as an instrument. When the voyage is over, it may leave for good. If it exercises its own functions properly, it may manoeuvre the ship in such a way as to further its own purposes, and to take it where it needs to go. But if it becomes confused or lazy, it may be lost at sea and thus become imprisoned. When this happens, as it often does, the fault lies not with the ship but rather with the steersman. The body is a subordinate instrument, not really a part of the whole human soul, which may be grievously misused, but is not bad in itself.

Since the soul has its own integrity, and so to speak lives its own autonomous and, for Plato, eternal life, it can enter into other bodies, as a pilot can steer many ships. Hence Plato adopted the eastern theory of reincarnation. Each soul is free to choose its own mode of life, but once the choice has been made, it must suffer the inexorable consequences. Thus a lazy soul will be punished by ignorance which will lead it into further wrong choices. Such an evil life will be punished by being born again into a lower form of human life and ultimately into a type of animal. On the other hand, souls which exercise their higher faculties and live wisely, will be reborn at higher levels, until eventually they are freed from the wheel of bodily life, 'and live henceforth without the body in mansions fairer still which may not be described.'[67]

(vi) *The Human Ideal and its Achievement*

Socrates' analysis of human reason as a power quite distinct from sense, which was able to unite immaterially with the stable formal structure of things as they are in themselves, enabled him not only to lay the foundations for science, but for a new kind of ethics as well. Each distinct mode of being has an invariable nature which determines its basic tendencies.[68] This

[67] *Phaedo*, 114 C.

[68] *Cf. Phaedo*, 75; *Tim.*, 72 B.; *Statesman*, 264 A, *Cratylus*, 339 C. 6–7; *Laws*, 927 B. 3. For a general discussion of the basic concepts of Plato's ethics, *cf.* Wild, *Plato's Modern Enemies and the Theory of Natural Law.* (Univ. of Chicago Press, 1953), Ch. V.

nature is accessible to inductive investigation, and can be expressed in a universal definition. From such knowledge, even though it be incomplete, we can also gain some understanding of the modes of action required to realize the nature. External influences which aid these tendencies are good for the entity; those that frustrate them are bad. Some knowledge of human nature and its essential tendencies can be attained. On the basis of this, we may formulate certain rules of action which must be followed if a genuinely human life is to be lived. Acts which agree with such rules (founded on the nature of man) are virtuous. They lead to the human good. Acts which disagree with these rules are vicious. They lead to frustration and destruction.

If this is true, scientific knowledge of the structure of a thing will enable us to understand its tendencies, how it acts in response to external influences, and how to control this action for our own purposes. This part of the Socratic thesis has now been verified in many fields. Modern engineering is based upon the theoretical sciences of physics and chemistry; modern medicine upon anatomy and physiology. But Socrates went even further. If this is true of the subordinate arts, it should be true of the master art of human living as well. A sound knowledge of human nature and its tendencies should shed light on the natural end of man, and what we ought to do to realize this end. This basic insight into the union of theory and practice was expressed in the famous formula *virtue is knowledge*, which lies at the heart of Socratic ethics. It is only through accurate, stable knowledge of the nature of things and especially of himself that man may attain the human good.

Plato deepened and developed this Socratic insight. He analysed human nature into three distinct aspects, each with a poetic and a dependent desiderative part: first, aspiration (now called *will*), which is guided by rational insight; second, *thumos* or spirit, guided by imaginative hope and fear; and third, desire (*epithumia*), which is guided by sense and short-range imagination.[69] Each individual is subject to a multitude of desires for sensory objects so that this third factor is by far the most variegated and impressive. Reason is of course invisible and intangible, but by far the most far-reaching and accurate of our apprehensive faculties. It can understand not

[69] *Rep.*, 581–7.

only itself and other invisible structures, but also the lower faculties of the soul and their objects. Hence it alone is fit to guide life to its natural end.

On the basis of this analysis, Plato worked out a penetrating theory of the four cardinal virtues as they are still called.[70] The sound guidance of human life certainly requires a knowledge of human nature. But man is dependent upon a multitude of external entities and upon the world order in general. Hence a sound understanding of this world order is also required. Such knowledge of course cannot be attained by sense and imagination alone whose horizons are very limited. Only reason has access to it, and to achieve any worthwhile knowledge demands arduous concentration and discipline. Those few who possess the requisite intelligence, and who are able to stand the prolonged strain, may gain some measure of that basic wisdom which underlies the other virtues. Courage resides primarily in that spirited element of the soul by which we feel shame and anger. It enables us to persist in our endeavours in the face of obstacles that can be overcome and lesser fears that should be withstood. But the man who rushes blindly into insuperable obstacles is not courageous but foolhardy, and he who fears nothing is a fool. Hence courage must be governed by a sound knowledge of what is and what is not truly fearful.

To act justly is to render to each thing and to each person, including ourselves, what is due to it by nature.[71] Thus it is unjust to treat an animal as a thing, or a human person as a brute animal, or a child as an adult. It is also unjust to devote one's major energies to something really trivial, or to dismiss what is of major importance with a wave of the hand. To act in this way, of course, requires a knowledge of the nature of each kind of being, and the hierarchical order of importance into which they fall. Justice is to reflect this order in our words and deeds. In the case of our own major faculties, it means that our voluntary aspirations (*eros*) will be guided by the insights of reason, that these will govern our feelings of anger and shame, and finally that reason and spirit together will impose discipline and order on the multitude of material appetites, allowing those that are necessary for the maintenance of life to be expressed in moderation, and doing away with the rest.

[70] *Cf.* especially *Rep.* IV and *Gorgias* 504.
[71] *Cf. Rep.*, 433 A.

Justice is the rule of the lower by the higher. Temperance is the agreement of the lower to this rule. The well-tempered soul is able to moderate its fits of rage, and to give up soothing and beloved objects when reason so requires. But such a soul does not attempt to wipe out all passion or to scorn the body as evil. The body is a necessary instrument for the living of life on the earth, and its *necessary needs*[72] deserve to be satisfied. The passions and appetites of the intemperate soul are constantly rebelling against the higher parts. If this rebellion is not corrected, the whole human life will first fall under the domination of unjustified passion and then of organized desire. Without the guidance of knowledge, however, each of these life patterns is unstable.[73] When the oligarchic pattern breaks down, the soul dissolves into a chaos of appetites, passions and aspirations where all are on a level, and no one is subordinate to any other. This chaotic condition of the democratic soul as Plato calls it, is maximally unstable. Disorder cannot last. It is bound to fall prey to some irrational obsession which comes to tyrannize over the whole of life, reducing it to the lowest stage of human misery, especially if given wealth and external means of realization. Virtue is the persuasive rule of reason which establishes a natural order in which each part receives its due. Vice is the inversion of this natural order.[74]

Plato also made a similar analysis of human technology (*technê*), where an analogous order is found.[75] In the living of life, man acts on himself; in technology on some object to give it an instrumental value. Here again genuine success will always depend upon knowledge. The artisan must first know something of the function which the finished instrument is designed to perform, and the general structure which will enable it to act in this way. By his operational technique, he must then be able to impose this general pattern on the indeterminate material before him. If his knowledge becomes unclear, he may be able to produce something which will please an uncritical agent, but which will no longer do the work, as a quack doctor may please and impress a patient by the elaborate show of technique without actually curing him. Plato held that many of the higher arts of his own time were affected by this disease of

[72] *Rep.*, 558 E–560.
[73] *Rep.*, Book VIII.
[74] *Rep.*, 444 C. ff.
[75] *Cf.* especially Gorgias, 463–6 and 501–2.

subjectivism which he called flattery (*kolakeia*), and gave a revealing analysis of it in the *Gorgias*. Such false or inverted art, instead of dominating its matter, leaves it essentially as it was before, and is really dominated by it.

Plato worked out an elaborate classification of the different arts which are required for the adequate living of human life,[76] and analysed the hierarchical order into which they naturally fall.[77] First come the basic techniques of possession which give us access to raw materials, and then the making arts which form them into useful instruments. The highest arts are those of therapy which care for the different powers of human nature, and help them to function in accordance with nature. First comes medicine, which is concerned with the body, then politics which attempts to maintain peace, freedom, and justice in the community, and finally the crucial art of education whose function is to train the cognitive faculties, and to keep knowledge alive in oncoming generations.

At the very top, are the pure sciences and philosophy which are devoted to the acquisition of knowledge, that pure insight which is required for the guidance of the whole enterprise. But these highest cognitive arts are very difficult, and subject to many mistakes and diseases. When they break down, lower arts like politics, production, and even military conquest try to exercise that ruling function which by nature they are unable to perform. Such technological diseases are correlated with basic inversions in the order of community life.

As we have pointed out, Plato held that the human community is not a substance with a life of its own, but rather a common life of its individual members.[78] The structure of this common life is, therefore, analogous to that of individual existence.[79] If it is to be sound, it must first of all be guided by a view of the world and a social plan that is coherent and true, provided by those who exercise the legislative function. In order to achieve social stability, this plan must be administered by those who are able to call forth sustained action in the facing of external and internal obstacles, and who corre-

[76] *Cf. Statesman*, 258 D. and *Sophist*, 219 A. ff.

[77] *Cf. Euthydemus*, 280 C.–281 C.; 290; and *Gorgias*, 517–20. For a fuller discussion of Plato's theory of *technê* see Wild, *Plato's Theory of Man* (Harvard Press, 1946), Ch. II.

[78] *Rep.*, 544 D.–E.

[79] *Cf. Rep.*, VIII.

spond to the spirited element in the individual. To achieve social justice every internal and external factor must be properly judged for what it is and given its due. The natural needs of every member must be satisfied by a common allotment of natural functions. From each according to his ability; to each according to his natural need.

Finally to achieve social harmony, all members must have some understanding of the purpose of community life, at least at the level of opinion. This alone will elicit voluntary devotion, and avoid internal conflict and rebellion. Hence ignorance and confusion concerning the common good is the most dreadful disease which can affect social life. When reason and education fail, the ruling function must be taken over by irrational bureaucrats, by oligarchs, then by a planless mob thinking only of its momentary desires, and finally by a despot who subordinates all to his fixed obsessions.[80] Sound order can be achieved not by the rule of any one party, one class, or one man, but only by the rule of reason in accordance with nature for the common good. There is one means alone that can approximate this goal. This means is education.

(vii) *Education*

If virtue is knowledge, then in some sense it can be taught. Socrates himself arrived at this conclusion, and devoted his individual energies to the task of stirring up the minds of his fellow citizens and leading them towards the truth. But this task, of course, transcends the powers of a single individual. In the end, he was sentenced and put to death by the Athenians. Plato's *Republic* is an attempt to describe a sound and rational community in which a man like Socrates could feel at home. In such a community education must be the central institution. Three whole books of the *Republic* (II, III and VII) and many further pages are devoted to this basic topic. Even in a sick society like his own, Plato felt that the only hope for betterment lay in the establishment of small circles and schools where sound ideas might be formulated, and healthy attitudes encouraged and strengthened by a common life. Hence at the age of forty, he abandoned his earlier plan for a political career and founded his academy, where he devoted the major part of his remaining life, as he puts it in the *Gorgias*, 'whispering

[80] *Rep.*, 565 B–580.

in a corner with three or four admiring boys.'[81] This is how it must have appeared to his friends and relatives who had been influenced by Sophistic theories.

But according to Plato, the human good is neither an unstable invention nor something automatic that will happen of itself. It is an ordered pattern of life whose changeless nature may be understood. The aim of education, therefore, is not merely to teach useful techniques but rather to elicit in the mind of the student a firm grasp of the good, and in his whole soul a sacrificial devotion to this end. The ideal scheme is worked out in the *Republic*.

The child cannot understand abstract argument. He is a creature of sense and imagination. Hence he must be surrounded with beautiful and harmonious objects which are visible embodiments of the pure forms he will later be able to apprehend by reason.[82] He must be told tales and stories which exemplify sound principles. In this way he will be led to form right opinions about important issues and intense moral attitudes before he can understand the reasons for them. During this early admonitory stage, to the age of eighteen or twenty, the role of the teacher is more active, that of the pupil more passive. He is taught the rudimentary disciplines and given a mastery of the tools for rational knowledge. Great pains must be taken to make the task an agreeable one, for no one can be expected to become proficient in any activity which seems painful and boring to him.[83]

At the age of twenty, he is ready for the pure scientific disciplines such as mathematics, physics, and astronomy.[84] Now his mind can be freed from the shackles which bind it to the confused and concrete images of sense. It is no longer limited to a particular triangle which can be seen, but is able to grasp the universal triangle, and to demonstrate theorems which apply to *any* given example. Penetrating to these formal structures, it can gain an understanding of the real causes of things. In many regions, right opinion is now replaced by rational insight into what is universally true, which not only believes the truth but can give the reasons why. But the special sciences simply assume their

[81] *Gorgias*, 485 D.
[82] *Rep.*, III, 401–3.
[83] *Rep.*, VII, 536 E–537 A.
[84] *Rep.*, VII, 522 C–531.

basic concepts and principles without critical examination.

These can be clarified and explained by the discipline of dialectic or philosophy, for which the ideal student of the *Republic* is ready at the age of thirty.[85] This discipline is able to achieve some understanding of the first source of all being which is goodness itself, and to see all time and existence in the light of this necessary first principle. The objects of the restricted sciences are now seen to fall into an all embracing pattern. Their basic concepts and principles are no longer passively accepted without criticism as in a dream.[86]

They are brought into relation with one another and explained in terms of what is more ultimate. The complex nature of man can now be clarified and the order of life which is required for its realization. Guided by such philosophic knowledge, the student of the *Republic* is now ready, at thirty-five years of age, to function as an administrator in the actual community, and to deal with living problems. At fifty, he is allowed to retire from this form of service, in order to engage in meditation and prayer, that pure contemplation of truth, and especially of the good itself which alone can satisfy our human aspiration.[87] But even this is only a beginning. A single human life is insufficient for the education of the human soul. When she leaves the body and all earthly things, however, the soul takes her training (*paideia*) with her.[88] If she has devoted her full energies to learning all that is possible in this life, she may die with good hope for further advances in the life to come.

Plato's reflections culminate in a complete philosophy of human culture, including the arts and techniques, the order of the human community, and the life of the immortal, individual soul. This is summarily expressed in the *Republic*, and in a more practical form in his last dialogue, the *Laws*. Rational wisdom is its very heart and core. This is the Greek view of man *par excellence*. Plato worked in his academy to train young men in pure science and philosophy so that they might then return to their cities and work for the reformation of Greek society. Many of his students, including Dion of Syracuse, did work in this way. But their attempts all failed. The Romans

[85] *Rep.*, VII, 531–537.
[86] 533 B–C.
[87] *Rep.*, VII, 540 ff.
[88] *Phaedo*, 107 D.

set up their empire, and ancient civilization in the West died a prolonged and tragic death.

The rationalistic ideas of Socrates and Plato were eventually taken over by the special sciences and arts which have now been brought to a flourishing state. But at the higher political and social levels of culture they have never exerted an important effect. Here the relativistic and materialistic ideals of Protagoras and his fellow Sophists have reigned supreme. Education provides us with a partial exception to this generalization. Since the time of Plato, many colleges and universities in the West have been founded on the model of his academy, with the pursuit of pure theory as their basic aim, and with the important corollary that such theoretical training is relevant to the practical problems of human life. No western community as a whole, however, has ever taken this idea seriously. In class rooms and universities here and there, Platonic theories and even the Platonic ethics still maintain, as ideals, a noteworthy but precarious existence.

4. ARISTOTLE

Aristotle was born in 384 B.C. at Stagira in Thrace, and studied for almost twenty years, 367–347 B.C., in Plato's Academy. He had a penetrating disciplined mind, and was certainly the most brilliant of Plato's students. During these early years, he was basically sympathetic with Plato's thought, and wrote several eloquent dialogues defending the rational and moral ideals of the Academy. These were read in the ancient world, which knew him as a master of rhetorical style. When Plato died in the year 347 B.C., he left the Academy to pursue his own studies, and finally (about 343) became the tutor of Alexander the Great. In 335 B.C. he returned to Athens, and founded his own school, the Lyceum, where he lectured, and directed the research of his associates in many different fields during a twelve year period of amazingly fruitful activity. After the death of Alexander, 323 B.C., he was forced to leave Athens because of local anti-Macadonian feeling, and died the next year on the island of Chalcis.

Ever since this time, a lively controversy has raged concerning the relation of his mature thought to that of Plato. His attack on the separate existence of the forms, with which

Plato had experimented in a certain phase of his development, and which had been intensively developed and defended by several of his disciples, has led many to believe that Aristotle's thought is essentially opposed to that of his master. The most influential ancient and medieval tradition, however, is ranged on the other side, for it tended to harmonize the two. Thus Albertus Magnus refers to the two points of view as two modes of one and the same philosophy. The thinkers of the Renaissance, with some justification, associated Aristotle with the scholastic thought against which they were rebelling. Seeking some anchorage in the classic tradition, they rediscovered and reinterpreted Plato, finding in him, especially in the style of his exoteric writings, exactly what they desired, the counterfoil to scholasticism. This tendency was strengthened in the nineteenth century by the emphasis on epistemology, and the consequent importance attached to Aristotle's critique of the theory of ideas.

Recent studies, however, especially those of Werner Jaeger in his book on Aristotle,[89] have tended once again to moderate this extreme view. Striking differences in the two accounts of human knowledge cannot be minimized. But when one takes an overall view, one can also see basic similarities. We cannot ignore the fact that Aristotle was nurtured during his formative years in a definitely Platonic atmosphere, with which he was intensely sympathetic. He reached his own position gradually through a careful and searching criticism of the ideas of his master. But the *basic* notions are the same. The world had an orderly structure which exists independently of human opinion or desire. This structure can be known, at least in part, as it really is by the rational faculties of man. Such insight offers us the only sound guidance for human life to which we have natural access.

Many mythical images and extravagant enthusiasms have been shorn away. The style of those lecture notes for advanced students, now called *The Works* of Aristotle, is very exact and condensed. Socrates was the first thinker in the West to discover the most distinctive features of the human soul, and especially its amazing power to grasp by reason the changeless structure of things. Hence it is not surprising that both he and his disciple, Plato, sometimes went too far in exaggerating

[89] W. Jaeger, *Aristotle*, (Tr. Robinson, Oxford, Clarendon Press, 1934).

the independence of the soul and the powers of reason. Aristotle carefully purged the doctrine of such exaggerations.

He was essentially a critical thinker, acutely aware of the limitations of human reason. He also recognized that this faculty could not operate without the aid of sense.

He lacked the synthetic capacity of Plato who could compress his whole vision of the universe within the compass of a single dialogue like the *Republic*, or even within a few pages. He analyses philosophy into its distinct branches, and deals with each of them very thoroughly, one by one. In each branch, he is able to deepen and refine the thought he had received by new insights and new distinctions. But in spite of these differences, the basic pattern remains the same. This is true of the theory of man.

Aristotle is more acutely aware of the limits and weaknesses of human nature and human knowledge. It is a more earthy and realistic view, following far more closely the given facts of experience, and distrusting speculation. There are many further refinements and developments. But the basic insights are still maintained. The soul is clearly distinguished (though not separated) from the body. Reason is the highest cognitive power, capable of grasping the immobile structures of nature. This is Platonic rationalism, but now more clearly formulated, and more firmly grounded on empirical observation and analysis.

This being the case, we can be more brief in our account of the Aristotelian theory of man. We shall presuppose that the reader is already familiar with the general Platonic view we have considered in section III. In each division of our analysis, we shall concentrate on these further criticisms and additions which come from Aristotle, and refer only briefly to the general framework which we have already considered. Under topics like *Man and Society*, and *Education*, where Aristotle adds nothing essentially new, we shall briefly remind the reader of the Platonic doctrines which need to be supplied.

(i) *Man and Nature*

Plato had made no distinction between logic and philosophy. In knowledge, the human mind by itself receives real entities exactly as they are. Hence our mental operations exactly reflect the structure of being. Plato even names philosophy by the word *dialectic*, which primarily signified a logical method. The universal forms by which we think must, therefore, exist outside the mind, precisely as we have to think them. They are combined and separated in reality precisely as they are combined and separated in our thought. These essences form a hierarchy in which the more universal are more perfect. The participation of the less universal essences in them is a physical fact with which the sciences are concerned.

Individual things of the material world are composed of an alien matter (identified with space in the *Timaeus*) and a limit derived from the pure forms. They are often regarded as copies of the pure forms in a foreign medium, like distorted images on a wind-rippled pool. When one form is replaced by another, there is change, which is thus reduced to succession. It is terminated by the acquisition of a different form. Physical entities do not exert causal efficacy. They simply pass on motion they have received. Souls, however, can move both themselves and others. They can be directly grasped by the human mind. Hence the Platonic literature is filled with imaginative speculations concerning the world-soul, demonic agencies higher than man, and the *demiourgos* who imposed form on the passive receptacle, and thus brought the world into being.

In Aristotle, the picture is altered in several important respects. The most significant advance is a far more detailed analysis of the process of human knowledge, from which there arises a profound sense of its limitations. Logic is sharply distinguished from first philosophy (ontology) and the sciences of nature.[90] The structure of an individual existent is immersed in matter, and hence unintelligible.[91] It must be first separated or abstracted from this individual matter before it can be understood. Our intelligence, therefore, is not wholly passive. It *acts on* the confused object of sense in order to construct its understanding of things.[92]

These things are understood by universal concepts in the mind, which are logically related in various ways. Each concept

[90] Logic is dealt with in separate treatises, the *Categories*, *On Interpretation*, *Prior* and *Posterior Analytics*. It is neither a theoretical nor a practical science (*cf. Meta.* VI), but rather the instrument by which we gain knowledge about beings. Hence it was later called the *Organon* or instrument.

[91] *Physics*, II, ch. I and 2; *cf. Meta.*, 1039 B 20 ff.

[92] *De Anima*, 430 A 14–19.

corresponds to some form in nature. But in nature, this form is always an aspect of some concrete individual, and is never abstract. The status of universality belongs only to the form in the mind. The way in which these universal tools of knowledge are logically related does not correspond to any real relations in nature.[93] Participation of this sort is a logical not an ontological phenomenon.

The act of universalizing is always an act of selection and omission. It is, therefore, an indication not of the power of our intellect, but rather of its incapacity to grasp concrete existence in its full richness. The more universal essences are not more perfect, but rather more abstract and indeterminate.[94] By means of this complex logical machinery, which Aristotle analysed with great care, the human mind is able to gain some understanding of reality. But this understanding is always very partial and incomplete, and subject to grave confusions, one of the gravest of which is the failure to distinguish sharply between logic and ontology.

This more self-conscious and critical attitude towards human knowledge is the most distinctive contribution of Aristotle to Western thought, and later on it exerted a profound influence on the course of mediaeval philosophy. It lies at the root of other specific alterations which Aristotle introduced in the Platonic view of nature. First of all, Plato's conception of a separate realm of universal forms outside the mind was subjected to an exhaustive and devastating polemic,[95] which has often been misunderstood. It has nothing to do with Ockham's razor. It is grounded rather on a more exact analysis of the logical tools of human knowledge, and a resulting sense of the transcendent richness and relative obscurity of being. Everything in nature is a concrete individual existent. Universals exist only in the mind as tools of understanding.

This leads to an important change in perspective. The world of nature is not the partial reflection of a pure realm of abstract universals. The truth is rather that the abstract universals in our minds are a partial reflection of the world of nature. This world is not an array of copies of other more real beings. It is rather a vast plurality of substances each of which exists in itself. We do not come to know these substances by first

[93] *Meta,* VI, ch. 4.
[94] *Physics,* 184 A 22.
[95] *Cf. Meta,* I, ch. 9, and VII ch. 13–16.

knowing other things. They are rather the primary objects of our human knowledge.[96] It is only by first understanding these material substances, with the aid of sense, that we may come to gain some understanding of other beings. These real beings are not individuated by something foreign to them, like space and time, but rather by a material principle that is not only an integral part but an essential part of their being.

Everything in nature is in flux. This is true. But change cannot be reduced to a mere succession of forms in an alien medium.[97] The material principle never exists alone by itself, but always together with some form by which it achieves its potency for other structures. Even in the union with form it still retains its potency for other structures. Change is the actualization of such potency, which always includes this factor of continuity as well as one of formal succession or discontinuity.[98] Natural substances not only suffer change; they also have active powers and exercise causal efficacy. Aristotle became deeply concerned with this phenomenon.[99] He distinguished four types of cause, which were implicit in Platonic thought, and analysed each in great detail.

In spite of these differences, Aristotle's view of the world is basically similar to that of Plato in his last dialogue, the *Laws*. For both of them, the universe is a cosmos, or order, of changing entities at different levels of being, inorganic things, plants, animals, and men. All are dependent on an ultimate first principle, which Aristotle held was in perfect act.

Though man possesses reason, and is, therefore, quite distinct from the other beings of nature, he is for Aristotle, like them, a hylomorphic being (composed of matter and form in union) who is subject to change, and who has arisen as the result of a long process of cosmic evolution.[100] The human soul is bound to its body, and even the power of reason cannot function without the assistance of the corporeal organs of sense. This reason is directed to the apprehension of the forms of surrounding bodily things about which it needs to know something in order to survive. Hence it is only with difficulty and indirectly that the soul can come

[96] *Meta*, VII, ch. 1.
[97] *Phys.*, I, ch. 7–9.
[98] *Phys.*, III, 201 A 10.
[99] *Cf. Phys.*, II, ch. 3.
[100] *De Anima*, 414 B 28 ff.

to understand the nature of itself and its non-physical operations.

Our human reason, chained to a body, is the lowest possible type. Hence Aristotle was very cautious about engaging in speculations concerning God, and purely spiritual beings above man. Nevertheless in spite of its serious limitations, he held that with the aid of sense, our rational faculty can gain accurate insight concerning physical things, a very broad though confused knowledge of being and its all-pervasive structures, and even some understanding of non-physical existence and God, the unmoved mover of nature.[101]

(ii) *Man and Society*

Aristotle held an earthier conception of man and was more keenly aware of the limitations of human reason. Hence he was less sanguine about philosophic attempts to describe the ideal constitution in detail, and devoted more of his time to studies of political history and concrete manifestations of social organization. He agreed with Plato that there is no super-individual group-substance, and that social unity depends upon common agreement with respect to a common good. But men are also bound together into families and other small groups by less conscious instinctive needs. He therefore criticized the idea expressed by Plato in the fifth Book of the *Republic* that these needs could be so rationally transformed as to make the family unnecessary.[102] He did not believe it possible that all children born at a certain time would ever be really considered as brothers and sisters, and the whole community as a single family. Flesh and blood cousins, he once remarked, were actually closer than these sublimated Platonic 'brothers' and 'sisters'. Human reason is bound to a body, and such oblivion to physical facts transcends the power of our nature.

There is a theoretical element in the deliberations of practical reason which should govern our active life. But this is not rightly conceived as a mere application of theory to special instances. In addition to theoretical insight, practical reason also involves a different sort of insight into concrete acts and situations, as well as a distinctive type of reasoning from means to ends.[103] To develop a sound practical judgment,

[101] *Meta*, XII, ch. 6–7.

[102] *Politics*, II, ch 2–3.

[103] *Nicomachean Ethics*, VI.

therefore, requires not only inborn intelligence of a certain kind, but long experience and discipline. Hence, like Plato in his older years, he was even more sceptical of such a pure science of government as Plato seemed to envisage in his *Republic*. All normal men have some political judgment, and Aristotle held that the combined judgment of many normal men in matters of this kind was often sounder than that of a few experts.[104]

According to him, the ideal state is one in which the citizens are really good, and those who rule are really the best. In such a genuine aristocracy, a good man would be the same as a good citizen. The chief aim of such a society, as in the *Republic*, is to enable the individual members to live well in accordance with reason and virtue. It can be achieved and maintained only by such a highly disciplined and developed system of education as Plato describes.[105] But this is an ideal which has never been remotely approximated. Following a suggestion of Plato in the *Politicus*, Aristotle enumerates five well-known forms of government.[106] Two of them, constitutional monarchy and aristocracy, the rule of a few who are the best according to some relative standard, are legitimate. But monarchy easily decays into tyranny, and aristocracy into oligarchy which are directed to special egotistic interests, rather than to the common good.

Aristotle also follows Plato in defining democracy, not as we do, but as the lawless rule of a crowd for 'freedom' which actually is license. But then, in consequence of his empirical observations, he introduces two 'mixed' forms, so-called *aristocracy*, a combination of oligarchy, democracy, and rule of those who are the best relative to some special standard, and something he calls *polity*, a combination of oligarchy and democracy. These compromise forms of social order are on the whole legitimate and good, and have often been realized in history. Aristotle carefully analyses them in the *Politics*,[107] and illustrates them by many examples.

But in spite of these critical refinements and additions, and the illuminating study of concrete data on which they are

[104] *Pol.*, ch. II.

[105] *Pol.*, VII, 13–VIII, 7, which unfortunately is only a fragmentary exposition of Aristotle's views on education.

[106] *Pol.*, IV.

[107] *Ibid.*

based, Aristotle's political theory is in basic agreement with that of Plato. Man cannot even exist as an individual by himself. He is by nature a political animal.[108] The fully developed society consists of individuals and families co-operating together for the sake of living well.[109] It is, therefore, not a substantial but a moral unity. If it is sound, it will lay down customs and laws directed towards the satisfaction of the natural needs of man. Extremes of wealth and poverty will be avoided. This general natural end can be achieved only through the overall guidance of theoretical reason, and of practical reason in particular. Otherwise, as Plato pointed out, natural justice, which is everywhere the same,[110] social stability, and social harmony cannot be attained. This is a cautious and critical form of Platonism, re-enforced by carefully analysed empirical observation.

(iii) *The Divine*

Aristotle believed that the human mind was able to gain some reliable information concerning physical things. But he was very sceptical about its capacity to attain trustworthy knowledge concerning spiritual beings higher than man.[111] Even the higher spiritual faculties of man, intellect and will, are very hard to grasp with any accuracy. It is clear that he believed in the existence of non-physical beings, or as he calls them *eternal substances*, not composed of matter and form, but of form alone. The writings that have come down to us contain very little on these topics, and the views which he expresses are cautious and reserved.

His careful studies of the basic structure of natural entities led him to see many respects in which they were dependent and require a first moving cause. Thus he agrees with Socrates and Plato that the order observed in nature cannot be explained without a first intelligent source of order.[112] Far from weakening this sort of argument, his penetrating analysis of chance[113] actually strengthened it.

He also accepted the argument from motion which Plato

[108] *Pol.*, I, 1253 A I.
[109] *Pol.*, I, ch. 1 and ch. 2, 1252 B 27–ch. 3.
[110] *Nic., Eth.*, V, 1134, B 18.
[111] *Parts of Animals*, 644 B, 22 ff.
[112] *Phys.*, VIII, ch. 5 ff and *Meta* XII, ch. 6–7.
[113] *Phys.*, II, ch. 4–6.

presents in the tenth Book of the *Laws*, but with certain significant alterations. He was deeply concerned with the acts by which natural tendencies are realized, and went beyond Plato in distinguishing different kinds.[114] Of these, change is the least perfect, for it involves the loss of some quality or character, and its replacement by one that is opposed. Thus when the leaf turns from green to red in the fall, the green is eliminated and the red acquired through the drop in temperature and other external causes. Here a passive potency is actualized, and a new quality (red) appears.

There are other processes, however, where internal factors play a more important role. Thus a stick of dynamite is already in act, or prepared to go off at the reception of a relatively slight external stimulus, though the process still moves from one contrary pole to another. At certain higher levels, this contrariety is eliminated. Thus when the eyes are closed, the visual sense is not seeing any actual colour at all. Nevertheless, it is already in act to see when the eyes are opened. When I come to see green, no opposite quality has to be removed. The visual power, already in act, simply moves into itself, as Aristotle puts it,[115] and realizes a further activity that belongs to it by nature, though the external stimulation of light is, of course, necessary.

At still higher levels, however, this external factor is no longer required, and the process is activated from within the active agent. This is true of the 'free' or spontaneous operations of intellect and will.[116] I can think and choose by myself alone. This observable hierarchy of increasingly active processes enabled Aristotle to conceive of a perfect act which would be completely stable and self-sustaining. The closest approximation to this in our experience is found in our adherence to a fixed purpose through changes of life and circumstance, and in the continuous contemplation of a single truth. These reflections enabled Aristotle to correct Plato's view that God is a self-*moving* cause.[117]

Motion is a most imperfect mode of activity which even man is able to transcend. It involves the transition from a state of potency to that of act. But potency is existential imper-

[114] *Meta*, IX, ch. 5–6.
[115] *De Anima*, 417 A 6.
[116] *Meta*, IX, 1048 A 8.
[117] *Meta*, XII, 1071 B–20.

fection which cannot be legitimately attributed to the first cause. Furthermore, that which is in a state of pure potency cannot activate itself, but requires an external cause in act. Hence this view is incompatible with the divine autonomy. God cannot suffer any change He is far more active than this He is, in fact, pure act.[118] This activity needs no external support and is entirely self-sufficient. This suggestion bore fruit in the Middle Ages, but Aristotle's remarks on theology in the twelfth Book of the *Metaphysics* are very brief, cautious, and condensed. The view of God here indicated is less anthropomorphic and more transcendent than anything in the writings of Plato.

All finite beings are dependent. The Divine Being, on the other hand, exists necessarily. It is, therefore, foolish to seek for His cause. He is rather that pure and self-sufficient act which causes all finite motions and changes, without having to undergo change, the unmoved, but intensely active mover of all. He must be intellectual. Otherwise He could not produce order, and would not be an appropriate object for worship. He must also be alive, a living God, for actual thought is a mode of life. Complete activity yields pleasure, and the purest pleasures are those of contemplation. Hence this is a life of joy.[119] But all our concepts break down when we attempt to describe such perfect existence. Our thought has to move from potency to act. But this thought is ever in act. Our thought is distinct from the reality it contemplates, an object with which it never becomes completely identified. But this thought *is* the being it contemplates.[120] Hence it is true to say that it is its own object, and that it contemplates itself.

At one point,[121] Aristotle drew the unfortunate conclusion that God, therefore, thinks only of Himself, and has no knowledge of lesser things. He failed to see that in knowing Himself and His active powers, God also must know these things. This mistake had to be later corrected. But in spite of their cautious brevity, his scattered remarks on theology are very profound, and their very incompleteness left the way open for further enrichment. This, together with their very incompleteness, led the way to further sound enrichments. The concluding

[118] *Ibid.*
[119] *Meta*, 1072 B 13 ff.
[120] 1072 B 22, *cf.* XII, ch. 9.
[121] 1074 B 20 ff.

D

sentence of a short discussion in Book XII of the *Metaphysics*[122] deserves quotation. 'We say, therefore, that God is a living being, eternal, most good, so that life, and duration continuous and eternal belong to God, for this is God.'

Like Plato, Aristotle did not sharply separate religion from philosophy. He believed in the existence of intermediate spiritual agencies, and thus took a tolerant view of polytheistic cults. But the purest forms of worship require the disciplined activities of our highest spiritual faculties, particularly reason which is by its immaterial nature closest to God, and therefore the most divine thing in us.[123] Our most intimate communion with the Divine, therefore, is achieved by meditative prayer and contemplation. Such activities are most akin to the Divine Act which, as Plato said, must be the ultimate pattern towards which we should strive so far as this is possible. Hence the crown of such activities, in which the animals have no part, is the highest part of human happiness.

(iv) *Evolution and Human History*

Aristotle rejected the theory of separate ideas and held that the hylomorphic substances of nature have an independent and fully real existence of their own. This led him to study their complex internal structure more carefully, and also the mysterious processes of change and evolution out of which they come into being, through which they endure, and to which they finally return. Change, in fact, was recognized by Aristotle as the most pervasive fact of nature,[124] and his categories can be understood only in the light of the role they play in different kinds of change.

There is a factor of indeterminacy, or potency, called matter, which is found everywhere in nature.[125] It is not nothing, but rather an incomplete mode of being which is not actual, yet able to become an indefinite number of forms. When one such determination is received, however, the matter still remains incomplete. It is able to lose this form, and to receive an indefinite variety of others. It is never found alone, but always united with some form.[126] Change is the actualization of some such composite entity, in so far as it is material or potential.

[122] 1072 B 28.
[123] *Nic. Eth.*, 1177 B 26 ff.
[124] *Phys.*, II, ch. 1.
[125] *Phys.*, I, ch. 9 and *Meta*, IX, ch. 3.
[126] *On Generation and Corruption*, 320 B 16.

Its further actualization, so far as it is *actual*, is that activity (*energiea*) which we have discussed in the preceding section.

Aristotle analyzes four types of change, generation and destruction, locomotion or change of place, growth and decrease or change in size, and finally alteration or change in quality.[127] The most fundamental of these is generation, by which a new substance comes into being. Such a substance exists not as a property in something else (an accident) but rather in itself. It includes the matter out of which it came into being, and an essential structure or form which makes it into the kind of thing it is. Hence the human mind defines each natural entity by means of a genus corresponding to its matter, and a difference corresponding to its last essential form.[128]

Spiritual beings have no matter, and do not evolve out of anything else. They cannot be understood in the usual way by means of genus and difference. Hence we cannot grasp them directly as they are. We have to approach them indirectly by comparing them with what they are not. This gives us only an analogous, negative knowledge of them which is expressed when we say they are immaterial. Material substances are, however, more accessible to our limited intelligence. They evolve out of preceding substances which are destroyed when the new essential form is received. These new substances are always individual, and are capable of enduring through the three modes of accidental change, locomotion, growth and alteration. Once a species becomes established, the individuals reproduce others like themselves.

But Aristotle's subtle analysis of change, and his careful biological observations led him to conclude that the higher and more complex forms of life are built up on the basis of the lower, as complex geometrical figures are based upon those more simple.[129] Thus he suggested that the lower species of life came first, and that from these evolved the later and higher forms.[130] He did not believe, however, that this was working towards some final end, since the cosmos is everlasting in time. Many such evolutions have happened before, and have ended in great catastrophes. Many will doubtless happen again after our particular history is finished.

[127] *Phys.*, V, 226 A 23 ff.
[128] *Meta*, VII, ch. 12.
[129] *De An.*, II, 414 B 28.
[130] *History of Animals*, 588 B 4–12.

The purposive change, which is due to rational reflection and spontaneous choice, is peculiar to man. Aristotle read everything he could lay his hands on, and made many acute observations on historic events that were known to him. But so far as we know, he never attempted to go beyond Plato in constructing an overarching philosophy of history. He certainly did not accept the Sophistic theory of automatic progress, nor the traditional theory of necessary decline. What happens in history depends upon the rational reflections, and the resulting free choices of men. Aristotle did not sympathize with Alexander's schemes for world conquest, and probably agreed with Plato that his own age was one of social decay and corruption. It would probably come to an end in a great world cataclysm, and then a new cycle would begin.[131] Aristotle made several comments of this sort, but never tried to work out in detail a coherent interpretation of the whole human history. He probably felt that this was something for the mind of God which transcends the capacities of our limited human intelligence.

(v) *The Human Individual*

Aristotle pushed much further the Socratic project of investigating the nature of the human soul, and his careful empirical methods led him to a conclusion far more earthy and realistic than that of Plato. As he expressed it, the human soul is the first animating form of a natural body,[132] and cannot as a whole exist without it, though, as we shall see, the rational part is separable and immortal. This organized body was prepared by a long process of evolution to receive the essential form of reason which is the differentiating feature of man. It was first of all a physical thing located in space, and subject to the laws of motion. Then such a body was endowed with a vegetative principle which enabled it to nourish itself and to grow. When this plant life became established, it was then infused with an animal form which was capable of sense and locomotion. Being material, this animal life retained the potency for a still higher form. At a certain stage in its accidental development, it became ready, and received the rational form of man.

This final rational form fused with the other lower patterns

[131] *Phys.*, 223 B 24; *Meta*, XII, 1074 B 8 ff.
[132] *De An.*, 412 A 29.

to which it was added, and bound them all into a higher unity, making this new organized body into a man. This is no mere set of separate properties strung together, for each is combined with a potential matter prepared to unite with a further matter, as the molten gold is able to receive the form of a ring. Thus body and soul are not two separate entities, but two interdependent principles, each of which exists only by virtue of the other.[133] It is as silly, therefore, to ask how the human soul can be combined with the body as to ask how the circular shape of the gold ring can be combined with the gold. The answer is that these are not two *things*, but rather two interdependent factors of *one* thing. Without the human body, there would be no soul, and without the soul, no human body. Each is distinct but not separable from the other.

The rational form fuses with the other lower forms in such a way as to give them a new unity, but in doing this, it also becomes dependent upon them, as we shall see.[134]

The vegetative soul is responsible for the function of nutrition, growth, and reproduction. Without these, the higher faculties cannot operate or even exist. But at the same time, they are under the general control of reason. Thus while we have to eat in order to live, we can choose when to eat and what food we shall take. The lower functions are necessary but always potentially open to further determinations from a higher source. Thus hunger and sexual need arise automatically in all men. But they can be controlled in an infinite variety of ways.

The animal factor in the human form provides us with faculties of sense and organs of locomotion. Aristotle gives an exhaustive account of sensation in the second book of the *De Anima*, which is far more accurate and penetrating than that of either Plato or Protagoras. The sense organ must receive an actual stimulation from physical pressures, sounds, colours, etc., but this is only the beginning—a first necessary condition for sensory feeling. The faculty attached to the organ is already prepared in the first act, like a stick of dynamite, to respond in an appropriate way.[135] All the visible colours are already in the eye in a state of virtual potency. When a stimulus of a certain type is received, this faculty assimilates the form without the

[133] *De An.*, 412 B 25–413 A 9.
[134] *Cf. Meta*, VII, 1041 A 33–1041 B 30.
[135] *De An.*, II, 417 B 2 ff.

matter, as wax receives the pattern of a seal without the iron.[136]

This pure form or sensible species is not physically received as a part of the organ. Thus if the eye were physically painted, it would not help us to see the colour. Not being physically received in the eye, this species is not individuated by the eye, and retains its identity with the physical form from which it came. Hence we see green as it is on the leaf, and we smell the rose fragrance as it is in the air around us.

In addition to those qualities, like colour and sound, which are peculiar to a single sense, there are others, like size, shape, and motion, which are discriminated, though far less accurately, by more than one sense.[137] Thus, the motion of the airplane is both heard and seen.

Sense enables us to become aware of physical things around us so far as they possess these special sensible properties. But it has three radical defects. In the first place, it is not under our control, but subject to physical conditions. Without physical light I cannot see. In the second place, it is jumbled and confused. What I see is not pure colour at all, but a coloured surface in a certain light, in a certain position, at a certain distance, etc.[138] By sense alone, I cannot distinguish clearly between colour and surface, and focus each form as it is in itself. In the third place, sense is always perspectival. It gives me a partial view or feeling of the thing as it is physically related to my organ, never the whole of the thing as it really is. Thus, when I look at a table, I see only one of its sides, and when I feel a penny, I touch only its surface, and not its inside.

The first and third of these defects are remedied by the faculty of imagination which is under our control to the extent that it can conjure up images of objects once sensed, and can alter and recombine them at will. [139] Thus, I can imagine a brilliant object even when the light is not physically shining. Also when I see only the front of a house, my imagination may be trained to supply me with the missing parts, if I have seen them before. But it cannot supply me with many important aspects of the object which are not open to sense at all. Hence this third defect is only partially remedied. The most

[136] *De An.*, II, 424 A 16 ff.
[137] 418 A 7–A 19.
[138] *De An.*, II, ch. 6.
[139] *De An.*, III, 428 A ff.

serious of all, the second, it cannot remedy, for the object of imagination is always an individual at some time and some place. As such, it is a confused blur of many distinct properties mixed together, and never clearly focused one by one.

Nevertheless, sensory awareness of such confused objects determines a new kind of appetite, quite distinct from the automatic tendencies of plants.[140] The animal's desires are not fixed in this way, but are subject to determination and direction by his sensory awareness. He can learn how to pursue and capture certain useful objects he sees, and how to escape from dangerous ones. Men also have appetites of this kind, which Aristotle calls passions, because they are at first under external control. Unless these natural appetites are finally brought under the control of reason, they are likely to become obsessive, and to upset the order of human life.

Aristotle's analysis of rational cognition is markedly different from that of Plato. Human intelligence is bound to a body, and dependent upon sense.[141] It can give us some insight into the composite nature of changing things, but with respect to immaterial beings, like the human soul, its knowledge is indirect and negative. Nevertheless it is by far the most penetrating of all our intellectual faculties, and is capable of revealing many aspects of being which are totally opaque to sense.

Plato had believed that there were universal intelligible entities outside the mind, which simply floated in to be passively received. Aristotle pointed out, however, that all the evidence indicates that everything in nature is concrete and singular.[142] The matter of such entities is opaque to reason.[143] Only form as such is intelligible. Hence before this structure can be understood, it must be separated from its material matrix. This means that reason is active, not passive. It grasps the structure, or nature, of a physical thing only by constructive acts of its own. The Aristotelian notion of an active reason (*Nous poietikos*)[144] is radically new.

When presented with a confused object of sense or imagination, this active power first breaks it down into its formal constituents, and focuses each of them one by one. Separating

[140] *De An.*, III, ch. 9.
[141] *De An.*, 432 A 6.
[142] *Meta*, VII, ch. 16.
[143] 1039 B 26 ff.
[144] *De An.*, III, ch. 6.

the pure nature from everything that is irrelevant to it, our active reason lifts it into a state of solitude where it can be compared with various instances, and predicated of them. This is the state of universality which is peculiar to the human intellect. By means of this, we are able to grasp some formal phase of a material entity. If this phase belongs to the matter out of which the thing has come into being, it is specific. If it has been gained by the thing through some process of change, it is accidental. This analysis of the sensory blur into its formal components is the first act of the mind, the formation of a universal concept. All concepts are either generic, specific, or accidental.[145]

After the object has been broken down by this sort of formal analysis, it must then be resynthesized as it really is. This is achieved by the judgment which predicates the definition (genus, subgenera, and difference) of the individual thing, and also such accidents as green, soft, loud, and fragrant. Single concepts are neither true nor false. They are either constructed or not. But judgments are true or false depending on whether the subject, reidentified with its artificially separated predicate and the predicate, are really one in nature.[146] Sometimes the mind discovers predicates that are causally connected with universal subjects, as mortality is connected with man. The propositions expressing such connections can be used to found further inferences. Thus if I know that all men are mortal, and if I can discover that a given object is a man, I may infer that this is mortal, thus deriving from what I already know, an item of knowledge that is genuinely new.

Concepts, propositions, and arguments are not found in *rerum nature*. A real entity is not universal but individual. It is not first separated from its *what*, and then reidentified with it. As long as it exists, it is what it is. One thing may cause another. But the effect is not a conclusion. These are not real beings but beings of reason *by which* we know real being, when we are fortunate, and think in a disciplined way. They are mental constructions, or tools, by which we may gain an abstract and always partial knowledge of the changing world of nature. Aristotle gave an exhaustive analysis of these noetic instruments in his *Prior* and *Posterior Analytics*.

[145] *Categories*, ch. 2.
[146] *De An.*, 430 A 26–430 B 5.

A major consequence of this analysis is a deeper sense of the partiality and weakness of human knowledge. We cannot unite with the thing directly, but only via elaborate constructions in the mind. A universal concept, even if truly predicated, is always abstract and partial. But all human knowledge is universal. This knowledge may shed some light on the composite things which have evolved in nature, and which are, therefore, built up out of a generic form with an added determination. But with respect to simple immaterial beings, it breaks down. Such beings did not evolve. Hence they cannot be understood in terms of genus and difference. Our knowledge is very weak and limited in range. When confronted with lofty objects of high intelligibility, it is blinded, like an owl gaping at the sun.[147] When confronted by lower objects immersed in matter, its light is too bright, and it misses their vagueness and indeterminacy. Nevertheless, this rational apprehension is beyond all question the clearest of our cognitive faculties, and far exceeds the range of sense.

Each distinct mode of apprehension elicits a corresponding mode of appetition.[148] Just as sensory apprehension calls forth desire for material objects, so does rational apprehension call forth voluntary aspiration for intelligible objects. Though these two modes of appetition are often confused in common discourse, they are really sharply and qualitatively distinct. Our desires are deliberately chosen. Hence they are called *voluntary*. If our desires clash, the stronger one wins. But if we reflect and deliberate, we may choose in favour of the weaker.

The basic moral issue confronting all men at all times is this. Can their finite and limited reason work out a sound and coherent view of the world and man, which is capable of eliciting modes of rational aspiration and of imposing order on the animal desires? Like Plato's great moral treatises, Aristotle's *Ethics* was written to clarify this crucial issue, and to strengthen the rational powers of man in meeting it.

(vi) *Human Ideals and the Ways of Achieving Them*

Aristotle's keener sense of the limits of human knowledge made him less confident concerning the possibility of working out a sound theoretical philosophy exhaustive enough to give specific guidance to human action. He also placed a far greater

[147] *Phys.*, 184 A 17 ff.

[148] *Meta*, XII, 1072 A 27–A 33.

emphasis on the distinctive features of practical reason. Otherwise he introduced no striking innovations into the framework of Socratic and Platonic ethics. His moral theory, like theirs, is founded on a dynamic ontology which he had refined and clarified, as we have seen. Human nature has an inherent tendency towards realization of its various capacities, which is the good for man. This good cannot be achieved unless certain general rules, grounded on nature, are followed in the different fields of action. Such rules can be theoretically understood and fused with appetite by deliberation and choice.

When a raw appetite is altered in this way and brought under rational control, it becomes a virtue (*arete*), which Aristotle defines as a firm habit of choice to avoid extremes in a certain field of behaviour, and to act in a rational way.[149] The first step in attaining the moral goal is to spread the influence of reason into every phase of human life, and thus to build up firm tendencies towards responsible action in the concrete. But this is only the first step. Firm tendencies are not enough. They must be actually energized in the concrete. Human happiness is activity (*energia*) *in accordance with virtue for the whole span of a human life.*[150]

Such a life must be ultimately directed by theoretical wisdom (*sophia*) concerning the nature of man and the world, though a given agent need not possess such knowledge in himself. He may accept it on faith from another, or simply hold it by connatural inclination in a semi-instinctive and inarticulate way. Nevertheless, such truth is the only stable and reliable guide. Hence practical knowledge (*phronesis*) is subordinate to theoretical wisdom (*sophia*).[151] The distinction between these is implicit in Plato. But in Aristotle it becomes far more clear and explicit. Theoretical knowledge is universal, and abstract from all appetition. Its object is what it is necessarily, or at least for the most part, and is, therefore, not subject to human control. Practical knowledge, on the other hand, is particular, since it concerns the concrete act, and fused with appetition.[152] Its object, lying in the future, is contingent, and subject to human control. These two modes of reasoning, theoretical investigation and deliberation, are quite distinct,

[149] *Nic. Eth.*, II, 1106 B 36.
[150] *Nic. Eth.*, I, 1098 A 16.
[151] *Nic. Eth.*, Vi, ch. 7.
[152] *Ibid.*, 1141 B 8 ff.

though one is ordered to the other. But a given agent may be profound and penetrating in theory but a fool in practice, and *vice versa.*

The aim of moral training is the acquisition of firm rational habits, or virtues, which fall into two major groups, the intellectual and the moral. The intellectual virtues enable us to understand being as it is.[153] They provide us with the ultimate directing insights, and when they reach their goal, which is very difficult, provide us with the purest and most lasting pleasure.[154] For this, three kinds of act are required: 1, clear insight (*nous*) into the meaning of terms, which enables us to grasp first principles; 2, a grasp of causal connections, which enables us to reason and to infer new conclusions from what we already know (*episteme*); and 3, wisdom (*sophia*), which is insight (1) and deductive power (2) applied to the most important objects, such as God, man and the human good. Such virtues have nothing to do with the control of passions, and, therefore, involve no mean.[155]

There are two basic genera of moral virtue: justice, which concerns the rational direction of our overt, social acts;[156] and passional virtue, which concerns the control of our own subjective passions.[157] The latter is a necessary condition for the former, which has no mean.

Justice is divided into three species. First of all, there is social justice in the broad Platonic sense of rendering to each distinct nature what is due, as this can be understood by reason. As Aristotle points out, this is the highest level of moral action, and in its actual exercise involves all the other virtues, including the intellectual.[158] In addition to this, however, advancing beyond Plato, Aristotle distinguishes two other specific types of justice. The first is distributive justice,[159] an equal sharing of common goods and common burdens by all individuals alike, or in proportion to real merit. This virtue has been ignored and neglected in modern times. The second is the commutative justice of exchange, where absolute equality should rule.[160]

153 *Nic. Eth.*, VI.
154 *Nic. Eth.*, 1177 A 23 ff.
155 *Nic. Eth.*, VI, ch. 6–7.
156 *Nic. Eth.*, V.
157 *Nic. Eth.*, III, ch. 6–IV, ch. 8.
158 *Nic. Eth.*, V, 1129 B 25 ff.
159 *Nic. Eth.*, 1130, B 30 off.
160 *Nic. Eth.*, V, ch. 4.

In the voluntary trade of valuable goods or articles of any kind, it is unfair if one receives more in relation to his needs than another. In extreme violations, the judge attempts to restore an equal balance by fines, and the imposition of other penalties on the offender.

Passional virtues are achieved by the deliberate control of those natural tendencies which are aroused in us by external objects and events. They fall into three major divisions[161] corresponding to the three main types of passional desire which are directed towards: 1, our own internal pleasures and pains; 2, external non-human goods; and 3, other human persons. Our human nature makes us necessarily subject to these passions. They cannot be entirely eliminated as the Stoics wished, but if unchecked, they can upset the whole order of life. Hence in each case, virtue will lie in the pursuit of a rational mean.

Each of us tends to desire those particular objects which have given him pleasure. We cannot eliminate this urge. Temperance consists in moderating it under rational direction, by pursuing those pleasures that are really good, and avoiding those apparent goods that are really only pleasant in relation to us.[162] Each person also tends to avoid objects which excite him to fear and terror. Courage lies first of all in clearly distinguishing those fearful things that need to be actively faced from those that do not, and acting accordingly.[163]

External non-human goods fall into two groups, material things that money will buy, and the honour bestowed by reason. Our subjective urge to the former needs to be toned down by the virtue of generosity.[164] That towards honour needs to be intensified by proper ambition and especially by that peculiar crown of the virtues which Aristotle calls *greatness of soul.*[165]

All men live in a social environment. Contacts with other persons excite desires in us which require certain social virtues. Aristotle devoted careful attention to these, though they have been neglected by the individualism of modern thought. The chief of these are deliberate sympathy, gentleness, truthfulness, and tact.[166]

[161] *Nic. Eth.*, KKK, ch. 6–IV, ch. 8.
[162] *Nic. Eth.*, KK, ch. 10–11.
[163] *Nic. Eth.*, KK, ch. 6–9.
[164] *Nic. Eth.*, IV, ch. 1.
[165] *Nic. Eth.*, IV, ch. 3–4.
[166] *Nic. Eth.*, IV, ch. 6–8.

The pathway to the good life lies through the cultivation of these moral virtues, which is the chief aim of sound statesmanship. How is this aim to be achieved? Here Aristotle would answer with Plato—education, though he would more sharply distinguish practical discipline from the theoretical, as we shall see. The same is true of moral virtue *vs.* art. The former concerns human acts each of which is an end in itself, whereas the latter is directed to the manufacture and use of mere instruments which are needed not *in* but *for* the living of human life. Hence in art, a voluntary mistake is preferable to an involuntary one. But this is not true of life.[167]

In his analysis of art and of the order of the arts, Aristotle did not go beyond the doctrines of his teacher. In its broad outlines, he accepts the rational ethics of Plato with many clarifications and refinements. This is also true of his political theory. Here he attempts to formulate an ideal grounded on human nature and the law of nature. As in Plato, the ultimate way of attaining this end lies in the practices and institutions of education.

(vii) *Man and Education*

Education should be the primary object of concern for the sound statesman, and should be under public control as the central institution of the well-ordered community.[168] Aristotle's discussion of education in the eighth Book of the *Politics* is unfortunately only a fragment. But from this and other occasional remarks scattered through his works, we may gather certain views concerning moral training and the order of learning in theoretical science. Some of these are significant additions to the Platonic theory which, in its broad outlines, Aristotle certainly accepted.

What happens in the earliest years is very important for the later development of the child. First of all, his body should be trained to be strong and resistant. Moderate athletic exercise is advisable, but should never become an end in itself.[169] Athleticism is extremely dangerous, since the body should not be trained for its own sake alone, but for the sake of the soul, which consists of a rational part (reason and will) and another that is sub-rational (sense, imagination, and desire). The

[167] *Nic. Eth.*, VI, 1140 B 20–30.
[168] *Politics*, VIII, ch. 1–2.
[169] *Pol.*, VIII, ch. 4.

former is ultimately more important, but it develops later. Hence education should begin with discipline in moral, passional virtue, with intellectual virtue ever in view. Aristotle's account of this early phase of moral training is very penetrating and worthy of comment.

Virtue is in accordance with nature, but no child is actually virtuous by nature. These habits have to be learned. They are learned by the performance of virtuous acts. But how can such acts be carried out by a child who as yet lacks virtue? Aristotle answers this question[170] by distinguishing the virtuous act which agrees with the moral rule, and the way in which it is performed. From earliest youth, parents and teachers should intervene in the life of the child, influencing him by rewards and punishments to perform virtuous acts. Thus he should first be led to carry out just, courageous, and generous acts, not spontaneously out of himself, but from the influence of a beneficent environment. He will give something of value to another child not because he is really generous himself, but in hope of some reward. Nevertheless, this will be a generous act, and will set up in him a habitual tendency which may grow into a genuine virtue.

This will depend upon three further steps which must be supplied by his education. First of all, he must learn *why* such an act is good. Then he must learn to choose it for its own sake alone (not for some extraneous reward). And finally, this mode of action must become so ingrained in him that he can perform acts of this kind at a moment's notice, and with lasting pleasure. If and when he reaches this stage, he will be actually and spontaneously virtuous, as is required for the good life.

After this essential moral training has begun, and after the child has learned the basic tools of theoretical activity such as reading and writing, the intellectual training of the child should begin. Here Aristotle's more careful and critical investigations of the noetic process led him to important alterations and clarifications of the Platonic view. Logic, for example, as we have noted, is sharply distinguished from metaphysics and ontology which study the real structure of being. Logic, on the other hand, is concerned with concepts, propositions, and arguments, the tools of knowledge, how they must be rightly arranged and used if truth about being is to be attained. This

[170] *Nic. Eth.*, II, ch. 4.

discipline is not easy. But since this instrument must be used in different ways in the acquisition of all the different types of knowledge, it should be taught before the factual sciences, though at first only in its barest rudiments, and by concrete example.

Since all knowledge involves abstractive acts of the mind, the different human sciences are distinguished not only by the kind of thing which is studied, but also by the kind of abstraction required. These levels of abstraction are three in number, mathematics, physical science, and ontology or *first philosophy*, as Aristotle called it.[171] Of these, mathematics is the most abstract and, therefore, the easiest for the human mind. Even young men can become very proficient in such disciples. This is because number, sets, and other forms of quantitative order can be studied in abstraction from matter and change. Nature, of course, is quantitative. Hence mathematics can be applied to the study of nature. But the mathematician can study it apart, along by itself,[172] without using sensory observation. His imagination is sufficient. Because of its relative simplicity and ease, this science should first be taught to the child.

Natural science and the philosophy of nature should come next. These disciplines seek general laws, and thus abstract from the concrete individual. All science is abstract in this sense. Unlike mathematics, the natural sciences are concerned not only with quantitative structure, but also with matter, change, and causation. These factors introduce many additional complications, and cannot be understood as they occur without the aid of sensory observation. Hence they are more difficult, and should follow the study of mathematics. But ontology, or first philosophy, requires a different point of view, or level of abstraction, which is far more difficult to carry through. It is interested in an entity not so far as it is quantitative, nor so far as it is changing, but in so far as it *is*. It asks such basic questions as whether it exists contingently or necessarily, in itself as a substance or in another as a property, potentially or actually. This mode of abstraction requires sense to begin with, but takes us beyond sense to objects which can be apprehended distinctly by reason alone. Hence it is the most difficult of the three theoretical disciplines, and should be studied last.[173]

[171] *Meta.*, VI, ch. 1.
[172] *Phys.*, II, 192 B 24 ff.
[173] *Cf. Meta.*, I, 982 A 20 ff.

After the mind has gained some abstract knowledge of the structure of the world and man, it may properly turn to the theory of human action and its grounds. The act itself is always concrete, but its reasons and grounds can be understood only in the light of natural science and metaphysics. Hence, as Aristotle points out, the youthful mind should not be encouraged to study ethics in a theoretical way, as it is studied in the *Nicomachean Ethics*. This should rather be postponed to a later age when the youth has gained control over his passions, and has gained some wisdom, which requires empirical observation and takes protracted intervals of time.[174]

Our review of the Aristotelian theory of man must now be concluded. He was the last of the great pioneers of Greek thought. Like Socrates and Plato also, he was an impassioned rationalist. He believed that reason is the most distinctive, the most penetrating, and the most far-reaching of all the human powers. Reason alone can guide our lives to individual and social fulfilment. It has a natural kinship with being, and is the most divine thing in us.

While he clarified and deepened these insights of his great predecessors in many ways, Aristotle also made a critical investigation of the nature of human knowledge which led him to revolutionary conclusions. This is his chief contribution not only to the Greek theory of man but to Greek thought as a whole. While he emerged with the same basic respect for reason as the most distinctive and important of all the human faculties, he was at the same time far more convinced of its weaknesses and limits. This profound sense of the limits of human knowledge, grounded as it was on an analysis that is empirically accurate and profound, was Aristotle's most original contribution to Greek thought.

5. THE INFLUENCE OF GREEK THOUGHT ON RELIGIOUS TRADITIONS

THE influence of Protagoras and the Sophists was definitely anti-religious. In later Hellenistic and Roman times, this influence merged with that of academic scepticism and materialistic epicureanism to form strong trends of secularist thought. In their own period, both Plato and Aristotle were tolerant of

[174] *Nic. Eth.*, I, 1095 A 2 ff.

polytheistic cults which were still active in the city states, but did not take them very seriously, since their philosophies pointed clearly in a monotheistic direction. This influence is apparent in those variegated and eclectic currents of thought which dominated the Roman world. Greek philosophy was here brought into relation with many alien influences. Hence we shall make only a few brief comments. But these may be helpful in understanding the important influence exerted later by both Plato and Aristotle on the development of Mohammedanism and Christianity.

(i) *Hellenistic and Roman Philosophy*

This period is characterized by two seemingly opposed but closely related tendencies. On the one hand, the intellectual life of the time is broken up into many diverse currents introduced by the many peoples and traditions brought together in the great empires of Alexander and of Rome. On the other hand, we also find them fusing together, especially later, in more inclusive eclectic combinations. Certain basic traditions, however, retained their identity through the whole period. The most important can be briefly characterized as follows.

In the fourth and third centuries B.C., certain thinkers in the Academic tradition of Plato began to interpret the Socratic method of questioning in a purely negative sense, and founded a sceptical school which attracted able adherents throughout the succeeding centuries.[174A] All 'knowledge' rests ultimately on sensory evidence, and sensation is unstable and relative to the individual observer, as Protagoras had pointed out. There is no proposition, therefore, which does not bear marks of uncertainty, and cannot be legitimately doubted. All philosophical propositions are only probable, though the later Academic sceptics often defended probable ethical statements as a sufficient guide for life. But there is, of course, no compelling reason for adopting one moral attitude rather than another. When consistently held, such scepticism must end in inactivity and silence. But few of these sceptics were so consistent. The general position was actively defended through the time of Sextus Empiricus (around A.D. 150). It exerted no direct influence on later philosophical or religious movements.

[174A] For a reliable account of Greek scepticism, *cf.* M. M. Patrick, *The Greek Sceptics* (N.Y.: Columbia Univ. Press, 1929). *Cf.* C. Bailey, *The Greek Atomists and Epicurus*, (Oxford: Clarendon Press, 1928).

The atomistic materialism of Democritus and its ethical corollary of hedonism were maintained by the earlier Cyrenaic school, (fifth and fourth centuries B.C.) and later on by Epicurus and Lucretius.[174B] From this point of view, man is a tiny material swirl, lost in a chaos of atoms moving through the void. The 'soul' is composed of finer round atoms which move with great speed. There are higher divine beings dwelling in the interstellar spaces, but they take no interest in human affairs. The swirl of the atoms is neither under intelligent control nor is it fixed by law. Hence they are apt to swerve in unpredictable ways, which makes what we call free will and ethical decision possible.

The good is identified with pleasure, and Epicurus developed on this basis a refined hedonistic theory which enabled him to prefer the more lasting pleasures of quiet discourse to the more violent delights of sense. He took over a theory of the early Sophist, Antiphon, about the nature of death. While we are alive, death is certainly non-existent. As soon as we are dead, we are non-existent. Therefore why should death concern us or worry us at all?[175] This mode of thought was constantly maintained until the Fall of Rome, and has been actively defended in varying versions ever since. In recent times, it has been strengthened by the rise of science, which is readily open to such materialistic interpretation.

In opposition to this hedonistic point of view, certain thinkers in the third century B.C. laid the foundations of an eclectic school known as Stoicism which persisted through the whole of Hellenistic and Roman periods.[175A] Influenced by Socrates and his great followers, these thinkers maintained that pleasure and goodness were sharply distinct and even opposed. The good lies rather in virtue, and virtue, as Socrates had maintained, is knowledge. No matter how weak or oppressed we may be, there is always some room for choice. Even when death inescapably confronts us, we may still choose how we are to die. In every exigency of life, the Stoic sage will remain oblivious to pleasure and pain, and will unswervingly perform his duty as wisdom requires. This doctrine demands a ruthless elimina-

[174B] *Cf.* Zeller, E., *The Stoics, Epicureans, and Sceptics*: (London: Longmans, Green & Co., 1892).

[175] H. Usener, *Epicurea*, pp. 15 ff and 391. Leipzig, 1887.

[175A] *Cf.* R. M. Wenley, *Stoicism and its Influence*, (Marshall Jones Co., Boston, 1924).

tion of human passions that goes far beyond the teaching of Plato and Aristotle.

But the Stoics took over from these predecessors the conception of an ordered cosmos, and an ethics grounded on ontology. Hence they expressed their moral idea as *life in accordance with nature*. They did not invent the idea of a moral law grounded on stable cosmic structure, as many text books now assert. But they constantly used the phrase *natural law*, spelled it out in greater detail, and applied it to jurisprudence. This influenced the great Roman jurists and codifiers who made it a basic element in the Roman Law. In their general philosophy of nature, they combined many elements taken from divergent sources into a syncretistic view. God is identified with the indwelling order of the cosmos. This led them into a pantheistic view which implied determinism, and sometimes conflicted with their defence of moral freedom.[176] Stoicism was a way of life embraced with passionate seriousness, and founded on a coherent view of the world based on fragments of Plato and Aristotle, which is hard to distinguish from religion. It persisted through the whole Roman period, and has continued to exert sporadic influences on mediaeval and modern thinkers.

Philosophy was taught at the Academy, founded by Plato, until A.D. 529 when its doors were closed at the command of the Emperor Justinian. While the traditional teaching underwent many changes throughout these 900 years, the writings of Plato were preserved, and his basic doctrines were studied, interpreted, and developed in many ways. In the third century A.D., certain of these interpretations were combined with elements taken from Aristotle to form a new and distinctive pattern of thought known as Neo-Platonism.[176A] Like Plato, these thinkers made no sharp distinction between logic and metaphysics. They also shared Plato's confidence in the capacity of the human mind to gain knowledge of God and superhuman agencies. Their writings are filled with speculations concerning the origin of the sensory world, and the higher spiritual agencies which are responsible for it.

They are not satisfied with Plato's anthropomorphic pictures of God, and show a marked tendency to stress His supreme and

[176] V. Arnim, *Stoicorum veterum fragmenta*, I, No. 175 ff.; II, No. 912 ff.

[176A] *Cf.* Pistorius, P. V. *Plotinus and Neoplatonism*, (Cambridge University Press, Howes, 1952).

perfect transcendence. Unity and goodness cannot be merely attributed to Him. He *is* oneness itself and goodness itself, beyond existence. Without losing anything of its Divine Perfection, this Supreme One emanates a second principle of reason which contains the ideas of all lesser beings within itself. By an inner necessity of nature, this being then pours further beings in an order of decreasing importance. Amongst the last of these are human souls, each with a perceived world of its own, and finally the realm of matter which is identified with evil.

The human soul has fallen into matter, but it can extricate itself by moral and intellectual exertion. Like most Hellenistic and Roman thought, Neo-Platonism took a very dim view of social life. Each individual must achieve his own salvation. To do this, he must first exercise certain moral and civic virtues, then the intellectual virtues, and finally mystical prayer and devotion. In this way, he may be able to gain freedom from the body and union with God.[177] The earlier Neo-Platonists were opposed to Christianity, but some of their later followers were converted to the new religion. St. Augustine was deeply influenced by it, and through his influence, it played an important role in the development of mediaeval Christian thought.

Aristotle's ideas were also preserved in a constant tradition which persisted through many transformations until the Fall of Rome. Indeed, it is fair to say that amongst the rich diversity of opposed philosophies, it was the thought of Plato and Aristotle that best survived the intensive conflict and criticism of this time. As we should expect, the Peripatetic tradition was able to preserve the more careful and empirical method of Aristotle until the very end.[177A] It devoted itself rather to the disciplined analysis of particular problems than to transcendental and far reaching speculations. Many Aristotelian commentators understood this restraint as derived from a sense of the limits of human knowledge, rather than from a denial of human freedom and transcendent being. But one very influential commentator, Alexander of Aphrodisias, in the

[177] *Cf.* Plotinus, *Enneades*, I, Book 8.

[177A] The most accurate account of the history of ancient Aristotelianism is still to be found in the German work, *Grundriss der Geschichte der Philosophie*, I, *die Philosophie des Altertums*, Praechter, Berlin, 1926, Mittler & Sohn, pp. 347–404, 483–6, 556–565, 655–9.

third century A.D. interpreted it in a more naturalistic sense. Man is an insignificant part of the material world and subject to natural determinism. This is the only world we can know, and speculations about divine things are altogether futile.

This early division of Aristotelian thought is most significant for the further development of Western thought. In later Roman times, various Neo-Platonic ideas were incorporated into the Peripatetic tradition, and each trend became more eclectic. By the eighth century A.D., many works of Plato and the Neo-Platonists as well as many works of Aristotle, had been translated into Arabic. As a result of this, they exerted a crucial influence on the history of Mohammedan thought, which we shall now briefly consider.

(ii) *The Greek View of Man in Mohammedan Thought*

Philosophic learning soon became firmly established in the Arabian schools, and the greater accuracy and penetration of the Aristotelian texts was clearly recognized. But many Neo-Platonic works were mingled with this Peripatetic heritage, and some of them were thought to be genuinely Aristotelian. Arabian culture was strictly dominated by the Mohammedan religion, divided into many different sects. Hence these thinkers were not satisfied with Aristotle's caution regarding metaphysical speculation relevant to religion, and supplemented it with Neo-Platonic ideas taken from a very different context. The result was a new kind of philosophical synthesis which was finally presented in two very different and influential versions by the great thinkers Avicenna (A.D. 980-1037) and Averroes (1126-1198).

The former is far more Neo-Platonic than the latter, who idealized Aristotle and eliminated many foreign elements from Avicenna's interpretation. Averroes' version is certainly not accurate, but it is far closer to the words of Aristotle than the Neo-Platonic constructions which had prevailed before his time. A few comments will enable us to suggest the diverse effect of the Platonic and Aristotelian traditions on Arabian religion.[178]

Avicenna rightly saw that the distinction between essence (what a thing is) and existence (its act of being) is implicit

[178] An accurate survey of the history of Arabian thought will be found in D. Gilson, *History of Christian Philosophy in the Middle Ages*, New York: Random House, 1955. *Cf.* Copleston, *Mediaeval Philosophy*, New York: Philosophical Library, 1952.

in the Aristotelian texts, and sharply distinguished between the two. All finite essences are mere possibilities until they are given existence by an external cause. There must, therefore, be a first necessary cause which gives existence to finite things. This first cause has no determinate essence. He is existence itself, and hence exists necessarily. By a necessity of his nature, he also gives being to a secondary rational principle, and then in the Neo-Platonic manner, through this being to others, down to the level of human souls and indeterminate matter or potency. In his philosophy of nature, however, Avicenna is a true disciple of Aristotle, identifying evil with privation rather than with matter which is good. This matter in fact, introduces a factor of indeterminacy into nature without which voluntary choice would be impossible.

Avicenna's view of man is probably closer to Aristotle's own thought, but lacks the latter's caution and restraint. He follows his Arabian predecessors in interpreting the active intellect of the Third Book of the *De Anima* as though it were not only separable from the body, as Aristotle says, but actually separate from it. This intellect, he thinks, is a higher intelligence which thinks for the whole human species. This is very dubious as an Aristotelian doctrine. But Avicenna held that a higher light is received by all human minds from the same source. There is, however, in each individual an immaterial capacity to receive this light. Hence the individual soul is distinct from the body, immaterial, and immortal. This soul can dominate the body, and choose its own acts voluntarily.

As Aristotle showed, most men have to abstract their ideas from sense and imagination without which they cannot think. But prophetic minds may gain direct access to the superhuman, active intellect, and thus be enlightened by supernatural knowledge. Hence religious cults and practices may be illuminating and important. Both philosophy and theology have a single end, the enlightenment and perfection of man. Each has a legitimate place. Aside from the supposition of a separate active intellect, this view of the nature of man is probably not far from the spirit of Aristotle.

His successor Averroes, however, while he pruned away certain Neo-Platonic extravagances, and stuck very close to certain texts of Aristotle, came out with a far more one-sided view. He completely rejected the distinction between essence and existence, which Aristotle certainly did not do. Pure possibility is a mental abstraction. Every real essence must exist. All finite entities have been necessarily produced by a first supreme principle through certain intermediate, moving agencies. But the whole world of nature is ruled by an inexorable necessity which leaves no place for indeterminacy or freedom.

Averroes' psychology is even farther from Aristotle's intent. The human individual is a purely material being. His imagination has a passive capacity to be worked on by a higher agency. Both the active and the possible intellect, which Averroes interprets as the first contact of the former with the material imagination, are separate and transcendent. Our choices are, therefore, determined by factors outside ourselves, and individual immortality is impossible. These doctrines led to conflicts with religious authority. Averroes himself, however, did not admit these conflicts. He held that philosophy was more exact and trustworthy in its demonstrative method than theology, which stated the very same truths in a popular and rhetorical manner accessible to the masses. His own personal views about religion are not known. His expressed views are readily interpreted in terms of a theory of double truth—one for philosophy and another for religion, though he never openly asserted such an opinion.

(iii) *The Influence of Plato and Aristotle on Christian Thought*

The early history of Christian thought in Western Europe is markedly similar.[179] The complete logic or *Organon* and a few other Aristotelian texts were known and carefully studied in the twelfth century. Because of their speculative daring, however, Plato's *Timaeus* and certain Neo-Platonic texts at first seemed more harmonious with religious tradition and practice. Hence until the middle of the thirteenth century, Christian thought was dominated by Augustinian philosophy which used Platonic theories from the very first, especially in its treatment of the human soul and human knowledge. It has in fact continued these notions down to the present day.

Hence when the Aristotelian texts on the human soul,

[179] *Cf.* Ueberweg, *Grundriss der Geschichte der Philosophie*, Berlin, Mittler, 1928; II, *Die Patriatische und Scholastische Philosophie* (ed. Geyer), pp. 287–325. Also Gilson *Hist.* (*cf.* 1178), and Copleston *op. cit.* (*cf.* 178) for brief surveys.

natural philosophy, and metaphysics, as well as the Arabian interpretations were translated into Latin, and introduced into Western Europe about the year 1200, major tensions were generated. The more Neo-Platonic Aristotelian thought of Avicenna was more easily integrated into a Christian framework. At the beginning of the thirteenth century, many syntheses of Avicenna with Augustinian thought were actually attempted. But owing to the confused state of the Aristotelian texts, and the metaphysical caution of their author, these texts were susceptible to another naturalistic and deterministic interpretation which Averroes, as we have noted, had worked out with great penetration and thoroughness.

When parts of his exhaustive commentaries were finally translated and studied by Doctors of the Faculty of Liberal Arts at Paris, they inaugurated a very lively movement known as *Latin Averroism*. The thinkers of this school claimed to base their ideas on the original texts of Aristotle, for which they had a most exalted respect. Appealing to his authority, they defended a philosophy which they claimed to be purely scientific, empirical, and rational. To win such knowledge is to attain the natural end of man.

The world is governed by necessary and determinate laws, and the human individual is a physico-chemical compound with no immaterial properties or powers. There is one separate, active intellect which is the same for the whole human species. The so-called 'will' is not free, and individual immortality is impossible. This one-sided interpretation of Aristotle was, of course, quite irreconcilable with the Christian Faith, as with any other religion, but it gained great headway. For many sober minds, it tended to discredit the use of disciplined empirical analysis, and even philosophy itself. Indeed, had it not been for a new approach to the original texts, the supremacy of Neo-Platonic speculative philosophy might have gone unchallenged, and the tentative spirit and disciplined empirical method of Aristotle himself permanently excluded from Western thought.

This new approach was inaugurated by Albert the Great in Cologne and Paris, where, even with the faulty texts at his disposal, he began to penetrate more accurately and profoundly into their real meaning. It was completed later on by Thomas Aquinas and his friend William of Moerbeke, who made a new and far more accurate translation from the original Greek. On this basis, Aquinas was able to work out a far less inaccurate and one-sided interpretation which he expressed in his penetrating and illuminating commentaries.

He was an original mind of the first order who was able to grasp certain implicit implications of the Aristotelian approach and to develop them in novel ways.[180] In his major works he showed that, when interpreted in this way, there is no conflict but rather a profound harmony between the disciplined and empirical use of reason with the aid of sense, and the Christian Faith. Since his time, this Aristotelian mode of thought, also using the great synthetic and moral insights of Plato, has remained very active in the West, and has been developed in many new ways.

[180] *Cf.* E. Gilson, *The Philosophy of St. Thomas Aquinas*, 3rd ed. St. Louis: Herder, 1939.

CHAPTER II

*The Concept of Man in Jewish Thought**

ABRAHAM JOSHUA HESCHEL

I. THE MEANING OF EXISTENCE

OUR theories will go away, will all throw dust into our eyes, unless we dare to confront not only the world but the soul as well, and begin to be amazed at our lack of amazement in being alive, at our taking life for granted.

Confronting the soul is an intellectual exposure that tears open the mind to incalculable questions, the answers to which are not easily earned. Modern man, therefore, believes that his security lies in refraining from raising such issues. Ultimate questions have become the object of his favourite unawareness. Since the dedication to tangible matters is highly rewarded, he does not care to pay attention to imponderable issues and prefers to erect a tower of Babel on the narrow basis of deeper unawareness.

Unawareness of the ultimate is a possible state of mind as long as man finds tranquility in his dedication to partial objectives. But when the tower begins to totter, when death wipes away that which seemed mighty and independent, when in evil days the delights of striving are replaced by the nightmare of futility, be becomes conscious of the peril of evasiveness, of the emptiness of small objectives. His apprehension lest in winning small prizes he did not gamble his life away, throws his soul open to questions he was trying to avoid.

But what is there at stake in human life that may be gambled away? It is the meaning of life. In all acts he performs, man raises a claim to meaning. The trees he plants, the tools he invents, are *answers to a need* or a purpose. In its very essence,

* In this chapter, the author has incorporated material from his three books, *Man is not Alone*, *Man's Quest for God*, and *God in Search of Man*.

consciousness is a dedication to design. Committed to the task of coalescing being with meaning, things with ideas, the mind is driven to ponder whether meaning is something it may invent and invest, something which ought to be attained, or whether there is meaning to existence as it is, to existence as existence, independent of what we may add to it. In other words, is there only meaning to what *man does*, but none to what *he is*? Becoming conscious of himself he does not stop at knowing: 'I am'; he is driven to know 'what' he is. Man may, indeed, be characterized as *a subject in quest of a predicate*, as a being in quest of a meaning of life, of all of life, not only of particular actions or single episodes which happen now and then.

Meaning denotes a condition that cannot be reduced to a material relation and grasped by the sense organs. Meaning is compatibility with an idea, it is, furthermore, that which a fact is for the sake of something else; the pregnancy of an object with value. Life is precious to man. But is it precious to him alone? Or is someone else in need of it?

Imbedded in the mind is a certainty that the state of existence and the state of meaning stand in a relation to each other, that life is assessable in terms of meaning. The will to meaning and the certainty of the legitimacy of our striving to ascertain it are as intrinsically human as the will to live and the certainty of being alivc.

In spite of failures and frustrations, we continue to be haunted by that irrepressible quest. We can never accept the idea that life is hollow and incompatible with meaning.

If at the root of philosophy is not a self-contempt of the mind but the mind's concern for its ultimate surmise, then our aim is to examine in order to know. Seeking contentment in a brilliant subterfuge, we are often ready to embezzle the original surmise. But why should we even care to doubt, if we cease to surmise? Philosophy is what man dares to do with his ultimate surmise of the meaning of existence.

Animals are content when their needs are satisfied; man insists not only on being satisfied but also on being able to satisfy, on *being a need* not only on *having needs*. Personal needs come and go, but one anxiety remains: *Am I needed*? There is no man who has not been moved by that anxiety.

It is a most significant fact that man is not sufficient to

himself, that life is not meaningful to him unless it is serving an end beyond itself, unless it is of value to someone else. The self may have the highest rate of exchange, yet men do not live by currency alone, but by the good attainable in expending it. To hoard the self is to grow a colossal sense for the futility of living.

Man is not an all-inclusive end to himself. The second maxim of Kant, never to use human beings merely as means but to regard them also as ends, only suggests how a person ought to be treated by other people, not how he ought to treat himself. For if a person thinks that he is an end to himself, then he will use others as means. Moreover, if the idea of man being an end is to be taken as a true estimate of his worth, he cannot be expected to sacrifice his life or his interests for the good of someone else or even of a group. He must treat himself the way he expects others to treat him. Why should even a group or a whole people be worth the sacrifice of one's life? To a person who regards himself as an absolute end a thousand lives will not be worth more than his own life.

Sophisticated thinking may enable man to feign his being sufficient to himself. Yet the way to insanity is paved with such illusions. The feeling of futility that comes with the sense of being useless, of not being needed in the world, is the most common cause of psycho-neurosis. The only way to avoid despair *is to be a need* rather than an end. *Happiness*, in fact, may be defined as the *certainty of being needed*. But *who* is in need of man?

The first answer that comes to mind is a social one—man's purpose is to serve society or mankind. The ultimate worth of a person would then be determined by his usefulness to others, by the efficiency of his social work. Yet, in spite of his instrumentalist attitude, man expects others to take him not for what he may mean to them but as a being valuable in himself. Even he who does not regard himself as an absolute end, rebels against being treated as a means to an end, as subservient to other men. The rich, the men of the world, want to be loved for their own sake, for their essence, whatever it may mean, not for their achievements or possessions. Nor do the old and sick expect help because of what they may give us in return. Who needs the old, the incurably sick, the maintenance of whom is a drain on the treasury of the state? It is, moreover, obvious that such service does not claim all of one's life and can therefore not be the ultimate answer to his quest of meaning for life as a whole. Man has more to give than what other men are able or willing to accept. To say that life could consist of care for others, of incessant service to the world, would be a vulgar boast. What we are able to bestow upon others is usually less and rarely more than a tithe.

There are alleys in the soul where man walks alone, ways that do not lead to society, a world of privacy that shrinks from the public eye. Life comprises not only arable, productive land, but also mountains of dreams, an underground of sorrow, towers of yearning, which can hardly be utilized to the last for the good of society, unless man be converted into a machine in which every screw must serve a function or be removed. It is a profiteering state which, trying to exploit the individual, asks all of man for itself.

And if society as embodied in the state should prove to be corrupt and my effort to cure its evil unavailing, would my life as an individual have been totally void of meaning? If society should decide to reject my services and even place me in solitary confinement, so that I will surely die without being able to bequeath any influence to the world I love, will I then feel compelled to end my life?

Human existence cannot derive its ultimate meaning from society, because society itself is in need of meaning. It is as legitimate to ask: Is mankind needed?—as it is to ask: Am I needed?

Humanity begins in the individual man, just as history takes its rise from a singular event. It is always one man at a time whom we keep in mind when we pledge: 'with malice toward none, with charity for all', or when trying to fulfil: 'Love thy neighbour as thyself'. The term 'mankind', which in biology denotes the human species, has an entirely different meaning in the realm of ethics and religion. Here mankind is not conceived as a species, as an abstract concept, stripped from its concrete reality, but as an abundance of specific individuals; as a community of persons rather than as a herd of a multitude of nondescripts.

While it is true that the good of all counts more than the good of one, it is the concrete individual who lends meaning to the human race. We do not think that a human being is valuable because he is a member of the race; it is rather the opposite: the human race is valuable because it is composed of human beings.

While dependent on society as well as on the air that sustains us, and while other men compose the system of relations in which the curve of our actions takes its course, it is as individuals that we are beset with desires, fears and hopes, challenged, called upon and endowed with the power of will and a spark of responsibility.

Of all phenomena which takes place in the soul, desires have the highest rate of mortality. Like aquatic plants, they grow and live in the waters of oblivion, impatiently eager to vanish. Inherent in desire is the intention to expire; it asserts itself in order to be quenched, and in attaining satisfaction it comes to an end, singing its own dirge.

Such suicidal intention is not vested in all human acts. Thoughts, concepts, laws, theories are born with the intent to endure. A problem, for example, does not cease to be relevant when its solution is achieved. Inherent in reason is the intention to endure, a striving to comprehend the valid, to form concepts the cogency of which goes on for ever. It is, therefore, not in pondering about ideas, but in surveying one's inner life and discovering the graveyard of needs and desires, once fervently cherished, that we become intimately aware of the temporality of existence.

Yet, there is a curious ambiguity in the way in which this awareness is entertained. For while there is nothing man is more intimately sure of than the temporality of existence, he is rarely resigned to the role of a mere undertaker of desires.

Walking upon a rock that is constantly crumbling away behind every step and anticipating the inevitable abruption which will end his walk, man cannot restrain his bitter yearning to know whether life is nothing but a series of momentary physiological and mental processes, actions and forms of behaviour, a flow of vicissitudes, desires and sensations, running like grains through an hourglass, marking time only once and always vanishing.

He wonders whether, at the bottom, life is not like the face of the sundial, outliving all shadows that rotate upon its surface. Is life nothing but a medley of facts, unrelated to one another; chaos camouflaged by illusion?

There is not a soul on this earth which, however vaguely or rarely, has not realized that life is dismal if not mirrored in something which is lasting. We are all in search of a conviction that there is something which is worth the toil of living. There is not a soul which has not felt a craving to know of something that outlasts life, strife and agony.

Helpless and incongruous is man with all his craving, with his tiny candles in the mist. Is it his will to be good that would heal the wounds of his soul, his fright and frustration? It is too obvious that his will is a door to a house divided against itself, that his good intentions, after enduring for a while, touch the mud of vanity, like the horizon of his life which some day will touch the grave. Is there anything beyond the horizon of our good intentions?

Despair, the sense of futility of living, is an attitude, the reality of which no psychologist will question. But just as real is our fear of despair, our horror of futility. Human life and despair seem to be incompatible. Man is a being in search of ultimate meaning of existence. But where is ultimate meaning to be found?

Ultimate meaning implies not only that man is part of a whole, an adjunct to greatness, but an answer to a question, the satisfaction of a need; not only that man is tolerated but also needed, precious, indispensable. Life is precious to man. But is it precious to man alone?

2. A NEED OF GOD

The Bible is a book about man. It is not a theology from the point of view of man but rather an anthropology from the point of view of God. And it is man who is becoming the central issue of contemporary thinking. His physical and mental reality is beyond dispute; his meaning, his spiritual relevance, is a question that cries for an answer.

It is the uniqueness of man that puzzles our mind. All other beings seem to fit perfectly into a natural order and are determined by permanent principles. Man alone occupies a unique status. As a natural being he is determined by natural laws. As a human being he must frequently choose; confined in his existence, he is unrestrained in his will. His acts do not emanate from him like rays of energy from matter. Placed in the parting of the ways, he must time and again decide which direction to take. The course of his life is, accordingly, unpredictable; no one can write his autobiography in advance.

Is man, who occupies such a strange position in the great realm of being, an outcast of the universal order? an outlaw, a freak of nature? a shred of yarn dropped from nature's loom, which has since been strangely twisted by the way? Astronomy and geology have taught us to disdain the over-weening vanity of man. Compared with the infinite universe, man is, indeed, a most insignificant speck.

However, if man's value and position in the universe are to be defined as one divided by the infinite, the infinite designating the number of beings which populate the universe; if man $= \frac{1}{\infty}$, how should we account for the fact that infinitesimal man is obviously the only being on this planet capable of making such an equation?

An ant is never stricken with amazement, nor does a star consider itself a nonentity. Immense is the scope of astronomy and geology, yet what is astronomy without the astronomer? What is geology without the geologist?

If we had to characterize an individual like William Shakespeare in terms of a measuring rod, we would surely avail ourselves of Eddington's description of man's position within the universe and say that Shakespeare is almost precisely halfway in size between an atom and a star. To assess his vegetative existence, it is important to know, for example, that man consists of a hundred million cells. However, to assess the essence of man, which alone accounts for the fact of his being anxious to assess his existence, we must discern what is unique about him.

Reflecting about the infinite universe we could perhaps afford to resign ourselves to the trivial position of being a nonentity. However, pondering over our reflection, we discover that we are not only carried and surrounded by the universe of meaning. Man is a fountain of immense meaning, not only a drop in the ocean of being.

The human species is too powerful, too dangerous to be a mere toy or a freak of the Creator. He undoubtedly represents something unique in the great body of the universe: a growth, as it were, an abnormal mass of tissue, which not only began to interact with other parts but also, to some degree, was able to modify their very status. What is its nature and function? Is it malignant, a tumor, or is it supposed to serve as a brain of the universe?

The human species shows at times symptoms of being malignant and, if its growth remains unchecked, it may destroy the entire body for the sake of its expansion. In terms of astronomical time, our civilization is in its infancy. The expansion of human power has hardly begun, and what man is going to do with his power may either save or destroy our planet.

The earth may be of small significance within the infinite universe. But if it is of some significance, man holds the key to it. For one thing man certainly seems to own: a boundless, unpredictable capacity for the development of an inner universe. There is more potentiality in his soul than in any other being known to us. Look at an infant and try to imagine the multitude of events it is going to engender. One child called Bach was charged with power enough to hold generations of men in his spell. But is there any potentiality to acclaim or any surprise to expect in a calf or a colt? Indeed, the essence of man is not in what he is, but in what he is able to be.

Yet the darkness of potentiality is the hotbed of anxiety. There is always more than one path to go, and we are forced to be free—we are free against our will—and have the audacity to choose, rarely knowing how or why. Our failures glare like flashlights all the way, and what is right lies underground. We are in the minority in the real realm of being, and, with a genius for adjustment, we frequently seek to join the multitude. We are in the minority within our own nature, and in the agony and battle of passions we often choose to envy the beast. We behave as if the animal kingdom were our lost paradise, to which we are trying to return for moments of delight, believing that it is the animal state in which happiness consists. We have an endless craving to be like the beast, a nostalgic admiration for animal within us. According to a contemporary scientist: 'Man's greatest tragedy occurred when he ceased to walk on all fours and cut himself off from the animal world by assuming an erect position. If man had continued to walk horizontally, and rabbits had learned to walk vertically, many of the world's ills would not exist.'

Man is continuous both with the rest of organic nature and

with the infinite outpouring of the spirit of God. A minority in the realm of being, he stands somewhere between God and the beasts. Unable to live alone, he must commune with either of the two.

Both Adam and the beasts were blessed by the Lord, but man was also charged with conquering the earth and dominating the beast. Man is always faced with the choice of listening either to God or to the snake. It is always easier to envy the beast, to worship a totem and be dominated by it, than to hearken to the Voice.

Our existence seesaws between animality and divinity, between that which is more and that which is less than humanity: below is evanescence, futility, and above is the open door of the divine exchequer where we lay up the sterling coin of piety and spirit, the immortal remains of our dying lives. We are constantly in the mills of death, but we are also the contemporaries of God.

Man is 'a little lower than the Divine' (*Psalm* 8:5) and a little higher than the beasts. Like a pendulum he swings to and fro under the combined action of gravity and momentum, of the gravitation of selfishness and the momentum of the divine, of a vision beheld by God in the darkness of flesh and blood. We fail to understand the meaning of our existence when we disregard our commitments to that vision. Yet only eyes vigilant and fortified against the glaring and superficial can still perceive God's vision in the soul's horror-stricken night of human folly, falsehood, hatred and malice.

Because of his immense power, man is potentially the most wicked of beings. He often has a passion for cruel deeds that only fear of God can soothe, suffocating flushes of envy that only holiness can ventilate.

If man is not more than human, then he is less than human. Man is but a short, critical stage between the animal and the spiritual. His state is one of constant wavering, of soaring or descending. Undeviating humanity is non-existent. The emancipated man is yet to emerge.

Man is more than what he is to himself. In his reason he may be limited, in his will he may be wicked, yet he stands in a relation to God which he may betray but not sever and which constitutes the essential meaning of his life. He is the knot in which heaven and earth are interlaced.

When carried away by the joy of acting as we please, adopting any desire, accepting any opportunity for action if the body welcomes it, we feel perfectly satisfied to walk on all fours. Yet there are moments in everyone's life when he begins to wonder whether the pleasures of the body or the interests of the self should serve as the perspective from which all decisions should be made.

In spite of the delights that are within our reach, we refuse to barter our souls for selfish rewards and to live without a conscience on the proceeds. Even those who have forfeited the ability for compassion have not forfeited the ability to be horrified at their inability to feel compassion. The ceiling has collapsed, yet the souls still hang by a hair of horror. Time and again everyone of us tried to sit in judgment over his life. Even those who have gambled away the vision of virtue are not deprived of the horror of crime. Through disgust and dismay we struggle to know that to live on selfish needs is to kill what is still alive in our dismay. There is only one way to fumigate the obnoxious air of our world—to live beyond our own needs and interests. We are carnal, covetous, selfish, vain, and to live for the sake of unselfish needs means to live beyond our own means. How could we be more than what we are? How beyond our own means? How could we be more than what we are? How could we find resources that would give our souls a surplus that is not our own? To live beyond our needs means to be independent of selfish needs. Yet how would man succeed in breaking out of the circle of his self?

The possibility of eliminating self-regard ultimately depends on the nature of the self; it is a metaphysical rather than a psychological issue. If the self exists for its own sake, such independence would be neither possible nor desirable. It is only in assuming that the self is not the hub but a spoke, neither its own beginning nor its own end, that such possibility could be affirmed.

Man *is* meaning, but not his own meaning. He does not even know his own meaning, for a meaning does not know what it means. The self *is* a need, but not its own need.

All our experiences are needs, dissolving when the needs are fulfilled. But the truth is, our existence, too, is a need. We are such stuff as needs are made of, and our little life is rounded by a will. *Lasting* in our life is neither passion nor delight, neither joy nor pain, but the answer to a need. The lasting in us is not our will to live. There is a need for our lives, and in living we satisfy it. Lasting is not our desire, but our answer to that need, an agreement not an impulse. Our needs are temporal, while our being needed is lasting

We have started our inquiry with the question of the individual man—what is the meaning of the individual man?—and established his uniqueness in his being pregnant with immense potentialities, of which he becomes aware in his experience of needs. We have also pointed out that he finds no happiness in utilizing his potentialities for the satisfaction of his own needs, that his destiny is to be a need.

But who is in need of man? Nature? Do the mountains stand in need of our poems? Would the stars fade away if astronomers ceased to exist? The earth can get along without the aid of the human species. Nature is replete with opportunity to satisfy all our needs except one—the need of being needed. Within its unbroken silence man is like the middle of a sentence and all his theories are like dots indicating his isolation within his own self.

Unlike all other needs, the need of being needed is a striving to give rather than to obtain satisfaction. It is a desire to satisfy a transcendent desire, a craving to satisfy a craving.

All needs are one-sided. When hungry we are in need of food, yet food is *not* in need of being consumed. Things of beauty attract our minds; we feel the need of perceiving them, yet they are not in need of being perceived by us. It is in such one-sidedness, that most of living is imprisoned. Examine an average mind, and you will find that it is dominated by an effort to cut reality to the measure of the ego, as if the world existed for the sake of pleasing one's ego. Everyone of us entertains more relations with things than with people, and even in dealings with people we behave toward them as if they were things, tools, means to be used for our own selfish ends. How rarely do we face a person as a person. We are all dominated by the desire to appropriate and to own. Only a free person knows that the true meaning of existence is experienced in giving, in endowing, in meeting a person face to face, in fulfilling other people's needs.

When realizing the surplus of what we see over what we feel, the mind is evasive, even the heart is incomplete. Why are we discontent with mere living for the sake of living? Who has made us thirsty for what is more than existence?

Everywhere we are surrounded by the ineffable, our familiarity with reality is a myth. To the innermost in our soul even beauty is an alloy mixed with the true metal of eternity. There is neither earth nor sky, neither spring nor autumn; there is only a question, God's eternal question of man: Where art Thou? Religion begins with the certainty that something is asked of us, that there are ends which are in need of us. Unlike all other values, moral and religious ends evoke in us a sense of obligation. They present themselves as tasks rather than as objects of perception. Thus, religious living consists in serving ends which are in need of us.

Man is not an innocent bystander in the cosmic drama. There is in us more kinship with the divine than we are able to believe. The souls of men are candles of the Lord, lit on the cosmic way, rather than fireworks produced by the combustion of nature's explosive compositions, and every soul is indispensable to Him. Man is needed, he is *a need of God*.

3. THE PARADOX OF DIVINE CONCERN

There are many things about man which are hard to understand. What is his nature? What is his purpose? What is his place in the universe? What is his relation to God? None of these issues is central in Biblical thinking.

The problem that challenged the Biblical mind was not the obscurity of his nature but the paradox of his existence. The starting-point was not a question about man but the distinction of man; not the state of ignorance about the nature of man and the desire to find an answer to the question, What is man? but rather a state of amazement at what we know about man, namely: Why is man so significant in spite of his insignificance? Not the question, Why is man mortal? but the question, Why is he so distinguished?

The problem that challenged the Biblical mind was not man in and by himself. Man is never seen in isolation but always in relation to God who is the Creator, the King, and the Judge of all beings. The problem of man revolved around God's relation to man. Two passages may serve as an illustration.

Lord,
What is man,
That thou takest knowledge of him?
Or the son of man,
That thou makest account of him?
Man is like unto a breath;
His days are as a shadow
That passeth away.
(*Psalms* 144:3-4)

When I behold Thy heavens,
The work of Thy fingers,
The moon and the stars
Which Thou hast established
What is man
That Thou shouldst be mindful of him?
And the son of man
That Thou shouldst think of him?
And make him
But a little lower than the Divine,
And crown him with glory and honour,
And make him rule over the works of Thy hands?
Thou hast put all things under his feet:
Sheep and oxen, all of them,
Yes, and the beasts of the field;
The fowl of the air, and the fish of the sea,
That pass through the paths of the seas.
(*Psalms* 8:2-9)

What gives the Psalmist the certainty that God is mindful of man? Is it inference from the facts of human existence namely that man was made 'a little lower than the Divine', that he was crowned 'with glory and honour', and that he was made to rule over the works of God's creation? Perhaps it was not such an inference but rather an immediate insight, a fundamental awareness, that was the source of the Psalmist's certainty.

The power and intensity of God's concern are at times beyond the endurance of man.

Therefore I will not refrain my mouth;
I will speak in the anguish of my spirit;
I will complain in the bitterness of my soul.
Am I a sea, or a sea-monster,
That Thou settest a watch over me?
When I say; 'My bed shall comfort me,
My couch shall ease my complaint';
Then Thou scarest me with dreams,
And terrifiest me through visions;
So that my soul chooseth strangling,
And death rather than these my bones,
I loathe it; I shall not live always:
Let me alone; for my days are vanity.
What is man, that Thou shouldst magnify him,
And that Thou shouldst set Thy heart upon him,
And that Thou shouldst remember him every morning,
And try him every moment?
How long wilt Thou not look away from me,
Nor let me alone till I swallow down my spittle?
If I have sinned, what do I unto Thee,
O Thou watcher of men?
Why hast Thou set me as a mark for Thee,
So that I am a burden to myself?
And why dost Thou not pardon my transgression,
And take away mine iniquity?
For now shall I lie down in the dust;
And Thou wilt seek me,
But I shall not be.
(*Job* 7:11-21)

Plants, stars, and beasts are expected to exist in conformity with the cosmic order, to continue to be what they are. Man, on the other hand, is expected to act in agreement with the will of the living God, to decide, to make a choice, to prevail. What man faces is not a principle but a living concern which expresses itself in God addressing man as well as in His guiding the history of man. God does not address the stars; He addresses man.

The insignificance of man compared with the grandeur of God underscores the paradox of God's concern for him. Neither Job nor the Psalmist offers an answer to the overwhelming enigma which thus remains the central mystery of human existence.

Yet the acceptance of that fact of Divine concern established the Biblical approach to the existence of man. It is from the perspective of that concern that the quest for an understanding of the meaning of man begins.

Nowhere in Plato's Socratic dialogues do we find a direct solution to the problem, 'What is man?' There is only an indirect answer, 'Man is declared to be that creature who is constantly in search of himself—a creature who in every moment of his existence must examine and scrutinize the conditions of his existence.'[1] The Biblical answer would not be that man is a creature who is constantly in search of himself, but rather that man is a creature God is constantly in search of.

The Greeks formulated the search of meaning as man in search of a thought; the Hebrews formulated the search of meaning as God's thought (or concern) in search of man. The meaning of existence is not naturally given; it is not an endowment but an art. It rather depends on whether we respond or refuse to respond to God who is in search of man; it is either fulfilled or missed.

The primary topic, then, of Biblical Thinking is not man's knowledge of God but rather man's being known by God, man's being an object of Divine knowledge and concern. This is why the great puzzle was: Why should God, The Creator of heaven and earth, be concerned with man? Why should the deeds of puny man be relevant enough to affect the life of God?

> Can a man be profitable unto God?
> Or can he that is wise be profitable unto Him?
> Is it any advantage to the Almighty, that thou art righteous?
> Or is it gain to Him, that thou makest thy ways blameless?
> (*Job* 22:2-3)

God takes man seriously. He enters a direct relationship with man, namely *a Covenant*, to which not only man but also God is committed. In his ultimate confrontation and crisis the Biblical man knows not only God's eternal mercy and justice but also *God's commitment to man*. Upon this sublime fact rests the meaning of history and the glory of human destiny.

[1] E. Cassirer, *An Essay on Man*, New Haven, 1944, p. 5.

There is only one way to define Jewish religion. It is the *awareness of God's interest in man*, the awareness of a *covenant*, of a responsibility that lies on Him as well as on us. Our task is to concur with His interest, to carry out His vision of our task. God is in need of man for the attainment of His ends, and religion, as Jewish tradition understands it, is a way of serving these ends, of which we are in need, even though we may not be aware of them, ends which we must learn to feel the need of.

Life is a *partnership* of God and man; God is not detached from or indifferent to our joys and griefs. Authentic vital needs of man's body and soul are a divine concern. This is why human life is holy. God is a partner and a partisan in man's struggle for justice, peace and holiness, and it is because of His being in need of man that He entered a *covenant* with him for all time, a mutual bond embracing God and man, a relationship to which God, not only man, is committed.

> This day you have avowed the Lord to be your God, promising to walk in His ways, to obey His rules and commandments, and to hearken to His voice;
> And this day the Lord has avowed you to be His very own people, as He has promised you, and to obey His commandments.
>
> (*Deuteronomy* 26:17-18)

Some people think that religion comes about as a perception of an answer to a prayer, while in truth it comes about in our knowing that God shared our prayer. The essence of Judaism is the awareness of the *reciprocity* of God and man, of man's *togetherness* with Him who abides in eternal otherness. For the task of living is His and ours, and so is the responsibility. We have rights, not only obligations; our ultimate commitment is our ultimate privilege.

In interpreting *Malachi* 3:18, Rabbi Aha ben Ada said: 'Then shall ye again discern between the righteous and the wicked,' meaning: 'between him who has faith and him who has no faith'; 'between him that serveth God and him that serveth Him not,' meaning: 'between him who serves God's *need* and him who does not serve God's *need*. One should not make of the Torah a spade with which to dig, a tool for personal use or a crown to magnify oneself.'[2]

[2] *Midrash Tehillim*, ed. Buber, p. 240.

E*

His need is a self-imposed concern. God is now in need of man, because He freely made him a partner in His enterprise, 'a partner in the work of creation'. 'From the first day of creation the Holy one, blessed be He, longed to enter into *partnership* with the terrestrial world'[3] to dwell *with* His creatures within the terrestrial world. Expounding the verse in *Genesis* 17:1, the Midrash remarked: 'In the view of Rabbi Johanan we need His honour; in the view of Rabbi Simeon ben Lakish He needs our honour.'[4]

'When Israel performs the will of the Omnipresent, they add strength to the heavenly power; as it is said: "To God we render strength" (*Psalms* 60:14). When, however, Israel does not perform the will of the Omnipresent, they weaken—if it is possible to say so—the great power of Him who is above; as it is written, "Thou didst weaken the Rock that begot Thee".'[5]

Man's relationship to God is not one of passive reliance upon His Omnipotence but one of active assistance. 'The impious rely on their gods . . . the righteous are the support of God.'[6]

The Patriarchs are therefore called 'the chariot of the Lord'.[7]

> He glories in me, He delights in me;
> My crown of beauty He shall be.
> His glory rests on me, and mine on Him;
> He is near to me, when I call on Him.
> (*The Hymn of Glory*)

The extreme boldness of this paradox was expressed in a Tannaitic interpretation of *Isaiah* 43:12: 'Ye are my witnesses, saith the Lord, and I am God'—when you are my witnesses I am God, and when you are not my witnesses I am not God.[8]

The God of the philosophers is all indifference, too sublime to possess a heart or to cast a glance at our world. His wisdom consists in being conscious of Himself and oblivious to the world. In contrast, the God of the prophets is all concern, too merciful to remain aloof to His creation. He not only rules the

[3] *Numbers Rabba*, ch. 13, 6; compare *Genesis Rabba*, ch. 3, 9.
[4] *Genesis Rabba*, ch. 30; unlike *Theodor*, p. 277.
[5] *Pesikta*, ed. Buber, XXVI, 166b; (compare the two versions).
[6] *Genesis Rabba*, ch. 69, 3.
[7] *Genesis Rabba*, ch. 47, 6; 83, 6.
[8] *Sifre Deuteronomy*, 346; (compare the interpretation of *Psalms* 123:1).

world in the majesty of His might; He is personally concerned and even stirred by the conduct and fate of man. 'His mercy is upon all His work.'[9]

These are the two poles of prophetic thinking: The idea that God is one, holy, different and apart from all that exists, and the idea of the inexhaustible concern of God for man, at times brightened by His mercy, at times darkened by His anger. He is both transcendent, beyond human understanding, and full of love, compassion, grief or anger.

God does not judge the deeds of man impassively, in a spirit of cool detachment. His judgment is imbued with a feeling of intimate concern. He is the father of all men, not only a judge; He is a lover engaged to His people, not only a king. God stands in a passionate relationship to man. His love or anger, His mercy or disappointment is an expression of His profound participation in the history of Israel and all men.

Prophecy, then, consists in the proclamation of the divine *pathos*, expressed in the language of the prophets as love, mercy or anger. Behind the various manifestations of His pathos is one motive, one need: The divine need for human righteousness.

The pagan gods had animal passions, carnal desires, they were more fitful, licentious than men; the God of Israel has a passion for righteousness. The pagan gods had selfish needs, while the God of Israel is only in need of man's integrity. The need of Moloch was the death of man, the need of the Lord is the life of man. The divine pathos which the prophets tried to express in many ways was not a name for His essence but rather for the modes of His reaction to Israel's conduct which would change if Israel modified its ways.

The surge of divine pathos, which came to the souls of the prophets like a fierce passion, startling, shaking, burning, led them forth to the perilous defiance of people's self-assurance and contentment. Beneath all songs and sermons they held conference with God's concern for the people, with the well, out of which the tides of anger raged.[10]

The Bible is not a history of the Jewish people, but the story of God's quest of the righteous man. Because of the failure of the human species as a whole to follow in the path of righteousness, it is an individual—Noah, Abraham—a people; Israel—

[9] *Psalms* 145:9.

[10] See A. Heschel, *Die Prophetie*, Cracow, 1936, pp. 56–87; 127–180.

or a remnant of the people, on which the task is bestowed to satisfy that quest by making every man a righteous man.

There is an eternal cry in the world: God is beseeching man. Some are startled; others remain deaf. We are all looked for. An air of expectancy hovers over life. Something is asked of man, of all men.

4. IMAGE AND LIKENESS

The Biblical account of creation is couched in the language of mystery. Nothing is said about the intention or the plan that preceded the creation of heaven and earth. The Bible does not begin: And God said: let us create heaven and earth. All we hear about is the mystery of God's creative act, and not a word about intention or meaning. The same applies to the creation of all other beings. We only hear what He does, not what He thinks. 'And God said: Let there be.' The creation of man, however, is preceded by a forecast: 'And God said: Let us make man in our image, after our likeness.' The act of man's creation is preceded by an utterance of His intention, God's knowledge of man is to precede man's coming into being. God knows him before He creates him. Man's being is rooted in his being known about. It is the creation of man that opens a glimpse into the thought of God, into the meaning beyond the mystery.

'And God said: Let us make man in our image (*tselem*), after our likeness (*demuth*). . . . And God created man in His image, in the image of God created He him' (*Genesis* 1:26 f).

These words which are repeated in the opening words of the fifth chapter of *Genesis*—'This is the book of the generations of man. When God created man, He made him in the likeness (*demuth*) of God'—contain, according to Jewish tradition, the fundamental statement about the nature and meaning of man.

In many religions, man is regarded as an image of a god. Yet the meaning of such regard depends on the meaning of the god whom man resembles. If the god is regarded as a man magnified, if the gods are conceived of in the image of man, then such regard tells us little about the nature and destiny of man. Where God is one among many gods, where the word Divine is used as mere hyperbolic expression; where the difference between God and man is but a difference in degree, then an expression such as the Divine image of man is equal in meaning to the idea of the supreme in man. It is only in the light of what the Biblical man thinks of God, namely a Being who created heaven and earth, the God of absolute justice and compassion, the master of nature and history who transcends nature and history, that the idea of man having been created in the image of God refers to the supreme mystery of man, of his nature and existence.

Image and likeness of God. What these momentous words are trying to convey has never ceased to baffle the Biblical reader. In the Bible, *tselem*, the word for image, is nearly always used in a derogatory sense, denoting idolatrous images.[11] It is a cardinal sin to fashion an image of God. The same applies to *demuth*, the word for likeness.

'To whom will you liken God? Or what likeness (*demuth*) will ye compare to Him? (*Isaiah* 40:18). 'To whom will ye liken Me, and make Me equal, and compare Me, that we may be like?' (*Isaiah* 46:5) 'For who in the skies can be compared unto the Lord, who among the sons of might can be likened unto the Lord?' (*Psalms* 89:7).

God is Divine, and man is human. This contrast underlies all Biblical thinking. God is never human, and man is never Divine. 'I will not execute the fierceness of Mine anger, I will not return to destroy Ephraim; for I am God and not man.'[12] 'God is not a man, that he should lie; neither the son of man, that He should repent.'[13]

Thus, the likeness of God means the likeness of Him who is unlike man. The likeness of God means the likeness of Him, compared with whom all else is like nothing.

Indeed, the words 'image and likeness of God' conceal more than they reveal. They signify something which we can neither comprehend nor verify. For what is our image? What is our likeness? Is there anything about man that may be compared with God? Our eyes do not see it; our minds cannot grasp it. Taken literally, these words are absurd, if not blasphemous. And still they hold the most important truth about the meaning of man.

Obscure as the meaning of these terms is, they undoubtedly denote something *un-earthly*, something that belongs to the

[11] *Numbers* 33:52; *I Samuel* 6:5, 6, 11; *II Kings* 11:18; *Ezekiel* 7:20; 16:17; 23:14; *II Chronicles* 23:17.

[12] *Hosea* 11:9.

[13] *Numbers* 23:19.

sphere of God. *Demuth* and *tselem* are of a *higher sort of being* than the things created in the six days. This, it seems, is what the verse intends to convey: Man partakes of an unearthly Divine sort of being.

An idea is relevant if it serves as an answer to a question. To understand the relevance of 'the Divine image and likeness', we must try to ascertain the question which it comes to answer.

Paradoxically, the problem of man arises more frequently as the problem of death than as the problem of life. It is an important fact, however, that in contrast with Babylonia and particularly Egypt, where the preoccupation with death was the central issue of religious thinking, the Bible hardly deals with death as a problem. Its central concern is not, as in the Gilgamesh epic, how to escape death, but rather how to sanctify life. And the Divine image and likeness does not serve man to attain immortality but to attain sanctity.

Man is man not because of what he has in common with the earth, but *because of what he has in common with God*. The Greek thinkers sought to understand man as *a part of the universe*: the Prophets sought to understand man as *a partner of God*.

It is a concern and a task that man has in common with God.

The intention is not to indentify 'the image and likeness' with a particular quality or attribute of man, such as reason, speech, power or skill. It does not refer to something which in later systems was called 'the best in man', 'the divine spark', 'the eternal spirit' or 'the immortal element' in man. It is the whole man and every man who was made in the image and likeness of God. It is both body and soul, sage and fool, saint and sinner, man in his joy and in his grief, in his righteousness and wickedness. The image is not in man; it is man.

The basic dignity of man is not made up of his achievements, virtues, or special talents. It is inherent in his very being. The commandment 'Love thy neighbour as thyself' (*Leviticus* 19:18) calls upon us to love not only the virtuous and the wise but also the vicious and the stupid man. The Rabbis have, indeed, interpreted the commandment to imply that even a criminal remains our neighbour.[14]

The image-love is a love of what God loves, an act of sympathy, of participation in God's love. It is unconditional and regardless of man's merits or distinctions.

[14] *Pesahim*, 75a.

According to many thinkers, love is induced by that which delights or commands admiration. Such a view would restrict love to those worthy of receiving it and condition it upon whether a person might invoke delight or admiration. It would exclude the criminal and the corrupt members of society. In contrast, to love man according to Judaism is not a response to any physical, intellectual, or moral value of a person. We must love man because he is made in the image of God. Said Rabbi Akiba: '*Love thy neighbour as thyself* is the supreme principle of the Torah. You must not say, since I have been put to shame (by a fellow man), let him be put to shame; since I have been slighted, let him be slighted. Said Rabbi Tanhuma: If you do so, know whom you put to shame, for in the likeness of God made He him.'[15]

Thus God loves Israel notwithstanding its backslidings.[16] His love is a gift rather than an earning.[17] 'The Lord did not set His love upon you, nor choose you, because ye were more in number than any people . . . for ye were the fewest of all peoples . . . but because the Lord loved you. . . .'[18]

Sparingly does the term 'image of God' occur in the Bible. Beyond the first chapter of *Genesis*, it comes forth in two instances: To remind us that every thing found on earth was placed under the dominion of man, except human life, and to remind us that the body of man, not only his soul, is endowed with Divine dignity.

The image of God is employed in stressing the criminality of murder. 'For your lifeblood I will surely require a reckoning; of every beast I will require it and of man; of every man's brother I will require the life of man. Whosoever sheds the blood of man, by man shall his blood be shed; for God made man in His own image.'[19]

The image of man is also referred to in urging respect for the body of a criminal following his execution. 'If a man has committed a crime punishable by death and he is put to death, and you hang him on a tree, his body shall not remain all night

[15] *Genesis Rabba*, 24, 8.
[16] *Hosea* 11:1 f.
[17] *Hosea* 14:5.
[18] *Deuteronomy* 7:7–8.
[19] *Genesis* 9:5 f. It is not clear, however, whether the last words of this sentence contain a condemnation of murder or a justification of man and the right to pronounce the death penalty for murder.

upon the tree, but you shall bury him the same day, for the dignity (or glory) of God is hanged (on the tree).'

The intention of the verse is stressed boldly by Rabbi Meir, an outstanding authority of the second century of the common era, in the form of a parable. 'To what may this be compared? To twin brothers who lived in one city; one was appointed king, and the other took to highway robbery. At the king's command they hanged him. But all who saw him exclaimed: The king is hanged! (For being twins their appearance was similar). Whereupon the king issued a command and he was taken down.'

Great, therefore, must be our esteem for every man. 'Let the honour of your disciple be as dear to you as your own, let the regard for your colleague be like the reverence due to your teacher, and let the reverence for your teacher be like the reverence for God.'[20] Thus, the esteem for man must be as great as the esteem for God. From this statement, a mediaeval authority concludes that our esteem for man must be as great as our esteem for God.[21]

(1) The observance of this law is apparently reflected in *Joshua* 10:26 f.

(2) Our translation assumes that *qelalah* is a euphemism for *kavod*. This assumption is implied in the Rabbinic interpretation of the verse and is similar in intention to Rashi's comment: 'It is a slight to the King, because man is made in the image of God.' *Qelalah* in the sense of reproach or insult is used in *Exodus* 21:17. A similar interpretation is found in *Pseudo-Jonathan*. Compare the rendering by Ariston of Pella: 'For he that is hanged is a reproach to God,' quoted by Jerome.[22] However, the *Septuagint* as well as the *Mishnah*[23] take the verse to mean 'for he is hanged because of a curse against God' . . . 'as if to say why was he hanged? because he cursed the name of God: and so (if his body be left hanging, thus reminding man of his blasphemy) the name of God is profaned.'

The divine likeness of man is an idea known in many religions. It is the contribution of Judaism to have taught the tremendous

[20] *Aboth*, 4, 15.

[21] Rabbi Meir be Todros Halevi Abulafia (1180–1244), quoted by Rabbi Samuel da Uceda, *Midrash Shemuel*, Venice, 1579, *ad locum*.

[22] Driver, *Deuteronomy* (International Critical Commentary), Edinburgh, 1895, p. 248 f. 'For man was made in the image of God,' Rashi.

[23] *Sanhedrin*, 6, 4, *Sanhedrin*, 46b; *Tosefta Sanhedrin*, 9, 7.

implication of that idea: the metaphysical dignity of man, the divine preciousness of human life. Man is not valued in physical terms; his value is infinite. To our common sense, one human being is less than two human beings. Jewish tradition tries to teach us that he who has caused a single soul to perish, it is as though he had caused a whole world to perish; and that he who has saved a single soul, it is as though he has saved a whole world. This thought was conveyed in the solemn admonition to witnesses, not by false testimony to be the cause of the death of an innocent man.[24]

No person may be sacrificed to save others. If an enemy said to a group of women, 'Give us one from among you that we may defile her, and if not we will defile you all, let the enemy defile them all, but let them not betray to them one single soul.'[25]

The metaphysical dignity of man implies not only inalienable rights but also infinite responsibilities. Stressing the idea that one man came to be the father of all men, the *Mishnah* avers: 'Therefore every man is bound to say, On account of *me* the world was created.'[26] That is, every man is to regard himself as precious as a whole world, too precious to be wasted by sin.[27]

In several ways man is set apart from all beings created in the six days. The Bible does not say, God created the plant or the animal; it says, He created different kinds of plants and different kinds of animals. In striking contrast, it does not say that God created different kinds of man, men of different colours and races; it says, He created one single man. From one single man all men are descended.

When the Roman government issued a decree that the Jews of Palestine should not study the *Torah*, should not circumcise their sons and should profane the Sabbath, the Jewish leaders went to Rome and marched through streets at night-time, proclaiming: 'Alas, in heavens' name, are we not your brothers, are we not the sons of one father and the sons of one mother? Why are we different from every nation and tongue that you issue such harsh decrees against us?'[28]

'Why was only a single man created? To teach you that he who destroys one man, it is regarded as if he had destroyed all

[24] *Mishnah Sanhedrin*, 4, 5.
[25] *Mishnah Terumoth*, 8, 12.
[26] *Mishnah Sanhedrin*, 37a.
[27] *Rashi, Sanhedrin*, 37a.
[28] *Rosh Hashanah*, 19b.

men, and that he who saves one man, it is regarded as though he had saved all men. Furthermore, it was for the sake of peace, so that man might not say to his fellow-man, "My father was greater than thy father".'[29]

The awareness of divine dignity must determine even man's relation to his own self. His soul as well as his body constitute an image of God. This is why one is under obligation to keep his body clean. 'One must wash his face, hands, and feet daily in his Maker's honour.'[30] Hillel, it is said, explained this obligation by a parable. Those who are in charge of the icons of kings which are set up in their theatres and circuses scour and wash them off, and are rewarded and honoured for so doing; how much more, who was created in the image and likeness of God.[31]

Indeed, Jewish piety may be expressed in the form of a supreme imperative: *Treat thyself as an image of God*. It is in the light of this imperative that we can understand the meaning of the astonishing commandment: Ye shall be holy, for I the Lord your God am holy (*Leviticus* 19:2). Holiness, an essential attribute of God, may become a quality of man. The human can become holy.

5. MAN THE SYMBOL OF GOD

From time immemorial man has been concerned with the question how to create a symbol of the Deity, a visible object in which its presence would be enshrined, wherein it could be met and wherein its power would be felt at all times.

That religious eagerness found an ally in one of man's finest skills: the skill to design, to fashion, and to paint in material form what mind and imagination conceive. They became wedded to each other, *Art* became the helpmate of *religion*, and rich was the offspring of that intimate union. It is alone through religion and cult that the consciousness of higher laws could mature and be imposed 'upon the individual artist, who would otherwise have given free rein to his imagination, *style*.' 'There, in the sanctuary, they took their first step toward the sublime. They learned to eliminate the contingent

[29] *Mishnah, Sanhedrin*, IVm, 5.

[30] *Shabbath* 50b, and Rashi *ad locum*.

[31] *Leviticus*, Rabba 34, 3; see *Aboth de Rabbi Nathan*, Version B, ch. 30, ed., Schechter, p. 66; *Midrash Tehillim*, 103; *Sheeltoth*, 1.

from form. Types came into being; ultimately the first ideals.'[32] Religion and cult inspired the artist to bring forth images of majesty, magnificent temples and awe-inspiring altars, which in turn stirred the heart of the worshipper to greater devotion. What would art have been without the religious sense of mystery and sovereignty, and how dreary would have been religion without the incessant venture of the artist to embody the invisible in visible forms, to bring his vision out of the darkness of the heart, and to fill the immense absence of the Deity with the light of human genius? The right hand of the artist withers when he forgets the sovereignty of God, and the heart of the religious man has often become dreary without the daring skill of the artist. Art seemed to be the only revelation in the face of the Deity's vast silence.

One is overwhelmed by the sight of the great works of art. They represent in a deep sense man's attempt to celebrate the works of God. God created heaven and earth, and man creates symbols of heaven and symbols of earth. Yet man is not satisfied with the attempt to praise the work of God; he even dares to express the essence of God. God created man, and man creates images of God.

A distinction ought to be made here between *real* and *conventional* symbols. *A real symbol* is a visible object that represents something invisible; something present representing something absent. A real symbol represents, e.g. the Divine because it is assumed that the Divine resides in it or that the symbol partakes to some degree of the reality of the Divine. A *conventional symbol* represents to the mind an entity which is not shown, not because its substance is endowed with something of that entity but because it suggests that entity, by reason of relationship, association, or convention, e.g. a flag.

An image is a real symbol. The god and his image are almost identified. They are cherished as the representatives of the gods: he who has the image, has the god. It is believed that the god resides in the image or that the image partakes to some degree of the power and reality of the god. A victor nation would carry off the god-image of the conquered nation, in order to deprive it of the presence and aid of its god. In the fifteenth century before the common era, a statue of the goddess Ishtar

[32] Jacob Burckhardt, *Force and Freedom*, New York, Pantheon Books, Inc., 1943, pp. 191, 318.

of Nineveh was carried with great pomp and ceremony from Mesopotamia to Egypt, obviously for the purpose of letting Egypt enjoy the blessings which the goddess by her presence would bestow upon the land.[33] As Durkheim remarked, the images of a totem-creature are more sacred than the totem-creature itself. The image may replace the Deity.

What was the attitude of the prophets toward that grand alliance of religion and art? What is the attitude of the Bible toward the happy union of priest and artist? Did Israel contribute toward cementing that matrimony? Did it use its talents to create worthy symbols of the One God it proclaimed by inspiring its artists to embody in stone the Creator of heaven and earth? Indeed, if a religion is to be judged by the degree to which it contributes to the human need for symbolism, the Decalogue should have contained a commandment, saying: Thou shalt make unto thee a symbol, a graven image or some manner of likeness. . . . Instead, the making and worshiping of images was considered an abomination, vehemently condemned in the Bible.[34] If symbolism is the standard, then Moses will have to be accused of having had a retarding influence on the development of man. It is not with a sense of pride that we recall the making of the Golden Calf, nor do we condemn as an act of vandalism the role of Moses in beating it into pieces and grinding it very small, 'until it was as fine as dust,' and casting 'the dust thereof into the brook that descended out of the mount.'

It is perhaps significant that the Hebrew word that came to denote symbol, *semel*, occurs in the Bible five times, but always in a derogatory sense, denoting an idolatrous object.[35]

Nothing is more alien to the spirit of Judaism than the veneration of images. According to an ancient belief, the prophet Elijah, 'the angel of the covenant,' is present whenever the act of circumcision is performed. To concretize that belief, a vacant chair, called 'Elijah's chair,' is placed near the seat

[33] Hugo Winckler, *The Tell-el-Amarna Letters*, Berlin, Reuther & Reichard, 1896, pp. 48 f.

J. A. Knudtzon, *Die El-Amarna-Tafeln*, *Vorderasiatische Bibliothek*, Leipzig, 1915, pp. 178 f, (no. 23) 1050 f.

[34] *Cf.* for example, *Deuteronomy* 27:15; *Leviticus* 4:15.

[35] *Deuteronomy* 4:16; *Ezeckiel* 8:3; 5:2; *Chronicles* 33:7, 15. However, by means of a metathesis, Ibn. Exra finds the word *selem* in *sulam* (ladder); *cf.* his interpretation of Jacob's ladder in his *Commentary* on *Genesis* 28:11.

of the *sandek* (god-father).[36] This is the limit of representation: a vacant chair. To place a picture or statue of the prophet on it, would have been considered absurd as well as blasphemous. To Jewish faith there are no physical embodiments of the supreme mysteries. All we have are signs, reminders.

The Second Commandment implies more than the prohibition of images; it implies the rejection of all visible symbols for God; not only of images fashioned by man but also of 'any manner of likeness, of any thing that is in heaven above, or that is in the earth beneath, or that is in the water under the earth'. The significance of that attitude will become apparent when contrasted with its opposite view.

It would be alien to the spirit of the Bible to assert that the world is a symbol of God. In contrast, the symbolists exhort us: 'Neither say that thou hast now no Symbol of the Godlike. Is not God's Universe a Symbol of the Godlike; is not Immensity a Temple . . .?'[37]

What is the reason for that sharp divergence? To the symbolists 'All visible things are emblems. . . . Matter exists only spiritually, and to represent some Idea and *body* it forth'.[38] The universe is 'a mechanism of self-expression for the infinite'. The symbol is but the bodying forth of the infinite, and it is the very life of the infinite to be bodied forth.[39]

Now, the Bible does not regard the universe as a mechanism of the self-expression of God, for the world did not come into being in an act of self-expression but in an act of creation. The world is not of the essence of God, and its expression is not His. The world speaks to God, but that speech is not God speaking to Himself. It would be alien to the spirit of the Bible to say that it is the very life of God to be bodied forth. The world is neither His continuation nor His emanation but His creation and possession.

The fundamental insight that God is not and cannot be localized in a thing[40] was emphatically expressed at the very

[36] See A. T. Glassberg, *Zikron Berith la-Rishonim*, Berlin, 1892, pp. 176 ff., 231 ff.

[37] Thomas Carlyle, *Sartor Resartus*, New York: Doubleday, Doran & Company, Inc., 1937, Book III, Chapter 7, pp. 253–254.

[38] *Ibid.*, Book I, Chapter 11, p. 72.

[39] H. F. Dunbar, *Symbolism in Mediaeval Thought and Its Consummation in the Divine Comedy*, New Haven: Yale University Press, 1929, pp. 15 f.

[40] See my, *The Sabbath, Its Meaning to Modern Man*, New York: Farrar, Strauss & Young, 1951, pp. 4 ff; 'Space, Time and Reality,' *Judaism*, 1, 3, July, 1952, pp. 268 f.

moment in which it could have been most easily forgotten, at the inauguration of the Temple in Jerusalem. At that moment Solomon exclaims:

> But will God in very truth dwell on earth? Behold, heaven and the heaven of heavens cannot contain Thee; how much less this house that I have built!
>
> (*I Kings* 8:27)

God manifests Himself in *events* rather than in *things*, and these events can never be captured or localized in things.

How significant is the fact that Mount Sinai, the place on which the supreme revelation occurred, did not retain any degree of holiness! It did not become a shrine, a place of pilgrimage.

The realization that the world and God are not of the same essence is responsible for one of the great revolutions in the spiritual history of man. Things may be *instruments*, never *objects of worship. Matza*, the *shofar*, the *lujav* are not things to be looked at, to be saluted, to be paid homage to, but things to be used. Being instruments they have symbolic meaning but, they are not primarily regarded as symbols in themselves. A symbol—because of its inherent symbolic quality—is an object of contemplation and adoration.

To a reverent Catholic the cross is a sacred symbol. Gazing at its shape, his mind is drawn into contemplation of the very essence of the Christian faith.

Thomas Aquinas taught that the cross was to be adored with *Latria*, i.e. supreme worship, and argued that one might regard a cross or an image in two ways: (1) in itself, as a piece of wood or the like, and so no reverence should be given to a cross or to an image of Jesus; (2) as representing something else, and in this way one might give to the Cross *relatively*, i.e. to the cross as carrying one's mind to Jesus—the same honour given to Jesus *absolutely*, i.e. in Himself. Adoration is also given to the Sacred Heart, as well as to images and relics of the saints.[41] In contrast, the image and shape of the scrolls, of a *shofar* or a *lulav* do not convey to us any inspiration beyond reminding us of its function and our obligation.

[41] William Edward Addis and T. Arnold, 'Latria,' *Catholic Dictionary*, Catholic Publication Society Company, London: Kegan Paul, Trench & Company, 1884, p. 505.

The spirit of Christian symbolism has shaped the character of church architecture, 'a noble church structure may be "a sermon in stone"'. According to Germanos, the Patriarch of Constantinople (715-730), the church is heaven on earth, the symbol of The Crucifixion, the Entombment, and Resurrection. From the fifth century, symbolism permeated the architecture of the Byzantine church building in all its details. 'The sanctuary, the nave and aisles were the sensible world, the upper parts of the church the intelligible cosmos, the vaults the mystical heaven.'[42] A similar spirit is to be found in Western Christianity, where, for example, the shape of church building is that of a cross, embodying the basic symbol of Christianity. The altar is often raised three or seven steps, signifying the Trinity or the seven gifts of the Holy Spirit.

In Jewish law, which prescribes countless rules for daily living, no directions are given for the shape of synagogue building.[43]

Any form of architecture is legally admissible. The synagogue is not an abode of the Deity but a house of prayer, a gathering place for the people. Entering a synagogue, we encounter no objects designed to impart any particular idea to us. Judaism has rejected the picture as a means of representing ideas; it is opposed to pictographic symbols. The only indispensable object is a Scroll to be read, not to be gazed at.

There is no *inherent* sanctity in Jewish ritual objects. The candelabrum in the synagogue does not represent another candelabrum either in Jerusalem or in heaven. It is not more than you see. It has no symbolic content. According to Jewish law, it is prohibited to imitate the seven-branched candelabrum as well as other features of the Temple in Jerusalem for ritual purposes. 'A man may not make a house in the form of the Temple, or an exedra in the form of the Temple hall, or a court corresponding to the Temple court, or a table corresponding to the table (in the Temple) or a candlestick corresponding to the candlestick (in the Temple), but he may make one with five or six or eight lamps, but with seven he should not make, even of other metals (than gold) . . . or even of wood.'[44] The

[42] Charles R. Morey, *Mediaeval Art*, New York: W. W. Norton Company, 1942, pp. 104 f.

[43] Rabbi Yeheskel Landau, *Noda be-Yehudah*, Second Series, *Orah Havim*, responsum 19.

[44] *Rosh Hashnah*, 242; *Avodah Zarah*, 43a.

anointing oil must not be produced in the same composition to be used outside the Sanctuary. 'It is holy and shall be holy unto you' (*Exodus* 30:32).

The purpose of ritual art objects in Judaism is not to inspire love of God but to enhance our love of doing a *mitsvah*, to add pleasure to obedience, delight to fulfilment. Thus the purpose is achieved not in direct contemplation but in combining it with a ritual act; the art objects have a religious function but no religious substance.

Jewish artists often embellished manuscripts and title pages with pictures of Moses and Aaron. Yet such decorations were regarded as ornaments rather than symbols.

And yet there is something in the world that the Bible does regard as a symbol of God. It is not a temple nor a tree, it is not a statue nor a star. The one symbol of God is *man, every man*. God Himself created man in His image, or, to use the biblical terms, in His *tselem* and *demuth*. How significant is the fact that the term, *tselem*, which is frequently used in a damnatory sense for a man-made image of God, as well as the term, *demuth*—of which Isaiah claims (40:18) no *demuth* can be applied to God—is employed in denoting man as an image and likeness of God!

Human life is holy, holier even than the Scrolls of the *Torah*. Its holiness is not man's achievement; it is a gift of God rather than something attained through merit. Man must therefore be treated with honour due to a likeness representing the King of kings.

Not that the Bible was unaware of man's frailty and wickedness. The Divine in man is not by virtue of what he does, but by virtue of what he is. With supreme frankness the failures and shortcomings of kings and prophets, of men such as Moses or David, are recorded. And yet, Jewish tradition insisted that not only man's soul but also his body is symbolic of God. This is why even the body of a criminal condemned to death must be treated with reverence, according to the book of *Deuteronomy* (21:23). 'He who sheds the blood of a human being, it is accounted to him as though he diminished (or destroyed) the Divine image.'[45] And in this sense, Hillel characterized the body as an 'icon' of God,[46] as it were, and considered keeping

[45] *Mekilta* to *Exodus*, 20:16.

[46] *Tselem elohim in Genesis*, 1:27 is translated in the Septuagint *kat' eikona theou*.

clean one's one body as an act of reverence for its Creator.[47]

As not one man or one particular nation but all men and all nations are endowed with the likeness of God, there is no danger of ever worshipping man, because only that which is extraordinary and different may become an object of worship. But the Divine likeness is something all men share.

This is a conception of far-reaching importance to Biblical piety. What it implies can hardly be summarized. Reverence for God is shown in our reverence for man. The fear you must feel of offending or hurting a human being must be as ultimate as your fear of God. An act of violence is an act of desecration. To be arrogant toward man is to be blasphemous toward God.

> He who oppresses the poor blasphemes his Maker,
> He who is gracious to the needy honours Him.
>
> (*Proverbs* 14:31)

Rabbi Joshua ben Levi said: 'A procession of angels pass before man wherever he goes, proclaiming: *Make way for the image* (*eikonion*) *of God*'.[48]

It is often claimed that 'Hebrew monotheism has ended by raising the Deity too far above the earth and placing Him too far above man'.[49] This is a half-truth. God is indeed very much

[47] *Leviticus Rabba*, 34, 3; see above (manuscript p. 41). Significant are the statements in *Jer, Berachoth III*, 8a, and *Moed Katan*, 83a.

[48] *Deuteronomy Rabba*, 4, 4; see *Midrash Tehillim*, chapter 17. That one lives in the company of angels, 'ministers of the Supreme', was something one is expected by *Jewish law* to be always conscious of. This is evidenced by the prayer *hithhabdu*, *Berachoth* 60b and *Mishne Torah*, *Tefillah*, 7, 4. The general belief, based on *Psalms* 91:11, is clearly stated in *Tacanith* 11a. According to *Exodus Rabba*, 32, 6, and *Tanhuma*, *Mishpatim*, end, angels are assigned to a person according to the good deeds he performs; *Seder Eliahu Rabba*, chapter XVIII, edition Friedmann, p. 100. Compare also the statement of the two 'ministering angels' that accompany a person on Sabbath eve on his way from the synagogue to his home, *Shabbath* 119b. 'Rabbi Simeon said: When a man rises at midnight and gets up and studies the Torah till daylight, and when the daylight comes he puts the phylacteries with the holy impress on his head and his arm, and covers himself with his fringed robe, and as he issues from the door of his house he passes the *mezusah* containing the imprint of the Holy Name on the post of his door, then four holy angels join him and issue with him from the door of his house and accompany him to the synagogue and proclaim before him: Give honour to the image of the Holy King, give honour to the son of the King, to the precious countenance of the King.' *Zohar*, III, p. 265a.

[49] 'It was left for the Christian religion to call down its god from the heights of heaven to earth, and to represent this god by means of art.' (A. D. Seta, *Religion and Art*, New York: Charles Scribner's Sons, 1914, p. 148). Indeed, this was not the way of Judaism which insisted upon its worship being independent of art. It is life itself that must represent the God of Israel.

above man, but at the same time man is very much a reflection of God. The craving to keep that reflection pure, to guard God's likeness on earth, is indeed the motivating force of Jewish piety.

The *tselem* or God's image is what distinguishes man from the animal, and it is only because of it that he is entitled to exercise power in the world of nature. If he retains his likeness he has dominion over the beast; if he forfeits his likeness he descends, losing his position of eminence in nature.[50]

The idea of man's divine likeness is, according to one opinion in the *Talmud*, the reason for the prohibition to produce the human figure. The statement in *Exodus* 20:20, 'You shall not make with Me (*itti*) gods of silver, or gods or gold,' should be rendered as if it were written, 'You shall not make My symbol (*otti; ot* means symbol), namely, man, gods of silver, or gods of gold'.[51]

What is necessary is not to *have a symbol but to be a symbol.* In this spirit, all objects and all actions are not symbols in themselves but ways and means of enhancing the living symbolism of man.

The divine symbolism of man is not in what he *has*—such as reason or the power of speech—but in what he *is* potentially: he is able to be holy as God is holy. To imitate God, to act as He acts in mercy and love, is the way of enhancing our likeness. Man becomes what he worships. 'Says the Holy One, blessed be He: He who acts like Me shall be like Me.'[52] Says Rabbi Levi ben Hama: 'Idolators resemble their idols (*Psalms* 115:8); now how much more must the servants of the Lord resemble Him'.[53]

And yet that likeness may be defiled, distorted, and forfeited. It is from the context of this problem that the entire issue of Jewish symbolism must be considered. The goal of man is to recognize and preserve His likeness or at least to prevent its distortion.

But man has failed. And what is the consequence? 'I have placed the likeness of My image on them and through their sins I have upset it', is the dictum of God.[54]

[50] *Genesis Rabba*, 8, 12.
[51] *Abodah Zarah*, 43b.
[52] *Deuteronomy Rabba*, 1, 10.
[53] See *Deuteronomy Rabba*, 5, 9.
[54] *Moed Kattan*, 15b.

The likeness is all but gone. Today, nothing is more remote and less plausible than the idea: man is a symbol of God. Man forgot Whom he represents or *that* he represents.

There is one hope. The *Midrash* interprets the verse *Deuteronomy* 1:10, as if it were written: 'Lo, today you are like the stars in heaven, but in the future you will resemble the Master'.[55]

6. IMAGE AND DUST

There are two ways in which the Bible speaks of the creation of man. In the first chapter of the book of *Genesis* which is devoted to the creation of the physical universe, man is described as having been created in the image and likeness of God. In the second chapter which tells us of the commandment not to eat of the fruit of the tree of knowledge, man is described as having been formed out of the dust of the earth. Together, image and dust express the polarity of the nature of man. He is formed of the most inferior stuff in the most superior image. The polarity of man may not imply an eternal contradiction. There is dignity to dust which, just as heaven, was created by God. There is, indeed, meaning and blessing in having been formed of the dust of the earth, for it is only because he is formed of the dust of the earth that he can fulfil his destiny to cultivate the earth. Yet while the duality of human nature may not imply an eternal tension, it does imply a duality of grandeur and insignificance, a relatedness to earth and an affinity with God.

The duality is not based on the contrast of soul and body and the principles of good and evil. Unlike the Pythagoreans, the Bible does not regard the body as the sepulchre and prison-house of the soul or even as the seat and source of sin. The contradiction is in what man does with his soul and body. The contradiction lies in his acts rather than in his substance. As nature is not the counterwork of God but His creation and instrument, dust is not the contradiction of the image but its foil and complement. Man's sin is in his failure to live what he is. Being the master of the earth, man forgets that he is servant of God.

Man is Dust

Dust thou art, and unto dust thou shalt return (*Genesis* 3:19) These words with which the Lord addressed Adam after he

[55] *Deuteronomy*, Rabba 1, 10.

sinned convey a basic part of the Biblical understanding of man. The fact of man having been created 'in the image and likeness of God' is mentioned as a Divine secret and uttered in a Divine monologue, while the fact of being dust is conveyed to man in god's dialogue with Adam. Nowhere in the Bible does man, standing before God, say, I am thy image and likeness. Abraham, pleading with God to save the city of Sodom, knows: 'Behold now, I have taken upon me to speak unto the Lord, who am but *dust and ashes*' (*Genesis* 18:27). Job prays: 'Remember, I beseech Thee, that Thou hast fashioned me as clay' (10:9). And his last words are: 'I abhor my words, and repent, seeing I am dust and ashes' (42:6; see 30:19). In this spirit, the Psalmist describes men as beings 'that go down to the dust' (*Psalms* 22:30). This miserable fact, however, is also a comfort to him who discovers his failures, his spiritual feebleness. The Psalmist is consoled in the knowledge that God understands our nature; He remembers that we are dust (*Psalms* 103:14).

God created man out of dust,
  And turned him back thereunto.
He granted them a (fixed) number of days,
  And gave them authority over all things on the earth.
He clothed them with strength like unto Himself,
  And made them according to His own image.
He put the fear of them upon all flesh,
  And caused them to have power over beasts and birds.
With insight and understanding He filled their heart,
  And taught them good and evil.
He created for them tongue, and eyes, and ears,
  And he gave them a heart to understand,
To show them the majesty of His works,
  And that they might glory in His wondrous acts;
That they might evermore declare His glorious works,
  And praise His holy name.
He set before them the covenant;
  The law of life He gave them for a heritage.
He made an everlasting covenant with them,
  And showed them His judgments,
Their eyes beheld His glorious majesty,
  And their ear heard His glorious voice;
And he said unto them, Beware of all unrighteousness;

And he gave them commandment, to each man concerning
his neighbour.

Their ways are ever before Him,
They are not hid from His eyes.
For every nation He appointed a ruler,
But Israel is the Lord's portion.
All their works are (clear) as the sun before Him,
And His eyes are continually upon their ways.
Their iniquities are not hid from Him,
And all their sins are (inscribed) before the Lord.
The righteousness of men is to Him as a signet,
And the mercy of man He preserveth as the apple of an eye.
Afterwards He will rise up and recompense them,
And will visit their deeds upon their own head.
Nevertheless to them that repent doth He grant a return,
And comforteth them that lose hope.
(*Sirach* 17:1-24)

Man is an artifact

That the end of man is dust is an indisputable fact. But so is the end of the beast. And yet, the Bible emphasizes an absolute difference between man and all other creatures. According to the first chapter of *Genesis*, plants and animals were brought forth by the earth, by the waters (*Genesis* 1:11, 20, 24); they emerged from 'nature' and became an 'organic' part of nature. Man, on the other hand, is an artifact, formed in a special act, created in 'an image', 'according to a likeness' (*Genesis* 1:26). In the language of the second chapter of *Genesis*, every beast of the field, and every fowl of the air, was formed of the ground. Man, however, was made not of the ground which is the source of all vegetation and animal life, nor out of water which is a symbol for refreshment, blessing, and wisdom. He was made of arid dust, the stuff of the desert which is both abundant and worthless.[56]

Thus, the statement that man was made of dust stresses not only his fragility but also his nobility. He owes his existence not to the forces of nature but to the Creator of all. He is set apart from both the plants and the beasts. The earth is not his mother. Man has only a father.

[56] *Zephania* 1:17; *Zacharia* 9:3; *Job* 22:24.

Other expressions of the uniqueness and magnificence of man come to us from the prophets. Isaiah proclaims:

> Thus saith God the Lord,
> He that created the heavens
> And stretched them out,
> He that spread forth the earth
> And that which cometh out of it,
> He that giveth breath unto the people upon it,
> And spirit to them that walk therein (42:5).

In the same way, Sechariah speaks of the Lord who stretched out the heavens and founded the earth and formed the *spirit of man* within him (21:1).

What is stressed about man in these passages is the forming of the spirit, the grandeur of which is made manifest by its juxtaposition with heaven and earth. The spirit in man is as much a creation of God as heaven and earth. What is the source of human understanding? 'It is a spirit in man, and the breath of the Almighty that giveth them understanding' (*Job* 32:8). The parallelism seems to imply that the spirit in man is a spirit of the Almighty. 'The spirit of God hath made me, and the breath of the Almighty giveth me life,' we read in the same speech (*Job* 33:4).

The word spirit in the Bible has more than one meaning. Of Bezalel it is said that he is filled with the spirit of God 'in wisdom, in knowledge, understanding, and in all manner of workmanship' (*Exodus* 31:4). Of the prophets we hear that the spirit of God comes upon them (*Isaiah* 61:1; *Ezekiel* 11:5). Of the Messiah we are told that 'the spirit of God shall rest upon him, the spirit of wisdom and understanding, the spirit of counsel and might, the spirit of knowledge and of the fear of the Lord' (*Isaiah* 11:2). The spirit in these passages denotes an endowment of chosen men. But, as we have seen, it is also an endowment of all men; it is that which gives them understanding.

Man holds within himself a breath of God. 'The Lord formed man of the dust of the ground, and breathed into his nostrils a breath of life; and man became living soul' (*Genesis* 2:7). It probably is this non-earthly aspect of human nature, the breath of God, that served as a basis for the belief in an after-life.

'And the dust returneth to the earth as it was, and the spirit returneth unto God who gave it' (*Ecclesiastes* 12:7).

7. THE SELF AND THE DEED

Many modern theologians have consistently maintained that the Bible stands for optimism, that pessimism is alien to its spirit.[57] There is, however, very little evidence to support such a view. With the exception of the first chapter of the *Book of Genesis*, the rest of the Bible does not cease to refer to the sorrow, sins, and evil of this world. As Maimonides pointed out (in a different context and order), the ideas that apply to the world in the state of its coming into being do not apply to the world that is in being. The design of the Creator was for a world that was to be good, very good; but then something mysterious happened, to which Jewish tradition alludes in many ways, and the picture of the world profoundly changed. When the prophets look at the world, they behold 'distress and darkness, the gloom of anguish' (*Isaiah* 8:22). When they look at the land, they find it 'full of guilt against the Holy One of Israel' (*Jeremiah* 51:5). 'O Lord, how long shall I cry for help, and Thou wilt not hear? Or cry to Thee "violence!", and Thou wilt not save? Why dost Thou make me see wrongs and look upon trouble? Destruction and violence are before me; strife and contention arise. So the law is slacked and justice never goes forth. For the wicked surround the righteous, so justice goes forth perverted' (*Habakkuk* 1:2-4). This is a world in which the way of the wicked prosper and 'all who are treacherous thrive' (*Jeremiah* 12:1); a world which made it possible for some people to maintain that 'Everyone who does evil is good in the sight of the Lord, and He delights in them', and for others to ask, 'Where is the God of justice?' (*Malachi* 2:17).

The Psalmist did not feel that this was a happy world when he prayed: 'O God, do not keep silence; do not hold peace or be still, O God. For, lo, Thy enemies are in uproar; those who hate thee have raised their heads' (*Psalms* 83:2-3).

The terror and anguish that came upon the Psalmist were not caused by calamities in nature but by the wickedness of man, by the evil in history:

[57] It was Schopenhauer who claimed that the Hebrew spirit was characteristically optimistic, whereas Christianity was pessimistic. *Die Welt als Wille und Vorstellung*, II, chap. 48; *Parerga and Paralipomena*, Gusbach ed., II, 397. *Samtliche Werke*, Franenstadt ed., III, 712 f.

Fearfulness and trembling come upon me,
Horror has overwhelmed me.
And I said, Oh that I had wings like a dove!
Then would I fly away, and be at rest.

Psalms 55:6-7.

These are the words of Moses in his last days: 'I know how rebellious and stubborn you are. . . . I know after my death you will surely act corruptly, and turn aside from the way which I have commanded you; and in the days to come evil will befall you, because you will do what is evil in the sight of the Lord' (*Deuteronomy* 31:27-29). It is not a sweet picture of man that Isaiah paints, saying: 'You have never heard, you have never known, from of old your ear has not been opened. For I knew that you would deal very treacherously, and that from birth you were called a rebel' (*Isaiah* 48:8).

There is one line that expresses the mood of the Jewish man throughout the ages: '*The earth is given into the hand of the wicked*' (*Job* 9:24).[58]

How does the world look in the eyes of God? Are we ever told that the Lord saw that the righteousness of man was great in the earth, and that He was glad to have made man on the earth? The general tone of the Biblical view of history is set after the first ten generations: 'The Lord saw the wickedness of man was great in the earth and that every imagination of the thoughts of his heart was only evil continually. And the Lord was sorry that he made man on the earth, and it grieved Him to His heart' (*Genesis* 6:5; *cf.* 8:21). One great cry resounds throughout the Bible:

The wickedness of man is great on the earth. It is voiced by the prophets; it is echoed by the Psalmist.

Sentimentality and unreality have often been considered a distinctly Biblical attitude, while in truth the Bible constantly reminds us of man's frailty and unreliability. 'All flesh is grass, and all the strength thereof is as the flower of the field. The grass withers, the flower fades . . . surely the people is grass' (*Isaiah* 40:6-7). 'Put not your trust in princes, nor in the son of man, in whom there is no help' (*Psalms* 146:3). Isaiah calls

[58] Raba, in *Baba Bathra* 9a, referred to the end of the verse as denying Divine Providence.

upon us not to trust the world; the Psalmist tells us not to rely on man.

What the rabbis thought about the nature of man may be shown in the following comment. We read in *Habakkuk* 1:14, *And Thou makest man as the fishes of the sea, and as the creeping things, that have no ruler over them*? 'Why is man here compared to the fishes of the sea? .... Just as among fishes of the sea, the greater swallow up the smaller ones, so with men, were it not for fear of government, man would swallow each other alive. This is just what we have learned: Rabbi Hanina, the Deputy High Priest, said, "Pray for the welfare of the government, for were it not for fear thereof, men would swallow each other alive".'[59]

According to Rabbi Jacob, 'This world is like a vestibule before the world to come; prepare yourself in the vestibule, so that you may enter the banquet hall'.[60] There is no reward for good deeds in this world.[61] The time for reward promised in the Bible is the life to come.[62] According to the *Rav*, 'The world was created for the extremely pious or the extremely wicked, for men like Rabbi Hanina ben Dosa (a saint who lived in the first century of the common era) or for men like King Ahab; this world was created for the extremely wicked, the world to come was created for the extremely pious'.[63] 'In this world war and suffering, evil inclination, Satan, and the angel of death hold sway.'[64]

In the Jewish mystical literature of the thirteenth century the doctrine is advanced that world history consists of seven periods (*shemitah*), each lasting seven thousand years, which in the Jubilee, the fifty thousandth year, will reach its culmination. The current period is one which is dominated by the divine quality of 'stern judgment'. In it the evil urge, licentiousness, arrogance, forgetfulness, and unholiness prevail.[65]

According to Rabbi Shneur Zalman of Ladi: Anything that refuses to regard itself as nothing beside God but, on the con-

[59] *Abodah Zarah*, 3b–4a; see also *Aboth*, III, 2.

[60] *Aboth*, 4:21.

[61] *Erubin*, 22a.

[62] *Kiddushin*, 39b.

[63] *Berachoth*, 61b. This world is often compared to 'night'; it is even called 'the world of falsehood'.

[64] *Midrash Vayosha*, *Beth Hamidrash*, ed. Jellinek, 2nd ed., Jerusalem, 1938, I, 55.

[65] *Temunah* (Koretz, 1784), p. 39b.

trary, asserts itself as an entity separate from God does not receive the light of its vitality, so to speak, from the 'hind-part' of his holiness, and only after it has gone through myriad channels of emanation and has been so obscured and contracted that it is capable of living 'in exile', apart from God. And that is why this material world is called a *'world of shells'* (*kelipoth*) *'the other side'* (*sitra abra*). And this is why all the things that happen in this world are harsh and evil, and this is why the wicked prevail.[66]

The pious Jews put no trust in the secular world. 'They realized quite well that the world was full of ordeals and dangers, that it contained Cain's jealousy of Abel, the cold malevolence of Sodom, and the hatred of Esau, but they also knew that there was in it the charity of Abraham and the tenderness of Rachel. Harassed and oppressed, they carried deep within their hearts a contempt for the world, with its power and pomp, with its bustling and boasting. . . . They knew that the Jews were in exile, that the world was unredeemed.'[67] Dazzled by the splendour of Western civilization, the modern Jew has been prone to forget that the world is unredeemed, and that God is in exile. The present generation which has witnessed the most unspeakable horrors committed by man and sponsored by an extremely civilized nation is beginning to realize how monstrous an illusion it was to substitute faith in man for faith in God.

We do not feel 'at home' in the world. With the Psalmist we pray, 'I am a stranger on earth, hide not Thy commandments from me' (119:19). Indeed, if not for our endless power to forget and our great ability to disregard, who could be at ease even for one moment in a lifetime? In the face of so much evil and suffering, of countless examples of failure to live up to the will of God, in a world where His will is defied, where His kingship is denied, who can fail to see the discrepancy between the world and the will of God?

And yet, just because of the realization of the power of evil, life in this world assumed unique significance and worth. Evil is not only a threat; it is also a challenge. It is precisely because of the task of fighting evil that life in this world is so preciously significant. True, there is no reward for good deeds in this world;

[66] Rabbi Shneur Zalman of Ladi, *Tanya*, p. 10b.
[67] A. J. Heschel, *The Earth Is the Lord's* (New York, 1950), p. 96.

yet this does not mean that the world is a prison. It is rather a prelude, a vestibule, a place of preparation, of initiation, of apprenticeship to a future life, where the guests prepare to enter *tricilinium*, or the banquet hall.[68] Life in this world is a time for action, for good works, for worship and sanctification, as eternity is a time for retribution. It is eve of the Sabbath, on which the repast is prepared for the Lord's day; it is the season of duty and submission, as the morrow shall be that of freedom from every law. More precious, therefore, than all of life to come is a single hour of life on earth—an hour of repentance and good deeds. Eternity gives only in the degree that it receives. This is why the book of *Ecclesiastes* pronounced the dead lion less happy than the living dog.[69]

More frustrating than the fact that evil is real, mighty, and tempting is the fact that it thrives so well in the disguise of the good, and that it can draw its nutriment from the life of the holy. In this world, it seems, the holy and the unholy do not exist apart but are mixed, interrelated, and confounded; it is a world where idols are at home, and where even the worship of God may be alloyed with the worship of idols.

In Jewish mysticism we often come upon the view that in this world neither good nor evil exists in purity, and that there is no good without the admixture of evil nor evil without the admixture of good. The confusion of good and evil is the central problem of history and the ultimate issue of redemption. The confusion goes back to the very process of creation.

'When God came to create the world and reveal what was hidden in the depths and disclose light out of darkness, they were all wrapped in one another, and therefore light emerged from darkness and from the impenetrable came forth the profound. So, too, from good issues evil and from mercy issues judgment, and all are intertwined, the good impulse and the evil impulse.'[70]

Ezekiel saw in his great vision that 'a stormy wind came out of the north, and a great cloud, with brightness (*nogah*) round about it, and fire flashing forth continually' (1:4). He first beheld the powers of unholiness. A *great cloud* represents 'the power of destruction'; it is called *great*, on account of its darkness, which is so intense that it hides and makes in-

[68] *Aboth* 4:22.
[69] *Shabbat*, 30a.
[70] *Sohar*, III, 80b; see also I, 156a.

visible all the sources of light, thus overshadowing the whole world. The *fire flashing forth* indicates the fire rigorous of judgment that never departs from it. *With brightness round about it* . . . that is, although it is the very region of defilement, yet it is surrounded by a certain brightness . . . it possesses an aspect of holiness, and hence should not be treated with contempt, but should be allowed a part in the side of holiness.'[71] Even Satan contains a particle of sanctity. In doing his ugly work as the seducer of man, his intention is 'for the sake of heaven', for it is for a purpose such as this that he was created.[72]

The great saint Rabbi Hrish of Zydatschov once remarked to his disciple and nephew: 'Even after I had reached the age of forty—the age of understanding—I was not sure whether my life was not immersed in that mire and confusion of good and evil (*nogah*). . . . My son, every moment of my life I fear lest I am caught in that confusion'.[73]

All of history is a sphere where good is mixed with evil. The supreme task of man, his share in redeeming the work of creation, consists in an effort to separate good from evil, and evil from good. Since evil can only exist parasitically on good, it will cease to be when that separation will be accomplished. Redemption, therefore, is contingent upon the *separation* of good and evil.

Judaism is also aware of the danger of evil's intrusion into the instrument of good. Therefore, at the great ritual on the Day of Atonement the high priest would cast lots upon the two goats: one lot for the Lord and the other lot for Azazel. He would lay both his hands upon the head of the goat, on which the lot fell for Azazel, 'and confess over him all the iniquities of the children of Israel, all their transgressions, all their sins'. While the purpose of the goat upon which the lot fell for the Lord was 'to make atonement *for the holy place,* because of the uncleannesses of the children of Israel, and because of their transgressions, even all their sins; and so shall he do for the tent of meeting, that dwells with them in the midst of their uncleannesses'.[74] At the most sacred day of the year the

[71] *Ibid.*, II, 203a–203b; see pp. 69a–69b. The *kelipoth*, or the forces of the unholy, are unclean and harmful from the aspect of man. However, from the aspect of the holy, they exist because of the will of the Creator and for His sake. A spark of holiness abides in them and maintains them. Rabbi Abraham Azulai, *Or Hahamah* (Przemysl, 1897), II, 218a.

[72] *Baba Bathra*, 16a.

[73] Rabbi Eisik Safran, *Zohar Hai*, I.

[74] Leviticus 16:16.

supreme task was to atone for the holy. It preceded the sacrifice, the purpose of which was to atone for the sins.

The ambiguity of human virtue has been a central issue in the lives of many Jewish thinkers, particularly in the history of Hasidism.

'God asks for the heart.'[75] Yet our greatest failure is in the heart. 'The heart is deceitful above all things, it is exceedingly weak—who can know it?' (*Jeremiah* 17:9). The regard for the ego permeates all our thinking. Is it ever possible to disentangle oneself from the intricate plexus of self-interests? Indeed, the demand to serve God in purity, selflessly, 'For His sake', on the one hand, and the realization of our inability to detach ourselves from vested interests, represent the tragic tension in the life of piety.[76] In this sense, not only our evil deeds, but even our good deeds precipitate a problem.

What is our situation in trying to carry out the will of God? In addition to our being uncertain of whether our motivation—*prior to the act*—is pure, we are continually embarrassed *during the act* with 'alien thoughts' which taint our consciousness with selfish intentions. And even following the act there is the danger of self-righteousness, vanity, and the sense of superiority, derived from what are supposed to be acts of dedication to God.

It is easier to discipline the body than to control the soul. The pious man knows that his inner life is full of pitfalls. The ego, the evil inclinations, is constantly trying to enchant him. The temptations are fierce, yet his resistance is unyielding. And so he proves his spiritual strength and stands victorious, unconquerable. Does not his situation look glorious? But then the evil inclination employs a more subtle device, approaching him with congratulations: What a pious man you are! He begins to feel proud of himself. And there he is caught in the trap (Rabbi Raphel of Bersht).

'For there is not a righteous man upon this earth, that does good and sins not' (*Ecclesiastes* 7:20). The commentators take this verse to mean that even a righteous man sins on occasion, suggesting that his life is a mosaic of perfect deeds with a few

[75] *Sanhedrin*, 106b.

[76] The essence of idolatry is to regard something as a thing in itself, separated from the holiness of God. In other words, to worship an idol does not mean to deny God; it means not to deny the self. This is why pride is idolatry. *Tanya*, 28b.

sins strewn about. The *Baal Shem*, however, reads the verse: *For there is not a righteous man upon earth that does good and there is no sin in the good.* 'It is impossible that the good should be free of self-interest.'[77] Empirically, our spiritual situation looks hopeless: 'We are all as an unclean thing, and all our deeds of righteousness are as filthy rags' (*Isaiah* 64:5).

'Even the good deeds we do are not pleasing but instead revolting. For we perform them out of the desire of self-aggrandizement and for pride, and in order to impress our neighbours.'[78]

Who can be trustful of his good intention, knowing that under the cloak of *kavanah* there may hide a streak of vanity? Who can claim to have fulfilled even one *mitsvah* with perfect devotion? Said Rabbi Elimelech of Lizhensk to one of his disciples, 'I am sixty years old, and I have not fulfilled one *mitsvah*'.[79] *There is not a single mitsvah which we fulfil perfectly* . . . except circumcision and the *Torah* that we study in our childhood,[80] for these two acts are not infringed upon by 'alien thoughts' or impure motivations.

The mind is never immune to alien intentions, and there seems to be no way of ever weeding them out completely. A Hassidic Rabbi was asked by his disciples, in the last hours of his life, whom they should choose as their master after his passing away. He said, 'If someone should give you the way to eradicate "alien thoughts", know he is not your master'.

We do not know with what we must serve until we arrive there (*Exodus* 10:26). 'All our service, all the good deeds we are doing in this world, we do not know whether they are of any value, whether they are really pure, honest or done for the sake of heaven—until we arrive there—in the world to come, only there shall we learn what our service was here.'[81]

The human will cannot circumvent the snare of the ego nor can the mind disentangle itself from the confusion of bias in

[77] Rabbi Yaakob Yosel of Plynoye, *Toldoth Yankov Yosel* (Lemburg, 1863), p. 150d.

[78] Rabbi David Kimhi, *Commentary on Isaiah*, ad locum. Similary, S. D. Luzatto in his commentary. *Cf.* N. J. Berlin, *Commentary on Sheeltoth*, sec. 64, p. 420. According to *Sheeltoth* the meaning of the verse is that our deeds of righteousness are as a cloth put together in patches, not woven together properly.

[79] Rabbi Yaakob Aaron of Zalshin, *Beth Yaakov* (Pietrkov, 1899), p. 144; Aboth 2:20.

[80] *Midrash Tehillim*, 6, 1.

[81] Rabbi Isaac Meir of Ger.

which it is trapped. It often looks as if God's search for the righteous man will end in a cul-de-sac.[82]

Should we, then, despair because of our being unable to attain perfect purity? We should if perfection were our goal. Yet we are not obliged to be perfect once for all, but only to rise again and again. Perfection is divine, and to make it a goal of man is to call on man to be divine. All we can do is to try to wring our hearts clean in contrition. Contrition begins with a feeling of shame at our being incapable of disentanglement from the self. To be contrite at our failures is holier than to be complacent in perfection.

It is a problem of supreme gravity. If an act to be good must be done exclusively for the sake of God, are we ever able to do the good? Rabbi Nahman of Kossov gave an answer in the form of a parable. A stork fell into the mud and was unable to pull out his legs until an idea occurred to him. Does he not have a long beak? So he stuck his beak into the mud, leaned upon it, and pulled out his legs. But what was the use? His legs were out, but his beak was stuck. So another idea occurred to him. He stuck his legs into the mud and pulled out his beak. But what was the use? The legs were stuck in the mud. . . .

Such is exactly the condition of man. Succeeding in one way, he fails in another. We must constantly remember: We spoil, and God restores. How ugly is the way in which we spoil, and how good and how beautiful is the way in which he restores!

And yet, Judaism insists upon the deed and hopes for the intention. Every morning a Jew prays, 'Lord our God, make the words of Thy *Torah* pleasant in our mouth . . . so that we study Thy *Torah* for its own sake.'

While constantly keeping the goal in mind, we are taught that for pedagogic reasons one must continue to observe the law even when one is not ready to fulfil it 'for the sake of God'. For the good, even though it is not done for its own sake, will teach us at the end how to act for the sake of God. We must continue to perform the sacred deeds even though we may be compelled to bribe the self with human incentives. Purity of motivation is the goal; constancy of action is the way.

[82] Moments of despair were known to the prophets. Elijah, fleeing from Jezebel, fled to the wilderness, and there he sat down under a broom-tree and said, 'It is enough; now, O Lord, take away my life, for I am not better than my fathers' (*I Kings* 19:4). Jeremiah exclaims, 'Cursed be the day wherein I was born' (20:14). *Cf.*, also *Psalms* 22, 39, 88; *Job* 9:21, 10:20 f; 14:6 f; *Ecclesiastes* 4:2.

The ego is redeemed by the absorbing power and the inexorable provocativeness of a just task which we face. It is the deed that carries us away, that transports the soul, proving to us that the greatest beauty grows at the greatest distance from the centre of the ego.

Deeds that are set upon ideal goals, that are not performed with careless ease and routine but in exertion and submission to their ends, are stronger than the surprise and attack of caprice. Serving sacred goals may eventually change mean motives. For such deeds are exacting. Whatever our motive may be in beginning such an act, the act itself demands an undivided attention. Thus the desire for reward is not the driving force of the poet in his creative moments, and the pursuit of pleasure or profit is not the essence of a religious or moral act.

At the moment in which an artist is absorbed in playing a concerto, the thought of applause, fame, or remuneration is far from his mind. The complete attention of the artist, his whole being, is involved in the music. Should any extraneous thought enter his mind, it would arrest his concentration and mar the purity of his playing. The reward may have been on his mind when he negotiated with his agent, but during the performance it is only the music that claims his complete concentration.

Similar may be man's situation in carrying out a religious or moral act. Left alone the soul is subject to caprice. Yet there is a power in the deed that purifies desires. It is the act, life itself, that educates the will. The good motive comes into being while doing the good.

If the antecedent motive is sure of itself, the act will continue to unfold, and obtrusive intentions could even serve to invigorate the initial motive which may absorb the vigour of the intruder into its own strength. Man may be replete with ugly motives, but a deed and God are stronger than ugly motives. The redemptive power discharged in carrying out the good purifies the mind. The deed is wiser than the heart.

This, then, seems to be the attitude of Judaism. Though deeply aware of how impure and imperfect all our deeds are, the fact of our doing is cherished as the highest privilege, as a source of joy, as that which endows life with ultimate preciousness. We believe that moments lived in fellowship with God, acts fulfilled in imitation of God's will, never perish;

the validity of the good remains regardless of all impurity.

Biblical history bears witness to the constant corruption of man; *it does not, however, teach the inevitable corruptibility of the ultimate in the temporal process.* The holiness of Abraham, Isaac, and Jacob, and the humility of Moses are the rock on which they rely. *There are good moments in history that no subsequent evil may obliterate.* The Lord himself testified to it. The integrity of Job proved it. Abraham could not find ten righteous men in Sodom by whose merit the city would have been saved. Yet there is not a moment in history without thirty-six righteous men, unknown and hidden, by whose merit the world survives. We believe that there are corners full of light in a vastness that is dark, that unalloyed good moments are possible. It is, therefore, difficult from the point of view of Biblical theology to sustain Nieburh's view, *plausible and profound as it is.*

If the nature of man were all we had, then surely there would be no hope for us left. But we also have the word of God, the commandment, the *mitsvah.* The central Biblical fact is *Sinai*, the covenant, the word of God. *Sinai* was superimposed on the failure of Adam. Is not the fact that we were given the knowledge of His will a sign of some ability to carry out His will? Does the word of God always remain a challenge, a gadfly? Is not the voice of God powerful enough to shake the wilderness of the soul, to strip the ego bare, to flash forth His will like fire, so that we all cry 'Glory'?

To the Jew, Sinai is at stake in every act of man, and the supreme problem is not good and evil but God, and His commandment to love good and to hate evil. The central issue is not the sinfulness but the obligations of men.

While insisting upon the contrast between God's power and man's power, God's grace and human failure, Judaism stresses a third aspect, the *mitsvah.* It is a *mitsvah* that gives meaning to our existence. The *mitsvah*, the carrying out of a sacred deed, is given to us as a constant opportunity. Thus there are two poles of piety; the right and the wrong deed; *mitsvah* and sin. The overemphasis upon sin may lead to a deprecation of 'works'; the overemphasis upon *mitsvah* may lead to self-righteousness. The first may result in a denial of the relevance of history and in an overtly eschatological view; the second in a denial of messianism and a secular optimism. Against both dangers Judaism warns repeatedly.

We must never forget that we are always exposed to sin. 'Be not sure of yourself till the day of your death,' said Hillel.[83] We have been taught that one may be impregnated with the spirit of the holy all the days of his life, yet one moment of carelessness is sufficient to plunge into the abyss. *There is but one step between me and death* (*I Samuel* 20:3). On the other hand, we are taught to remember that we are always given the opportunity to serve Him. Significantly, Jewish tradition, while conscious of the possibilities of evil in the good, stresses the *possibilities of further good in the good*. Ben Azzai said, 'Be eager to do a minor *mitsvah* and flee from transgression; for one *mitsvah* leads to (brings on) another *mitsvah*, and one transgression leads to another transgression; for the reward of a *mitsvah* is a *mitsvah*, and the reward of a transgression is a transgression.'[84]

Judaism, in stressing the fundamental importance of the *mitsvah*, assumes that man is endowed with the ability to fulfil what God demands, at least to some degree. This may, indeed, be an article of prophetic faith: the belief in our ability to do His will. 'For this commandment (*mitsvah*) which I command thee this day, it is not too hard for thee, neither is it far off. It is not in heaven, that thou shouldest say, Who shall go up for us to heaven and bring it unto us and make us hear it, that we may do it? Neither is it beyond the sea that thou shouldest say, Who shall go over the sea for us, and bring it unto us, and make us hear it, that we may do it? But the word is very nigh unto thee, in thy mouth and in thy heart, that thou mayest do it' (*Deuteronomy* 30:11-14). Man's actual failures rather than his essential inability to do the good are constantly stressed by Jewish tradition, which claims that man is able to acquire 'merit' before God. The doctrine of merits implies the certainty that for all imperfection the worth of good deeds remains in all eternity.

It is true that the law of love, the demand for the impossible, and our constant failures and transgression create in us grief and a tension that may drive us to despair. Yet, is not the reality of God's love greater than the law of love? Will He not accept us in all our frailty and weakness? 'For He knows our nature (*Yetsen*); He remembers that we are dust' (*Psalms* 103:14).

[83] *Aboth* 2:5.
[84] *Ibid.*, 4:3.

Judaism would reject the axiom, 'I ought, therefore, I can'; it would claim, instead, 'Thou art commanded, therefore thou canst.' It claims, as I have said, that man has the resources to fulfil what God commands, at least to some degree. On the other hand, we are continually warned lest we rely on man's own power and believe that the 'indeterminate extension of human capacities would eventually alter the human situation.' Our tradition does not believe that the good deeds alone will redeem history; it is the obedience to God that will make us worthy of being redeemed by God.

If Judaism had relied on the human resources for the good, on man's ability to fulfil what God demands, on man's power to achieve redemption, why did it insist upon the promise of messianic redemption? Indeed, messianism implies that any course of living, even the supreme human efforts, must fail in redeeming the world. In other words, history is not sufficient to itself.

Yet the Hebraic tradition insists upon the *mitsvah* as the instrument in dealing with evil. At the end of days, evil will be conquered all at once; in historic times evils must be conquered one by one.

CHAPTER III

The Concept of Man in Chinese Thought

WING-TSIT CHAN

1. INTRODUCTION

WHETHER a Chinese is a Confucianist or a Taoist, a conservative or a radical, a scholar or an illiterate, he is a humanist. To him, man is the measure of all things. Following Confucius (551-479 B.C.), he believes that 'It is man that makes truth great but not truth that makes man great.'[1] And following Mencius (371-289 B.C.?), he is convinced that good men can make good laws but 'Laws alone cannot operate themselves.'[2]

2. THE IMPORTANCE OF MAN IN CHINESE CULTURE

The all-importance of man can be seen in the Chinese concepts of government. When his pupil Tzu-kung asked about government, Confucius said, 'People must have sufficient to eat; there must be a sufficient army; and there must be confidence of the people in the ruler.' When the pupil asked that if he was forced to give up one of three objectives, what would he go without first, Confucius replied, 'I would go without the army first.' And when the pupil asked which of the remaining two he would give up if he was forced to, Confucius said, 'I would rather go without food. From time immemorial there have always been deaths, but a nation without the people's confidence in the ruler will collapse.'[3] In a similar vein, Mencius said that in a nation 'The people are the most important element; the spirits of the land and grain are the next; the sovereign is the slightest.'[4]

Not only in government but also in art has man been the

[1] *Analects*, 15/28.
[2] *The Book of Mencius*, 4A/1.
[3] *Analects*, 12/7.
[4] *The Book of Mencius*, 7B/14.

centre in China. From its earliest day Chinese poetry has been concerned with man's fortune and misfortune, his joys and sorrows, and his family and friends. It is man's sentiments that poets aim to express. This idea is stated more than once in the Classics. In the *Book of History*, it is said that 'Poetry is to express the will.'[5] This dictum is repeated in Tso's *Commentary* on the *Spring and Autumn Annals*.[6] And in the *Book of Propriety* it is declared that 'Poetry is to express the Will.'[7] When Confucius said that 'the odes can arouse the mind, can help us observe social conditions, can assist us in living as a group, can express our feelings of dissatisfaction, and can help us fulfil the more immediate duty of serving one's father and the remoter one of serving one's ruler as well as becoming acquainted with the names of birds, animals, and plants,'[8] he was describing the function of Chinese poetry that has been accepted as true in Chinese history ever since his time. It is true that there have been nature poetry and religious poetry in China, but they are exceptions rather than the rule. While it has been the convention for poets to devote the first half of a poem to the description of natural scenery, the purpose is chiefly to create a mood for the expression of human sentiments in the latter half.

Like drama in many lands, Chinese drama had a religious origin and, consequently, in its early stages had supernatural characters and supernatural themes. But as it developed, it quickly gave way to the portrayal of historical events and social life and the expression of sentiments. What is true of Chinese poetry and drama is true of Chinese music, for it has always been a part of the poetic and dramatic arts.

It may be argued that in Chinese painting man occupies a rather insignificant place. In the traditional classification of painting, landscape and flowers-and-birds come ahead of people-and-things. Landscape is the crowning art of China, in which the fundamental principles of art are embraced and the

[5] 'Books of YU,' Bk. 2; see English translation by James Legge, *The Shoo King*, London; Henry Frowde. *The Chinese Classics*, Vol. III, 1865, p. 48.

[6] *Tao's Commentary on the Spring and Autumn Annals*, Duke Hsiang, twenty-seventh year, sec. 5. See English translation by James Legge. *The Ch'un Ts'ev', with The Tso Chuan, The Chinese Classics*, Vol. V, London: Henry Frowde, 1892.

[7] The *Li chi* ('Book of Propriety'), ch. 19, sec. 15; see English Translation, Vols. XXII and XXVIII, by James Legge, *The Li Ki*, *Sacred Books of the East*, Oxford: Claredon Press, Vol. XVII, 1885, p. 112.

[8] *Analects*, 17/9

greatest artistic talents have been immortalized. It is truly the representative art of China. Here man seems to be subordinated to Nature, for human figures are usually very small, often incidental, and sometimes totally absent. This fact has led some western writers to conclude that man in China is not important.

To understand the true meaning of Chinese landscape paintings, however, one must understand its relation to poetry. It is well known to students of Chinese art that in Chinese painting there is poetry and in Chinese poetry there is painting, or, as Ko Hsi (*c.* 1085) put it, 'Poetry is formless painting and painting is poetry in visual form.' In short, the two arts are not only related but identical as far as their ultimate functions are concerned. What is their function? It is none other than to express human sentiments of joy and sorrow, happiness and anger, and feelings of peace, nobility, loneliness, and so on. Chinese artists paint landscape for the same reason poets describe scenery in their poems. Their purpose is to refine the feelings, stimulate the mind, and create a mood so that when the reader or onlooker comes out of it, he becomes a nobler soul, a loftier spirit, a friendlier neighbour, a more filial son, in short, a better human being. There is no subordination of man to Nature in Chinese landscape painting. Neither is there escape from the human world.

Not only is man the centre in Chinese government and the arts, but even in religion, which is supposed to be otherworldly and transcendental. This is not to deny that most Chinese Buddhists aspire to go to Paradise, the 'Pure Land'. But significantly, one of the most important transformations of Buddhism in China has been the change from the doctrine of salvation in Nirvana after death to the doctrine of salvation on earth and 'in this very body'. In spite of its acceptance of Buddhist concepts of heavens and hells, the Taoist religion has always held to the goal of everlasting life on earth. Immortals are believed to inhabit the high mountains. They may ascend to heaven, but more often than not, they roam this earth and move among men, guiding them and helping them. The centre of religion is the human world, where even man's own body becomes important. In humanistic Confucianism, salvation, as we shall see, consists in the full realization of human nature, for it is tantamount to serving Heaven.

The emergence of man as the most important being took

place very early in Chinese history, probably even before Confucius. During the Shang Dynasty (1751-1112 B.C.), as is well known, spiritual beings, whether spirits of nature, spirits of ancestors, or the highest spirit, the Lord on High (Shang-ti), exercised direct control over men and their affairs, sending down rain or drought, a good or poor harvest, fortunes and misfortunes, as rewards and punishments. No expedition was undertaken, no city or capital was built, no marriage was contracted, and indeed no decision was made without first consulting the spirits through divination by the use of tortoise shells. In the early Chou period (1111-256 B.C.), this custom continued, and, in addition, divination by the use of stalks of plants came into practice. In spite of this, however, the spirits became not more, but less, prominent in the Chou. According to the *Book of Propriety*, 'The people of Yin (Shang) honour spirits. The rulers led the people on to serve them and put them ahead of ceremonies. . . . The people of Chou honour ceremonies and highly evaluate the conferring of favours. They serve the spirits and respect them but keep them at a distance. They remain near to man and loyal to him.'[9] Students of Confucianism will be reminded of the Sage's famous saying, 'Respect the spirits but keep them at a distance.'[10]

Gradually even the Lord on High lost his influence. The Mandate of Heaven, by which a ruler obtained his power to rule, used to be absolute but now came to be looked upon with misgiving. 'The Mandate of Heaven is not constant,' an Early Chou poet declared.[11] 'Heaven is hard to depend on. . . . Heaven is not to be trusted,' announced Duke Chou (d. 1121 B.C.).[12] Even ancestors lost their power! 'Never mind your ancestors! Cultivate your virtue,' were the words of a bold poet.[13] The new

[9] *Li chi*, ch. 32, sec. 13; *cf.* translation by Legge, *The Li Ki, Sacred Books of the East*, Vol. XXVIII, p. 342.

[10] *Analects*, 6/20.

[11] *The Book of Poetry*, Ode No. 235 (or III, I, I), verse 5.

[12] *The Book of History*, 'The Book of Chou,' Bk. 18, secs. 4 & 6. See translation by Legge, *The Shoo King*, pp. 476–477.

[13] *The Book of Poetry*, Ode No. 235 (or III, I, I), James Legge's translation: 'Every thing of your ancestors!' (*The Shoo King, The Chinese Classics*, Vol. IV, London: Henry Frowde, 1871, p. 431). Author Waley's version: 'May you never thus shame your ancestors!' (The book of Songs, Beston, Houghton Mifflin, 1937, p. 251). Bernhard Karlgren's version: 'Should you not think of your ancestors?' (*The Book of Odes*, Stockholm; The Museum of Far Eastern Antiquities, 1950, p. 186). If we realize that humanism was now growing strong, there is no need to twist the original and obvious meaning of the text to conform to the earlier or later custom of ancestor worship.

emphasis is now man and his virtue. The destiny of man or that of a dynasty no longer depended on the pleasure of God or the spirits but on man himself, especially his virtue. As one poet said, 'The calamities are simply caused by man.'[14] Whether the Mandate of Heaven was given to or taken away from a ruler depends on his moral character. As Duke Shao told King Ch'eng (reign 1115-1079 B.C.), 'The fact was simply that the Mandate easily fell to the ground (in the case of the Shang Dynasty) because there was no reverence for virtue.'[15] The emphasis on human virtue instead of the power of spirits represented a radical transition from the Shang to the Chou Dynasty. The term *te* (virtue) does not appear in the oracle inscriptions of the Shang but is a key word in Early Chou documents. The conquest of the Shang must have required a great deal of human ingenuity and ability, and the importance of man could not have failed to impress thinking men. Besides, the growth of new trades and trade centres inevitably bred many new talents. Experts, whether or not nobility by blood, were needed to consolidate the kingdom and to fight the barbarians. Later, when the feudal structure began to crumble, individual merit played a greater and greater role. Time finally came when a slave became a prime minister. The upshot was humanism, which eventually reached the climax in Confucius. Neither the Mandate of Heaven nor the spirits were abandoned, but their personal power was supplanted by a self-existing moral law. The Lord's rewards or punishments depended on whether man obeyed or violated moral principles. Through his moral deed man could now control his own destiny.

3. DOCTRINE OF HUMAN NATURE

Is man by nature capable of this moral responsibility? This raises the key problem in the history of Chinese thought: What is the nature of Man? This question was asked very early in history and controversy over it has been more persistent than any other problem and has lasted for 2000-odd years. We shall examine it at some length.

Generally speaking, the fundamental belief of the Chinese is that human nature is basically good. This is of course a broad

[14] *The Book of Poetry*, Ode No. 193 (or II, IV, 9), verse 7.

[15] *The Book of History*, 'The Books of Chou,' Bk. 14, sec. 17. See Legge, *The Shoo King*, p. 430.

statement, but it is essential to appreciate this viewpoint before one can understand certain aspects of Chinese life. For example, one reason for the proverbial reasonableness of the Chinese is the belief that every human being is basically good. Negotiation, arbitration, and compromise have became general practices in China not only because they have been proven to be effective but also because the belief in the original goodness of human nature dictates these approaches. The strong Chinese sense of optimism cannot be adequately explained without this belief. It was because of this firm conviction that the Christian doctrine of original sin has been unacceptable to the Chinese intellectuals. More important than all of these, the belief in the goodness of human nature has led to the conviction that the development of one's moral nature is the way to perfection, as we shall explain later.

This doctrine of the original goodness of man was primarily the contribution of the Confucian school. If the Taoist and Buddhist schools had anything to offer to it, they did so only indirectly. To these two 'heterodox' schools man was beyond good and evil both in his original state and after he reached the stage of the Sage or the Buddha. To the Confucianists, however, the idea that man's nature is originally good has been taught every school child. In the traditional educational system, the beginning sentences of the first primer read, 'Man's nature in the beginning is good.'

While it is correct to say that this doctrine has been the contribution of the Confucian school, at the same time several things must be noted that will qualify the statement. The first of these is that the doctrine was not taught in the ancient Confucian Classics. Secondly, it was not originated by Confucius but by Mencius. Thirdly, Mencius' doctrine did not become orthodox until the Neo-Confucianists of the eleventh century advocated it and elaborated it. And fourthly, his doctrine was not accepted without serious modification. We shall now take up these points separately.

4. HUMAN NATURE ACCORDING TO THE ANCIENT CLASSICS AND CONFUCIUS

The word *hsing* (nature) does not appear in the oracle inscriptions of the Shang, the earliest records of Chinese writing.

In the ancient Classics, however, it appears many times. Examples of these are 'the nature endowed by Heaven'[16] and 'regulation of nature'.[17] But in the first place, the dates of the Classics are still matters of dispute. While portions of them belonged to the sixth century B.C. or earlier, much of the rest was not written until centuries later. In the second place, from the short phrases as have just been quoted no definite conclusion can be drawn whether the ancient doctrine of human nature was one of original goodness or original evil. Of course the saying in the *Book of Changes*, 'What issues from the Way is good and that which realizes it is the individual nature. . . . The realization of nature . . . is the gate to truth and righteousness,'[18] points to the doctrine of original goodness, but the traditional date of the book is now rejected by most scholars in favour of a later date. Most important of all, according to Fu Sju-nien (1896-1950), all instances of *hsing* used in ancient Classics mean *hseng*, that is, what is inborn in man.[19] From all these it is clear that the doctrine of the original goodness of man is not found in ancient Classics.

Likewise the doctrine did not originate with Confucius. On the one hand, we may say that he was the first in Chinese history to have formulated a definite proposition about human nature. As every school child used to know, Confucius said, 'By nature people are near one another but through practice they have become apart,'[20] and this saying was quoted immediately following the first sentences of the school primer referred to earlier. On the other hand, one of his pupils is recorded to have said that 'our Master's discussions on nature and the Way of Heaven cannot be heard.'[21] Clearly there seems to be a contradiction between these two sayings. What is worse, Confucius also said, 'The most intelligent and the most stupid do not change.'[22] This does not seem to agree with either of the preceeding quotations!

[16] *Ibid.*, 'The Books of Shang,' Bk. 10, sec. 3; Legge, *The Shoo King*, p. 271.

[17] *Ibid.*, 'The Books of Chou,' Bk. 12, sec. 15; Legge, *op. cit.*, p. 429.

[18] The *Book of Changes*, *hsi-tz'u*, I, chaps. 5 & 7. See English translation by James Legge, *Yi King*, *Sacred Books of the East*, Vol. XVI, Oxford: Clarendon Press, 1882, pp. 355, 359. See also pp. 213, 422 and 423 for additional instances of the use of the 'nature'.

[19] *Hsing-ming ku-hsün pien-cheng* ('Critical Studies of *Classical Interpretations of Nature and Destiny*'), Shanghai; Commercial Press, 1940, 1/1a, 4b, 17b, 23a.

[20] *Analects*, 17/2.

[21] *Ibid.*, 5/12.

[22] *Ibid.*, 17/3.

To resolve these conflicts, Chinese scholars throughout the centuries have tried to attribute to Confucius a specific doctrine on human nature which he did not teach. Some have argued that, since some Confucian pupils have taught that in human nature there are both good and evil elements and that it is the cultivation of these diverse elements that set people apart, they must have reflected the ideas of Confucius. It is true that, according to Wang Ch'ung (27-100?), 'a certain Shih Shih held that human nature is mixed and that if the good element is cultivated it becomes increasingly good and if the evil element is cultivated it becomes increasingly evil; other thinkers like Tzu-chien and Kung-sun Ni also discussed human nature although they differed from Shih Shih somewhat; and all of them held that in human nature there is that which is good and that which is evil.'[23] But whether these philosophers were pupils of Confucius is by no means certain.[24] Even if they were, to infer Confucius' own doctrine from his pupils' remarks runs the risk of speculation. In any case, Confucius did not advocate that human nature is originally good.

There has also been the attempt to attribute to Confucius the concept that there were several categories of human nature, that is, the nature of some men is good while that of others is neutral or evil, on the basis of his saying that the most intelligent and the most stupid' do not change. But as Ch'eng I (1033-1107) has said, 'in spite of what Confucius said, there is the principle by which people can change.'[25] And as Juan Yuan (1764-1849) has pointed out, this saying refers to intelligence while the problem of human nature is one of good and evil. A man with the greatest intelligence, like the man with the greatest stupidity, may be good or evil. Further, he said, Confucius did not say that they *could not* be changed; he merely said that they did not change.[26]

Instead of trying to pin on Confucius what he did not teach,

[23] *Lun-heng* ('Balanced Inquires'), Bk. 3, ch. 4; *cf.* English translation by Alfred Forke, *Lun-heng, Mitteilungen des Seminars fur Oreintalische Sprachen.* Vol. X (1907), p. 165, also *Lun-heng*, London: Luzac, 1907, p. 384.

[24] Ch'ien Mu, for example, does not believe they were. See Ch'ien's *Hsien-Ch'in chu-tzu hsi-nien* ('Interlinking Chronology of Ancient Chinese Philosophers'). Shanghai: Commercial Press, 1935, pp. 458–460.

[25] *I-shu* ('Literary Remains'), in the *Erh-Ch'eng ch'uan-shu* ('The Complete Works of the Two Ch'engs'), *Szu-pu pei-yao* editions, Shanghai: Chunghua Book Co., 1933, 18/17b.

[26] *Yen-ching shih chi* ('Collections of the Classics-Studying Studio'), First Series, *Szu-pu ts'ung-k'an* edition, Shanghai: Commercial Press, 1929, 10/16b.

it is far better to accept on face value the report that he did not discuss, that is, extensively, human nature or the Way of Heaven. Confucius was not a metaphysician. He was not interested in the metaphysical problem of what human nature originally is. Rather, he was interested in what to do with man's nature. To him, it is *practice* that sets people apart. If the most intelligent or the most stupid do not change, it is not because they cannot be changed but because they lack the will to change. In other words, Confucius was first and foremost an educator. His spirit was that of a reformer and was entirely consonant with the doctrines of 'regulating nature' and 'realizing nature' in the ancient Classics, regardless whether they were earlier or later than he.

From the above it is clear that Confucius did not teach any doctrine about the original character of human nature except to note that by nature men were near to one another. As to the doctrine of original goodness, there is not even a slight suggestion in him. The father of this doctrine was not Confucius but a follower some two hundred years after him, namely, Mencius.

5. MENCIUS' DOCTRINE OF HUMAN NATURE

There were several reasons why Mencius had to discuss this question. One reason was that, while Confucius had taught what the good was and how to achieve it, he did not explain why. The time had come for Mencius to do so. His simple answer was that goodness is original with man. Furthermore, while Confucius never undermined the importance of the individual, his attention was chiefly directed toward social relations. Mencius continued this emphasis, but he had to investigate into the moral nature of the individual who, after all, is the basic unit of social relations. To him, a good society depends on the moral consciousness of the individual. Take government for example. If the ruler has a heart that 'cannot stand the suffering of the people,' this moral quality will permeate the entire government.[27] The upshot of this line of thought is the celebrated saying, 'All things are complete in me.'[28] Besides, between the time of Confucius and Mencius, there was a vigorous religious development as evidenced by

[27] *The Book of Mencius*, 2A/6.

[28] *Ibid.*, 7A/4.

the religious nature of the *Doctrine of the Mean*[29] and the religious teachings of Mo Tzu (fl. 479-438 B.C.).[30] It was inevitable that the problem of human nature engaged the attention of philosophers at this time.

A variety of doctrines of human nature grew up in this period.[31] There were those who believed that 'man's nature may be made to practise good and it may be made to practise evil,'[32] and there was those who believed that 'the nature of some is good while the nature of others is evil.'[33] Mencius rejected both of these propositions. But it was the doctrine of philosopher Kao Tzu that he attacked with particular bitterness. Philosopher Kao said, 'Man's nature is like whirling water. If a breach in the pool is made to the east, it will flow to the east. If a breach is made to the west, it will flow to the west. Man's nature is indifferent to good and evil just as water is indifferent to east and west.' To this, Mencius countered, 'Water, indeed, is indifferent to the east and west, but is it indifferent to high and low? Man's nature is naturally good just as water flows downward. There is no man without this good nature; neither is there water that does not flow downward.'[34] To Kao Tzu's argument that 'Man's nature is like the willow, and righteousness is like a cup or a bowl. To treat human nature as love and righteousness is similar to treating willow as cups and bowls,' he replied and said, 'In making cups and bowls, do you follow the nature of the willow or violate it? If you must do violence to the willow in order to make cups and bowls with it, then you must in the same way do violence to humanity in order to fashion from it love and righteousness!'[35] And to Kao Tzu's contention that 'What is born in man is called his nature,' he asked, 'When you say that what is born in man is called his nature, do you mean that it is like saying that a white substance is called White? . . . Then is the whiteness of the white feather the same as the whiteness of snow? Or again, is the whiteness of snow the same

[29] Traditionally attributed to Confucius' grandson, Tzu-szu (483–402 B.C.?). Some modern scholars have dated it later. For its religious ideas, see chaps. 22 to 32.

[30] See *The Ethical and Political Works of Motse*, trans. by Y. P. Mei, London: Arthur Probsthain, 1929, chaps. 26–31.

[31] See *The Book of Mencius*, 6 Ap 4–5.

[32] *Ibid.*, 6A/6.

[33] *Ibid.*

[34] *Ibid.*, 6A/2.

[35] *Ibid.*, 6A/1.

as the whiteness of white jade? . . . Is the nature of a dog the same as the nature of an ox, and the nature of an ox the same as the nature of a man?'[36]

There is more oratory than logic in Mencius' utterances, but his position is perfectly clear. It is that man's nature is originally good. To support his own position, he pointed to the fact that 'When men suddenly see a child about to fall into a well, they all have the feeling of alarm and distress, not in order to gain friendship with the child's parents, nor to seek the praise of their neighbours and friends, nor because they dislike the reputation (of being unvirtuous).' From this he concluded that 'a man without the feeling of mercy is not a man; a man without the feeling of deference and complaisance is not a man; a man without the feeling of shame and dislike is not a man; and a man without the feeling of right and wrong is not a man. The feeling of commiseration is the beginning[37] of love; the feeling of shame and dislike is the beginning of righteousness; the feeling of deference and complaisance is the beginning of propriety; and the feeling of right and wrong is the beginning of wisdom. Men have these four beginnings just as they have their four limbs.'[38] 'These four, love, righteousness, propriety, and wisdom,' he added, 'are not drilled into us from outside. We are originally provided with them.'[39]

He went even further and said that not only is goodness inherent in man's nature but also man does not require any learning to practise it or any thought to know it, for man does so intuitively. In his own words, 'the ability possessed by man without the necessity of thought is native knowledge. Children carried in the arms all know to love their parents. As they grow, they all know to respect their brothers. To have filial affection for parents is love, and to respect elders is righteousness. Their feelings are universal in the world, that is all.'[40] They are universal because innate goodness and intuitive ability to know and do good are common to the human species. 'All things of the same kind are similar to one another,' he observed, 'and why should there be any doubt about men? The sage and I are the same in kind. . . . Men's mouths like the same relishes; their ears like the same sounds; and their eyes like the same beauty. Can it be that only their minds do not like the same

[36] *Ibid.*, 6A/3.
[37] Or 'seed.'
[38] *Ibid.*, 2A/6.
[39] *Ibid.*, 6A/6.
[40] *Ibid.*, 7A/15.

thing? What is this that their minds all like? I say, the principle of reason and righteousness.'[41]

If man's nature is originally good, why does he practise evil? Mencius' answer to this question is both simple and direct. He said, 'If we follow our essential character, we will be able to do good. This is what I mean in saying that man's nature is good. If man does evil, it is not the fault of his original endowment. . . . Therefore it is said: Seek and you will find them (love, righteousness, propriety, and wisdom), neglect and you will lose them. Men differ from one another by twice as much, or five times, or an incalculable amount, because they have not fully developed their original endowment.'[42] As to why man does not fully develop his original endowment, Mencius again turned to man himself. The failure is due to one's 'losing the originally good mind',[43] 'self-destruction and self abandonment',[44] 'lack of nourishment',[45] 'failure to develop the noble and great elements in oneself',[46] 'failure to preserve one's mind',[47] 'lack of effort',[48] or simply lack of thought.[49] It is clear that man is the cause of his own downfall. Not that Mencius ignored the influence of environment. In explaining why water could be forced uphill, he said that it is not the nature of water, but the force applied from outside that made it.[50] And to explain the inequality of products, he recognized the difference of the soil and the unequal nourishment afforded by the rains and dews.[51] Nevertheless, his emphasis on man's own responsibility is unmistakable. This, in brief outline, is the doctrine of the original goodness of human nature that eventually came to dominate Chinese thought and became accepted as Confucian orthodoxy.

6. DOCTRINES OF HUMAN NATURE IN LATER CHOU AND MEDIAEVAL TIMES

This orthodoxy was not established, however, until the doctrine had faced much competition and was finally elaborated and modified by the Neo-Confucianists of the Sung period (960-1279) some fourteen centuries later. In the meantime, Confucianists offered many and diverse theories of human nature.

[41] *Ibid.*, 6A/7.
[42] *Ibid.*, 6A/6.
[43] *Ibid.*, 6A/8.
[44] *Ibid.*, 4A/10.
[45] *Ibid.*, 6A/8.
[46] *Ibid.*, 6A/5.
[47] *Ibid.*, B4/28, 6A/8.
[48] *Ibid.*, 6A/7.
[49] *Ibid.*, 6A/6.
[50] *Ibid.*, 4A/2.
[51] *Ibid.*, 4A/7.

The development may be divided into four periods. In the latter part of the Chou Dynasty, notably during and immediately after Mencius' time, human nature was considered either originally good or neutral, as we have seen. In addition to this, there was the doctrine of Hsün Tzu (fl. 298-238 B.C.), who held that human nature was originally evil. In the Earlier Han period (206 B.C.-A.D. 9) human nature was described in dualistic terms, that is, that nature was good but feelings were evil, or that human nature was both good and evil. From the later Han period through the Wei and Chin times (A.D. 25-419), the representative theory was that there were three grades of human nature; namely, the highest, which was wholly good, the medium, which was neither good nor evil but could be made to be good or evil, and the lowest, which was wholly evil. And in the fourth period, that of T'ang (618-907), there were the doctrines of Han Yu and Li Ao who opposed each other. A brief survey should reveal the direction of Chinese thinking with reference to the problem under discussion.

(i) *The Later Chou Period* (*to* 256 *B.C.*)

We have already referred to the contemporary schools of Mencius. In ancient China, Confucianism may be said to have grown along two opposite directions, one led by Mencius and the other by Hsün Tzu. In the matter of man's nature, they were diametrically opposed. Hsün Tzu, Mencius' junior who evidently never met him, strongly attacked his doctrine of the original goodness of human nature. In his famous essay on 'the evil nature of man', he said:

'The nature of man is evil; its goodness is the result of nurture. By nature, man is born with the desire to seek for gain. If this desire is followed, strife and rapacity will arise and deference and complaisances will disappear. Man is born with envy and hatred. If these are followed, injury and destruction will result and loyalty and faithfulness will disappear. Man is born with the desires of the ear and the eye and with fondness for pleasant sound and beautiful colour. If these desires are followed, excess and disorder will result and propriety and righteousness and refinement and orderliness will disappear. Therefore, to bow to the nature of man and to follow his feelings will surely result in strife and rapacity, amounting to a violation of refinement and orderliness, and result in chaos. Hence, there must be the transforming influence of education and law and the guidance of propriety and righteousness. Only then will it result in deference and complaisance, conform to refinement and orderliness and culminate in peaceful order. From this, it is clear that man's nature is originally evil and his goodness is the result of nurture. . . .

'Mencius said, "The fact that man is teachable shows that his nature is originally good."[52] I say that this is not true. Mencius did not thoroughly know the original nature of man, nor did he examine into the difference between nature and nurture. Human nature is completed by Heaven; it cannot be learned or attained through practice. On the other hand, propriety and righteousness are created by sages and can be achieved through learning and attained through practice. That in man which cannot be attained through learning or practice is called original nature. That in man which can be attained through learning or practice is called nurture. This is the difference between nature and nurture. . . .

'Someone may ask, "If man's nature is originally evil, where did propriety and righteousness come from?" In answer, I say, All propriety and righteousness were created through the nurturing by the sages, not the original product of human nature. . . .

'Mencius said, "The nature of man is good." I say that this is not so. Throughout the world, whether in the past or at present, goodness means true principles and peaceful order and evil means depravity, maliciousness, perversion, and disorder. Herein lies the distinction between good and evil. If the nature of man were really that of correct principles and peaceful order, then why was the necessity of sage-kings and propriety and righteousness? What could sage-kings and propriety and righteousness have added to these true principles and peaceful order? It is not true that man's nature is good. Rather, it is evil. Consequently, the ancient sages realized that man's nature was evil, that the people were depraved, dangerous, and uncorrected, and perverse, disorderly, and not disciplined, and, therefore, for their sake, established the authority

[52] This and the following quotation from Mencius do not appear in *The Book of Mencius*, but they faithfully express Mencius' ideas.

of the ruler to deal with them, made clear propriety and righteousness to transform them, instituted laws and government to govern them, and accentuated punishments to restrain them, so that the entire world would come to good order and accord with goodness. Such is the result of government by sage-kings and the transforming influence of propriety and righteousness. . . . It is clear that man's nature is originally evil and that his goodness is the result of nurture.'[53]

Needless to say, Hsün Tzu's arguments are as arbitrary as those of Mencius. Both of them selected certain facts in human society to suit their theories. However, in spite of the direct opposition to each other, and in spite of the fact that they both departed from Confucius so far as the question of human nature is concerned, they have been the two arch Confucianists in Chinese history. This is so far the simple reason that their common objective is the same as that of Confucius, namely, the desirability and possibility of perfection through moral training and social education. As an outstanding leader of ancient Confucianism, Hsün Tzu exerted tremendous influence on Chinese history and thought from the third century B.C. to the first century A.D. But eventually he was supplanted by Mencius as the chief and orthodox Confucianist. Perhaps his doctrine of evil nature, more than anything else, accounts for his eclipse. Because of this doctrine, he advocated strict discipline. Of course, his forms of discipline, namely, music, rules of propriety, 'rectification of names,' and benevolent government, were essentially consonant with basic Confucian teachings. But his pupils, Han Fei (d. 233 B.C.) and Li Ssu (d. 208 B.C.), who were leaders of the Legalist School, advocated and enforced strong governmental control, stringent laws, ruthless punishments, and absolute and extensive standardization, including that of thought. The latter, as prime minister of the newly established and unified empire of Ch'in (221-207 B.C.) achieved for the state unchallenged authority and instituted an airtight dictatorship. The harshness of his concepts, the severity of his measure, and the cruelty of his treatment of fellow human beings ultimately led to his own execution and the downfall of the Ch'in Dynasty. It is unfair to hold

[53] *Hsun tzu*, ch. 23; *cf.* English translation by Homer H. Dubs, *The Works of Hsuntze*, London: Arthur Probisthain, 1928, pp. 305–308.

Hsün Tzu responsible for this violent episode of Chinese history, but there is always the possibility that his lack of faith in the original goodness of human nature was a contributing factor to the harsh disciplinarianism of the Legalists. At any rate, the Chinese had not only suspicion, but fear, of the doctrine of original evil, and it died with the Ch'in Dynasty, never to be revived.

(ii) *The Former Han Period* (206 B.C.—A.D. 9)

As Legalism declined, Confucianism assumed supremacy. It became a state cult, and its Classics formed the basis of the education for all civil servants. Confucianists in this period agreed in their major doctrines but in the matter of human nature, they differed widely. As mentioned before, they interpreted human nature in dualistic terms, to the effect that nature is good but feelings are evil.

The representative Confucianist in this tendency, perhaps the originator of the theory, was Tung Chung-shu (*c.* 179-*c.* 104 B.C.), the very Confucianist who was instrumental in establishing Confucianism as the state cult. He drew an analogy between human nature and the rice plant. Just as the plant may produce rice, he said, so human nature may produce goodness. But in both cases such product is not absolutely certain, and both require external help. These facts, according to him, show that human nature is not completely good. To him, in man's nature there are both good and evil, just as there are the two cosmic forces in the universe, namely, the *yin*, or passive or negative force, and the *yang*, the active or positive force.[54] He equates nature with *yang* and feelings with *yin*, thus making nature the source of goodness and feelings the source of evil.

This theory did not gain universal acceptance. For example, Yang Hsiung (53 B.C.—A.D. 18), who came a little later than Tang, believed, like Kao Tzu, that 'man's nature involves both good and evil, and that if one cultivates the good element, he will become a good man and if he cultivates the evil element, he will become an evil man.'[55] And he added, 'the material force is like a horse that pulls man toward good or evil.'[56] The

[54] *Ch'un-ch'iu fa-lu* ('Luxuriant Crown Gems of the *Spring and Autumn Annals*'), ch. 35.

[55] *Fa-yen* ('Model Sayings'), ch. 3; *cf.* German translation by E. von Zach, '*Yang Hsiung's Fa-yen* (*Worte strengen Ermahung*)', *Sonilogische Beitrage*, Vol. IV, No. 1 (1939), p. 11.

[56] *Ibid.*

difference between him and Tung is that with him, material force (*ch'i*), to which later Confucianists and Taoists alike ascribed feelings, is not evil but may lead to good or evil. Nevertheless, the dualistic theory remained the dominant one throughout the Earlier Han period and extended into the Later Han (25-220). This can be seen in the *Comprehensive Discussions in the White Tiger Hall*, which sums up the prevailing opinions in the first century A.D., and immediately before, where it definitely says that 'nature is the application of *yang* while feelings are the transformations of *yin*,' and, quoting a work now non-existent, that 'the material force of *yang* means love while the material force of *yin* means greed. Hence in feelings there are selfish desires while in nature there is love.'[57] There is no doubt that the dualistic view was widely held.

(iii) *From the Later Han through the Wei and Chin Times* (A.D. 25-419)

There was an obvious attempt in the dualistic theory to compromise or synthesize the two cardinal Confucian doctrines as represented by Mencius and Hsün Tzu.[58] The attempt was continued in the next period, that is, from the Later Han through the Wei and Chin times. The controlling thought in this period was that the natures of men may be classified into several categories, usually three.

The theory of three grades has been traditionally identified with Han Yu (768-824), who has been generally credited with originating the theory. Actually that was not the case. It is true that he was the first to apply the term 'three grade' (*san-p'in*) to the theory of human nature. But the term is found in several places in the Classics, and Hsün Yüeh (148-209) six hundred years before him had propounded the theory of three grades of human destiny.[59] The theory of three grades of human nature itself had been taught in Buddhism, specifically in the *Treatise on the Completion of Ideation-Only*, or the *Ch'eng wei-shin lun* (*Vijñaptimātratāsiddhi*), which was translated into Chinese by Hsüan-tsang (596-664) some fifty years before.

57 *Polhu t'ung*, ed. by Pan ku (32–92), *Szu-pu ts'ung-k'an* edition, 1929, 8/1a; see English translation by Tjan Tjoe Som, *Po Hu T'ung, The Comprehensive Discussions in the White Tiger Hall*, Leiden: E. J. Brill, 1949, Vol. II, 1952, p. 565.

58 See, for example, the *Book of History*, 'Books of Hsia,' Bk. I, sec. 44; Legge, *The Shoo King*, p. 110.

59 *Shen-chien*, ch. 5.

In chapter five of that treatise it is stated that there are the good nature, the neutral nature and the evil nature. This is not to suggest that Han Yu borrowed his idea from Buddhist Idealism, for there is no evidence that he had studied the Buddhist text. But the Buddhist doctrine was a very common one among the Buddhists whom Han Yu vigorously attacked. The actual source of Han Yu's theory, according to Fu Szu-nien, is Wang Ch'ung (b. A.D. 27).[60] In his *Lun-heng* ('*Balanced Inquiries*') Wang Ch'ung wrote, 'I believe that when Mencius said that human nature was originally good, he was thinking of people above the average; when Hsün Tzu said that human nature was originally evil, he was thinking of people below the average; and when Yang Hsiung said that human nature was mixed with both good and evil, he was thinking of average people.'[61] Like the Confucianists of the Earlier Han period, Wang Ch'ung was trying to compromise Mencius and Hsün Tzu and to combine their theories with that of Yang Hsiung, which is itself a compromise. Furthermore, the theory seems to offer an acceptable solution to the conflict between the Confucian saying that in nature men are near to one another and his saying that the most intelligent and most stupid do not change. In fact, looked at from a different angle, the theory is not so much a compromise of Mencius and Hsün Tzu as an effort to go back to Confucius himself.

(iv) *The T'ang Period* (618-907)

It was in this spirit that Han Yu claimed to defend and represent the 'correct transmission' of Confucianism and propounded the theory of three grades at the same time. In his well-known essay *Yuan-hsing* (*An Inquiry on Human Nature*) he said, 'Nature comes into existence with birth, whereas feelings are produced when there is contact with things. . . . There are three grades of nature, namely, the highest, the medium, and the lowest. The highest is good, the medium may be led to be good or evil, and the lowest is evil. Nature consists in five virtues; namely, love, righteousness, propriety, good faith, and wisdom. Men of highest nature abide by the first and act according to the other four virtues. Men of medium nature do not possess much of the first but do not violate it, and are

[60] *Op. cit.*, 3/7b.
[61] *Lun-heng*, Bk. 3, ch. 4; Forke, *op. cit.*, X, 171.

mixed in the other four. Men of lowest nature violate the first and oppose the other four. . . . The three philosophers—(Mencius, Hsün Tzu, and Yang Hsiung), in discussing human nature, referred only to the medium grade and neglected the highest and the lowest.'[62] Incidentally, it is interesting to note that just as Mencius, who claimed to represent the 'correct transmission' of Confucius, did not follow the sage in the matter of human nature, so Han Yu, who claimed to represent the 'correct transmission' of both Confucius and Mencius, opposed the former and did not actually follow the latter.

From the above it will be seen that Han Yu merely echoed Wang Ch'ung; there was nothing new in him. As a matter of fact, there was nothing new in the entire T'ang period so far as doctrines of human nature are concerned. While Han Yu echoed Wang Ch'ung's doctrine of three grades, his friend or pupil, Li Ao (A.D. 798) echoed the dualistic doctrine of Han Confucianists. In his treatise on recovering nature, he said that 'it is man's nature that enables him to become a sage and it is his feelings that lead his nature astray.'[63] Unlike Han Yu's theory which came out of the Confucian tradition, Li Ao's definitely reflects Buddhist influence.[64] Such utterances as 'when there is neither cognition nor thought, then the feelings will not arise' and 'to stop feelings by means of feelings is to aggravate feelings' might well have come from the mouth of a Zen Buddhist. However, this influence is one of stimulation, not of origination. The source of Li Ao's theory is also Confucianism, not Buddhism. What happened was that since the Earlier Han Confucianists developed the theory that human nature and human feelings form two separate levels, for several hundred years there was nothing new in the field of human nature. In this period, both Buddhism and Taoism soared to great heights in their discussions on this question. Under the stimulation and challenge of Buddhism and in order to compete with it, Li Ao sought a comparable doctrine and found it in the Earlier Han Confucianists, and combined it with Mencius's idea of originally good human nature, the idea of

[62] *Yuan-hsing*, in *Han Ch'ang-li ch'uan chi* (Complete Works of Han Yu'), ch. 11; ch. English translation by James Legge, 'An Examination of the Nature of Man,' *The Chinese Classics*, Vol. II, Oxford: Clarendon Press, 1895, pp. 89–91.

[63] *Li Wen-kung chi* ('Collected Works of Li Ao'), *Szu-pu ts'ung-k'an edition*, Shanghai; Commercial Press, 1929, 2/5a.

[64] *Ibid.*, 2/8a–b.

tranquil nature in the *Book of Changes*[65] and in the *Treatise on Music*,[66] and the idea of full development of human nature in both Mencius and the *Doctrine of the Mean*.

7. NEO-CONFUCIAN IDEAS ON HUMAN NATURE AND ON THE EMERGENCE OF EVIL

We have now surveyed the development of Confucian doctrines of human nature through the four periods. The diversity is amazing even if the reasoning is unsatisfactory. Of all the different theories, it was that of Mencius that triumphed and became *the* Confucian teaching.[67] Several reasons may be offered to explain this interesting phenomenon. The terrible effect of the doctrine of evil nature has been recounted. To say that human emotions are the source of evil is too unrealistic as well as too Taoistic and Buddhistic for the Confucianists to accept. To them, emotions are the natural expressions of life and are essentially good as they can and should be harmonized. To combat the Taoist and Buddhist contempt for the emotions, the Neo-Confucianists of the Sung period had to show that they were natural and good. Wittingly or unwittingly, Taoists and Buddhists themselves helped to bring the doctrine of original goodness into prominence. They had dominated Chinese religious life for many centuries and exerted vast influence on various aspects of Chinese culture.[68] The Taoist teaching that all men possess Tao in their nature and therefore could attain sagehood and the Buddhist teaching that all men had Buddha-nature in them and therefore could become Buddha, had been universally accepted. Perhaps their doctrines were partly a result of Mencius' teaching that all men could be Yao and Shun (sages).[69] Certainly they had in turn influenced the Neo-Confucianists. If all men could become Taoist sages, Buddhas, or Yao and Shun, it is necessary to hold that they had the original goodness in them. The doctrine of three grades may not stand in direct conflict with the ideal of sagehood for all, for even men originally evil may be transformed. But there is always the danger for such men to be considered beyond

[65] *The Book of Changes, hsi-tz'u* I, ch. 10; Legge, *Yi King*, p. 3870.

[66] Forming chapter 19 of the *Book of Propriety*. See Legge, *The Li Ki*, p. 96.

[67] *The Book of Mencius*, 7A/1.

[68] *The Doctrine of the Mean*, chaps. 21–22.

[69] *The Book of Mencius*, 68/2.

salvation, as were the *iccāntikas* in Buddhism, who, so the early Chinese Buddhists thought, were forever condemned, until Tao-sheng (d. A.D. 434) challenged the belief and, at the cost of excommunication, advocated the doctrine of universal salvation.

The most important reason for the triumph of the doctrine of original goodness, however, is to be found in the very essence of Confucianism itself. The central interest of the school, as already pointed out, is education. During the Han and Y'ang times, education had already been made the chief avenue through which talents were to be discovered and developed, and social and political leadership to be recruited, and man's moral nature was to be cultivated. By the time of the eleventh century, printing had been highly developed and libraries were growing up in various parts of the country. The concept of education was now considerably enlarged. Books could now reach the common man. The ideal that all men could become Yao and Shun is now real and alive. It is only natural, and logical, to believe that man's nature is originally good. No wonder this doctrine came to be accepted as the true and orthodox teaching of Confucianism. It has remained so ever since.

However, Mencius' doctrine, like all others, failed to explain one concrete fact in human life and society, namely, the existence of evil. To say, as did Mencius, that man's evil is due to his failure to develop his capability fully, or his foolishness in destroying his own moral nature, or laziness, or unfavourable external environment,[70] is to beg the question. It is no more satisfactory to divide human nature into several categories, one of which is evil. To say that feelings are evil is even worse, because, in the first place, it is not true to fact, and in the second place, it contradicts the central Confucian doctrine that feelings, when harmonized, are good.

There was no logical answer to the question, Whence comes evil? until the Neo-Confucian philosopher Chang Tsai (also called Chang Heng-ch'u, 1020-1077). According to him, evil arises with the emergence of physical nature, that is, nature associated with Material Force (*ch'i*). He said, 'Nature in man is never evil. . . . With the existence of physical form, there exists the physical nature. If one skilfully recovers the Nature

[70] *Ibid.*, 6A/1–8.

of Heaven and Earth (that is, the original, good nature before the endowment of Material Force), then it will be preserved. Therefore in the physical nature there is that which the superior man denies to be his original nature.'[71]

For an explanation of the above statement, we must turn to an earlier passage in Chang's work, which reads, 'In its original state of Great Vacuity (*hsu*, Void), Material Force is absolutely tranquil and formless. As it is acted upon, it engenders the two fundamental elements of *yin* and *yang*, and through integration gives rise to forms. As there are forms, there are their opposites. These opposites necessarily stand in opposition to what they do. Opposition leads to conflicts, which will necessarily be reconciled and resolved. Thus the feelings of love and hate are both derived from the Great Vacuity.[72] In other words, when the original state of being, the Great Vacuity, assumes form, differentiation necessarily follows. As it is expressed in his famous dictum, 'Reality is One but it differentiates into the Many.' In the state of differentiatedness, there is bound to be opposition, discrimination, and conflict, which gives rise to evil. Furthermore, in the process of differentiation, our endowment often lacks harmony and balance, and this lack leads us to deviate from the Mean. This deviation is evil. Thus physical nature gives rise to two types of evil: first, setting the self against the other, and second, lack of harmony and balance. In the words of the greatest of all Neo-Confucianists, Chu Hsi (1130-1200), 'the Nature of Heaven and Earth is the Principle (*li*). As soon as, and where *yin* and *yang* and the Five Agents (of Water, Fire, Wood, Metal and Earth) operate, there is physical nature. Herein are the differences between intelligence and beclouding, and the heavy and the light.'[73] 'The two forces (of *yin* and *yang*),' he said, 'sometimes mutually supplement each other and sometimes contradict each other. . . . Sometimes their operation is even and easy but sometimes unbalanced. Hence there is evil and there is good.'[74]

The process of differentiation itself is not to be regretted, for it is a matter of necessity. Chang Tsai said, 'The Great Vacuity of necessity consists of Material Force. Material Force of

[71] *Chang-meng* ('Correct Discipline for Beginners'), *Cheng-i-t'ang ch'uan-chi* edition, 3/8a.

[72] *Ibid.*, 2/10a.

[73] Commentary on the *Cheng-meng*, 3/8a.

[74] *Chu Tzu ch'üan-shu* ('Complete Works of Chu Hsi'), Palace edition, 1713, 42/4a.

necessity integrates to become the myriad things: Things of necessity disintegrate and return to the Great Vacuity.'[75] Chu Hsi put it later, 'Without physical forms, Principle (that is, the Great Vacuity) would have nothing to adhere to.'[76] That is to say, the Great Vacuity or Principle would be abstract and unreal unless and until it becomes concrete through its being differentiated into the many. This is the reason why the Ch'eng brothers, Ch'eng Hao, also called Ch'eng Ming-tao (1032-1085), and Ch'eng I, also called Ch'eng I-ch'uan (1033-1107), say that 'it will not be complete to talk about the nature of man and things without including the Material Force, and it will be unintelligible to talk about Material Force without including the nature.'[77] It is important to note here that with Buddhism and Taoism, the world of differentiation, the world of multiplicity with all its discriminations and conflicts, is to to be ignored, forgotten, or transcended. With the Neo-Confucianists, however, it is not only to be accepted as fact but also as an essential aspect to the reality of the Ultimate Being. As to why in the world of differentiation there is lack of balance, lack of harmony, conflict, or inequality, the Neo-Confucianists went right back to Mencius, who declared, 'It is the nature of things that they are not equal.'[78] Ch'eng Hao said, 'It is unreasonable to expect that all people in the street are superior men or that they are all inferior men.'[79]

We should note that the Neo-Confucianists did not say that differentiation resulting from physical nature as such is evil. That would be following the Buddhist doctrine that the world is an illusion. What they meant is that in differentiation is the occasion for evil. Here we have a logical explanation of the emergence of evil. No wonder Chu Hsi said, 'The doctrine of physical nature originated with Chang and Ch'eng. It made a tremendous contribution to the Confucian school and is a great help to us students. No one before this time has enunciated such a doctrine. Hence with the establishment of the doctrine of Chang and Ch'eng, the theories (of human nature) of all previous philosophers collapse.'[80]

[75] *Cheng-meng*, 2/3b.

[76] *Op. cit.*

[77] *Ts'ui-yen* ('Pure Words'), in the *Complete Works of the Two Ch'engs*, 2/21b.

[78] *The Book of Mencius*, 3A/4.

[79] *The Complete Works of the Two Ch'engs.*

[80] Commentary on the *Cheng-meng*, 3/8a.

As already suggested, the Neo-Confucian attempt to find an explanation of evil is not only to provide an answer to the question but also to preserve Mencius' doctrine of original goodness. However, while the Neo-Confucianists generally remained true to Mencius, they did not agree with Mencius that evil originated with man. To them, it originated with physical nature. This does not mean that to the Neo-Confucianists evil is a natural phenomenon and not a moral one. Although they confused natural evil and moral evil, there is no doubt that to them moral good and evil arise only in human society. This is the reason why Ch'eng Hao declared that 'nothing can be said about the state before birth.'[81] The problem of good and evil becomes real only when one's moral life has begun, when in a man-to-man relationship one has to deal with physical nature which is unbalanced and therefore causes him to deviate from the Mean, and which puts him in the position of isolation, discrimination, and opposition, thus setting himself against another. The moral problem, then, is what to do with our physical nature. Chang Tsai's answer is, 'Transform it'.

This phrase, 'Transform the physical nature', has been hailed by Neo-Confucianists as an outstanding contribution and has remained a golden teaching in the Confucian school. To Chang Tsai, as already pointed out, nature to man is never evil. 'It depends on whether or not man can skilfully recover the Nature of Heaven and Earth.'[82] If we can skilfully recover the Nature of Heaven and Earth, then physical nature will be transformed. For ways and means of transformation, he urged study. 'There is a great benefit in study,' he said, because it can transform our physical nature.[83] He also urged virtue. 'When virtue does not overcome the Material Force, our nature is determined and controlled by the Material Force. But when virtue overcomes the Material Force, then our nature is determined and controlled by virtue. . . . Only life, death, longevity, and premature death are due to the Material Force and cannot be transformed.'[84] But the most important way to transform physical nature is what he called 'enlarging the mind'. 'When one enlarges his mind,' he said, 'one can

[81] *The Complete Works of the Two Ch'engs.*

[82] *Cheng-meng*, 3/7b.

[83] *Ibid.*

[84] *Cheng-meng*, 3/9a.

embrace all things in the universe. As long as there is something not yet embodied by me, then there is still something outside my mind. The mind of the common man is limited to the narrowness of what he has heard and seen. The sage, on the contrary, does not allow his limited knowledge to restrict his mind, but regards all things in the universe as part of himself.'[85]

This passage should call to mind Chang Tsai's famous essay, 'Western Inscription', in which he declares that 'Heaven is my father, Earth my mother, and all human beings my brothers.' When all discriminations and oppositions and distinctions between the self and the non-self are eliminated, men and Heaven will become one body.

But what makes it possible for the mind to enlarge itself? To go back to Mencius' doctrine of native ability to do good is useless, because such ability itself needs an explanation. In this respect, Chang Tsai offered only an unsatisfactory and what might even be called a negative explanation although philosophically it is extremely important. This is his concept of the Great Vacuity. Only when reality is a Vacuity can the Material Force operate, and only with the operation of the Material Force can things mutually influence, mutually penetrate, and mutually be identified. Thus the Great Vacuity is the necessary condition for the removal of oppositions and conflicts.

This doctrine of the Great Vacuity is extremely important because, unlike the Taoist Vacuity, which is pure Void in which individual things are transcended, it is the very thing that makes individual things possible and real, achieve harmony among themselves, and attain their full being. Thus Chang Tsai's concept of the Great Vacuity is not a blind borrowing from the Taoists, as sometimes asserted. Rather, it is a conversion of the Taoist concept from something negative to something positive.

But so far as goodness of human nature is concerned, if the doctrine of Vacuity is negative because it only provides the necessary condition for the transformation of physical nature but does not explain why human nature is good, what makes it good, and what makes it possible to grow and extend so as to overcome all the imbalance and conflicts. The answer to these questions lies in the Neo-Confucian concept of *Jen*, which was chiefly developed by the Ch'eng brothers.

[85] *Ibid.*, 3/11b.

8. THE CONCEPT OF JEN

It is impossible to discuss Chinese concepts of human nature in particular or of man in general without taking into consideration the Chinese concept of *jen*, a word perhaps best translated as love. The two words, *jen* as love and *jen* as man used to be interchangeable, and in some cases still are. The word *jen* as love is written with two parts, the radical *jen*, meaning man, on the left and two strokes on the right. The two words have the same pronunciation. Most important of all, as the *Doctrine of the Mean* and the *Book of Mencius* have it, '*jen* (love) is *jen* (man)'.[86] For this reason, *jen* has been considered the highest good in the Chinese scheme of values. This being the case, it is necessary to trace its development in some detail.

The word *jen* is not found in the Shang Dynasty oracle inscriptions.[87] It is only occasionally mentioned in pre-Confucian texts, and in all these cases it denotes the particular virtue of kindness, more especially the kindness of a ruler to his subjects.[88] With Confucius, however, all of this is radically changed. Instead of perpetuating the ancient understanding of *jen* as a particular virtue, he transformed it into what James Legge very appropriately translated as 'perfect virtue' and Arthur Waley as 'Goodness'.[89] It denotes the general meaning of moral life at its best. It includes filial piety, wisdom, propriety, courage, and loyalty to government.[90] It requires the practice of 'earnestness, liberality, truthfulness, diligence, and generosity.'[91] A man of *jen* is 'respectful in private life, earnest in handling affairs, and loyal in his association with people.'[92] In short, *jen* precludes all evil and underlies as well as embraces all possible virtues, so much so that 'if you set your mind on *jen*, you will be free from evil.'[93]

[86] *Doctrine of the Mean*, ch. 20; *The Book of Mencius*, 7A/16.

[87] According to Tung Tso-pin, 'The Word *Jen* in Archaic Script' (in Chinese), *Academic Review*, Vol. II, No. 1 (Sept. 1953), p. 18.

[88] For Example, *The Book of Poetry*, Ode No. 77 (or Part I, Bk. 7, Ode 3), Ode No. 103 (or Part I, Bk. 8, Ode 8); *The Book of History*, 'Book of Chou,' Bk. 2 (Legge, *The Shoo King*, p. 292).

[89] See James Legge, trans., *Confucian Analects*, *The Chinese Classics*, Vol. I, Oxford: Clarendon Press, 1893, *passim* Arthur Waley, trans., *The Analects of Confucius*, London: Allen & Unwin, 1938, *passim*.

[90] *Analects*, 17/21, 5/18, 12/1, 14/5, and 5/18.

[91] *Ibid.*, 17/6.

[92] *Ibid.*, 13/19.

[93] *Ibid.*, 4/4.

When one has fully realized *jen*, one becomes a sage.[94]

But what is this general virtue in concrete terms? Confucius offered neither a precise definition nor a comprehensive description. However, when a pupil asked him about *jen*, he replied, 'It is to love men.'[95] We have here the key word to the Confucian doctrine, namely, love (*ai*). It is on the basis of this meaning, no doubt, that the standard Chinese dictionary, the *Shuo-wen* (A.D. 100), define *jen* as affection (*ch'in*). It is also on the basis of this that ancient Chinese philosophers, whether Confucian, Taoist, Mohist, or Legalist, and practically all Han Confucianists, have equated *jen* with love.[96]

By love all these philosophers meant love for all. Confucius definitely said, 'Love all men comprehensively.'[97] Mencius said, 'The man of *jen* embraces all in his love,'[98] and this theme runs through the *Book of Mencius*. Han Yu even explicitly used the term 'universal love' (*po-ai*). 'Universal love constitutes *jen*,' he declares in the very beginning of his celebrated essay on the Confucian Way.[99] These are the traditional concepts and Han Yu's use of a new term represented no departure from the Confucian tradition. It is not true that traditional Confucianism lacked the idea of universal love and Han Yu had to broaden the concept in order to match Taoist and Buddhist concepts of love for all.[100]

However, the Confucian concept of *jen* did undergo an im-

[94] *Ibid.*, 6/28, 7/33.

[95] *Ibid.*, 12/22.

[96] For example, The *Li chi*, '*Jen* is to love.' (Legge, *The Li ki*, p. 98); the *Hsün Tzu*, '*Jen* is love,' ch. 27 (the chapter not translated in Dubs' *The Works of Hsüntze*); the Mo Tzu, '*Jen* is to embody love,' ch. 40, '*Jen* is to love . . .' ch. 12, see Herbert A. Giles, trans., *Chuang Tzu*, Shanghai; Kelly & Walsh, 1926, p. 137, the *Han Fei Tzu*, '*Jen* means that in one's heart one joyously loves others,' ch. 20, see W. K. Liao, trans., *The Complete Works of Han Fei Tzu*, London: Arthur Probsthain, 1939, Vol. I, p. 171; Tung Chung-shu, *Ch'un-ch'iu fan-lu*, ch. 29, '*Jen* means love in man,' ch. 30, '*Jen* is to love mankind,' Yang Hsiung, *T'ai-hsuan ching* ('great Mystery Classic'), ch. 9, '*Jen* is to see and love' and 'To love universally is called *jen*'; Wang Pi (226–249). *Lun-yu shih-i* ('Explanation of the *Analects*'), I, '*Jen* is to extend one's love to all creatures.'

[97] *Analects*, 1/6.

[98] *The Book of Mencius*, 7A/46.

[99] 'Yuan-tao' ('An Inquiry in the Way'), *op. cit.*, ch. 11. See English translation by Herbert A. Giles in his *Gems of Chinese Literature: Prose*, London: Bernard Quaritch, 1923, p. 115, and French translation by George Marguolies, in his *Le Kou-Wen chinois*, Paris: Geuthner, 1926, p. 177.

[100] This question is extensively discussed in my 'The Evolution of the Confucian Concept *Jen*' *Philosophy East and West*, Vol. IV, No. 4 (January, 1955), p. 259 ff.

portant extension in Neo-Confucianism. We have already referred to Chang Tsai's 'Western Inscription'. It seems to be an insignificant piece, but it marks an important step in the advancement of Chinese thought. 'Heaven is my father and Earth is my mother,' it begins, 'and such a small creature as I find an intimate place in their midst. . . . All people are my brothers and sisters, and all things are my companions.'[101] Although the inscription is very short, it exercised tremendous influence on the thinking of Chinese philosophers at his time and has ever since. Its primary purpose, as Yang Kuei-shan (1053-1135) pointed out, is to urge the student to seek *jen*.[102] Here we have an important development, that is, that *jen* not only means the love of all people but the love of all things as well. In other words, love is truly universalized.

There is no doubt that this idea reflects Buddhist influence, for hitherto Confucian love had been confined largely to the mundane world, whereas the object of moral consciousness in Buddhism is the entire universe. Yang Kusi-shan thinks that Chang Tsai's doctrine comes right out of Mencius' saying, 'the superior man is affectionate to his parents and is *jen* toward all people. He is *jen* toward all people and loves (*ai*) all things.'[103] But 'thing' in the quotation refers only to living beings, whereas Chang extends *jen* to cover the whole realm of existence. The result of this extension is the all-important doctrine of 'forming one body with the universe'.

This doctrine received strong impetus in the Ch'eng brothers. In his famous treatise on *jen*, the *Shih-jen p'ien* (*On Understanding the Nature of Jen*), which has been a *vade mecum* for many a Chinese scholar, Ch'eng Hao begins, 'The student must first of all understand the nature of *jen*. The man of *jen* forms one body with all things comprehensively.'[104] Elsewhere he says, 'The man of *jen* regards the universe and all things as

[101] *Hsi-ming* ('Western Inscription'). *Cf.* German translation by Werner Eichhorn, 'Die Westinschrift des Chang Tsai, ein Beitrag zur Geistesgeschichte der Nordlichen Sung,' *Abhandlungen fur die Kunde Des Morgenlandes*, Vol. XXII (1937), pp. 33–73; French translation by Ch. de Harles, 'Le Si-ming, Traité philosophique de Tschang-tze, avec un double commentaire,' *Actes du Congres International des Orientalistes* (1889), pp. 35–52; English translation by P. C. Hsü, *Ethical Realism in Neo-Confucian Thought*, Peiping, privately published, 1933, Appendix, pp. xi-xii.

[102] *Kuei-shen yü-lu* ('Recorded Conversations of Yang Kuei-chan'), *Szu-pu ts'ung-k'an* edition, 1934, 2/18b, 3/28a.

[103] *The Book of Mencius*, 7A/45; *Kuei-shan yü-lu*, 2/18b.

[104] *I-shu* 2A/3a.

one body.'[105] His brother Ch'eng I also said, 'The man of *jen* regards Heaven and Earth and all things as one body.'[106] Their utterances have become so familiar that they have come to be regarded as the originators of the doctrine rather than Chang Tsai.

From the time of Chang Tsai, every Neo-Confucianist has elaborated or at least repeated the idea. Among them, Wang Yang-ming (also called Wang Shou-jen, 1472-1529) has been generally recognized as the strongest champion of the doctrine. He said, 'The great man regards Heaven and Earth and the myriad things as one body. He regards the world as one family and the country as one person. As to those who make a cleavage between objects and distinguish between the self and others they are small men. That the great man can regard Heaven, Earth, and the myriad things as one body is not because he deliberately wants to do so, but it is natural with the loving nature of his mind that he forms a unity with Heaven, Earth, and the myriad things.'[107]

But what makes it possible for man to extend this love to cover the entire universe? As has been said before, Chang Tsai's theory of Vacuity only provided a negative condition. For a positive explanation, we have to go to a new concept of *jen*, namely, *jen* as a dynamic process of creativity. This new concept was chiefly developed by the Ch'eng brothers. This is what the elder brother has to say:

> 'Books on medicine describe paralysis of the four limbs as absence of *jen*. This is an excellent description. . . . If things are not parts of the self, naturally they have nothing to do with it. As in the case of paralysis of the four limbs, the vital force no longer penetrates them, and therefore they are no longer parts of myself. Therefore, to be charitable and to assist all things is the function of the sage.'[108]

This analogy of paralysis may sound naïve, but it contains an exceedingly significant idea, namely, that *jen* is a life force.

[105] *Ibid.*, 2A/2a.

[106] *Ts'ui-yen*, 1/7b.

[107] *Yang-ming ch'üan-shu* ('Complete Works of Wang Yang-ming'), *Ssu-pu pei-yao* edition, Shanghai; Chunghua Book Co., 1934, 26/lb; *cf.* English translation by Frederick Goodrich Henke, The Philosophy of *Wang Yang-ming*, Chicago; Open Court, 1916, p. 107.

[108] *I-shu*, 2A/2a.

If *jen* is merely something comparable to the feeling of pain in the case of illness, it would be nothing more than a state of mind. But what is in operation is not merely feeling, but the life force, the dynamic element behind all production and reproduction.

The idea of life force (*sheng*) goes back to the *Book of Changes* where it is declared, 'The great virtue of Heaven and Earth is to give life.'[109] But to make *jen* and life-giving synonymous was definitely an innovation of the Ch'eng brothers. Ch'eng Hao said, 'The will to grow in all things is most impressive. . . . This is *jen*.'[110] And according to Ch'eng I, 'the mind is like seeds. Their characteristic of growth is *jen*.'[111] And their pupil, Hsieh Liang-tse (1050-1103) said, 'The seeds of peaches and apricots that can grow are called *jen*. It means that there is the will to grow. If we infer from this, we will understand what *jen* is.'[112] To call the seeds of fruits *jen* and the dynamic creative moral force also *jen* is not just a pun. It means that whereas hitherto *jen* meant love or universal love, to the Ch'eng brothers the fundamental character of *jen* is to grow, to create, to produce and reproduce, to give life. All virtues spring from it. Because by nature *jen* is creative and therefore expansive and increasingly inclusive, it will not stop until it covers the entire universe. Let Chu Hai elaborate on this idea of creativity:

'(The Ch'eng brothers said), "The mind of Heaven and Earth is to produce things."[113] (They also said), "In the production of man and things, they receive the Mind of Heaven and Earth as their mind."[114] These sayings describe the moral qualities of the mind in a most comprehensive and penetrative manner and leave nothing to be desired. Nevertheless, one word will cover all, namely, *jen*. Let us explain. The Mind of Heaven and Earth has four characteristics, namely, Origination, Development, Adaptation, and Correction. But Origination covers them all. In its operation, it becomes the sequence of spring,

[109] *The Book of Changes, hsi-tz'u.* II, ch. 1; *cf.* translation by James Legge, *Yi King, Sacred Book of the East,* Vol. XVI, Oxford: Clarendon Press, 1882, p. 381.

[110] *I-shu,* 11/3a–b.

[111] *Ts'ui-yen,* 1/4b.

[112] *Shang-ts'ai yü-lu* ('Recorded Sayings of Hsieh Liang-tso'), *Cheng-i-t'ang ch'üan-shu* edition, 1/2b.

[113] *Wai-shu* ('Additional Works'), in the *Erh Ch'eng ch'üan-shu,* 3/12.

[114] This saying is not found in their existent works.

summer, autumn, and winter, but the vital force of spring penetrates them all. Similarly, the mind of man has four characteristics, namely, love, righteousness, propriety, and wisdom, but love embraces them all. . . . For the way of *jen* is the Mind of Heaven and Earth to give life . . . it is the source of goodness and the basis of all conduct. . . .'[115]

Elsewhere Chu Hsi said, '*Jen* as the principle of love is comparable to the root of a tree and the spring of water.'[116] 'Wherever *jen* is in operation the idea of righteousness becomes the reality. . . . It is like the will to grow, like the seeds of peaches and apricots.'[117] In other words, since the Mind of Heaven and Earth is to produce and reproduce, and man receives this Mind to be his mind, therefore his original nature is good because it is the original character of his mind to give life. *Jen* as the life-giving force is therefore natural to him. It is this dynamic, creative life-giving quality that makes the growth and extension of the good inevitable. In the light of this new concept of *jen,* we may reinterpret the saying in the *Doctrine of the Mean* and the *Book of Mencius* that '*Jen is man*' to mean that the nature of man is life and to give life. Similarly, we can reinterprete the Han period saying, 'In man's nature there is *Jen,*'[118] to mean that in man's nature there is native to it this life-giving force.

To sum up, evil is a natural fact, because as Reality assumes forms and becomes differentiated, it gives rise to a state of unbalance and a state of bifurcation between the self and the non-self. But man has the ability to change this state of affairs. Indeed it is his mandate from Heaven, for his original nature is *jen,* to grow, to give life. This force he has received from Heaven and Earth whose great virtue is to produce and reproduce. This is the original goodness of his nature, and the force is not totally operative until he forms one body with the universe.

9. THE INDIVIDUAL

Two questions may now be asked: Is this unity with the universe a pure one so that there is only an 'undifferentiated

[115] *Chu Tzu ch'üan-shu,* 47/22a–b.
[116] *Ibid.,* 47/37a.
[117] *Ibid.,* 47/3a.
[118] *Po-hu t'ung,* 8/1a.

continuum' without distinctions and man does not exist as an individual? Secondly, what does unity mean in terms of man's relationship with society, animals, Nature, and God?

With reference to the first question, the answer is decidedly no. In Chinese thought there cannot be One without the Many, and there cannot be the Many without the One. This principle was most clearly formulated by Chang Tsai: 'The Principle is One but its function is differentiated into the Many.' As he said, 'The Great Vacuity is the essence of the Material Force. . . . It is in reality one. When the active and passive Material Forces (*yang* and *yin*) are disintegrated, they become the many.'[119] This is not an undifferentiated continuum, but a unity full of clear distinctions. 'The Great Harmony is called the Way (Tao, Moral Law),' he said, 'It embraces the nature which underlies all counter processes of floating and sinking, rising and falling, and motion and rest. It is the origin of the process of fusion and intermingling, of overcoming and being overcome, and of expansion and contraction.'[120] While he asserts that 'Nothing stands isolated,'[121] he at the same time maintains, 'No two of the products of creation are alike.'[122] This doctrine of 'The Principle is One but its function is differentiated into the Many' has become a keynote in the entire course of Confucianism during the last eight hundred years. In the principle, one identifies with the universe but at the same time retains his own identity, very much like a light in a group of lights or a note in a chorus. This is why Taoism and Buddhism were rejected in China as a guiding philosophy of life, for they either deny individual identity or consider it as an illusion. It is true that the Chinese insistence on synthesizing the universal and the particular has forced the Buddhist schools to develop a similar approach in equating the One and the Many as Ocean and Waves. It cannot be denied, however, that in the minds of Taoists and Buddhists, the waves are after all secondary.

It is sometimes asserted that in Chinese thought the individual loses his ultimate identity because he does not enjoy immortality. This is not true. For many centuries the major effort of the Taoist religion was to find a formula by which man could live forever on earth. To this day, longevity is still

[119] *Cheng-meng*, 4/27b.
[120] *Ibid.*, 2/2b.
[121] *Ibid.*, 3/2a.
[122] *Ibid.*, 2/10b.

among the highest values for the Chinese in general and for Taoists in particular. In popular Buddhism, everlasting life in Paradise is the final refuge. But in traditional Chinese thought, which has been more or less identified with Confucianism, immortality does not mean the survival of the individual soul in eternity. The ancient belief was that at death a white (*po*) light leaves the human body and joins the moon's light. To this was added later the concept of *hun*, which etymologically includes the element of *yun* (cloud). Since cloud is more active than light, *hun* came to represent the active or positive part of the soul, corresponding to *yang*, and *p'o*, the passive and negative, corresponding to *yin*. *Hun* is the soul of man's vital force (*ch'i*) which is expressed in man's intelligence and power of breathing, whereas *p'o* is the spirit of man's physical nature expressed in his body and his physical movements. When *hun* predominates, the spirit of man becomes *shen*, or heavenly spirit, and when *p'o* predominates, it becomes *kuei*, or earthly spirit. This is the general supposition of the masses. It is reinforced by the Buddhist belief in heavens and hells inhabited by *shen* and *kuei*, respectively.

The educated Chinese, however, totally reject this popular understanding as superstition. They believe with Chang Tsai that '*kuei* and *shen* are the natural function of the principles of *yin* and *yang* . . . in the sense that coldness is an example of *kuei* while hotness is an example of *shen*.'[123] '*Shen* means to expand,' he said, 'and *kuei* means to return.'[124] According to Chu Hsi, '*kuei* and *shen* are the increase and decrease of two universal forces of *yin* and *yang*.'[125] 'From the standpoint of the two forces,' he added, '*shen* is the efficacy of *yang* and *kuei* is the efficacy of *yin*. From the standpoint of the one universal force, what has become and extended is *shen*, and what has departed and returned (to its origin) is *kuei*.'[126] In short, what has become and is unfathomable is *shen* and what has gone is *kuei*. These interpretations of *kuei* and *shen* are entirely different from the concept of spirits roaming the universe as believed in by the ignorant masses.

But, it may countered, these interpretations seem to show that there is no individual immortality, for the two forces of

[123] *Cheng-meng*, 3/8a–b.
[124] *Ibid.*, 3/1a.
[125] *Chu Tsu ch'üan-shu*, 51/2b.
[126] *Ibid.*, 51/5b.

which everything is made up are always part and parcel of the universal forces. Man as an entity consisting of the two forces does not survive as a distinct individual. The answer to this comment is that the Chinese do not believe in immortality in this sense. Instead, they believe in the immortality of worth, work and words. This is best stated by an ancient teacher who said, 'I have heard that the best is to establish virtue, the next best is to establish achievement, and still the next best is to establish words. When these are not abandoned with time, it may be called immortality.'[127] The individual survives. But he does not survive in Paradise enjoying eternal bliss, which is considered by the educated Chinese as selfishness. Instead, true survival is conceived in terms of everlasting influence in society.

10. MAN AND SOCIETY

This leads us to the relation between man and society. Man exists as an individual, but he does so only in society. Because the ultimate goal of Buddhism is Nirvāna, it is a renunciation of the human world and for this reason has been constantly under Confucian attack since the T'ang period. But it must be remembered that what is truly *Chinese* in Buddhism is a rather earthly sort of religion. Salvation is to be attained here on earth and in one's own body. Taken out of context, the *Lao Tsu* (the *Tao-te ching*)[128] seems to forsake society, especially in chapter eighty, where it is said that the ideal community is the place in which 'though there be neighbouring states within sight, and the voices of the cocks and dogs therein be within hearing, yet the people there may grow old and die without ever visiting one another.' Taken as a whole, however, the *Lao Tsu* is essentially a book on how to govern. According to it, the ideal government is one that governs the least, follows the principles of non-interference and simplicity, and rejects the use of law and punishment.[128A] The ideal being is the sage, who 'always saves man in the most perfect way, and consequently no man is neglected.'[129] It is true that Chuang Tzu (bet. 399

[127] *Tso chuan* ('Tso's Commentary on the *Spring and Autumn Annals*'), Duke Hsiang, twenty-fourth year.

[128] For English translations, see J. J. L. Duyvendak, trans., *Tao Te Ching; The Book of the Way and Its Virtue*, London: John Murray, 1954; Arthur Waley, *The Way and Its Power*, London; Allen & Unwin, 1934.

[128A] Chaps. 2, 10, 29, 31, 37, 51, 57.

[129] Ch. 27.

and 295 B.C.) taught men to roam the universe freely, like a bird that 'flies up 9,000 miles', or like a mythical being who 'rides the wind', so as to 'wander in Infinity'.[130] But to him after all the ideal being is one who knows how to 'nourish his life', 'live in the human world', and 'administers the government'.[131] The Neo-Taoists were more explicit. As Kuo Hsiang (d. A.D. 321) says, a sage governs by taking no action. But that does not mean that 'only when a man folds his arms and closes his mouth in the mountain forests' that 'we can call him a man of taking no action. . . . Responsible officers insist on remaining in the realm of action without regret.'[132] However, 'although the sage is in the midst of government, his mind seems to be in the mountain forest. . . . His abode is in the myriad things, but it does not mean that he does not wander freely.'[133]

The great emphasis on society, of course, came from the Confucianists. It will be recalled that the word *jen* (love) consists of two parts, meaning man and two. The latter part, 'two' or rather plural, denotes society.[134] If we remember the equation of man with *jen*, it follows that man is meaningless unless he is involved in actual human relations. This is the reason why Cheng Hsüan (127-200) defines *jen* as 'people existing together'.[135] This is also why Juan Yuan insisted that *jen* connotes human beings living together in society. He emphasized this point more than anyone else, saying, 'To explain the word *jen* it is unnecessary to employ many terms or offer many examples. It is sufficient to cite the passage in chapter 54 of the *Book of Propriety of the Elder Tai*, which says that "*jen*" denotes people dealing with one another, like boats and carriages helping people to reach their destination . . . and to give Cheng Hsüan's definition.'[136]

It is clear that in the Chinese view no man exists in isolation. From birth till death he exists in social relations. These relations

[130] *Chuang Tzu*, ch. 1; see English translation by Herbert A. Giles, *Chuang Tzu*, Shanghai: Keely & Walsh, 1926, pp. 1 and 5.

[131] These phrases are titles of the *Chuan Tzu*, chaps. 3, 4, and 7.

[132] Commentary on the *Lao Tzu*, ch. 1, *Nan-hua chen-ching.*/*Szu-pu ts'ung-*

[133] *Ibid.*, 1/14b.

k'an edition, Shanghai: Commercial Press, 1929, 1/9b-10a.

[134] Some have interpreted 'two', that is, the two horizontal lines, as meaning Heaven and Earth or as parents. Such interpretation is arbitrary.

[135] Commentary of the *Doctrine of the Mean*, ch. 20.

[136] Juan Yüan, *op. cit.*, La-b; *Ta-tai li-chi*, *Szu-pu ts'ung-k'an* edition, Shanghai: Commercial Press, 1929, 5/2a.

have traditionally been divided into five. As described by Mencius, 'between father and son there should be affection. Between soveriegn and minister, there should be righteousness. Between old and young there should be a proper order. And between friends there should be good faith.'[137] These are the Five Relations that have governed Chinese society from the first millennium to the present day. Western critics have asserted that this set is incomplete because it includes neither the stranger nor the enemy. But logically speaking, a stranger does not enter into any relation, and when a person does, he is no longer a stranger, but should become a friend. The same may be said of the enemy. Of course in a modern society man has different relations, such as that between an employer and an employee. Even the traditional Five Relations have been radically changing in contemporary China. For example, in old Chinese society, 'separate functions' between husband and wife has meant not only 'man's function being outside the home whereas woman's function being inside the home' but also a double standard. Today, not only the double standard is dying out but women are assuming responsibility in government and industry. Nevertheless, the basic ideas remain unchanged, namely, that man exists only in social relations and these relations must be defined in moral terms.

II. MAN, ANIMALS, AND THINGS

Similarly, the distinction between man and animal is a moral one. The central difference between the two lies in the fact that while man is a moral being, an animal is not. The idea that man and animals belong to two different categories of being was quite clear in Confucius. When a stable was burned down, he asked whether any man had been hurt, but did not ask about the horses.[138] Not that Confucius was unkind to animals, but his first concern was with human beings. About religious sacrifices with animals, he said when a pupil of his recommended doing away with the offering of a sheep, 'You love the sheep; I love the ceremony.'[139] What is at issue here is not the animal but religious ceremonies, indicating that moral matters must take priority over all.

[137] *The Book of Mencius*, 3A/4.
[138] *Analects*, 10/12.
[139] *Ibid.*, 3/17.

In Mencius the difference between man and animal is categorically stated. When it was said that nature is simply what was given at birth, he asked, 'Is the nature of a dog like the nature of an ox, and the nature of an ox like the nature of a man?'[140] His own answer was decidedly, No. He clearly stated that dogs and horses are not the same in kind with man.[141] What is the difference between them? This is Mencius' answer: 'That whereby man differs from the lower animals is but small. The mass of people cast it away, while superior men preserve it. (Sage-Emperor) Shun clearly understood the multitude of things, and closely observed the relations of humanity. He acted according to the principles of love and righteousness.'[142] Thus what is present in man, but not in animals, is the 'mind of love and righteousness', which a superior man knows to preserve. If one is not able to preserve this mind, 'one's nature becomes not much different from that of the animals.'[143] From these Confucian teachings has come the Chinese conviction that moral sentiments and ethical standards, absolutely essential for the well-being of mankind, should not be applied to the animal world. Only when this conviction is understood can we comprehend the meanings of such Confucian sayings as these: 'In regard to inferior creatures,' Mencius said, 'the superior man is kind to them, but not loving. In regard to people generally, he is loving to them but not affectionate. He is affectionate to his parents, and lovingly disposed to people generally. He is lovingly disposed to people generally and kind to creatures.'[144] Mencius also said, 'To feed (a scholar) and not love him, is to treat him as a pig. To love him and not respect him, is to keep him as a domestic animal.'[145] If these sayings seem to conflict with the doctrine of universal love, including love of animals, it should be pointed out that, while there should be love for the entire universe, the expression of such love differs in degree and kind according to the various relations. This is the social application of the principle of the One differentiated into the Many.[146]

[140] *The Book of Mencius*, 6A/4.
[141] *Ibid.*, 6A/7.
[142] *Ibid.*, 4A/19.
[143] *Ibid.*, 6A/8.
[144] *Ibid.*, 7A/47.
[145] *Ibid.*, 7A/37.

[146] This question of the Confucian doctrine of love with distinctions *versus* the Moist doctrine of universal love without distinction has been discussed in some detail in my article on the 'Evolution of the Confucian Concept *Jen*', referred to in note 100.

The distinction between man and animals, then, is a moral one. For logical explanations of this distinction, we have to go to the leading Neo-Confucianist, Chu Hsi. Let us quote from his works at length:

'Chi submitted to the Teacher (Chu Hsi) the following statement concerning a problem in which he was still in doubt: The nature of man and the nature of things are in some respects the same and in other respects different. Only after we know wherein they are similar and wherein they are different can we discuss their nature. Now as the Great Ultimate begins its activity, the Material Force (*yin* and *yang*) assume corporeal form, and as they assume corporeal form, the myriad transformations of things are produced. Both man and things have their origin here. This is where they are similar. But the two Material Forces and the Five Agents (of Water, Fire, Wood, Metal, and Earth), in their fusion and intermingling, and in their interaction and mutual influence, produce innumerable changes and inequalities. This is where they are different. They are similar in regard to Principle, but different in respect to Material Force. . . . Therefore, in your *Dialogue on the Great Learning*, you said, "From the point of view of Principle, all things have one source, and therefore man and things cannot be distinguished as higher and lower creatures. From the point of view of Material Force, man receives it in its perfection and unimpeded while things receive it partially and obstructed. . . . Thus consciousness and movement proceed from the Material Force while love, righteousness, propriety, and wisdom proceed from the Principle. Both men and things are capable of consciousness and movement, but though things possess love, righteousness, propriety, and wisdom, they cannot have them completely. . . ." Is it correct?'

'The Master commented, "On this subject you have discussed very clearly".'[147]

Elsewhere, when Chu Hsi was asked whether man embodies all the Five Agents while things embody only one, he answered, 'Things also embody all the Five Agents, except that they embody them partially.'[148] He also said, 'Man possesses the

[147] *Chu Tzu ch'üan-shu*, 42/27b-29a; *ch.* English translation by Percy Bruce, *The Philosophy of Human Nature* by *Chu Hsi*, London: Arthur Probsthain, 1922, pp. 62–64.

[148] *Ibid.*, 42/25a; Bruce, *op cit.*, p. 56.

principle that can penetrate the obstruction of physical nature, whereas in birds and animals, though they also possess this nature, it is nevertheless restricted by their physical structure, which creates such degree of obstruction as to be impenetrable.[149] In the case of love, for example, in tigers and wolves . . . or in righteousness in bees and ants, only the obstruction to a particular part of their nature is penetrated, just as light penetrates only a crack. As to the monkey, whose bodily form resembles that of man, it is the most intelligent among other creatures except that it cannot talk.'[150]

It is interesting to note that Chu Hsi allows a limited degree of moral qualities to animals. If this is taken to contradict the general statement that the distinction of man and animals is a moral one, it must be remembered that in the Chinese view the transition from animals to man is a gradual evolution. The evolutionary scale is such that with animals the love in tigers and so forth are exceptions whereas moral nature in man is the rule. It is also interesting that Chu Hsi considered that there is a direct relationship between physical structure and moral qualities. This is a metaphysical question he did not go into. His primary interest was the moral consciousness of man.

This pre-occupation with the moral distinction between man and things has to some extent prevented the Chinese from the scientific approach to them. So far as man is concerned, neither anthropology in general nor evolution in particular has been developed in Chinese thought. In the *Chuang Tsu* we do find the passage saying, 'All species come from germs. Certain germs, falling upon water, become duckweed . . . become the dogtooth violet . . . produces the horse, which produces man. When man gets old, he becomes germs again.'[151] But this is no evolution, for the concept was arrived at through intuition instead of postulation, and the Chinese term *chi* may not mean germs at all. In the *Hsün Tzu*, we read, 'water and fire gave the Material Force but not life. Grass and trees have life, but no consciousness. Birds and beasts have consciousness but no sense of what is right. Man has the Material Force, life, consciousness, and also the sense of what is right, and therefore he is the highest being on earth. His strength is not comparable

[149] *Ibid.*, 42/25a; Bruce, *op. cit.*, p. 61.
[150] *Ibid.*, 42/27b; Bruce, *op. cit.*, p. 228.
[151] *Hsün Tzu*, ch. 9; *cf.* translation by Dubs, *op. cit.*, p. 136.

to that of the ox, and his ability to run is not comparable to that of the horse, and yet the animals are used by him. Why? The answer is that men are able to form a society whereas they cannot. How is it that men can form a society? It is because they have distinctions (in social relations). How can the distinctions be carried out? The answer is because of the sense of what is right.'[152] Here we have a definite scale of things. But this is no science. The basis of distinction, in the final analysis, is moral.

12. MAN AND NATURE

The same moral attitude characterizes the Chinese reaction to man's total environment, Nature. This is not to deny that to some extent Nature to the Chinese is a mystical entity with which man ultimately becomes identified. Such mystical union is what Chuang Tzu and other Taoists meant when they spoke of 'Becoming one with Heaven,' or 'Heaven and Earth coexist; the myriad things and I are one.'[153] This is what Buddhists mean when they speak of the 'ocean'. But significantly the Mystic School of Buddhism, which considers the whole universe as the body of the Buddha with which man comes into a mystical union, did not develop in China—it has only one temple in China proper today, in Peiping. The Taoist unification with the universe is more aesthetic than religious. Its keynote is harmony with Nature. In fact, practically all major schools of Chinese thought advocate harmony between Nature and man. These theories may now be briefly outlined.

The first is the theory of correspondence between man and Nature developed by the Yin Yang School; it was adopted by both the Confucian and Taoist Schools, and vastly influenced Chinese thought, especially in the Han era. The best representative of this line of thought is Tung Chung-shu, the most outstanding Confucianist in the former Han. According to him, 'In man's body, his head is large and round, like the shape of Heaven. His hair is like the stars and the constellations. His ear and eye are brilliant and resemble the sun and moon. The inhaling and exhaling of his nostril and mouth resemble the wind and air. The penetrating intelligence that lies within his breast resemble spiritual beings. . . . The alternating opening

[152] *Chuang Tzu*, ch. a; Giles, *op. cit.*, p. 23.
[153] *Tung Chung-shu*, *op. cit.*, ch. 56.

and closing (of his eye) correspond to day and night. The alternation of hardness and softness correspond to winter and summer. The alternation of sorrow and joy correspond to *yin*, the negative or passive principle, and *yang*, the positive or active principle. The thinking and deliberation in his mind correspond to the calculation and measure (in the universe). And there being principles of social relations in his conduct corresponds to (the relationship of) Heaven and Earth. . . . They all correspond to Nature.'[154] Quite aside from the interesting viewpoint that the universe is regular and rational, the theory led to the belief that because man and Nature correspond to each other, they can influence each other. Human behaviour was believed to be able to exert a direct influence on the operation of Nature and *vice versa*. This means that man's nature and behaviour are in some ways determined by natural events. At the same time, by directing his conduct, man can also alter the course of nature. When the correspondence is out of balance, it was believed, there will be misfortune, and when the correspondence prevails, the result is auspicious. Most probably, when the Han Confucianists propounded this theory, their motive was to acquire the right, as philosophers, to interpret natural phenomena and so control or influence the rulers. By so doing, they contributed in no small degree to the nondevelopment of the doctrine of divine right in Chinese political thought. But the theory of correspondence also enhanced superstition. To this day, many Chinese consult geomancists before building a house or a grave to make sure that the correspondence between man and Nature will prevail and their harmony undisturbed. The educated Chinese have long rejected this theory of correspondence as too close to superstition.

The second theory is that of harmony of Nature and man. There is some suggestion of this in Confucius' aphorism, 'The man of wisdom enjoys water; the man of love enjoys mountains.'[155] However, this doctrine is usually associated with the Taoist School. In some respects Chuang Tzu seems to advocate submission to Nature instead of harmony. 'Those inwardly upright,' he says, want to be 'followers of Nature.'[156] 'They do not want to assist Nature with man.'[157] However, totally speak-

[154] *Analects*, 6/21.

[155] *Chuang Tzu*, ch. 6; Giles, p. 73.

[156] *Ibid.*, ch. 6; Giles, p. 112.

[157] *Ibid.*, ch. 4; Giles, p. 41.

ing, Chuang Tzu's objective is harmony with Nature and not submission. 'Be a companion with Nature,' he urges.[158] 'The pure man of old,' he said, 'did not know what it was to love or to hate death. He did not rejoice in birth nor resist death. Spontaneously he went; spontaneously he came; that was all. He did not forget whence he came; nor did he seek to know where he would end. He accepted things gladly, and returned them to Nature without reminiscence. This is not to violate Tao with the human heart, nor to assist Nature with man. . . . Being such, his mind was free from all thoughts. . . . He was in harmony with all things, and thus on to Infinity.'[159]

Chuang Tzu actually lived with Nature, for he loved to 'move among the deer and swines'. The Neo-Taoists, especially the celebrated Seven Worthies of the Bamboo Groves of the third century A.D., went even further. They went to Nature, disregarded conventions, drank, sang, and made merry, displaying their wits in 'pure conversations', that is, conversations that are elegant, refined, transcendental, carefree, and entirely free from the vulgarism of politics and worldly values. They were fatalists and escapists, to be sure, but in them man and Nature become completely harmonious.

It is, of course, in Chinese landscape painting that the ideal of harmony is best illustrated. This is not the place to go into this delightful subject. Suffice it to say that the Chinese look upon it as the highest of the arts. It has achieved this lofty position partly because the Chinese spirit can find its best abode in 'mountain and water', as this art is called, not as mere physical objects but as the expression of 'life movements and universal rhythm', in which everything has its being and attains its glory. Nature is not a place to lose oneself but the place where the human spirit enjoys its tranquility and peace. It means self-realization in the best sense.

The Third theory is that of the Confucian 'forming a triad with Heaven and Earth'. When was this doctrine first advocated is difficult to determine. Both the term and the theory are found in the *Doctrine of the Mean*, Chapter 22. But scholars are not agreed whether the Classic, originally a chapter of the *Book of Propriety*, was the work of Confucius' grandson, Tzu Szu (483-502 B.C.?), or was of a century or two later. Centuries

[158] *Ibid.*, ch. 4; Giles, p. 70.
[159] *The Book of Mancius*, 6A/2.

afterwards, it became the doctrine of 'forming one body with Heaven and Earth', which has already been discussed. In the meantime, the two great ancient Confucianists, Mencius and Hsün Tzu, had something different to say. The former seems to have felt that while man is affected by environment, he may transcend it so far as his moral development is concerned. In his discussion on human nature, he recognized the influence of external forces, as we have already seen. It should not be forgotten, however, that Mencius, as do all Confucianists, laid the chief emphasis on the human factor. 'When Shun was living amid the deep retired mountains,' dwelling with the trees and rocks, and wandering among the deer and swine, the difference between him and the savages was very small. But when he heard a single good word or saw a single good deed, he was aroused and inspired like a stream or river bursting its banks and flowing out in an irresistible flood.'[160]

Haün Tzu, however, definitely advocated the control of Nature. To him, 'the Way is not the Way of Heaven, nor the Way of Earth, but the Way of man.'[161] 'Therefore the superior man is serious with what lies within himself,' he added, 'and does not adore what lies with Nature. Hence he progressed every day. The inferior man is careless with what lies within himself and adores what is from Nature. Hence he degenerates every day.'[162] Finally, he asked, 'Instead of glorifying Nature and adoring her, why not domesticate her and control her? Instead of obeying Heaven and praising it, why not regulate the Mandate of Heaven and use it? Instead of hoping for good seasons and waiting for them, why not respond to them and employ them? Instead of depending on things to multiply themselves, why not develop them by applying your own ability? Instead of longing for things to materialize, why not manage them so as not to waste them? Instead of vainly seeking the cause of things, why not bring about the conditions which cause their development? Therefore, I say, to neglect man and wishfully think about Nature is to misunderstand the nature of things.'[163]

Hsün Tzu's doctrine of the control of Nature is as explicit as it is vigorous. Nowhere else in the history of Chinese thought

[160] *Ibid.*, 6A/7.
[161] *Ibid.*, 7A/17.
[162] *Hsün Tzu*, ch. 8; *cf.* Dubs, *op. cit.*, p. 96.
[163] *Ibid.*, ch. 17; *cf.* Dubs, *op. cit.*, p. 179.

has a similar idea been put forth so strongly. This hostile attitude toward Nature is probably another reason why Hsün Tzu has been considered heterodox in the Confucian School. As has been repeatedly stated, the ideal is to form unity with Heaven and Earth.

13. MAN AND GOD

Is Nature equivalent to the Divine Spirit? The Chinese term *T'ien* is literally Heaven, but it has been used both to denote Nature and the Divine Spirit. When someone asked him about the difference between Heaven (*T'ien*) and the Lord (*Ti*), Ch'eng I answered, 'Heaven is so-called because of its corporeal form and substance. From the point of view of divine sovereignty, it is called the Lord. From that of profound mystery, it is called Spirit. From that of its function, it is called heavenly and earthly spirits (*kuei* and *shen*). From that of its manifestations in feelings and nature, it is called the Heavenly Principle. But in reality all these are one and the same.'[164]

This belief is representative not only of Confucian scholars but the educated Chinese in general, whether Confucianist or not. The Divine Spirit they believe in is sharply different from that worshipped by the common masses, be it called The Lord on High (Shang-ti) as in the traditional religion, Jade Emperor as in the Taoist religion, or the Buddha. To the multitude, this deity is anthropomorphic, supervising their actions and controlling their destiny, accepting their offerings and listening to their prayers, and sending down reward or punishment in accordance with their thoughts and deeds. To the educated Chinese Heaven is the Spiritual Reality with which man forms a unity, in which a man will become a sage.

14. THE FULL REALIZATION OF HUMAN NATURE

How can this unity be achieved? The answer to this question was given long ago, in the *Doctrine of The Mean*, where it said, 'It is only the one who is absolutely true to himself that can develop his nature to the fullest extent. Being able to develop his nature to the fullest extent, he will be able to develop the nature of others to the full extent. Being able fully to develop

[164] *Ibid.*, ch. 17; *cf.* Dubs, *op. cit.*, p. 183.

the nature of others, he will be able fully to develop the nature of things. And being able fully to develop the nature of things, he will then be able to assist Heaven and Earth in their transformation and nourishment. Being able to assist them in their transformation and nourishment, he can form a triad with them.'[165]

The key to the whole process is the full realization of human nature. Generally speaking, there are two ways to achieve this end. One is the subjective method of cultivating the mind. According to Neo-Confucianism, all things in the universe are manifestations of the Principle, which is good because it is the sum-total of moral values in the universe. But it is the mind that embraces the Principle. Since it is Principle that is endowed in man's nature, he can realize his nature fully by cultivating his mind. This is the thesis of the Idealistic wing of Neo-Confucianism, initiated by Ch'eng Hao but firmly established by Lu Hsiang-shan (1139-1193) and later elaborated by Wang Yang-ming. Lu Hsiang-shan said, 'The mind is one and the Principle is one. Perfect truth is reduced to a unity and the essential Principle is never a duality. The mind and the Principle cannot be bifurcated as two.'[166] He further said, 'There is only one mind. My friend's mind, the mind of the sages thousands of years ago, and the mind of sages thousands of years to come are all the same. The reality of the mind is infinite. If one can completely develop his mind, he will become identified with Heaven. To acquire learning is to appreciate this fact.'[167] His ways of developing the mind include 'learning the fundamentals.' 'If in our effort to learn we know the fundamentals, then all the Six Classics are my footnotes.'[168] It also includes 'establishing yourself'. 'Establish yourself and respect yourself,' he said, 'and don't follow other people's footsteps nor repeat their words.'[169] It includes 'building up the nobler part of your nature'.[170] And it includes 'gathering your own spirit' and 'being your own master'.[171] These are simple words but they not only represent a vigorous way of

[165] *Ts'ui-yen*, 2/1b.

[166] *The Doctrine of the Mean*, ch. 22.

[167] *Hsiang-shan ch'uan-chi* ('The Complete Works of Lu Hsiang-shan'), *Szu-pu pei-yao* edition, Shanghai: Chunghua Book Co., 1934, 1/3b.

[168] *Ibid.*, 35/10a.

[169] *Ibid.*, 35/1b.

[170] *Ibid.*, 35/22a.

[171] *Ibid.*, 34/5a.

life with deep insight and broad perspective, but also started a movement to get at the fundamentals, that is, to get at the innermost of the mind, a movement that lasted for several hundred years in Chinese history.

Wang Yang-ming was more specific. He said, 'In the matter of serving one's parents, one cannot seek for the principle of filial piety in the parents. In serving one's ruler, one cannot seek for the principle of loyalty in the ruler. In the intercourse with friends and in governing the people, one cannot seek for the principle of good faith and love in friends and the people. They are all in the mind, for the mind and the Principle are identical. When the mind is free from the obscuration of selfish desire, it is the embodiment of the Principle of Heaven, which requires not an iota added from the outside. When this mind, which is purely the Principle of Heaven, emanates to be service of parents, there is filial piety; when it emanates to be service of the ruler, there is loyalty; when it emanates to be intercourse with friends or governing the people, there are good faith and love. The main thing is for the mind to make effort to get rid of human desires and preserve the Principle of Heaven. . . . Why not endeavour to practise them? The main thing is to use the brain. . . . For instance, to endeavour to provide warmth for parents in the winter is none other than the extension of the filial piety of this mind to the utmost. . . . It is merely to endeavour to practise this mind.'[172]

This line of thought is obviously Idealistic and as such represented the Idealistic wing of Neo-Confucianism. The opposite wing, represented by Ch'eng I and Chu Hsi, prefer the rationalistic, objective method. According to Ch'eng I, 'the investigation of the Principle to the utmost, the complete development of human nature, and the fulfilment of destiny are one and only one. As the Principle is exhaustively investigated, our nature is completely developed, and as our nature is completely developed, our destiny is fulfilled.'[173] He also said, 'A thing is an event. If the principles underlying the event are investigated to the utmost, there is nothing that cannot be understood.'[174] As to concrete methods, he advised us in these words: 'To investigate things in order to understand

[172] *Ibid.*, 34/5a.

[173] *Ch'üan-hsi lu* ('Record of Instructions for Practical Living), in the *Yang-ming ch'üan-shu*, 2/2a–b; *cf.* translation by Henke, *op. cit.*, pp. 50–52.

[174] *I-shu*, 18/9a.

the Principle to the utmost does not require the investigation of all things in the world. One has only to investigate the Principle in one thing or one event exhaustively and the Principle in other things or events can then be inferred. For example, when we talk about filial piety, we must find out what constitutes filial piety. If the Principle cannot be exhaustively understood in one event, investigate another. One may begin with either the easiest or the most difficult, depending on one's own capacity.'[175] He recommended 'reading about and discussing truth and principles', 'talking about the people and events of the past as well as the present', 'distinguishing which is right and which is wrong', and 'handling affairs' and 'settling them in the proper way', all of which he considered to be proper ways to investigate the Principle of things exhaustively.[176]

Chu Hsi followed Ch'eng I closely. However, he was careful to emphasize both observation and intuition. Elaborating on Ch'eng I, he said, 'If we carry our knowledge to the utmost, we must investigate the principles of all things we come into contact with, for the intelligent mind of man is certainly formed to know, and there is not a single thing in which the Principle does not inhere. Only because all principles are not investigated that man's knowledge is incomplete. For this reason, the first step in the education of the adult is to instruct the learner, in regard to all things in the world, to proceed from what knowledge he has of their principles, and investigate further until he reaches the limit. After exerting himself in this way for a long time, he will suddenly find himself possessed of a wide and far-reaching penetration. Then, the qualities of all things, whether external or internal, the subtle or the coarse, will all be apprehended, and the mind, in its total reality and in its relations to things, will be perfectly intelligent. This is called the investigation of things. This is called the perfection of knowledge.'[177]

These two methods—the cultivation of the mind and the investigation of things then—are the two ways to realize one's nature to the fullest extent, one stressing the moral nature of man and the other the rational principle of things. The two should be understood as complementary, not mutually

[175] *Ibid.*, 15/1a.
[176] *Ibid.*, 15/11a.
[177] *Ibid.*, 18/5b.

exclusive. Few Chinese follow only one of them. Indeed, they prefer to follow both of them at the same time, believing that one reinforces the other. In fact, this spirit of balance, or synthesis rather, characterizes the entire Chinese concept of man. He is the highest of creatures, but he does not seek to dominate or control things. Instead, he wants to be in harmony with all Nature. He enjoys a high degree of individuality but finds its full meaning in an active life in human society. He forms one body with Heaven and Earth, but he does so only through realizing the goodness that is the virtue of Heaven and Earth and the entire universe. This he does by realizing fully his nature, because his nature, being endowed with this goodness and the creative energy to give life, cannot fail to encompass all with love if he makes the proper effort and has the proper education. In short, just as his original goodness comes from a balanced and harmonious combination of universal force in accordance with the Principle, so his ideal lite consists of a balanced and harmonious relationship with all, in which he will attain full manhood, that is, become a sage.[178]

[178] Commentary on the *Great Learning*, ch. 5.

CHAPTER IV

The Concept of Man in Indian Thought

P. T. RAJU

I. INTRODUCTION

IN a book including the treatment of the Greek tradition, the writer on the Indian tradition has to note that Indian philosophy started sometime around 2000 B.C. and has lasted up to the present day, whereas the writer on Greek philosophy starts usually with Thales of the seventh century B.C. and ends with the Alexandrians of the third century A.D. It is true that Greek philosophy was absorbed into the Mediaeval and the modern: the Platonic and the Aristotelian traditions continue up to the present in some form or other. Yet they are so much modified by the Christian thought of the Middle Ages and the rationalistic and scientific thought of modern times that we do not call the mediaeval or modern thought Greek. But Indian thought is still called by the same name. The ideas of the twentieth-century Indians are greatly influenced by western thought; but they still refer to the Vedas and the Upaniṣads as the source of their inspiration and call their thought Indian, claiming that theirs is only an interpretation. While Indian thought has had a continuity of about 4000 years—or even more, if we include the Mọhanjo-Dare civilization—Greek thought had a continuity of only about a thousand years. The Greeks who were the authors of Greek thought belonged to a different race from that of the present Greeks, and we hear very little of the thought of the latter.

Chinese thought also has continued for about 3000 years, and we do not yet know whether contemporary communist China will break away completely from her Confucian tradition or will continue it in some modified form. This difference in length of time may place the presentation of Greek thought at some disadvantage. But the approach of the Greeks, being both rational and humanistic, gives Greek philosophy an advantage so far as philosophy goes; for Greek philosophy, or at least its way of approach to the philosophical problems, has become the standard for philosophical judgments in the East also; and even when Greek philosophy is criticized, it is its own standards which are often applied.

The ancient and the classical Indian philosophies continued without being influenced either directly by western philosophy or indirectly through Islamic philosophy until the advent of the British. Islam entered India nearly six hundred years before the Europeans did; but that Islam was not the reflective and philosophical Islam of Arabia or North Africa, but the militant and conquering Islam that brooked no questionings, and produced no effect upon the philosophical thought of India. So classical Indian philosophy remained purely Indian until the West stepped in. Since this chapter is intended to present views which are peculiarly Indian, the ideas of modern Indian philosophers, who are all influenced by western thought in one way or other, are omitted.

Again, when dealing with the concept of man, it is difficult for the writer on Indian thought to confine himself to what is generally called philosophical literature. The main aim of almost all the Indian systems is to show the way to salvation; and they were written after the ideal of renunciation (*sannyāsa*) took definite shape. Not even one out of ten thousand take to renunciation; so the philosophical literature of the systems cannot be said to represent the whole life of every Indian, although the life of renunciation is presented as an ideal for everyone. For a complete philosophy of man one has therefore to turn not only to the systems, including the Mīmāmsā, but also to the early Vedas, the ethical codes, and the epics: then only can one get a complete picture. The Mīmāmsā is out and out humanistic and activistic; and the ethical codes and epics are meant for all men, as they tell men what to do and how to do it in this world. The early Mīmāmsā did not care even for God and for salvation (*mokṡa*), which is existence above birth and death. Only later were the ideas introduced into the system somewhat surreptitiously and as a concession to the general outlook of the time. If one asks me how could India's culture and civilization survive, I should say that they did not only because of the transcendental ideal of the Brahman and the confidence it gave the people in times of stress and strain but also because of the intensively active life which the Mīmāmsā preached, the injunctions of which were never questioned by any school so far as mundane life was concerned. The Mīmāmsā is the most orthodox of all the orthodox systems, accepted by every school so far as man's relations to society, forefathers, teachers, and gods are concerned. Without the Mīmāmsā, the orthodox Vedānta would have disappeared or been modified and absorbed by the non-Vedantic schools, just as Greek philosophy was modified and absorbed into the Christian and the Islamic. Not that everything which the Mīmāmsā preached was accepted by the other schools, but that its spirit guided their followers in their mundane life. This is sometimes pointed to as a contradiction in the life of Indian culture. How can India, with its ideal of peace and quietism, react vigorously in times of crisis? How is she able in contemporary time to welcome technology and industrialization? The Mīmāmsā, which also permeates India's outlook, furnishes the answer. This world is a world of action (*karmamayam*); if one wants life, one must act. It is unfortunate that the importance of the leaven of the Mīmāmsā in Indian culture and philosophy has not been properly recognized even by Indian writers and has not been brought to the notice of the western thinkers who are interested in understanding Indian culture.

What may be considered to be a split in the philosophy of the Vedas has not been given its proper value; for it is this split that has kept India's culture alive. If life is a bundle of contradictions and if it can exist only by cutting through them when it cannot resolve them with the help of accepted methods, then this split has proved to be an advantage to India's life. The Vedas are generally divided into four parts: the Samhitas (hymns), the Brāhmaṇas (ritual texts), the Āraṇyakas (forest treatises), and the Upaniṣads. The Mīmāmsā deals with the first two parts and the Vedānta with the next two. Almost all interpreters say that the whole Veda is one and has only one philosophy of life. Then why does the Mīmāmsā metaphysics differ so basically from the Vedānta metaphysics? To give two important differences: The Mīmāmsā is pluralistic and the Vedānta monistic; the former preaches action and the latter non-action. None can say that these differences are unimportant. Then, how can two such disparate systems of metaphysics belong to the same Veda? I have not come across a satisfactory answer until now. Because the Vedānta is extolled, foreigners think that it represents the whole philosophy of life for India, which is misleading. The main answer given is that the Mīmāṁsā is meant for immature minds, while the Vedānta is for the mature. But how can we have two systems of metaphysics, if metaphysics itself is meant for the mature? Are we to say that the Mīmāṁsā metaphysics is to be considered *as if* true at certain levels of mental development? One may as well tell an immature mind: 'You cannot understand the truth now; do your duties and come again.' Instead, a whole system of metaphysics is presented, with elaborate reasoning, categorization, etc. And what do the Mīmāṁsakas themselves say? They do not say that their philosophy is only *as if* true; they say 'absolutely true'. For metaphysics there can be no levels of maturity. If the whole Veda teaches one philosophy of life, we have to remove the split and have one consistent philosophy of life. What, then, is the way out of this difficulty? I think it is this: The thesis that the two philosophies belong to two levels of maturity means that man is the starting point of philosophy. So let us affirm the reality of man first and let us then see what is implied in his reality. The Vedas have an essentially humanistic approach, which is often forgotten. What I have been advocating elsewhere finds a justification here: a humanism that does not shun metaphysics, because man's being has very deep foundations.[1] These foundations can be discovered only after affirming man. Without restoring man to his original central place in philosophy, it is impossible not only to bridge the gap between the Mīmāṁsā and the Vedānta but also to reconcile the difference between any two philosophics.

This introductory digression is necessary for the present topic of the concept of man, lest we should get a one-sided picture. The epics and the ethical codes had to give a complete picture of the life of man, since they were meant for all men; and all of them are unsystematic. They, too, did not attempt to remove the split except in terms of intellectual maturity. The ethical codes are not philosophies of ethical conduct, but lay down the duties of castes and stages of life (*āśramas*). The

[1] 'Activistic Tendency in Indian Thought,' *The Vedānta Kesari*, October 1955.

epics taught the Vedic ideal of life with the help of stories, anecdotes, histories, etc., interspersed with popular expositions of philosophical schools and religious sects. But they cover the whole life of man. Both the epics and the ethical codes hold the Mīmāmsā and the Vedānta sacrosanct and do not attempt to criticize or reconcile the metaphysical theories.

It is from this context that we have to get the idea of man. One who likes to make a detailed study has to keep in mind what the ancient sages said about sacred literature. This will be rather fully explained later, but a little acquaintance with it will be useful. The main literature for the ancients is the Vedas. They are four in number: Ṛk, Yajus, Sāma, and Atharvan. They need 'six subsidiary studies' or limbs (*aṅgas*): *śikṣā* (phonetics), *kalpa* (ceremonial), *vyākarana* (grammar), *nirukta* (explanations of obscure Vedic terms), *chanda* (prosody), and *jyotiṣa* (astronomy and astrology). In addition, there are four 'secondary subsidiaries' (*upāṅgas*): *purāṇa* (epic), *nyāya* (logic), *mīmāmsā*[2] (rules of textual investigation), and *dharma-śāstra* (ethical code). Sometimes the six orthodox systems of philosophy—the Nyāya, Vaiśeṣika, Sāṅkhya, Yoga, Mīmāmsā, and Vedānta—are also called the 'six secondary subsidiaries'.[3] Later, other forms of literature grew up to teach the Vedic way of life. Even poetry was originally meant to teach the Vedic way of life in a pleasant way to the common man. Out of all these sources, if one is to present a detailed conception of man, one has to take the Vedas, the epics, the ethical codes, and the systems also into consideration. In this chapter it is possible only to give an outline.

For the sake of clearness, the present chapter will be divided into three parts dealing with the concept of man in the Vedas, including the Upaniṣads, in the heterodox schools of Jainism and Buddhism, and in the orthodox systems. There will be some unavoidable repetitions, because most of the orthodox systems are elaborations of the ideas of the Vedas and even the heterodox systems contain much that is Upaniṣadic.

2. THE VEDIC CONCEPTION OF MAN

The Vedas: Much has been written on Vedic culture and civili-

[2] The word *mīmāmsā* is the name of a school as well as of a method for interpreting the Vedic texts. Its etymological meaning is discussion.

[3] *Sanātana Dharma*, p. 30 (Madras: The Theosophical Publishing House, 1940).

zation, and the majority of the scholars believes that the early Ṛgvedic culture is marked by an optimistic outlook. The early Ṛgvedic Aryans, when they entered India (about 2000 B.C.), were full of zest for life and were not very much worried about life after death.[4] Of the four Vedas which have already been referred to, the Ṛgveda is the earliest, and a part of it might have been brought by the Aryans into India from outside. The hymns are generally addressed to natural entities and forces—the sun, the moon, the dawn, the wind, sky, etc.—conceived as so many gods. The Aryans, scholars believe, destroyed the Mohenjo-Daro settlements of the pre-Aryan settlers, who were of several races but predominantly Dravidian. The latter knew agriculture and trade but were not good warriors like the Aryans. They were worshipping some form of the Mother-Goddess and knew also some forms of yogic meditation. Thus the Aryan religion, in which nature worship was predominant, came into contact with the yogic type. Nature worship is outward-looking for its deities, but yogic meditation is inward-looking; but out of the combination of these two was developed the Atharva Veda, the main feature of which is magic, incantations, etc. not only to propitiate gods but also to harm enemies. After the Atharvan, the Sāma and the Yajur Vedas seem to have been developed. The elaborate ritual of the Vedic sacrifices needed detailed organization, and so the *Brāhmanas* were composed for each of the Vedas. After a time the people seem to have realized the meaninglessness of ritual and become reflective. The result was the *Āranyakas*. Some of the ancient thinkers took also to secluded and reflective life in the forests and thought over the problems of life; the *Āraṇyakas* contain their thoughts. When these thoughts took a definite form, the Upaniṣads resulted. The four Vedas were chanted by four kinds of priests who officiated at the sacrifices and handed down their profession, father to son and teacher to pupil.

Āśramas: It is not clear whether the Upaniṣads were originally meant only for the *sannyāsins* (i.e. for those who renounce the world) or for everyone only when he made up his mind to renounce the world; for many of the Upaniṣadic personalities were good householders, like King Janaka and his teacher

[4] *The Vedic Age*, p. 381, (edited by R. C. Majumdar and A. D. Pusalkar, London: Allen & Unwin, Ltd., 1951).

H

Yājñavalkya. We read also that for some time life was not formally divided into four stages or *āśramas*. Dr Kane says that the word *āśrama* does not even occur in the Samhitās and the Brāhmaṇas.[5] In the *Chāndogya Upaniṣad* we find mention of only three.[6] All this shows that it took some centuries to develop the idea of *āśramas*. It is very likely that the early Aryans thought of only two stages of life, the student's and the householder's; and a third stage might have been added when the Āraṇyakas were composed and that stage was the forest-dweller's; and by the time of the Upaniṣads, the fourth stage, the sannyāsins, could have been accepted. During the student's stage man gets all information about the world from his teachers. During the householder's stage man performs sacrifices with his wife—for without the wife the sacrifices could not be performed—and pays back his three debts: to the forefathers, by having children; to the gods, by performing sacrifices; and to the sages, by transmitting the learning he has obtained from them. Thus, procreation, sacrifice and teaching, were obligatory. During the forest-dweller's stage he entrusts the duties of the family to his children, retires to the forest with his wife, and reflects on the life he has lived and the values of the world he has enjoyed. During the last stage he gives up all worldly connections and lives the rest of his life in quiet detachment and surrender to the Divine Spirit.

Formation of castes: The formation of the caste system was a very complicated process. Several factors contributed to it. The conquering Aryans were small in numbers when compared to the conquered people; and something like the caste system must have been found convenient for establishing a stable society in which the Aryans could place themselves at the top. Much has been written on the subject; but I believe this to have been the process: The pre-Aryans knew agriculture and trade and had also their own priests. The Aryans knew the art of fighting and also had their own priests. The Aryans would not accept the priests of the conquered; and so priesthood was assigned to Aryans only and was given the highest place. Again, the Aryans would not allow the conquered to learn the art of fighting; so the warrior (*kṣatriya*) caste also remained

[5] *History of the Dharmaśāstra*, Vol. II, part I, p. 418, (Poona: The Bhandarkar Oriental Research Institute, 1941).

[6] II, 23, 1.

Aryan. Since the Aryan priests and the warriors could both live on the wealth produced by traders and agriculturists, there must have been some mixing of Aryans and non-Aryans at the traders (*vaiśya*) level; and the Vaiśyas were entrusted with the production of wealth through both trade and agriculture. The fourth caste, Sūdras, though often described as meant for service, were mostly agriculturists, so that, later, the Vaiśyas came to be identified with trade and the Sūdras with cultivation. As a sort of compromise between the rulers and the ruled, the Vaisyas, who must have been composed of both Aryans and non-Aryans, were allowed to study the Vedas and wear the holy thread.

Again, not even all the Sūdras were non-Aryans. There was, for example, an Aryan tribe, Sydroi, inhabiting the northern Arachosia.[7] Further, the word Aryan came to mean a way of life rather than a race; and some Aryans who entered India but did not accept the orthodox way were at first left out of the four-fold caste system, but later, through inter-marriages, entered the higher castes. Members of the same race became Kṣatriyas in some parts of India and Sūdras in other parts. Moreover, the castes were fluid at first, not rigid. There were both inter-marriages and inter-dining. Then inter-marriages disappeared, but inter-dining continued. Then inter-dining also was stopped. Still, a higher caste boy was allowed to marry a lower caste girl, but it did not often occur.[8]

The early Ṛgvedic reference to castes was a reference to facts without any theological or philosophical basis. We may say that two principles worked in the distinction, though not separation, of castes: colour and profession. Long afterwards, a theological and ethical justification was formulated. The Brahmins were supposed to have been born from the forehead, the Kṣatriyas from the shoulders, the Vaiśyas from the thighs, and the Sūdras from the feet of the Godhead. Next, the *Bhagavadgītā* said that the castes were created by God according to the character and activities of men. But on this basis the birth of cruel and wicked people in higher castes and of saints in the lower castes cannot be explained. However, once the castes were formed, man's duties were fixed in them.

[7] See the writer's *India's Culture and Her Problems*, p. 7 (Jaipur: University of Rajputana, 1951).

[8] For a detailed account of these practices, see P. V. Kane, *History of the Dharmaśāstra*, Vol IV.

Puruṣārthas or values of life: It has already been observed that the early Ṛgvedic Aryans did not bother much about life after death or about salvation (*mokṣa*) conceived as a state of existence beyond the reach of birth and death. But Indian thought now recognizes four values of life: wealth (*artha*), enjoyment (*kāma*), duty (*dharma*), and salvation (*mokṣa*). The early Aryans were mindful of only the first three. For a long time the controversy must have been carried on as to whether there were two, or three, or four basic values. The Cārvākas would accept only the first two. Vātsāyana (100 B.C.?), the author of *Kāmaśāstra* (*Science of Erotics*), salutes the first three, not the fourth. Up to the time of the Āraṇyakas, the Aryans seem to have known only the first three values. But by the time of the Āraṇyakas, the fourth may have been recognized. Then the four sciences may have been elaborated, the science of wealth (*arthaśāstra*), the science of enjoyment (*kāmaśāstra*), the science of duty (*dharmaśāstra*), and the science of salvation (*mokṣasāstra*). Vātsāyana says that Bṛhaspati was the original author of the first, Nandi was the original author of the second, and Manu was the original author of the third. Whatever is studied as philosophy proper, that is, all the systems, except the Mīmāmsā and the Cārvāka, constitutes the fourth.

One can easily see that the scheme of values is well rounded out. Wealth, which does not mean merely cash but any means of sustenance, is needed for life itself and is its very foundation in this world. But wealth, however, is not meant for accumulation but for enjoyment, and enjoyment is not to be disorderly but ethical, and morality becomes aimless without the ideal of salvation. Why should man follow ethical injunctions and care for the other members of society in his accumulation of wealth and enjoyment? There is a higher good than the ethical, and that is self-realization, unity with the Supreme Spirit, understood differently by the different systems later. Thus wealth is subordinated to enjoyment, enjoyment to duty, and duty to salvation. As originally conceived, the lower value, though instrumental, is a necessary means to the higher.

But later, after the rise of Jainism and Buddhism, the lower value ceased to be considered as necessary for the higher. Jainism and Buddhism started the practice of giving initiation into the life of the monk (*sannyāsa*) to young boys and girls and did not consider the repayment of the three debts to forefathers, gods, and sages as important or necessary. Until then ethics was understood as following the injunction of the Veda, which included sacrifices also. But sacrifices were condemned by the new schools. Further, if the highest ideal, salvation, can be attained by meditation, why not teach the boys and girls the methods of meditation and why impose on them the other kinds of activity? The orthodox schools also were influenced by this argument, and Sankara in particular said that one could take to (*sannyāsa*) whenever one felt disinterested in the world, whether one went first through the first three stages of life or not and whether one realized the first three values of life or not. The three debts are automatically paid up when one renounces the world. Rāmānuja does not seem to have accepted this view; for, in his commentary on the first of the *Brahmasūtras*, he says that the nature of the Brahman should be inquired into only after one understands the nature of *dharma* or duty.

Man and religion: The early Vedic religion, as the worship of natural forces, was polytheistic. Scholars believe that there was no idol worship and there were no temples, for the early Aryans worshipped nature directly. For instance, they offered prayers and oblations to the sun when it rose and when it set. Nature was conceived as fully animated. And this was a natural conception; for when man did not distinguish between spirit and body within himself, he could make no distinction between them in nature either. But later, when he drew that distinction within himself, he made it within nature also; and the idea of presiding deities (*adhiṣṭānadevatās*) arose. These two stages of development in India may be called animatism and animism coming under polytheism. Then the tendency of what Max Müller called henotheism grew. When each of the gods was worshipped, he was called the Supreme God. Thus Varuṇa (god of the oceans or of the mythological waters which surrounded the world, the encompassing god who later became the god of the earthly seas), Prajāpati (the lord of created beings), Viśvakarman (the architect of the universe) and others, became supreme one by one, and the other gods were subordinated to them. By this time the Aryans may have realized that the world was an ordered cosmos and that independent natural forces, unrelated and uncontrolled by a single entity, would work against each other and shatter the world to pieces. Henotheism became a stepping stone from polytheism to monotheism.

The further step in the development cannot be appreciated without referring back to the two forms of religion, the outward-looking and the inward-looking. The tendency to see order in external nature, to unify the world and place it under the control of one God, can result only in seeing God somewhere external, either in space or beyond space. But then, how can He control man, who has an inward mind? Can He do it by controlling only man's external circumstances? Here the inward-looking religion supplied an answer: He does it by controlling man's inward nature also. God controls man both from outside and from inside. The *Bṛhadāraṇyaka Upaniṣad* says that the light of the *ātman* is the same as the light of the sun; the self within is the same as the sun without. The subordinate gods became the presiding deities of mind (which the Upaniśads always distinguished from the *ātman*) and the senses, on the one hand and of their objects on the other. Thus a correlation was established between man's psychological nature and the physical world outside. For instance, the presiding deity of the eye and the light which it sees is sometimes given as the sun and at other times as fire; the presiding deity of touch and of the object of touch is air, and so on. This correlativity is best illustrated in the semi-mythological narrative of the *Aitereya Upaniṣad*. The *Ātman* once existed alone and wanted to create the lords of the worlds. It then created the upper and the lower worlds. Then it wanted to create the lords of the worlds. It created a form (world-person) and meditated on it. The mouth of the form opened; from the mouth speech and from speech the god of fire came forth. Its nostrils opened; out of the nostrils came life (*prāna*) and out of life air came forth. Its eyes opened; out of eyes sight and out of sight the sun came forth. Similarly, other gods came out of the other senses and out of mind. The gods wanted a habitat and sustenance. The *Atman* gave them first a cow and then a horse. They said that the animals were not enough. Then they were given man and were satisfied. Thus the senses and the mind of man and their corresponding objects became the realms (bases, *āyatanas*) of the gods of the world. And all the gods were subordinated to the *Ātman*.

This narrative is full of significance for philosophy, for it supplies the reason why the Vedānta became essentially idealistic. The narrative further says that fire became speech and entered the mouth of man; the sun became sight and entered the eye; and in that way all the gods became the functions of man's organs and entered him. The external gods became internal to man. Philosophy may ignore the theological and mythological aspect; but the correlativity between the senses and the objects, based on their being due to the division of the principle into the subjective and objective poles of man's experience, is accepted by all orthodox philosophies, be they monistic, dualistic or pluralistic, realistic or idealistic. Even Buddhism retained this correlativity in its doctrine of *āyatanas* or bases of experience. But the implications of this correlativity are brought out fully in the idealistic culminations of the Vedānta and Buddhism.

Man thus became the meeting point of the gods of the universe or its controlling forces. The highest controlling power was the *Ātman* the source of light, both internal and external, as finally accepted. All gods were once and for all subordinated to the *Ātman*, the Supreme Spirit dwelling within all men, and Prajāpati, Varuṇa, etc., were relegated to a lower place. A fullfledged monotheism emerged with the concept of the Supreme Spirit as the most inward reality of man. Later the question was rasied whether or not the Supreme Spirit could be personal in the ordinary sense, and monotheism was developed into monism. But it is not clear whether the Upaniṣads are monistic as opposed to monotheistic; no exact formulation can be found. In any case, they accept the idea that God is the innermost Spirit within man. The philosophical thought of the Upaniṣads once and for all became inward looking in its effort to find explanations.

Creation of man: As shown above, man is created as the habitat, the abode, of the lords of the universe, the meeting point of their realms of activity and fields of enjoyment. Gods of the external natural forces were made gods of the psychological activities of mind and the senses also, and were brought under the supervision of the *Ātman*.

But how does the *Ātman* create man? The words we usually come across are *kāma*, which may be translated as wish, desire, or will, *kratu*, which may be translated as sacrifice or desire, and *tapas*, the English equivalents for which are penance and intense willing. The *Ātman* desired, willed, did penance and performed sacrifice, which is meant for strengthening the creativity of desire. Man is the result of the creativity of the *Ātman*.

Epistemological discussions of the later Vedānta have created the impression that the *Ātman* is a static existence, that it is without activity and, therefore, uninteresting. But epistemology, concerned mainly with truth and falsity, is not the same as the whole of philosophy and is not religious thought. In the Upaniṣads the *Ātman* is clearly conceived as dynamic and as full of bliss and consciousness. Indeed, it is not merely dynamic, it is also static, because it is self-subsistent. Or as some commentators put it, it is neither dynamic nor static. If the *Ātman* is the whole of reality and if it is inactive, why do the Upaniṣads speak of its activity and creation of the world? Whatever conclusions some later philosophies drew, the original conception of the *Ātman* was not merely static.

Although the Vedas thought of man as created by the *Ātman* in a complex way for a complex purpose, some heterodox materialistic conceptions also prevailed at the time. The founder of the Lokāyata school, which is also called the Cārvāka school, was a person of the Vedic times, who maintained that man is a product of four material elements, earth, water, fire and air. When particles of these elements come together and constitute a particular structure, life and consciousness emerge; and when the particles are separated, life and consciousness disappear. Thus both the conceptions, creation of man out of Spirit and creation of him out of matter, were present in Vedic times. But the materialistic conception did not make much headway in the philosophies of India.

Man and his environment: Man in the early Vedic and even in the Upaniṣadic times did not think that he was living in an alien environment which he had to quit for ever. He thought of it as his own, to be controlled by *karma* or action. *Karma* in the early Veda does not have any fatalistic implications. It meant only action. Man thought that he could determine his own destiny, make it or mar it: he was its master. He had no conception of salvation, of an existence beyond the life of action. He had no need even of God, whom he had to beg for boons. Everything, happiness and misery, heaven and hell, depended on his own actions. He performed actions on earth, accumulated merit, part of which he enjoyed here and the rest in heaven, exhausted his merit, came back to the human world and performed actions again in order to accumulate merit. He found joy in life and in action themselves; and *joi de vivre*, which is so conspicuously absent in some of the renderings of later philosophy, finds a strong emphasis in the early Vedic thought. This topic will be elaborated in the subsequent sections also.

Karma and activism: The question how the world conforms to the merits and demerits of action did not trouble the early Vedic thinker. The world is a world of action, meant for action and sustained by action—by prescribed action, of course, not by prohibited action. For what is *Dharma* (duty), towards the explanation of which the whole philosophy of the Mīmāmsa is directed? It is action prescribed by the Veda. *Dharma* literally means that which sustains and supports and, by implication, that which sustains man and the universe: *Dharma* is *karma*, according to the Veda. Meritorious *karma* sustains and supports the universe. *Karma* is necessary for the universe: the significance of the world is understood only through *karma*. According to its virtues, human action can transform the nature of the universe. not only the mundane but also the supra-mundane. No greater faith in the potency of human action can be found in any other philosophy. This is highly activistic faith.

But the sustaining action was not just any action; it was action according to the Vedic injunctions. The Veda itself was eternal, not composed by any person (*apauruṣeya*), not even by God. God was superfluous; the Veda was enough, and action according to it was enough. But how? Man was at that time living in a hylozoistic world in which the opposition of spirit and matter was not felt. As a philosophical system the Mīmāmsā drew the distinction; but the Samhitās, the first part of the Veda, did not feel the opposition acutely. We have seen that the early

Ṛgvedic Aryans treated the natural forces as animated and, later, placed a presiding deity in each. So material nature conformed to the spiritual forces. After some time the latter were regarded as controlled by the *Ātman*. However, even earlier there was no conflict between the spiritual forces and the natural over which they presided. Man was thus living in a world of animated natural forces or in a world of presiding deities, all born of *karma*, which was at first associated with sacrifice. Sacrifice is a form of desire. *Karma* is born of desire, and so the presiding deities were born of desire. Sacrifice is the external manifestation of desire. It strengthened desire and controlled the world. Yet sacrifice is a necessary manifestation and so action has to be performed. Only then are gods pleased, proper enjoyment is obtained for them, and the natural forces and the world yield to man's wishes.

The philosophy[9] of sacrifice is too complicated to discuss further in the present context. Few of us now are prepared to accept the world of the early Aryans. But what is of philosophical importance is the conception of *karma* as central to the explanation of the universe. The parts of the world are brought together by human action, for human action, and for the sake of enjoyment. In the early Vedic hymns, one should not expect the atomic theory; but when once the theory was formulated, the Mīmāmsā said that the atoms were brought together by *karma* and for future *karma*. Thus the creation of the world was due to *karma*. Later the Nyāya-Vaiśeṣika adopted this view and said that God was prompted to bring the atoms together for creating the world by the *karma* of the individuals. The Mīmāmsā, when it later introduced God as the supervisor of *karma*, propounded a similar doctrine. One point has to be noted here: past *karma* determined the present nature of the world; but present *karma* may determine the future form of the world and may change its present form. So the doctrine of *karma* is not pure fatalism: man has the power to change his environment through action. This aspect of the *karma* doctrine has not been clearly brought to the attention of the western philosophers; but I think it is very important.

Because of the importance of the doctrine of *karma* and because of too many one-sided interpretations and criticisms

[9] See K. R. Potdar: *Sacrifice in the Ṛgveda*, particularly Chapters X and XIII (Bombay: Bharatiya Vidya Bhavan, 1953).

of Indian philosophy as purely passive and lacking all activism, I shall dwell a little more on the problem. The early Aryans conceived the world as a world of action (*karmamayam jagat*). But action produces effects. If under specific conditions we combine hydrogen and oxygen, water will be formed immediately. In the ethical world, however, effects appear frequently only after long intervals and at times only after several years. The difficulty which this fact entails did not trouble the early Aryans, although they believed that heaven could be obtained through action performed several years before. But the difficulty troubled the Indian thinkers of a later period. The action performed is ethical and concerns both men and gods; and the gods are the presiding deities of the natural forces. Therefore, no action is ever lost. If it does not produce immediate effects, it remains in a latent form until the proper occasion for fructification appears. It becomes what we now call potential energy. It is this that produces the required forms of existence in the ethical world; and the whole world—earth, heaven and hell—was ethical for the Vedic Aryans. When right action is performed, gods are satisfied; when they are satisfied, the natural forces over which they preside yield to human desires. Even gods are born of desire in the *Ātman*. And when desire, sacrifice, and penance were associated, the *Ātman* itself was believed to have performed sacrifice and to have done penance for the creation of the world.

Later the doctrine of *karma*, which originally meant action and then action according to the Vedic injunctions, was related to the doctrine of transmigration. Scholars[10] believe that very likely, the early Aryans had no idea of transmigration, but that they may have taken it over from the pre-Aryan inhabitants. It is difficult to verify the doctrine: we cannot have definite proofs for or against it. By the time of the Upaniṣads, however, the doctrine of transmigration, was definitely accepted by the Aryans.

Man's environment was thus an environment for action. Material nature was there; but it was animated or controlled by presiding deities or gods who, like man, were intelligent beings. Like men, gods were born of desire; and desires were satisfied by action. Every action, however, was a sacrifice;

[10] See P. S. Deshmukh: *Religion in Vedic Literature*, pp. 214–8, (Bombay: Oxford University Press, 1933); and also Potdar: *Sacrifice in the Ṛgveda*, p. 276.

animal sacrifices performed for pleasing some gods were not the only sacrifices. For the gods themselves were the forces acting through man. They chose man as their habitat in order to enjoy themselves; and so it came about that every action performed by man was indirectly an action performed by the gods themselves. If man sees, then it is the sun that is seeing through him; if he touches, then it is the god of wind that touches through him. Again, the objects seen and touched are the objective aspects of the respective gods. As I said above, we may ignore gods for philosophy; but the correlativity accepted between senses and their objects led Indian thought in the Vedānta into a metaphysical idealism.

Scholars believe that the Vedas had an important foundation for morality in the conception of Varuṇa as the controller of Ṛta (right), and when Varuṇa fell from the highest throne of the Supreme God, the concept of Ṛta was given up and that of *Dharma* was reinstated in its place. It is true that, in time, *Dharma* obtained greater importance than Ṛta; but I doubt that this charge resulted in the loss of the foundations for an active morality. Western ethical theories are woven around two basic concepts, the Right (Ought) and the Good. Kant's name is particularly associated with the former and Plato's with the latter. But, even before Kant, Jewish ethics was based mainly on the Right: God gave the commandments and it is man's duty to obey them without questioning. If man obeys them, he will attain happiness in the world; otherwise God's wrath will condemn him to misery. Since Christianity was generally influenced by Judaism, one can appreciate the criticism of the Indian ethical outlook by Christian philosophers and their regret that the concept of Ṛta fell into disuse.

Actually, however, it did not fall into disuse, although the word Ṛta was not used as often as the word *dharma*. *Dharma* is the central concept of the Mīmāmsā, and, as I have said, the Mīmāmsā is the philosophy of the first two parts of the Veda, which are intensively activistic. By the time the *Mīmāmsāsutras* were composed by Jaimini (about 400 B.C.), *dharma* became the central concept of ethical activity. But the Right was not yet differentiated from the Good; and *dharma* included both. The question, Which is primary, the Right or the Good? engaged the thought of some thinkers until about the seventh century A.D., when two followers of the school, Prabhākara and

Kumārila, clearly took opposite sides. Both of them accepted the view that the Veda was eternal and that even God did not compose it. But the question arose as to why we should follow the injunction of the Veda. Prabhākara said that action according to the injunctions was good because the Veda commanded it; but Kumārila maintained that the Veda commanded it because it was good. Prabhākara thus gave primacy to the Right and Kumārila to the Good. But in either case, what is good and right is *dharma*. Thus *Ṛta* did not disappear, but was absorbed by *Dharma*.

In later literary language *Ṛta* became synonymous with *satyam* or truth. But the Upaniṣads still distinguished the two terms. Sankara (about A.D. 800), who is a younger contemporary of Kumārila, explains the word *ṛta* as meaning that which accords with the Veda and with duty, and is well considered by reason.[11] We may translate it as 'practical truth' in opposition to 'theoretical truth', or, more freely, as truth of practical reason as distinct from the truth of theoretical reason.

Forms of explanation: By the time of the Upaniṣads different kinds of explanation of the world became current and of these the explanation in terms of the *Ātman*—that is, the view that the world derives from the *Ātman*—became important. The *Taittiriya Upaniṣad* says that the Upaniṣads are of five kinds. They are concerned with physical processes, with processes of gods, with processes of knowledge (*vidyā*) obtained through sacrifices, penances, and teachers, with processes of creation through cosmic sexes, and with processes of the *Ātman*. Correspondingly world processes can be explained as due to natural processes, actions of gods, effects of sacrifices, penance, and incantations, processes of cosmic sexes, and the creative processes of the *Ātman*.

Man himself can be viewed under any one of these five aspects. Ultimately, however, the fifth perspective superseded the rest and was regarded as the highest form of explanation. In its pursuit of this form of explanation the Upaniṣadic reflection attained deep inwardness. But even then, outwardness was not completely subordinated or treated as unimportant: a balance was struck between inwardness and outwardness,

[11] *Yathāsāstram yathākartavyam buddhau suparinis citam.* Commentary on the *Taittiriya Upaniṣad*, I, 1.

between striving for salvation through contemplation and a life of activity. This world is a world of names, forms, and activity. Names and forms arise through activity, and this activity is the activity of the *Ātman*, the activity of gods as the presiding deities of senses and their objects, and the activity of man for satisfying his own desires and the desires of gods. That action is to be shunned is not obvious in the Upaniṣads. *The Iśāvāsya Upaniṣad*, for instance, asks man to perform actions, saying that they do not taint him when performed rightly, although Saṅkara tries to give the meaning of the passage a new twist. What we find in the Upaniṣads is the exhortation of man to realize the *Ātman*, and the view that the *Ātman* is the same as the Brahman, the highest reality, the source and creator of the world. The *Ātman* within man himself is the same as the Brahman. Then, why endeavour to please the lower gods, who are inferior to the *Ātman*? Just as one's *ātman* supervises the activities of one's senses, so the Brahman supervises the activities of gods. Just as the perfection and satisfaction of the senses is not the same as the perfection and satisfaction of one's self, so the propitiation of gods is not the same as the propitiation of the Brahman. The realization of gods is not the same as the realization of the Brahman. Whether the Brahman is the same as the *Ātman* or different from it, it is within man and so can be realized through inward contemplation. Then, is activity necessary and indispensable, or is it unnecessary and dispensable? The Upaniṣads are not clear in their answer. The Vedāntins later gave different answers. The idea that the world is a vale of misery and that one should free oneself from its fetters is not emphasized in the early Upaniṣads, such as the *Bṛhadāraṇyaka*. But the idea of salvation had entered Indian thought and, in time, was given the highest place.

The constitution of man: The inchoate ideas of the early parts of the Veda regarding the nature and constitution of man are present in a fairly clear form in the Upaniṣads. It has already been said that the Vedic man does not find himself in an alien environment. In the early Ṛgvedic hymns, in the *nāsadīyasūkta* (one of the hymns), for instance, we find man asking how the world came into being, whether it came into being from Being or Non-Being. But such doubts slowly ceased to trouble him and finally disappeared when the universe was conceived as the product of his own innermost Spirit, the *Ātman*, and when he thought that all the gods were its products and that he himself was created as the field of their activities and enjoyment.[12] Had man not been born, gods would have been without an abode. From the standpoint of philosophy, it may be repeated, this theological perspective may be ignored, and we may say that man discovered the correlativity of his senses and their objects, and that he thought that it was due to the polarisation of the same elements. Man was one with the world, not a stranger dropped into it by an unknown agency.

Although man was called the abode of gods, this did not mean that man was first created and then offered as an abode to gods; it means, rather, that he was a form created out of the being of gods: he was the unifying principle of the activities of gods or, in other words, of the processes of the natural elements and forces presided over by gods. In non-theological language, man is the unifying principle of the processes of sense organs (like vision and audition), of organs of action (like hands and feet), and of their corresponding objects.

The *Taittirīya Upaniṣad* gives an account of the structure of man. Already by the time of the Upaniṣads, the distinction was drawn between body and spirit, between man's physical body and his *ātman*. The *ātman* is one's real and ultimate self. But is not one's self the body? Do we not identify ourselves with the body and say: I am the son of so and so and the father of so and so? The Upaniṣad says: No. From the *ātman*, which is the Brahman, aether (*ākāṣa*) is born; from it air; from air fire; from fire water; and from water earth. From earth are born plants and from plants food is derived; and from food man is born. But this is only the physical body to which we refer as 'I'. This 'I' disappears at death, although the physical body may remain for some time. Hence, body is not the true 'I'. What disappears at death is life, the vital principle; then the vital principle, *prāṇa*, must be the *ātman*, the 'I'. But even now we have not penetrated to the true *ātman*; for when a man is asleep, his life is present, but he does not answer if we call him. The 'I', therefore, is absent here; more specifically, however, what is absent here is mind (*manas*). Mind, therefore,

[12] See Belvalkar and Ranade: *Creative Period*, pp. 71 fol. (Poona: Bilvakunja Publishing House, 1927).

may be the *ātman* and life its body. But we cannot stop even here. A lunatic may say: I am dead long ago, and yet his mind is operating. What is lacking in the lunatic is reason. So reason is the *ātman* and mind is its body. Even here, however, we cannot stop. Man may be in deep sleep when his reason does not work. We do not say that his self has disappeared. It exists. We therefore have to say that there is something still deeper than reason, and that it is the unconscious bliss in deep sleep, in which man attains the unity of subject and object and intensity of being. Bliss is intensity of being. Because this is unconscious and the *ātman* has to be conscious, even the unconscious bliss is not the *ātman* but only its body. Thus we get the following levels: *ātman*, the unconscious bliss body, reason, mind, life, and matter. The lower is the body of the higher, and the higher is the *ātman* of the lower. Matter is not the *ātman* of anything; and the ultimate *ātman* is not the body of anything.[13]

Man, as he exists, is an integral unity of all these bodies and *ātmans*, which may be interpreted as different levels of reality accepted by the Upaniṣads. Modern philosophy has still not solved the problem of the relation of matter, life, mind, and spirit. In addition to these four levels, however, the Upaniṣads accept two more. Certainly, the Upaniṣads also have not solved the problems we now raise. In fact, they do not seem to have felt the acuteness of the problems. They saw that all the levels were unified and integrated in man and they were content with viewing the relation between them as the relation between body and the controlling spirit. This way of solving the problem may not be completely satisfactory to modern science. But at least it lessens the acuteness of the problems. As a result the study of man becomes not only the noblest of studies but also one that is basic for philosophy. Nature has solved the problem for herself by uniting all the levels of reality in man. For us, therefore, man alone provides the clue to nature's mysteries.

The main interest of the Upaniṣads centred in that entity

[13] In interpreting this doctrine commentators differ. The words used by the Upaniṣad are body and *ātman*. The Advaitins introduced the word *kosa* (sheath) and called each lower one as a sheath of the higher. Again, some identify the 'blissful' with the highest *ātman* itself. The Upaniṣad indeed does not use the word 'unconscious'. But I am following Sankara's interpretation, which seems to be quite reasonable. Here we need not enter into the controversy.

which, precisely, is called the 'I'. The word *ātman* in its general usage refers to the 'I' in the third person. When we say, 'I am happy', it is not the body that is happy, it is not even life, mind, or reason. We speak of 'my mind' and say, 'I observe my mind's activities'. The 'I' is farther back than is mind. This is the significance of the *Taittiriya* account.

The *Maṇḍūkya Upaniṣad* raises the question about the various states of the 'I', which ultimately is identified with the *Ātman*. The 'I' in me lives through the three states of waking, dream, and deep sleep. In both the first two states, man experiences that he is seeing, hearing, talking, walking, etc. In both states, therefore, his senses and organs of action are operating. One may ask how this is possible. When I am awake, my senses are open and my hands and feet move; but in my dreams my senses are shut and my hands and feet are at rest. But the Upaniṣad says that we should not identify our senses and organs of action with the gross material parts so called. They have subtle forms also, which operate in dream. After all, dream experience also is an experience. Surely, we call it unreal, not because the dream 'I' has no continuity with the waking 'I', but because the dream objects have no continuity with the objects of the waking state. The 'I' remembers the experience of the dream. The question whether the dream objects are due to impressions left on the mind by the experiences of waking consciousness or not is here not the point. The Indian thinkers accepted that they are due to such impressions. But why does man suffer and enjoy in dreams? Why does he think, so long as the dream lasts, that the objects are real objects? Why does he not think he is only reviving past impressions? Obviously man, or something within man, is able to bipolarize itself in dream into the subject and its objects. The Upaniṣad says that it is psychic force (*tejas*) that creates the world of dreams, and that this psychic force includes in subtle forms the senses, the organs of action, and the corresponding objects: touches, sounds, tastes, etc. The body of man in dream is the subtle body. All this may look like going back to the conceptions of primitive man. But dreams are a testimony of the inwardness of man's being, which includes the subjective and objective poles.

In deep sleep the bipolarization of man's experience into

subject and object is cancelled; the subject and object become one, and their unity is shrouded by ignorance or unconsciousness. We cannot appreciate Upaniṣadic psychology, if we take deep sleep as nothing but becoming unconscious. In deep sleep, mind and the subtle forms of senses and organs of action, which are active in dream, are all present but in a latent form, gripped in the unity of subject and object. In dream and waking consciousness, the being of man is diffused through senses and their objects, his personality is spread out; but in sleep this diffused being is brought to a centre or focus, the spread out personality is completely brought into a unity, and man's being attains the utmost intensity. The state, therefore, is called bliss or *anada.* So long as the objective world is felt to be separate, man feels unhappy until he makes it his own. But when it is taken into one's self, nothing is left out to be attained, and so man feels his completeness and is happy. I am not here justifying this theory, as against the psychological doctrines of the West; I merely present it as the Upaniṣadic view. And I feel that there is some truth in it which is worth considering when we discuss the psychological and epistemological conditions of happiness and of value even from the usual point of view of western philosophers, who have generally taken the stand-point of waking consciousness and ignored the states of man in dream and sleep, which are also essential states of his being.

One may here say that sleep is not a state of the 'I'; that the 'I' is completely wiped out in sleep, since otherwise we could be conscious. Some Indian thinkers say that we are conscious; for man says, after he wakes up, 'I slept well'. If the 'I' was swept out, how can he say, 'I slept well'? How does he *know* that he slept well. It is the nature of the 'I' to be conscious; therefore man is conscious of the fact that he slept well. But is not consciousness always directed towards an object? And what is the object towards which consciousness is directed in sleep? This question is not discussed by the Upaniṣads but is taken up by the later commentators, who differed from one another. But all agree that the 'I' is present in sleep. Some, like Śaṅkara, say that the 'I' is conscious but is conscious of Nothing, which, like Hegel's Nothing, is the undiversified positive Being of objectivity. Others, like Rāmānuja, say that, although the 'I' is self-conscious, it is not conscious of any objectivity.[14] On the face of it, however, the view of the Upaniṣad seems to be that objectivity is withdrawn into the being of the 'I', because mind and senses are withdrawn. Since mind, senses, and their objects are correlates, when one correlate is withdrawn, the other is also withdrawn. We must remember, furthermore, that the being of the 'I' is not understood by the Upaniṣads as a bare point but as dynamic and creative. The *Ātman* is the creator of everything.

When the shrouding and the overwhelming unconsciousness is removed, the 'I' is seen as the *Ātman* shining in its purity. It is at this stage that man knows, directly and without reference to anything else, his original conscious being. It is a stage which transcends both subjectivity and objectivity. It is wrong to think that it is a subjective stage. Subjectivity lasts only so long as objectivity lasts. But both are transcended when mind, senses, and their corresponding objects are withdrawn. This is the limit of man's inwardness, at which he touches again, or as Sankara says, becomes one with the Supreme Brahman, which is the same for all.

A western epistemological realist may find it difficult to appreciate the idea of the withdrawal of objectivity. He will say that even when man withdraws his mind and his senses, their objects can remain outside. The Upaniṣadic thinker will answer that they can remain outside for the other minds and senses. If the correlativity referred to above is accepted, then the withdrawal of the objects also has to be accepted. Man's being is not merely his consciousness limited to his body but extends to the objects also. The experience of dreams shows that the separateness of objects from the subject does not exclude the creation of both, subject and object, by the same principle. Mind is the foundation of both. That the same object is experienced by different subjects has to be reconciled with this fact of experience and should not be allowed simply to negate it. Dream and sleep testify to the privacy of man's being, and waking consciousness to his living in a common world.

In dream and sleep man retains his connection with the physical world through the vital principle or *prāna*. It is this principle that holds together the different parts of the body

[14] These differences of view gave rise to important technical problems into which we cannot enter here.

and it is responsible for the synthetic vital processes. It is of five kinds and the processes also are of five kinds. The five *prānas* are: *prāna*, *apāna*, *samāna*, *udāna*, *vyāna*. All are called *prānas* and the first of the five also is called *prāna*. It is difficult to translate these terms because no similar division of the vital principle is found in western philosophy. Of the five, *prāna* resides in the heart and is responsible for respiration; *apāna* resides at the anus and performs excretory functions; *samāna* has its abode in the navel, keeps up the heat of the body and controls the digestive and assimilative processes; *udāna* is in the throat and controls the activities of speech and the functions of the upper parts of the body; and *vyāna* pervades the whole body and co-ordinates the functions of the different parts of the body. All the five together thus constitute the life process of the individual.

We saw that in the original semi-mythological conception of the *Aitareya Upaniṣad*, man was created as the centre of the activities of the cosmic gods, who were the presiding deities of the cosmic elements, and who burst out of the original mass created by the *Ātman*. This was the mythological basis of the theological and philosophical conception of the microcosmos and the macrocosmos. Man with the three states is the microcosmos and, at the fourth stage consciously realizes[15] his relation with the macrocosmos. The microcosmos is the *ātman*, and the macrocosmos is the Brahman. Sometimes the Brahman is called the Supreme *Ātman* (*paramātman*) or simply *Ātman*. Corresponding to the three states of the microcosmos, there are three states in the macrocosmos. The states of the latter are not discussed by the *Māṇḍūkya Upaniṣad*; but commentators, particularly the Advaitins, developed the theory with the help of the other Upaniṣads.[16] The various states may be given thus:

States	Microcosmos	Macrocosmos
Waking consciousness	Viśva	Virāṭ
Dream	Taijasa	Hiraṇyagarbha (also called Sūtrātman)
Sleep	Prājña	Īśvara
Pure State	Ātman	Brahman

[15] This relation is identity according to Śaṅkara, similarity according to some, nearness according to some others, and identity in difference according to the rest.

[16] See Radhakrishnan: *Indian Philosophy*, Vol. I. p. 169 fol. (London; Allen & Unwin Ltd., 1948).

In every state the microcosmos is thus connected with the macrocosmos. Virāṭ is the physical cosmos. Hiraṇyagarbha is the vital principle that binds all the parts of the universe, and the Taijasas are connected together through it. Īśvara is the self-conscious entity that, like mind, controls the universe. And the Brahman is the self-effulgent Spirit that comprehends the whole. That the physical man is part of the physical cosmos is easily understood. In their dream state all men are bound together by the thread of the bio-psychic principle, Hiraṇyagarbha. Except for this tie, they are allowed each to create his own dream world. In the deep unconsciousness of their sleep, they are the objects of Īśvara, who is eternally and without intermission conscious, is not overwhelmed by sleep, and for whom sleep is an object consciously known. In the fourth state, the microcosm and the macrocosm are one, although this one-ness is explained in different ways by different commentators.

The idea seems to be implied in Upaniṣadic thought, that the states of the macrocosmos explain how the individuals, although having their own private lives, are bound together by a common world. The epistemological implications are not worked out by the Upaniṣads or by the commentaries. But the suggestion is there that the objective bearings of men's private experiences are to be explained in terms of the macrocosmos, which has some similarity to the Objective Mind of the western idealists.

Salvation, which is attainment of complete bliss, lies in reaching the fourth state. How can this be accomplished? The difference between the third and the fourth states of the microcosmos lies in the presence and absence respectively of the unconscious. The third state is the cancellation of the bipolarity of experience and the withdrawing of the two poles, subject and object, into one's self. This withdrawal can be achieved by withdrawing mind and senses, and their objects. The whole Yoga is a technique developed for this withdrawal and for reaching the limit of inwardness. This is given succintly by the *Kaṭha Upaniṣad*.[17] The subtle elements or objects are higher than the senses, mind (*manas*) is higher than the objects, reason (*buddhi*) is higher than mind, Cosmic Reason (*Mahat*, the Great, Logos) is higher than reason, the Unmanifest

[17] I, 3, 10–11.

(*Avakta*) is higher than Cosmic Reason, and Puruṣa (*Ātman*) is higher than the Unmanifest. The 'higher' means the more inward or deeper. Man has to withdraw the lower into the higher; for the lower came out of the higher. In his waking state man contains all in their full unfoldment. His ideal is presented as pushing the outward into the inward until the limit is reached.

For a proper appreciation of Upaniṣadic thought, it is useful to be clear about what mind, ego, reason, soul, and self (*ātman*) mean. In modern western philosophy mind is all that these five terms mean in Upaniṣadic thought, but for the latter they have different meanings. Often the Upaniṣads mix up mind (*manas*) and reason (*buddhi*). The *Aitareya Upaniṣad*, for instance, gives mind, reason, memory, desire, will, etc. as synonyms. But the *Kaṭha Upaniṣad*[18] places reason higher than mind. The function of mind is association and dissociation, synthesis and analysis. The function of reason is assertion (*niścayātmika*). Again, that reason is higher than mind means, for the Upaniṣad, not merely a higher function but also a higher reality. Reason is as different from mind as mind is from life. But it is through reason that man is a part of Cosmic Reason, of the Mahat, the Logos. That man is peculiarly one with the Logos is common to both Greek and Indian thought.

In Indian philosophy, the ego is called *ahaṁkāra*[19] but it is not particularly mentioned in the Upaniṣads. The soul is the *jīva*. This also is not discussed in the Upaniṣads but is discussed by the commentators. The *jīva* consists of the vital principle (*prāna*), of mind (*manas*), of reason (*buddhi*), of the subtle elements and of the bliss body. This is so according to Saṅkara; but according to Rāmānuja, the bliss body is the same as the *ātman*. The *jīva* is thus the ethical personality which enjoys and suffers the fruits of its actions and which also transmigrates from one birth to another. It is also called the subtle body (*sūkṣmaśarīra*). In philosophical discussions *Ātman* means the self. But the Upaniṣads use the word to mean several things; the physical body, the vital principle, mind, reason, the bliss body, and the metaphysical principle as well as the Brahman. In popular literature, it means also one's own nature, striving, and steadfastness.

[18] See Śaṅkara's *Commentary* on II. 10.
[19] This will be explained later.

In this connection one should understand what is usually called the causal body (*kāraṇaśarīra*). As the *Māṇḍūkya Upaniśad* says, deep sleep is not blank unconsciousness but the potential being of the *jīva*, who withdraws into a unitary state. He is still connected with the physical body by the vital principle, which preserves this connection in dream also. In dream, psychic force or *tejas* is active and divides itself into the subject and its objects. This subject assumes the form which one sees as one's body in dream. Through introspective analysis the Upaniṣadic thinkers discovered that the subject is more comprehensive than the physical body and that it is not the same as the physical body. And this is the reason why, in dream one can perceive himself as dead and his dead body carried to the cremation ground. Unless the subject is more extensive than the dream body, it cannot see the body as dead. Similarly, in the waking state also, the subject transcends the physical body and the physical body is one of its objects. Of all the objects one's own body is chosen by the ego for identifying itself for the sake of activity and enjoyment. This analysis may seem counter to the usual ways of thinking but cannot easily be gainsaid. If the ego is completely identical with the physical body, why does the ego perceive its own body as an object? One's own back and face cannot be seen by oneself; yet they can be touched; and even otherwise one can feel their objectivity through one's mind. I can experience my whole body, even my head, face, and back, as my object. The I, as the knowing subject, cannot be any of these objects. Yet, in action and enjoyment I identify myself with the body. I say: 'I am so many feet tall', although such words are referred to the body. This analysis of the situation has to be recognized, and whatever necessary implications it has have to be accepted. If Indian thinkers drew some wrong conclusions, their errors may, of course, be pointed out. But the analysis itself, I think, is not contrary to experience.

In the dream state the subject assumes the forms of one's body as well as the forms of one's objects. For this reason the 'I' is called self-revealing (*svayamjyoti*).[20] The light with which man sees the objects is his own. In this state, to create the objects and to perceive them is one and the same, and Berkeley's principle, *esse* is *percipi*, holds good. For the dream object

[20] IV, III, 14, *Brahadāraṇyaka Upaniṣad*.

exists only so long as it is seen. The moment it is not seen, it goes out of existence and becomes merged in the ego's psychic force (*tejas*) as waves merge in the sea. In the waking state also, in order to perceive the object, the same psychic force must be taking the form of the object, since otherwise it would be inaccessible to the ego's mind. The difference is that in the waking state the form taken by the psychic force is not determined merely by the impressions of the ego.

In deep sleep the dynamic psychic force withdraws itself into a potential state, which is called the causal state or the causal body. Some of the misunderstandings of this doctrine are due to the fact that the ego is taken to be a static and inactive entity,[21] which is regarded as being annulled in the unconscious. Although the ego is submerged and becomes latent, it is not annulled. In addition, it is not merely one pole of experience that is submerged but both. One may go even farther: what is usually called the subject is only one pole of the ego, the other pole being the object. The ego includes not only the 'I' but also the 'mine'; and the 'mine' includes not only the objects experienced in dream and waking states but also the physical bodies with which the 'I' identifies itself.[22] For instance, the colour I see in the waking state is part of my experience; a colourblind person does not see it. From this fact, to be sure, one-sided conclusions have been drawn in the history of philosophy, like Berkeley's *esse* is *percipi*. But this is not a sufficient reason for us to deny the factual data themselves. The dynamic creative nature of the ego is an important doctrine of the Upaniṣads.

In deep sleep the dynamism of the ego is suspended and the different poles of activity and experience into which the ego is spread out in dream and waking states are collected into a unity; the ego itself becomes submerged in the unconscious. When the waking state dawns again, the ego spreads out and becomes active. In sleep the urges, forces, instincts, etc., in accord with which the ego is spread out in the dream and waking states, are kept latent, and so the state of the ego in deep sleep is called the causal body of the *jīva*.

[21] The philosophical importance of dream has not been brought out by any one so far. It has real epistemological implications also.

[22] The western philosophers perhaps will say that Indian philosophy has not made a scientific study of this aspect of experience, but I feel that western philosophy has not made even that much of study. If we are properly to understand man, this study cannot be avoided.

The *Bṛhadāraṇyaka Upaniṣad*[23] shows us the way for reaching the *ātman*, which is higher than the *jīva* or personality, but which does not exclude the *jīva*. The *jīva*, as has already been pointed out, is the ethical personality; and according to the general trend of the Upaniṣadic thought, the *ātman* transcends this ethical personality, not by exclusion but by inclusion. Among the later commentators, however, there is a tendency to exclude the *jīva*. But if everything originates from, and is the *Ātman*, how can the *Ātman* exclude anything? We have seen that, in dream, the ego knows every object by its own light. And this light is not some physical light but the psychic light (*tejas*). This means that the psychic force itself takes various forms; and, since it is psychic, it knows its own forms. There is, therefore, no difference between this psychic creative force and the light in which its created objects are seen. And this is what the Upaniṣads mean when they say that the *ātman* is everything. The psychic force is the same as the objects created. When the Upaniṣads give the example of the clay and the pot made of it and say that clay is the truth of the pot, they have this psychic force in mind. In sleep this psychic force withdraws all the forms it creates and becomes submerged in the unconscious. The *Bṛhadāraṇyaka Upaniṣad* exhorts man to get at this psychic force, which is his essential being, apart from the forms it creates, which is the same as the psychic force at its uncreative stage. There, in one's own being, one gets the light as such of the *ātman* and becomes one with the Brahman, although the oneness is interpreted differently by different commentators. When unity with the Brahman is realized, man knows that he has the whole world within himself, that he has no need to desire anything, and he is consciously blissful. But the Brahman, too, is not pale static consciousness; it is eternal creative being. Even when one realizes the Brahman, creation goes on and the world continues to exist for those who have not the realization. Here, one may say, is mysticism and spiritual experience. Here one transcends the world of action and is no longer within it. Until this realization is achieved, the causal body retains the potency of creation and does not cease to act. The causal body is the result of the tendencies produced by man's actions. It is the medium of the Brahman's creativity. The Upaniṣads

[23] IV, III.

believe that this causal body goes from birth to birth in transmigration. The tendencies are brought together, tied into a knot, and constitute the individual's inner core (*hṛdayagranthi*). The individual is created and acts according to these tendencies, with the possibility of always rising above them, for the *ātman* is the origin of this creativity and is therefore above the forces of which it is the origin. Man, therefore, can alter himself and his environment, provided he understands himself well.

Regardless of whatever the Advaitins maintain, as far as the general trend of the Upaniṣadic thought is concerned and in order to be in consonance with the first two parts of the Veda, we must say that rising above the world of action, penetrating one's causal body, is possible only through ethical action. Ethical action is necessary; it is not dispensable. The Upaniṣadic seers in general went through *dharma* (duty), preached by the first two parts of the Veda, and then began their inquiry into the Brahman. There are instances of persons who renounced the world during early boyhood; but this phenomenon is explained generally as being due to such persons having gone through dutiful activity in their past lives.[24] Most of the great sages of the Upaniṣads—Yajñavalkya, King Janaka, King Ajātaśatru, Bhṛgu, for example—were householders. Hence, to say that the *Ātman* is the highest reality and its realization is the highest good is one thing; to preach against ethical action is another.

Here I may add another point. The Upaniṣads speak of the *Ātman* as the Truth and of the rest as other than truth, which came to be identified with falsity. But if the *Ātman* is everything and everything issues out of it, how can falsity come out of truth? Does truth generate falsity? Why are the two words found in the Upaniṣads? I think that the reason lies here: The problem of the Upaniṣads is to find out what the 'I' ultimately is. Ultimately, it is the *ātman*, not the physical

[24] The story is given of Vyāsa and his son Śuka. When Śuka, as a naked youth, approached a lake in which some damsels were bathing naked, the latter did not care to put on their clothes but approached and talked to him. A little later, Vyāsa, the old man, approached the lake, but the ladies rushed for their clothes and put them on. Vyāsa was surprised and asked them why they did so before a very old man and not before a youth. They replied that Śuka was unconscious of any sex, whereas Vyāsa, in spite of his old age, was conscious of it. Śuka is said to have realized *Dharma* in his past lives. But how many Śukas are there at any time in this world? Philosophy is for the average thinking man, not for Śukas. And how many of those who claim to be like Śuka are really so?

body. But, in general communication, we use the word "I" to designate our physical body. That the 'I' is the same as the physical body is obviously false. But the body itself, as a material body, is not false. It is not false that there is a physical body and that we identify ourselves with it. One friend remarked that, whether God is a fact or not, it is a fact that there are proofs in the history of philosophy for the existence of God as a fact. Similarly, whether the identity of the body with the *ātman* is a truth or not, it is a truth that many of us identify ourselves with the body, and it is also a truth that the body is regarded as material.[25] I do not think that the material body is treated as unreal by the Upanisads; only one's complete equation to it is treated as false.

Man and evolution: One naturally does not expect to find the doctrine of evolution, as expounded by Darwin and other scientists, in the Upanisads which belonged to a time long before Christ. But the doctrines of the creation by God out of Himself, not out of Nothing, and the doctrines of the origin of the universe out of the *Ātman* may be treated as theological and philosophical forms of the doctrine of evolution. Of all the Indian schools, the Cārvāka alone believed that life and mind appeared when material particles came together and assumed some structural patterns, although even this school did not inquire into the nature of the structures; it was interested mainly in the problem of what to do with this life and held that, because life and mind disappear when material particles are separated as happens necessarily at death, man had to make the best of life here on earth and enjoy whatever enjoyment is possible. It is not surprising, however, that in the intensely spiritual milieu of India, this school did not wield much influence and was very little developed. The other doctrine, therefore, that everything came out of the *Ātman*, came to be more generally accepted, even though the Nyāya-Vaiśeṣika, in particular, could not reconcile it with its atomic theory.

Philosophically the doctrine of evolution has importance in inter-relating matter, life, mind, and spirit. The Upaniṣads

[25] In the further development of the Upaniṣadic ideas, later commentaries got into insoluble difficulties, as they carried over these conceptions of truth and falsity into their epistemologies. This two-valued logic, when they had to deal with several levels of man's being with intimate inter-connections, did not serve them.

have other levels of reality, such as finite reason, Cosmic Reason, and the Unmanifest. Now, one may begin with matter and derive from it other levels, up to and including spirit, as evolutes; or one may begin with spirit and derive the rest from it. Theoretically both derivations have a claim to be called evolution, and there is no *a priori* reason to reject the claim. The question as to which derivation is true remains open and must be answered on other grounds. Personally I believe, that, in our present state of ignorance concerning the world and man, it is at least useful to accept and work with both alternatives. As a source of ethical principles, spirit is necessary as the foundation of the world and of human life and activity; but as a basis of man's physical life and as a field of his activity, we want matter. Each kind of derivation, therefore, will check the excesses and mistakes of the other; for we cannot regard man as a conglomeration of material particles only; neither can we view him as nothing but spirit. He cannot live and act merely as the one or as the other.

Of course, it is not usual to call the derivation of matter from spirit evolution; other terms—creation, emanation, transformation, etc.—have been used. Yet there is a significant similarity between these processes and evolution. Scientists and philosophers have attempted to work out the details of the form of evolution from matter; but an equally detailed and rationally interesting method of derivation from spirit has also been worked out by some Indian philosophers. However, in the West such explanations have been rejected as not rational, because generally speaking, spirit has been treated as being beyond reason by philosophers who accept its truth; and a rational explanation in terms of a principle which is itself beyond reason is considered to be impossible. In any case, however, evolution is derivation from some principle which is accepted as ultimately true and as objectively common to all men. And there are philosophers who do not doubt the reality of matter (or of space-time), just as there are some who do not doubt the reality of God or Spirit. If the world of matter is common to all according to some, Spirit or God is common to all according to some others. So both are justified, so far as their ultimate objective principles go, in deriving other forms of reality from the ultimate principle, whether it is matter or Spirit.

Here I may add another point. If matter evolved life, did

it push up what it originally contained or did it create something new? If it pushed up what it contained, then the logical assumption that nothing comes out of nothing is satisfied. But if matter contained life potentially, how can it be pure matter? In accordance with the assumption that originally there was pure matter, it is said that matter created a new form. But, again, if the new form is really new, then the implication is that it did not exist before and nothing has become something. The concept of evolution, it is thought, lifts us above this dilemma. Evolution is the same as creativity: matter is not static but dynamic, and is creative of higher forms. All that is needed for explanation is that there must be something out of which something else can come; the latter need not be also present in the former.

If the creativity of matter is evolution, then why should we not call the creativity of Spirit also evolution? The only answer is that we cannot observe the creativity of the *ātman* or Spirit and therefore, cannot study it in detail in the way in which we study the creativity of matter. But have we been able to study even the latter in all detail? Therefore, is it not necessary, for ethical and spiritual purposes, to work with evolution out of Spirit? These are questions which the rival philosopher can justifiably ask.

However, the Upaniṣads spoke of the creativity of the *Ātman* and of the evolution of the world out of it. There is an ultimate inexplicable mystery about this creation, and we know only the results. The *Taittirīya Upaniṣad*, we have seen, says that ether (*ākāśa*) came out of the *Ātman*, air out of ether, fire out of air, water out of fire, and earth out of water. Plants came out of earth, food out of plants, and man out of food. This, of course, is not a systematic account. We are not told how man comes out of food. The particular Upaniṣad speaks also of the levels of the *ātman* in man: matter, life, mind, reason, bliss body, and spirit. But these levels are not given as products of evolution, although a modern philosopher can work them out into an evolutionary pattern.

Here we see also a circular process of creation, which includes the withdrawal of the world by the *Ātman*. The cosmos is created first and is withdrawn through man, that is, through the efforts of those men who want salvation. Thus, from the side of the *Ātman*, there is an evolution of the world; creation; and an involution; withdrawal through man. What is involution from the side of the *Ātman* includes the evolutionary process accepted by science.

The details of the cosmic process are not worked out in a systematic form by the Upaniṣads. Even the Cārvākas did not do it from the side of matter. How do the material particles come together? What is the force that first pushes them together and later separates them at death? The Cārvākas say that it is natural for particles to do so, and do not inquire further. But the orthodox systems which accepted the atomic theory explain the process in terms of man's ethical merit and demerit. The accumulated potency of man's ethical activity brings the atoms together and separates them. Even those systems which do not accept the atomic theory say that creation was pushed out of the *Ātman* by the potency of ethical actions. The theory may or may not be satisfactory; but that the creative force behind creation is an ethical force seems to be implied by the Upanisads. This point will be elaborated later.

Influence on religious traditions: India's religious traditions are many; but those founded on the Veda and connected with it are considered to be the most high. Here we might bear in mind what an Indian calls religion. With the exception of Buddhism and Jainism, none of the old important religions was founded by a person. Even in the case of these two exceptions, the founders do not claim exclusive revelation of spiritual truths which are not vouchsafed to their followers. Any one who follows Jina, also called Mahāvīra (original name Vardhamāna), the founder of Jainism, or Buddha (original name Gautama), the founder of Buddhism, can become a Jina or Buddha. Jina means the conqueror (of one's self) and Buddha means the enlightened. But what is called Hinduism in the narrow sense has no founder. It is based on two kinds of scripture, the Vedas and the Āgmas. There are three forms of this Hinduism: Smārtism, Saivism and Vasnavism. Saivism identifies the Brahman of the Upanisads with Siva, Vaiṣṇavism identifies it with Viṣṇu, and Smārtism follows the pure Vedic tradition and generally calls the Brahman by that name only. Orthodox followers of Saivism do not enter the temples of Viṣṇu, and orthodox followers of Vaiṣṇavism do not enter the temples of Śiva; but the followers of Smārtism do not mind going to both the temples. They treat Śiva and Viṣṇu as only personified conceptions of the Brahman. All the three sects have a worship of the Mother or Mother-Goddess, called Śakti, although this worship is more common in Śaivism. Śakti is the material creative energy of the Brahman or the Supreme Spirit; and when the Supreme Spirit is worshipped, Śakti also has to be worshipped. But some persons give more importance to Śakti than to the Supreme Spirit, for, after all, the world is due to its creative energy, which is Śakti. Such worshippers are called Śāktas, and their sect is called Śāktism and, sometimes, Śāktaism.

One peculiarity of India's religions is the absence of all dogmas in the strict sense of the term. For instance, a Christian has to believe in the Virgin Birth, and this is laid down as a dogma. Hence, dogmatics is peculiar to Christianity. In spite of the fact that much of Greek philosophy, Platonic and Aristotelian, was introduced into Christian thought, it retained the dogmas as its very life. Christ himself might or might not have believed in them as codified Christianity did. But in the Indian religions, so far as spiritual revelation goes, there is no dogma; but only an appeal to reason and experience, as in Greek thought. Sometime before the Christian era the caste system assumed rigidity. And although, until modern times, caste was adhered to as if it were a dogma, it was not considered to be essential for spiritual realization. The Supreme Spirit was called by different names such as Śiva and Viṣṇu; but the name, unlike a dogma, was not considered to be important. The Yogic techniques or methods of realization were different for the religions; but they were not expounded as dogmas but in rational and psychological terms. There is evidence for strong sectarian prejudices, but even these were not laid down as dogmas.

This peculiarity of Indian religions can be appreciated if we understand how the religions grew. The Aryans entered India with their religion of nature gods and sacrifices.[26] It seems that, after they entered India they elaborated and systematised their sacrificial religion. Then they formulated the idea that God was inward to man, that natural forces were presided over by some spiritual beings, and that, therefore, the forces had their own cosmic inwardness, that their inwardness was

[26] Potdar seems to hold that the religion of sacrifice grew out of the religion of nature worship in India. This theory is in accordance with the view that the *Brāhmaṇas* are later than the *Samhitas*. See his *Sacrifice in the Ṛgveda*, Ch. XIII.

somehow centered in the inwardness of man, that true worship was inward and was inward realization, and that outward forms of worship were therefore to be interpreted as symbolic of inward forms. Once this symbolic theory was accepted, it was applied to the non-Aryan forms of external worship also, some of which were barbarous. As the Aryans organized the whole Indian society into one fold through the caste system, they incorporated all the religions of the earlier races and tribes, allowing each to continue its own forms and interpreting them as symbolic of the one true inward form. This method allowed each group to follow its own cult and yet united all cults as different symbolic forms of the one true cult. Since in those times religion was intimately associated with social forms and conferred sanctity on them, each group was able to follow its own social forms also without interruption.[37] The practice prevented unnecessary bloodshed, gave freedom to the social groups to follow their own ways, and yet enabled them to realize that the inward way was the purest and the highest. The Aryans encouraged only members of their own race to officiate as priests, even at the ceremonies of non-Aryans, except in the temples of some outcastes and untouchables. This practice also helped to unify the heterogenous cults by conferring upon them some recognition by the Aryan priesthood. But spiritually it conferred on them an inwardness of which they were at first not aware. That is why a foreigner sees in India the most varying forms of religion, ranging from the worship of wood and stone to the highest and purest philosophical mysticism of the Vedānta. But if religion is essentially spiritual realization, then its pure form can be had in inward psychological technique. If man is essentially interrelated with the rest of the world, then the world also must have its inwardness: this is what the Aryans of the Upaniṣadic times thought. Their view is similar to the western philosophical view that mind and matter are two aspects of one and the same reality. Techniques of Yogic inwardness lead to the realization of the cosmic inwardness of the physical world, but they do so only through man. Other creatures are incapable of this realization, for they do not yet have that freedom of mind from matter necessary for the purpose. Man's inwardness is given to him as a microcosm; but the microcosmic

[37] See the author's *India's Culture and her Problems*.

inwardness can be pushed by man's own efforts into the macrocosmic. Man is thus a privileged creature.

Of the important religions[28] of India, Śaivism and Vaiṣṇavism had their roots in the Veda. Śāktism can be traced to the same origin. But all three composed their own Āgamas or sacred texts. Some say that the Āgamas are authoritative because they are based on the Veda; others hold, however, that they are independently authoritative also. Some say that both the Vedas and the Āgamas are equally authoritative, but a few sects give a higher place to the Āgamas. Śaṅkara, who was a Smārta, gives all authority to the Vedas only. The Śaiva Āgamas are also called Pāupata Āgamas; and the Vaiṣṇava Āgamas are also called Pañcarātra Āgamas. In any case, the Āgamas are later than the Vedas, and the earliest of them seem to belong to the second or the third century B.C.

For our purpose it is not necessary to go into the details of these cults. It is sufficient to point out how Upaniṣadic thought influenced the Āgamas. The Āgamas are, on the whole, theistic; but the Upaniṣads sometimes speak in theistic terms and at other times in non-theistic terms. In either case, the attitude to the Supreme Spirit is naturalistic: Spirit is a continuation of mundane reality, and this continuation can be seen in man. The spirit in man is one with the Supreme Spirit in the cosmos. But this oneness can be variously understood. It may mean only similarity (*sādṛśya*), or only nearness (*sāyujya*); or it may mean identity in form and difference in being, or difference in form and identity in being: in all these cases, the Supreme Spirit is distinct from the finite spirit, and theism is maintained. But the oneness may be understood as absolute. In that case, pure spiritual monism is reached. Even then, however, the mysterious power or energy of the Supreme Spirit, through which it creates the world, may be regarded as real or unreal. But the Āgamas do not treat it as unreal. If the energy is real, then God becomes an active agent and so a person: theism is still retained. We find all these views in the different Āgamas.[29] All the Āgamas call the Supreme Spirit Ātman and

[28] For religions of India, see J. N. Farquhar: *Primer of Hinduism* (The Christian Literature Society for India, London, 1912), Louis Renou: *Religions of Ancient India* (University of London Press, 1953), Macnicol: *Indian Theism* (Oxford University Press, 1915), and D. A. Pai: *Religious Sects of India* (published by the author, Victoria and Albert Museum, Bombay, 1928).

[29] See F. Otto Schrader: *Introduction to the Pāñcarātra and Ahirbudhnya-saṃhitā* (Madras: Theosophical Publishing House, 1916).

the Brahman and also Śiva or Visnu. The Śākta Āgamas do the same. The view that the Supreme Spirit, whatever its nature (in understanding which the Āgamas show differences of opinion), is inward to man is accepted by all the Āgamas. The idea was developed in different ways by the followers when the various systems were developed.

Mahāvīra, the founder of Jainism, was an older contemporary of Buddha (Sixth Century B.C.). Jainism traces its origin to Ṛṣabha, who is a Vedic personality. The Veda teaches *ahimsā* or non-injury, although, at the same time, it preaches injury at the time of sacrifices. But Ṛṣabha teaches non-injury without exception and so turns against Vedic sacrifice. By 600 B.C., salvation came to be recognized as the highest ideal, and any person who did not care for it was pitied as misguided and ignorant. The ideal depended only on inward realization. If salvation is the highest ideal, then why should one care to propitiate the gods, who were the presiding deities of the natural forces contributing to the bondage of man? And why should one perform sacrifices for those gods? The traditionalists pointed to the injunctions of the Veda, which preached sacrifices. Mahāvīra and Buddha, therefore, had to reject the Veda as an authority in guiding man's life towards salvation. It should be noted, however, that they did not reject the Vedic gods. Even superficial acquaintance with Jaina and Buddhist literature shows that the gods were retained, but they were given a secondary place. They themselves had to struggle for salvation and had to learn at the feet of Mahāvīra and Buddha. Thus, Brahma, the creator of the worlds, and Indra, the lord of heaven, are represented as coming from their abodes to pay homage to Buddha. The usual separation of Jainism and Buddhism from Hinduism is wrong. Both are but reform movements within Hinduism—just like Vīraśaivism, Sikhism, the modern Brahmosamaj, Aryasamaj and Satsang—except that they are called after their founders. They are part and parcel of Hinduism.*

For the early Aryans religion was a way of life, *dharma*,

* It should be noted that Hinduism is not an Indian word and is not to be found in any Sanscrit, Pāli, or Prākṛt dictionary. The word is derived from a corrupted form of the word 'Sindhu,' which is the Sanscrit name of the River Indus. The Persians could not distinguish S from H, and mispronounced the word as Hindu. They called the people living near the river Hindus, and the religion of the people they called Hindu religion—whatever it was. Even today in Rajasthan the letter S is pronounced as H. The word 'Indus' also is a further corruption of the word Hindu.

which sustained and supported man and the universe. They called their religion Arya Dharma and also Vedic Dharma, and equated the two. When the ideal of salvation was introduced, it also became part of Vedic Dharma and Arya Dharma. Sacrifices were preached by this Dharma. But, later, doubts arose about the validity of sacrifices, and Vedic Dharma and Arya Dharma came to be distinguished. Buddha and Mahāvīra used the term Arya Dharma for their ways of life and preached against Vedic Dharma. Both were Aryan by race.[30] For both, realization of the most inward reality, whether called by the name *ātman*, *jīva* or *nirvāna*, was the highest aim of life. But the ideal is given at first in the Upaniṣads themselves. We must therefore, say that Jainism and Buddhism took over the inwardness of the Upaniṣads and elaborated and intensified it. They said that this highest doctrine should not be withheld from any person, high or low, man or woman, and with missionary zeal associated with excesses of pacifism and non-injury, they propagated their doctrines throughout India. It must be said to the credit of these two religions, however, that the proverbial Hindu pacifism and abhorence of bloodshed are due to their teachings. It was after the rise of these two religions, Jainism and Buddhism, that the inwardness of India's outlook became intensified and even onesided. It is now the responsibility of India to restore the balance of inwardness and outwardness, which is characteristic of early Upaniṣadic times.[31] To be sure, the influence of the early Upaniṣads on these two religions is great; but the influence of these religions on the later Upaniṣads is also great. Even Śaṅkara, the *smārta* follower of the Veda, was called by his critics a Buddhist in disguise (*pracchannabauddha*). The Jaina and Buddhist doctrines will be presented later.[32]

Education: The Vedic theory of education, as it ultimately shaped itself, is to be found in the Upaniṣads. By the time of the

[30] It is a pity that western Aryanism preaches hatred and contempt of the non-Aryan humanity, while in India it preached against every destruction of life, even insects.

[31] All the Upaniṣads which over-emphasized renunciation like the *Paramahamsopaniṣat*, *Bhikṣukopaniṣat*, *Sannyāsopaniṣat*, etc., are regarded as being influenced by these two religions. Even the *Muṇḍakopaniṣat* is thought to be so.

[32] See *India's Culture and Her Problems*, p. 64. It is not the aim of the author to bring the paper up-to-date, but present what is purely Indian before the advent of Islam and the West.

Upaniṣads Vedic culture became reflective, formed concepts of ideals and practices, ends and means, and attempted to give explanations of the world and man. Not that we do not find some explanations in the pre-Upaniṣadic Veda; but they are rather mythological and immature, although a few are profound. But by the time of the Upaniṣads, a definite conception of man's ideal as salvation was formulated, and salvation was understood as self-realization—which again meant realization of one's pure *ātman*. Whatever else is realized has to be given up either in this life or in some other; but the realization of one's self is not something that can be lost. Whatever is gained in this world is gained for one's self. But if this is so, then what is the self for which everything is gained? Without knowing it, we remain in the realm of uncertainty and doubt. But if we obtain that which, after having been gained, can never be lost, we shall reach certainty.[33]

The early Upaniṣads do not think of the world as a vale of misery but as a training ground for man's self-realization. Indeed, one may forget that it is only a training ground and may get completely entangled in it. But against this attitude the Upaniṣads give a warning. The warning, however, is in terms of the more, the better, the higher in man's inwardness, not in terms of a pessimistic wail over the imperfections of the world or in terms of downright condemnation of the world as absolutely evil. Man's life is meant for the realization of the inward reality; if he wilfully neglects to realize the truth within himself, he loses an opportunity. Education, therefore, has its final aim in helping man to realize his true inwardness. Like birth, death was accepted as a certainty. Birth brings man into society, and death takes him out of it. He may not be taken out of the society of gods and ancestors but only out of that of human beings; but he may be reborn again in human society.

The cosmos consisted of living beings including men, gods who presided over the natural forces, and ancestors. Man had relations to all, duties to all, and was born again and again according to his merits. It was his duty to keep all satisfied so that their relations to him could equally be satisfactory. He had therefore to learn how to keep them satisfied. There thus arose the idea of three debts,[34] debt to gods, debt to

[33] Cp. *Bṛahadāraṇyaka Upaniṣad*, II, IV, and IV, V.

[34] See *Śatapada Brāhmaṇa*, 1, 5, 5 and also *Taittirīya Saṃhitā*.

ancestors, and debt to sages. Gods were satisfied when sacrifices were performed, ancestors were satisfied when progeny was left, and sages were satisfied when knowledge was transmitted. Hence it was one of the duties to learn and to educate oneself, and to educate others.

But while performing one's duties, one must not forget the highest aim of life, namely, the realization of self. Performance of duties has to be oriented towards this self-realization. Performance of duty is thus a means. The early Upaniṣads do not say that it is a dispensable means. I am inclined to think that the word 'means' is misleading; for it may mean instrument; but an instrument may be neglected after the end is attained. But duties are performed for the realization of one's essential relationship with the cosmos and for the deepening and expansion of one's self. By the performance of duties the way is cleared thus for self-realization. But the way is the way of inwardness; and, in order to be put on the path of inwardness, man has to perform duties and enjoy the values of the world. Action and enjoyment open up the inward paths of the spirit. But, again, this is only a way of speaking; for the path is not different from man's own being. One may, of course, enjoy worldly values without knowing or understanding their inward significance. It is against this mistake that the Upaniṣads warn us.

It is only later, when the influence of Buddhist and Jaina monasticism spread, that what the Vedic Aryans considered to be indispensable means was regarded as dispensable. If this interpretation is not accepted, I do not see how we can reconcile, even as philosophies of life, the teachings of the first two parts and the next two parts of the Veda.

Thus the whole life of man was meant to be education for self-realization. What is learnt from teachers is meant to help this self-realization. Man is part of this cosmos: but he has his own individuality and personality, which apparently transcend all relationships. He must therefore still learn how far this transcendence reaches and what he himself is in that transcendence. If he learns this, he will know what is beyond and, therefore, what is beyond death. Such knowledge will satisfy all inquisitiveness and remove all worry about death. The attempt to obtain such knowledge will intensify one's individuality, deepen one's being, and strengthen one's will and character; and this deepened individuality is then surrendered before the Supreme Spirit directly. Compared with the Socratic conception of education as bringing out what is already within, this Indian conception makes man realize what is originally within and what he is in his pure form, which is described as the *ātman*. Knowledge of the *ātman* therefore is the highest kind of knowledge (*parā vidyā*).

Once this highest kind of knowledge was recognized, other kinds of knowledge were regarded as lower, and knowledge was classified into two kinds, higher and lower (*parā* and *aparā*).[35] The *Chandogya Upaniśad*[36] says that Nārada studied the Vedas and everything else in the world; yet he was depressed and dissatisfied, and therefore approached Sanatkumāra to be taught the nature of the *ātman*. He had had only lower knowledge. But how is higher knowledge to be obtained? The usual answer is: Through penance (*tapas*). Another method is meditation (*dhyāna*). But for either method a life of renunciation (*sannyāsa*) was not prescribed as necessary, not even the life of a bachelor (*brahmacārin*). Since many of the Upaniṣadic personalities were householders and young people, we may conclude that penance and meditation could be practised by young and old. Bhṛgu's son, who was young, practised them. Usually students practised them at their teachers' houses. It was only later that renunciation was considered necessary. The practice of remaining a life-long bachelor at the teacher's house was also introduced; but such bachelors were ridiculed by the followers of the earlier two parts of the Veda, the Mīmāmsakas, as eunuchs hiding their impotency under the garb of spirituality.[37] The *Taittirīya Upaniṣad*, for instance, advises the student who finishes his studies to perform all the duties of a householder.

Although the Upaniṣads distinguished between two kinds of knowledge, they did not explain the positive relation between them but took it for granted. They simply asserted that man has to have both, and that he must direct his life according to both. The implication seems to be that life knows how to relate them. Since men were living according to the two, the necessity of inter-relating the two was not felt. This fact, however, led later on to a split in doctrine, and the later Upaniṣads over-

[35] *Muṇḍakopaniṣat*, I, I, 4 and 5.
[36] Chap. VII.
[37] I, XI.

emphasized higher knowledge and treated the lower as insignificant. The early Upaniṣads took it for granted that man would go through the four stages of life, but the later Upaniṣads felt otherwise.

It is in conformity with this idea of life as the training ground for self-realization that the whole curriculum of education was framed. The Vedas, of course, were the main subject of study. But for their study many accessories were needed. There are six main accessories or subsidiaries (*aṅgas*), which have already been given. Four sub-accessories also (*upāṅgas*) have been mentioned. They are *purāṇa* (often translated as epic), Nyāya or logic, *mīmāmsā* or the science of the methods of interpretation, and *dharmśāstra* or the science of duty, i.e. ethics.

Of these four, the word *purāṇa* needs some explanation. It is generally translated as epic. But what the West calls epic includes all the three Indian classifications, *purāṇa*, *itihāsa*, and *mahākāvya*. Roughly translated, *purāṇas* are world histories, *itihāsas* are narratives of the past, and *mahākāvyas* are what the West would strictly call epic poems. The *purāṇa* has five characteristics: it describes creation, dissolution, some geneology, the activities of persons belonging to it, and the progenitors of mankind. The *Bhāgavata*, for instance, is called a *purāṇa*; some call it *mahā* (great) *purāṇa*. A *mahāpurāna* has eleven characteristics: description of creation, dissolution, maintenance, and control of the world, nature of action (*karma*), and of its potency, information about the world, the succession of the progenitors of mankind, deluges, salvation, praise of the Supreme Spirit and of the different gods. The *itihāsa* is described as the narration of what happened in the past along with the teaching of the four ideals of life, wealth, enjoyment, duty and salvation. The *Mahābhārata* is an instance of *itihāsa*. The *mahākāvya* is meant to preach the Vedic ideal of *dharma* (duty) in a pleasant, enjoyable and appealing way so that the reader may identify himself with the hero of the epic. In the *mahākāvya* we come across the ethical conception of poetry.

It should, however, be mentioned that these distinctions were of a later date. The Upaniṣadic times seem to know only of the *purāṇa*. The sub-accessories were meant for a systematic and logical understanding of the Vedic ideal of life and for its propagation through philosophy and literature even among those who were not allowed to study the Vedas. The *purāṇas* contain philosophical disquisitions and nice literary poems about persons, men and women of all castes, who were devoted to the Vedic ideal of life. Often the narrators belong to the fourth caste, as did Suta. By such study and by transmitting the learning to the next generation a man could pay back his debt to the sages. Education was associated with the debt to the sages.

It is important to note that, when self-realization was recognized as the highest aim of life, all forms of culture in the arts and sciences were directed towards it. Politics, economics, erotics, ethics, fine arts (like dance and music), poetry, drama, and social organization, although in some cases not completely remodelled, were interpreted and given a bias towards the ideal.[38] In these spheres, the ideal was not interpreted as austerity and asceticism, but as enjoyment of the bliss of the *ātman* in a reflected form. Through cultivation of sound in music, one was said to realize the bliss of the Logos (*Nāda Brahman*) as the primeval sound or Word. The attempt also was made to raise the state of sex enjoyment to the level of the Brahman; but this was condemned by many as being too risky. And the ascetic ideal, in a mild form, was encouraged.

The aim of education thus was to enable man to realize the highest in him, and that was the *ātman*. The world itself was the training ground, but the teachers enabled man to understand more readily the inter-relationships of its parts and thus accelerate the process of realization through a proper grasp of the situation. There were philosophers like the Cārvākas[39] who did not recognize this ideal. Their theory of education was therefore worldly in orientation. Some say that the Cārvākas developed sixty-four kinds of arts and sciences. Unfortunately, however, most of the literature of this school is lost, and whatever we learn about them comes mainly from the references made to them by rival schools. It is difficult to believe that mundane arts and sciences belonged to them only and not to the orthodox schools also. The latter also developed them and taught them; but, naturally, they gave them a spiritual orientation.

[38] See the author's *India's Culture and Her Problems*, first two chapters.

[39] Some think that Vātsāyana, the author of *Kāmaśāstra* (Science of Erotics), was associated with the Cārvākas. But it is difficult to accept this view; for he bows to *Dharma* as expounded by Jaimini, the founder of the Mīmāṃsā school, which intepreted the first two parts of the Veda.

Spiritual orientation, however, was not given by making every man follow the same way of life but rather by directing all ways of life towards the same goal. Society was already divided into four castes, and each caste was assigned some profession. So the members of any caste could follow only the profession assigned to it; and education in that profession only was given to them.[40] The first three castes were allowed to study the Vedas; the fourth was not. Again only the first three were allowed to pass through the four stages of life; the fourth had to be satisfied with the first two stages only. These restrictions naturally prevented some persons from educating themselves along lines of their own choosing. But surely, education for worldly life was not neglected. It received every attention and was perfected up to the degree possible at the time.

A modern philosopher of education may ask: How can the different ways of life of the different castes lead to the same goal? How are we to explain the relation between these different kinds of activity and self-realization? Such questions did not trouble the thinkers of the time. They felt that, if one performed the duties according to one's station and caste and surrendered his soul to God, one could attain salvation. But one may now ask: Should one not pass through the same hierarchy of values to realize the highest value? Should one not be educated through the same hierarchy? Answers to these questions were given later. They are two: First, the lower castes, through meritorious action, would be reborn in the higher castes and then attain the highest ideal; and, second, whatever be his caste, if man performed his duties according to its requirements and surrendered his self to God, he would attain salvation. This wavering answer may not satisfy us now. But we can see that such an answer was a historical and sociological requirement, since otherwise the only alternative left would have been to wipe out the lower castes and establish only one caste, which would, of course, mean a casteless society. Freedom for the groups to follow their own ways of life required safeguards for those who considered themselves superior, so that they might preserve their purity. These requirements necessitated the assignment of different professions to the different

[40] For details, see A. S. Altekar; *Education in Ancient India* (Nand Kishore and Bros., Benares, 1951), and R. K. Mookerji: *Ancient Indian Education* (London: Macmillan and Co., 1951).

groups, which, in their turn, brought about differences in education. However, so far as general education for worldly life is concerned, the differences do not seem to have been great in the case of the first three castes. And I might say again that even in the methods of spiritual training, the differences were later reduced to the minimum of externals; for when, through *purāṇas*, etc. the Vedic spiritual ideal was spread among the members of the fourth caste, they took over the ideal with enthusiasm and practised penance, austerities, and asceticism with even greater zeal than did the orthodox. And the orthodox did not forbid any caste to acquire worldly education in the arts and sciences.

3. MAN IN JAINISM AND BUDDHISM

Introduction: It was in the Upaniṣadic atmosphere of spiritual and social life that Jainism and Buddhism made their appearance. Mahāvīra and Buddha are sometimes called social reformers; but they are really religious reformers. Both of them were Aryans and had the greatest respect for the word Aryan. It had no racial meaning for them; it meant, rather, the noble, the sublime. The Aryan path was the noble path, and the Aryan was one who followed the path to salvation. For Jainism, anyone is an Aryan who follows the path of absolute non-injury[41] (*ahimsā*); and every student of Buddhism is acquainted with the Buddhist Aryan truths (*āryasatyas*). If both Jainism and Buddhism are Arya Dharmas, and if the Vedic religion also is an Arya Dharma, then what is the difference? What is common to all three is the spiritual path of self-realization. What differentiates the last from the first two is the Vedic insistence on the performance of sacrifices and leading the householder's life, both of which comprised the socio-ethical life of the time. Although the Vedas preached self-realization in the Upaniṣads, they preached sacrifices also as a duty. And in this latter respect, both Jainism and Buddhism rejected the Veda. For them self-realization is possible only through renunciation. Since everyone, irrespective of one's caste, creed, or sex, is capable of self-realization, members of all sexes and castes can become monks and nuns. In the monastic order distinctions were thus abrogated. But neither Mahāvīra nor

[41] See *Abhidhānarājendra*, the Jaina Encyclopaedia, for the word *ajja*, which is the Prākṛt form of the word *ārya*.

Buddha seems to have preached against the caste system in the lay society. They seem to be indifferent to it. Both of them believed in transmigration and in rebirth in different castes according to one's actions. The *Dhammapada* of Buddhism gives a rational interpretation of the word Brahmin in ethical and spiritual terms, just as, in China, Confucius gave a rational meaning of the term 'superior man'. This rationalization must, of course, have worked against the idea of privileged birth, but no definite attack seems to have been made upon caste as such. The fact that Buddhism spread to countries without caste systems shows only that it was indifferent, rather than antagonistic to the caste system. The interest of Jainism and Buddhism was centred mainly in the monastic order. Jainism, as it is now found, has no caste system within its fold; but its followers allow intermarriages with the third caste of the orthodox society,[42] and, thus, for practical purposes, have became part and parcel of the Hindu society.

But why should not everyone become a monk or nun for the sake of self-realization? Why should the fourth *āśrama* be restricted to the higher castes only? The adherents of orthodoxy gave the answer that the fourth caste was spiritually immature; they even drew a distinction between monks of the Brahmin caste, monks of the Kṣatriya caste, and monks of the Vaiśya caste. But if a monk is above caste and even above society itself, why should the distinctions be made? And if everyone, at least theoretically and in principle, can have self-realization, and if self-realization can be had through penance and austerities, then why should the lowest caste or even the untouchable be prevented from practising them? Attainment of worldly values may be possible through propitiation of gods through sacrifices; but those who do not care for worldly values but only for salvation need not and should not perform them. Further, if self-realization is to be the ideal of every man, then sacrifices should not be performed, because they lead men astray towards worldly values. Such were the motive and the reasoning of Jainism and Buddhism, which turned religion into a pure spiritual discipline and encouraged and popularized monasticism. Those who were previously either prevented or discouraged from taking to the life of renunciation

[42] In Rajasthan, which is a stronghold of Jainism, the Jaina monks are called Baniya monks or Vaisya monks.

took to it with enthusiasm, and the number of monks and nuns swelled by thousands.

It is indeed wrong to think that there were no monastic orders before Buddha and Mahāvīra; indeed, for some time, both of them were disciples of non-Buddhist and non-Jaina ascetics. But the restrictions on taking to the monk's life were very great; and men from castes which were forbidden to take to that life but did so anyway, were not respected. Further, very few women took to it. But Buddhism and Jainism made the monastic life highly respectable and removed caste and sex restrictions. Monastic orders, therefore, became popular, increased, and even became a burden to society. Too many men and women, who might otherwise have been a great asset to society, became monks and nuns; and too many persons who were unfit for monastic life entered it. The missionary zeal of the monks expressed itself not in the question, how many have we been able to convert to Jainism or Buddhism, but in the question, how many have we been able to turn into Jaina or Buddhist monks and nuns?

Buddhism and Jainism thus shifted the emphasis from interest in the whole life of man and society to interest in the monk's life and society. The life of the monk or ascetic was included in the orthodox scheme of life, but generally it was meant for the old; and the fourth stage of life was not considered to be indispensable. The ceremonies at the time of initiation into the fourth stage show that the person has to offer final oblations to gods and ancestors and to himself also, as if he were dead, at least, for all social purposes—a fact expressive of the sense of social and cosmic responsibilities which the Upaniṣadic Aryans had. But Jainism and Buddhism set all that at naught and freed man from this sense of responsibility. And only after these two religions made their appearance did the practice of turning young boys and girls into monks and nuns entered the orthodox tradition also.

However, one important idea which Jainism and Buddhism emphasized is the separation of spiritual life from the social and, therefore, the political life also. Not that the orthodox did not develop the idea that spiritual practices could lead a man, whatever his caste or stage of life, to self-realization; but they considered it to be very difficult unless man went through all four stages. The idea of the fourth *āśrama* arose as a natural outcome of the development of inwardness, but was associated with social and cosmic awareness, as expressed in the social order of castes and the cosmic order of gods and ancestors. But Jainism and Buddhism weakened this awareness and intensified inwardness. For these two religions the centre of interest was the life of the monk, whereas for the orthodox it was the life of the householder, which was regarded as the sustainer of the cosmos. For instance, Jainism and Buddhism have nothing comparable to Manu's ethical code or *Dharma-śāstra*, giving detailed duties of every lay man and woman—a fact which shows that they did not take as much interest in the lay society as they did in the monastic order. Scholars attribute the disappearance of Buddhism from the place of its birth to this very fact: it was confined to monasteries and had no roots in society. When monasteries were destroyed or when support was withdrawn from them, Buddhism had to leave. The pale preachers of compassion had to leave for the remote parts of India or for other lands. Jainism would have shared this fate, had it not associated itself with the third caste and, for many practical purposes, become part and parcel of Hinduism. Even now Brahmin priests officiate at Jaina marriages.

But the separation of spiritual life from social life had its advantages also. Buddhism could spread outside India, because it did not have to carry with it any set of social laws. As a religion and philosophy of pure spiritual discipline, it could be suited to all social and political forms. This is why Buddhism is religion *par excellence*. But this intense inwardness is its greatness as well as its weakness. It is its greatness because Buddhism could suit all social and political forms. It is its weakness because Buddhism could have no roots in any social structure. For instance, while Buddhism ended in pure passivity in India, it is the *samurai*, the warrior class of Japan, that accepted and utilized it. It suited the polyandry of Tibet and the caste system of India. One of the great contributions of Buddhism, we may therefore say, is the divorce of religion from political and social life, and the purification of spiritual discipline.

Man and his environment: So far as the environment of man living on earth goes, the Buddhist conception differs little from the Vedic. A Supreme God is not accepted, but all the other gods, and the natural forces which they control, are accepted. Man is considered to be a wayfarer, and the way is the way of the development of his own being towards inwardness. This is the same as the Upaniṣadic idea. But Buddhism overemphasized inwardness and said that man, if he is intent upon self-realization, need not bother about pleasing gods and ancestors. To a man of self-realization, gods themselves pay homage, as they did to Buddha.

For Jainism also, man's environment was the same as that of the Veda, and, like Buddhism, it overemphasized inwardness. This overemphasis by Buddhism and Jainism naturally resulted in a condemnation of the world, whether Buddha and Mahāvīra foresaw it or not.

Scholars differ on the question of whether or not Buddha himself condemned the world in strong terms. Mrs Rhys Davids thinks that he did not and that the monks, who came later, did it in order to justify their life. But it is difficult to be certain about what Buddha himself said.[43] Jainism also showed and encouraged extreme disregard for the world and its values. Greater austerity and self-mortification cannot be found in any philosophy and religion other than in Jainism. In these respects, Buddha showed great moderation, although Buddhism preached that the world is misery. That the world is misery later crept into the orthodox philosophies also—for instance, into the Sāṅkhya.

Some scholars believe that Buddha did not deny the reality of the ultimate self (*ātman*) but merely kept silent when the question was raised. His followers, however, interpreted his silence as denial and held that the *ātman* does not exist. What one realizes through self-purification is pure *nirvāṇa*, some nonmoving indescribable essence, which is not the same as the psycho-physical being. Jainism, on the other hand, gave a positive answer: the object of realization is *jīva* in his transcendent purity and glory. For Jainism, also, there is no God; there are only gods, who are inferior to the man of self-realization.

Man and evolution: It has already been said that classical Indian philosophy does not have the modern scientific conception of evolution, and that the idea of evolution can be traced, if at all, only in the Cārvāka system and, to a less

[43] See the author's *Idealistic Thought of India*, the first chapter on Buddhism.

extent, in the atomistic philosophies of the Nyāya and the Vaiśeṣika. Only the Cārvāka, however, can be regarded as scientific because it starts with pure matter and says that the higher forms of reality are due to structural relationships into which material particles enter. The other two schools introduce God and the potential state of *karma* as supervising and moving the atoms, and although they say that *karma* brings the atoms together, they do not say that higher forms, such as life and mind, are also due to *karma*. The tendency is to regard everything—matter, life and mind—as produced together, and matter and mind as eternal. Mind also is an atom or, rather is atomic in size.

How is man formed according to Jainism? Unlike Buddhist metaphysics, Jaina metaphysics did not undergo much change. It first classifies the world into two categories, *jīva* or spirit or soul, and *ajīva* or matter. Both of them are substances. Jainism uses the word *jīva* itself for the *ātman*, saying that the *ātman* of the orthodox schools is the *jīva* itself in its pure original state, and that their *jīva* is the *jīva* in its impure state. The difference is between the pure and the impure.

The impure *jiva* is bound by matter. *Ajīva* or matter is of various kinds: time, space, motion, rest and atoms. All are substances and, except time, are extended. Even *karma* is conceived as a material substance.

Man is the *jīva* bound by matter and assuming the gross physical body. In its pure state the *Jīva* is unbound and omniscient and, though not infinite, is only a little less than infinite. But then *karma* enters it and binds it, i.e. gives it a determinate form. This entering of *karma* is said to be due to the *avidyā* (ignorance) of the *jīva*. But how the *jīva*, which is originally pure, becomes ignorant is not known. It is usually said that the ignorance is *anādi* (beginningless); then the original nature of the *jīva* must also be ignorant. How and why *karma* first enters the *jīva* thus remains unexplained. However, this is an ultimate problem which no Indian system has been able to solve satisfactorily. Modern evolutionism may say that the *jīva* is formed spontaneously by incessant activity within matter towards inwardization. Such a theory, however, would be foreign to the Jaina conception of the *jīva*, which is originally pure, omniscient, and eternal.[44]

[44] Cp. the first *Sāṅkhyakārikā*.

Human *karma* is the bond that binds the *jīva* and the world of action. Performing both good and evil actions, the *jīva* goes from birth to birth, assuming various forms and limiting itself to the bodies of those forms. In an elephant the *jīva* is as big as the elephant, and in a mosquito it is as small as the mosquito. The atoms constituting the bodies enter the corresponding structures.

The conception of the formation of man found in Buddhism is more complex than is that found in Jainism.* Though Buddhism was at first pluralistic in its metaphysics, it retained from the beginning a line of thought which, in the derivation of the world from some spiritual principle, is akin to the Upaniṣadic. The Upaniṣads derived everything from the *Ātman*. The Buddhists refused to call the ultimate principle *ātman* but *nirvāna*, the indescribable and unmoving, and derived the world from it. Although in the Hīnayāna this line of thought is not strong, the Mahāyāna emphasized it strongly; and an impartial reader can see that the Vijñānavādins, one of the schools of the Mahāyāna, conceived it nearly in the same terms as those of the *ātman* and the Brahman of the Upaniṣads.[46]

Buddha is said to have preached the four Aryan (noble) truths: the world is misery, it has a cause, misery can be stopped, and there is a way for stopping it. It is the second truth that is important for our purpose, for it gives the cause of the world, which is misery. The Buddhists accepted causal occasionalism or *pratītyasamutpāda*: the cause is only an occasion for the appearance of the effect, it does not enter the effect. They had to develop this occasionalism because of their doctrine of momentariness. Everything in the world is momentary. The cause, therefore, being momentary, cannot continue to exist in the effect. The effect is a different entity. Even the pot is a different existence from the clay of which it is made. Yet the effect can come into being only with reference to the cause. Hence the cause is necessary, but it acts only as the occasion for the effect to appear.

* Buddhism is first divided into two main branches, the Hīnayāna or the Lower Vehicle, which is really the early Buddhism, and the Mahāyāna or the Greater Vehicle, which is the later Buddhism[45] Each vehicle has many schools and on some point or other they differ from each other. But what is generally common to all schools may be given here.

[45] See *Idealistic Thought of India*, the two chapters on Buddhism.

[46] See *Idealistic Thought of India*, the section on *Asaṅga*.

Understanding causation thus, the Buddhists said that there are twelve links in the process of the causation of the world. They are Ignorance, Impressions, Initial Consciousness, Body-Mind, Senses, Sense Contact, Sense Experience, Thirst (Desire), Clinging (to objects), Tendency to be Born, Rebirth, and Old Age and Death. Somehow, due to Ignorance (*Avidyā*), Impressions (*samskāras*) are born. By impressions the Buddhists mean inner forces, instincts, latent urges, dispositions, etc. Out of the Impressions an embryonic consciousness is born, called *vijñāna*; out of it the embryonic organism (Body-Mind or *nāma-rūpa*) is born; out of it the six senses (mind also is called a sense by the Buddhists); and out of them sense-contact is born and so on. This is how man's coming into being is explained by Buddhism.

What is common to the Upaniṣads and Buddhism is the derivation of man from the infinite and ineffable *nirvāṇa* through ignorance. But the reader can easily notice the important difference between the motives behind the derivations. The Upaniṣadic account is that of the lower coming out of the higher. The motive here is to exhort man to realize the higher. The Buddhist account is that of the derivation of misery. The Buddhists are not interested in forms of reality like matter, life, mind, reason, and *ātman*; they are interested in showing how misery has come to be. Further, we have to say that this derivation is not a strict evolutionary process but a psycho-ethical causal process. For instance, we cannot say that old age and death come chronologically after rebirth; even in the first birth they have to be experienced.

However, a more evolutionary idea was later adopted by the Vijñānavādins. They called ultimate reality by the name Vijñāna (Consciousness, Reason, Mind). It is of two kinds, *Ālayavijñāna* or Storehouse Consciousness, and *Pravṛttivijñāna* or activity consciousness. It is the latter that transforms itself into the world of man and his environment. But how does it arise, if *Ālayavijñāna* is the original reality? It arises through Ignorance.[47] Ultimately Vijñāna is the original principle out of which the world comes, and it comes through man, through his mind and senses.

Structure of the human individual: The Jaina conception of the

[47] *Ibid.*, the sections on Asaṅga, Vasubandhu and the Bhūtatathatā school.

structure of the human individual is not as clear as that of the Upaniṣads. For instance, the concept of *prāna* (vital principle) does not seem to have been given any importance. The Buddhists call it *jīvitīndriya* (sense of life) but do not say much about it. For Jainism, the *jīva* bound by *karma* constitutes man. Mind is of two kinds: *bhāvamanas* or the psychic mind, and *dravyamanas* or substantial or physical mind. This distinction is not very clear. The former, we may say, is the activity of consciousness. But all activity is due to *karma*, which is matter, and is different from the *jīva*. Then, if *bhāvamanas* or psychic mind is a product of *karma*, it also must be material. If this is so, then the only distinction will be that one is subtler than the other. For instance, the Nyāya-Vaiśeṣika school maintains that the perceiving sense is different from the physical organ. But a similar distinction in the case of mind is rare; for mind is always psychic and subtle.[48]

Karma binds the *jīva* to the material world through false knowledge (*mithyādarśana*), incontinence (*avirati*), negligence (*pramāda*), passion (*kaṣaya*: anger, egoity, deceitfulness and greed), and action (*yoga*,[49] that is, taking in *karma* which is found all round). Instead of burdening the reader with more technical terms, I shall give only the central idea of Jainism. The idea is that *karma* is the agency that binds the *jīva* to matter. But as already indicated, the idea does not provide a satisfactory explanation. The whole world is pervaded by *karma*; and the *jīva*, like a wet cloth taking in dust from the air, takes in *karma*. According to Jainism, 'karma is an aggregate of material particles which are very fine and are imperceptible to the senses.'[50] Why should these particles enter the pure *jīva*? If they can enter of their own accord, what is there to prevent them from entering again even after liberation? These questions are raised here only to show the mystery that is involved in all explanations which derive man from a higher principle such as *ātman*, *jīva*, *nirvana*, God, or the Brahman.

But taking the usual scientific theory of evolution according to which man comes out of some material elements, we may

[48] Mr Tatia says that one writer, Akalaṅka, equated *manas* to *ātman*. *Studies in Jaina Philosophy*, p. 62 f.n. (Benares: Jaina Cultural Research Society, 1951).

[49] This term *yoga* should not be confused with the other term which means control of mind, etc. for self-realization.

[50] M. L. Mehta: *Outlines of Jaina Philosophy*, p. 134 (Bangalore: Jaina Mission Society, 1954).

explain him as a new structural form into which the elements enter. Actually, however, even the scientist cannot tell us why the material elements evolve life, and why life evolves consciousness. He finds them in this world, and thinks that the process is natural. Those who derive man and matter from the *ātman* may also say that the process is natural. But the difficulty now is that, even after liberation, the *ātman* will evolve matter and man, because it is natural for it to do so. Or the *kārmic* matter of Jainism can enter the pure soul, because it is natural for it to do so. However, according to Jainism, the five causes (false knowledge, etc.) constitute man. He is the *jīva* full of *kārmic* matter. He has a mind, the five senses, and organs of action.

The Buddhists have given us a clearer conception of the constitution of man. He is essentially *nirvāṇa*, according to all schools of Buddhism; Śunya, according to the Mādhyamikas (one school of Mahāyāna); and Vijñāna also, according to the Vijñānavādins (another school of Mahāyāna). In addition, man is also a *pudgala*, a psycho-physical person. Somehow, through ignorance, the psycho-physical personality is formed; and when it is analysed away, the original *nirvāṇa*, Śūnya, or Vijñāna is realized.

The psycho-physical personality consists of five aggregates or *skandhas: rūpaskandha* or the aggregate of matter, *vedanāskandha* or the aggregate of feelings and sensations, *samjñāskandha* or the aggregate of ideas, *samskāraskandha* or the aggregate of instincts, propensities, impressions, etc. and *vijñānaskandha* or the aggregate of consciousness. The last, of course, cannot be the same as the original pure Vijñāna of the Vijñānavādins. It is a product of *pravṛttivijnāna* or active consciousness.

The idealistic conception that the senses and their objects are correlates and are due to the same elements assuming the subjective and objective forms seems to be common to most of the Indian schools. We saw it in the semi-mythological explanations of the Upaniṣads. Jainism and Buddhism do not seem to have elaborated this idea, but have assumed it. In the doctrine of the *āyatanas* or bases of experience, for instance, Buddhism correlated the senses to their objects. The bases of experience are twelve in number, the five senses and mind, and their objects. In the semi-mythological and semi-philosophical atmosphere of the time, Buddhism and Jainism seem to have accepted the current ideas.

Both the schools believed in transmigration. It is the subtle body that transmigrates; and it consists of everything in man except the physical body. Like Jainism, Buddhism showed very little interest in the principle of life, calling it *jīvitīndriya* or the organ of life. The reason seems to be that both schools were more concerned with what man ought to become than with what he is. The Upaniṣads gave equal thought to both problems. The general cosmology of the Vedas was assumed by Jainism and Buddhism, which built up their ethico-religious philosophies on it as the foundation. Much of Jainism and Buddhism cannot be understood without assuming the mythological and philosophical atmosphere created by the Vedas. Though rebels against the Veda, they are daughters of the Veda.

Buddhism also accepted the doctrine of *karma* and said that the soul is born again and again according to it. The world is a world of *karma*, and there must have been the assumption that the aggregates (*skandhas*) come together when impelled by the latent forces of *karma*, which produces the *samskāras* (impressions). But Buddhism did not believe, like Jainism, that *karma* is a material substance pervading the whole world and entering the soul somehow.

One point needs to be clarified before closing this section. The Vijñānavādins among the Buddhists called the highest reality by the name Vijñāna. Generally the word is translated as mind and also as consciousness. Other Sanscrit terms used are *manas* and *citta*. Now, according to classical Sanscrit, none of these words means the *ātman*. The orthodox schools explain *vijñāna* and *citta* as reason and *manas* as mind, as we saw in explaining the categories of the *Kaṭha Upaniṣad*; both are lower than the *ātman*. But Asaṅga, one of the Vijñānavādins, used the word *ātman* also for *vijñāna*.[51] We may therefore say that the Vijñānavādins approached the Upaniṣadic conception of the *ātman* in their own way, although the words they used created some confusion. The Vedāntins thought that the reality as conceived by the Vijñānavādins was lower than theirs; but the Vijñānavādins held that it was as high as that of the Vedāntins and better conceived than theirs. It seems to me that the

[51] See *Idealistic Thought of India*, Section on Asaṅga.

quarrel between the two schools was due to each giving the usual and popular meanings to the terms of the other.

Life's ideal: The reader does not have to be told now about life's ideal according to Jainism and Buddhism. It is the realization of the essential reality within man, and becoming one with it. By the time of the Upaniṣads, according to all schools of philosophy, both orthodox and heterodox, the ideal was to rise above the world of action. Only the Mīmāmsakas hesitated to accept the ideal for a time; but later they also followed suit, though insisting that rising above action was possible only by performing right action. This is the teaching of the *Bhagavadgītā* also. The *Bhāgavata*[52] also says: The Veda which speaks of imperceptible entities teaches immature minds; it teaches them to perform actions only to be freed from actions. The *Vācaspatya Encyclopædia* quotes from Bhṛgu to the effect that action preached by the Veda is of two kinds, aiming outwards and aiming inwards, but both are actions. All this teaching is the teaching of the way of action (*karmamārga*) for the realization of the Supreme Being. But Buddhism and Jainism overstressed life above action; and their doctrines gave rise to the idea that action is detrimental to salvation. This view entered the orthodox schools also. If man is to rise above action, why should he perform action at all? The life of the monk, therefore, became the ideal.

Jainism, as a consequence of its theory that man is the *jīva* into which *kārmic* matter entered, exhorted him to get rid of *karma*. As a philosophy of life, it gives the following concepts or categories: *jīva* (soul), *ajīva* (matter), *āsrava* (inflow of *kārmic* matter), *bandha* (bondage), *samvara* (stopping the inflow), *nirjara* (decaying or exhausting the accumulated *karma* through penance, etc.), and *mokṣa* (salvation).

For separating the *jīva* from *karma*, Jainism exhorts man to practise three methods: right views, right knowledge, and right conduct.[53] Right views are interpreted as right faith (*śraddhā*) because one can be taught right knowledge through right faith. Right knowledge is grasping things as they are and leads to right conduct; for one who knows the truth can act according to it. Right conduct is of five kinds: *ahimsā* (non-

[52] XI, III, 44.
[53] Umāswāmi: *Tattvārthasūtra*, I. 1. (Mysore: Govt. Branch Press, 1944).

injury), *satya* (truthfulness), *asteya* (non-stealing), *brahmacarya* (celebacy), and *aparigraha* (non-acceptance of gifts, etc.). The monk has to observe all the five strictly. He has of course to have right views and right knowledge also. The householder also is expected to observe all but is allowed some latitude. But the ideal life remains that of the monk.

Buddhism advocated a similar ideal of life. Man is a product of ignorance and *karma* and so must get over them. He wrongly thinks that he is the same as the psycho-physical personality (*pudgala*), formed out of the five aggregates. He can know the truth about his essential nature by analysing the aggregates away. Buddhist philosophy and psychology showed great acuteness in this analysis. However, the Buddhist schools differed from each other in their answers to the question, What is the remainder after this analysis? To be sure, all said *Nirvaṇa*. But what is the nature of *nirvāṇa*? The Mādhyamikas said: It is Nothing, Void, Śūnya, which is neither positive nor negative. The Vijñānavādins said: It is the highest Vijñāna or Consciousness.

The way to the highest realization was pointed to by Buddha as the eight-fold noble path, which is the fourth of the four noble truths. It consists of right views, right resolve, right speech, right conduct, right livelihood, right effort, right mindfulness, and right concentration of mind (*samādhi*). All the eight may be followed by the householders also but are mainly meant for the monk. By practising them, laymen and laywomen rise in the path, but ultimately they have to become monks and nuns. The path to *nirvāṇa* is highly ethical, in the sense of absolute self-control—control of mind, body, and speech. But this self-control is not enough: the highest kind of concentration and self-analysis are needed for the final result.

So far as ethics is concerned, Buddhism and Jainism emphasized subjective self-control to the utmost, but not man's self-expression through right activity. Activity has itself to be transcended; and this transcendence is possible when human individuality as such is transcended. Transcendence of active individuality is an ideal common to almost all the Indian schools. But it need not always be a demerit. Man has to die and after death activity, for all we know, is transcended. This, however, is not the important point. Philosophy may consider the soul as continuously existing in this life and in the next.

All great religions postulate life after death, although they differ in their views about its nature. They take death as part of the process of a soul's life. When the essence of man is understood as transcending this process, then transcendence of activity as an ideal follows. But we have also to note that man, so long as he is man, has to lead a life of action, and that a radical application of the ideal may do violence to his nature.

The ideal of salvation was preached by Jainism and Buddhism with missionary zeal, and the latter propagated it beyond India. In India this ideal was a supplementary to what already existed. But because it could be distinguished and separated from other ideals, Buddhism could carry it to other lands and engraft it on the life of the communities. However, those communities in India that took to the ideal solely and seriously lost their bearing to the life of this world and its ideals; and when the monasteries disappeared, Buddhism waned away.

But Buddhism has a lesson and a problem for the modern world. On the one hand, we say that religion should be divorced from political and social life, and we welcome the separation of political and religious headships; on the other hand, we maintain that spirituality should be expressed in social and political institutions. For both the East and the West, this problem is an acute one. I mention it here, because of its particular relevance to Buddhism, but shall discuss it in the concluding chapter.

The missionary zeal of Buddhism rose so high that it resulted in the Bodhisattva ideal. The Bodhisattva is a man of realization, who postpones his own salvation (*nirvāṇa*) and works in the world until all the living beings obtain their salvation. This is a peculiarly Mahāyānist ideal. The Bodhisattva practises six *pāramitās*. A *pāramitā* is a virtue carried to the utmost peak of perfection. They are: *dānapāramitā* or the virtue of charity, *śīlapāramitā* or the virtue of character, *kṣāntipāramitā* or the virtue of forbearance, *vīryapāramitā* or the virtue of exertion, *dhyānapāramitā* or the virtue of meditation, and *prajñāpāramitā* or the virtue of knowledge.[54] The Mahāyāna, on the whole, treated the last of these as the highest and as basic to the rest. It is also likely that the orthodox idea of the way of knowledge leading to salvation or *Jñānamārga*

[54] See Prajñākaramati's *Bodhicaryāvatārapañcika*, for details (edited by la Vallee Poussin, 1902).

was given definite shape at first by the Buddhists, with *prajñāpāramitā* as the basis. Asaṅga, a Vijñānavādin Buddhist who lived long before Gauḍapāda, the grand-teacher of Śaṅkara, uses the word *jñānamārga* and speaks of the pure way of knowledge.[55]

Sometimes these perfect virtues are given as ten: charity, character, non-activity, knowledge, exertion, forbearance, truthfulness, persistency, friendliness, and disinterestedness. In other contexts they are given as the six above plus tactfulness, earnestness, strength of mind, and general knowledge. All of these virtues have to be practised to perfection. Often the perfection advocated seems to be an excess. But only in its excess do we find the peculiarity of a religion or philosophy. Jainism, for instance, preached non-injury to excess; and that is the reason why we identify the ideal of non-injury with Jainism. Almost all religions preached the ideal, but did not carry it to its logical extreme, as Jainism did. The reader may note that non-injury is not a separate virtue for Buddhism; but we may say that it is the highest *pāramitā* for Jainism.

It seems that by about the second century A.D. several paths leading to salvation were recognized and formulated. Buddha himself made *mārga* or path one of the four Aryan truths. But he explained it only as the eight-fold noble path and did not give it a name. Other schools took up the idea, and each distinguished the path it preached from those of the others, and gave them names. Of the paths thus recognized *karmamārga* or the way of action, *bhaktimārga* or the way of devotion and *jñānamārga* or the way of knowledge became important. They will be explained in the sequel.

Influence of Jainism and Buddhism on religious traditions: Jainism and Buddhism spread very quickly throughout India. The orthodox tradition recognized the ideal of *sannyāsa* (renunciation), but did not encourage too many people to take to it. This tradition insisted also that man should first pass through the earlier stages of life and thus excluded the majority, which consisted of the fourth caste, from the fourth stage. But Jainism and Buddhism removed these restrictions. The general masses, who had been eager to know about this

[55] See *Idealistic Thought of India*, Section on Asaṅga.

life and had been prevented from knowing it, therefore welcomed Jainism and Buddhism. Monastic life came to be admired, and the orders of monks and nuns increased. So long as enthusiasm was high, the compassionate life of Buddha and the austere life of Mahāvīra were strictly adhered to; and the life of the orthodox, which did not exclude worldly enjoyments or performance of worldly duties, must have been looked down upon as unspiritual and misguided. Because of the Jaina influence, many orthodox Brahmins had to give up meat and become strict vegetarians. It is not known definitely whether or not there were orthodox monasteries, like the Buddhist and the Jaina—there were indeed *āśramas* or hermitages run by sages who were householders—before Śaṅkara; there were perhaps a few, though no big ones. But regular orthodox monasteries began to play an important role in the social life of the country after Śaṅkara, who divided India into four parts and gave one monastery to each.[56]

Both the religions again intensified the inward outlook of man. The aim of life is the realization of spiritual inwardness. One who is after worldly values is outward-looking and therefore cannot realize the true nature of spirit. Self-control along socially prescribed channels and positive ethical virtues, therefore, were re-interpreted as stepping stones to detachment from the world. Buddha, indeed, preached against unnecessary austerities and self-mortification. He had practised them and had discovered their uselessness. Yet he popularized the life of the monk. Mahāvīra, on the other hand, practised and encouraged both self-mortification and the life of the monk. How can a man who is pursuing worldly values be spiritual? This was a common question raised by the people, and a negative answer was implied. The orthodox tradition, particularly the Mīmāmsā school of Jaimini, which at first preached that the performance of positive duties was the highest aim of life, had to fight hard against the new teaching. The tendency to subordinate its philosophy to that of the Vedānta, which was greatly influenced by Buddhism in its monistic interpretations, became strong. But the influence of Buddhism on the Vedānta is stronger than that of Jainism.

Buddhist philosophy, it has been said, had a chequered

[56] At present the influence of these monasteries on the life of the community is not great.

development. The earlier schools were mostly pluralistic and were mainly concerned with ethics of self-discipline leading to absolute detachment and *nirvāṇa*. They were also individualistic; and for this reason, the Hīnayāna was also called Khadgayāna or the Vehicle of the Rhinoceros, because the rhinoceros is an animal living and moving alone. Salvation was for the individual, not for the whole world. The ideal was called the ideal of Arhatship or Pratyekabuddahood. The Arhat or Pratyekabuddha is an individualist, caring only for his own salvation. And it is his creed that all cannot become Buddhas or one with the Buddha-principle. As against this doctrine, the Mahāyānists held that all could become Buddha, the perfect transcendental principle. They formulated the ideal of the Bodhisattva who, though perfect, would not enter *nirvāṇa* until all living beings were saved. By that time Buddha became identified with the all-pervading reality towards which all living beings were attracted, just as, according to Aristotle, all things are attracted towards God. Thus the essential nature of Buddha became similar to that of the Brahman of the Upaniṣads. The Hīnayāna called the ultimate reality *nirvāṇa*, and *śūnya* (the unmoving and the void). The Mahāyāna accepted both the terms and used them to describe the ultimate Buddha nature, which became monistic, being the same for all. The Buddha nature is the origin of the world, and into it the world returns when it is perfected. The Mādhyamikas called it *śūnya* only, because it was devoid of all determinations. But the Vijñānavādins said that there must be consciousness in it in order to know that it was devoid of all determinations, and called it Vijñāna also.

I have said elsewhere[57] that the logical connotation of both *śūnya* and *māyā* are the same, that sometimes the Buddhists used the word *māyā* also, and that we find this logical connotation given first in the Buddhist *Prajñāpāramitās*. The connotation is that the world is neither existent, nor non-existent, nor both, nor neither. Since the *Prajñāpāramitā* literature is earlier than Śaṅkara and his teacher's teacher, Gauḍapāda, we have to conclude that it is the Advaintins who took over the connotation from the Buddhists. The ultimate ideal of knowledge, *prajñāpāramitā*, according to the Buddhists, is to know that the essence of the world is neither

[57] See *Idealistic Thought of India*, pp. 109 and 142.

existence nor non-existence. Again, the word *śūnya* was incorporated even by the Śaiva and the Vaiṣṇava schools, although they used it for a reality lower than the highest.[58] For these two schools, however, it is not the logical connotation that is important but the stage of experience which the meditator on the Brahman reaches. The *śūnya* is a stage of experience without any form whatever, and is absolutely indeterminate. According to Śaivism, it is a stage of latent urges, which are not yet active. According to Vaiṣṇavism, it is a stage when Viṣṇu is about to create the world but has not yet started creation. It is similar to the causal body (*kāraṇaśarīra*) of the Advaitins and also to the creative power of Īśvara when the latter is still inactive. According to these schools, there is a reality which is still higher than the Śūnya, and which can be realized by carrying meditation further. All these concepts can be traced to the principle of Avyakta (Unmanifest) given in the *Kaṭha Upaniṣad.*

The Buddhist Vijñānavādins maintained that Vijñāna is higher than Śūnya. But here also the orthodox gave the popular meaning to the word *vijñāna*, that of reason, and treated it as lower than the Brahman. These differentiations were made to justify the position and superiority of each. But Asaṅga[59] called Vijñāna both *Sat* (Existence) and *Ātman*, and the path leading to self-realization he called *jñānamārga* or the way of knowledge. Many scholars believe that Gauḍapāda, the grand-teacher of Śaṅkara, was greatly influenced by the Vijñānavādins, and some scholars even maintain that he was once a Buddhist who later became a Vedāntin. The debt of Vedānta to Buddhism has not yet been properly assessed; but it seems to be very great. I feel that it is difficult to deny that the later development of the Upaniṣadic thought owes much to Buddhism, just as Buddhist Mahāyāna owes much to the original Upaniṣadic ideas. Only sectarian bias can deny mutual influence.

Some of the main reasons for the disappearance of Buddhism from the land of its birth are important to notice in an essay on man. In the first place, zest for life, vigour, and activity became weak because of the purely pacifist, meek monkish ideal. The country could not face the invader, as there were

[58] See Abhinavagupta: *Īśvarapratyabhijñāvimarśinī*, Vol. II, p. 234; and *Ahirbudhnyasamhitā* of the Vaiṣṇavas.

[59] *Idealistic Thought of India*, p. 266.

few who were willing to fight. Life was badly enervated. Secondly, the Buddhists founded a large number of huge monasteries; and the best and the ablest men and women became monks and nuns. Society was the poorer and weaker for it. The great kingdom of Magadha was so full of monasteries that it came to be called Bihar, the land of *vihāras* or monasteries. In the third place, the monkish ideal provided an opportunity even for those who merely wanted to escape the responsibilities of life to enter the monasteries, although ethically and intellectually they were unfit for the life of the monk. Corruption thus entered monasteries, and they became a burden upon society, which deteriorated economically, politically and morally. These effects have to be pointed out in a study of man in order to gauge the effects of one-sided and unbalanced spirituality on the life of the individual and of society. In the fourth place, Buddhist philosophy, through free self-development, approached the Vedānta very closely and was easily absorbed. Buddhism could then give no justification for separate existence. In order to resuscitate zest and vigour of life, Kumārila started his attack from the side of the Mīmāmsā and its philosophy of action, and Śaṅkara did so from the side of the Vedānta and its philosophy of salvation. Both belonged to about the eighth century. The decline of Buddhism started.

Education: Education for Buddhism and Jainism, as for the orthodox schools, was meant to enable man to realize the highest within him. But for the orthodox tradition, the world had a positive value; it was man's training ground; and he was to learn how to utilize the world. We may even say that, for the early Ṛgvedic Aryans, education consisted in training man how to enjoy the values of this world and the next. This is clearly reflected in the Mīmāmsā ridicule of life-long bachelors, who remain religious students in order to conceal their lack of virility.[60] Even later, when some Mīmāmsā writers preached salvation and rising above action, they said that the ideal could be attained only through action and by passing through all the four stages of life. But Buddhism and Jainism tended to treat the world and its values with contempt. And a system of education which dispensed with the necessity of

[60] *Śabarabhāṣya*, Vol. I, p. 95 (Eng. tr. by Ganganatha Jha, Gaekwad Oriental Series, Baroda, 1933).

passing through all four stages of life would consequently give little or no importance to training for worldly life. An explicit social orientation to education can be found only in the orthodox tradition, provided we allow that society could be understood as cosmic, consisting of gods, ancestors, sages, and ordinary men.

The orthodox system of education was centred not in monasteries but in *pāṭhaśālas* or schools, and in *āśramas* or hermitages. In both, the pupil had to live with the teacher. The word hermitage may give the idea that they were run by monks. But they were not. They were run by sages, most of whom were regular householders with families. The sons of both the rich and the poor went to the same schools and hermitages, and studied what they wanted. The study of the nature of the Brahman was, of course, considered to be the highest. But all arts and sciences useful for society were taught. The ideal of education can be understood from what may be regarded as the convocation address given by the teacher to the pupil in the *Taittirīya Upaniṣad*,[61] after the pupil finished his studies. The address insists upon four injunctions: Speak the truth; Do your duty (*dharma*) to gods, ancestors, and sages; Do what is useful, and Do not miss the opportunity of becoming great. No one can say that this is an ascetic ideal of education.

The Jaina and the Buddhist systems of education, like the Christian system of education in the Middle Ages, centred in monasteries, for which initiation and training of monks and nuns were primary and of lay men and women were secondary. Certainly, in the Buddhist universities worldly arts and sciences were taught, but the whole system of education was geared to monastic life and not to worldly life. The Jaina centres of education do not seem to be as renowned as the Buddhist; but both were equally monastic.

In this chapter, it is possible to give only the central idea of the philosophy of education, but not the methods used by the orthodox and the heterodox institutions.[62] On the highest ideal both the orthodox and heterodox agreed. But the orthodox insisted that the world and its values had to be utilized

[61] I, II.

[62] For which see R. K. Mookerji: *Ancient Indian Education*. This book omits Jainism. But the Jaina ideal was also to turn man into a monk and woman into a nun. The Jainas are not as famous as the Buddhists for their universities.

positively in the training of man. The Mīmāmsā tradition completely affirmed man and human values.

Let me interpret in my own way Dewey's remark that the test of every philosophy lies in its theory of education. If the remark means that every philosophy must be consistent with its theory of education, then the Jaina and the Buddhist philosophies and their theories of education are consistent with each other. Once morality is interpreted as self-control oriented towards detachment from life and attachment to the supreme goal of salvation, education becomes moral and psychological training in self-discipline; and the Jaina and Buddhist monastic education worked this out systematically and thoroughly. But the orthodox theories of education also are consistent with their philosophies.

Dewey, however, may have had something else in mind, when he used the word test. How does a theory of education test a philosophy? By its human usefulness, social and individual. If this is the test, then the heterodox theories fail; for by human usefulness they do not understand worldly usefulness but usefulness for salvation only. The orthodox theory, on the other hand is, on the whole, inclusive of the whole life of man; it is both this-worldly and other-worldly. Historically the effects of Buddhism and Jainism on life have not all been favourable. Yet their technique of spiritual discipline is one of the highest. I am inclined to think that as far as the theory of education of the common man is concerned, they have added little to the orthodox tradition. But they certainly have intensified the training of the monk and the nun and have made it more systematic and thorough.

4. MAN IN THE EPICS

One finds in the epics a more comprehensive survey of man—of his life, thought, and action—and of his relation to the world than in the schools, because the epics never try to be systematic, but give all systems of philosophy in a popular way. As the epics are meant for those also who are not permitted to read the Vedas, and so for every person, they have explained every aspect of life. They are not meant merely for the man intent upon renunciation; and in this respect, they are unlike the Upaniṣads and the *Brahmasūtras*, out of which all the Vedāntic systems grew. Though they contain philosophical expositions also, they are not classed as philosophical literature, but rather as popular literature. They are popular expositions of the Aryan way of life.*

Because of the suitability of teaching the Aryan ideal through epics, the Jainas and the Buddhists also composed them. But there seem to be more Jaina epics than there are Buddhist; perhaps some of the Buddhist epics are lost. The Jainas, for instance, re-wrote the *Mahābhārata* in which they extolled their own teachings.

So far as the philosophy of man and the world is concerned, we find in the epics almost all that is found in the systems. But since the epics are addressed to all people, they preach mostly the life of action (*karmayoga*). Now and then they preach also the way of devotion (*bhaktiyoga*) and the way of knowledge (*jñānayoga*). Of the three, there is more emphasis on the first two; for performance of duties and devotion and self-surrender to God are more suitable to ordinary men than is the way of knowledge, which depends greatly on self-effort and self-analysis.

By about the first century B.C. or A.D., the controversy over the way of action, the way of devotion, and the way of knowledge may have taken a definite shape. A possible split between the way of action and the way of knowledge is implicit in the Veda itself, if we take all four parts together. After the rise of Jainism and Buddhism, which rejected the whole of the Veda but accepted the ideal preached by the Upaniṣads, namely, salvation by removing one's ignorance and obtaining knowledge of the Supreme, the gap between the two ways must have been widened. The orthodox also were influenced by the split, for later we find it in the Advaita of Śaṅkara, who preached the way of knowledge and gave a low place to the way of action.

Meanwhile, by about the first century B.C., Śaivism and Vaiṣṇavism became active. The cults of these two religions are indeed as old as the Vedas. But the Āgamas, which are the main

* As I have indicated already, there were epics even during Vedic times. Śaṅkara refers to them. But they are lost. The available epics are all of a later period. The *Mahābhārata*, which is the earliest available, belongs perhaps to about the fifth century B.C. The story may have to be dated much earlier; and there may have been later interpolations and additions. The story of *Rāmāyana* seems to be earlier than that of the *Mahābhārata*, but its composition is later.

source of their inspiration, are of a later period. Their language is classical, not archaic. Vaiṣṇavism is based on the Pāñcarātra Āgamas, and Śaivism on the Pāsupata Āgamas. Vaiṣṇavism, on the whole, preached the way of devotion or *bhaktimārga*, but Śaivism preached also the way of knowledge or *jñābamārga*.

Now, religion is meant for the general run of mankind; and so the majority of people among the Hindus are either Śaivas or Vaṣṇavas. Those who follow the Vedic tradition alone are fewer in number and are called Smārtas. The epics or *purāṇas* are written either from the Śaiva or Vaiṣṇava point of view. That the epics are treated as accessories to the Veda indicates that they also were accepted by the Vedic tradition as a necessary means for propagating the Vedic ideal. This means that the Vedic tradition accepted all the three ways—action, devotion and knowledge—as reliable ways leading to salvation.

But there came a time when the followers of each began to claim superiority over the others. Controversies started; reconciliations and syntheses also were attempted. Some preached both knowledge and action, some preached devotion and action, and the others preached all the three.

We can present here only the general differences. When once salvation as the highest ideal was accepted by the Mīmāmsā also, the tendency to subordinate action either to knowledge or to devotion became strong. The Mīmāmsā, however, did not and could not follow this trend but maintained that salvation was possible only through action. Salvation was indeed above the world of action; still it could be reached only through action. All the ethical codes, like that of Manu, accepted this view. Debts to gods, to ancestors, and to sages can be paid back without the desire for anything in return as reward: then action leads to salvation. But if the payment is made with some desire for wealth or enjoyment, one has to be reborn and salvation cannot be had.

Both the way of devotion and the way of knowledge treat the way of action as a means or a stepping stone; but the former treats the means as necessary. For instance, Rāmānuja, who preached the way of devotion, said that one should inquire into the nature of the Brahman—which leads to salvation—only after understanding the nature of duty[63] (*dharma*) as

[63] Commentary on the first *Brahmasūtra*.

given by the Vedas. But Śaṅkara said that one could inquire into the nature of the Brahman the moment one felt detachment from the world.[64] So the way of knowledge does not treat active life as even necessary, though its usefulness for producing detachment (*vairāgya*) is recognized.

The way of knowledge is generally preached by those philosophies that accept the ultimate identity of the inward essence of man with the Supreme Reality. Devotion needs distinction between the devotee and the object. Absolute identity cannot allow such distinction. Since the nature of the Supreme Reality is knowledge, the way of knowledge is the highest for those who accept absolute identity. So long as the identity is not realized, the distinction lasts and devotion becomes helpful. Devotion can be practised by surrendering one's individual self and its activities, without refraining from activity. When action thus is surrendered to God, devotion increases. That is why the *Bhagavadgīta*, which is part of the epic *Mahābhārata*, preaches self-less action or, more literally, desire-less action (*niṣkāmakarma*). Desire involves egoity; but in self-less action man works only as an instrument of God.

Those who preach the way of devotion subordinate knowledge to devotion. They emphasize the aspect of love of the Supreme and maintain that it can be realized only through devotion, which is an aspect of love. One who is devoted to a person always makes the latter an object of continual knowledge without break, just as a woman deeply in love with a man always has him in mind. So devotion is a kind of knowledge, which, as a continual and uninterrupted flow, is higher than knowledge as such, which is but intermittent and changing. Such devotion to the Supreme marks the state of salvation and permits the distinction between the devotee and his object. To achieve this end, action is necessary in this world. Life necessarily involves action, which must support devotion. But it can support devotion only if it is surrendered to the Supreme. The followers of the way of devotion maintain that the *Bhagavadgīta* preaches the way of devotion.

These three ways are also called yogas, *karmayoga*, *bhaktiyoga* and *jñānayoga*. *Yoga* means joining and by extention, the joining of the finite spirit with the Supreme Spirit. Later, the word came to mean the method that leads to such joining.

[64] *Ibid.*

Since all the three ways (*mārgas*) are such methods, they are called *yogas*. Psychological, physiological, and even medical techniques were later developed as spiritual disciplines, and all were called *yogas*. The technique developed by Patañjali is often called *the yoga*; to distinguish it from the other forms, it is called Pātañjala *yoga*. Its philosophy is similar to that of the Sāṅkhya which will be discussed later. It was thought that salvation could be had by complete control of the vital processes; and, as a result, what is called Hatha Yoga was developed. By practising it man obtains salvation by a sort of *tour de force*. Next, the Śāktas developed Laya Yoga or the technique of completely dissolving one's ego in the Supreme Being through control of nervous plexus. There is Rāja Yoga, which is practically the same as Pātañjala Yoga, but practised by one who is curious about the mysteries of the inner Spirit. Then there is Mantra Yoga or the *yoga* leading to salvation through uttering *mantras* or sacred syllables. Lastly, there is the curious Auṣadha Yoga or medical *yoga*; for some persons thought that salvation could be had by taking some herbs or other drugs. For instance, some thought that mercury was the origin of the world and that by making one's body full of it, one could attain salvation. However, such views had very little popularity and were ridiculed. Of all these yogas, Mantra Yoga and Pātanjala Yoga are accepted now only as aids. All *yogas* have their own philosophies. Mantra Yoga believes that the Sound (or Sabda) Brahman is the first evolute out of the Supreme Brahman, that all sacred syllables are forms of that Supreme Sound (Logos, Word), and that one can reach the Supreme Brahman through the Sound Brahman.

But there are still other forms of Yoga. The doctrine of the Sound Brahman, for example, developed into the philosophy of music, which is called the Yoga of the Nāda (Sound) Brahman. The notes of music, when properly ordered, reflect the transcendental sound of the Nāda Brahman. So music became not merely an art of enjoyment but also a Yoga for self-realization. Then the idea that, if the Brahman is *sat*, *cit* and *ānanda* (existence, consciousness and bliss) and can be realized through knowledge, it might also be realizable through bliss (as found in the human enjoyment of sensual pleasures) struck some thinkers, and they tried to develop techniques for sublimating sensual pleasures and a corresponding philosophy of salvation. This philosophy is found in some Tantric works, but is condemned by many thinkers.

Of all the Yogas the most respected are Karmayoga, Bhaktiyoga and Jñānayoga. The Yoga of Patañjali, Hatha Yoga, and Mantra Yoga are accepted by most only as aids. The epics advocate the first three, whereas the ethical codes explain and advocate mainly Karmayoga.

Regarding educational ideals, the epics do not contain anything which cannot be found in the Vedas and the schools. But we must not forget that the epics are meant only to propagate the doctrines of the Veda.

5. MAN IN THE ORTHODOX SCHOOLS AND SYSTEMS

Introduction: It may be mentioned here that the Indian systems of philosophy did not grow out of each other but, starting more or less simultaneously, developed through mutual criticism and clarification of concepts. One should, therefore, not think that the Vedas came first, then Buddhism and Jainism, then the epics, and then the schools. The main schools—Nyāya, Vaiśeṣika, Sāṅkhya, Yoga, Mīmāmsā and Vedānta—are nearly as old as the Upaniṣads. Their aphorisms (*sūtras*) may have been composed between 400 B.C. and A.D. 400. It is difficult to fix their dates; but the logical nature of the development of the schools may be indicated.

The early Ṛgveda is assigned to approximately 2000 B.C. Its ideas were superposed on the Mohenjo-Dare culture and thought, which is assigned to some time between 3000 B.C. and 4000 B.C. The sacrificial and activistic religion and thought of the Ṛgveda became blended with some of the inward forms of religion and thought of the earlier culture, which may have impressed on the Aryan mind the significance of the inward elements contained in the Ṛgvedic religion itself and brought them into prominence. The result was the Upaniṣads, which identified the reality within man with the reality without. Of them, the *Bṛhadāranyaka Upaniṣad*, which is generally assigned to the ninth century B.C., is the earliest.

Then, since the Upaniṣads preached the necessity of transcending *karma* or action and the Brāhmaṇas the necessity of performing it according to their injunctions, a split appeared in the Vedic teaching itself and two schools of thought arose.

These schools may roughly be assigned to the fourth century B.C., or even earlier. But then the need for systematizing the thoughts of the two schools was felt. Jaimini composed his *Dharmasūtras*, which is also called *Mīmāṃsāsūtras*, and Bādarāyaṇa composed his *Brahmasūtras*, which is also called *Vedāntasūtras*. The former inquired into the nature of *dharma* or right action, whereas the latter dealt with the nature of the Brahman or the Supreme Spirit. Such, briefly, is the nature of the growth of the two Vedic systems of thought.

But the Vedāntic or Upaniṣadic thought—the Upaniṣads are called the Vedānta, because they form the ending part of the Vedas—developed further. Vedānta means not only the Upaniṣads but also the systems of philosophy based on them. I have mentioned already that, besides the Vedas, another class of sacred literature, called the Āgamas arose. Many scholars say that it grew out of the Vedas; but a few hold that it is an independent development. In any case, it is later than the Vedas. The Āgamas are mainly of two kinds. Śaiva or Pāsupata, and Vaiṣṇava or Pāñcarātra; but a third is added, namely, Śākta. The first makes Śiva identical with the Brahman of the Upaniṣads, and the second gives that high place to Viṣṇu. The third, although accepting the Brahman generally as Śiva but now and then as Viṣṇu, emphasizes the importance of Śakti or the energy aspect of the Godhead, considering it to be the feminine aspect. The Brahman has to produce the world out of itself and yet be unaffected by the act of production. How can this be possible? It is possible only if the Brahman creates the world through its Śakti or mysterious energy. Without Śakti, the Brahman is incapable of creation. We are directly in contact with Śakti, and through Śakti only can we realize the Brahman.

The Āgamas, therefore, cannot treat Śakti, which is an essential part of the Brahman, as unreal. The world, therefore, is real. Furthermore, as the creator of the world, as an agent, the Brahman becomes a person and an object of devotion and worship. The Śāktas make Śakti the wife of the Brahman and worship her. The Āgamas thus satisfied the general human urge for devotion and worship. But since the Supreme Person is identified with the Brahman of the Upaniṣads the followers of the Āgamas found it necessary to reinterpret the Upaniṣads and the *Brahmasūtras* in conformity with their own theories.

There arose, therefore, several systems of the Vedānta as expounded through commentaries. Śaṅkara and Bhāskara alone among the commentators did not utilize the Āgamas; all others did. And all the others whose commentaries are now available are later than Śaṅkara. The works of the earlier commentators are not available. Thus, after the period of the Sūtras or aphorisms, there comes the period of commentaries, lasting until the fifteenth century A.D.

But, alongside the main Vedic tradition of the Mīmāmsā and the Vedānta, there were other philosophical traditions, both orthodox and heterodox. The heterodox traditions are Jainism and Buddhism. The independent orthodox traditions are orthodox in the sense that they did not reject the Vedas as a scriptural authority. However, they did not accept either the Mīmāmsā or the Vedānta metaphysics, but thought about man and the world independently and accepted the Vedas wherever it suited them to do so. Such schools are the Nyāya, Vaiśeṣika, Sāṅkhya, and Yoga.

The Cārvāka is really heterodox in an extreme sense, in that it accepted neither ethics nor soul, nor God, nor the Veda. But it is said to have been propounded by Bṛhaspati, the orthodox priest of gods, in order to mislead the demons. The orthodox tradition has respect for the founder of the school but not for his philosophy. Another view is that it was expounded by Loka, after whom the school came to be called Lokāyata. This is a purely materialistic and Epicurean school.

All these schools have their *sūtras* or aphorisms, which may have been composed during the same period, sometime between 400 B.C. and 400 A.D. But the ideas may have been earlier; whereas some interpolations may have been later.

The epics, too, belong to about the same period. The sects and schools were criticising one another and were developing their doctrines; and the epics were being written to popularize the latter.

Man and his environment: In understanding man and his environment, the schools, except the Cārvāka, do not differ much from the Vedic conception. The idea that the world is a world of action and that, if man wants to be part of the world, he has to live a life of action according to the laws of duty was accepted by all schools, both orthodox and heterodox, except the Cārvāka. The Cārvāka materialists did not believe in the law of *karma*, in the soul, in rebirth, and in God, and taught that man should make the best of the situation.

Among the orthodox schools, the Sāṅkhya[65] (founded by Kapila, 400 B.C.) did not accept God. However, it accepted the minor gods as part of man's environment, and it accepted the Vedic injunctions about duties and sacrifices, if man wanted to remain a member of the cosmos. If man wanted salvation, he should give up everything and realize his inner spirit. What is given up is the material world. In this respect, the Sāṅkhya is similar to the Nyāya and the Vaiśeṣika. The difference lies here: whereas the Nyāya and the Vaiśeṣika left the world as a pure plurality of atoms, of time and of space, the Sāṅkhya unified all phenomena and treated them only as forms of one unconscious principle, Prakṛti. Naturally, there are no independent atoms for the Sāṅkhya. 'To give up the world' has a literal meaning, therefore, for these schools. Matter is not transformed into spirit: spirit frees itself from matter, and leaves it behind.

The Yoga of Patañjali (400 B.C.?) accepted almost every doctrine of the Sāṅkhya and, in addition, also the reality of God. The two schools are generally grouped together and are called Sāṅkhya-Yoga. Vijñānabhikṣu of the fifteenth century A.D. wrote a commentary on the *Brahmasūtras* from the point of view of the Sāṅkhya; but he could do so only by identifying the Prakṛti of the Sāṅkhya with the Sakti of the Brahman of the Upaniṣads, thereby combining the theism of the Yoga, the dualism of the Sāṅkhya, and the monism of the Upaniṣads. But the atheism of the Sāṅkhya had to be given up.

The orthodox schools which did not unify the plurality of man's environment as forms of one principle are the Mīmāmsā of Jaimini, the Nyāya of Gautama (400 B.C.?), and the Vaiśeṣika of Kanāda (600 B.C.?). All of these accepted the reality of qualitatively different atoms. Impelled by the *karma* of the souls, the atoms come together to form the world. At first the Mīmāmsā did not accept God even for supervising the process of *karma*, but later it did. The other two schools accepted God for the purpose, although the Vaiśeṣika was a little hesitant. Atoms, time, space, etc. and human *karma* in its potential and

[65] The Sāṅkhya, as expounded in the epics, accepts God and is practically the same as the philosophy of Patañjali.

kinetic states are the essential constituents of man and the world. All schools accepted the reality of the *ātman*. The environment is necessarily the world of action. From their very beginning, the Nyāya and the Vaiśeṣika preached the desirability of rising above the world action; the Mīmāmsā did so only later.

The Vedāntic schools followed the Upaniṣads, each school interpreting them in its own way. According to these schools, man's environment consists, on the whole, of the Brahman within and the material world outside. Like the Sāṅkhya, all the Vedāntic schools unified the material world into one principle, Prakṛti, and made it part and parcel of the Brahman. The Advaita of Śaṅkara said that the world had no distinct reality of its own apart from that of the Brahman, but the other Vedāntic schools gave it a distinct, and some even a separate, reality. The Advaita called it Māyā and, like the Buddhists, defined it as neither existent, nor non-existent, nor both, nor neither. But the other schools made Prakṛti a form of the Śakti of the Brahman, distinguished Māyā from both, and treated Māyā as a real form of Śakti, issuing from, and evolving Prakṛti. This will be explained in the sequel.

Thus man's environment is not merely material but also spiritual and ethical. Men are bound together in a common world either by human *karma*, or by Prakṛti, or by God, or by any two, or by all the three. For early Mīmāmsā, it is *karma* only, for the Sāṅkhya it is Prakṛti only, and for the other systems it is all three. The Sāṅkhya accepts *karma* also. In fact, no system denies the role of *Karma*. Only the Cārvāka accepts the single role of material particles. Since it does not accept the reality of anything imperceptible, even the atom, if imperceptible, is not accepted.

What is important to note here is the attempt of the Vedāntins who approached the Vedānta from the side of the Āgamas to incorporate systematically and constructively the Nyāya-Vaiśeṣika and the Sāṅkhya-Yoga into a philosophy of the Brahman. The Nyāya-Vaiśeṣika left the pluralistic material world as a mere plurality of space, time, ether and atoms. But the Sāṅkhya-Yoga reduced all of these to one principle, Prakṛti. Even then, however, the Puruṣa or *Ātman* and Prakṛti remained different and opposed; and the Puruṣas constitute a plurality, unrelated to one another. But the Āgamic Vedāntins unified them again into one Śakti and made Śakti part and parcel of the Brahman, thus conferring a unity of inter-relatedness on all the categories. This attempt led to the rejection of ultimate, independent, eternal atoms and also of the independence of space and time. The atomic theory is accepted by the Jainas, some Vaibhāṣikas who belonged to the Buddhist Hīnayāna, the Mīmāmā, the Nyāya, and the Vaiśeṣika, but not by the other Indian schools. The Cārvākas accepted something like atomism; but, consistently with their principle that nothing imperceptible is to be accepted, they could not accept imperceptible atoms.

Man and evolution: As already indicated, evolution, as understood and explained by science, is practically absent from classical Indian thought. But if the word can be used for the issuing of the world from some ultimate principle or principles, then there are some theories of the evolution of man. The Upaniṣadic account has already been given. It is accepted by all the Vedāntic schools, but with some modifications introduced from the side of the Āgamas of the Pāśupata and the Pāñcarātra. The Mīmāmsā, Nyāya, and Vaiśeṣika, which are strongly pluralistic, could not say much except that man and the world came into being when the atoms were brought together by human *karma* existing latently even during the time of the dissolution of the world. Theistic systems accepted the supervision of the workings of *karma* by God; non-theistic systems held that *karma* by itself was enough to perform the function of producing the world.

It will be useful to present the Sāṅkhya conception of evolution in some detail, because it is incorporated in all the Vedāntic schools and in the Yoga of Patañjali. The Sāṅkhya accepted two qualitatively different principles, Puruṣa or Spirit, and Prakṛti or Primeval Matter. This dualism corresponds to the qualitative dualism of Mind and Matter of Descartes. Spirits are many; but Matter is one and therefore explains the commonness of the world to all men. Spirit throws its reflection into Matter; and the latter begins to evolve the world. Matter is composed of three Guṇas (attributes): purity (transparency), activity, and lethargy, *sattva*, *rajas* and *tamas*. In its original state Matter contains these three attributes in equilibrium; but when it receives the reflection of spirit, the equilibrium is destroyed, each quality tries to dominate over the others and a series of evolutes come into being. The first evolute is Reason (*Buddhi* or *Mahat*). It is cosmic in nature and is above individuality. Out of it comes Ego (*Ahaṁkāra*). This is individuality, the centre of experience. Out of it come Mind (*manas*), the five senses (eye, ear, nose, taste and touch), the five organs of action (hands, feet, speech, the generative organ, and the excreting organ), and the five subtle elements (earth, water, fire, air, and ether). Out of the subtle elements comes the world of gross elements, which we experience in our waking state.

It is evident that the evolution given by the Sāṅkhya is not the same as that given by the *Kaṭha Upaniṣad*; yet the two have important similarities. The Yoga of Patañjali accepts the Sāṅkhya theory as it is and, though it accepts the reality of God, it leaves the relation of God to Spirits and Matter undefined and vague.

The Vedāntic schools which approach the Upaniṣads from the side of the Āgamas make the relation between God or the Brahman, on the one side, and Spirits and Matter, on the other, clearer than it is in the Yoga. The Pāñcarātra Āgamas identify the Brahman with Viṣṇu and the Pāśupata Āgamas with Śiva and derive the world, each in a slightly different way, from the Supreme Being. Both derivations incorporate the Sāṅkhya evolution with some modifications. Again, each group of Āgamas contains differences of view; but certain common general features can be given here.

According to both the Pāśupata and Pāñcarātra, evolution is of three stages, pure, mixed (pure and impure), and impure. In the last of these materiality dominates. According to the Pāśupata, the highest reality is Siva, including his creative energy, Śakti. The first act of creation is the freeing of Śakti by Siva. Śakti is of three kinds; knowledge (*jñāna*), will (*icchā*), and activity (*kriyā*). Each of these forms dominates the process in succession, and so we get three evolutes: Sadāśiva, in which desire dominates; Iśvara, in which activity dominates; and Sadvidyā, in which knowledge dominates.[66] Up to this point creation is completely pure, since ignorance has not entered the process. Now, however, there begins a creation which is both pure and impure. This is due to Māyā, which comes out of

[66] These categories (*tattvas*) cannot have English equivalents.

Sadvidyā and divides itself into five forms; Limit, Time, Attachment, Partial Knowledge, and Partial[67] Ability. These five categories—six if Māyā also is included—are called sheaths (*kañcukas*), because they sheathe the purity and infinity of the individual spirits.

Next comes the evolution of impure categories. Out of Māyā originates the distinction between Spirit and Matter, or Puruṣa and Prakṛti. Subsequent evolution follows the line of the Sāṅkhya.

The Pāśupata evolution may be given thus:—[68]

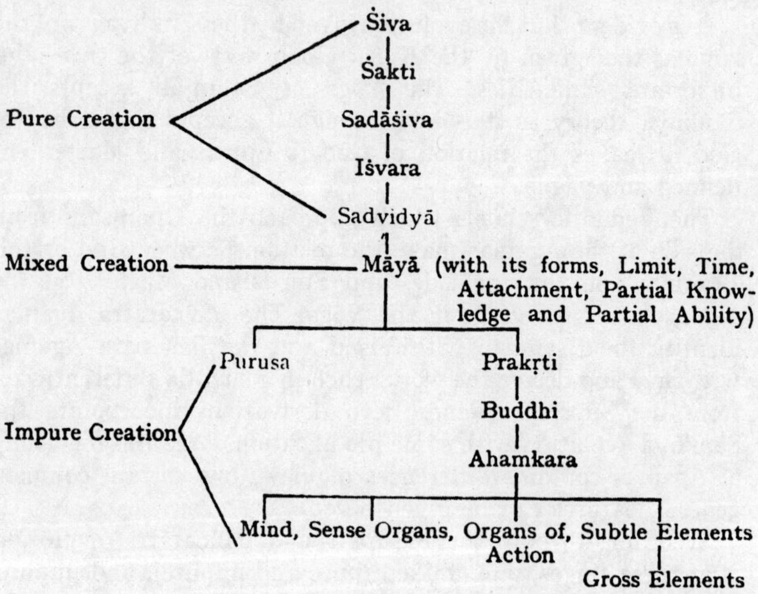

The Pāñcarātra evolution follows a similar line. The highest reality is Viṣṇu. He has six auspicious qualities: Knowledge, Lordship, Ability, Strength, Virility, and Splendour. Viṣṇu first separates his Śakti from himself; then the creation follows. In each of the subsequent three evolutes, two of the above qualities dominate. In Saṅkarṣaṇa, knowledge and strength dominate; in Pradyumna, lordship and virility dominate; and in Aniruddha, ability and splendour dominate. So far creation is pure.

[67] *Niyati*, *kāla*, *rāga*, *vidyā*, and *kalā*.
[68] See *Idealistic Thought of India*, pp. 141–4.

But at the stage of Aniruddha, the duality of Puruṣa and Prakṛti becomes manifest. Aniruddha contains not only the three qualities of *sattva*, *rajas* and *tamas*, but also Limit, and Time. This is mixed creation; it is both pure and impure. Next comes impure creation, which is similar to the evolution given by the Sāṅkhya.

The Pāñcarātra table of categories may be given thus:—[69]

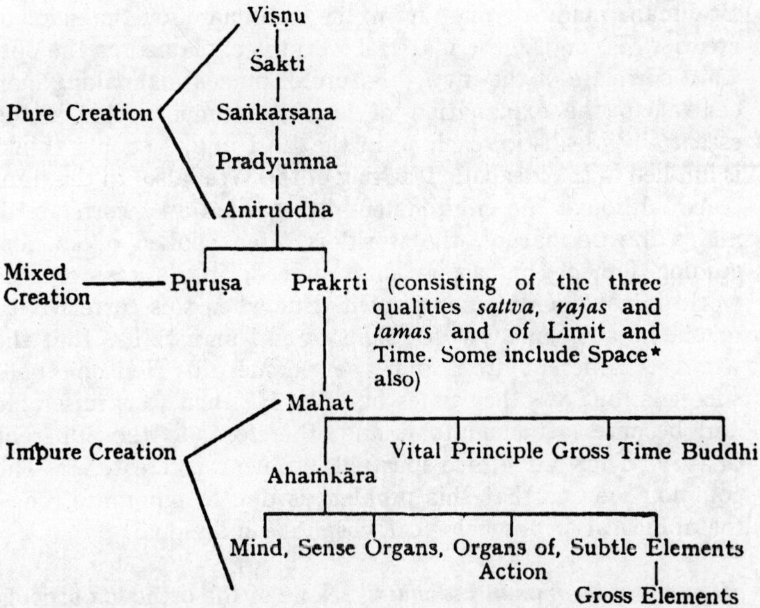

Corresponding to the doctrine of evolution, the Sāṅkhya and and Vedāntic systems have a doctrine of involution. According to the Sāṅkhya, of course, gross matter is withdrawn, through the very stages by which it came down, into the original Matter, Prakṛti; but according to the Vedāntic systems, it is withdrawn into the Absolute Spirit. Thus the downward and the upward movements constitute a cyclic process. The descent is beyond the powers of man; but once man is created, the ascent depends upon man himself, upon his desire and his efforts for self-realization. Evolution, as recognized by science, is objective evolution, the factors of which are not controlled by man. Once man is created, further process of inward reali-

[69] *Ibid.*, pp. 146–7. * Space is generally identified with aether.

zation depends on man's own efforts and belongs to the sphere of religion or spiritual development. What science calls evolution is thus a part only of involution, which, in its totality, is one half of the circular process in the Absolute Spirit.

There are a few important points to be noted here. First, the Vedāntins who interpret the Upaniṣads from the side of the Pāśaputa or the Pāñarātra do not view the world as not real. The world is a transformation of the very energy of the Brahman, made distinct from the Brahman for the sake of creation. Secondly, the material world is explained as the outward correlate of the inward nature of man, thus making man central to the explanation of his environment. This is the essentially idealistic teaching in the East and, I should think, is implied in the idealistic teaching of the West also. In the third place, although the environment is regarded as a correlate of man's inward nature, the world is often spoken of as misguiding him in his aspirations. Indeed, in its essence, the world is not alien to man's spirit. But when this correlativity or one-ness is somehow lost sight of and man thinks that the world is different from him, he pursues it. He sometimes succeeds, but at other times he fails. He then feels miserable and becomes attached to it and, therefore, to the apparent duality. Thus an ethico-spiritual problem is created.[70] The common view is that this problem is due to ignorance, be it metaphysical or psychological, cosmic or individual.

Structure of the human individual: None of the orthodox schools openly contradicts the views of the Vedas including the Upaniṣads, but all differ from each other and each interprets the Vedic utterances in its own way. So far as the constitution of man goes, the Sāṅkhya view is generally accepted by the Yoga and the Vedāntic schools whereas the Mīmāmsā view is similar to the Nyāya and the Vaiśeṣika. Each school differs from the rest on some points; and even the Mīmāmsā has similarities to the Vedānta.

Taking the former group first, since it is more in consonance with Upaniṣadic thought, we find that man is a spiritual and psycho-physical individual. But the nature of spirit,

[70] This problem is implicit in all idealism including Berkeley's. For if *esse* is *percipi*, why should man struggle for obtaining material things? Why should there be an ethical problem, if my mind is everything? Similarly, why should there be a spiritual ideal at all like the realization of God?

mind, and body is differently understood by each of these schools.

The Advaita of Śaṅkara accepts, on the whole, the evolution of man as given in the *Taittirīya Upaniṣad*, but it treats the explanation as of secondary importance because it is the explanation of a product of Māyā. The Advaita conception of the constitution of the individual also is the same as that given by the Upaniṣad in its doctrine of the levels of the *ātman* and body. These levels are interpreted by this school as sheaths (*kosas*). The original pure *ātman* is encased, first, in the sheath of bliss; this is encased in the sheath of reason, this in the sheath of mind, this in the sheath of life, and this, finally, in the sheath of matter. The original nature of the *ātman* is *saccidānanda*, existence, consciousness, and bliss. It is the same as that which, in religion, is called spirit.

In some of their works, the Advaitins combine reason (*buddhi*) and mind (*manas*) into one principle, called the inner instrument (*antahkaraṇa*), and divide it into four parts according to the functions each performs. As mind (*manas*), it analyses and synthesises the internal and external perceptions; as the ego (*ahaṁkāra*) it appropriates those experiences as its own; as reason (*buddhi*) it asserts them through affirmative and negative judgments; and as apperception (*citta*) it unifies all experiences into an interconnected whole.

The conception of the vital principle is also the same as that of the Upaniṣads. The physical body consists of the five elements. The senses and their corresponding objects are correlates.

The other Vedāntins also accept the *Taittirīya* account. But some, like Rāmānuja, do not regard the sheath of bliss as a sheath at all but say that it is the same as the *ātman*.

The Sāṅkhya conception of the nature of man is more in accordance with the *Kaṭha* categories than with the *Taittirīya* account. As the centre is to the circumference, so man is the correlate of the external world. But the centre of both man and the world is the ego, or rather, the ego comprehends both, because both issue out of it. The ego itself comes out of reason, which comes out of the Primeval Matter, Prakṛti. Some Vedāntic systems make Prakṛti part and parcel of the Brahman. The important difference between the Sāṅkhya and the *Kaṭha* is that the former leaves the opposition between spirit and matter unreconciled, whereas the latter makes matter[71] only a derivative of spirit. It is along the lines of the *Kaṭha* that some of the Vedāntic schools have reconciled the opposition by making the material principle a form of the energy aspect of the Brahman.

There is another important difference between the Sāṅkhya and the Vedānta. According to the former, the five elements come simultaneously from the ego; but according to the latter, they come out of one another: earth out of water, water out of fire, fire out of air, and air out of ether. Again, according to the *Taittirīya* account, ether comes out of the *ātman;* but according to the Sāṅkhya, all the elements come out of the ego and not out of the *ātman.*

The Sāṅkhya understands the inner instrument (*antahkaraṇa*) as consisting of three parts: mind (*manas*), ego (*ahaṁkāra*), and reason (*buddhi, citta* or *mahat*). The function of reason is asserting and determining. It has two aspects, the *sāttvika* or the pure or transparent, and the *tāmasika* or the lethargic. To the former are due merit (*dharma*), knowledge (*jñāna*), detachment (*vairāgya*), and lordship (*aiśvarya*); and to the latter are due the opposite qualities. The functions of mind and ego are the same as those of the Vedānta. By including reason in *antahkaraṇa*, the Sāṅkhya seems to maintain that, in possessing the inner instrument, man transcends his private individuality.

Another peculiarity of the Sāṅkhya doctrine of *antahkaraṇa* is that it carries the potency of both merit and demerit. Reason (*buddhi*), as included in it, is both theoretical and practical; it is both consciousness and conscience in the usual meanings of these terms.

The Sāṅkhya conception of the vital principle is different from that of the Upaniṣads, which speak of it as different from mind. As indicated previously, for both the Sāṅkhya and and Upaniṣads it is of five kinds; but the Sāṅkhya says that the vital principle is the common function of the three forms of the inner instrument (*antahkaraṇa*). Each of the three has its own function to perform; but together they perform the function of biological activity.

According to the Yoga of Patañjali, the functions of reason

[71] Matter is the *avyakta*, the unmanifest, indeterminate and unconscious principle.

(*citta*, *buddhi*) are knowledge, illusion, objectless verbal knowledge (*vikalpa* like that of the meaning of the 'of' in 'the son of X'), sleep, and memory.[72] It should be noted that sleep also is one of the functions of reason. Even if the word *citta* is equated to the whole of the inner instrument, this peculiarity of the conception of its functions is important. For the *Taittiriya*, on the other hand, sleep is deeper than reason, not one of its functions.

The Sāṅkhya understands the nature of the *ātman* as *sat* (existence) and as *cit* (consciousness) only, and does not include *ānanda* (bliss). The Vedāntic conception includes bliss also. According to the Sāṅkhya, bliss is a characteristic of the inner-instrument, particularly of reason, when it becomes pure (*sāttvika*). But the *ātman*, when it exists by itself, has no relation with reason. Reason, after all, is a product of Prakṛti; but the *ātman* is independent of Prakṛti.

The Nyāya and the Vaiśeṣika conception of the *ātman* does not include even consciousness. The *atman* in its original state is only existence (*sat*). Consciousness is merely an adventitious quality which the *ātman* gets when mind (*manas*) comes into contact with it. Reason (*buddhi*) is not an entity distinct from mind as in the Sāṅkhya, but only a quality which the *ātman* acquires now and then. Furthermore, the Sāṅkhya distinguishes reason (*buddhi*) from the *ātman*, and treats the *ātman* as conscious even when separated from reason. But the Nyāya and the Vaiśeṣika equate consciousness to *buddhi* and therefore say that, if the *ātman* is separated from *buddhi*, it becomes unconscious. Similarly, bliss (*ānanda*) does not belong to the *ātman*, because bliss also is an adventitious quality.

Mind (*manas*), according to the Nyāya-Vaiśeṣika, is atomic in size. One of its functions is synthesis of impressions and individualizing the group into a unity. For this purpose, mind has to rush from sense to sense with infinite speed; and this infinite speed is not possible unless mind itself is infinitesimally small.

The Nyāya-Vaiśeṣika treats the vital principle (*prāṇa*) as an

[72] For Indian psychological theories, see the writer's articles, 'Nature of Mind and its Activities', and 'Indian Psychology', in *Cultural Heritage of India*, Vol. III (The Ramakrishna Mission Institute of Culture, Calcutta, 1953, 2nd edition). Vācaspati is not definite in his explanation; he says that the word may mean *antahkaraṇa*. See *Pātañjala-yogasūtras* with the commentaries of Vyāsa and Vācaspati, p. 8 (Poona: Anandasrama Press, 1932).

imperceptible striving, called *jīvana-yoni-yatna*, which correspond to the conatus in Spinoza's philosophy. It is imperceptible because it works even in sleep, when mind (*manas*) does not work.

According to the Nyāya-Vaiśeṣika, the inner sense or inner instrument (*antahkaraṇa*) is only one, namely mind (*manās*). The Mīmāmsakas held a similar view, but later they introduced several differences. The most important followers of the Mīmāmsā are Prabhākara and Kumārila. According to Prabhākara, the *ātman* is just the same as it is according to the Nyāya-Vaiśeṣika; that is, it is many and, by itself, unconscious. But Kumārila holds that the *ātman* is conscious also. In this respect, his position is similar to that of the Sāṅkhya. But some Mīmāmsakas[73] like the Vedānta attribute bliss also to the *ātman*. According to Prabhākara, but not according to Kumārila, mind is atomic.

The Mīmāmsaka view on the nature of the vital principle is not clear. Perhaps they did not hold any particular view.

According to both the Mīmāmsā and the Nyaya-Vaiśeṣika, the physical body of man is a group of atoms brought together by the latent *karma*. Atoms are of four kinds, earth, water, fire, and air. While the Nyāya-Vaisśeṣika treats ether (*ākāśa*) and space as different, the Mīmāmsā treats them as one.

It is not possible in a chapter to give all the detailed differences between the schools concerning the spiritual and psycho-physical nature of man. But it will be useful if a few details are given about the relation between the *ātman* and the Brahman, particularly as understood by the Vedāntic schools. According to the Nyāya-Vaiśeṣika, Yoga, and the later Mīmāmsā—early Mīmāmsā was indifferent to the idea of the Supreme Being—the Brahman is a personal God and is completely different from the individual *ātman*. This view is accepted by Madhva, one of the Vedāntins. According to Rāmānuja, all the *ātmans* constitute, along with the material world, the body of the Brahman. According to Śaṅkara and Vallabba, the *ātmans* in their essence are completely identical with the Brahman. The other conception is that they are both identical with the Brahman and also different from it. Some Vedāntins say that they are identical in being but different in form; others maintain that they are different in being but identical in

[73] See Radhakrishnan: *Indian Philosophy*, Vol. II, p. 423.

form (similar); and the rest hold that both identity and difference obtain both as regards being and form. Bhāskara held the view that the *ātman* in its essence is the same as the Brahman; but matter is different and is also real.

Ideals of life according to the systems: The systems, because they claim to be systematizations of ideas found in the Vedas and Upaniṣads, did not present a new set of ideals. The same four—wealth, enjoyment, duty and salvation—were recognized as the highest values of life. On the nature of the first three and the methods of realizing them, the systems did not differ from each other, but accepted what was taught in the current treatises. There were works on wealth, enjoyment and duty. The last was discussed by the Mīmāmsā and the ethical codes. Whatever was prescribed in these treaties was accepted without much criticism, except where some philosophical doctrines were involved.

The question was raised whether there are four ideals of life or only three or only two; but, generally, the orthodox schools accepted all four. All the schools accepted the view that the nature of future births depends on the nature of actions performed by man in his present and past lives. But the question as to how the actions determine future births was answered differently by the different schools. On this point the Mīmāmsā and the Nyāya carried on a long controversy. The Mīmāṃsā, particularly as interpreted by Prabhākara, holds that action performed now produces in the *ātman apūrva* or *adṛṣta*, the Unseen, that the latter remains as a latent force and produces the effects when the opportunity comes. But the Nyāya does not accept the principle of the Unseen, and says that the qualities of merit and demerit of actions themselves enter the soul, and that, according to these qualities, God apportions the results when the occasion comes.

This difference looks as if it were verbal and unimportant. But I think that there is something more to it. The early Mīmāmsā did not accept God but said that human action itself was enough to create the necessary circumstances for the enjoyment of its fruits. Action itself, therefore, has to enter the *ātman*, though in a subtle form. Or it has to produce a righteous creative force in the *ātman* itself. But according to the Nyāya, God supervises the creation of the world and future births according to the merit and demerit of man's actions. Merit and demerit are qualities of the *ātman*. So action itself need not enter the *ātman*, but only its quality of merit or demerit. However, later Mīmāmsā accepted the reality of God. But Prabhākara argued according to the original Mīmāmsā.

As regards the nature of salvation, the schools differed from one another in very important respects. First, it has been the general view of the Vedas and many Vedāntins that one should take to the fourth *āśrama*, that is, *sannyāsa*, and renounce the world only after going through the first three. But Śaṅkara, very likely influenced by Buddhism and Jainism, maintained that one could renounce the world even without going through the first three *āśramas*, if one felt disinterested in the world. In the second place, the nature and methods of salvation differed according to the conception of the relation between the *ātman* and the Brahman. If the relation is one of complete identity, as in the Advaita of Śaṅkara and Kasmir Śaivism, the way of knowledge (*jñānamārga*) is preached; for what is needed for salvation is the conscious realization of the identity and the removal of that difference which is but the result of the ignorance of the identity. If the relation is difference or contains an element of difference, then, generally, the way of devotion (*bhaktimārga*) is preached. Even here, however, the realization of one's original nature is necessary, but this nature contains an element of difference. The realization is possible by removing the ignorance of one's original nature. But this removal is again possible only through devotion and self-surrender to the Supreme Being, which is the Brahman. Vallabba, among the Vedāntins, preached identity and yet advocated the path of devotion; for love enables man to become one with the object loved. Early Mīmāmsā did not believe in God. Even the later Mīmāmsā placed the path of action (*karmamārga*) over the other two; for it believed that the life of the individual is necessarily a life of action. But this action has to be performed in complete self-surrender to the Divine Spirit and without any appropriation of the agency and the results. It has already been mentioned that this teaching is the usual one given by the epics and the ethical codes.

Even those thinkers who emphasize the way of knowledge insist upon ethical preparation of the individual. Śaṅkara classifies the main ethical qualities of the individual seeking salvation into four: discrimination between the eternal and the non-eternal, renunciation of enjoyment in this world and the next, the group of six qualities, and desire for salvation. The six qualities are: first, tranquility, which consists of keeping the mind in a controlled state by withdrawing it from the objects of enjoyment; second, subduing the activities of both the sense organs and the organs of action and keeping them in their proper places; third, withdrawing the mind from all external functions; fourth, endurance of all miseries without grief and retaliation; fifth, faith in the teachings of the teacher and the scriptures; and sixth, fixing the mind, without giving it any induglence, in the pure Brahman. The four main ethical qualities are also the means for attaining salvation.

Influence of the schools on religious traditions:—As already mentioned, there are several sects of which Śaivism, Vaiṣṇavism and Saktism are important. All religious sects preach salvation as the highest aim of life and all say that it lies in the realization of the original nature of the *ātman* and its relation to the Brahman. Only a few misguided sects believed that salvation could be had by taking drugs, such as mercury. To the three important sects we should add the Smārtas, who do not form a really religious sect but are the Brahmins who accept the scriptural authority of the Vedas only. For instance, there are Śaivas, Vaiṣṇavas, and Śāktas among all the castes; but I have not come across any Smārtas except among the Brahmins.

Man's life is understood by all as containing misery, though they will not accept that life is nothing but misery. All say that the imperfections and shortcomings of life can be removed completely only by realizing one's relation with God or the Brahman. Salvation means gaining eternal life.

On the whole and in general, the followers of the Nyāya and the Vaiśeṣika are Śaivas, whereas the followers of the Sāṅkhya (theistic) and Yoga are Vaiṣṇavas. The Vedāntins include both and the Smārtas. The followers of the Mīmāmsā are also Smārtas, whether they do or do not accept God or the Brahman. In fact, the Vedānta also is called Mīmāmsā; but the Mīmāmsā as expounded by Jaimini on the basis of the first two parts of the Veda is called Pūrva (Prior) Mīmāmsā and that expounded by Bādarāyaṇa on the basis of the last two parts of the Veda is called Uttara (Posterior) Mīmāmsā.

Again, every religious sect has its own philosophy, which is either non-dualism of the *ātman* and the Brahman, or qualified non-dualism, or dualism, or dualism-cum-non-dualism. These differences of view can be found among the Śaivas and the Vaiṣṇavas. The Śāktas generally seem to be non-dualists. The schools thus contributed philosophies to the sects.

Furthermore, Śāktism in one form or another is associated with both Saivism and Vaiṣṇavism; for both accepted Śakti as the creative energy of Śiva and Viṣṇu and made it their consort, giving different names. The consort of Śiva is called Durga, Kali, etc.; and the consort of Viṣṇu Lakṣmi. For devotees, the wife is as real as the husband; often she is more important, because a woman's heart can be more easily appealed to. In philosophy, too, the creative energy is as real as the creator. Only the Advaita of Śaṅkara denies separate reality to Śakti.

In spite of elaborate external worship and ritual developed by these religious traditions, by all of them, the Brahman or the Divine Spirit, whatever be its relation with the individual *ātman*, is conceived to be the innermost core of the human individual. Prescribed religious practices are meant to turn man's outwardness inward. The schools added nothing to the original religious thought except by way of clarification and systematization. It should be kept in mind that in India, not only did philosophy originate in religion but also that it has remained religious. One may therefore well say that the religious sects contributed the schools.

One more point needs to be mentioned. What is the nature of salvation in the religious sects? The Vedāntic systems contain theories about the relation between the *ātman* and the Brahman. There are very few people who follow the atheistic Sāṅkhya as a religion. And no one has been found who follows the Nyāya and the Vaiśeṣika as religions. The followers of these two philosophies, it has been said, are generally Śaivas, that is, they worship Śiva. But they do not seem to think, in their religious beliefs, that their *ātmans* will be without consciousness and bliss if they attain salvation. On this point, they follow perhaps some pluralistic Āgamas of the Pāśupata rather than the strict Nyāya-Vaiśekika philosophy. Salvation, according to all the schools which treat matter as different from spirit, consists in freeing spirit from matter; but, according to those schools for which matter is somehow part and parcel of spirit or has no reality apart from spirit, it consists in transforming matter into spirit or into its original form as part of spirit. The former schools may be interpreted as preaching escapism, and the latter as preaching transvaluation and sublimation. Popular renderings of philosophies often saw no difference between these forms of salvation. Particularly after the idea that the world contains much misery came to be widely accepted, popular renderings of philosophies treated both kinds of salvation as giving up the world of misery. But there has been a great change in the philosophical outlook of the present.

Education:—The orthodox schools did not develop a new theory of the nature and ideals of education. They accepted what was contained in the Vedas and later literature. Man has to be trained for realizing the four ideals of life, the highest of which is salvation. The philosophies of the schools are concerned with the nature and method of salvation, and not with the first three ideals. The only exception is the Mīmāmsā school of Jaimini, which is concerned with the nature of duty or right action.

6. CONCLUSION

I have abstained from giving many details of the philosophies, which would be needed for a systematic and detailed study of the concept of man in Indian thought. Even then the foreign reader will find a number of new terms and new concepts. But they cannot be avoided in any book on comparative philosophy, which has to include all the four great traditions. However, to facilitate understanding, I may present the general trends of thought concerning man, found in ancient and classical literature. I have given some details so that the reader may have some knowledge of the concepts and doctrines in their contexts, and his feeling that I might be misleading him may not be too strong. Some western philosophers may be impatient with many of the details given. But there have been many hasty generalizations, wrong interpretations, and vague reading of western doctrines into the Indian even by Indian writers. It is safer therefore to give some details, however strange the terms and concepts look. Their strangeness itself may make one pause, and prevent him from rushing to a hasty conclusion. India is acquainted with western philosophy but not with the Chinese, in spite of China being a next-door neighbour, absorbing and preserving Buddhism for a long time. The Chinese terms and concepts are as strange to the Indian reader as the Indian are to the western reader. The aim of comparative philosophy is to remove this strangeness and enable people all over the world to appreciate each other's way of life and thought. But for this appreciation to be possible, some details need to be studied.

(i) Whatever be the earliest conception of man in the Ṛgveda, the idea that he is a wayfarer, a *mārgayāyin*, has been made popular after Buddha enunciated the doctrine of the Way (*mārga*) as one of the four noble truths. Asaṅga, a Buddhist of about the second century A.D., called the Buddhist way *jñānamārga* or the way of knowledge. Jainism, the other heterodox school, and the orthodox schools formulated their own ways. Ultimately, three ways have been accepted as important; the way of knowledge, the way of devotion, and the way of action.

For all the schools, man is a wayfarer; the way, however, lies not from one point of space to another, but from the world of outward reality to the inward realm. The direction of the process of the world is from the outward to the inward. Life is the inwardness which matter attains; and mind is the inwardness which life attains in the process of the world we observe. The being of man belongs to this process, and the success of life is proportional to the inwardness he deliberately pursues and attains. For philosophy of life, this process of the world from the outward to the inward is most important.

(ii) According to the Mīmāmsā, which is the philosophy of the first two parts of the Veda, and according to Buddhism, which did not accept the authority of any part of the Veda, the concept of Dharma is the most important concept of philosophy. It is difficult to translate the word. In the terminology of the Indian schools, it has many meanings: quality, entity, nature, duty, merit, religion, law, justice, and even reality.[74] The

[74] See *Idealistic Thought of India*, pp. 281 foll.

important meaning for the Mīmāmsā is action (*karma*) according to the injunctions of the Veda; and according to Buddhism, it is the ultimate law and nature of the universe and is above action. There is a very significant connection between these conceptions. According to the Mīmāmsā, what binds man and the universe together and supports them is action (*karma*) according to the Vedic injunctions; and this *karma* is the same as Dharma. The world and man's being contain material particles or atoms; but these are brought together and supported by Dharma. According to Buddhism, the essential nature of the universe is Dharma, which is sometimes also called Tathatā (Suchness), which means the way of the process of the world and, therefore, of man. The nature of man is his *dharma*, the way of the process of his being. Thus, to act according to Dharma is, for man, to act according to his essential nature.

But while the Mīmāmsā conceived Dharma as action and so the essence of human nature as containing activity, process (*karmamayam puruṣah*), Buddhism conceived Dharma as the way of this process, as an adverb of this activity, which is itself permanent and fixed, while everything else changes. Ultimately, it is *nirvāṇa*. Thus Dharma, whether it is *karma* (activity) or is beyond activity, constitutes the essence of man; and so man has to act according to Dharma. However, the higher conception of Dharma is not elaborated by the orthodox schools,[75] only by Buddhism.

Because Dharma is the highest reality, the realization of which is the same as salvation, and because it is also one of the four values of life, it includes in some of its usages all the four values of life. Thus, to acquire wealth also belongs to the nature of man.

(iii) All the Indian schools of thought, except perhaps the Cārvākas, exhort man to know his true self. Even the Cārvākas may be said to make the same exhortation, if we consider that, according to them, the self is the physical body. Man goes after the values of this world and of the next. For whom are these values meant? They are, for the self. At death the physical body is left in this world and, therefore, cannot be the

[75] It is interesting to note that the word *dharma* is used by the Jainas in the sense of motion also, and the interpretation can be appreciated by us in this context.

self which enjoys the values of the next world. Then, what is it? At this point the Socratic ideal, 'Know thyself', becomes also the ideal of Indian philosophy.

But there is a difference. Perhaps Socrates would not have said: 'Know thy self', thus separating 'self' from 'thy'. But the Indian thinkers separated them; for, according to them, the self is ultimately not the body. There is indeed a sense in which, according to Socrates, it is not the body. If the distinction between the rational soul and the irrational is Socratic and if the rational soul alone is eternal, then the true self will be the rational soul, not the lower; and in that case, man's true self will not be the body, but reason. Even then, however, according to Indian thought, the self (*ātman*) is higher than reason.

(iv) Although both spiritual life and rational life are universal, according to Indian thought, the former is higher than the latter. Spiritual life is universal because spirits (*ātmans*), even for the schools that accepted their plurality, have the same nature. Rational life is universal because reason (*buddhi*), according to all schools, has the same objective reference. According to the Sāṅkhya, reason is cosmic and is called *Mahat* (the Great, Logos). All the Vedāntic schools give it a higher place than they give the ego (*ahaṁkāra*). The *Kaṭha Upaniṣad* gives it a higher place than to mind, but postulates a Cosmic Reason even higher than the individual's reason. Even so, however, both have rationality in common. The Nyāya-Vaiśeṣika gives rationality a higher place than to the process of mind, but does not treat reason as an entity.

Another important point to note is that reason (*buddhi*) is not understood by the Indian schools as merely intellectual but also as ethical and even aesthetic. Only in the Nyāya, the Vaiśeṣika, and the Mīmāmsā, do we find a purely intellectual conception. According to the Sāṅkhya, the characteristics of *Buddhi* include not only cognitive assertion but also *dharma* (merit), and *adharma* (demerit). The Vedāntic schools follow the Sāṅkhya on this point. According to both, the aesthetic pleasure which man enjoys belongs to reason. On all these points there are differences of view, but the general tendency is to treat the highest rational life as ethical and aesthetic also. In the language of the Sāṅkhya and the *Bhagavadgīta*, such a life will be *sāttvika* existence, as distinct from the *rājasika* and the *tāmasika*. *Sāttvika* existence is the existence in which the *sattva* quality of Prakṛti, Māyā or Śakti predominates. In such life, virtue is knowledge and knowledge virtue.

(v) If there is a sense or a state of life for which knowledge is virtue and virtue knowledge, then there is a sense in which to know is to become. Certainly, if I *know* the pen in front of me, I do not *become* the pen. But the Upaniṣads say that he who knows the Brahman becomes the Brahman.[76] This can be true only when 'to know' implies 'to transform one's being'; and this again can be true only when the object to be known is one's innermost self. Where knowledge implies transformation of one's being, it comes to have ethical and spiritual significance. When we see this point, we can appreciate the significance of *jñānamārga* or the way of knowledge. Knowledge in this sense is not a pale hovering awareness but is also the being of the object known. But such knowledge cannot be had without inner ethical and spiritual transformation. And this is the reason for laying great emphasis on the ethical qualities of the person following the way of knowledge.

(vi) If we take the general trend of the schools of Indian philosophy, the highest aim of life is not necessarily the realization of the highest personality, as usually understood. According to the Advaita of Śaṅkara, the highest reality, that is, the Brahman, is suprapersonal, and the individual is exhorted to realize his oneness with it. But according to Rāmānuja, the Brahman is a personal God and is different from the individual *ātmans*. Man is still being exhorted to realize the *ātman*; but the *ātman* is now not a personality in the psychological sense in which the word is generally understood. It is not, for instance, an integration of all the characters which a human being possesses. These characteristics are, rather, forms of Prakṛti, and man is exhorted to disentangle himself from Prakṛti.

I believe that the question of personality and its development through integration is outside the scope of the problem of salvation as understood by Indian philosophers. This is certainly true not only of the Sāṅkhya and the Vedānta, but also of the Nyāya and the Vaiśeṣika, and of Jainism and

[76] *Brahmavidbrahmaiva bhavati.*

Buddhism. For the Nyāya and the Vaiśeṣika, the *ātman* or self in its pure state is beyond the reach of mind (*manas*) and intellect (*buddhi*), and so is not a personality, as psychology understands the word. Jainism exhorts man to get rid of all *karma* (action) and the jiva in such a state can hardly be called a well-integrated unity of psychological characters. For Buddhism, salvation lies in the liquidation of personality (*pudgala*), not in its integration.

But the question of personality is relevant so far as rational life is concerned; and rational life includes the ethical also. Personality extends from matter up to the stage of *buddhi*—or, at the most, up to what the Advaitins call the causal body; but it has little significance beyond. Sometimes the Upaniṣads speak of the knot of the heart (*hṛdayagranthi*), which is a knot of the urges, instincts, etc. working through man and making him what he is. But he is exhorted to cut the knot and go beyond. Personality is the limitation of man's conscious being to this 'knot of the heart'.

(vii) But it may be said that the central aim of Indian philosophy is the discovery of the true nature of the 'I', of the basis of the experience of the 'I'. The 'I' is ultimately regarded as the inwardness of the physical body. It maintains itself through a process of inwardness, the 'I' consciousness being the activity of this inwardization. It should be pointed out, however, that the Upaniṣads do not say that inwardness is a process. Had they done so, they would have propounded something like the modern theory of evolution. But we shall not be far wrong in deriving such a theory from the Upaniṣadic doctrine.

(viii) If we take Indian philosophy as a whole, then the most important of the developments show that the general trend is towards idealism and monism. Idealism is obvious in the almost universal acceptance of the correlativity of the senses and their objects. This correlativity is accepted both by the pluralistic and the monistic schools. The same element polarises itself into the sense and its object. The monistic systems go farther and derive the elements themselves from the *Ātman* or the Brahman. This correlativity and the drive towards monism are found even in Buddhism.

The western distinction between epistemological idealism and epistemological realism, is of secondary importance in Indian philosophy because both views have been found to be compatible with the correlativity mentioned. For instance, both are found among the sub-schools of the Advaita of Śaṅkara.[77] Although it is accepted that the object experienced is different from the sense experiencing it, it is also accepted that both are polarized forms of one and the same element. In Greek philosophy Democritus held this view but did not draw the idealistic implications involved. The idealism of the Vedānta is a metaphysical idealism, which was developed out of a kind of theological or theistic idealism found in the Vedas.

The significance of this idealism for a study of the nature of man and his place in the universe is that, although man feels himself an alien in the universe, his feeling is only apparent, not true. Philosophically he is the link between the Supreme as the inward reality and matter as the outward reality. Theologically he is the field of the activity of the gods of the universe, the agency through which the Supreme Deity wished to control the activities of the lower deities. The theological aspect of the doctrine may be ignored by us. Its philosophical import, however, i.e. the centrality of man, is of great significance for philosophy: man is the centre of the universe.

(ix) Another idea which Indian philosophy brings to the forefront is that evolution can be explained in two ways. Matter can be derived from the Infinite Spirit via the finite spirit, mind and life; or the Infinite Spirit can be derived from matter via life, mind and the finite spirit. There is no *a priori* reason why evolution should be explained only in one direction. No scientist will now say that matter is perceived by our senses; nor will a theologian say that God can be perceived by the senses. Men differ from one another in their emotional experiences and in the perspectives of the objects they see; yet the material world is said to be the same for all. Similarly, God or the Supreme Spirit is the same for all. Thus, if matter exists, it is the common ground for inter-subjective intercourse; and if God exists, He is also the common ground for intersubjective intercourse. For our experience both are equally objects of inference, not of perception. We have the forms:

[77] *Idealistic Thought of India*, pp. 103 foll.

Spirit, Mind, Life, and Matter; and we have to understand their relation in terms of evolution. Then evolution can theoretically be explained in either direction. Explanation from spirit to matter meets our ethical and spiritual requirements; and the opposite explanation meets our scientific requirements. Thus each serves a useful purpose. Until human knowledge is perfect and absolute, I do not see how either can be rejected.

(x) So far as its social orientation goes, Indian ethics seems to be less developed than the western. But the psychological discipline needed for self-control, as developed in Yoga, is more systematic and elaborate than it is in western philosophy. Discipline is all geared to self-realization, and is, therefore, mainly individualistic. This observation holds true particularly of all developments of thought after the early Vedic period. On the whole, however, Indian ethical discipline may be interpreted in two ways: positively it is the realization of one's self (*ātman*); negatively it is liquidation or complete surrender of the ego and its activities. Except for the Nyāya, the Vaiśeṣika, and the Mīmāmsā, the ego is different from the *ātman*, and so realization of the *ātman* is compatible with liquidation of the ego. For these three schools as well as for Jainism, the aim of discipline is to lift the ego above all activity. For Buddhism, the goal is liquidation of the ego, whatever be the remainder after liquidation.

(xi) The avowed aim of traditional Indian education is spiritual realization. Yet, neither the orthodox nor, to a degree, the heterodox institutions neglected secular education. But the gulf between the two kinds of education grew wider in later thought because the systems cared very little about secular life and concerned themselves with the theories of salvation. Search for truth and search for salvation were considered to be identical.

However, we may detect some important ideas. In the conception of *jñānamārga* (way of knowledge), we may notice the idea that the more the knowledge acquired, the greater is the transformation of man's being towards the Supreme, and so the greater also is the surrender and the attuning of oneself to the ways of the Supreme. Thus, the more the knowledge one has, the greater is the self-surrender and *vice versa*. The latter, of course, is implied in *bhaktimārga* (way of devotion) also. *Karmamārga* (way of action) does not imply that knowledge necessarily leads to this transformation, which will be the transformation of one's character also. It insists, therefore, upon performance of action, and regards this as the proper index to whatever knowledge motivates action.

During the Vedic period, the whole universe was regarded as the training ground of man, for producing inwardness. Deliberately planned education was to help accelerate the natural inward process. Man was to realize that he was intimately connected with the world of gods and men. But, later, when intensified spiritual individualism developed, man was taught how to be indifferent to the many relationships. Even then, however, a feeling of intimate and ultimate one-ness with the universe was fostered.

(xii) After the Upaniṣads were composed, a split in Vedic philosophy developed, the first two parts of the Veda preaching a way of action and the other two parts teaching a life above action. The attempt to remove the split was made, not with the help of metaphysics, but with the help of the ideas of maturity and immaturity of man's mind. Thus, man is brought in to justify the teachings of the Veda. But the implication of reinstating man at the centre of Vedic thought has not been fully brought out. One implication is that Vedic philosophy is a guide to life *for man*. That it is a philosophy *of man* is also involved in treating man, both in religion and philosophy, as the meeting point of gods and cosmic forces. It is now necessary to have one system of metaphysics which reconciles the Mīmāmsā and the Vedānta; otherwise, we cannot have one philosophy for all the parts of the Veda. Here arises the need for possible new developments of philosophy in India.

(xiii) In the philosophies, as finally articulated and systematised, the highest kind of education is that which enables man to realize his deepest inward self. We have seen that the process of this realization corresponds to the process of involution of the material world into spirit, which corresponds roughly to the direction of the process of evolution given by science. If matter evolved life, and life mind and so man, then what is the next step in natural evolution? Philosophers like S. S. Alexander spoke of Deity. But traditional Indian philosophy says that Deity is already there and is therefore not something to come into being. Nature's process, it would say, stops with man; man has now to push the process upwards by his own efforts. The process can be pushed up not by producing a new kind of being but by deepening man's inwardness. The Upaniṣads will support this way of understanding evolution.

The role of nature in evolution is to produce inwardness, after bringing together some material particles. Life is the inwardness of matter, and mind is the inwardness of life. By deepening inwardness, man can realize the spirit within himself and bring it to the level of Deity. The highest education is that which helps man in deepening inwardness and is therefore that which completes the process of natural evolution. What the Sāṅkhya, the Upaniṣads, the Pāśupata, and the Pāñcarātra call involution is something to be produced deliberately by man. Prakṛti withdraws herself from Purusa only after man realizes that he is essentially Puruṣa, but not any of the evolutes of Prakṛti.

For the Upaniṣads, the Pāśupata, and the Pāñcarātra, evolution and involution are the two halves of a circular process, starting from Deity and ending with Diety. For the Sāṅkhya, Prakṛti or Primeval Matter occupies the place of the Deity, and the process starts and ends with Prakṛti. Spirit is outside this process, although necessary for it. It supplies only its reflection to Prakṛti for starting the process.

(xiv) Man is thus a highly privileged creature with the power to move up to the Diety, on the one side, and to resolve himself into matter, on the other. The latter power is explicitly accepted by the Sāṅkhya in its idea of *prakṛtilaya* or merging in Primeval Matter. Such merging, however, is not considered to be salvation. But what is man? Is he the spirit (*ātman*), the soul (*jīva*), mind, life, or physical body? I think that, in the opinion of the Upaniṣads, he is all these put together in an integral form. But the word *puruṣa* may be misleading; for it means both the *ātman* and man. One may then jump to the conclusion that, according to the Upaniṣads, man is the *ātman*. It is a paradox that man, as containing spirit, is more than spirit. But pious philosophers may say that the welfare of man is the welfare of spirit, or something similar to it, which may sound sublime but unhelpful so far as the life of man as man is concerned. The safest interpretation seems to be that man is an integral unity of the levels given in the *Kaṭha* and the *Taittiriya Upaniṣads*, and to say that it is the duty of science to study how the integrality is attained, and that it is the duty of religion to show how it can be utilized for raising man's consciousness to the level of the Supreme Deity. Ethics and all the other sciences incidental to the life of man in society have also to show how this integrity can best be utilized in the different spheres. Indian philosophers might not have accomplished this varied task adequately and to the satisfaction of the twentieth-century man, but that is no reason for reading too much into the classical philosophies. To do so—a practice, which unfortunately has become very widespread, particularly in response to western criticisms—will lead one to miss much that is peculiar to Indian thought, and much of what is thus missed may contain elements of permanent value.

CHAPTER V

Comparisons and Reflections

P. T. RAJU

I. INTRODUCTION

READERS of the preceding four chapters may have seen that the aim of man's life on earth is not conceived in the same way by the four traditions. There are similarities and differences. Each tradition itself contains many views. In this chapter on comparisons it is not possible to consider every view, but only the characteristic ones. For almost every doctrine of Indian philosophy, it has been observed, there is a corresponding doctrine in Western thought, and vice versa. But while some views are well developed in the one tradition, others are well developed in other traditions. Almost all doctrines are, however, touched by each in one way or the other. Even those views which are well developed in both India and the West are developed often in the context of some major problems, which frequently are not the same. Again, from different doctrines the same conclusion is drawn; and other times from the same doctrine different conclusions are drawn. For comparative philosophy this is a very significant fact to note. It may look illogical; but life and experience are so complicated that the veins of thought running through them may take devious and opposite ways and yet arrive at the same terminus; or they may take the same or parallel ways and, entering a little knot somewhere, branch off towards opposite ends.

We should not forget that a philosophical tradition is not one system of philosophy but several. It is very easy to forget this and ask what does Chinese, Indian or Greek philosophy say about this or that problem. I am not sure that even Jewish philosophy constitutes one system; for even if we consider only the orthodox Jewish philosophers, we can find differences of view. But, on the whole, Jewish thought seems to be more compact than are the others and contains not as many opposing schools as do they. The chapter can take only some dominant and characteristic views into consideration, and only with reference to the problem of the concept of man. It is an open question as to what are the characteristic views. On this the reader may disagree with the author. Even then, however, it will be useful to compare what the author considers to be characteristic, in choosing which he has followed the opinions generally expressed by recognised authorities. Others interested in the problem may make other comparisons. If they do, it is hoped that this chapter may be helpful as a stimulus.

2. AIMS OF PHILOSOPHY

If we take the utterances of the important philosophers of each tradition into consideration, the aim of philosophy is expressed in different ways, although every philosophy claims to be rational. 'Man, know thyself'; this may be said to be the first advice of all four traditions. Socrates said it in so many words. The Upaniṣads did the same when they exorted man: *ātmānam viddhi* (know thy self). *Ātman* does not mean merely the metaphysical self but also reason, mind, the vital principle, and the physical body. This advice would not have been given if it had been thought that man was right in taking himself to be what he was in his unreflective moments. Confucius also gave the same advice. He said that in order to organize one's state well, one had ultimately to study the nature of things. But 'things' meant for the Chinese philosophers human relationships originating out of the nature of man. So the study of things meant the study of the nature of man. Similarly, the Jewish thinkers wanted to know the meaning and significance of man with reference to God; man is a subject in search of a predicate, in the words of Dr Heschel; he is a 'That' in search of a 'What'. So all philosophies aim at understanding the meaning of man and the significance of his life.

We may say that, in the above sense, all philosophies aim at finding out a way of life. The recent differentiation according to which Western philosophy is a mode of thought and Indian philosophy a way of life does not seem to be accepted by many

Western philosophers. The differentiation came into vogue because of some recent conceptions of philosophy as a mere intellectual pursuit, as nothing more than an attempt at a conceptual reconstruction of the world; and it is being narrowed down to an intellectual understanding of thought only. But from the time of the Greeks to Bertrand Russell, the idea that philosophy is to inspire and infuse a way of life has repeatedly been expressed, although some philosophies are only indirectly connected with that aim and do not take it seriously. But one would hardly maintain that Greek philosophy is not directly concerned with a way of life. The Sophists, to be sure, ridiculed the earlier philosophers for being too preoccupied with questions about the origin of the world. For what and how does it matter to man and his life if the world originated out of water, fire, or air? It is not very important for man and his life to be informed about this. But, as Cornford says,[1] even for the earlier philosophers the quest for the origin of the world is a religious quest in order to have communion with the origin. When Empedocles jumped into Mount Etna—if the story is true—he was searching for communion with his creator, however wrongly and physically conceived. Communion with the creator is a life's aim. Hence, Greek philosophy in its beginnings also can be viewed as inculcating a way of life and not merely as a mode of thought.

Another differentiation that has become popular recently is that philosophy, as the word connotes, is only love of wisdom for the West, but that the corresponding word in Sanskrit, *Darśana*, means direct perception, which is perception of the Supreme Being. I think that the etymological meaning of the words is misleading. Not all Indian philosophers claim to have direct perception of the Supreme Spirit. No one will say that Cārvāka materialism, although called a *darśana*, exhorts man to perceive the Supreme Spirit, because it denies such a being. *Darśana*, of course, means perception. Even supposing that all schools of Indian philosophy preach direct perception of God, preaching is not the same as perception. No theory is needed if God can be directly presented. The meaning of the word *darśana*, when it means philosophy, is 'view'; hence, a view of the world, of man and his life, and of God, if He is accepted. Just as 'view' means perspective, opinion, theory, etc., *darśana*

[1] See *Greek Religious Thought* (London: J. M. Dent & Sons Ltd., 1923).

also means perception, perspective, opinion, theory, and doctrine. The synonymous words for ***darśana*** are ***mata, siddhānta***, etc. which mean doctrine, theory, opinion. ***Darśana***, when referred to the systems, does not mean perception of God, but a vision of reality. ***Darśana***, one may add, is what leads to the perception of reality; and if reality is God, then it is what leads to the perception of God. However, we should not depend too much on the etymological meanings of words, which may lead us to seeing differences even where they do not exist. Why do we not say that the philosophy of Plotinus, which is very similar to that of the Vedānta of India, is the same as the perception of God? Philosophy, whatever words are used in the different languages, means a theory of man, of his life, of the world, by possessing which man becomes wise and can plan his life accordingly.

But the question now is: wise for what purpose? Here the philosophies seem to give different emphases on different ideals of life. Greek philosophy, on the whole, wants man to be wise by cultivating knowledge. Dr Wild writes that, according to Socrates, 'the chief obligation of every man is first to tend his own soul, and then, so far as this is possible, to help others in tending theirs.'[2] Tending one's soul, for Socrates, is cultivating knowledge; for virtue is knowledge. For Confucius the aim of philosophy is to make men virtuous. He speaks of 'illustrous virtue', 'supreme virtue', and of cultivating virtue. Indeed, Confucius says that one can know what it is to be virtuous by studying human relationships. Thus virtue, one may say, is based upon knowledge. But while the Greeks developed a systematic theory of knowledge and of the methods of obtaining it, Confucius and the later Chinese philosophers did not care to develop any elaborate theory of knowledge.

While the aim of Greek philosophy is to make man wise and that of Chinese philosophy is to make him virtuous, the aim of Indian philosophy is to enable him to obtain salvation, which is communion with the Supreme Spirit, or realization of the *ātman*. This is a characteristic of the major philosophies of India. These schools regard philosophy as *ātmavidyā* or *adhyātmavidyā*, that is, the science of knowledge of the *ātman*, which is the highest self in man. Wisdom or virtue is not excluded; for one who is serious about the realization of the *Ātman* has to

[2] Chapter I, p. 62 (the present work).

be wise and virtuous. But *ātmavidyā* may be exclusive of the knowledge of things other than the *Ātman*; whereas one who is wise, in the general sense of the term, is supposed to know much about the world and about men; and the virtuous man, according to Confucius, is expected to know much about human relationships.

The aim of Jewish philosophy is to find out the meaning of man in relation to God. As Dr Heschel[3] puts it, it is not enough that man knows God; it is necessary that he is known to God. What is emphasized is not merely man's knowledge of God but also God's knowledge of man and man's knowledge that he is known to God. One may say that communion is a relation which holds both ways; man in communion with God and God in communion with man. The Jewish religion lays particular emphasis on the latter relation. Dr Heschel[4] says that the Jewish religion may be defined as the awareness of God's interest in man. This emphasis is not found in Greek or Chinese thought, and even in Indian thought it is not strong. That God loves man is enunciated by philosophies like those of Rāmānuja and Madhva; but that man should know that God is interested in him is only implied, not explicitly propounded. All religious philosophy implies that, in his ethical activity, man is watched by God, but this idea is not brought to the forefront equally by all.

3. THE IDEAL MAN

The ideal man for Greek philosophy is the lover of wisdom, even if not the wise man. There are indeed differences of opinion as to who exactly is such a man, even if we take Socrates, Plato, and Aristotle as the only representatives of Greek thought. All three exhort man to tend his soul, by which they mean the development of the rational part. Aristotle differs from Plato on some points; but even then both attach the highest importance to rational knowledge and its cultivation. Aristotle subordinates practical knowledge to theoretical knowledge.[5] Plato not only places reason far above sense but also wants that the lower parts of the soul be guided by reason.

Just as we speak of the wise men of Greece, so we speak of

[3] Chapter II, pp. 119 and 122 (the present work).
[4] Chapter II, p. 123 (the present work).
[5] Chapter I, p. 92 (the present work).

the saints of India. Christianity has its saints and Greece, too, must be having them, whatever be their appellations. But saintliness does not seem to be placed before all Greeks as the ideal to be attained. In India it is the ideal of all. It is associated with the realization of one's innermost self, the *Ātman*. The man of realization is indeed virtuous but develops a detachment from the world and its values. He is wise also in the sense that he is able to discriminate between the eternal and the transient, and that he longs for the former.

For Jewish thought, the ideal man is one who is assured of God's interest in him. 'Man is needed, he is a need of God.'[6] The need is the 'need for human righteousness.'[7] It is often said that man is created as an image of God. But what is the nature of God in whose image man is created? The divine pathos is expressed as love, mercy, and anger. But behind all of these is God's concern for human righteousness. If man is righteous, he becomes holy and acquires the attribute of holiness, which is an essential attribute of God. We may, therefore, say that, according to Judaism, the ideal man is the ideal image of God; and he becomes an ideal image if he embodies ideal righteousness.

One feels like commenting on the doctrine of the image. This idea is not completely new to Greek thought or to the Indian. Plato spoke of the objects of sense perception as images or copies of Ideas and even spoke of man as likeness[8] to God. The rational part of the soul, at least, must be a likeness to God. In Indian philosophy man's consciousness is said to be the reflection or image of the *Ātman* or the Supreme Spirit. But the image theory in Greek and Indian thought is developed in a different context and with different emphasis. Indian thought does not say that the whole man is an image of God, and Greek philosophy also assigns this attribute to the rational aspect of the soul. Furthermore, the idea of ethical concern is not so dominant in either as it is in Jewish thought. God is essentially righteous; and man can be His image only by being righteous.

For Chinese thought the ideal man is a sage. He is interested in everything human, including government. The philosopher-king of Plato accepts kingship when pressed to do so; but the

[6] Chapter II, p. 119 (the present work).
[7] Chapter II, p. 125 (the present work).
[8] Chapter I, p. 60 (the present work).

sage-king of Chinese thought willingly goes after it,[9] since it is his duty to take interest in human affairs. Thus, the philosopher of Plato is something of an individualist, deeply interested in developing the highest in him; but the primary concern of the Chinese philosopher is for society. As Fung Yu-lan says, 'the purpose of the study of philosophy is to enable man, *as man*, to be a man, not some particular kind of man, and the character of the ideal man is sageliness within and kingliness without.'[10] Thus the tone of Chinese philosophy is more human and humanistic than that of the Greek. The Chinese philosopher does not aim at God-realization or at righteousness with reference to God, but only with reference to man. *Jen* (love, human-heartedness), which is derived from the Chinese word for man, is the highest virtue. Man should cultivate it to the highest degree possible. He who is fully and truly man is the sage. His primary concern is with man, not with God.

Does this peculiarity of Chinese philosophy mean that the other conceptions do not contain man's concern for man? Judaism insists on man's usefulness to society or on what we call love of one's neighbour. But that is not all. Is man's worth lost if society does not care for his usefulness?[11] Is society itself a value? Is it needed?[12] Only when society finds that it is

[9] Fung Yu-lan: *A Short History of Chinese Philosophy*, p. 9. (New York: Macmillan & Co., 1950; London: Allen & Unwin, Ltd., 1952) Dr Fung's works on the subject are still the best works available to the non-Chinese knowing reader. He has now changed his views and I understand that he is planning to re-write the history of Chinese philosophy from the new communist point of view. But his two-volume *History* and his *Short History* were written and translated into English before he changed his views and may therefore be taken as fairly authentic representations of Chinese philosophers without being biased.

Attempts are being made and have been made to write histories of nations and histories of their philosophies from this or that point of view. But such attempts lose objectivity of approach. The important question is whether the leaders of men and thought of the former epochs had the new point of view at all. If they do not have it, we shall be unfair to them if in any way we attribute to them our new point of view and judge whether they were consistent and their ideas adequate. To present their ideas as they thought them from their own point of view and then criticize them is one thing; and to assign our point of view to them and then present them and criticize them is another. I do not know what exactly Dr Fung will do in the works he projected; but in the works referred to *supra*, he may be taken as having followed the tradition, except for minor differences of interpretation. So far no other sizeable work on the history of Chinese philosophy is available than Dr Fung's, in English.

[10] *Ibid.*, p. 8.

[11] Chapter II, p. 111 (the present work).

[12] *Op. cit.* (the present work).

needed by God does it get a meaning, a value. Man's concern for man gets a revaluation in the light of the mutual concern of man and of God. But in Chinese philosophy man's concern for man is basic and final. Man is man only if he has that human concern (*jen*). *Jen* as a virtue (love, human heartedness) is higher than *yi* (righteousness). Some Chinese philosophers derive righteousness from human-heartedness.[13] It does not require a supra-empirical divine being for being derived from. Human nature itself is enough and can be relied upon. 'The fundamental belief of the Chinese is that human nature is basically good.'[14]

In spite of the comparative individualism of the Greek philosophers, no one will accuse them of lack of interest in society and its problems. The treatises of Plato and Aristotle are the first on social and political thought of the West. Plato explicitly said that the individual is the microcosm of the macrocosm that is society. The Cynics are the only group who can be accused of lack of social interest. Yet the Greek faith in the goodness of man and in its self-sufficiency is not as strong as that of the Chinese. But the interest of Greek philosophy is wider than that of the Chinese and comprehends the whole cosmos. Man is in relationship not only with society but with the whole cosmos. If a little over-simplification is allowed, one may say that, for the Chinese, the essence of man is human-heartedness and that, for the Greeks, it is reason.

Indian thought goes farther and maintains that the essence of man is even beyond reason: it is the *Ātman*. In pointing this out, I do not mean that Indian thought is truer or higher but only that it regards the *Ātman* as higher than reason and as transcending all human relationships. I think that a wrong conclusion is drawn by some Indian writers to the effect that, because the essence of man is beyond all human relationships, man himself is beyond human relationships and is therefore free from them. Pseudo-saints can justify their unsocial activities on this theory.

We may also say that if the essence of man is the *Ātman* and is the highest good, then man is essentially good. But the Chinese do not mean that something within man is essentially good, but that man, as man (human nature), is essentially good.

[13] Chapter III, p. 188 (the present work).

[14] *Ibid.*, p. 162 (the present work).

Naturally man's concern for man does not get as much emphasis in Indian thought as it does in the Chinese.

4. MAN AND NATURE

The problem of philosophy arises only because man finds himself in an environment which he wants to understand. Even those philosophers, like Mencius, who said that the 'universe is within me' do not mean thereby that man has no environment but, rather, that it can be understood by understanding one's own mind. The environment, so far as our life goes, is of three kinds: the natural, the social, and the divine. In our activities we do not separate the three completely. In the history of thought, ethics, for instance, has had to deal with both society and God; but man sustains himself by meeting his needs from nature's products, and this sustaining activity also is not beyond ethical concern. However, for purposes of study these three kinds of environment may be separated.

In Greek philosophy man is one with nature. Neither is nature set over against man nor is man set over against nature. Early philosophers, like Thales, did not conceive of any dichotomy of man and nature, not even of mind and body. Protagoras, the Sophist, said that man is the measure of all things, and nature is thus what man perceives it to be. This is not a sound doctrine but contains the hopeful belief that nature is not opposed to man and can even be what man makes it to be. While for Protagoras nature is what man's senses represent it to be, for Socrates it is what human reason says it is. Human reason is part of the universal cosmic reason[15] and, as universal, is the same for all men. Reason grasps the stable structure of nature, *being* within the flux of *becoming*.[16] Through reason, therefore, man is not only one with nature but also one with other men. Plato's views are practically the same as those of Socrates.

Aristotle differed from Plato in not admitting the wide gap between reason and sense-perception. But the toned-down idealism[17] of Plato's *Laws* is basically the same as Aristotle's position. Reason is embodied in sense-perception and is not something set over against it. So, through both reason and sense,

[15] Chapter I, p. 55 (the present work).
[16] *Ibid.*, p. 56 (the present work).
[17] *Ibid.*, p. 78 (the present work).

man is one with nature. Even in the Stoic and Cyrinaic schools, man is one with nature and has to live according to nature.

Is nature meant to be controlled and transformed by man? A clear and affirmative answer can be given only by a technological age. The Greek answer does not seem to be clear. The Stoic and the Epicurian answer is more in the negative than in the affirmative: man is to live according to nature. Plato would say that physical nature is Non-Being but is capable of reflecting Being. Aristotle would say that it is pure potentiality, which can take various forms. But neither taught that forms can be, or ought to be, imposed on matter, although both emphasized the importance of a rational life. Man has to tend his rational soul, not transform nature. But one may interpret their teachings as meaning that man has to transform his own physical non-rational nature into the rational. And one may add that forms have to be imposed on physical nature, which means transforming nature.

In Jewish thought 'image and dust express the polarity of the nature of man.'[18] Man is not only the image of God but also a product of physical nature. But nature is subservient to man; the world is created for man by God so that man can show his righteousness in it. The Jewish thinkers did not care to elaborate further the concept of nature.

In Chinese thought 'nature' has a meaning of its own. To some extent, it is a mystical entity[19] with which man ultimately becomes identified and with which he ought to identify himself. In this sense, nature is not what we nowadays call physical nature. It is, at the lowest, human nature, but not again human nature with all the evil we find in it, but human nature at its highest and best. When Mencius asked man to realize his original nature, he was thinking of the best in man, because he thought that the original nature of man is essentially good. Similarly, when Lao Tze said that original nature is the *Tao*, he thought of it as the highest and the best. On the whole, it seems to me, the Chinese philosophers understood by 'nature' human nature or what is inward to man, just as they understood by the 'study of things' the study of human relationships. So, when we speak of the nature mysticism of the Chinese, we have to be careful about the meaning of the word 'nature'.

[18] Chapter II, p. 141 (the present work).

[19] Chapter III, p. 197 (the present work).

The peculiar conception of nature given by the Chinese should make us pause and think about the meaning of the words 'nature', natural', and 'naturalism'. Do the Chinese understand by 'nature mysticism' absorption in physical nature or in nature comprising the material, plant and animal world? Indeed, they distinguish between the world of nature and the world of culture. Even in the West there are philosophers, like the Stoics in Greece and Rousseau in modern times, who exhort man to return to nature and live according to nature; and they are opposed to the artificialities of civilization which have no value in themselves, and make over-statements about the noble savage roaming in the forests. Yet their nature is idealized nature, not the crude and brute nature, red in tooth and claw. Chinese philosophers, like Mencius, thought of nature as human nature and as originally ideal and perfect. If this ideal human nature is natural to man, why should not the *Tao*, which is in man and yet transcends him, also be natural to him? This is what can be meant by saying that the *Tao* is nature. If the *Tao* is natural, why should not spirit or *Ātman* of Indian philosophy be also natural? Spirit is within man as naturally as his body is made of matter. Some forms of modern naturalism narrowed down the meaning of nature to physical nature, which, at the most, includes entities from which the idea of value can be dissociated. It includes at the most the world of plants and animals. But what can be the reason for excluding spirit within man from nature? Is it because man considers spiritual realization to be a value? Science proposes to itself the exclusion of the study of values; but is it or is it not excluding thereby the study of many things valuable? If the accepted scientific method is not suited to the study of spirit, are we then justified in saying that spirit is not a natural entity? Are we justified in *a priori* finding the meaning of the word natural? Science depends on observation and experiment; but should all observation and experiment be of the same type? Some experiments in physical science may take a few hours, some a few days, and some others a few weeks. Our experiments with plants and animals may take years. In the political and social fields, they may take a decade or more and in the religious field a few centuries. And observations in each area may not be of the same kind. Again, astronomers can do far fewer experiments than can physical scientists. I think that, if science broadens its outlook and reassesses its methods, spirit will not appear to it supernatural in the sense that it is completely disconnected with what we call nature.

If spirit can be natural and is not disconnected with what we narrowly define as natural, then what the Chinese philosophers call nature, particularly the *Tao*, may be regarded as spirit. The *Tao* is not defined exactly as the *Ātman* of the Upaniṣads, or even as the rational soul of the Greek philosophers. But the *Tao*, the *Ātman* and the rational soul are within man like the *nirvāṇa* and the *śūnya* of the Buddhists. The various philosophies are groping for a description of what is ultimately inward to man and which is as natural to him as that which is ultimately outward, his material world. How we evaluate these concepts, which of them is higher and which lower or whether they all belong to the same level but are concepts of different aspects of the same reality, is a different question and must be decided on other considerations. What we have to note here is that, irrespective of the name which the various traditions employ, all spiritual and rational aspects are considered to be naturally connected with man and are not supernatural entities.

In a situation like this, in which we have different conceptions of the ultimately inward in man, what should comparative philosophy do? Should it say that man is the same everywhere and that therefore the spirit within man is the same and that the different conceptions are conceptions of different aspects of the same spirit, complementary to one another; or should it say that the different conceptions correspond to different kinds of spirit, and that the spirit within man is not the same everywhere and that therefore man is not the same everywhere? I think that comparative philosophy, if it is to be of value, should adopt the first alternative. The question is of both theoretical and practical importance. It is theoretically important for our method: Has comparative philosophy a theoretical and *a priori* justification for the assumption that man is not the same everywhere? If it has not, is it justified in assuming that man is the same everywhere? I think that it is. Thought works with the assumption of its own universality; whether it can prove it or not, it works with the principle of the uniformity of nature. The question is practically important because humanity is now anxious that man should utilize all the values of life enjoyed, formulated and achieved everywhere. If man is not the same everywhere, he cannot even appreciate these values. If he cannot appreciate them, he develops an indifference, which is sometimes pathetic, towards them, and even a hostility towards these values and the people who appreciate and enjoy them. Leaders of men, who are sincere in their desire for world peace, are therefore very much concerned about making all of life's values accessible to all men. The aim, although it started and gained force in international politics, has now become practically a moral responsibility. And even if one cannot accept theoretically the principle of the uniformity of nature with reference to man, one's practical reason has to accept the principle.

There are three main theories in Chinese philosophy about the relation between man and nature. The first is the theory of correspondence between man and nature, originally developed by the Yin-Yang school and later adopted by the Confucian and the Taoist schools.[20] The correspondence is said to hold between parts of man's body, on the one side, and the planets, the natural forces, and the heavens, on the other. The second theory maintains the harmony of man and nature. 'The man of wisdom enjoys water; the man of love enjoys mountains.'[21] However, the Taoist school understood this relation not as submission to nature but as harmony with it. The third theory is the Confucian doctrine of 'forming a triad with Heaven and Earth.'[22] This was explained later as 'forming one body with Heaven and Earth.' The idea, although stressing the unity of man with Heaven and Earth (both of which may be called 'nature'), is somewhat vague and gave rise to different interpretations, Mencius stressing the human factor and harmony with rivers, and mountains, and Hsün Tzu exhorting man to control nature.

The idea of the unity of man and nature reminds us of the Greek idea, particularly that of Democritus, that man's senses and the physical elements like fire, water, air, and earth have some correspondence and correlativity. This correlativity is more explicitly worked out in Indian thought by the Upaniṣads. Not only corresponding to man's senses but also corresponding to his mind, to his waking, dream and sleep states, there are cosmic realities. Man, as a psycho-physical being, is therefore

[20] *Op. cit.* (the present work).
[21] *Ibid.*, p. 198 (the present work).
[22] *Ibid.*, p. 199 (the present work).

very intimately one with nature. He is the centre of the field of the activities of the cosmic forces. In the semi-mythological languages of the Upaniṣads, he is the instrument, the means, the medium of the enjoyment of the deities presiding over the cosmic realities. They obtain their enjoyment through man, and man obtains his enjoyment through them. Philosophically this correlativity and mutual dependence is the important idea. We may say that control and transformation of nature are implied by the idea, for nature is meant for enjoyment. However, the idea of controlling nature is not explicitly formulated; on the contrary, self-control is the dominant trend in Indian thought.

5. MAN AND SOCIETY

In Greek philosophy, although the individualistic trend is strong, concern for human society is not weak and is one of its important strands. For Socrates and Plato, if man is the microcosm, then society is the macrocosm.[23] The pre-Sophist philosophies did not say much about man's relation to society, although we should not think that therefore they had no idea about society. The Sophists were more individualistic, being mainly devoted to training leaders of men who would influence society and use it as means to their own ends. Society and its laws were a necessary evil.[24] Each man was the measure of things for himself, not only of things cognized but also of good and evil in society. But Plato and Socrates were opposed to this radical individualism and relativism of the Sophists. Man, the measure of things, is not to be the particular man, but the universal man. The structure of society and the structure of man's soul reflect each other, and are interdependent. The essence of man is reason and is found in a rationally ordered society. The modern idea that the individual cannot be studied apart from society[25] and that the personality of man is formed by society and grows in society,[26] is not strong in Greek thought.

[23] *Republic*, Book II. Socrates indeed thought that justice could be seen in larger letters in society than in the individual, but held that social justice 'is simply the social expression of the conditions of the soul.' (See A. D. Lindsay's Introduction to *The Republic*, p. xxxvii, London: J. M. Dent & Sons Ltd., 1926).

[24] Chapter I, p. 46 (the present work).

[25] Lapierre and Farnsworth: *Social Psychology* (New York: McGraw Hill Book Co., Inc., 1949).

[26] G. H. Mead: *Mind, Self and Society* (Chicago: University of Chicago Press, 1952).

However, approaching the relation of man to society from the side of the individual after universalizing him, Socrates and Plato showed that society is a projection of human nature on a vast canvas or is a much enlarged reflection of human nature. Man cannot live without society and can have full life only within it. So the more the organization of society corresponds to human nature, the fuller and better will be the life lived in it by the individual. Aristotle also was a rationalist, but less idealistic and more realistic than was Plato. He was more conscious of the shortcomings and weaknesses of human nature than Plato, who thought that reason can transform everything in man. However, Aristotle accepted[27] the main principles of Plato. Man cannot be man without society. The ideal state is one in which all citizens are really good and which enables each to live the fullest life possible. So the structure of society must be in accordance with human nature. And, we may add, if man is necessarily a political animal and can realize his potentialities only within society, then society must be reflected in human nature just as much as human nature is reflected in society.

In spite of the keen interest which Greek philosophy took in man's relation to society, the idea that man transcends society in some way is also evident in it. Man is essentially rational, but reason is not confined to society only. It has a cosmic reference and transcends society. As part of the Logos, which is Cosmic Reason, it has reference beyond society. It is what enables man individually to be in communion with the Divine. Socrates is reported to have entered trance. Russell[28] tells us that the word 'theory' originally meant a spiritual concept, that which lifts man to the universal *Theos* or God. But this idea of man's transcendence is not clearly worked out in Greek thought, although the Stoic teaching of man's oneness with the Cosmos may be interpreted as this transcendence and communion with the Divine. Even then, however, its psychological aspects are not definitely enunciated.

[27] Chapter I, p. 81 (the present work).

[28] *History of Western Philosophy*, p. 33. (London: Allen & Unwin, Ltd., New York; Simon and Schuster, 1945). Cornford interprets the word theory, says Russell, as 'passionate sympathetic contemplation.' Cornford says that the Pythagoreans divided the soul into three parts, intelligence (nous), reason (phrenoe) and the heart. The rational part is immortal and the others are mortal. (*Greek Religious Thought*, p. 67).

In Jewish thought man's concern for society is very strong, although it was confined to the Jewish society. And this concern was made a categorical imperative and God's command and chief interest. Man's concern for man derives its value from the fact that all men are creatures of God and constitute His main concern. Righteousness, which is the keynote of Jewish ethics, gets its meaning from God's concern for all men. But explaining society in terms of human nature is not the fashion of Jewish thinkers; it is the Greek fashion. Left to himself, man is selfish; he wants a reason for being ethical. Thus, ethics needs a foundation, which is found in God's concern for man.

In Chinese thought, man's concern for man is the strongest and is considered to be almost self-sufficient. Quite often we read of man, Heaven and Earth, and their unity; but the interest in Heaven and Earth is far less than is that in man; and how to have the best kind of state and society in which man can be virtuous is an ever-recurring question in the history of Chinese philosophy.[29] 'Study human relationships in order to organize the state well' is the Confucian advice; and human relationships are ultimate basic facts, not derived from Heaven or Earth, or accepted as commandments of God as in Judaism. The Yin-Yang school and some later Confucians and Taoists tried to correlate them to cosmic forces; but their attempts are inchoate and unsystematic. Indeed, virtue cannot be realized except in society; but the roots of virtue are to be found in man himself. When Mencius says that the universe, which is the universe of human relationships, is to be found within mind, he meant that this universe can be found within man and is not to be derived from any reality outside man. Hsün Tzu differed from Mencius and said that man is essentially selfish and evil and therefore needs education and culture in order to become good. Even then, however, he does not derive the principles of virtue from a divine being but from culture, which is a social phenomenon. If a self-sufficient and well developed humanism is to be found anywhere in classical thought, it can be found in Chinese philosophy. Man is essentially a social creature and can live a virtuous life only in a society of men, whether God exists or not.

In this respect, Indian philosophy offers a contrast to the other three traditions. This does not mean that no Indian

[29] Fung Yu-lan: *A Short History of Chinese Philosophy*, p. 70.

thinker was interested in the problems of men and society. But the classical philosophers, who are studied as representative thinkers, gave little thought to these problems. Only the authors of ethical codes, the law-givers, were concerned with the problems of society. The Vedic thought handed down the idea that man lives in a society of men, ancestral spirits, the deities of the universe, and the Supreme God. Since this wider society is not so concrete as the human society, a kind of strong individualism developed, each man being concerned with this wide circle individually. As far as human society was concerned, by the time philosophers began to think about it, it had already been divided into castes. The caste system was taken for granted as the final structure of society and all social theorising was based upon it. The idea that, whatever be one's caste, one can realize the supreme spiritual ideal, became strong and made a strong appeal. Thus, man's relation to God became more important than man's relation to man. Philosophically, the social nature of man did not receive the thought it deserved, although in practice it was accepted as a working principle. The ideal, as theoretically formulated, is how to become a saint, not how to embody social virtues. In Jewish thought man is primarily concerned with God; but he is necessarily concerned with other men as God's creatures and cannot transcend this concern. Greek thought also stresses man's concern for man, but accepts also transcendence of that concern. Chinese thought does not, on the whole, care for this transcendence, if we take Confucianism as representative of Chinese life.

Each tradition emphasizes those aspects of the relation of man and society which raised special problems in the context in which man lived. The Greek understanding of the relation is philosophical and rational. Even when Greek thought analysed the psychological factors of man's soul, it held that those factors had to be controlled and transformed by reason and in accordance with the ideals of reason. Even Aristotle held this view, although he doubted the power of reason to accomplish the task. Even when something supreme in man was admitted by the Greeks, the admission was based upon proof and analysis of mind. Jewish thought allowed no such analysis and proof. The reality of God is not to be proved but accepted. Man, his nature and powers, are not to be relied upon. Both the Greek and Jewish philosophies are interested in state and society. But, in theory, the Jewish state is theocratic. For both traditions, however, morality can be realized only in society. But according to the Greeks, virtue is to be based upon knowledge, even if it is not the same as knowledge itself; virtue is not to be derived from a transcendent God. The Jewish thinkers, on the other hand, did not trust man's knowledge and derived virtue from God. Morality is righteousness in accordance with God's dictates. The right is the good because God has dictated it. But the Greeks would reverse this principle and would say that the good is the right because it is good for man; and what is good for man is to be understood in terms of man and society. For the Greeks the basis of the good is not God's commandments but human nature, which may include factors transcending society. All factors are to be rationally understood before we frame our conception of virtue.

Chinese philosophy, like that of the Greeks, bases its conception of virtue on the study of human nature and does not derive it from anything external to man and society. But there is a difference. For most Greek philosophers, particularly for Socrates, Plato and Aristotle, virtue is rational. The soul has different parts or aspects, and a rational ordering of each part constitutes a virtue. Plato analysed the soul into three distinct parts, the rational, the spirited, and the vegetative. The last consists of desires and urges. Wisdom corresponds to the first, courage to the second, and temperance to the third. But justice is the harmony of the three parts. Thus it is reason which orders itself, which orders each of the other parts of the soul and orders them with reference to one another. Virtue, therefore, is the work of reason. But the Chinese philosopher would say that virtue, apart from reason, is an innate psychological disposition in man. Indeed, reason also is innate to man. But, according to the Greek philosophers, a disposition becomes a virtue only when organized by reason; whereas, according to the Chinese philosophers, even apart from such organization, there are certain dispositions in man which, by themselves, are virtues. Thus, Mencius says: 'The feeling of commiseration is the beginning of human-heartedness. The feeling of shame and dislike is the beginning of righteousness. The feeling of modesty and yielding is the beginning of propriety. The sense of right and wrong is the beginning of wisdom. Man has thus the four beginnings.' For the Chinese philosophers, therefore, virtue belongs to the innate psychological nature of man.

Now, is the view of the Chinese philosophers wrong? I see no *a priori* reason for saying that it is. First, if human nature is originally good, then virtue must belong to this original nature. Secondly, if ethical experience has to have its own autonomy, its own distinctive character, then it must be as original in man as the usually accepted instincts, like pugnacity. The contribution of Chinese thought to ethics is the recognition of this autonomy. Kant was impressed by the starry heavens above and the moral law within, each claiming to be as hard and irrefutable a fact as the other. For him also moral experience has its own autonomy. Yet the Chinese philosophers do not go along with Kant in placing the right above the good. Kant is in line with the Jewish thinkers in giving primacy to the right over the good; but the Chinese would follow the Greeks in placing the good above the right. I wonder, however, whether the Greeks gave ethics the autonomy which the Chinese gave it.

It is possible to say that ethical experience has its factors: reason, emotion, instincts, sentiments, etc. To admit that it has factors and that they are not systematically analysed by the Chinese philosophers is one thing; but to say that the experience can be completely analysed into such factors is another thing. Ethical experience has a quality of its own, like religious experience. If we grant uniqueness to the latter, we must grant it to the former also.

Furthermore, there is no reason why ethical experience should be analysed only in the way the Greeks analysed it, and not also in the way the Chinese did. The two modes of thought are complementary. For preserving the autonomy of ethical experience, the Chinese method is helpful; but for analysing it and correlating it with reason and other aspects of the human mind, the Greek method is useful.

Indian philosophy, on the whole, exhorts man to rise above social virtues. Social virtues are necessary so long as man lives within society. But a distinctive feature of Indian philosophy is its exhortation that man should rise above society. This feature is associated with the life of renunciation, the fourth stage of life, through which every man ought to pass. Here man's concern is only with God or the Supreme Spirit. In Judaism, also, we find the idea of communion with God; but here it is meant as an inspiration of righteousness and its justification rather than as communion itself.

6. MAN AND THE DIVINE SPIRIT

Consideration of man's relation to society and of the ethical situation naturally leads us to the question of man's relation to God. We have noticed already that Jewish thought does not separate man's relation to man from man's relation to God, the latter being an intensely ethical relation. The Greeks separated the two relations. The Chinese paid little attention to the relation of man to God. The Indians also separated the two relations, but regarded the relation of man to man as leading to the relation of man to God. The latter was considered to be higher than the former, with the result that less thought was bestowed upon its problems.

According to Cornford,[30] when the Ionins were searching for the origin of the universe, they were searching for God, however physically they conceived Him. Man, then, according to them, would be a transformation of that original reality. The Sophists ridiculed these attempts and were sceptical about the existence of God. But Socrates not only advanced arguments for the existence of God, but also said that his inner warning voice was something numinous and divine and, according to Xenophen, was Divinity[31] itself. Plato went farther and said that God is the self-moving cause and that man is the image[32] of God. Aristotle also believed that God is the first cause of the universe, the unmoved mover, consciousness of Himself only, pure form without matter. The clue to the Greek understanding of God can be found in their conception of reason as the universal factor in man, lifting man above his particularity and making him one with the Divine Spirit, which is universal and one.

Yet we cannot say that this conception of reason is without ethical significance; for the rational is the good. We may say that this principle holds true even in Aristotle's philosophy;

[30] See his *Greek Religious Thought*.
[31] Chapter I, p. 59 (the present work).
[32] *Ibid*., p. 60 (the present work).

for according to him, the aim of everything is to realize its proper form, and form is the universal or idea of reason. We would not say, with Plato, that form alone has being and not matter. According to Aristotle, the Divine Spirit must be pure actuality, form, reason. So far as man possesses reason, he is divine; through reason man can be in communion with the Divine Spirit.

This aspect of Greek thought is opposed to the spirit of Jewish thought, for which man is in communion with God through righteousness. Reason doubts, questions, formulates concepts, modifies some, and discards some others; but righteousness is a passion for obeying the dictates of God. Communion with God is to be sought; but it is to be sought only through and for righteousness.

The Chinese philosophers, particularly the Confucians, did not elaborate the concept of God or of the Divine Spirit. The early Chinese worshipped God as Shang Ti; but it is not known what exactly He was. Later Chinese spoke of T'ien, meaning Heaven; but the word does not mean exactly the Divine Spirit. As Ch'eng I said, it is nature, Lord, and Spirit, all in one.[33] A concept more helpful in this connexion is the *Tao*. The *Tao* is not a concept of the Taoists only but belongs to all the Chinese schools and, later, after Buddhism entered China, was associated with *Tathatā* and *nirvāṇa*. *Tao* means the way, the way of man, of Heaven and Earth, and of everything else. Every school wanted to define *Tao*, the Taoists defining it in a negative way even before they came into contact with Buddhism. The Confucians were interested only in man and so in the *Tao* of man. The *Tao* of man is the way of man, which is ultimately the ideal and virtuous human nature. It can be realized only in society. But the Taoists, following Lao Tze, said that the *Tao* transcends man, and yet the ideal of man is to realize it. He realizes it within himself by living according to nature and avoiding the artificialities of civilization. Realization consists in becoming one with it, in a kind of mystic union.

As a philosophy of life, Confucianism is more representative of China than is Taoism. In any country, whatever be the philosophy professed, actual and practical mystics are far fewer than are men who seek a decent life in society. Now,

[33] Chapter III, p. 201 (the present work).

Confucianism did not depend on God for deriving its ethical relationships; neither did it care for communion with Him. Communion with the *Tao* would actually be communion with society through virtue, although union with Heaven and Earth is also spoken of. Taoism, on the other hand, did not care for ethical relationships; for, according to its law of reversal,[34] the good can become evil and evil good: opposites pass into each other. This is really a form of ethical relativity. The Absolute is the *Tao* only. It is beyond all human goods and evils, and is the ultimate good for every man, who therefore should not worry about relative goods and evils. The ultimate good of man lies beyond ethics, in union with the *Tao*. This union is not ethical communion, as in Judaism, or rational unity, as in Greek thought. It is a mystic union beyond description, as in Indian thought.

Indian philosophy presents a more complicated picture of the relation of man to God than do the other philosophies. From the time of the Upaniṣads this relation is its main problem, and on it the Indian thinkers expended much thought. In this respect, it is like Jewish thought. But Jewish thought is almost exclusively concerned with the ethical relationship between man and God; and the relationship is pre-eminently ethical. In Indian thought, this ethical relationship is transcended and transmuted into that of blissful communion. The joy derived is not a result of having performed one's duties; rather it is through that joy, and because of it, that one performs one's duties. If a little exaggeration be allowed to pinpoint the difference, one may say that the Indian mystic would tell God, 'I love you and therefore I follow your laws of duty,' whereas the Jewish mystic would say, 'I performed my duties, therefore love me.' But this is an exaggeration for the sake of clarifying the difference only. As a matter of fact, even the Jewish mystics, when they realized that they could not follow God's commandments to the letter, prayed for forgiveness and also for love. Hence, the difference between Indian and Jewish thought is one of emphasis, not one of substance. The Indian mystics also say that without ethical endeavour mystic union is not possible. It is sincere endeavour that is insisted upon, not actual perfection. Intense love of God makes man incapable of being unethical. Love of God and the consequent self-

[34] Fung Yu-lan: *A Short History of Chinese Philosophy*, p. 97.

surrender, which in extreme cases becomes self-negation and absorption in God, are helpful to ethics; and absence of unethical activity is one of the tests of true love of God. But Indian thought often emphasizes transcendence of ethics by love. This transcendence does not mean that a person who loves God obtains a licence for being unethical. On the contrary, if we love God, we must love His creatures; and if we love them, we shall not only be not unfair to them but shall show our love in active relationship.

However, the difference between Jewish and Indian thought brings out certain important points. First, it seems to me that all religions which have a tribal origin lay a strong emphasis on ethical conduct, at least a stronger emphasis on man's relation to man, than do religions which are naturalistic and cosmic in their origins and which lay the same emphasis on man's relationship to the lord of the cosmos. When I speak of naturalistic origins, I do not mean that kind of naturalism which is more or less materialistic and calls everything falling beyond the recognized field of science supernatural. I mean those religions which start with cosmic forces rather than with tribal societies as the first objects of concern. Indian religion is naturalistic in this sense. Now, both kinds of religion develop ethics and ethical thought. But one religion starts with the laws and conventions of tribal society as the basis; its interest is in the tribe, in the discipline of its members, in their welfare and prosperity. Discipline, righteousness in terms of certain fixed laws, becomes therefore important; and God will reject the prayers of those who do not follow the accepted laws of tribal discipline. The tribal religion may later become universal; but it carries with it the spirit of fixed and unquestioning moral discipline.

But the other kind of religions develops the laws of conduct in terms of the laws of cosmic forces, which include man as a cosmic entity. There were tribal gods in the Vedic times; Indra was a tribal god of the Aryans. But as philosophy progressed, he was dethroned and given a subordinate place. Then the Brahman became the Supreme God. All ethics and laws of self-control were formulated with reference to Him. But He lost even personality and became an It, a neuter gender, like any cosmic force. Nevertheless, reverence for the Brahman did not decrease at all. However, fixed ethical laws were not associated with it, and ethical relativity was accepted. But it was enunciated, as a primary principle, that one who is in search of God cannot be unethical.

In the second place, the attempt to derive moral laws from the nature of God or His substance leaves a serious doubt unresolved. I do not refer merely to the abuses to which the idea is put. There have been many persons in the history of the world who claimed to know the nature of God and who dictated how men should behave, and who persecuted those who conscientiously did not obey them. Science revolted against them and exposed not only their views of the cosmos but also their moral pretentions. There may be men who, knowingly or unknowingly, committed such mistakes, brought misery to many, and hindered the progress of mankind. But this does not distract the value of the principle. What I wish to ask is: Can we deduce moral laws from an absolutely transcendent God? If man with his finite intellect conceived God, his conception cannot be perfect and complete, and if he deduces moral laws from that incomplete conception, his deductions cannot be true. What, then, is the test and check? Are science and humanism totally wrong if they revolt? If we view the conflict with a spirit of detachment, both parties seem to be committing excesses.

If, on the other hand, man does not merely conceive God and frame a concept, but is in direct communion with Him, then where does the communion take place? Only in the mind of man, because God cannot be seen as an external figure. In that case, God must be immanent in man. Of course, immanence cannot mean that He is completely within the mind of any particular man, but that He is in all men whether they feel His presence or not. Because He is in all individuals. He transcends each and is therefore both transcendent and immanent for each. Even then, however, man cannot have a complete grasp of God and cannot, therefore, deduce ethical laws from His nature. All that man experiences in this communion is love, joy, infinity, indescribability, etc.; and whatever ethical laws can be deduced from these experiences are the only ones that may be called deductions. For instance, we can say that, because the nature of God is love and He is the unifying principle of our souls, man must love man and not hate him. But many other details of human conduct have to be decided by an empirical study of human nature. They must be correlated with the inward experience.

The third point to which I wish to refer is that mysticism is not very favourable to ethics, unless it is ethical mysticism. There is some truth in what the critics of mysticism say. Except in the case of a few great mystics of the world, mysticism tends to produce a disregard of ethical values. The majority of men belong to the class of lesser minds. Even with the best of intentions, the mystic, when obliged to act in certain ethical situations, becomes confused and uncertain. And when the intentions are not the best, he can always have ready at hand the principle of ethical relativity to excuse and support himself. He is generally unsteady and undisciplined in social action. If religion preaches nothing but communion with the Divine Spirit, mysticism, when preached to all grades of men, becomes a danger to ethics and a danger to disciplined social life. This argument has much force and is not without support from the history of societies. But that mysticism can be abused is not a final argument against it. It is an argument, however, that has to be considered seriously by religious leaders. Just as scientific concepts are not merely confined to the laboratory but enter our social, ethical, and religious life, so the concepts of mysticism enter our social and ethical life and can deeply influence it for good or for evil.

But this is only one side of the problem. Any religion which is detrimental to ethical discipline needs re-modelling. But what ethical discipline is strengthened by ethical religions? We have seen that it is difficult to deduce an absolutely valid and detailed set of moral laws from the nature of God. No set of laws revealed to any prophet is now found to hold good without apologetics, modification, subterfuges for legal violation, and grammatical and scholastic gymnastics for changing the meaning of the laws. When these methods are not adhered to, we have only ethical and religious fanaticism, which is detrimental to human progress.

If one considers both religions with sufficient detachment and without any bias, one will find, I think, that there is truth in what both say. Then, what is the solution? Ethical relativity does not mean a divine licence for immorality, permission to do anything one likes. To whichever ethical system one belongs, it is one's duty to observe its laws. Even if we suppose that a person finds an existing system defective, God does not prevent him from communion if he does not violate the system. Mystics are born in all kinds of ethical systems, some of which, we now say, contain injustices. Should not man fight for the reform of a defective ethical system? But what should be his guide in that case, if he is not to depend on ethical revelation? It seems to me that the only guide is the question: Do I want this ethical reform without any egoistic motive? Or am I colouring an egoistic motive as divine revelation? Self-lessness, self-surrender, self-negation, non-egoity is the only test and the final test which one can perform on oneself but which one should apply only after very careful self-analysis. Ordinary human beings without this ethical passion cannot become ethical reformers, because man cannot work without a motive.

This self-surrender or self-negation brings us again to mysticism, for mysticism generally aims at complete surrender of egoity. Mysticism, therefore, has ethical usefulness, but only at a very high level. It is for this reason that Indian thought insists upon training in ethical purification as a primary step in mystical or yogic training.

In the fourth place, what does immanence of God mean? This idea is carefully worked out by Indian thought. According to Chinese thought the *Tao* is immanent in man. According to Greek thought God, as the Supreme Cosmic Reason, is immanent in human reason. For Buddhism, *nirvāṇa*, *Tathatā* or *Śūnya* is immanent in man. Man's realization of it is possible because of its immanence. It also is vast and infinite and transcends man. Yet, since it is immanent, man can realize it in his inwardness. In this respect Indian philosophy, in several of its systems, differs from Greek philosophy in saying that the highest in man is not reason but spirit (*Ātman*), which is above reason. Yet the *Ātman* is not irrational; it is supra-rational* For all the orthodox schools in India, spirit (*Ātman*) is higher than reason. All the orthodox schools, except one form of the Sāmkhya, accepted God in some sense or another; and of these schools the Vedānta laid the greatest emphasis on communion with God.

Should communion mean necessarily complete absorption

* In Greek philosophy also one may find evidence for a similar conception; but it is not conspicuous.

in the Infinite? Some Western critics mistakenly think that, at least according to Indian philosophy, it does. They say that this idea of complete one-ness with God cuts at the very roots of ethics and is false to religious experience, in which man is face to face with God as an object. It may be admitted that, if fools and rogues are convinced that they are God, they become shamelessly and dangerously immoral. But I have shown that the idea of one-ness does not necessarily falsify ethics, but that it is necessary for ethics in so far as it encourages true self-lessness. As regards the other criticism, it has to be admitted that, to the extent to which man is finite, the Supreme Infinite remains an Other to him; and it is safer to say that in the experience of communion, if the experience of one's egohood is completely lost, the situation becomes indescribable. If we admit that it is beyond reason, it is unreasonable to attribute definite rational categories to the experience. But in this context it is also necessary to correct the other mistake of the western critics. Only a few schools of the Vedānta, particularly that of Śaṅkara, uphold the complete one-ness of the spirit in man and God; and even they do not say—and I think that no true mystic says—that man, as man, is the same as God and that man's mind, with all its evil propensities and shortcomings, is divine. However, all the other Vedāntins—Rāmānuja, Madhva and Nimbārka—maintain that the spirit in man is different from the Divine Spirit. All say that the Divine Spirit is the *Ātman* immanent in man. Śaṇkara says that the Divine Spirit is the *Ātman* of man himself. But Rāmānuja and others say that it is the *Ātman* within the *ātman* of man. This is an important difference and one which we should not miss; and we should not be misled by the repeated use of the word *ātman*. What all schools accept is the immanence of the transcendent spirit. But even when we say that God is the *Ātman* within the *ātman* of man, fools and rogues may find justification for being immoral. In that case, we have to give up immanence altogether. But if we do this, then as I have already pointed out, we have other difficulties to face.

The fifth point which the idea of immanence suggests is the deep inwardness of man. Man's outwardness has its limit, the world of matter, which is common to all men and is called the common world. But is there also a limit of inwardness? Is the inwardness of man limited to feelings and emotions only or reason only? We say: 'I reason'. The 'I' is deeper than reason. Here is needed an existential analysis of our conscious being. The physical body does not reason and is an object of my consciousness. In certain moments I even speak of 'my ego'. One's consciousness, therefore, extends beyond the ego and even beyond reason. One may call such consciousness the pure witness consciousness which, in a way, detaches itself from the ego and reason. But when this recession reaches its limit, it reaches the core of our conscious being, the self as such. By whatever name we call it, there is a limit to this inwardness beyond which the 'I' vanishes. But is the limit different for each man? Concerning the limit of outwardness, we say that, in spite of the fact that the sensations of each man are different from the sensations of other men, the yellow colour seen by one man is yellow also to other men, and that behind all the sensations and perceptions there is the material world, which is the same for all men. Similarly, can we say that the inward limit is the same for all men? All religions aver that God is one and the same for all men and resides in their hearts. But if He is inward and immanent in all men, then, like the material world forming the limit of man's outwardness, God or the Divine Spirit must form the limit of man's inwardness. If the outwardness of all men is to have a common limit, then their inwardness also must have one. If the ethical values of all men are the same, if man's religious experience and communion with something higher than himself is to have a factual basis, then there must be something inward which is also common to all men. This is the Divine Spirit. Thus men are different, each having his own private experience; but their existence involves two common points, the material world outside and the Divine Spirit within.

There is another line of approach to the common inward limit. The Greeks maintained that human reason derives its truth and universality by partaking of Cosmic Reason. Through reason man rises to the level of Being, to objectivity as distinct from subjectivity. The Pythagoreans even thought that through reason or theory man could lift himself to the abstract level of unity with *Theos*. Reason is deeper and higher than sensations, feelings, and emotions. That it is deeper and higher is implied by its being called abstract and universal. At the level of his reason man becomes one with the Logos. The implied

Cosmic Reason within human reason is thus common to all men. When something deeper than Cosmic Reason is accepted —some Greeks seem to have accepted it, and Plato sometimes speaks of God as higher than the Logos—and if man can have communion with it, then it is the same for all men and forms the common inward limit for all. We say men's sensations, feelings, and emotions work similarly. But reason, we say, is the same for all. Indeed, we may say that reason works similarly in all men. But if similarity implies sameness and identity, then there must be the selfsame principle working through all men and their reason. This principle was regarded as divine by the ancients both in India and Greece. Whether it is Cosmic Reason or something higher than that it is the limit of inwardness and is common to all men.

We come now to the sixth point. Man's environment does not consist merely of nature and society but also of the Divine Spirit. Man does not live alone; neither are the worlds of Spirit and matter alien to him. The sameness or, rather, similarity of all men is the ground for saying that there is something inwardly common to all. This sameness may be explained as due to man having evolved out of the same kind of matter; and because of the similarity of men, it may be said, ethical values are the same for all. Even then the question will be asked: Why should man be moral? Why should he practise self-control, be not selfish and be good to others? The only answer can be: Prudent self-interest requires man to be moral. Then ethics becomes little different from diplomacy, prudent self-aggrandizement. If this is to be avoided, ethics must transcend itself, not downwards towards matter, but upwards towards spiritual experience. The Spirit within all is ultimately the same and binds individual spirits together in love; for its very nature is love. It seems that, if we want a stable foundation for the inwardness of man as we want it for his outwardness, there is no escape from accepting the essential validity of spiritual experience.

In the seventh place, the discussion brings out an important aspect of man. His conscious being has two directions, the outward and the inward. It has been usual in traditional thought to call them the inner and the outer, as if one were placed within the other. But although mind is placed within the physical body, it is not placed like a box within a box;

it is rather the inward direction of the body and has its own inwardness also. This is evident from man's ability to turn his consciousness towards the external objects of sense and also inwardly, not only psychologically but also spiritually, towards deeper objects within himself. Just as matter becomes the final object of his outward direction, so the object of spiritual experience becomes the final object of his inward direction.

7. MAN AND EVOLUTION

The idea of man's inwardness brings us to the problem of evolution. Accepting the view that man evolved out of matter, what has evolution placed in man as distinct from matter? A large majority of educated men now accept the theory of evolution, and it has become unfashionable to question its truth. Men have tended to treat it as a fact of nature, an agent like man or God manipulating nature, experimenting on it and producing new forms out of inorganic matter. But as a process it is a fact of nature, one of the various forms of nature's becoming.

If we put together all the evidence collected by science, it seems that the evidence in favour of the theory is stronger than against it. Man is the highest product of evolution. Other animals also might feel that they are the highest products, but they do not reflect like man, have perhaps no moral struggles, and do not support their conduct by a philosophy. Man alone is a rational and ethical being and he alone is worried about the meaning of the universe and of his life. For this reason, man considers himself to be the highest of animals. And every philosophical tradition, whether it had any idea of evolution or not, has treated him as the highest of creatures. The Indian tradition treated him as higher even than gods; for the gods have to come back to human life if they wish to obtain salvation.

Indeed, none of the classical traditions produced a theory corresponding to the modern scientific theory of evolution, although every tradition regards man as the highest of creatures. The idea that some primitive form of life became an ape and that the ape became man was not even conceived by them. But some rudimentary conceptions and forms of the theory can be traced in the ideas of creation, emanation, transformation, and the cyclic succession of political and social forms.

The pre-Sophist philosophers of Greece thought that the forms of the world, including man, were the products of some original substance, water, air, etc. The Sophists were interested in the evolution of human history and not in the question of how man evolved out of some original stuff. Human history is a history of culture and civilization; the golden age lies in the future.[35] Plato, also, associated evolution with human history. Gods are interested in human affairs and endow men like Socrates with special gifts in order to guide men along right paths.[36] The best that we get in Plato in this connexion is the procession of political forms. Aristotle was more realistic and naturalistic than Plato. His theory of matter and form as potentiality and actuality brings us near to the conception of evolution. He graded the forms of life into the higher and the lower but did not say whether and how the lower becomes the higher. Up to spirit the higher is built on the lower; but spirit, which is pure forn, does not develop out of matter.[37] Change below man is not purposive; purposive change, which is a result of rational reflexion, is peculiar to man.[38] Even then, if we consider Aristotle's view that God, as pure form, acts as an attractive force on matter, we may say that at least in the background of Aristotle's thought the idea of a continuous process of evolution from matter to God is latent. In Plotinus we find a completion and explicit enunciation of this idea. Becoming is a circular process from the Infinite One to matter and back again from matter to the Infinite One.[39] Of course, none of these theories in its details corresponds to the modern scientific theory. But we can see that, when we take the total circle of this process as in Plotinus, the modern theory is confined to only one part of it, the stretch between matter and man and history.

Jewish thought is little concerned with the doctrine of evolution. It has a theory of creation by God; God created the world out of nothing and gave man nature to live on. He created man also directly and not through the process of evolution.

[35] Chapter I, p. 49 (the present work).
[36] *Ibid.*, p. 61 (the present work).
[37] *Ibid.*, p. 85 (the present work).
[38] *Ibid.*, p. 86 (the present work).
[39] W. P. Montague: *The Great Visions of Philosophy*, p. 189. (Chicago: The Open Court Publishing Co., 1950).

Chinese thought contains much less of the idea of evolution than does Greek thought. Its main interest is in man and history but not in how the world is created. But as far as history is concerned, Chinese philosophy, like Greek thought, supplied a theory of the cycle of political forms. Tsou Yen, in the third century B.C., developed a philosophy of history. He said that historical changes take place according to the revolution and transformation of the five Powers of Elements —Earth, Wood, Metal, Fire and Water. Each of the five elements predominates in succession; and whenever there is a change in predominance, a new dynasty arises.[40] But, Tung Chung-shu, in the second century B.C., rejected this theory and said that the succession of the dynasties corresponds to the succession of the 'Three Reigns,' black, white and red.[41] Neither of the theories is based upon a study of human nature in politics and society but upon some cosmological speculations, particularly of the Yin-Yang school. Yet both contain the truth that human history is not absolutely independent of cosmological factors.

Confucius was not very much interested in explaining the process of creation. Taoism derived everything from the original *Tao* and preached a return to the *Tao*. It contains also the interesting principle that 'reversal is the movement of the *Tao*',[42] which is like the Hegelian principle that each concept by its very nature passes into its opposite. Perhaps the Taoists were thinking that history proceeds, in a like manner, each form passing into its opposite. But this idea was not worked out clearly by them. In the Yin-Yang school we find attempts at explaining the creation of the world. And when some later philosophers incorporated the ideas of this school, they tried to derive the Yin and the Yang also from the *Tao*. Chou Tun-yi, in the eleventh century, is an example. Thus the circle of derivation from the *Tao* to the world and then back again to the *Tao* became complete.

In Indian philosophy also the general tendency is to complete the circle. Indeed, no clear ideas of the modern theory of evolution are found in it. The Upaniṣads themselves contain the idea of the circular process of creation reaching back to the *Ātman*. Matter comes gradually out of the *Ātman* and goes

[40] Fung Yu-lan: *A Short History of Chinese Philosophy*, p. 136.
[41] *Ibid.*, p. 199.
[42] *Ibid.*, pp. 19 foll. and 97 foll.

back to the *Ātman* through man's realization of the *Ātman*. Like Aristotle, Indian thought does not consider spirit as a new entity that comes into being through the process of evolution. Neither does Indian philosophy know that some lower forms of life have ultimately developed into man. It knows only that man is the highest creature. It does not speak also of a cyclic evolution of political history. If Indian thought has any idea about it, it can be found only in the epics, particularly in the theory of the Four Ages (*Yugas*). They are the *Kṛta* Age, the *Treta* Age, the *Dvāpara* Age, and the *Kali* Age. Each later Age follows the former in a circle; when the *Kali* Age ends, the *Kṛta* Age begins again.[43] The classification of the Ages is based upon the moral strength and goodness of man. *Dharma* (virtue) is divided into four parts. In the first Age, man is fully virtuous; in the second he is three fourths virtuous; in the third, half; and in the fourth, only one fourth. When there is fear of man losing even that one fourth, some incarnation of God destroys the vicious and starts the first Age again.

There is one peculiar application of the concept of evolution made by the Sāṅkhya philosophy and incorporated by some Vedāntic schools belonging to the Pāñcarātra and the Pāśuputa. Taking man's conscious being and experience as they are and without raising the question as to how man himself is evolved, matter is explained as an evolute out of the conscious being of man. It is a product of man's mind (*antahkaraṇa*). This sounds like idealism; but this idealism is common to all the orthodox

[43] *Śrīmadbhāgavata*, XII, 3–30. Another description of the Ages may interest the reader. *Dharma* (virtue) has four feet, Truth, Compassion, Self-control and Charity, and walks on them. In the Kṛta Age each foot is strong and perfect. In the Treta Age each loses one fourth of its strength, in the Dvāpara Age another one fourth and in the Kali Age still another one fourth. This means that humanity will not be completely devoid of virtue. Again, the Kṛta Age is that in which men are *sāttvic* by temperament and are devoted to self-control and salvation. In the Treta Age men are devoted less to salvation and more to duty, wealth and enjoyment; and their temperament is *rājasic*. In the Dvāpara Age human temperament is a mixture of the *rājasic* and the *tāmasic:* men are full of greed, discontentedness, egoity and arrogance; they have strong desires and are actively interested in fulfilling them. The Kali Age is *tāmasic;* men are full of deceit, untruth, lethargy, sleepishness, cruelty, pain, temptation, fear and dejection. *Sattva*, *Rajas* and *Tamas* are attributes that correspond to pure, agitated and dull; rational, active and lethargic. *Sattva* is the highest and is not only rational but also good. The three attributes roughly correspond to the three divisions of the soul made by Plato. This similarity is interesting. As the four Ages succeed one another, the Golden Age is not only in the past but will also be in the future.

schools except the Nyāya, the Vaiśeṣika, and the Mīmāmsa. Let us strike the entities, Prakṛti and Puruṣa, out of the Sāṅkhya categories; then everything that remains is man, the psycho-physical being. The highest in him, then, is reason (*buddhi*, *mahat*), which is universal and cosmic in significance. It corresponds to either the Logos or the rational soul of the Greeks. Out of it evolves the ego (*shaṁkāra*), which, unlike reason, is not universal and cosmic. Out of the ego evolves mind (*manas*), the senses, and the organs of action on the one side, and the world of material elements, on the other. Man becomes ultimately aware of the world through reason, ego, mind, senses, and the organs of action.

What does the Sāṅkhya mean by calling this process evolution (*pariṇāma*)? To call it evolution sounds absurd. We do not find that reason is first born, then the ego and then mind, the senses, and the physical body. On the contrary, we find that the reverse process accords more with the modern doctrine of evolution. Consequently, the Sāṅkhya must have some other meaning. It must refer to developed awareness, the mature mind. One may verify the theory by observing the stages by which one comes to be aware of the world immediately after sound sleep. First, one is aware of one's pure being, something like 'am-ness' in 'I am' without the 'I'. This is pure awareness of one's self in which one's ego is not concretely felt. It is a pure affirmation, assertion, without any particular object being asserted. Then one feels one's ego, the 'I-ness', and then one's senses and their objects. Pure rational consciousness must be involved in the first awareness after sound sleep; it is rational consciousness without differentiation; for the function of reason is primarily assertion.

It seems to me that this analysis has an interesting similarity to the analysis of cognition into indeterminate and determinate stages. When I perceive an object, say, the paper in front of me, there is first pure awareness of sensation, which is indeterminate. The object is known vaguely as 'something', not definitely as a paper. Next it is known as a paper, a member of the class of papers, and so as determined and made determinate by the universal paper (paper-ness). The first is indeterminate cognition and the next determinate. It is of course very difficult to catch and fix the stage of indeterminate cognition; but we can say that it must have been the first stage.

Similarly, in the awareness of one's being also, after sound sleep, the stages, whether exactly the same as those given by the Sāṅkhya or not, are passed through before one comes to a definite cognition of oneself and the objective world. Then the question will be whether the earliest stage is reason. Whatever be the answer, if this explanation or something similar to it is not given, the Sāṅkhya theory of evolution looks absurd. Evolution, for the Sāṅkhya, is the process of concretization of, or of conferring determinateness on, the pure affirmative experience, called *buddhi*, *mahat*. Reason is the highest in man; but it comes to know the world through the ego, the mind, the senses, and the organs of action.

The different applications of the concept of evolution, of the idea of the one transforming itself into the many, given above, raise some important points for philosophy.

First, if evolution is true, can man be the measure of things? If the starting point is God or the Absolute, then it may be said, that man has to be explained in terms of God or the Absolute; and if the starting point is matter, then he is to be explained in terms of matter. In either case, however, it would seem that man is not the measure of things. But if we accept either position, many difficulties crop up. First, to explain man in terms of God or matter should not be the same as reducing him to either. Secondly, we do not know how God thinks, except in an imperfect way, and we take it that matter does not think. When we take man as God and expect him to act as God, or take him as matter and treat him as a material object, we do him injustice; for in either case he ceases to be man. Thirdly, man should be explained in terms of what man ought to be as man, which Aristotle and Chinese philosophy in general hold, and not in terms of what is below him or above him, neither of which may be man at all. Fourthly, even evolution is true *for man:* but man has to be affirmed even apart from evolution; for if the doctrine of the evolution is false, the existence of man still has to be affirmed. If man himself does not exist, there will be no doctrine of evolution. It is possible to imagine a process of nature producing newer and newer forms; yet it is still man who imagines the process. So man is still the measure of things. Even the proposition that the Absolute is beyond man and his reason has to be asserted by man.

The second point that arises is: Should the doctrine of evolution be limited to the phase of the process which leads from matter to man? Science is studying this phase, because science is able to elaborate its methods only within the limits of that phase. But there is no *a priori* reason why reality and its processes should be limited to this phase. If mind can come out of matter, we are naturally obliged to ask whether there is an inner drive in matter to evolve mind. If there is such a drive, from where does it come? We may refrain from asking this question and arbitrarily stop with matter. We may even say that the fact that matter has the drive is a mere matter of chance. But to ask the question is not irrational. The circle of the descent of matter from spirit is as plausible a hypothesis as is the evolution of mind out of matter, and is more suitable and explanatory for a philosophy of life than is the incomplete circle.

A philosophy of life requires a factual basis for the aims of life. The material world, however, is not enough as such a basis; otherwise Man could not be differentiated from animals, if both had the same factual basis. If scientific experience has its own autonomy, religious experience also must have its own; and the facts of religious experience have as much importance for philosophy of life as have the facts of science. If we do not accept the truths of religion, ethics becomes the art and theory of prudent self-aggrandizement. But our experience is not satisfied with such ethics. In Greece, in India, and in China we find, therefore, tendencies to present a completed circle of evolution from Spirit to matter and back again to Spirit.

We now come to the third point. Although the evolutionary circle is complete, man is exhorted to make special efforts for completing the circle. If we accept the thesis that matter evolved out of Spirit and man evolved out of matter, then can man depend on the evolutionary process itself to push his being up again to the level of Spirit? Both affirmative and negative answers have been given to the question. But the more common answer is in the negative. Man should not allow his nature to work as it likes. He has a lower and a higher nature. The higher is nearer Spirit than is the lower. He should subordinate the lower to the higher and for the purpose practise self-control. So long as the conflict between the higher and the lower lasts, man continues to struggle to realize ethical values which are still unrealized. Ethical values realized become spiritual facts. Man has to do his part and struggle hard to make evolution reach its destination.

The negative answer is expressed in two other forms, which are sometimes understood to mean the same. 'Return to your original nature,' and 'Do nothing.' Taoism in China understood both as meaning the same. Man's original nature is the *Tao,* which is working through man. He goes astray by forgetting his original nature. Then what is he to do? Do nothing. Even for doing nothing he has to struggle hard. If he does anything, he takes an initiative; but if he does nothing, the *Tao* works through him. By not doing anything, he allows his original nature to do everything and so he returns to his original nature. This advice is often understood as quietism, and Taoism is interpreted, in addition, as nature mysticism. Buddhism, some forms of the Vedānta, and some mysticism of the West also are interpreted as quietism. But what about the ethical endeavour which Buddhism and the Vedānta insist upon? And why is ethical endeavour needed in order to regain one's original nature?

After identifying the *Tao* with the *nirvāṅa* of the Buddhists and absorbing it into their own philosophy, the later Confucians raised an interesting question. How does a man who has realized the *Tao* or the *nirvāṅa* live? He lives according to nature. But what does he do? He draws water from the well, cuts wood, cooks his meals and eats them. It is natural for him to live that way. Then why is it not natural for him to take part in political and social activities? Is it not natural for him to have a political and social life? Ethical life is as natural for man as are cooking food and eating it. Only through ethical activity does he gain entrance into spiritual reality. Insight into spiritual depths is gained through ethical living. That is why Buddha called the highest reality Dharma. The circle from man to Spirit can be completed only through man's ethical endeavour.

In the fourth place, we may ask: What is evolution trying to accomplish? What is the nature of the evolution of Spirit out of matter? If evolution is trying to reach its final objective through man, and if Spirit is the inward reality in man, then evolution must be aiming at producing inwardness. Life is the inwardness which matter attained; mind is the inwardness of life; and Spirit is the inwardness of mind. Then evolution must be aiming at producing deeper and deeper inwardness in matter, until inwardness becomes completely self-conscious. Then matter, life, and mind are not to be understood as layer upon layer of reality like one sheet upon another; not even as qualities of each other. They are to be understood as the inward and outward forms of the same reality.

The fifth point is the conflict between ethical and spiritual realization. Ethical realization is a becoming, a transformation of one's being into something higher and deeper, the actualization of a value which has been only in idea.[44] But spiritual realization is the recognition of one's original nature; God, *Ātman*, soul, etc. are not produced by man but are only to be recognized as essentially constituting his inwardness. How is this conflict to be removed? It can be removed only if in the deeper levels of inwardness 'to become' can be 'to know' and 'to recognize', and *vice versa*. The Upaniṣads in India and some forms of mysticism in the West accepted this identity. Taoism in China also seems tacitly to accept it. But at the lower levels, this identity is not found: 'to know' is not the same as 'to become'. One may know virtue but may not become virtuous, and one may be virtuous without knowing that one is virtuous. The divergence between knowing and becoming can be removed only when both can be identical. Instead of making one-sided formulations of this identity, it will be safer and truer to experience if we recognize and admit a change in knowledge situation from level to level. There are levels at which to know is to become and there are levels at which to know is not the same as to become.

The sixth point concerns the relation of evolution, that is, of all becoming and transformation, to the two principles *ex nihilo nihil fit* and its opposite, both of which have been accepted in some form or other by some philosopher or other in all the traditions. This relation is closely connected with the fifth point: On the one hand, man transforms himself completely into Spirit, into something which he is not as mere man; on the other hand, the transformation is said to be recognition of

[44] See the author's article in *Radhakrishnan: Comparative Studies in Philosophy Presented in Honour of His Sixtieth Birthday* (London: Allen & Unwin Ltd., 1951) and also *Idealistic Approaches: Eastern and Western* (Baroda: M.S. University, 1956).

what man is in his essence. From the side of evolution, the question assumes a slightly different form. If life evolved out of matter, mind out of life, and spirit out of mind, if the new entities are really new, then they must have come out of nowhere, and the principle, *ex nihilo nihil fit*, is violated. If they are not new, then what appears to be new must already be existing in a latent form in matter; and the principle is not violated. Even then, however, we have to answer the question: Is the appearance new or not? If it is new, as it must be, the principle is again violated. We have then to modify our principle and to reinterpret it as meaning that something can come only out of something but that the two need not be the same. It follows that, except in a purely mechanistic explanation, the principle in its literal sense cannot be accepted. But, then, can everything come out of everything? If it can, then the very law of causality is violated. We therefore need a law for every happening.

But even now one problem remains. The forms of life, mind, and spirit, it may be said, are quite accidental to matter, and matter may have no purpose in manifesting them. But if man is really the result of the transformation of matter, he cannot but take cognizance of the direction, because that is the direction which he experiences and in which he lives. This direction is a problem for him and he cannot but ask: Whence comes this push and this drive? The drive towards inwardness must be inherent in matter and must be directed towards complete manifestation of spirit. Acceptance of the drive can, to a certain extent, meet our demand for a law. So far as our observation goes, this spontaneous drive has stopped with man, leaving to man's own efforts the further push inwards towards the complete actualization and realization of Spirit. Man can then understand that this achievement is due to his own causality. It thus seems to be man's responsibility to push his inwardness to the greatest depths made possible by evolution itself.

Then a further question will have to be asked. Is this transformation possible if matter itself is not the outwardization or externalization of Spirit? We may accept the transformation of matter into Spirit but not the existence of Spirit in matter like one box within another. But even then transformation needs a push, a direction, a drive towards something. And the question is, whence comes this push? It must be from Spirit which is inwardly latent in matter.

As man stands, he has to become that something towards which the drive is directed. Again, man finds that in the realm of the inward, after certain stages, the transformation is recognition of something deeper: at these deeper levels, to know is to become, and to become is to know. That is why God, the Supreme Spirit, is, by all religions, mystic or otherwise, said to be eternally present in man. God is not a product of the process but an object realized through the process as eternally present all along. If this experience has any truth, then matter has to be regarded as the result of the outward push from within God, and the spirit in man is the result of the inward push in matter. The starting point of the first process and the end of the second process meet in God. The second process is sometimes treated as the pull which God exercises over matter.

In the seventh place, from the point of value of evolution, the question of whether or not the spirit in man and the Supreme Spirit or God are ultimately identical is of secondary importance. The answers given by religious thinkers and mystics are various. Even the mystics are not unanimous in their views, when details are concerned. Some say that the spirit in man and the Supreme Spirit are absolutely identical; others hold that they are both identical and different—identical in form and different in being, and so forth. St. Thomas used analogy to explain their relationship: they are analogical but not completely one. The Vedāntins also gave much thought to this problem. Śaṅkara upheld absolute identity; but Rāmānuja and others maintained similarity of different kinds. But since all schools maintain that God is inward to man, I think that the quarrel over the relationship may be treated as of secondary importance. From the human point of view, we can assess only the value of these positions for man and human affairs; but we cannot assess their truth precisely, as all schools hold that the relationship is beyond ordinary sensuous and rational experience. The attempt to determine logically what is acknowledged to be beyond logic is illogical.

For the same reason, I should think, the controversy between theists and pantheists is of secondary importance. It is self-deception to think that man as such is the same as God. But if something deep within man is the same as God, then the very fact that it is universal and is the same for all men implies that it transcends each individual. That this something is also the creator of matter and supplies matter with the inward drive shows that it is wider than humanity and matter put together. The controversy between theism and pantheism had its origin in the conception of God as external, i.e. as an agent existing somewhere outside man and so remote from his experience that man can understand nothing of Him. The insoluble question here is: How can such a transcendent God enter human experience at all? If communion with God is a legitimate and possible experience, then He must be immanent in human experience. Yet neither Śaṅkara nor Lao Tze nor Mencius nor the Buddhists nor Plotinus maintained that the mind of man is the same as God. Aristotle's distinction between man as a combination of form and matter and God as pure form is not an absolutely transcendentalist conception. As form, which is reason, man partakes of God's nature; and so God is immanent in man. The only step needed to make Aristotle's position complete and rounded out is the possibility of matter transforming itself completely into form; but this possibility of matter transforming itself completely into form is only hinted at by Aristotle and is not explicitly accepted, for he separated the rational soul from the lower.

In this context one may mention a ninth point. The transformation of man into Spirit, it is said, is also the recognition of the eternal presence of Spirit. This conception has led to the doctrine of the illusoriness of the world. The object of recognition is said to be an eternal truth in man; what is apparently transformed into that truth can only be an appearance, an illusion. When truth and falsity are the only two values applied to spiritual transformation, which is the highest value and the end of all ethical process, the struggle for one's ethical uplift tends to be regarded as belonging to the sphere of falsity and is therefore considered to be valueless. Consequently, a negative attitude develops towards the world of matter and ethics. It is against this attitude that ethical leaders like Schweitzer protest. But those who develop this attitude forget one point: the recognition dawns only after the completion of ethical and spiritual transformation. They forget another point: man has to struggle for spiritual transformation, and the struggle is not meaningless. The result, although a recognition, is also the positive result of a positive effort. The conclusion then follows that the two-valued logic is not adequate to explain the process. It is not from falsity to truth that we go, but from one kind of truth to another. Or else not even ordinary transformation can be adequately explained: When an object O changes from state A to state B, we would have to say that A was false and B true.

It is in this context that the negative logic developed by the Buddhists and the Advaitins in India becomes significant. When life develops out of matter, we may ask: Is life the same as matter? The answer given by these philosophers would be: It is neither the same as matter, nor is it different from matter, nor is it both the same and different, nor neither same nor different. The truth is that we do not see life apart from matter and yet they are not the same. Thus whenever there is transformation, the novelty has to be recognized as such; and the novelty and that which is transformed into it do not fit into the two-valued logic.

What should not be overlooked is that we have to explain, if at all, spiritual transformation from the standpoint of man and not from that of the final result by attaining which man ceases to be man and becomes pure Spirit. And from the standpoint of man, transformation is true, it is not an illusion. And man also must be true; for, if he is false, there is no *a priori* reason for saying that what falsity implies must be true. As modern logicians say, a false proposition may imply a true as well as a false proposition. We have no justification to say that the implied proposition is necessarily true. But if man is true, what his being implies must necessarily be true; for every true proposition implies only true propositions. Further, if man is false, why should we give any thought to what he says? The reality of man has to be accepted by every philosophy of life.

As a tenth point we may note that ideals and values belong to the higher reaches of evolution, which are attained by man when he pushes deeper the inwardness produced by nature. When the higher values are attained, they become spiritual facts; and when they are not yet attained, they remain values, ideals to be realized. The field and origin of values is this inwardness, which acts as a lure for man's ethical and spiritual struggle. Nature here does not help man spontaneously. Some philosophers in the East and the West exhorted man to live according to nature; but by 'nature', as already indicated, they must have meant the inward reality, not the brute nature of animals and plants. By the lure of outwardness man is drawn away from his inward nature, and has therefore to struggle for regaining his inwardness and push it to its deepest limits. Man's ethical and spiritual struggle is thus a continuation of the processes of nature's evolution. Man feels the struggle, because he is self-conscious to a high degree. Ethics can have a naturalistic basis only when 'nature' includes man's inwardness. Physical and animal nature cannot be an adequate basis for ethics. Evolution, when man's inwardness is recognized, thus gets ethical significance.

8. NATURE OF THE HUMAN INDIVIDUAL

Jewish thought, with its intense and overwhelming ethical passion, is concerned more with man's relation to God than with an analysis of the psycho-physical individual. In the history of ethical thought we find many attempts to base ethics on the nature of man without reference to God; on his emotions and sentiments, and on his reason. But Jewish thought furnishes an example of a different type. It cared less to analyse the nature of man than Greek thought did; and whatever later Jewish thought said about the nature of man was due to the influence of Greek thought. The primary concern of Jewish thought was with man's responsibility to God, and it was content with propounding that responsibility. The greatest contribution it made to Western thought is the idea that man, the whole man, not merely his reason, is the image of God. 'The image is not in man; it is man.'[45] 'The Greek thinkers sought to understand man *as a part of the universe*; the Prophets sought to understand man as a partner of God.'[46] Indeed, the Prophets were aware of death, of the transiency of human life; yet they were not interested in immortality but in sanctity.[47] The need for sanctity arises because, although man is made in the likeness of God, he is of dust. Man is made of dust, and yet he is an image of God, and dust has to be sanctified: this analysis was enough for the Jewish prophets.

If the word sanctity epitomizes Jewish ethics, virtue epi-

[45] Chapter II, p. 128 (the present work).
[46] *Op. cit.* (the present work).
[47] *Op. cit.* (the present work).

tomizes Chinese ethics. The word virtue has a peculiar applicability in Chinese thought. Man can be virtuous *by virtue of* being man, i.e. the true man. Virtues constitute the nature of man; they are 'natural forces' in man, if we understand 'nature' in the widest sense, not merely in the sense of physical and animal nature. Indeed, I do not see much reason for not calling human nature by the word nature, if we can call physical nature and animal nature by it. If animal nature has its own peculiarities as distinct from physical nature, then human nature may have its own peculiarities as distinct from animal and physical nature. The Chinese emphasized that human nature as such is ethical. This emphasis is particularly true of Confucianism. The roots of pity, compassion, sympathy, righteousness and *jen* are found in man as such and are not conceptual formulas of prudence. They are not reduced to something below or above man.

Although such is the general view of Chinese philosophy as a whole, the Yin Yang school made an attempt to correlate virtues with some forces of nature called Powers or Elements.[48] The idea of correlation is pre-Confucian.[49] But the correlation of virtues to Elements is occult and mystical rather than rational and empirical, and therefore cannot easily be accepted as a philosophical basis for ethics and cannot supply a proper analysis of the human individual. It is therefore understandable that Chinese philosophers refer more to the Confucian analysis, particularly to that of Mencius and Hsün Tzu, than to that of the Yin Yang school, although this school also made its own contribution.

In Chinese thought *hsing* (nature) means 'the nature endowed by Heaven.' This has some similarity to the Jewish conception that man has a divine spark. But the Chinese idea of Heaven is vague and undefined, though often used. Confucius said that 'by nature people are near to one another, but through practice they have become apart.' He therefore upheld that, by nature, men are social, i.e. human nature is essentially social; but that, in practice, man becomes individualistic and self-centred. Rousseau said that man is born free but is everywhere in chains. Rousseau's conception of freedom has thus a ring of individualism. But for Confucius

[48] Fung Yu-lan: *A Short History of Chinese Philosophy*, pp. 131–2.
[49] Fung Yu-lan: *A History of Chinese Philosophy*, Vol. I, p. 27.

man is born into a social nexus, i.e. into definite relationships with other men—which is one of the essential characteristics of man. Confucius did not analyse human nature further. The chief interest of Chinese philosophers does not lie in such analysis but in understanding how and why man is good or evil. Mencius said that human nature is essentially and originally good. The roots of the four virtues, human-heartedness (*jen*), righteousness (*yi*), propriety (*li*) and wisdom (*chih*), are the feelings of commiseration, of shame, of modesty, and of right and wrong, which are found in human nature itself. Hsün Tzu, unlike Mencius, said that human nature is essentially and originally selfish and evil. Some later philosophers maintained that nature is good but feelings are evil. Some classified human nature into three kinds: good, neutral and evil. Han Yu expressed the view that men above the average are good, those below the average are evil, and those at the average are neutral. Some Neo-Confucians wanted to explain the origin of evil. If human nature is originally good, whence comes evil? They did not accept, unlike the Buddhists, that evil is due to emotions and feelings. So Chang Tsai maintained that evil is due to the emergence of physical nature (*ch'i*). *Ch'i* in its original nature of Vacuity is tranquil. But when acted upon, it engenders the two elements, *Yin* and *Yang*,[50] and through integration gives rise to various forms. And whenever these two elements contradict each other, evil arises. Hence physical nature has to be transformed into pure Vacuity.

We see thus that human nature, when analysed, is analysed only from the ethical point of view. Even the function of reason is understood to be that of distinguishing between right and wrong. The constituents of human nature are ethical constituents, like human-heartedness and righteousness. Even when explanations of human nature are sought in terms of Vacuity, *Ch'i*, *Yin* and *Yang*, these cosmic principles are pressed into service as producers of ethical constituents.

The Greek analysis of the human individual is made from a different point of view. The interest of the Greek thinkers, particularly that of Socrates, Plato and Aristotle and the founders of the Socratic schools, is also ethical and human. The aim of none of the traditions in explaining man's nature can be said to be disinterestedly scientific in the modern sense

[50] Chapter III, p. 179 (the present work).

of the word. All wanted to evolve a way of life. But the way of life and the ideals to which the way leads must be workable; and they can be workable, only if they agree with the nature of reality. Hence the study of reality becomes important. But it can be fruitful, only if it is true and unbiased by preconceived ideals. Thus the study of 'things' was the first condition laid down by Confucius for a good ordering of society. But by 'things' most of the Chinese philosophers meant, as mentioned *supra*, human relationships, that is, feelings, and emotions, socially relevant. The Greeks, on the other hand, had a wider conception of 'things'. Although the Sophists and Socrates were not much interested in cosmologies, Plato and, to a greater degree, Aristotle were cosmologists also, so much so that the Stoic conception of nature included the whole ordered universe, and man was asked to live not merely according to his own nature but according to the nature of the cosmos. So one would be right in saying that Greek thought took man as part of the universe, not merely as part of society. Man may be part of society, but society itself is part of the cosmos. Furthermore, the nature of man is to be understood not in terms of the nature of society but *vice versa*. So man as part of the cosmos becomes the starting point. The Chinese philosophers also explained man as part of the cosmos; but their explanations remained occult, mystic, rationally unsystematic, and did not contribute much to a psycho-physical analysis of the human individual.[51]

The pre-Sophists said very little about the human individual. We know very little even about the views of the Sophists except that man consists essentially of sensations. Even the soul is nothing but sensations. Reason is meant for practice, for gaining victory in debate and controversy, not for truth. There is nothing sacred in reason. The idea was current among the Orphics, particularly among the Pythagoreans, that reason lifts man towards God; but the idea was not accepted by the Sophists. They did not draw any distinction between soul and body. But the distinction was made definitely by Socrates. The soul is not merely the guiding part of the human person[52] but also survives death.[53] The human individual is a compound of soul and body. Plato carried farther the analysis

[51] Russell: *History of Western Philosophy*, p. 33.
[52] Chapter I, p. 62 (the present work).
[53] *Op. cit.* (the present work).

given by Socrates. The soul has three parts, factors or aspects, the rational, the spirited, and the vegetative. The rational is the highest and has to control the others. In addition to the three parts, Plato recognized fantasy or imagination, the power that paints pictures in the mind. Again, the rational is the good.

Aristotle's analysis is similar to Plato's; but he is more empirical and realistic than Plato. The soul has three forms, the rational, the animal and the vegetative. The vegetative provides us with the functions of nutrition, growth, and reproduction; and the animal form provides us with sense organs and organs of locomotion. The soul cannot exist without the body, although Aristotle thinks, somewhat inconsistently, that the rational part is immortal and survives death.

Through Orphism, Pythagoreanism, the philosophies of Socrates, Plato and Aristotle the idea runs that rational life is the highest life and constitutes the highest good, that through reason man is one with the highest principle in the universe, the Logos or *Theos*, and that man, by lifting himself to the level of reason, becomes universal and immortal. The third aspect of the idea is an implication of the second. Universality, rationality, immortality—these three may be said to be aspects of the same entity. Thus the rational is the good also. The highest Idea for Plato is the Idea of the Good, which is an Idea of Reason. Rational life is the same as good life. Aristotle did not accept Plato's theory of Ideas; yet for him also the highest reality is pure form, Thought of Thought, Consciousness of Consciousness. Hence the highest good is the contemplative life. This great faith in reason, in its universality, immortality, and its power to take man nearer God is not found in Chinese and Jewish thought.

Writers on comparative philosophy sometimes pointed out that for western thought the basic idea is that man is the measure of all things, whereas for Indian thought it is the Brahman, the Supreme Spirit that is the measure of all things. Therefore, it is said that western philosophy is individualistic, whereas Indian thought has no faith in man. But they seem to forget that the greatest of the Greek philosophers—Socrates, Plato and Aristotle—universalized man by lifting him to the level of reason and made him one with cosmic reason, and only then did they accept the Protagorean principle that man is the measure of all things. It is faith in reason, but not faith in individual man, that motivated Western philosophy and culture. There is no individualism in our faith in reason. Faith in man is due to his possessing reason.

We may say that, for Mencius, faith in man is not due to his possessing reason, but due to his possessing the roots of morality in his feelings. But was he wrong? We should say that, for good life, the possession of ethically significant feelings is as important as the possession of reason. We should say that Jewish thought also was not wrong. For man may possess both feelings and reason, and yet he may deceive himself through what the psychologists call rationalization. A higher source, whatever it is called, than man's reason and feelings is necessary as the guiding and controlling principle of good life.

That good life is rational life, although rational life is not necessarily good life, is accepted by Indian thinkers on the whole. Faith in reason is quite strong in Indian thought. The Sāṅkhya theory of personality is generally accepted by all the Vedāntic schools. It attributes good (*dharma*) and evil (*adharma*) to reason (*buddhi*). But the Nyāya-Vaiśeṣika and the Mīmāmsa attribute them to the *Ātman* itself. The admission that the good belongs to reason implies that good life is rational life; but rational life may be evil also, for reason can be pressed into the service of evil. Again, the Sāṅkhya regards reason as universal and cosmic in significance. At this point some Vedāntins who closely follow the Upaniṣads differ from the Sāṅkhya by distinguishing between individual reason and cosmic reason. Evidently they feel that the individual's reason may err and be evil. But Cosmic Reason does not err and is not evil. To be sure, the Sāṅkhya cannot explain why, if the individual reason is cosmic and universal, it can be evil. However, the faith in the universality of reason and in the goodness of universality is common to the Sāṅkhya, the Yoga and the Vedāntic schools.

Another important similarity is that between the Greek division of the soul into the rational, the spirited, and the vegetative and the Sāṅkhya division of the inner sense (*antahkaraṅa*) into reason, ego, and mind. The similarity is not exact but significant. Reason is pure, transparent; the ego is active and appropriating; and mind synthesizes and divides sensations. The Advaitins added another division, *citta*, the function of which is to collect together all the rationally organized ideas of finite reason into an apperceptive mass or unity, and which is therefore above reason. *Citta* is not exactly the same as Kant's trascendental unity of synthetic apperception, which is the same as the transcendental 'I'; but is similar to that unity. The ego is lower than *citta* according to the Advaita. But *citta* itself is lower than the cosmic reason. The latter is the *Mahān Ātmā* (The Great Ātman) of the *Kaṭha Upaniṣad,* which distinguishes between finite reason and Cosmic Reason.

To the three divisions of the soul given by Plato correspond the three attributes (*guṇas*), *sattva, rajas* and *tamas* of Prakṛti, as propounded by the Sāṅkhya. But the attributes are not attributes of the soul but of Prakṛti, the Primeval Matter. However, *sattva* corresponds to the rational soul, *rajas* to the spirited soul, and *tamas* to the vegetative soul. Often when classifying men according to their nature, it has been the practice of many philosophers to say that some men are *sāttvic,* i.e. intellectual, wise and good, some are *rājasic,* i.e. active and spirited, and the others are *tāmasic,* i.e. dull, unthinking and inactive.

Another analysis of man which we find in Indian thought is that he is matter, life, mind, reason, bliss body and *Ātman.* As he is, man is a unity or synthesis of all of them. And he has three states: waking state, dream, and deep sleep.

The Chinese and the Jewish thinkers, particularly the earliest of them, were not very much concerned with the problem of life after death and so with that of the immortality of the soul. The idea of immortality entered the thought of the Chinese along with Buddhism, and it entered the thought of Judaism after the Jewish thinkers came into contact with Greek thought. Although Epicurus said that the problem of death should not worry man, as there was no death so long as he lived and no life after death; Socrates, Plato and Aristotle believed in soul's immortality. Yet immortality belongs only to the rational soul. According to the Indian thinkers—except the Cārvākas who do not accept the reality of the soul at all, and so reject immortality—immortality belongs not to the rational soul but to the *Ātman,* which is still beyond the soul. Yet the soul, both rational and affective, survives death and undergoes transmigration. This idea is accepted by Plato. Actually, the soul—which for the Sāṅkhya and the Yoga and the Vedāntins is the *jīva*—is the ethical personality, which.

according to the merits and demerits of its actions, takes on new births. One who wants to be free from rebirth has to realize that one is not the *jīva* but the *Ātman*. For the purpose of showing the reality of the *Ātman*, the Indian thinkers made an existential analysis of man's conscious being until the *Ātman* was obtained. Thus the transcendence of the rational soul by the *Ātman* becomes a peculiar contribution of Indian thought.

This conception of transcendence is found not only in the Sāṅkhya-Yoga and the Vedānta but also in the Nyāya-Vaiśeṣika, Jainism, the Mīmāmsa and Buddhism. All schools except Buddhism explicitly maintain that the transcendent principle is the *Ātman*, although Jainism calls it *jīva*, distinguishing the transmigrating *jīva* from the eternal *jīva*. Buddhism calls the transcendental principle *nirvāna*, the unagitated, *śunya*, void or vacuity. The Nyāya-Vaiśeṣika, Jainism, Buddhism, and the Mīmāmsa do not show in reason as a cosmic principle that faith which the other schools show, but the faith is implicit in their philosophies. On the whole, they regard reason as belonging to the individual.

In its Mahāyāna developments Buddhism forms an interesting exception. The Vijñānavāda school upheld the doctrine of *manomātratā*, *vijñaptimātratā*, and *cittamātratā*, all the terms meaning mind-only or reason-only. The only reality is mind (*manas*) or reason (*vijñāna* or *citta*). Do the Buddhists mean by *manas*, *vijñāna*, and *citta* the same as the orthodox schools mean by *ātman*? The rejection of the reality of *Ātman* by the followers of Buddha made the rival schools think that the Buddhists could not have meant the *Ātman* by any of the three words. If the rival schools are right, we may be tempted to draw the conclusion that, for the Buddhists, mind or reason is the absolute reality, and that their faith in reason is as strong as that of the Greeks. But the Buddhists say that reason cannot comprehend pure *Vijñāna*, just as the Vedāntins say that reason cannot comprehend the *Ātman*. Furthermore, the the Vijñānavādins say that *vijñāna* is *śūnya* or void. This assertion seems to be significant. Did they feel at the back of their minds that this pure reason, without any determination and devoid of all empirical content, can say nothing about the world, just as some modern mathematical logicians say that pure logic and mathematics can tell us nothing about the empirical world? Perhaps, as Bosanquet said, even extremes meet in philosophy. Formal logic, which started with the Greeks with a strong faith in the powers of reason to disclose the mysteries of the world, has ended with a frank admission that it can say nothing about the world; reason ended in an admission of complete failure. Similarly, the Buddhist search for the ultimate nature of reality or existence ended in the admission that ultimate reality has no nature (*nissvabhāva, śūnya*), because reason itself, the highest reality in man, has no nature. This is a very strange meeting of extremes, and quite surprising. For comparative philosophy such meetings of extremes are very significant.

With the same spiritual motive as that of the orthodox schools of India, Buddhism analysed man into five aggregates: matter, feelings, ideas, instincts and consciousness. Each of these aggregates is also an aggregate. Man's psycho-physical personality is an aggregate of these aggregates. The unity of his personality can be analysed away into these aggregates. The remainder after analysis is *śūnya, nirvaṅa*, which is not many but one. Another analysis is that of *āyatanas* or bases of experience: the five sense organs, and their objects, mind and its objects, which together make up twelve entities. An interesting difference between the analysis of the orthodox schools and that of Buddhism is that in the latter the five organs of action do not find a place. It seems that Buddhism did not give importance to man's activity.

For all the schools of Indian philosophy except the Cārvaka, the question is: What is the reality reached when human personality is transcended? The answer is: There is something, although differently called and understood. Thus what is immortal is not the human personality as such, but something that transcends it and yet is immanent in it. It is doubtful whether the Greeks believed in the immortality of the human personality as such, although they spoke of the immortality of the rational soul. The rational soul is universal and is part of the cosmic reason. Even if one rational soul is different from another, there is nothing to differentiate the two except their supposed difference. But how that difference can be known is a difficult question to answer.

Indian thought accepted not only the universality of reason but also that of the *Ātman*. Just as we assume that reason is the same for all men, the Advaita maintains that the *Ātman* is the same for all. Many other schools do not accept such absolute one-ness. Even then they have to say that all *ātmans* are exactly alike, although each has an individuality or particularity of its own. But the universality of the pure *Ātman*, like that of pure reason, is an ultimate problem which reason itself is unable to solve. Is reason the same or different in different individuals? Certainly, it works more efficiently in some individuals than in the others; but when it is correct, it gives the same results. Then, are we to say that it is the same or similar? Whatever be the answer, a similar answer can be given to the question whether the *ātmans* are the same or similar. If the individual reason partakes of the Logos or the Cosmic Reason, what is the nature of this partaking? Religious leaders and mystics have given different answers to these ultimate questions. But from the human point of view, we may treat this question as ultimate and leave it to be answered by man for himself when he has that experience of partaking. But the conviction that the results of reason have objective and cosmic meaning and applicability, that good life is essentially rational life—whether the man who lives it knows it or not—and that man should not be allowed to fall below good life seems to be common to both Greek and Indian philosophy, although the latter claims that the highest kind of life transcends rational life even. To live a rational life is to live a non-egoistic universal life, because reason is above the ego. This seems to be implicit in Greek thought, though not clearly expressed.

That man is a knot of the forces and urges acting through him is accepted by the Indian schools. The Upaniṣads speak of the 'knot of the heart' (*hṛdayagranthi*), which is untied as soon as man realizes that his conscious being is essentially the *Ātman*. They say also that man is the field, basis (*āyatana*), of the activity of the cosmic forces, although he thinks that he is the agent and the enjoyer. Buddhism also places *samskāras* (innate forces) above the individual; he is their product. Even in Greek thought, the spirited and the vegetative factors of the soul would constitute the particularity of the individual, and would have to be controlled and guided by the rational part. Reason is universal, and is therefore higher than the individual and is nearer the Divine Spirit than is the individual himself. This is the faith of the Orphics and the Pythagoreans, and even of Socrates, Plato and Aristotle. The word *theos*, from which the word theory is derived, indicates that, for the Greeks, God is essentially a rational being.

Several points emerge in the discussion of this topic. First, none of the great traditional philosophies analysed the nature of man with what we now call a pure scientific dispassionate attitude, that is, with mere scientific curiosity. Their aim was ethical and spiritual. They had a motive, an objective in pursuing the analysis. Logic and epistemology, as pure scientific disciplines, were developed quite vigorously both in Greece and India. But the development was not disinterested. The Greeks, with their ultimate faith in reason, tended, on the whole, to give primary importance to their logic and epistemology, which they applied to their study of man, society, and the cosmos. The Indians, with their faith in something above reason, gave their experiences first, and then accordingly developed their logic and epistemology. This difference explains why ancient and classical India was not interested in the development of pure formal logic. Jewish and Chinese thought paid very little attention to logic and epistemology. The former was primarily interested in the sanctity of man and the latter in social solidarity. And in none of the traditions is philosophy the result of mere scientific curiosity or of what is sometimes called wonder. It is only because of the Greek faith in dispassionate reason that Greek thought is often regarded as a result of wonder.

Secondly, we may say that faith in reason is not a peculiarity of Greek thought. As has been pointed out above, we find it in Indian thought, which also conferred cosmic status on reason. But in Greek thought we find the highest and the strongest faith. Socrates, in particular, said that virtue is knowledge and knowledge is virtue, and in the beginning he refused to recognize that the bad, the false, and the ugly have corresponding rational ideas. His refusal means that evil cannot have an Idea; only the good can have an Idea; which, again, means that only the good can have a place in reason, but not evil. The Indians have no corresponding theory about this aspect of the problem.

In the third place, whether the claim of reason to absolute reality is admitted or not, the idea that good life is universalized life, life raised to the level of universality, is common to all the traditions. The roots of the idea can clearly be seen in the Greek and the Indian doctrines that reason is cosmic and universal. Confucius explicitly enunciated the Kantian principle: Do to others what you wish to be done by them to you. The commandments of God for good life, in Jewish thought, are universal rules. God is the same for all, and His commandments have universal applicability. Reason is right when it rises to the level of universality. But the rational aspect of these rules is not so much emphasized in Chinese and Jewish thought as in Greek and Indian thought.

In the fourth place, man, for all traditions, is a combination of 'Heaven and Earth', 'image and dust', *ātman* and body, soul and body. Yet there are differences. In Chinese thought it is not very clear what Heaven means; and nature endowed by Heaven and Earth is distinguished from physical nature. One may say that nature endowed by Heaven and Earth means that human nature is a combination of the Divine and the earthly, and physical nature is merely earthly. Human nature is psycho-physical and is essentially ethical. In Jewish thought man as such, as a whole, is divine from one point of view, i.e. as the image of God, and dust from another point of view. But the idea that man has a spark of the Divine is also current in Jewish thought—which means that not the whole man but only a part of man is divine. Since man contains both the divine and the earthly, ethical conflict stages in him, higher ideals pulling him upwards and lower desires dragging him downwards.

In the fifth place, Greek and Indian thinkers accept reason, not as a function or aspect of mind as we find in modern philosophy, but as a distinct part of man's being. Modern interpreters are averse to calling it a 'part'. But Plato called it a part of the soul that could exist by itself apart from the other parts. Aristotle might have objection to dividing the soul into separate parts; but actually he said that the rational soul could survive death and could exist separately from the other parts. Many Indian thinkers also say that reason is an entity distinct from mind. It is usual also with the Sāṅkhya and the Vedānta to club together reason, ego and mind and call the totality by the name *antahkaraṇa* (inner instrument); yet they say that reason is an entity distinct from the other two. It is not my intention to defend the division of the soul into three parts. I wish only to show the similarity between Greek and Indian thought. Modern philosophy and psychology may not accept either theory. But the truth seems to be that, for both Greek and Indian thought, reason is a substantive, not an adjective of mind.

The sixth point to note is that, for Indian thought, reason is not the same as spirit (*ātman*). Reason is a product of the contact of spirit and an insentient principle, which is the root of matter. Reason, although universal, has an element of insentience (*jaḍatā*) in it. The contact of spirit with the etherial matter is variously explained; but in every case, reason is the first product of the contact.

The seventh point is that Indian thought has not given as much analysis of man's social nature as Chinese, Greek or Jewish thought. When personality is analysed, it is the individual, apart from society and without reference to it, that is analysed. This omission of reference to society is not due to any unawareness of the existence of society in the Indian thinkers. But their interest in the individual's salvation is dominant; and that salvation is individualistic is also their main doctrine. If those thinkers were to give a list of human rights, they would include what Del Vecchio[54] calls the 'right to solitude' in the literal sense of the term.

However, there are exceptions. The Mahāyāna Buddhists, although they do not deny the possibility of individual salvation, exhort man not to enter *nirvāṇa* until the rest of the world enters it. Some of the Advaitins say that salvation can only be universal, not individual. No individual can obtain complete salvation if a single soul remain without obtaining it. The individual souls are products of Iśvara, a principle corresponding to the Logos of Greek and Hellenistic thought. They can obtain salvation only when Iśvara merges into the Brahman. Until then they have to remain at the level of Iśvara, who cannot become the Brahman if each of his creatures does not return to him. There is another interesting idea in the Pāñcarātra, according to which all the *ātmans*, which are different from one another, together constitute a society like a beehive,[55] and hang on to God. Even at the

[54] Giorgio Del Vecchio: *Justice*, p. 116 (Eng. tr. University Press, Edinburgh, 1952).

[55] See the author's *Idealistic Thought of India*, (London: Allen & Unwin, Ltd., 1953, p. 146).

highest metaphysical level, they constitute a society. However, this idea has not been systematically worked out down to the empirical level. But in the Pāñcarātra we find roots of a social philosophy.

9. LIFE'S IDEALS AND THEIR ATTAINMENT

It is obvious that the four traditions gave different pictures of life's ideals. But we should add that all the ideals are equally important for all men, and pass and repass into one another. The Jewish tradition extolled sanctity of life, detailing every act of man and turning it into a ritual. But this is not peculiar to Jewish thought. Orthodox Indian life is as much a ritual in every aspect—in bathing, cooking, eating and dressing—as orthodox Jewish life is. But the ideal presented by Indian thought is salvation, *nirvāṇa*. Chinese thought maintained the ideal of social solidarity and virtue, and said that the ideal of life is life according to nature. This 'nature', via its association with the *Tao* of Taoism, became the *nirvāṇa* of Buddhism after it entered the country. The Chinese wanted social stability, good government and virtuous men; and men could become virtuous by following their *tao*, which was identified by the Taoists with their *Tao* and by the Buddhists with their *nirvāṇa*. The Greeks also aimed at the ideal of producing virtuous men, a stable society, and a good government. Both the Greek and the Chinese philosophers analysed man for the purpose. The constituents, for the former, are the constituents of the human mind individually considered; but the constituents, for the latter, are the social relationships themselves based upon social feelings of the individual. The Chinese philosopher will say that man will be virtuous by being a true man; that he can be a true man by cultivating his truly human feelings and emotions; and that the truth of those feelings and emotions can be tested by their relevance to social solidarity based on human love and affection. The Greek philosopher will say that man will be virtuous if he controls his lower nature by his higher nature, reason. The Jewish philosopher will say that man will be virtuous, if he knows that God is interested in him and that he is answerable to God for his actions. Indian philosophy also wants to make man virtuous; but it held that he can be virtuous by complete self-surrender, through non-egoity. But to surrender one's ego and yet to live the highest life is to become one with the Supreme Being, whether this one-ness means similarity or sameness.

All the ideals are true and need each other. Are we to think that God gave commandments which are harmful to the nature of man? They must be for the good of man; whatever is for the good of man must agree with his essential nature. And man's essential nature does not consist merely of reason, but also of feelings and emotions. If man's rational nature is completely opposed to his affective nature, then man cannot be ethical unless he jumps out of his skin. Here the Chinese philosophers have a strong point. Ethical nature is not merely rational nature; it is emotional nature as well. Even moral emotions are emotions. Yet mere reliance on man's moral feelings is not enough. Feelings are turbulent, clash with one another, and overwhelm man. So reason, with its universal standards, has to guide and control them. Indeed, it cannot do so unless man develops a strong inclination to be guided by reason. The question, whether or not reason, if it can move man like any other emotion, belongs to his affective nature, is still an open one. If it does not belong to his affective nature, it needs the help of his affective nature in order to move man. Even then reason may end in mere rationalization of evil, unless there is some definite authoritative commandment as Jewish thought maintains, and unless man feels that he is answerable to God. The idea of the right, i.e. of the categorical imperative, acts as a check. But after all, even this idea is an idea in the mind of man and may be wrongly understood. The question, Why is it right? will naturally be raised, and has to be answered in terms of the good. But whose good? Each individual, in such crisis, thinks of his good alone, and finds it difficult to rise to the level of universality. Then the only criterion left is non-egoity, disinterestedness, detachment. Here Indian thought supplies the answer.

Not only the ideals but also the ways of achieving them, as given by the different philosophical traditions, are mutually complementary. One may depend on divine revelation for ethical laws. But the laws are revealed to a finite human mind, which interprets them. The interpretations are necessarily coloured by the imperfections of finitude. The interpretations need checking by historical experience and the nature of man.

When we say that the laws are for the good of man, we imply that they agree with human nature and are meant for perfecting and completing human nature. The same is the implication of Kant's assertion that 'thou oughtest' implies that 'thou canst'. Ethical laws are not meant for making human life dry and miserable. Only when our emotions and feelings are directed along ways pointed out by ethics, can our life be both ethical and happy. Here is the contribution of Chinese ethics, which insists on cultivating virtue through the development and strengthening of the relevant emotions and feelings, without destroying them. Of course, when we speak of *relevant* emotions and feelings, reason necessarily comes in to distinguish between relevant, irrelevant, and opposed. The emphasis on reason is the specific contribution of Greek thought. To prevent the abuse of reason from conscious and unconscious rationalization, the Indian contribution of non-egoity is helpful.

But non-egoity by itself, though ultimate, is not enough for the positive guidance of man. One may surrender egoity and may be very watchful about its intrusion. But what else is he to do then? It is sometimes observed that even the teachings of the *Bhagavadgītā*, so far as definite action goes, are not enough. It asks Arjuna to follow the movement of the Cosmic Person (Viśvarūpa), to swim along the currents of the cosmos, not against them, and to be only an instrument in the hands of God, not an agent appropriating all action to himself. But an earnest seeker will ask: What are the movements of the Cosmic Person, which way do the currents of the cosmos flow? In Western language, Arjuna is asked to act according to the nature and movements of the Logos. But what are the nature and movements of the Logos? We have no answer. The injunction is positive, not negative; yet it is not concrete enough. All that Arjuna could get is that he should perform his duties according to his station and caste. The crux of the problem lies here. Are the duties handed down by custom and tradition true? How are we to judge their truth? One may say that they should accord with the Cosmic Reason or Person. But how are we to know that they do? Do we know the nature of the Cosmic Person? The reference then, so far as human powers go, must not be to the Cosmic Person but to the human person. Our question can then be: Do the duties accord with human nature? If they do, then our faith is that they must accord also with the nature of the Cosmic Person. What is wanting in the Indian ideal and practice can be supplied by the Chinese and Greek ideals and practice.

One warning may be repeated in this discussion. When we are speaking of the Jewish, Greek, Chinese, and Indian ideals, we should not think that each did not take at all into consideration the other ideals and practices. The difference between them is a difference between emphases or over-emphases. Indian thought may preach non-egoity; yet Indian literature contains practical advices and concrete rules of conduct. Greek thought might have stressed reason; yet it has elements of thought supporting the ideal of lifting oneself to the level of the Cosmic Reason or Logos. Mysticism and the idea of self-surrender are not new to Greek thought. Similarly, reason and mysticism are not complete strangers to Chinese thought. Hsün Tzu and the School of Names are rationalistic and Taoism is mystic. Man, in all the cultures, obtained what he needed for good life. But the cultures developed consciously towards ideals most highly admired, and obtained their peculiarity from them.

The way of achieving the ideal of life, for Jewish thought, is following the *Torah* and *mitsvah.* They include man's relations to God, to other man and to nature. Life is highly rigorous, controlled by rules and regulations at every step. Such ethics is very strict, although not ascetic. Public and private morality within society is very high. But the Greek way is rational. Public and private morality is controlled by reason. The possibility of examining both is allowed. There is naturally more liberalism, change and progress than strict adherence to fixed laws. But is not human reason itself to be controlled by some higher principle? We have no definite answer in Greek thought, except that human reason must agree with Cosmic Reason. We cannot definitely know how and when there can be such agreement. The way of the Chinese is the cultivation of *jen* and the other virtues associated with it. It is development of the affective nature of man; the ideal of man is to be fully humane, it is not to become a god or an angel or pure reason. If reason is to be used, it is to be used mainly as an instrument for the proper development of man's affective nature. This is a positive humane ethics, which does not make life miserable. The only difficulty is that, in Chinese thought, man is made a judge of himself, and he has to judge himself with his affective nature as the standard. Greek thought placed reason above affective nature, though it did not advise suppression of the latter. But Chinese thought, on the whole, did the opposite. Indian thought preached non-egoity, which lacks positive content. A truly non-egoistic man cannot be immoral; but in positive morality he lacks guidance. Where non-egoity is over-emphasized, public morality becomes weak, and even private morality becomes infirm, irresolute and inconstant, and even evasive. To attain non-egoity, practices of the Yogic type are developed, and the tendency to treat them as enough and to treat public and private morality as of secondary importance also grows. All the ideals of the traditions are great; but each by itself, when applied to human life, shows the need for the others, because human life is not fixed but fluid and creative.

Here we may raise a few questions.[56] First, what is the ideal which we are to place before man? Should philosophy ask him to become a full man or something other than man, although higher? On this point, philosophies have differed from each other. On the whole, the Jewish, the Greek, and the Chinese philosophies asked man to become a full man; Indian philosophy exhorted him to become something higher. Greek philosophy has a tendency to lift man above himself; but it is not strong. Taoism also has the same tendency; but Confucianism, as we have noticed, is more representative of the Chinese mind than Taoism. Jewish thought, except in its Hellenistic developments, has no such tendency. One may of course say that, unless man tries to be something higher than himself, he cannot be completely himself. But one may apply the golden mean advocated by Aristotle and Confucius; but man's inclinations may be such as to make the application result in making him something below the norm. Yet philosophy has no right to insist that man has to be more than man, but only a perfect man. If man chooses to be something higher, it is his choice. But he cannot escape the ethical demand that he should be a full man.

Secondly, some religions justify themselves in exhorting man to become something higher than man. Almost all religions have done so. Strongly ethical religions demand that man

[56] None of the points is new to Western thought, which is richly varied in its history. Yet they have to be mentioned.

should be a perfect man. But strongly spiritual religions place before him the ideal of something higher. Then what is the relation between ethics and religion as a purely spiritual attainment? We see merits and demerits in each. The minimum that society requires of spiritual life is that it should not be unethical. Similarly, ethics should not be a bar to spiritual communion. If both ethics and religion are true, then they must not come into conflict. We have to say that, wherever and whenever there is conflict, then at least one is wrong.

In the third place, we say that religion should be divorced from politics. In the history of culture and civilization, the divorce has been found to be advantageous. Yet we say that spirituality should be embodied in our social and political institutions. We seem to be asking for the fulfilment of contradictories. But the apparent contradiction is due to the ambiguity of the word religion. We mean by religion, spirituality, communion with God, and self-surrender to Him; and we mean also any institutionalized religion like Hinduism, Judaism, Islam, and Christianity. When we speak of life according to religion, we tend to think of *Torah*, *Sunna*, or *Manu*, and say that our social institutions must accord with them. We get protests when we wish to modify them. But we feel the need to modify them. Hence political and social institutions are made independent of religion, and religious institutions are becoming part of social institutions. Social institutions have thus become wider than the religious; and social laws have begun to control religious institutions instead of *vice versa*. But how then are social institutions to be controlled and guided? Religions have only been partly successful in this guidance. They have not been able to change *pari passu* with the growing knowledge of man and nature. Hence arose distrust of religion. Hence the answer that social institutions should be based upon a scientific study of man and nature. Spirituality has become a taboo; at the most it is explained as emotional and aesthetic development, and the word spirituality is retained, although spirit is discarded. But there can be no spirituality without the reality of spirit. If spirit is real, is it not to be a component of the constitution of man?

Supposing spirituality also is not retained, what can be the basis of man's ethical institutions? All social institutions including the political are ethical. If spirituality is not accepted, then the ethical criterion will be prudent self-interest. Or it may be some traditionally accepted law, which cannot itself offer a basis for its own change and modification, when they are necessary. It is said that when Felix Adler started the American Ethical Union, and placed moral character above theology, he had actually in mind the *Torah*. '. . . his ultimate reality, his absolute moral law or order, was only his father's Torah, the Divine Law, handed down by Yahweh to Moshah on the Mount, the eternal unchangeable Torah, sublimated in Adler's Ethical Idealism into a mystic ineffable Moral Order.'[57] Here is exactly the modern difficulty. If the Jews accept *Torah*, the Muslims *Sunna*, and the Hindus *Manu*, which is right? It is not enough to accept whatever is common to all three. We want a basis for testing the truth not only of the differences but also of the common points, for even the common points may be mistaken. Criteria, like social welfare, adaptability to the environment, survival of the fittest and so on, have been offered by social philosophers and natural scientists. The ethical criterion must take into consideration social welfare, which is therefore a necessary component of the criterion; but it is not enough. If the criterion is social welfare alone, its application may lead to complete totalitarianism and may be detrimental to the individual welfare. And if the individual's welfare alone is the criterion, it can justify selfishness and can, at the most, lead up to prudent self-interest. Next, those persons who can adapt themselves to the environment may not be the ethically fittest, but may know only how to tackle men and nature, treating both alike as instruments for their self-aggrandizement. So ethics, for its basis, has to look upwards and inwards to something higher and deeper than man and society. This something is the spirit in man, demanding his self-surrender, non-egoity.

But this non-egoity cannot be extinction or pure negation of oneself, but transformation of man into the universality of Spirit. The moment when a particular individual is universalized, he ceases to be egoistic. This is the essence of the teaching of all religions, which said, 'surrender yourself to God', 'die to live', 'become one with the Brahman', 'enter *nirvāṇa*', and so forth, although their teachings have been

[57] Charles Francis Potter: *The Faiths We Live By*, p. 197. (The World's Work (1913) Ltd., 1955).

differently interpreted and practised. This teaching is a completion of ethics, not its negation. That is why ethical training is considered by the Vedānta and Buddhism to be a requisite of spiritual practice. It is wrong to think that spiritual realization can be had by a *tour de force* or by a mechanical practice of some psychological discipline (*yoga*), just as chemical compounds can be produced in a laboratory by mixing some components. There is no psychological or physiological chemistry for spiritual realization. Ethics opens the way for spiritual inwardness, which man can push farther by spiritual practices. Ethics by its demand for universalization lifts man above egoity, and paves the way for spiritual inwardness. This universalization is inwardization, the deepening of the self.

The universality of Spirit, being common to all, is naturally that which unites all men, and is expressed by religions as the love that unites God and men. Even the early Greek philosophers thought that the components of the universe are brought together by love and separated by hate. One of the concrete expressions of Spirit is love. As a universal principle, it is called Law or Dharma by the Buddhists, who said that Dharma unifies the world by interconnecting its parts like the intersecting roads of a city.[58] Yet the Buddhists say that Dharma is indescribable, for it transcends man, though it is in man, and man cannot give a complete description of it. All that we know is that it contains the best in human nature, love and its various forms, like sympathy, compassion, friendliness, etc. Hence religions ask us to cultivate these qualities.

Then how is spirituality to be embodied in social institutions? Non-egoity, which is identical with positive spiritual universality, can only be the ultimate guiding principle, but cannot give positive content to social institutions consisting of individuals, who have to act and who therefore cannot completely be devoid of the ego. The content of Spirit, so far as we understand it, must be embodied in human institutions; and embodiment means expression in action. Wherever religions failed, they failed because they could not find out the proper mode of this expression in action. Both action and its proper mode are necessary at the human level. Without them any talk of the spiritual will be meaningless except in the case of saints who transcend society and even humanity.

[58] See *Idealistic Thought of India*, p. 262.

The expression of Spirit in man, we may say, is *jen*; or rather Spirit as embodied in man is the true *jen*, a word derived from the Chinese word for man. It is a more concrete and inclusive idea than love, righteousness, compassion, etc. It is the norm of man, not merely of his rational part, but of the whole man. The Greeks would have called it the idea or concept of man and the Indians man-ness, but neither word can have such a concrete import as that which *jen* can have. Indeed, Confucius did not bother about Spirit, although the realization of *jen* is sometimes spoken of as being one with Heaven and Earth. But in the light of comparative philosophy, we may re-interpret it as the embodiment of Spirit in man. *Jen* brings men together into a common bond of love. The Buddhists said that the function of bringing men together in love is performed by Dharma; but *Dharma* is a less humane word than *jen*. But because the concrete nature of Spirit is beyond man's comprehension, man has to use reason for realizing *jen* in his actions. The Greeks therefore are right. But virtue, in the human situation, cannot be mere knowledge; it is knowledge of the true *jen* plus its cultivation. But because reason may be corrupted and may deteriorate into rationalization, it needs control by the principle of non-egoity. But neither *jen* nor reason works in a vacuum or on a vacuum; it works in some society with some established laws considered to be sacred, meant to be obeyed and, of course, to be modified if necessary; and it works on the instincts, urges, desires, and emotions of individuals. Thus spirituality is embodied in *jen*, and is guided by reason, which, in its turn, is guided by non-egoity; and *jen* is to be expressed in the laws of society and its institutions, which it obeys and, if necessary, modifies. When we ask for the embodiment of spirituality in social institutions, we need not mean that they should be embodiments merely of the *Torah*, the *Sunna*, or *Manu*. Otherwise, there is no hope for the unity, harmony and peace of mankind.

We are now brought to the fourth point. Spirit is supposed to be supernatural; embodiment requires that it should be natural. The supernatural cannot be embodied in the natural. But can Spirit be natural? That it is as natural an entity as matter and life is the teaching of Indian thought and, to some extent, of Greek thought. It is therefore connected with matter, life, and mind. When we speak of Spirit transcending the mind of man, the word transcendence has only a relative significance. Spirit transcends mind, just as much as life transcends matter and mind transcends life. The Jewish conception of absolute transcendence taken over by Christian philosophy is responsible, in western thought, for the rise of naturalism as opposed to the supernaturalism of Spirit. If Spirit is natural, how can it be an ideal? The clue to the answer is found in the process of evolution. If matter becomes life, then life is the ideal of matter; if life becomes mind, then mind is the ideal of life; and if mind can become Spirit, then Spirit is the ideal of mind. All are there in Nature; yet one is the ideal of another. We cannot explain why there is this transformation. An ideal is not something that is to remain always an ideal without being realized. An unrealizable ideal is not a true ideal; 'thou oughtest' must imply 'thou canst'. Indian philosophers said that the transformation is the play (*līla*) of the Supreme Spirit; but they mean nothing more than that Spirit is there as a fact and we have to accept it as such. Any higher natural entity can be an ideal for the lower. To be an ideal is not necessarily to be unattainable or unreal. We have to broaden our concept of the natural.

The fifth point to be noted is that the admission of the reality of Spirit is necessary as a basis for a truly democratic way of life. Spirit expresses itself in social institutions through the individual. It has no other way. Man's contact with Spirit is through his own mind. Whitehead described religion as what man does in his loneliness; and Del Vechio speaks of the 'right to solitude'. There is a sacredness in the privacy of man's life; from this privacy he derives his own individuality and his transcendence of society; and yet this privacy does not make him anti-social, but makes society the nobler for him. Without this transcendence, the individuality of man is reduced to a point formed by the inter-crossing of social forces. If man cannot transcend society, he cannot react to it. And he can transcend society because of his contact with his inward Spirit. Without accepting this transcendence, democracy reduces itself to pure totalitarianism. The privacy of the individual has a core, spiritual in essence.

As a sixth point, we may ask: Is Spirit real? Does not this transcendence belonging to the individuality of man bring back egoistic ethics? It has been the teaching of all religions that God, the Supreme Spirit, is the same for all. Early Jewish thought did not raise questions about individual immortality but only about sanctity. Yet it accepted the reality of one Supreme Spirit. Greek thought accepted the reality of Universal Reason or Logos, with which individual reason was to be one. The Vedānta, Buddhism and Taoism accepted an ultimate principle with which man was to become one. This becoming one with the Supreme Spirit is common to all religions; some took it literally; others took it metaphorically. Becoming similar to God is implied in the Jewish idea that man is made in the image of God and has to justify that he is an image. In order to become something higher, man has to rise to a universal point of view. Thus this higher individualism is not egoistic but universalistic. Man can find justification for differing from society, only when he can identify himself with the Supreme Spirit. Thus politics, social thought, ethics, and religion are practically unanimous in stressing the need for this transcendence. And if man's experience has any truth, then Spirit must be true. And if we do not deny the reality of man, then the reality of Spirit cannot be denied. Much depends on how we understand it. If we treat it as supernatural, as completely cut off from what is generally called natural, there is no way for accepting its truth except that of faith. But Spirit can be real only as a natural entity, not as a supernatural entity.

And why should we call Spirit supernatural? Is it because we cannot explain its processes in terms of physics that we call Spirit supernatural? Then life cannot be explained in terms of inorganic matter and has to be called supernatural. Similarly, from the standpoint of life, mind will be a supernatural entity. If we do not regard life and mind as supernatural, we have no justification for calling Spirit supernatural. It is not our ability to explain with the help of a certain method that should distinguish the natural from the supernatural, but experience and its implications. Our methods of explanation should be changed according to the nature of the entity to be explained. Spirit can be explained only in terms of spiritual experiences, not in terms of physical experiences. When once it was found that the physico-chemical methods could not explain life, the reality of even life was denied. But now the science of life has developed its own methods. Similarly, the study of Spirit should have its own methods.

10. INFLUENCE ON RELIGIOUS TRADITIONS

Does the philosophy of man influence religion or does religion influence the philosophy of man? History shows that the influence has been mutual. Jewish thought framed the concept of man as the image of God; and the concept is ethico-religious. Judaism is the root of Christianity, and along with Christianity it influenced Islam to a great extent. The mythology of the three religions, like the stories of creation, have many common elements. Greek thought also later entered Christianity and Islam and to a degree even Judaism, and made them philosophical. For all the three religions, although they distinguish between body and soul, the main question is: What is man and what is he to do? For Indian philosophy, the question is: What is the nature of the 'I'? It is not the body, not life, not mind, not even reason, but Spirit. Thus the philosophical quest has become the religious quest. It is in Chinese thought that the influence of the concept of man on religion is the most clearly seen. After Buddhism entered China and the *Tao* and 'nature' were identified with the *nirvāṇa* of the Buddhists, some Neo-Confucians asked: What does a man of realization do? He lives according to nature. The minimum he has to do will be drawing water from the well, cutting wood, cooking his food and eating it. If such activities accord with the *Tao*, why does taking part in social and political activities also not accord with the *Tao*? Man has to live according to his nature, which is his *tao*. To take part in social and political activities is also according to his *tao*. Thus the Chinese philosophy of man drew back to itself the Taoist and Buddhist religions. Chinese philosophy is mainly socio-ethical, and religion is made to subserve its ends.

Religions influenced the philosophies of man by supplying ultimate ideals. This observation may not be true of early Chinese philosophy; but Taoism following Buddhism, became a religion later, and even Confucianism tended to be a religion. And generally when an idea of man gets the approval of religion, and the highest in man is analysed and postulated, the tendency is to exhort man to realize it; consequently the difference between one religion and another can finally be traced to the difference between the highest in man according to the one and that according to another. We have already seen that these conceptions need each other; religions therefore have something to contribute to each other.

II. EDUCATION AS THE DEVELOPMENT OF THE HIGHEST IN MAN

Whatever be the actual practice, the methods, and the programme of education, ideals considered to be the highest gave them a bent and a guiding principle. The ideals considered to be supreme were theorized, not those considered to to be less important. For instance, the Indian ideal of the realization of the Brahman or of communion with God was elaborated into a theory of practice, and it became the central theory of education. Yet that man should learn how to be great, how to be a useful member of his community and of the wider humanity, and how he should develop the virtues of love, compassion, charity, wisdom, etc. is also given as advice and exhortation. But this advice is not properly systematized into a theory based upon human nature. That man is essentially a social animal, rational and political, is a conception not so seriously considered in Indian thought as in Greek thought; and consequently that human personality has social reference is also not definitely formulated. This is accepted either directly or indirectly by Jewish and Chinese thought. But in Indian thought it is ignored, although tacitly implied in the advices given. Hence the ideal of education, with the aim of social usefulness, did not obtain explicit recognition. The ancient Buddhist universities were monastic. But so also were the universities of mediaeval Christendom. The ideal was to make man higher than man. Naturally both taught the suppression of emotional life, the Indian universities doing it more methodically than the Christian. Even Christianity cannot be regarded as being free from this practice. Montague tells us how the Christian Church impeded not only the advancement of science but also humanitarian work, on the ground that man ought not to interfere with nature created and guided by God.[59] However, the humanitarian work done by the Church is great indeed. Here religion seems to be preaching contradictories, at the one extreme preaching charity, love, friendliness and alleviation of human suffering, and at

[59] *The Great Visions of Philosophy*, p. 172.

the other extreme preaching man not to interfere with the processes of nature, including suffering, but to subdue and suppress human nature and emotions. This is true of Indian religions also, although they have never asked man not to interfere with nature in the alleviation of human suffering. But on the one hand, they preached complete suppression of man's emotions and propensities; and on the other, they exhorted man to construct tanks, build hospitals, do charity, cultivate love, non-injury, friendliness, and compassion.

An explanation is offered for this contradiction. Virtues like Charity are said to make man less egoistic and to lift him to the level of universality. They control emotions and urges in the individual by sublimating them. But why should we regard the process of sublimation as supression? Why should we not regard it as canalization, transformation, universalization? I believe that the latter understanding and interpretation is more correct. Transformation is the nature of evolution directed inwards. It is the attainment of deeper and deeper inwardness. The universality, which man attains in his inward struggle, is an inward universality. In it egoity, which is particularity, becomes thinner and thinner. Ethical rules, like love and charity, are meant to lift man's emotional nature to the level of universality. Ethics therefore has a positive role to play in helping spiritual communion. It is not something to be discarded but to be transformed and elevated. At the spiritual level, perfection of personality lies in its complete universalization and therefore in transcending personality. This transcendence is understood, by Indian Vedānta and Buddhism, as depersonalization. But as we have seen, non-egoity is an essential aspect of the ethical and spiritual ideal; but it has to be re-interpreted.

Education therefore was not wrong in attempting to train man in non-egoity. But it may miss the other aspects of the ideal life, and may be concerned exclusively with non-egoity. Here is the danger that a man, trained accordingly, may not become a useful member of society; he may become a social cynic and anti-humanitarian; and when unable to appreciate the ideal, he may become even anti-social. The Chinese insistence, therefore, on the cultivation of emotions and *jen* is a necessary complementary to the ideal of non-egoity. Otherwise, non-egoity lacks content, even when interpreted as universality. It is interesting to note that both Confucius and Plato taught that music is an important part of education and produces harmony of emotions. And this harmony should be made the basis of non-egoity or universalization of the ego.

Greek thought, on the whole, felt that harmonization is the power of the rational soul, and so taught tending the rational soul. Tending it involves tending the lower parts also, as reason otherwise will have no content. Emotions should become rational in the sense of being rationally canalized and directed.

Education should thus aim at the development of the whole man including his emotions and urges, under the guidance of reason properly cultivated towards the ideal of universalization. It is the transformation of man's particularity into universality. To this universalization belong virtues like justice, wisdom, etc. They are the expression of the universality given inwardly to every man. Man can attain their universality by controlling his emotions and urges and by giving them a proper direction. He cannot suddenly transform himself into spirit without transforming his urges and emotions. To this end the different philosophies of education belonging to the traditions are contributory. And for attaining this end, they are complementary to one another.

12. CONCEPTIONS OF MAN COMPLEMENTARY

The reader might have seen that the conceptions of man, sometimes apparently strange to each other, are brought together as complementary. This bringing together has been possible, because man is essentially the same everywhere and is in need of all values. In some parts of the globe he might have seen the importance of some values and formulated theories about them only; but he has tacitly been accepting and working with the others also. What he needs in the present age is consciously to recognize the importance of all, to co-ordinate them, and to plan his life accordingly. Ages-old differences, suspicions, and animosities make some values appear strange, although they may have been involved in his activity all the time. He may wonder at the idea that they have been involved in his life; but the wonder will rouse him from his dogmatic self-sufficiency, and widen the horizon of his intellect and experience.

The conceptions are complementary because the man of one culture is not really strange to the man of another, although some writers picture him otherwise. It has been said that the West is expansive, extensive, and objective, whereas the East is self-centred, inexpansive, intensive, and subjective. Even if we take the differentiation to be true, each needs the other and cannot be a stranger to the other. There is no subject without an object and there is no object without a subject. Cultivation of each needs a corresponding cultivation of the other; otherwise there is danger for both. The balance of exclusive self-centredness is easily destroyed by any external factor which has not been taken into the being of the subject; and mere other-centredness dissipates the subject. And if the subject is lost, what is the use of the object? One may say that the eastern cultures have been able to survive only because the subject is not lost. In other words, the inwardness of man, in the East, is intensely developed and is able to rise above the conflicts created by new incoming objective factors. East and West are complementary to each other; the Eastern man has something to teach the Western man and the Western man has something to teach the Eastern. But the truth, as it seems to me, is neither the West is completely dissipated in objectivity nor is the East completely absorbed in subjectivity. The difference is only a difference of emphasis. Leaders of thought, both in the East and the West, raise their voice whenever there is loss of equilibrium, and humanity adjusts itself.

Only when we understand the need of the subject for the object and of the object for the subject, can we reconcile science and ethics. Like ethics science is not an authority dictating what natural laws are. From the human point of view, science is an activity unconcerned with human values. It is an activity of man, all the same, directed towards understanding and controlling the object; and it assumes that this control makes no difference to the object and that the object has no value for itself. Such an object we call physical nature. Human nature has a value for itself, and external control makes a difference to it. Although physical nature has no value for itself, its control is directed towards human values. It is the duty of man to see that this control is directed towards right values, and that it is not aimless or misdirected. In terms of the above distinction, I may say that, the wider the objectivity attained, the deeper should be the subjectivity. If subjectivity confers meaning on objectivity, objectivity guarantees the truth and reality of subjectivity. Only apparently is science unconcerned with human values; for it is really meant to be an instrument of human values. Values are excluded from scientific study, because we want that nature should be understood as it is—so that we can know its laws and, through them, control and utilize it—but not because we want science for itself as an end in itself. The crisis in Western culture, however it is explained and by whatever name it is called, is due to the conscious or unconscious forgetting of the instrumentality of science for obtaining power over objectivity in order to force it to conform to human values. The crisis in Eastern culture is due to a similar forgetting that inwardness cannot be true unless its correlativity with outwardness is retained. Spirit is not mere subjectivity, but is polarized into the other pole, objectivity, also. Science is originally meant for man and his values. What he and his values are is given in the great philosophical traditions.

In conclusion, I might say that philosophy does not seem to belong to No Man's Land between science and theology. Philosophy, first and last, is philosophy of life. There is no theology in India and China. The moment the word 'life' is uttered, some may say that the subject belongs to biology; but biology is not the same as philosophy. Philosophy then may be called the discipline which brings together facts and values and which brings to light values involved in facts. Russell says that even philosophies of analysis are meant to inspire a way of life. But what way of life do they inspire? Because reason is primarily concerned with analysis of facts, the way of life it inspires has led to the denial of reality to values, not explaining them but explaining them away or rather exposing them. Plato also separated reason from perception, as the modern school of analysis has done; but it did not lose its content, its content was idealized perception. But reason, in the modern school, has tended to be empty. It has lost the characteristic of the good. But that the rational is the good is the faith and teaching of the grand tradition of Western philosophy. One can therefore see how far modern reason has strayed from the way paved by her mother in the grand tradition. Rational life can no longer claim to be good life. Philosophy is useful, and can justify its existence by keeping in touch with the life of man. And what the life of man is can be seen in the great philosophical traditions of the world. They might have committed mistakes, ignored some aspects of experience, and over-emphasized some others; but they have not lost their importance and usefulness.

As some philosophies have not ceased to be religious, comparison becomes a very delicate affair. Every religious philosophy claims to be self-sufficient and wishes that others should say so. I hope that I shall be excused if I have not said so. I have high regard for every religious and philosophical tradition. But the more I think about them, the more I feel that, although each contains an essential and undeniable truth, it has, at the same time, its own shortcomings which are due to the limitations imposed upon its ideas by the conditions of space and time. The great traditions are complementary to each other and have to be completed further by the addition of the results of the conflict between science on the one hand and religion and ethics on the other. The great traditions bring us back to man and his values, which the modern scientific temper has left in the background, ignored or even denied.

There seems to be a feeling that bringing together the truths and values of the different traditions will end in eclecticism. But if it is necessary to bring them together and if such work must end in eclecticism, then eclecticism will be the only adequate philosophy of man. But I do not think that it will necessarily end in eclecticism. If the different truths are truths and the values are true values and all belong to the same reality, then there must be a way of integrating them without being eclectic. The truths are truths for man and values are values for man: man becomes the centre of reference for all. A new standpoint for philosophy has to be recognized. Man becomes the common denominator of all truths and values and therefore of all philosophies. All truths and values have to be integrated without losing sight of their reference to man, who is already an integrality given in reality. This integration has therefore to be done critically, determining carefully how each truth and value can be a completion of the others. Such work will lead to a new kind of humanism, which is critically systematic and which, at the same time, does not ignore the integrality of man. A new standpoint in philosophy will be the result of such work.[60]

[60] For the new standpoint, see *The Personalist* (Vol. 32, No. 5, July 1951), *The Philosophical Quarterly* (Vol. XXIV, No. 1, April 1951), and *The Proceedings of the International Congress of Philosophy* (Vol. VIII, 1955), and *Revue Internationale De Philosophie*, (Fascicule 3, 1956), for the author's articles. See also the author's *India's Culture and Her Problems* (University of Rajputara, 1952) and 'The Concept of the Spiritual in Indian Thought', (*Philosophy: East and West*, Vol. IV, No. 3, October 1954).

CHAPTER VI

The concept of Man in Christian Thought[1]

ERNST BENZ

I. THE SOURCES OF CHRISTIAN ANTHROPOLOGY

NO presentation of the Christian understanding of man in this age of the ecumenical movement can be satisfactory, if it only gives again the anthropology of any particular Christian denomination. However, the theological efforts of the Christian churches are to-day directed towards working out a common understanding of the essence and status of man, of his relation to God, to the universe, and to his neighbours, through joint reflection on the common biblical foundations of the Christian dogmas.

But such a commonly acknowledged Christian concept of man is the goal of the ecumenical endeavour, and the endeavour to reach the goal is only in its infancy. It is not our aim to speak of the theologically binding expressions in which the endeavour shows itself and on which the following exposition can be based. Whoever tries to grasp the Christian concept of man is, therefore, directed, as always, to fall back on the Old and New Testament sources and to add to them the various statements in which the tradition of the Early Church and the main forms of the Christian Church and denominations have expressed themselves on the theme of Christian anthropology and the types of the Christian concept of man which they in particular realized in the development of Church history.

[1] Translated from the German manuscript into English by P. T. Raju with the help of Prof. Wm. Schreiber of the Department of German and Prof. H. B. Smith of the Department of Religion in The College of Wooster. Dr Ernst Benz, with the help of his assistant, Mr E. L. Lashlee of Harvard Divinity School, gave the final reading and touches to the English version. Dr Raju is thankful to all of them.

However, it is advisable, in presenting Christian anthropology, not only to consult the dogmatic texts of the Christian faiths, which represent, more or less, the typical interpretations of the Old and New Testaments. Of equal importance are the spontaneous expressions of the Christian mystics for whom the question of the understanding of the Christian concept of man in connection with their own religious experiences was important. The religious experience of the mystics is one of the strongest creative impulses of the Christian history of the spirit. While the anthropological chapters of the dogmatic texts have, for a great part, a conventional character and, in the process of the development of Church history, showed very few new ideas, in the anthropology of Christian mysticism, surprisingly new, fresh, and revolutionary aspects came to the fore. In the field of anthropology one is, therefore, quite dependent on the Christian mystics.

This anthropology is all the more important because, for centuries, some themes of Christian anthropology have, under the domination of one-sided dogmatic conceptions, either receded into the background or have been forgotten. So the question of the Christian understanding of nature and of the relation of man to the universe faded away in European Christianity during the period of Reformation of the sixteenth century. As a result, the religious question was reduced to that of man's personal relationship to God and that of faith and its vindication. Here above all stand the mystics who, through the centuries, have carried forward the knowledge of the inner connection of God, man, and the universe, and have interpreted it in ever new forms, according to their own unique experience of God and Christ.

2. MAN, THE IMAGE OF GOD

The starting point of the Christian understanding of man is the knowledge that man has been created in the image of God. This idea of the creation of man after the image of God[2] has become so generally familiar in the centuries-old theological tradition that few understand that incomprehensible mystery or even imagine that a mystery is expressed or shows itself in this

[2] Genesis i. 27. So God created man in His own image, in the image of God created He him.

conception of man. But nothing more and nothing less lies enclosed in it than that the incomprehensible, immaterial, almighty God, who transcends all existence, all power, and all knowledge, wanted to become a copy of Himself in His creatures and that of all His creatures, He chose man to form a copy of Himself in him. This does not mean that He simply impressed His image like a seal on some plastic material, but also that He raised man to a creature in which He recognized His own image and came to the consciousness of Himself and that man then, in a completely decisive way, belongs to the self-manifestation of God, that the history of humanity is theogony. In man God works out His own image; God, as He is, makes His appearance in man. As He reflects Himself in man, He not only allows man to partake of His image, but also makes him a partner in His self-realization, His self-manifestation. So closely do man and God belong to each other that one can say that they are designed for each other. Here the statements of the mystics have their significance. Those who have had the experience of *unio mystica* have time and again expressed the thought that man and God are designed for each other

> I know that without me God cannot live even for a moment.
> If I were destroyed, He would give up His spirit in distress.
> (Angelus Silesius)

This is perhaps the most radical interpretation of the idea that man has been created after the image of God. Man finds his fulfilment in God, his prototype; but God also comes to the full consciousness of His own Being in man. In the *unio mystica* the longing for God by man fulfils itself, and so too the longing for man by God.

No other mystic has perceived the relation between God and man as a two-sided one so strongly and understood the mystery lying in the image-relationship between God and man so profoundly as Meister Eckhart. His view is expressed clearly in the following thought: The innermost essence of God is love; but the lover can fulfil himself only in a freely returned love; God created man after His image and thereby conferred on him freedom so that he could turn his full love to Him and return God's love; but with that freedom God opened for man the possibility to turn away from Him. Man has, in fact, proved his freedom in its negative possibility; he has loved himself, instead of turning his love towards God. But God cannot allow it to pass that He loves man without expecting the fulfilment of His love through a free return of love. He awakens divine love in man in that He begot and brought forth His Son in him. The divine abyss and depth is that abyss out of which the divine love wells up, flows over, and floods human love to fulfil itself in it.

The idea of man as the creature made after the image of God was already interpreted in a two-fold way by the Early Church. First, it was held that man, like the other creatures of the universe, is, in essence, a creature of God; that is, he is not divine in his own nature, he is created out of Nothing and, as a creature, stands in simple dependence on God; as a creature, he has nothing by himself, but owes everything, even his existence, to the will of his divine creator. Thereby the special relationship of man to his fellow-creatures comes into the open. Man stands in a solidarity of universal brotherhood with all his fellow-creatures, who, like him, have received their life and form from God.

In modern Western theology, the idea of the solidarity of the created beings with one another in the light of their common creatureliness through God, to whom they owe their nature, life, and form, is overshadowed by the idea of the special place of man and his specific commission to rule the world. Only rarely and only by a few charismatic personalities in the spiritual history of the West is the idea of the solidarity of man with the rest of the creatures realized and expressed. One of those few charismatic persons who have felt the creaturely brotherhood with other fellow-creatures in an original way was Francis of Assisi, who expressed this experience in his *Song of the Sun*:

> Praised be thou, my Lord, with all your creatures,
> particularly with our Sister Sun.
> Praised be thou, my Lord, through our Brother Moon,
> Praised be thou, my Lord, through our Brother Wind,
> Praised be thou, my Lord, through our Sister, Mother Earth,
> who cares for and nourishes us,
> Praised be thou, my Lord, through our Brother, the bodily
> Death.

There are few statements in modern theology in which this

awareness of the solidarity of man with his fellow-creatures comes to expression as a dominant motive of Christian thought and Christian practice; and moreover, they lack the insight that this loss of the consciousness of solidarity is one of the results of the revolt of man against God that has basically changed man's relationship to God, the universe, and his fellow-creatures.

The second aspect of the idea of man as the image of God is much more impressively pushed into the foreground: The fact that God has created man after His image determined man's special status before all the other creatures. God created man after His image: through this a unique position is assigned to man with reference to God and also an absolutely special assignment with regard to the other creatures. In the fact that one sees the image of God in man, which is only suggested in the other creatures, is founded the unity of humanity, within which the biological and racial, the geographical and historical differences—as individuations of that unity—are the common characters of the *imago dei* for all men. The image of God in man is the true sign of his divine destiny and calling, and the ground of the future integration of humanity. For the sake of this destiny and calling, 'all men should, with one another, consider themselves as one man, and should maintain with one another the greatest unity and peace'. (Johann Arndt.)

In what does this being the image of God consist? Christian theology, under the influence of the dualistic philosophy of Plato, has sought for some time to see the idea of man as the image of God restricted simply to the rational faculty of man and to his means of cognition. Augustine's great work on the divine Trinity, which has inspired the whole theology of the Middle Ages, began with the basic idea that, if man were created after the image of God, then some traces of the inner triune nature of the life of God should be capable of being found in man, and that these traces should be discovered in the spiritual life of man. Thus Augustine sought to establish, in an analysis of the process of sense perception these traces of the divine triunity—*vestigia trinitatis*—and thereby to grasp metaphysically and psychologically God's image in man.

Here also Christian mysticism has gone further than the dualistic understanding of man and has understood him in his unity of body and spirit as the image of God. The image of God impresses itself right into the sphere of man's corporeality.

Behind the idea of the creation of man after the image of God lies already the basic notion and the basic intent of incarnation, the descent of God into flesh, the self-manifestation of God in man. Moreover, in the creation of man after the image of God the will of God to manifest Himself in the body of history demonstrates itself. Furthermore, man exists according to his bodily constitution; he is that universal being in whom the forces, the formative principles, and the forms of manifestation of the whole universe hold together in a personal unity.

3. MAN AND THE UNIVERSE

From the outset, man's relation to the universe also has been held in view in the idea of man as the image of God; for the universe, the cosmos, is also an image of God, the creative ideas of God are represented in it also, and the spiritual forms, which existed in the consciousness of God, have realized themselves in it physically. God is an *ens manifestativum sei*, a being who forces Himself towards His own manifestation, presentation, and incarnation, and whose place of work, self-manifestation and self-realization, is the whole realm of the created universe.

Man and the universe, therefore, stand at the same time in an image-relationship between themselves. To determine this relationship in detail, Christian anthropology took an ancient idea of Neo-Platonic mysticism and changed its meaning, viz., the idea of man as the microcosmos, the little world. This idea signifies that man, according to his body-spirit nature, is the representation of a synoptic combination of all the life-forms and formative principles. The whole realm of life of the creatures is nothing else than the unfolding of man. All these formative elements and forces, which find a final, definitive form in man, are displayed, so to say, in an experimental, artistic, and playful way in the whole realm of the animal and plant world and in the organic and mineral world. The idea of man as the microcosmos in the Christian exposition, as compared to the Neo-Platonic understanding, is so transformed that the idea of creatureliness and the essential difference between God and man is nowhere abandoned, and that a distinctive hierarchy of worship, love, service, and responsibility was derived out of man's special place. This idea was the most clearly expressed by Johann

Arndt, who gave the gist of the whole mystical experience of Western Christianity in his *Four Books of True Christianity*.

Worship:

Man should 'use the creatures of God—for the knowledge, praise, and value of God so that God will be praised in all things through our Lord, Jesus Christ'. The creatures among whom man is placed are understood as the 'hands and messengers of God', 'which shall lead us to God'.

Love:

A look at the wonderful order of nature should exhort man to love God, who has drawn in every single form of His creation the 'sign of His living hand-writing and direction'. To every believing man, the universe opens itself as a realm 'of every perfect gift coming down from the Father of lights',[3] and exhorting man freely to love God.

Here shows itself the insight into a typically Christian understanding of the universe and the conception of man's place in it: The world, as the creation of God, is understood as the realm of divine order, which has its validity through the will of God. Therein is grounded a great inner confidence of man in the world, which is understood as the realm of self-realization of divine order and providence as well as the basic awareness that the world, as it is, is right. Here in the sphere of the relation of man to the world is the dualism overcome. Man is not thrown into an evil, hostile, and naturally sinful and wicked world; he stands in the world as a creature of God, as a microcosmos in the middle of a great cosmos, which likewise has issued forth as a creature of God, and which has been built according to the same laws and regulations as those that form the inner constitution and spirit-body structure of man.

Service:

The same hierarchical order shows man his special service. Man is the 'noblest' creature: while all the other creatures are created to serve man, man is created to serve God. For the reason that all the other creatures are directed towards man, find their end

[3] James i. 17.

and their highest aim in him and 'all their works' rest 'in one single man as the highest and noblest creature',[4] and those creatures are without rest to serve the most noble of creatures among them, 'so is it against all nature and against all creatures that man, who is the noblest creature, should not serve the one God as one who is far higher and nobler than man' himself. Thus the consideration of the other creatures leads man himself to the knowledge of his own place in the universe and with reference to God.

Responsibility:

The peculiar responsibility also of man with reference to God is herein expressed now. It is nowhere separated from the position of man within the togetherness of the creatures and the universe. It is very definitive for the founding of Christian anthropology that the view-point of responsibility is superposed on the viewpoint of lordship. Just because the creatures have received what they have, not for their own sake, but for the sake of man, man also has obligation not only to himself, but also to the world with reference to God. So 'the better and the more noble the creatures are, the more man is under obligation to God'.

Only from this idea of the obligation of man with reference to all the other creatures on the basis of his peculiar position within the hierarchy of creatures is to be understood the commission of lordship, which God assigned to man over the whole hierarchy of creatures lying under him, with the words to the first created human pair: 'You subdue the earth!'

4. THE LORDSHIP OF MAN OVER EARTH

This is perhaps the point at which Christian anthropology and cosmology differ sharply from the great non-Christian religions of Asia. Above all, it is to Buddhism that such a commission of God to man to subjugate all creatures below himself is particularly unacceptable and offensive in view of the relation of man to the universe, which is not domination, but identification.

It is precisely here that the connection of the secularization of Christianity and Christian culture with God's commission to man to rule the world is founded. The whole development of

[4] *Buch* 4, *Teil* 2, *Kapital* 3.3.

industrial revolution and modern technology has ended in terms of a secularized proclamation of this commission of domination —a proclamation that has been detached from its religious roots. This process of secularization was possible because the technological revolution and the emancipation of the natural sciences were complete at a time when the Christian Church itself, in its proclamation, almost completely neglected the Christian anthropology. The Christian proclamation has very much forgotten to point out to man with all emphasis that the commission of God to man—'You subdue the earth!'[5]—was directed to him before the Fall, i.e., before the abuse of his freedom to rise against God; and that this mighty commission to dominate was connected with a no less comprehensive obligation to the world entrusted to man. The commission to dominate, which was given to the primordial man, was tied up from the first with the assignment of the highest obligation to the world before God. It is fulfilled, since the Fall, only in those men who are regenerated by Christ. The farther the lordship of man reaches, the wider will be the obligation before God to the creatures which have been entrusted to man; and this obligation is known and carried out to the fullest extent by him who has received again the renewal of God's image from Christ and in Christ. This is the only knowledge by which the mistake of modern technological development and the misuse of the domination exercised over the world by man through his technics can be overcome to-day.

5. THE PROBLEM OF EVIL

The Christian understanding of evil is directly connected with the basic idea of man as a being created in the image of God. It is false to think that the Christian idea of evil and sin is derived from the dualistic presupposition of the contradiction between spirit and body, mind and matter. The triumph of evil is not identical with the conquest over spirit by matter, 'by the flesh'. It is true, such a dualistic interpretation has been suggested, for the Christian understanding of sin among many teachers of the Church was for centuries influenced by the philosophical presuppositions of the Neo-Platonic dualism. Moreover, Manichaenism had its influence on Augustine, who had been in

[5] Genesis i. 28.

the end fed on the dualistic ideas of the Zoroastrian religion and who saw, above all, in the sexual concupiscence the primary drive of the power of sin.

One also bars the entrance to the inner understanding of Christian anthropology, if one starts from a metaphysical dualism. The only right starting point is the idea of freedom, which is founded in the idea of man as the image of God. God has created man in His image. As God, the creator, is a person, whose personality unfolds itself in His unfathomable and mysterious inner life, the character of being a person comes, therefore, to man, as His image. Man is a person because God is a person and man is made after God's image. The personality of man is the actual stamp (impress) of his being God's image; and here lies the real nobility (dignity) of man, who is distinguished from all the other creatures. If the Christian faith differentiates itself from all the other religions by the fact that God is a person for all the Christians, then this faith finds its dynamic realization and its creative influence in the consequence that follows, viz man is also a person.

Now, along with the acceptance of the idea that God has made man after His image, i.e., as a person, an immense risk is also taken. The proper mark of God's personality is freedom. When God made man after His image, He gave him the noble characteristic, freedom; and this freedom surely makes the only presupposition of love, the only possibility that man, as a partner of God, brings to God his love in return.

Here we come upon the inner kernel of the *imago*-idea, the Christian view of love. Love in its perfect form is possible, according to Christian understanding, only between persons; and inversely, a person can fully realize himself only in love to another person. But the fundamental presupposition of love is freedom.

Here a mystery suggests itself, which only mystics of the rank of Meister Eckhart dared to speak out: Why has God after all created man? Why has He taken this risky step to make a creature created by Himself be an image of Himself and to impress the stamp of His own personality on it? The mystics have, out of their innermost experience, only the one answer to this question: God willed not to be alone; He wanted to realize His essence, which is love, in a meeting with another being that is in a position to meet divine love through its own free love.

Man should be a partner of God; he should be one in whose free love of God the innermost being of the creator is fulfilled.

> God is to me so much as I am to Him,
> Him I help for His Being as He mine cherishes.
> (Angelus Silesius)

6. THE RISK OF FREEDOM

The risk which God undertook in the creation of man, as He created him after His own image, lies in that He entrusted man, as a person, with freedom. Man can use this freedom to bring to God his love in return, to offer himself in free love to Him, his creator, and to unite himself with Him.

In the gift of freedom lies hidden the other possibility, viz., man may decide against God and make himself the object of his love. The occurrence, which is pictured in the Mosaic history of creation as the so-called Fall of sin, is in its innermost nature the decision of man, which lies in trying his freedom, the free decision of man, against God, his creator. This rebellion of man against God is rooted in the fact that he made a wrong application of the peculiar nobility of his nature, the noble gift of his personality, the proper seal of his being the image of God, by setting himself as the centre of his will and love as against God and by being himself 'like God'.

The essence of sin as the rebellion of man against his creator is very significantly brought out in modern Christian anthropology. 'God and His rebel' is a frequent subject in modern theology used for characterizing the relation of God and man, which has been disturbed by sin. Thereby is still recognized that the problem of sin is essentially tied up with the freedom of man and this freedom, in its turn, is tied up again with the image of God in man.

On the other hand, in modern theological anthropology the knowledge has long been lost, viz., that with the abuse of freedom and of the sharing of personality by man, in the sense of directing it against the divine prototype, the relation of the whole universe to God has fallen into disorder. Yet the Early Church has known something of the mystery that, with the rising of man against God, the cosmos also and the hierarchy of the rest of the creatures were drawn into the rebellion of man against God; and the effects of this rebellion reached up to the physical sphere of man, his bodiliness. The mystic theology of Jacob Boehme also knew something of it, viz., that the revolt of the men of paradise against God had its effects right up to the coarsening of the corporeality of man and the materiality of the world and gave death dominance over man. Only through the disturbance of the original relationship of God and man did the conflict arise between spirit and body,—which does not go back to an original dualistic structure of nature, but is connected with the rebellion of man against God. Primarily through this rebellion is the 'indissoluble life' of man changed into 'a dissoluble life.'

7. THE CHRISTIAN UNDERSTANDING OF GOD BECOMING MAN

The peculiar understanding of sin as the rebellion of man, abusing his freedom, against God makes understandable the Christian conception of the salvation of man and the conception of Jesus Christ as a historical being that represents the guarantee of the salvation of man.

It becomes difficult especially for the great Asian non-Christian religions to understand the basic idea of Christian revelation, viz., the idea of the incarnation of God in the historical form of Jesus Christ. The religious person of the East is inclined to understand the Christian idea of incarnation as an anology to the Hindu idea of Avatar (incarnation), which follows from the idea that again and again the Divine descends to earth and again and again clothes Himself in a human form in order to manifest the heavenly truth to every epoch and every people in an understandable and accessible way. So it becomes very easy to think of the figure of Christ as such an Avatar, as an image of the descent of the Divine into humanity; and so in the sphere of Hinduism are found repeated the attempts to understand Christology in this sense. However, a fundamentally different kind of presupposition lies at the basis of the Christian understanding of incarnation, without which the whole Christian human image and the specifically Christian conception of the human person, human society, and human ethics are not understandable. The proper meaning of incarnation lies in the simple expression of the Gospel of John:[6] '*O Logos sarx egeneto*'—'The Logos has become flesh.'

The intent of this idea can be best demonstrated in its opposition to the Avatar-idea. While the Avatar-idea presupposes that the Divine clothes itself in ever new earthly clothes and thus the single divine form comes out, in a cyclical process of ages, always in earthly cover, the peculiarity of the incarnation-idea is two-fold: first the absolute and definite uniqueness of the event and secondly the extreme materialistic aspect that is present in it, viz., that here it is not a transcendent divine being that puts on the appearance of an earthly body, but God Himself enters in the bodily, fleshy, and material nature of human history and in its midst starts and begins a comprehensive transformation of the ways of man's existence—a transformation that comprehends and penetrates likewise all spheres of his existence—material, mental, and spiritual. The incarnation is not a special case of the cyclical, self-perfecting descent of God, always renewed; it is rather the unique intervention of God in human history, in which God Himself, in an act of unimaginable condescension, gives Himself in the historical, material, fleshy conditions of man, in the form of a unique historical person who suffers completely the conditions of human existence and who in himself overcomes the roots of their corruptibility and thereby founds the beginning of a transformed, renewed, and exalted form of that human existence.

One cannot emphasize this opposition to the Avatar-idea strongly enough; it is, therefore, necessary to accentuate rightly the material, indeed, materialistic element that lies in the idea of incarnation. In Jesus Christ a man has set foot on our earth, into whose command God Himself delivered the conditions of human existence and in whom God confronted the corruption that crept into human nature through its rebellion against God. In this act of complete self-surrender, God set His creature in a position to fulfil his destiny—a creature which He Himself created after His image, which should offer itself to Him in free love and free worship, and which turned against Him through the abuse of the divine freedom. The idea of man as the *imago dei* is the foundation and presupposition of the idea of incarnation.

[6] i. 14.

8. THE SUFFERING SERVANT OF GOD

Only from this point is the idea of the suffering, sacrifice, death and resurrection of Jesus Christ to be understood in its fullest and deepest sense. God Himself, in the historical form of Jesus Christ, fathomed fully the depths of human existence, was exposed to all the suffering of man, took upon Himself all the guilt of man that grew out of his rebellion against God, and, though guiltless, suffered death, the most severe punishment for that guilt. The incarnation of such nature did not have the character of the concealment of God in a human form that made it possible for the Divine Being to speak to man in human words; for here it was not only spoken of, but also suffered, endured, expiated, atoned in all the dimensions of human existence, the spiritual, the mental, and the physical. Here not only the spiritual search, the spiritual doubt, the temptation, despondency, and despair of the soul, but also the physical pain in the extreme and the spiritual suffering in the greatest despair—'My God, my God, why hast thou forsaken me?'[7]—were suffered and seen through; here was a bloody sacrifice offered and a terrible death undergone.

Now, in this context arises the decisive question about the status and place of suffering in Christian anthropology, which is, in the last analysis, the question about the meaning and significance of the cross of Golgotha.

Christianity has often been reproached by its opponents and by the representatives of the great religions of Asia for glorifying suffering, instead of overcoming it. This reproach is not wholly unjustified. There have been, in the history of Christian piety, epochs in which suffering as such experienced a pure ecstatic glorification, particularly in some periods of the Middle Ages in which the Christian Church was shaken by strong inner and outer crises. To me the experience is unforgettable and is repeated with a certain regularity, when I have the opportunity to take Asian friends around old churches or museums of medieval art: the Asians who have come out of the inner resting peace of Buddhist piety and who have before them the picture of Buddha in deep absorption with the smile of conquest of the world on his lips, are scared, bewildered, and even shocked by the brutal gruesomeness of medieval art, which above all in the

[7] Matthew xxvii. 46.

representation of horrible scenes of martyrdom, in the fondly detailed picturing of all kinds of flaying, beheading, and burning of holy men, comes to be expressed and by which a certain intentional sadistic feature cannot be belied. The observation of the medieval representations of the man of sorrows, which show Christ in terrible depths of suffering, calls forth the same reaction from my Buddhist friends. Indeed, I should here make the confession that, after my long stay in a sphere of Buddhist art and under the deep impression of the great Buddha figures of Japanese art, it was hard for me on my return to Europe to accept again from within myself this aspect of Christian art, which evidently brings to expression an element of the essence of the Christian message.

Precisely because modern Church art, under the influence of the destruction of the human image through a series of world wars and revolutions in the recent past, pushes to the foreground this element of the glorification of suffering again in a consciously shocking form, it is necessary to speak on the original meaning and place of suffering in the Christian understanding of man. Here the starting point can only be the messianic self-understanding of Jesus.

The expectation, in later Judaism, of the end of time, as the ushering in of the Kingdom of God awaited the Son of Man, the Messiah, who would come down with the power and splendour of God, who would conquer his enemies with the breath of his mouth, and who would gather around himself his followers, the selected companions of the Kingdom and, after receiving the throne of glory, would use his enemies as a stool for his feet. The image of the Bringer of Salvation in the expectation of the end of time in later Judaism is an image of power and glory. The disciples of Jesus also at first lived with the expectation of this powerful image of salvation, which would open the Kingdom of God; and they were prepared to play, with their founder, the role of judges and commanders in that Kingdom.[8] Thus there lay a temptation of power and self-aggrandisement in this promise of the coming of the Son of Man, the Messiah.

The Gospel of Matthew gives clearly a right perception again, when it describes the temptation of Jesus in the desert, which entered him, immediately after the baptism in Jordan and the call that followed it, as a temptation of worldly power. Dos-

[8] Matthew xxiii. 11.

toevsky had, without doubt, a deep grasp of the meaning of the history of this temptation, when he understands the temptation as an attempt of the Satanic perversion of the mission of Jesus into the role of a political, social, and magical sovereignty of the world, as the temptation for self-exaltation in the role of the ruler of the world.

This interpretation finds a confirmation in the fact that Jesus himself was filled with a completely different image of his mission, an image that deeply disappointed the disciples who were full of the ideas of power and exaltation. He taught them something that disturbed their expectations of the Kingdom, God, and Son of Man, viz., 'the Son of Man must suffer many things'.[9] He tied to the image of the Son of Man the image of another great being of the prophetic promise, the image of the suffering servant of God. He saw as his mission that he should undergo the humiliation and meanness of the suffering servant of God on earth, himself live through and test all the misery of men, and indeed submit to the might of the terrible enemies of man in order to be installed, after he first fathomed the whole depth of human misery and death, in the position of the sovereign and to return in glory. Here, therefore, suffering right up to physical death in the fate of the Son of Man is consciously accepted. Thus the utterances of Jesus over the fate of the Son of Man are always tied up with the proclamation of suffering and death.

Nevertheless, the pronouncements on the characteristic significance of suffering for the Christian image of man have already been made: Suffering is not the ultimate end and ideal of life in the realization of the destiny of man, but characterizes the great turning point towards resurrection.

9. THE SECRET OF THE CROSS

This idea receives its deepest clarification from the Christian understanding of sin itself. Sin is indeed understood, as we have already shown, as an abuse of freedom by man. Created by God as a co-worker of His Kingdom and as a companion of His love, man has abused his freedom to place himself at the centre of creation and to oppose God as a rebel and usurper. This self-chosen alienation has led man into opposition to God, who,

[9] Mark viii. 31.

therefore, gave man over to death. The turning to God can, therefore, occur only after the results of this rebellion, which affect the deepest roots of the physical body and reveal themselves in suffering and death, are overcome at all stages of human existence down to the physical.

The iconography of ancient Christianity has expressed this idea in an unusually concrete and eternally true manner by painting the skull and the crossed thigh-bones of Adam under the cross in Golgotha. In an apocryphical tradition of the second century, the place of the erection of the cross of Jesus in Golgotha is pointed out as the place in which Adam was buried. Where the first-created suffered death as the punishment for his rebellion, there was he crucified who, as a representative, took upon himself the guilt of the death of Adam, and as a resurrected new Adam, as the 'first-born from the dead',[10] inaugurated the new humanity of the Son of God.

In a remarkable way, the picture of Christ as that of a man of suffering is completely foreign to the Old Church. Christ died a most painful and disgraceful death to experience in this way, to the utmost depths, the humiliation, in the spiritual, mental, and physical sphere, of the life of the fallen men found in the condition of the rebellion against God, and to implant afterwards the roots of a new spirit-body form of existence in man, including the sphere of his physical body.

The cross of the Early Church did not, therefore, aim at the conquest of suffering as such: it was rather a mark of victory in the sense of the ancient sign of victory that pointed to the place at which the great turn of the battle was reached, to which the great sacrifice was brought, resulting in the great victory, and which sealed the defeat of the enemy. The inscription on the cross of the Early Church marks the cross as the 'Terror of the Demons', for it has been erected as the sign of victory, which shows the beginning of the rule of God and which infuses terror into the earlier demoniac powers; the tree of crucifixion tells them, through its very presence, that their rule has ended and that they have come up against a new Lord. The glory of the Kingdom of God emerged at the point of deepest humiliation and spread out progressively from the moment of the resurrection of the 'first-born from the dead'.[11]

[10] I. Colossians i. 18.
[11] *op. cit.*

The cross is likewise named in the Hymn of the Cross of the Early Church 'The Cross of the Beauty of the Kingdom of God'. Christ appears in the representations of the cross given by the Early Church as the crowned victor who manifests himself, at the tree of the cross, as the lord of a new aeon. It has now to be understood also that the emperor who observed the profound transformation of the spiritual and political structure of the Roman Empire brought about by Christianity, Emperor Constantine the Great, attached and sewed the cross to the standards of the imperial legions and raised it as an emblem of his military victory over the legions of his enemies who gathered under the emblems of old gods—the cross which, for the Christians persecuted till then by the Roman Empire, was held as the consoling sign of victory and which had still stood the test of such terrible persecutions. Constantine introduced thereby, at any rate, an epoch in Church history, in which the temptation to abuse power—that very temptation which stood in the beginning of the messianic self-consciousness of Jesus and was overcome by him—crept into the Church and in later centuries, under the signs of the growing world-domination of the Church, would spread in an ever stronger form.

Therefore, suffering appears in Christian understanding not as an end in itself, but as a factor of conquest; it is also not, as in Buddhism, a suffering under the universal conditions of man's existence in the world, but is connected with the specifically Christian idea of freedom. The rebellion against God, which is chosen in freedom and which is the will to self-assertion in man against God, can only be overcome through self-conquest, self-surrender, and through sacrifice of the will to self-assertion by the acceptance of suffering. Every individual Christian is called upon to become the successor of Christ; the incorporation into the body of Christ is effected through the complete fulfilment and execution of the destiny of Christ. The designation of the Christian in the Old Church is 'Christophorus'—the Bearer of Christ. Self-conquest, as free self-surrender unto death, is contained in this idea; suffering is an element in the great drama of freedom, which, seen by God and worked out by God, is identical with the drama of salvation.

It is from the above that the difference from the Buddhist idea of suffering can be understood. Again, it is here not a question of flight from the materiality of the earthly body, which is understood as a prison of the spirit and as an entanglement in the wheel of birth, death, and rebirth, but the question of entering into a new spirit-body existence in which the destructive powers of the rebellion against God, working at all levels of human existence, are overcome through transformation into a new form of spirit-body nature. The overcoming of suffering does not follow the mere declaration of the non-existence of suffering—as in Buddhist meditation—but is effected through the fact, viz., that suffering, in the very act of facing it, which God Himself, for the sake of us men, has taken on Himself and at every moment takes on Himself, is endured faithfully to the end and is understood as the beginning of a profound transformation of man and as the root and source of a new imperishable form of human existence.

10. THE SIGNIFICANCE OF RESURRECTION

Equally clear is the real, indeed, materialistic significance, which is closely connected to the Christian understanding of resurrection. A dualistic understanding of man, which presupposes in man a sharp difference in essence between the spiritual and bodily sides of his existence, leads necessarily to the idea of the immortality of the soul; and so indeed, the feature of imperishability belonging to existence falls only to the share of the spiritual nature of man. The Christian hope aims not, however, at the immortality of the soul, but at the resurrection of the body. The spiritual strives for embodiment; and its ultimate and eternal form is a bodily form. The great theologians of the Eastern Church have often unambiguously expressed what Solowjow has expressed in the following words: 'Of what avail is the highest and greatest moral conquest, if the last enemy, death, which lies in wait in the deepest depths of the physical, corporeal, material sphere, is not overcome?'

Here the non-dualistic, indeed, anti-dualistic conception of the Christian image of man becomes clear. The end of salvation is not the separation of the spirit from the body; it is not the freeing of the spirit-nature of man from the realm of sense-nature and material corporeality; the end of salvation is rather a new man in his wholeness and totality of spirit, mind, and body. The Christian image of man has an essential bodily aspect, which is founded on the idea of incarnation and which finds its strongest and most sensuous expression in the idea of resurrection. Corporeality is not something that is removed from the perfection of God. The spiritual is not given in an abstract, but concrete bodily manifestation. 'Corporeality is', as one of the great mystics of Protestantism says, 'the end of the ways of God.' As against the dualistic attempt to tear asunder God and the world, spirit and body, the central point of the Christian message is the descent of God into human history and in a human body with the aim of renewing man in his human nature, which is forced into perishability and mortality and is diseased through the rebellion against God, with the aim of leading man through resurrection to a new, imperishable nature. The period of the new man will be inaugurated through the incarnation, through the coming of the 'second Adam'.

The life, suffering, death, and resurrection of Jesus Christ are the beginning of a new age, in which forces of spirit and life are at work to transform the 'old man' and to establish anew the image of God, which has fallen from its prototype. Here emerges a new realm, in which the negative possibility of freedom is cancelled through an act of complete self-surrender found in God's own self-sacrifice, and in which a new humanity is brought into being for the purpose of establishing the realm of free love, which is worthy of the communion between God and man. This intervention of God in history, 'in the fulness of time', in the form of Christ is not a singular, static event; neither is it an occurrence that repeats itself in the cyclical process of time. It is the prelude to man's transformation, working right into the sphere of man's corporeality; and it comes only at the end, when God will be 'all in all'.[12]

The idea of the incarnation elucidates the completely unique position of man which the human person occupies within the Christian religion as against all other religions. First it sets the idea of the creation of man in the image of God in its true light. If we have found the content of this idea, viz., that in being created after the image of God is rooted the peculiar status of man, his peculiar nobility, his peculiar relation to God, and his peculiar place in the universe, then this idea will be brought to its truest possible significance through the fact that God Himself did not take it lightly to take the form of man and 'to be

[12] I Corinthians, xv. 28.

born in the likeness of man',[13] and that He identified Himself completely with His copy in the truest form right up to corporeality and decay in order to take back through this identification the deformed image of God and to renew and transform it.

II. CHRIST, THE NEW ADAM

Primarily out of this significance of Christ as the new 'last' Adam,[14] as the 'first to rise of the dead',[15] as 'the first-born from the dead',[16] as the 'first fruit of them that slept',[17] the Christian understanding of man shows itself in its full light. The Christian man understands himself as the 'first fruit' because the Son is the 'first fruit'. The peculiar and unique status of man, whom He admitted into the ranks of His creatures is confirmed, renewed, and secured for ever in the Kingdom of God. God made man 'in the beginning' after His image and made him the last created in the series of His creatures and the goal of all the previous creations; for He entrusted him with the sovereignty over the earth and over other creatures. Only now is man, who is renewed in Christ, the first fruit, confirmed anew in his rank. 'The Father of Lights—has brought us forth by the word of truth, that we should be a kind of first fruits of His creatures.'[18] These 'first fruits' are the elected of the realm of God; out of them the élite are formed, who stand around 'the throne of the lamb' and sing the 'new song'. 'These are bought from out of men to be the first fruits of God and the lamb.'[19] They are not first fruits from birth, for they have betrayed their nobility of birth through the fall from their Lord, but the first fruits of election, 'redeemed' from among men. Here lies the relevancy of the aristocratic élite-consciousness, which is expressed theoretically in the teaching of predestination,[20] a teaching not based on a heightened human self-consciousness and pretension, but on a complete self-surrender and self-offering, on the crucifixion and death of the 'old man'.

[13] Philippians ii. 7.
[14] I Corinthians xv. 45.
[15] Acts xxvi. 23.
[16] Colossians i. 18.
[17] Corinthians xv. 20; Colossians i. 18; Acts xxvi. 23.
[18] James i. 18.
[19] Revelation xiv. 4.
[20] s.u.S.

Christian anthropology was for a long time dominated by static thought. Man appeared in the theological view as a ready-made being, set in a ready-made world like a tenant provided according to a plan with a prefabricated, new apartment building, ready with keys. Similarly static were the ideas of sin and salvation. The Fall by sin was understood as an event that transplanted man into unmitigated misery; through man's disobedience of God, the image of God appeared deformed once for all; the capacity for true knowledge of God was likewise corrupted through the fall along with the capacity to be good and the propensity to love God. The fallen man appeared as being in the hopeless situation of 'a lost son'—a situation that has not changed in the history of humanity.

Salvation was likewise understood statically: Salvation appeared in the dogmas of the Church as restitution and restoration of the lost divine image and more frequently, no doubt, as a patch of broken pieces, as a true, new creation through the Church's means of salvation. This static conception of man, of his prototype, his fall, and his salvation permitted itself well to be utilized for the legitimation of the institution of the Church and of its sacramental management.

Such a static understanding of man and such a purely restorative understanding of the working of salvation corresponds in no way to the original concern of the Christian image of man. The New Testament knew something of the progression of salvation in history and, indeed, as much of single men as of humanity, of a progressive perfection of man.

Already in the preaching of Jesus, this feature comes forth. He promised his followers: 'Then the righteous will shine like the Sun, in the Kingdom of their Father. He who has ears, let him hear.'[21] This announcement of a wonderful exaltation of existence is found already in the promises of salvation in the later Jewish prophetic sayings. Already in Daniel 12. 3 it is said about the position of the just after the rising of the dead: 'Those who are wise shall shine like the brightness of the firmament, and those who turn many to righteousness like the stars for ever and ever.' In the same Gospel of John, Jesus promises his disciples an increase of their divine power, which will surpass the measure of his own spiritual strength. He says

[21] Matthew xiii. 43.

to his disciples in his farewell speech:[22] 'Truly, truly, he who believes in me will also do the works that I do and will do greater works than these; for I go to the Father; and whatever you ask in my name, that will I do, that the Father may be glorified in the Son.' The spiritual authority of the disciples of Jesus is, therefore, not limited to the measure of spiritual authority that worked on the earth during his life-time. Jesus promised his disciples a spiritual power by which they would be qualified to do a greater work than he himself. That the workings of the power of the Holy Spirit are here referred to comes out of this, viz., that directly from this promise of a mighty increase of the charismatic powers of the disciples follows the proclamation of the coming of the Paraklete (Holy Spirit).

Similar expectations of a mighty rise in existence along with the happenings at the end of time are expressed in the Epistle I of John: 'My beloved ones, we are God's children now; it does not yet appear what we shall be. But we know, that, when it will appear, we shall be like Him, for we shall see Him as He is.'[23] The believing Christians are already just children of light, God's children; but this stage does not yet represent the last: it has not yet appeared. But the Christians know that the last stage will usher in a further unimaginable exaltation of existence: the similarity of form to the exalted Christ, the raising of the copy to the prototype.

Paul too knows clearly about this increase in existence, which brings rebirth with it. The action of the spirit is not what happens only once; a constantly progressive, creative effort proceeds from it and raises and transforms man step by step. In II Corinthians 4. 16 it is said: 'Though the outward man perishes, the inward man is renewed day by day.' That this renewal is not the restoration again of a former condition lost through the Fall, but presents a progress in the form of the opening up of a higher glory, is shown by the statement of II Corinthians 3. 18 which is addressed to the same community: 'But we all, with open face beholding as in a glass the glory of the Lord, are changed into the same image from glory to glory, even as by the Spirit of the Lord.' Here also the Spirit appears as the force of a progressive transformation into the image of the Lord Himself.

[22] John xiv. 12.
[23] I John iii. 2.

The idea of the Christian 'Übermensch' is a consequence of this understanding and was expressed by the prophet Montanus, the founder of the Montanist Movement, of the Early Church.

In connection with the break-through of the idea of evolution through Darwin in the field of biology, zoology, and anthropology, the tendency is prevalent in American theology of the nineteenth century to explain Christian anthropology in the sense of an evolution and to expect the future perfection of man in the form of attaining higher and higher charismatic stages and ever higher means of spiritual knowledge and communication. These ideas have recently been given their usual formulation and dissemination through Teilhard de Chardin, who, as a paleontologist, sought a completely new conception of Christian anthropology. In truth, his idea is not so new as now thought, but can be traced back to the old ideas of an evolutionary Christian anthropology, given already long ago in the Pauline and Johanine theology and in the mystic theology of a Jacob Boehme, F. C. Oetinger, and Robert Fludd, who sought to overcome the static, restorative image of man in the Christian texts through a renovation of the dynamic anthropology of the New Testament: For them Jesus Christ is only the visible manifestation of the embodiment of God in the form of a historical human person. But God's becoming a man is not a singular entry of God into human history 'straight from above', but is also the beginning, the starting of a new form of life and way of existence, into which humanity, according to the measure of its spiritualization, personification, and Christianization, will be drawn. Christ is not merely the form in which incarnation becomes a historical event; he is at the same time the goal of becoming a man, in which becoming the changed, spiritualized, reborn, and perfected humanity finds its summation, the goal at which God's becoming a man and the Christification of man converge. This larger Christ is the focus not only of the individual but also of the collective salvation of the 'living stones' joining together in his body.

Thus the new spiritual interpretation of the evolutionary theory discovered again, in its understanding of man, what for a long time was veiled by a purely static and restorative thought of dogmatic anthropology. Paul describes the goal of the evolution of Christianity to the community in Ephesus in these words: 'Till we all come in the unity of faith and of the knowledge of the Son of God unto a perfect man, unto the measure of the stature of the fulness of Christ.'[24] 'To become a perfect man', 'to the measure of the stature of the fulness of Christ'—that is the future goal which Paul sees fixed for the evolution of the history of the salvation of man, that inner growth in the perfection of the greater Christ, who himself grows in and with the history of humanity, takes humanity into himself until at the end he has penetrated and transformed humanity into the 'perfect man', who he himself is and will be.

Nevertheless, this evolutionary interpretation of Christian anthropology brings nearer the dangerous temptation to understand the story of salvation itself as a kind of 'process' of natural law, which itself takes place with an unavoidable necessity in the history of mankind. This understanding offends against two basic ideas of the Christian image of man: first, the Christian understanding of freedom, and second, the dramatic, fundamental concept of history as the history of salvation. The concept of evolution can be applied to the Christian image of man and the Christian understanding of the history of salvation only in a completely spiritualized and reinterpreted sense; and only in the sense that with Jesus Christ a new stage of evolution begins, which in turn bears, on its side, the characteristically new presaging sign of the dramatic self-realization of the spirit in the sphere of freedom—a presaging sign through which this evolution differentiates itself from that in the realm of animal life already known. The new form of evolution lies in the sign of the cross, of the break in the naturalistic line of evolution and in its leap into a higher form of evolution in which the law of freedom, of self-surrender, and of self-conquest prevail.

12. THE MAIN SCHEMATA OF THE CHRISTIAN CONCEPT OF MAN

It is from this understanding of Christ, which saw in Jesus Christ the incarnated divine Logos, the descent of God in Flesh, in history, in the form of a man, the second Adam and inaugurator of a new humanity, that the different conditions of human existence will become understandable, in which the specifically Christian self-understanding of man, his specifically Christian sense of life, and his specifically Christian form of self-realization express themselves.

[24] Ephesians iv. 13.

(i) *Justification:*

Since the Reformation of the sixteenth century, Christian anthropology has oriented itself primarily to the schema of justification: the Christian man is the man to whom the righteousness of God—to the great credit of Jesus Christ, which he has earned through atonement at the cross—is imputed in faith and who in faith is imputed with the righteousness of Christ.

This schema of justification is characteristic of the strong juridical thought which has prevailed in the Latin West and which is understandable either when one lives—as was the case with the Jews and the Jewish Christians of the first centuries—wholly under Mosaic law, sees his daily process of life determined by the commands of Mosaic law, and experiences in the course of his daily life, now and again anew, its difficulties and impossibilities as well as the demands of this complicated and comprehensive law or when one lives under a system of atonement stamped with rules, as it prevailed in Roman Catholicism under the influence of the legalism of the ancient Roman religion and led to a strong juridical conception of sin, atonement, and sacrament and thus made the problem of the justification appear as the central concern of the Christian religion.

The schema of justification as the starting point of Christian anthropology is, however, no longer understandable in the contemporary situation; for the concept of law presupposed by it as well as the reduction of the relationship between God and man to a juridical relation no longer finds a presupposition in the religious consciousness of our times. The schema of justification has become pale for us, as it seems no longer relevant to our life and outlook.

The resulting withdrawal from the traditional schema commends itself so much the more in our present ecumenical situation, for this schema never had a universal Christian value to show. In the whole realm of the Eastern Orthodox Church, the schema of justification has found little respect. It plays no role in the liturgy of Eastern Christianity. In the classical representation of the orthodox theology, in the 'Fount of Knowledge' of John of Damascus, the concept of justification does not come to the fore. This concept was of little concern to Greek thought; for the idea of law—*nomos*—had a cosmological content for Greek thought and comprehended the whole sphere of natural law. Furthermore, ethics showed a cosmological foundation, whereas in the teaching of justification, which permeated Roman Catholicism, the whole cosmological aspect was omitted and the religious function of the juridical relation of God and man was reduced to the question: 'How can I find a merciful God?'

This holding back of the schema of justification is, therefore, required, because for Paul, the theologian of justification, it was not the only schema for interpreting the relation of God and man and the work of Christ. Moreover, Paul used the schema only when he spoke to predominantly Jewish-Christian communities, which still lived under Mosaic law and which, like him, came from the Mosaic juridical thought. Paul speaks of justification when he, a Jew, speaks to the Jews. But when he speaks to the heathen Christians, he is a Greek speaking to the Greeks, gives up this schema and uses for his purpose schemata and images that conform to the Greeks oriented to the idea of mysteries. He speaks to them of a new man, of a liberated and redeemed man, of new creation, of resurrection with Christ, of man as being changed, of undergoing transformation, of being transfigured, and of being the son of God and friend of God. In the following phenomenological description of the Christian image of man, these schemata may be drawn and examined.

(ii) *The New Man:*

Really no thought, no feeling, dominates so radically the Christian's sense of life as the consciousness of the newness of the life in which man, through his participation in the life and body of Christ, sees himself transplanted. The novelty of the Christian message of salvation appeared as the dominant element of the Christian proclamation, an element that not only filled the hearts of the faithful, but also attracted the non-Christian environment. When Paul entered Athens, the followers of the Epicurian and Stoic philosophy had, according to the information of the history of the Apostle, the impression 'as though he will announce new gods'. In the strongest reproach made by the non-Christian environment against the Christians —they are godless, *atheoi*—the fact expresses itself in a distorted mirror that the Christian message did not fit into the old schema of the traditional religions, into the traditional world of gods, and that to that annunciation stuck the character of something new at first unintelligible to the environment.

This claim of complete novelty could be raised in the second century to a basic dogma of a new Church. Mark himself can only so explain the novelty of salvation, which appears with Christ in the world, that here a completely new, till now unknown, strange god manifests himself, who breaks into the domain of sovereignty of the previous lords of the world, the creator gods of the Old Testament and liberates the souls held back by force in the world ruled by a Demiurge. The Gospel of Mark about a strange 'god' is founded on the idea of a simple novelty of salvation revealed through Christ and on the simple novelty of the revelation mediated by him. The new God is the strange, previously unknown, true, and highest God, who is not identical with the wicked, wrathful and righteous God of the Old Testament,

What has been done by Mark in a one-sided way for contrasting the new and the old God, the New and the Old Testament, and for splitting up the history of salvation into a series of 'antitheses', is to be seen as a counterpoint throughout the whole New Testament. God's working of salvation is understood as the creation of a new man in a new universe, on a new earth, under a new sky. In the twenty-first chapter of the Revelation of John the seer John sees 'a new heaven and a new earth', and he sees 'the new Jerusalem', the holy city, 'descending from heaven, prepared like a bride adorned for her husband', and the great voice of Him who sits on the throne speaks: 'See, I make all things new!' The jubilation of the elect to God's Kingdom, the 144,000, unites in a powerful 'new song', which is sung before the 'throne of the lamb'.[25]

The 'new man' experiences and knows the newness of his life as the life of Christ, which begins to flow in him. This new life expresses itself as the overwhelming experience of a condition already reached. So Paul can write to the faithful in Corinth: 'If anyone is in Christ, he is a new creature.'[26] He thereby establishes the presupposition of human salvation and, on the whole, for the first time the existence of the new man. He can, however, write to the Ephesians, imperatively admonishing

[25] Revelation v. 9 and xiv. 3.
[26] II Corinthians v. 17.

them:[27] 'Put on the new man, who is created after the likeness of God!', and describes the new life as a goal of the future.

Still more significant is the relationship of creation, true humanity, and renewal of man in the words which Paul writes to the community in Colossia:[28] 'Put off the old man with his deeds, and put on the new man who is renewed in knowledge after the image of Him that created him; there there is no Greek, no Jew, no circumcision, no uncircumcision, no barbarian, no Scythian, no slave, no freeman, but Christ is all and in all.'

Here it becomes obvious how deeply the Christian image of man is dominated by the idea of the creation of man after the image of God. The first man is created in God's image, but has abused his freedom in his rebellion against God, his creator. In Jesus Christ, the image and reflection of the Father, the original image of God among men, was again set up; in him, the second and last Adam, men can now 'put the new man on' like a new dress, into which they themselves change and with whose shining ornaments they can cover up the old torn coat of the body and cover up the nakedness of the 'lost son', abandoned in the service of the swineherd.

In all these statements, the eschatalogical, indeed one may say here, evolutionary character is distinctive: the question is not about a ready-made, final, new state, into which man will be transplanted through grace, but about a beginning, an anticipation of a prelude to the coming of a new state, the fulfilment and completion of which will first come in the future, which itself in its completeness must be led up to, a break that first points to the goal, an arrow of evolution that speeds towards the goal but has not yet reached it. The new man is one who is caught up in the process of renewal; the new life is an element in the growth of Christ ripening towards perfect humanity.

The new man, on his side, works again as yeast, as effervescing 'leaven' within the old man. He works as a 'fresh dough'[29] and contributes thus to the transformation of the old society into the state of the Kingdom of God by fermenting with the help of a new leaven. The eschatalogical, disturbing, and, one

[27] Ephesians iv. 24.
[28] Colossians iii. 9–10.
[29] I Corinthians v. 7.

may say, revolutionizing element in this process of the onward growth and becoming oi the new man is not to be overlooked.

(iii) *The Regenerated Man:*

The idea of rebirth has been frequently misunderstood, precisely because 'rebirth' became identified with 'conversion' in an exact, temporally datable and spatially fixable way. The Christianity of the pietists and of the different forms of revivalism has, in particular, contributed to a certain universalizing and thereby also compromising of the idea.

Now, there are indeed, in the history of Christian piety, a series of eminent personalities who have experienced their rebirth in the form of a temporally and locally fixable conversion-experience, as the case was, for instance, with John Wesley, the founder of the Methodist Church, and with the spirituality of the much transformed August Herman Francke, the founder of German Pietism.

But this explanation of rebirth as a single type of psychological experience is absolutely not allowable and is actually unjustified. There are numerous and, presumably, innumerable individual forms of the maturing of that mysterious process of renewal, transformation, and creation anew of man—a process that is designated by the term rebirth. Already Zinzendorf, in order to introduce, as against the tendencies of August Herman Francke, his own type of conversion as the standard type of Christian rebirth, referred to the fact that God 'has many ways to draw His own to Himself' and that the ways of gradual evolution also lead to the goal like the ways of sudden upheaval. This only is definite that a re-creating effect goes from God to man and that man receives from God a new life and a new form. The form of the experience of rebirth itself is as various as the individuality of man, as the form of his appearance, and as his peculiar intellectual and emotional aptitude. The various types of rebirth differ from one another not only on the ground that the experience may come in suddenly with overwhelming surprise or as a result of a slow process, a 'growth', a 'ripening', an 'evolution', but also on the ground of the dominant faculty of the soul and spirit assuming the command. In the process of rebirth, the natural pre-disposition of the endowments, the personal disposition, and the psychological type of experience and of self-realization are not extinguished, but are filled with a new content, a new setting of the goal, and a new dynamism.

In the voluntaristic type, rebirth calls forth a new directing of the will to the goal, which is in its content surprising, which sets free absolutely new forces and aptitudes, and which has not been noticed hitherto in the persons concerned; in some others, rebirth activates the means of knowledge, it works that break-through into a new 'view', it awakens surprisingly new and deep insights; in some others, it produces the discovery of a new unsuspected beauty in the order of nature or in the process of the history of salvation; in still others, it produces new ethical visions and a new love of the neighbour, who in the light of the Father of Light suddenly appears as God's man, as the present Christ, and urges him to a new kind of relationship to his fellow-men.

Obviously the old man continues to exist in his definite personal structure based on inheritance, education, and experiences of previous life history; but he senses his life in Christ as a new life, he experiences his inner change as a new birth. From the many testimonies about the experience of rebirth, it follows that all the stages of the human person are covered by this process of a new creation. The Gospel does not permit the least doubt that all the spheres of human life are permeated and transformed by the power of the spirit of Jesus Christ, from the bodily sphere to the highest spiritual 'gnosis' and 'wisdom'. Characteristically enough, the 'afflicted holy' are also the 'cured by faith', who were related to the forgiveness of sin, i.e., to the restoration of the image of God in man that was disfigured by sin. Equally frequently appear the cures connected with exorcisms of the demons. The evil spirit is—or the wicked spirits are—driven out from the heart of man, in whom the divine Word sets itself down, and in whom 'the Son is born'. The newly creative power of the spirit works through the bodily, mental, and spiritual spheres of man; it produces cure in the bodily sphere, purification of the demonic powers and regeneration of will and love in the mental sphere, and 'gnosis', the knowledge of God, the 'face to face' in the spiritual sphere.

It is important to hold before one's eyes this radical power of the renovating spirit of Christ—a power that penetrates all the dimensions of human existence. Rebirth was understood frequently in the exclusive sense of a 'conversion of the heart' in the circles of the so-called revivalist movement, which were characterized by a strongly anti-intellectualistic and anti-scientific attitude. This interpretation conceives the anthropological range and dimensions of depth too narrowly: there is not only a change of heart, which works with a new ethical attitude, but also an illumination of the understanding, which leads to a new knowledge and an exaltation of human consciousness, reaching the realm of the supra-mental. Here lie the additional points of the Christian gnosis, which was and is of very great importance for the growth of Christian anthropology and for the experience of what Jacob Boehme characterized as the 'glimpse into the essence of all beings' and George Fox described as the 'inner light'.

In rebirth the old man is, therefore, activated anew, receives a new physical power, a new direction of will, a new object of his love, a new light of knowledge. What is thereby psychologically surprising is that, along with this process, not only the previously present and activated qualities and already developed talents come forth strengthened, but also talents till now slumbering are aroused, just as a stricken man is brought into a state to break off from his habits of life grounded into him for a long time and apparently unsurmountable and to begin a new life which is led by a new sense of life and a new attitude of spiritual consciousness and which seeks new spiritual forms of expression. For 'whatever is born of God overcomes the world'.[30]

(iv) *The Free Man:*

No other idea determined the peculiar sovereignity of the Christian idea of man than the Christian idea of freedom, the real seal, as we saw, of his being the image of God. In the original meaning of the word, God alone is free; He has the sovereign ability to will Himself and actualize Himself with a free decision, in a world willed by Himself. As He made man after His own image, He endowed his created image with the highest nobility of His essence, viz., freedom.

As described already, the Christian understanding of sin and salvation is connected very closely with this idea of freedom. Sin is the abuse of freedom by man, born of the will to assert

[30] I John v. 4.

himself against God, the will that wills itself, the will to have for himself the world entrusted to him and thereby to set himself in the place of God.

This abuse of freedom has entangled man in slavery. The state of the fallen man is designated in the New Testament as slavery at its worst. It is the slavery to self-will, which wants to have all the things for itself and enjoy them, which wants to appropriate everything and fit everything to its own plan and desire. It is the slavery to alienated love, which is no longer turned towards God, but subjects the things of the world and also fellow-men as means of self-seeking, wilfulness, and exploitation.

Furthermore, this understanding of sin was reinterpreted in the sense of the Platonic and Manichean dualistic thought in that one explained the drives stemming from the sphere of the body, of the 'flesh', as the chief drive to sin and saw its peculiar roots primarily in sexual appetite. This is an additional falsification, a backward interpretation in terms of the dualism already overcome in the idea of incarnation—an interpretation that produced fateful consequences. The servitude of sin is not identical with the dominance of sensual appetites; nor is it identical with the overwhelming of the spirit by the 'love of life', as Buddhism teaches it; but it is the loss of divine freedom which was proper to man as the image of God and which should fulfil itself in the free, loving surrender of man, in his totality of spirit and body, to God, his prototype.

The servitude of men fallen away from God is more burdensome than slavery to sensuality and love of life. It is a fall to wilfulness, the compulsion to indulge one's selfishness, the necessity to war with God, the necessity to involve oneself with spirit, with soul, and with body, more and more in the rebellion against God, the inflaming of the whole centre of life or, as it is said in the Letter of James, of the 'wheel of life', which revolves only around the centre of its own ego and inflames itself into opposition to God. The slavery of fallen men is the enslaving of the whole man, not merely of his 'flesh', but of all the levels of his human existence, also of his 'most spiritual'. In a Christian reinterpretation of the language of Platonic dualism, Luther has expressed it thus: The whole man, not reborn, is flesh, also in his spirit; and the whole reborn man is spirit, also when he eats and sleeps. The man whose life-force, in opposition to God, turns only round the centre of his own ego is absolutely enslaved and cannot free himself from this slavery, for the opposition against God springs from the innermost centre of his life's stirrings.

It is from here that the term, 'freedom of the Christian man', first receives its full, sovereign ring. The freedom which the Christian receives is the freedom for which Christ has fought on his behalf, in that Christ has overcome sin and death, in that he has completed the sacrifice of full self-surrender to God, in that he has surrendered himself to God in free love and has taken upon himself persecution, suffering, and death freely and without guilt, and in that he, as the Son of God, has freely realized in his own life the prayer: 'Father, not as I will, but as Thou willest', 'Father, let Thy will be done', and fulfilled it at the cross. The freedom of the Christian man is a freedom in Christ, it is the freedom of the first-born obtained again in Christ, the second Adam, in whom the possibility of abuse of freedom, the possibility of choosing against God, is surmounted. It is the freedom of the reborn men, now at last to fulfil the original destiny of man and surrender themselves to God in free love. For love is possible only in freedom, one cannot compel love. Full communion between persons can be attained only in free devotion. In Christ and freed by Christ, man can fulfil his destiny as the image of God.

Freedom alone can make possible a truly fulfilled communion. Communion comprehends even the neighbour, in whose form God faces us. Thus freedom realizes itself in the free service of love. Luther has most appropriately expressed the paradox of Christian freedom, which includes the both, love and service:

> A Christian man is a free lord over all things and is the subject of none;
> A Christian man is a subservient servant of all things and is the subject of every one.

One should not overlook the fact that a peculiar significance came to the evangelical schema of liberation—and to the corresponding schema of ransoming—in the first centuries of the Church in a society that was built, according to its social structure, completely upon the system of slavery. In the society of the late antiquity lived, on the one hand, whole layers of population in a permanent state of slavery; on the other hand, the free population also was, however, continually exposed, according to the prevalent rights of war, to the danger that, in case of the conquest of their political community by a victorious enemy, it would go over as slaves into the possession of the victor and, according to the laws of the prevailing rights of war, would be distributed. The schema of 'liberation' was, therefore, made particularly appealing to the men in their deepest anxieties and counted upon their spontaneous understanding.

This was all the more the case, for the legally proposed liberation of slaves, according to the practice of the Greek and—in a modified way—Roman law, could take effect only when one delivered the emancipated slave to a god and the freed man henceforth considered himself as the freed man of that particular god and also in part took on the name of the liberating god. Redemption and liberation through Christ derived thus their actual and realistic meaning and underscored the peculiar aspect of freedom in the religious anthropology of the Christians.

From this it is understandable why Christian freedom is not to be understood purely individualistically, as implied in a secularized meaning of Christian freedom. Similarly, it is not to be understood in a collective sense, as suggested in many modern attempts to formulate a socialistic 'theology of revolution' in the churches of the Eastern Bloc. The personal and the social elements are inseparably connected with each other through the idea that every man is for himself an image of God, that at the same time he recognizes, to that degree, his being an image of God in Christ, the new Adam, and also finds that image of God in the neighbour, that he revives his love of the neighbour in his love of God, renewed through Christ, and that he begins actually to practise that love.

Again, the eschatalogical, evolutionary element of this 'process' is not to be misunderstood. The Christian does not see himself set in a 'static' state of freedom, but feels himself entangled in a dramatic process of liberation, in which Satan endeavours always anew with new methods to enslave him, while God struggles to liberate His children from the prison and establish them in the promised glorious 'freedom of the children of God'. No wonder that this evolutionary element of the struggle for liberation has operated as a spiritual stimulus to the social and racial manumission, as it was demanded by the Christian champions of human rights in the eighteenth, and the nineteenth, centuries and pursued and established under unspeakable hardships.

(v) *The Man of Joy:*

Friedrich Nietzsche has summed up his criticism of the Christian man: 'More redeemed must they look to me, these disciples!' He expressed thereby that the form of the physiognomical expression of the soul's attitude in the Christians does not correspond to the theoretical picture, which the Christian teaching of the liberated, reborn men drew, that the actual, actually lived 'picture' of the Christian does not fit his theological understanding of the *imago dei*. Without doubt, Nietzsche's criticism is relevant at this point. From this type and from this attitude to life of the Christian man many features became lost or were alienated—features that belonged to the original picture and type of life of the Christian man and still appear to-day only sporadically and in an underdeveloped form, but at first sight in any case no longer to bear the characteristic distinguishing marks.

Here belongs the element of delight, cheerfulness, and joy. Joy is the conspicuous and distinguishing mark of the Christian. In the history of the Apostles, it is named always with new variations by the Christians gathering: 'They praised God with joy and simple heart and had grace on all the people';[31] they were 'full of joy and the Holy Spirit.'[32] Joy is the spontaneous result of being filled with the Holy Spirit; indeed, it counts as the chief gift of the Holy Spirit along with justice, love, and peace.[33] The Apostles characterize themselves as the 'helpmates of joy' of the Christians of their community.[34] Above all, the Gospel of John is wholly tuned to this note of joy. Jesus promises his disciples in his farewell speech that their grief 'shall be changed into joy'. 'These things I have spoken unto you, that my joy might remain in you, and that your joy might be full.'[35]

[31] Acts ii. 41.
[32] Acts xiii. 52.
[33] Galatians v. 22.
[34] II Corinthians i. 24.
[35] John xv. 11.

'No one will take your joy from you.'[36] This joy will increase itself in the meeting of the community, and become jubilation, exaltation—*agalliasis*.

This joy has a specifically Christian character. It is drawn from the knowledge that the superiority of the wicked has already been broken in principle by the power of Christ—'I saw Satan fall like lightning from the heaven'[37]—, that death, devil, and demon no longer possess any claim on man, that man is no longer delivered to calamity, damnation, and destruction, that the great turn to new existence has already been opened up, and that the 'first-born from the dead' has already appeared, and the forces of forgiveness, atonement, resurrection, and transfiguration have already begun to work in men.

This element of joy in the Christian is preserved most strongly, if anywhere, in the liturgy of the Eastern Orthodox Church. Above all, the Eastern liturgy is wholly attuned to the note of joy over the beginning of resurrection, over the antecedental beginning of the Kingdom of God, and over the fact that the renewal of man is already in process; and it brings to expression in its hymns this joy in an often strongly ecstatic way. In these hymns of rejoicing is summed up the spiritual experience of the greatest charismatic persons, holy men, and mystics of the Eastern Church of over a thousand years.

Later, the marks of this charismatic joy again broke in, above all, in the radical ecstatic Pentecostal Movements (*Pfingstbewegungen*) of Christendom; again in the pietistic revivalist movements, the break-outs of charismatic joy are frequently found. So a clergyman of Württenburg, Preziger by name, founded a new 'joyful Christianity' in the eighteenth century. The Christian is the 'joyful man', who knows that death and devil can have nothing to do with him, that Christ, the 'perfect man', has given back to him the perfect joy of the 'new Adam'. This joy sets the Christian free to realize active love.

> Whoever finds salvation in the Lord
> And rejoices, as it is becoming,
> He holds himself obligated
> To lead another to the Lord.

[36] John xvi. 22.
[37] Luke x. 18.

In this joy lie, again, the roots of the specifically Christian humour, which obtains its peculiarity from the fact that it is in a position, in the middle of the conflicts of life, to look upon all sufferings and afflictions from its point of view of future conquest, which, in a situation in which other men feel the bitterness and hopelessness of life, sees the coming conquest, already completed in Christ, of suffering and the coming change of sorrow into joy. In the Christian humour, joy is coupled with the 'freedom of a Christian man', who does not allow himself to be entangled and challenged by the cross and suffering, but sees in the cross and suffering themselves the mark of triumph and joy. To-day one often refers to Kierkegaard, when one speaks of Christian humour. But Kierkegaard's humour is too intellectual, too dialectical and bilious to exhaust all the fulness of Christian joy. More of this joy is found in the 'Halleluja' of the unadulterated Negro spirituals than in the tormented performances of Kierkegaard over humour.

(vi) *The Charismatic Man:*

Generally in the New Testament, where the living reality of the Christian communal life is described, the Christian man is represented as the charismatic man, as the man who is full of the powers of the Holy Spirit, as the man through whom the gifts of the Holy Spirit are realized. Is there a connection between the idea of the Holy Spirit and the statements about man as the image of God and about Christ as the second Adam, the founder of the new humanity? Or do we come across a completely new realm of ideas, standing independently and unrelated, alongside other ideas basic for a Christian understanding of man?

Here it may at first be pointed out that the effusions of the Holy Spirit belong to the promises of salvation of the Old Testament, which were bound very closely with the expectation of the Kingdom of God and of the coming of the Messiah—as the Son of Man. Already in the expectation of the end of time in later Judaism, the Holy Spirit plays a decisive role: the Kingdom of God is the expected, coming Kingdom of Wonder, in which the spirit of God fills men and the whole of human life will be transformed through its miraculous powers. The Holy Spirit, the Kingdom of God, and the harbinger of the Kingdom belong together, they are elements of the sphere of salvation.

The Christian community of Jerusalem understood the beginning of the charismatic phenomena in their midst as the fulfilment of the promises about the end of time by the prophets of the Old Testament. The account in the history of the Apostles about the precedents of the Pentecost is characteristic. At the participation in the meeting by the disciples of Christ in the upper room, the Holy Spirit comes out in the shape of fiery tongues accompanied by a powerful tumult, as a result of which the population runs together. The signs of ecstatic excitement which came upon the disciples were taken to be symptoms of drunkenness by the onlookers below in the street. But Peter, in an apologetic address, turned to the people gathered and said: 'Men of Judea,—let this be known to you,—these men are not drunk, as you suppose—but this is what was spoken by the Prophet Joel: "It shall be in the last days, says God, that I will pour out my spirit upon all flesh, and your sons and your daughters shall prophesy, and your young ones shall see visions, and your old men shall have dreams; and on my menservants and on my maidservants I will, in the same days, pour out my spirit, and they shall prophesy. And I will do wonders in the heavens above and signs on the earth below—and it will happen that whoever will call the name of the Lord shall be saved." '[38] The descent of the gifts of the spirit, occurring in such a wonderful way at the Pentecost in the midst of the community is here understood as the fulfilment of the prophecy of Joel, as the sign of the beginning of the end of time, as the sign with mysterious powers.

The anthropological aspects of the gifts of the spirit are extraordinarily manifold and comprehend a whole wide spectrum of multi-coloured radiations of the spirit; the gifts of the spirit are realized not only in the realm of the intellect, but reveal themselves as the bestowing of powers in those spheres of human life in which openly the irrational, ecstatic phenomena, among which the numerous break-throughs of the parapsychological sphere came up, predominate.

The uncontrollability and spontaneity of the spiritual gifts represented a highly disturbing element in the original Christian community. Thus in Paul are found absolutely contradictory tendencies immediately juxtaposed. On the one side, the effort is found in him to clear the way for the break-through of the

[38] Acts ii. 14–21.

Holy Spirit—'Quench not the spirit! Do not despise prophecy!'[39] But this very tendency led to an increase of ecstatic and irrational element in the community thus multiplying the chances of the starting of tumultuous scenes, and promoted orgiastic ways of behaviour.

For this reason the opposite tendency is the more strongly noteworthy—the intention, viz., to push into the foreground rational expressions of the spirit and to devalue the irrational ones, forces the latter into the background and suppresses them completely, where possible. Thus the enumeration of the gifts of the spirit in I Corinthians[40] presents a list of descending importance, which begins with the gift of utterance about wisdom and then the gift of utterance about gnosis and ends with the gift of tongues (different languages) as the last. Even so, in Paul the tendency is predominant throughout to place the gifts of the spirit under the control and tests of rational consciousness: 'Test everything and hold fast that which is good.'[41] Such a direction presupposes already a critical outlook against the gifts of the spirit. When further it is said to the prophets that they should not prophesy simultaneously in the meeting of the community, when it is said to the hymn-singers that they should not sing at the same time, but one after another, therein the principle of a control through intellect and will is set forth. 'The spirits of prophets are subject to prophets'[42]—this statement says basically the exact opposite of the direction: 'Quench not the spirit!'

This return to a conscious control of the expressions of the spirit works still more clearly in another area: speaking is entirely forbidden to women, to whom, in the service of God in the Synagogue, only a silent help was allowed and who first made use, on their side, of the freedom of God in the Christian meeting of the community to come out as charismatics (prophets, visionaries, teachers, and speakers of languages); and now the synagogal principle: '*mulier taceat in ecclesia*'[43] is reaffirmed again. The subjection of the charismata to the control of consciousness signifies already an effective tendency towards rationalization of the whole charismatic field.

[39] I Thessalonians v. 19.
[40] xii. 7–12.
[41] I Thessalonians v. 21.
[42] I Corinthians xiv. 32.
[43] The woman is quiet in the church.

No wonder, that from the end of the first century a quick process of elimination of free charismatics and of the free practice of the gifts of God is carried out: in place of the free charismatics come the occupants of the different church offices—bishops, presbyters, deacons—and the teachers of theology.

The question remains decisive: In what relation does the manifestations of the Holy Spirit stand to the fundamental idea of Christian anthropology, the understanding of man as the *imago dei*, and to the fundamental idea of the understanding of Christ, the idea of incarnation?

An answer to this question is found in *The Gospel of John*. There Jesus himself promises in his farewell speech the coming of the Holy Spirit, who will be sent to the disciples as a comforter and counsellor—Paraklet—when the Son goes back to the Father. The Holy Spirit steps into the place of Christ returning to the Father. At the time after the ascension of Christ to heaven, the Holy Spirit is the form in which God, with His mysterious power, continues to be present in His community. This conception presented no difficult theological problem for the believing Christian of the early times of the Church: for him the Holy Spirit, which showed itself in the form of the charismata in the midst of the community in such a demonstrative and wonderful way, was the spirit of God, the spirit of Jesus Christ, who, in his body, which is the wonderful element of life of the new aeon, showed himself to the community of believers still in the midst of the old aeon. Paul completed this identification in words with magnificent power: 'Now the Lord is the spirit; and where the spirit of the Lord is, there is freedom. But we all, with open face beholding as in a glass the glory of the Lord, are changed into the same image from glory to glory, even as by the Spirit of the Lord.'[44]

The Holy Spirit, as the spirit of freedom, has been the leaven in the history of the Church throughout all the centuries—all great reformations and numerous foundings of new Churches and sects stand as the distinguishing marks of new charismatic break-throughs and are called forth from charismatic personalities. The great creations of church-history issued forth from the charismatics, who have appeared in every epoch. The history of the Church and of the heretics is, as Gottfried Arnold has

[44] II Corinthians iii. 17–18.

rightly seen, fundamentally a history of Christian charismatics and of the ever new eruptions of the gifts of the Holy Spirit.

(vii) *The Perfect Man:*

We turn only hesitatingly to the last aspect of the Christian image of man; this aspect is of significance in this context; it is the idea of the perfect man. Yet we enter here upon a field that was accessible only to the deepest spiritual experiences and is presumably, on the whole, closed to a purely conceptual understanding. On the other hand, this reference to the perfect man is so frequently repeated in the New Testament and has played such a significant role in the history of Christian spirituality that it is impossible to avoid or conceal it.

In the Gospel of Matthew, Christ directs this demand to his disciples: 'You shall be perfect like your Father in heaven.' This demand, which God Himself lays down as the criterion of human perfection, sounds frightful; considering human nature, it appears to demand too much from men, and exceeds the measure expected of man. If, from the first, one does not proceed from the thought that such a statement is a poetical exaggeration, an exuberance of the religious way of speaking, when one attempts to understand this demand in its proper, literal meaning as a demand directed to men like us, then one may well be amazed by it. Evidently, this demand is literally meant; for it is very often made in the letters of the Apostles, for instance, by Paul:[45] 'A man of God may be perfect,' and by James:[46] 'That you may be perfect and complete.'

In the letters of the Apostles, the perfection of God is not expressly mentioned as the measure of the perfection demanded of man; but it is assumed to be that measure here also: the apostolic demand does not fall short of the demand by Christ.

A disclosure of the content of the meaning of this claim can—if at all—follow from the understanding of man as the image of God and that of Jesus Christ as the 'new Adam' and renewer of the *imago dei*. The perfection of man is that perfection by which the image of God is reflected. Man has indeed disfigured this image through his rebellion against God, through his wilful

[45] II Timothy iii. 17.
[46] James i. 4.

abuse of his original image; but in Christ he received back the perfection of God's image.

The Early Church was closer to this theology of the image—which has many more deeper strata to point out than can here be indicated—than we are to-day. Origen, the great teacher of the Alexandrian school of catechism, has brought this out, in an unsurpassable way, in his explanation of the works of Ezekiel. The Prophet Ezekiel speaks in Ch. 14. 4, of 'Man-men from the house of Israel' in a completely unique re-duplication of the idea. Origen explains this re-duplication of the concept of man as a reference to the perfecting of man in the history of salvation: 'All of us men are born as men, but all of us are not man-men.—Only when we are good and pious, do we duplicate the name of man, so that in us lives no longer the mere man, but man-man. So long as man is externally present, while a snake lives within, he is no man-man, but only a man. But when the inner man always corresponds to the image of Him who has created him, then will the true man be born, and the outer and inner man will together be harmoniously held to the man-man.'[47]

In a bold exegesis, the idea of man-man was used to unfold the whole theology of the *imago dei*. 'Man' is the fallen man, the rebel who has turned his mind away from God, his archetype, and in whose heart the serpent 'has nestled down'. Only the man-man, in whom the perfected image of God is restored, is the perfect man, in whom the perfect harmony of the 'inner man' i.e., the *imago dei*, and the 'outer man' is established. Thereby is presupposed for ever the incarnation, the descent of God in flesh, the act of liberation bringing salvation, and the annunciation of Christ, the 'first-born from the dead', the 'last Adam'.

In the same direction of the theology of the *imago dei* points also the not less bold idea of the 'deification' of man. The Post-reformation theology has erased this audacious idea, which stemmed from the practice of mystical experience, almost completely from its vocabulary for fear of mysticism. But one should remember that the idea of deification—behind which lies a corresponding spiritual experience—formed, in the first one and half thousand years of the Christian Church, a central

[47] Hom. in Ezekiel iii. 8.

idea of Christian soteriology at a time when the Church found genuine mystics among the ranks of great theologians.

Athanasius, the great Bishop of Alexandria, provided the fundamental formula for the theology of deification: 'God has become man, therefore we shall be God.' He has thereby in no way introduced a new idea into Christian soteriology, but has only expressed in one formula what has completed the thought and the religious experience of many Fathers of the Early Church.

Besides, the idea of deification of man developed among the Church-fathers in an exegesis of a biblical statement and indeed in the words of Psalm 81. 6: 'I have said: "You are gods, and all at once children of the Highest—*Ego dixi, Dei estis et filii excelsi*".'

Already in the Gospel of John, this word plays a decisive role in the Johanian image of man, and in the messianic self-explanation of Jesus. John reports how Jesus refers to this statement of Psalm 81. 6, in a conversation with the Jews in the Hall of Solomon;[48] and exactly when the Jews reproached him for the words: 'I and the Father are one', and saying that he was making himself God, wanted to stone him, Jesus replied to them: 'Does it not stand written in your law: "I have said, you are gods?" If he calls gods those men to whom the word of God has come—and the scripture cannot be broken—do you then tell him whom the Father has sanctified and sent into the world: "You blaspheme God?" ' Here, therefore, Jesus in no way rejects the great claim that lies in the designation of men as gods in the words of the Psalm quoted by him, but expressly stresses the validity of these words. When God calls those to whom the word is spoken by the name gods, then this designation is applicable to them and they are truly 'gods'. Jesus quotes, therefore, the words of the Psalm for a justification, in conformity to the scriptures, of his own statement: 'I am the Son of God.'

In the theology of the Early Church, this statement made to the men: 'You are gods', became the basis of theological anthropology. The perfection of man worked out by Christ is identical with the deification of man. In men's perfection is fulfilled God's promise of salvation to them: 'You are gods—*dei estis*.'

Clement of Alexandria writes thus about the perfection of the

[48] John x. 34.

true gnostic: 'The same happens to us, the archetype of which the Lord has been:

> Through baptism we are enlightened,
> Through enlightenment we receive the sonship,
> Through the sonship we are perfected,
> Through perfection we obtain immortality.

He says: 'I have said: "You are gods and sons of the highest, all together".' The same Clement of Alexandria writes at another place: 'This gnosis leads to an endless and perfect goal in that you have beforehand taught what kind of life will be allotted to us, in accordance with the will of God, in the community of "gods", after we are freed from every chastisement and punishment which we, on account of our violations, have to suffer for the sake of correction that brings salvation. After this liberation, the prize and honours will be conferred on us; for we shall have become perfect, i.e. because purification will have been done to us and, indeed also, all other service will have come to an end. Then when we have become "pure in heart", there awaits us the restoration to our Lord through eternal presence; and such people obtain the name of "gods", as they shall be enthroned together along with other "gods" who have attained the first place below the redeemer.'

Generally, therefore, where the perfection of man is spoken of in the New Testament, it is associated with the idea of the creation of man after the image of God, but obtains its peculiar meaning through Christology: the perfection of man is reached 'in Christ'. This perfection is not an individualistic ideal, which aims at the ethical and spiritual perfection of individual men, but is understood always with a view to the collective growth of the believers towards the love of Christ. At many places in the letters of the Apostles, the promise of perfection appears to have a predominantly individualistic ring: '. . . teaching every man in all wisdom; that we may present every man perfect in Jesus Christ',[49] or as Paul in the same letter later writes:[50] 'For in him [Christ] dwelleth all the fullness of the Godhead bodily and ye are complete in him, who is the head of the principality and power.' But these passages, apparently having an individualistic

[49] Colossians i. 28.
[50] *Ibid.*, ii. 9–10.

tone in their expression, receive their peculiar significance from the thought that the community of saints is the body of Christ which is forming itself in history and is growing up and is growing as a whole, and in which 'we shall become a perfect man, who will be there to the degree of the completed age of Christ'.

This idea of perfection in man, laid out in accordance with the creation, betrayed by man himself, and obtained again in Christ, makes another upgrading in the conception of man understandable, as it appears in the history of Christian piety: the raising of the sonship of God to the friendship of God. The friendship of God appears as the highest form of society that will be attained between God and man—in it love is sublimated to the highest form of personal communication between the prototype and the image.

The fine sensitivity for the difference of the levels between the sonship of God and the friendship of God has been brought to expression by Joachim de Fiore, the prophetic Abbot of Calabar. This founder of spiritualism has understood the history of salvation as the process of a successive self-development of the divine Trinity in three holy periods of salvation, in the first of which God the Father, in the second of which the Son, and in the third and last of which the Holy Ghost steps forth as the Divine Power taking a form. In his long enumeration of the particulars of the sequence of the periods of the history of salvation, the first stage, the age of the sovereignty of the law of the Old Testament, is described as the stage of the servant; the second stage, the age of the New Testament, as the stage of the Son; but the third stage, the age of the Holy Spirit, as the stage of the friend. Here appears the friendship of God as the finale and climax of the development of the relation between God and man. The friendship of God is more than the sonship of God; for it presupposes a higher state of freedom. It is the last, highest, and final form of a loving, personal meeting of God and man. The third, the highest age of salvation is the age of the 'friendship of God', in which the relation of man to God is raised to a level appropriate to the status of freedom. But therewith is concerned a sphere of spiritual life and inner experience, a sphere that lies on the other side of the bounds of the speakable.

13. THE NEIGHBOUR AS THE CHRIST PRESENT

Primarily from the establishment of the Christian anthropology in the *imago dei* is the revolutionary idea, which is the foundation of Christian ethics, understandable, viz., that for the eye of the Christian faith God is present in every man, even in the degenerate. One of the most impressive places of the New Testament in which this new, specifically Christian evaluation of man comes to the forefront is Matthew 25. 31. There Jesus, in his speech on the last judgment, describes the surprise of the judged at the statement that they owe the judgment passed on them—consignment to and banishment from the Kingdom of God, of the heirs and of the accursed respectively—to their attitude towards the Son of God. The Son of God says to them on his right: 'Come, you blessed of my Father, inherit the Kingdom prepared for you from the beginning of the world. For I have been hungry and you have given me food—I have been thirsty and you have given me drink. I have been a guest and you have taken me in. . . .' Surprised, the righteous say to the Son of Man: 'Lord, when have we seen you hungry and fed you or seen your thirsty and given you drink? . . .' In answer to their surprised question, they heard from the mouth of the world-judge: 'Indeed, I say to you: What you have done to one of these, my poorest brothers, that you have done to me.'[51] Similarly, the accursed heard from the mouth of the Son of Man the grounds of their damnation: 'Whatsoever you have not done unto one of the least of these, that you have not done unto me.'[52]

In a very close connection with this potent word is found another word in the Fathers of the Early Church, a word that does not exist in the canonical Gospels, but is cited as an independent noble word (*Herrenwort*) and yet brings impressively the basic idea of Christian ethics to expression: '*Vidisti fratrem, vidisti dominum tuum*'—'Have you seen your brother, so have you seen your Lord.' For the Christian, the neighbour is the Christ himself present. The Christian sees also, under the guise of the miserable, the degenerate, the suffering, and the disgraced, the image of the Lord visible, who became man, who suffered, and was raised to the cross, who died and was

[51] Matthew xxv. 34 fol.
[52] *Ibid.*, xxv. 45.

resurrected, in order to lead men back to his Kingdom and to complete his Kingdom with them.

Here is a characteristic ethic which, in its norms, is not based upon distinctions, social, biological, psychological, physiological, spiritual, or educational, but which understands man in his deepest basis as the image of God, not in an abstract, theoretical remoteness, but in final identification with the brother in whom it sees Christ, the God that became man, the 'new man', as actual. The Christian ethics does not, therefore, aim at a pure ethics of the individual, but sees every single man always in his relationship to his next, his neighbour, and his fellow-men.

Here lies, again, before us one of the significant differences from the other great religions. Hinduism as well as Buddhism aims, in its highest and most spiritual experiences, which are comparable to similar Christian experiences, to liberate the individual from his entanglement in suffering and death and from the causality of earthly transience, and to unify him with his transcendent origin. The religious ethics of Hinduism and Buddhism is, to the last, an individualistic ethics. There also, where it expressly underlines the Bodhisattva ideal as in the case expressly of Mahāyāna Buddhism, it is found that the man striving for liberation renounces the desire for its highest stage, the entering into Nirvāṇa, in order to lead other men on to the path of liberation.

14. COMMUNITY OF THE BELIEVERS AS THE BODY OF CHRIST

The novelty of Christian ethics lies further in that the idea of identification with the brother is connected with the conception of the community of Christians as the body of Christ. No single believer understands himself as a separate individual who has found a new spiritual and ethical relationship to God. He understands himself as a 'living stone'[53] or, as we would say to-day, as a living cell in the living body of Christ; for this ethics represents the community of believers as the body of Christ, in which the forces of God's Kingdom are already powerful and in which the blood of Christ circulates.

Here again, a surprisingly physical, material, indeed, materialistically fundamental feature presents itself. The idea

[53] I Peter ii. 5.

of the community of the believers as the real body of Christ, whose head is Christ himself, the body which is permeated thoroughly by his spirit and blood, is the authentic and only foundation of the Christian social metaphysics and social ethics.

How little this idea of the community of the believers as the body of Christ is meant in a purely metaphysical sense, how concrete and real this idea of the belongingness of the believers as 'living stones' to the body of Christ is, follows from the fact that within the organism of the body of Christ a peculiar communication stands among the single cells and organs. And so there is within this body an intercession of one for another; but there is also a vicarious suffering of one for another; there is an answerability of one for another, in which one carries the burden of another and one allows his gifts of grace to devolve on another. It is an organism in which Christian love leads to a proper exchange of gifts and suffering, elevation and degradation, defeat and victory—which is possible only in a corporeal organization in which the individual can even contribute, through self-sacrifice, to the development of the whole. 'I fill up that which is behind of the afflictions of Christ in my flesh for his body's sake, which is the church.'[54] When we take upon ourselves the suffering of humanity at death, indeed, of the whole creation, just as Christ has done at the cross, then we complete his work of salvation, then we become Christ. Thus can the individual, through his suffering, really actuate and accelerate the growth of the body of Christ and the development of the community of believers into the 'perfect man'.

On this fundamental thought of the community of believers as the body of Christ are based all the different forms of the church-community and the different social and political forms in Christendom. By this basic idea are stamped also the numerous forms of secularization of the Christian society, even where to-day they actually repudiate their Christian origin or even adopt an anti-Christian attitude.

Obviously, in the pre-Christian world in the past and in the non-Christian world to-day, the significance of the human body is understood as that of an image and copy of the political community of a kingdom, a state, or a city. But generally this idea of the body is changed by them into an unauthentically similar meaning and surprisingly nowhere with reference to a

[54] Paul's words in Colossians i. 24.

religious community. But the sacral and sacramental application of this idea is of an absolutely new kind, when it appears in the conception of the community of believers as the real body of Christ. The emphasis is laid by this realistic understanding not only on the idea of the organic coherence of the single cells within a body and not only on the idea of the differentiation of the single organs of the body into parts—and herein lies the beginning of a completely new metaphysic of society and of a completely new social ethic based on the idea of corporation—but also equally on the idea of a progressive growth of this body within history through continuous inclusion of new 'living stones' into it.

The so-called 'eschatological aspect' of the Christian history of salvation appears here revived in all its force. It means basically nothing else than that in the community of believers the newly creative, transformative, and regenerative powers of the Kingdom of God are already now at work, which have come forward, for the first time in the history of the world, in the form of Jesus Christ and which, coming from him, the 'first-born from the dead', the 'first among the resurrected', operate progressively in humanity, in that they build, by a mysterious selective process, the community of the Kingdom of God among men, which is the body of Christ. Thereby is opened up an unexplorable, unceasing process of the growth of the Kingdom of God in history, a kingdom that is expressed with the utmost clarity in the numerous comparisons of Jesus with the sower, with the self-growing seed, with the varied fate of the scattered seeds, but also with leaven.

Nevertheless, here is noticeable a peculiar state of tension, which, till now, has not found its definite solution and resolution within the historical forms of the Christian Church. From the beginning, in the self-understanding of the Christian community, two tendencies come into conflict with each other, which lead to different consequences in the basic adjustment of the Christians to fellow-Christians and fellow-men.

The first adjustment lies in the predominant idea of election. God is He who Himself elects His own out of the humanity that lives in opposition to Himself and builds His Kingdom out of those elected by Him. This idea emphasizes the aristocratic character of the Kingdom of God, which consists of the élite of the elected. This idea of the élite is expressed in the Apocalypse of John in a hardly surpassable exclusiveness: 'The picked troops of the Kingdom consist of the 144,000, who have not defiled themselves with women.'[55] The object of the immense effort of the history of salvation is so small a number, the beneficiary of the cosmic drama is so small a community that played out the struggle of the storming armies of the Kingdom of God and of Satan in the heavens and on the earth! Even for Augustine, the community of the elect is restricted in numbers: their number corresponds to the number of fallen angels, which must be made up again by a corresponding number of liberated men, by whom the Kingdom of God will again be restituted according to the number! The Church is, in a true sense, understood as elective, as the selection of a few out of *massa perditionis* of all too many, who will never partake of the Kingdom and who form the jetsam of the history of salvation.

In this attitude is hidden a great danger to society: into the way of the aristocratic, exclusive consciousness of the elect are drawn easily self-righteousness and self-security, which are the roots of self-love, and thereby the death of the love of God and the neighbour.

The other attitude lies in the opposite direction: it stems from the idea that the aim of salvation, opened up through Christ, can only be the regeneration and saving of all humanity, and the love of God, as the immense drama of his self-surrender and self-sacrifice for the sake of man shows, is greater than righteousness, which demands the eternal damnation of the sinful. According to this conception, the infinite love of God must be in a position even to cancel the greatest sin of man, to overcome through love the rebellion against God by the first authors of the fall, and to bring all mankind again into the Kingdom of God.

The second attitude is often found expressed in the great mystics of the Early Church and the Eastern Church; it has found its apostles in many charismatics of the western Christendom as well. For it the object of salvation is humanity as a whole; the history of salvation is ultimately identical with the history of humanity, the body of Christ is identical with humanity integrated into a single community. In spite of the Church's condemnation of the teaching of universal atonement, as Origen has taught, the great theologians and mystics of the

[55] Revelation; John xiv. 4.

Eastern Church have actually remained secretly the followers of his teaching and have been of the innermost conviction that only the salvation of all, finally of Satan himself, is commensurate with the complete triumph of divine love.

That the teaching of universal salvation—*apokatastasis*—is nevertheless pushed often into opposition to Church dogmas in all Christian confessions goes with the fact that such a universalistic conception of salvation easily leads to the opinion that views salvation as an unavoidable event, as a kind of soteriological process of nature from which man cannot escape in the long run. Such an attitude can have only one result, viz., the consciousness of ethical responsibility of man before God and his neighbours will be lost. If man cannot escape salvation in this or a later life, then there will be no necessity of the struggle for salvation. Thus in the idea of *apokatastasis* lies the temptation of a dangerous spiritual and ethical indolence and certainty.

15. CHRIST IN THE WORLD: CHRISTIAN ASCETICISM

The peculiarity of Christian asceticism is not easy to grasp, particularly for the followers of any of the great non-Christian religions. At many points, Christian asceticism appears to be identical with the Hindu or Buddhist method of flight from the world, the methodical overcoming of the desire for self-preservation, of the love of life, of the will to enjoy the physical gifts of human life like lust, power and prestige. Indeed, the Christian asceticism of the early centuries of Christendom was strongly influenced by the old ascetic traditions of the regions of the Essenes, Manicheism, and also Hinduism and Buddhism, and certainly right up to the details of the method and practice of asceticism. It easily appears—and a great part of the polemic against asceticism on the part of the reformers of the sixteenth century is due to this semblance—as though the foundation of Christian asceticism is the same dualism between spirit and flesh, soul and body, form and matter, idea and substance, as that which forms the presupposition of the asceticism in Hinduism and Buddhism. The fact that the fathers of the Early Church founded their ascetic theology on a Christian Platonism has further strengthened this identification.

Nevertheless, Christian asceticism has absolutely different

presuppositions. These are not to be sought, indeed, in an ontological dualism, but in Christian eschatology, in the expectation of the imminent coming of the Kingdom of God, in the expectation next of the breaking in of the descent of the 'fulness of time', which is really an anticipation of the coming itself. Christian asceticism has, in its original form, an extraordinarily strong, dynamic element of hope, indeed one may almost say, an element of violence, an element of the confirmation here of the breaking in of the Kingdom of God itself. The Christian community prays for the end of the world. Its prayer sounds: 'Lord come! *Maranatha!*' It means an imploring desire that the Lord may no longer delay His return, He may come straight away, immediately, at once, at this spot. The prayer: '*Maranatha!*' is a prayer for the accelerated end of the world. In the supper-prayer of Didache, the community prays: 'May grace come, may the world vanish. Hosanna to the God of David—*Maranatha!*' The community prays, therefore, to Christ to lead the old world speedily to its destruction and to introduce the new aeon as rapidly as possible, in which the children of the Kingdom will celebrate the messianic meal with the Son of Man.

Christian asceticism is to be understood from this pressing expectation. It is the anticipation of the approaching fulfilment, the attitude to the coming in the form of an anticipation of the coming here and now; it will quicken the arrival of the coming new aeon. Asceticism is the transition to active abolition of the old aeon and is the means of accelerating the setting of the old aeon and the rising of the new. The normal conditions of the now ruling aeon are knowingly ignored, compromises for possibilities are avoided and only permitted to the 'weak' as cases of exception casuistically and exactly fixed. The martyrs and ascetics press for the quickening of the coming of the fulfilment. Tertullian writes: 'Our sighing wishes stretch themselves towards the decline of this age and therewith also towards the passing away of this world, towards the great day of the Lord, the day of wrath and retribution.'

The time-moment and the eschatological tension present, therefore, a completely new kind of feature in Christian asceticism. Of an equally new kind is the second characteristic feature of Christian asceticism: the tendency towards asceticism of the inner world. Christian asceticism does not lead man away from the world, but calls him into the world for transforming it under the commission of God. Actually this feature has so long been used that it should prevail against dualistic elements. The differentiation during the Middle Ages between *vita contemplativa* and *vita activa,* a higher and a lower form of Christian life, was nevertheless founded on a complete dualism. But in the same sphere there prevailed also the basic thought of incarnation: the end of the spirit shall not be to withdraw from the corporeal sphere, to turn itself back on itself and to break all bonds that binds the spirit to material and corporeal existence. It shall be the aim of the spirit to raise matter and corporeality to the status of means to its self-development and to represent itself bodily. 'For Christendom, matter exists as the vehicle of the spirit; and the material stuff fulfils its true function only when it is this vehicle.'[56]

This shows itself also clearly in a mystic like Meister Eckhart, who comes entirely out of an ascetic tradition stamped by dualism and Neo-Platonism. Eckhart has recoined the whole medieval tradition of asceticism and mystical theology in that he speaks of the pre-eminence of Martha (the type of *vita activa*) over Mary (the type of *vita contemplativa*). For him asceticism is not a flight from the world, but the self-realization of man, who, for working in the world, was liberated by God Himself through the birth of God in the soul.

The slogan is no longer: The fulfilment of existence through detachment from time; but it is the fulfilment of the meaning of time through work for the Kingdom of God. Thus Christianity became the religion that discovered the value of time, the religion of the clocks. The pre-Christian cultures knew the sun-dial, which showed only the bright and clear hours and which reflected the cosmic return of the similars, and in addition also the klepsydra and the sand-clock, which showed the passage of a fixed time-measure. It was from the Christian eschatological understanding of time that the human spirit was given the call: 'Redeem the time! Work while it is day',[57] to divide time more and more exactly, to cut out time into smaller and smaller units, and to bring before the eye the fleetingness of the seconds, technically represented by the 'unrest' of the clock, and the dwindling of time and value appearing through this 'unrest'.

[56] Archbishop Temple.

[57] Ephesians v. 16; John ix. 4.

The beginnings of the watch-industry are associated closely with monasticism and its liturgical rhythm of *ora et labora* and its further development in the later centuries are associated with the movements of Calvinistic puritanism and that of pietism—a movement which, in turn, shows a series of puritanical features. The virtue of punctuality shows a still greater significance. He only is punctual who knows something of the value of time, who knows that time is apportioned by God as a measure, at our call, of every moment of our co-work in the Kingdom of God, and who knows that the precious time is to be filled with valuable actions and that the waste and dissipation of time is a sin against God and the neighbour.

Similarly, frugality is a specifically Christian virtue, which is associated with the same eschatalogically basic attitude. He who expects the quick decline of this aeon, the quick coming of judgment, and who knows that the end is imminent and yet will burden himself only with the most necessary things, will use nothing more for himself than what he absolutely needs for the fixed span of time of his life. He will collect no treasures, which 'the moths and rust eat up',[58] but will seek to make both ends meet with the minimum and allow all else to the share of his brothers.

If this eschatalogical virtue is, however, alienated from its basic spiritual intent, it transforms itself into its opposite: it becomes the drive of acquisitiveness, which ever goads egoism strongly and leads to the accumulation of saved up goods. To economize means originally to consume as little as possible in order to have as much as possible for a free disposal to the brothers; but in its degenerate form, economizing means: to accumulate for oneself as many as possible of the unconsumed goods. Here perhaps lies the point of approach of the thesis of Max Weber, however much abused and highly one-sided: Calvinism is the father of capitalism.

To this eschatalogical consciousness of time, which has determined Christian asceticism, belong also the 'vigil' and sobriety (fasting). The clock on the church-tower, the church-clock, and the church-bell, which 'strike the hours', belong together. 'Let us watch and be sober!'[59] 'Be sober and watch!'[60]

[58] Matthew vi. 19.
[59] I Thessalonians v. 6.
[60] I Peter v. 8.

'Watch and pray.'[61] 'You do not know at which hour the Lord will come.'[62] 'I come like a thief, blessed is he who watches!'[63] This watching along with sobriety leads to a new form of the use of time, not only for the liturgical prayer but also for work, for study, for science. Along with the burning candle on the altar, which burnt during the night long service of God by the monks—*Pannichide*—in the Eastern Church, stands the candle in the study room of the savants and the researchers. The clock became the awakener, at first in the form of the *simandron*, the beating stick (bat) with which the monks were torn from their short sleep with the hammer, through a quickly accelerated knocking sound, for the service of God, but with which also the beginning of the work of hand and labour was signalled, and to which the monk was bound; and later this sound became all the many mechanical forms of the awakener, which till to-day the technical instrument, against which human nature mostly rebels, represents.

16. CHRISTIANITY AND SECULARIZATION

The asceticism of the inner world has led, through its peculiar connexion with the expectation of the end of time and acceleration and exaltation of work, to a unique result, which for the non-Christians, especially the Asians, remains often unintelligible—namely, to the fact that the visible results, emerging before our eyes, of this attitude lead to a tremendous rise in material power and to the surprising consequences of its manipulation. Christianity has brought forth some absolutely unique, but for it essential, forms of secularization of its spiritual and ethical impulses and thereby has drawn the wide-spread rebuke of 'materialism' upon western civilization developing within the sphere of Christianity. In the contemporary situation, it is really of decisive importance to hold this phenomenon before our eyes! Often the precedent of the secularization and the Christian spiritual and ethical values have been pilloried in a one-sided way—actually by non-Christians—and judged as an unholy symptom of the decline of Christian religion and culture.

[61] Matthew xxvi. 41.
[62] *Ibid* xxiv. 42.
[63] Revelation; John xvi. 15.

But this criticism does not touch the essence of the thing. In a certain sense, Christianity, according to its nature, is set towards secularization; for it stands upon the fundamental idea —or better to say, as said by the believers, the fundamental fact—of incarnation. God Himself wanted, indeed, to be a man, wanted to embody Himself; God Himself, as the first, took the step towards self-realization, self-representation, self-manifestation, in the material, corporeal, and carnal world and has more and more let Himself into the sphere of the process of the history of humanity. Secularization belongs, therefore, to at least a part of His intention in the great process of incarnation. No other religion, according to its essence, could go through a profound process of secularization and actually outlast it than this religion, whose gospel proclaims the Logos and is derived from the Logos that became flesh. While Buddhism, for instance, has, in an essential measure, a tendency towards flight from the world, Christianity shows an inherent tendency towards secularization.

But in no other religion is it so difficult to establish the point at which secularization passes from the measure of God's intended embodiment, turns into the anti-godly, leads to the estrangement of the original Christian point of departure, and makes itself self-sufficient, and takes an anti-theistic, anti-Christian turn. Basically all movements of secularization stand exposed to the danger of estrangement and the danger of perversion into the anti-Christian. Thus the technical and commercial exploitation of the earth and of man came from God's commission to the integral man before the fall: 'Make the earth subject to you!' Thus the idea of the communist society came from the idea of the sovereignty of the approaching Kingdom of God. Thus revolution came out of the expectation of the imminent; organization out of the idea of the corporation of the Christian community; the commissar and the functionary out of the watching ascetic; the stop-watch of the supervisor of the work time out of the church-clock and the simandron; democracy out of the Kingdom of God; and human rights out of the rights of God over man. In every one of these individual developments within the total process of secularization there lies somewhere a point at which the turn towards alienation begins or at which at least the danger of alienation enters—a danger to which men at times succumb with a regularity almost frightening. The limiting point is obviously reached there where man loses sight of his *imago dei* and knowledge of it, where the heavenly *sophia* leaves him, and when the life-bringing connection with the second Adam, the renewer of the image of man, is cut off completely.

CHAPTER VII

The Concept of Man in Islamic Thought

IBRAHIM MADKOUR

I. INTRODUCTION

THE concept of man is as old as man himself. From the start man was aware of his existence as a separate entity, different from nature and the universe. In attempting to secure his sustenance, this feeling became clearer and stronger; he experienced hope and pain, success and failure in his struggle against nature and other creatures. As his struggle became harder, his self-confidence increased, and he began to understand his rights and duties.

The concept of man is closely connected with the notion of human values, which have been created by successive generations of men, the precious outcome of various religions and philosophies. They increased and developed in the course of time, their waymarks became clear and well defined. These values flourished at times, but at times they degenerated also; they were sanctified beyond all things at certain periods, and swept away almost completely at certain others. Though the eighteenth century is known as the century of human rights, the twentieth century does not seem to uphold these rights or enshrine them as it should. The world wars with their barbarism and tyranny were very hostile to them and they became, to a certain extent, subjected to doubt and confusion. Much of the honour and dignity of man was overflown by obstinate materialism. In the name of the community, the existence and independence of the individual were desecrated; but a society whose component elements have lost their personality is useless.

Islam is the religion of humanity, a mercy for the world; it appeals to man and addresses its message to him. It preaches his dignity and announces his superiority to many other creatures, and considers him the representative of God on earth. It is his duty to populate the earth and to direct its affairs according to his own wisdom. He was thus entrusted with these duties—and they are enormous indeed. He was charged with responsibilities which were burdensome and excessive. But by the gift of his reason man lifts the veils and rules over nature and learns what he has not mastered.

Islam is a religion as well as a civilization; it encompasses teachings, behaviour, doctrine and philosophy. Its basic doctrine is that glory is proper to God the One; there is no deity beside Him; nothing is to be worshipped besides Him. Thus man is diverted from idolatry and even from devotion and submission to his fellow men. The basis of man's civilization is this Islamic fraternity in which there is no discrimination on grounds of noble birth, race, or colour. The Muslim is the brother of the Muslim, and an Arab cannot have precedence over a non-Arab Muslim except by his piety. It is a kind of brotherhood similar to that which has been propagated by the ancient Stoics, and which we are trying to re-establish to-day under the name of world-citizenship.

Before we discuss the concept of man as such, we may refer to some of the human values proclaimed by Islam.

2. HUMAN VALUES

In the Koran man is addressed clearly, and with great care. Almost every *Surah* addresses him either in the singular or the plural form. If the word 'prophet' or 'apostle' is used several times, the word 'man' or 'men' occurs scores, if not hundreds of times.[1] No subject is mentioned in the Koran more often than this one. The creation of man and his origins are referred to more than once. All these references indicate the care and the perfection with which he was created: 'Surely We have created man most beautifully erect.'[2] 'No wonder, for he has been created by God's own hands.'[3] This last metaphor clearly implies the honour bestowed upon man. Adam, the father of all

[1] The word 'man' occurs in about 45 *Surahs* and the word 'men' about 240 times. There are two *Surahs*, one entitled 'The Man' (76) and the other entitled 'The Men' (114).

[2] *Surah* 95, verse 4.

[3] *Surah* 38, verse 75.

men, was created from 'potter's clay, of mud ground down'.[4] And this in turn contains admonition and warning against pride and false greatness but without any depreciation of man's dignity. In the teachings of Islam human values such as justice and equality, honour and dignity are defined. We have to mention these briefly at this point.

(i) *Preference of Man and Prohibition of Bloodshed:*

In the Koran there are eloquent verses indicating preference of man to other beings: 'And now we have honoured the children of Adam, by land and by sea have we carried them, food have we provided them of good things, and with endowments beyond many of our creatures have we endowed them.'[5] The position of man is obvious in other contexts also, particularly in Adam's relation to the angels, for we are told that he knows more and occupies a higher position than they. 'And He taught Adam the names of all things and then set them before the angels, and said: "Tell me the names of these if you are endued with wisdom." They said: "Praise be to Thee. We have no knowledge but what Thou hast given us to know. Thou art the knowing, the Wise".' He said: 'O Adam, inform them of their names.'[6] 'When your Lord said to the angels, I create man of dried clay, of dark loam moulded, and when I shall fashion him and breathe of my spirit into him, then fall you down and worship him.'[7]

Islam emphasized man's dignity by prohibiting bloodshed, especially in an environment where killing and vendetta were permitted. It prohibited the burial of female children alive,[8] and the killing of children for fear of want.[9] Islam threatens with eternal punishment, wrath and malediction whoever destroys the life a fellow-man. 'Whoever shall kill a believer of set purpose, his punishment will be hell, forever shall he abide in it; God shall be wrathful with him, and shall curse him, and shall make ready for him a great torment.'[10] Islam has fixed retaliation, penalties, bloodmoney, and polltax to prevent

[4] *Surah* 15, verse 26, and *Surah* 23, verse 12.
[5] *Surah* 17, verse 70.
[6] *Surah* 2, verses 31–33.
[7] *Surah* 15, verse 29.
[8] *Surah* 81, verse 8.
[9] *Surah* 17, verse 33.
[10] *Surah* 4, verse 93.

bloodshed and to protect life. 'In this law of retaliation is your [security for] life, O men of understanding! to the intent that you may fear God.'[11]

In all this we find respect for human life, which is regarded as holy. No life can be destroyed unjustly, and even in war the teachings of Islam decree that enemies must not be taken by surprise, nor should they be mutilated. Likewise, prisoners of war are to be treated with mercy and pity.

(ii) *Succour of the Feeble and Emancipation of Slaves:*

The language of the *Hadith* does not differ from that of the Koran in any way. It exalts man and prefers him to other creatures. It asserts his freedom and dignity, and explicates all the noble ideas which occur in the Koran. The life of Muhammad is a living example of the aid and support that can be extended to man. He strove against the lords and the highborn and succoured the weak and the oppressed. He never cherished rank or wealth and often warned against adherence to rank, noble birth and tribalism. When Mecca was conquered, a man came to Muhammad trembling with fear, and Muhammad said to him: 'Do not worry, I am not a king, but the son of a Qoraishite woman who eats dried meat.'[12] Once the emigrants (Mohājirin) and the defenders (Ansārs) dissented and each party tried to call for help saying: 'O, for so and so!' and the Prophet's answer was: 'Do not repeat such words, they smell of evil.'[13]

Slavery was an institution recognized all over the world before Islam. The Greeks had their slaves, and regarded all non-Athenians as barbarians. The Romans had many more slaves, and in some of their provinces the number of slaves was three times the number of free men. The Arabs had slaves in pre-Islamic times, and had slave-markets as well. When Islam came, the slaves, men and women, were among the first to respond to its appeal, and they suffered greatly for it. The new religion made it imperative that they should be well treated. It favoured their emancipation and made it a proper atonement for many crimes. 'And whoso killeth a believer by mischance

[11] *Surah* 2, verse 179.

[12] Muhammad al Khodari: *Nūr al Yaqīn fi sīrat Sayyid al Morsalīn*, pp. 397–399, Cairo 1910.

[13] *Ibid.*, p. 208.

shall be bound to free a believer from slavery.'[14] 'God will not punish for a mistaken word in your oaths, but He will punish you in regard to an oath taken seriously. Its expiation shall be to feed ten poor persons with such middling food as ye feed your own families with, or to clothe them, or to set free a captive'.[15] 'And those who thus put away their wives, and afterwards would recall their words, must free a captive.'[16] Muhammad gave the first example in Islam when he set free his slave Zaid ibn Hāritha, whom he had received as a present from his wife Khādija. Many of his companions followed in his footsteps, and those emancipated slaves became lords and *imāms*. They commanded the armies, and carried the banners of learning. They played an important part in the Islamic scientific movement.

(iii) *Women's Rights:*

Islam addressed women as it addressed men, and treated them almost equally. A woman has the same rights and duties as a man. Burying newborn daughters alive was strictly forbidden—a custom which was widespread before Islam. 'For when the birth of a daughter is announced to any one of them, dark shadows settle on his face and he is sad. He hides himself from the people because of the ill tidings. Shall he keep it with disgrace or bury it in the dust? Are not their judgments wrong?'[17] The woman has to pray, give legal alms, fast, and perform the pilgrimage to Mecca. She can inherit and be inherited. She is both rewarded and punished like man. 'And their Lord answered them: I will not suffer the work of him among you that worketh, whether male or female. The one of you is the issue of the other.'[18] When she comes of age, nothing can be done without her consent; she cannot be forced to marry or made to sell or purchase. She disposes of her affairs, and her financial rights are complete. Women in Islam have had these rights long before they were granted them by modern legislation.

In Islam women teach and are taught; they can give also legal opinion on religious matters. Some of the wives of the Prophet were authorities in religious law and *Hadith*. The

[14] *Surah* 4, verse 92.
[15] *Surah* 5, verse 89.
[16] *Surah* 58, verse 3.
[17] *Surah* 6, verses 58–59.
[18] *Surah* 3, verse 195.

Muslim woman takes an active part in public life too and undertakes responsibilities as Arab women did in pre-Islamic times. She is entitled to her own opinion, and even takes part in war. The wives of the Prophet accompanied him during his campaigns and proved their bravery in war. Their help was invaluable, for they tended the wounded, gave the thirsty to drink and the hungry to eat, and took part in the fighting sometimes. Muslim women followed their example. It would be sufficient here to mention Al Khansā (664), the famous poetess, who encouraged her four sons to fight in the battle of Qādisīya and praised the Lord who had honoured her by their death on the battlefield. A'isha (698) shouldered great responsibilities during the revolt against Othman (655). She was the first Muslim woman to direct the major policies of the state, and to lead armies in battle in defence of her beliefs. The veiling of women was not an Arab custom in pre-Islamic times, nor was it a religious precept in Islam; it was the custom of some of the nations which embraced Islam.

(iv) *Brotherhood, Justice and Equality:*

Muhammad established brotherhood among his companions, and taught them to love one another. 'The community of believers is like a structure whose parts are fully integrated.' He ordered the emigrants from Qoraish to live with the defenders in Medina as their guests, making them into one family in spite of all that has separated them in the past. On the occasion of the 'Farewell Pilgrimage' he said: 'O men, your Lord is one, and your Father is one, you are all the sons of Adam, and Adam was made of dust. The most pious among you is the most honoured by God. An Arab does not have precedence over a non-Arab Muslim except by his piety.'[19] He treated Muslims equally in his pronouncements and never discriminated between them in loss or gain. He saw to it that justice was done even if he himself was involved. He never took into account either friendship or noble birth. Once he struck one of his companions with a rod on the belly in order to make him toe the line during the holy war. The man complained to him. He did not hesitate to bare his belly and said to him: 'Retaliate, O Sawad!'[20] When his uncle

[19] Al Khodari: *Nūr Al Yaqīn*, p. 352.
[20] *Ibid.*, p. 156.

Abbas and his cousin Oqail ibn Abu Tālib were captured in the battle of Badr, he required the same ransom from them as he required from the other prisoners.

Islam propagated equality, and rejected the classification of people into masters and slaves, noblemen and commoners. Men are brothers, all are the offspring of Adam, and Adam was made of dust. Islam opposed tribal and racial discrimination, and established amity among nations and peoples. 'O men, verily we have created you of a male and a female, and we divided you into peoples and tribes that ye might have knowledge of one another. Truly the most worthy of honour in the sight of God is he who feareth Him most.'[21] Islam made consultation imperative, and rejected oppression and dictatorship. 'And consult them in the affair'[22] 'and whose affairs are guided by mutual consent.'[23]

(v) *Consultation:*

Muhammad used to consult his companions in serious matters and encouraged them to express their opinions. He accepted their decisions without partiality or despotism. The first problem he faced was the question of the prisoners of war in the battle of Badr. He presented it for discussion, and one party proposed their extermination, while the other voted for their ransom. The Prophet consented to their ransom, since this was the decision of the majority, and in spite of the fact that he suffered a great deal from the hands of the Qoraish.[24] Many tribes plotted to invade Medina, and strong armies marched towards it, and this came to be known as the 'war of the trench' (*Khandaq*). Muhammad put the whole matter before his companions. In the discussion a proposal was put forward by a man who was neither a lord nor a nobleman and not even an Arab; his name was Salmān the Persian (655). His proposal, in a nutshell, was to dig a trench around Medina in order to protect it against the attack. The idea was adopted, and Muhammad insisted on participating with the other Muslims in digging

[21] *Surah* 49, verse 13.
[22] *Surah* 3, verse 159.
[23] *Surah* 42, verse 38.
[24] Al Khodari: *Nūr Al Yaqīn*, pp. 261–272.

the trench. In this way, Muhammad and his companions won the battle.[25]

This customary procedure of consultation had its impact on the investiture of *'Saqifa'*, when the first Caliph was elected. The emigrants and defenders could not agree on a successor to Muhammad after his death. But they soon voted unanimously for Abu Bakr (634) in a plebiscite. We wish that plebiscite had become a permanent institution and its method had been codified; it would have saved the Muslims from many disastrous and successive controversies. The caliphate can be regarded as the first schism through which evil befell the Muslims and caused their power to be divided. It revived tribalism and racism. Instead of consultation and election, the whole matter was turned into a hereditary monarchy within fifty years after the decease of the Apostle.

Scholars have tried to settle the matter in vain. In so doing they put forward different opinions concerning the election of the *imām* or the Caliph. Some of these opinions are marked by perfect impartiality and absolute frankness. They have in fact left us studies that can be considered an important chapter in the history of political philosophy; they are perhaps the oldest ever written on the subject of the selection of the head of the state. In short, absolutism and dictatorship are alien to the teachings of Islam. They are only a creation of some Muslim dictators who try to cover them with religious cloak.

(vi) *Socialism in Islam:*

Islam has fixed for the poor and destitute a formal claim on the funds of the Muslims, and assigned part of these funds for the weak and disabled. It has made the poor-tax imperative, and indicated its expenditure. 'And observe prayer and pay the legal impost; and whatever good things ye have sent on before for your soul's sake, ye shall find it with God.'[26] 'But alms are only [to be given] for the poor and the needy and to those who collect them, whose hearts are won [for Islam] and for ransoms and for debtors and for the cause of God and for wayfarers.'[27] Omar succeeded, though independent judgment, to amend the expenditure of the impost according to circumstances and situations.

[25] Al Khodari: *Nūr Al Yaqīn*, pp. 217–221.
[26] *Surah* 2, verse 110.
[27] *Surah* 9, verse 50.

Islam has not stopped at the legal impost, for it encourages donations and charity for the common good, without setting a limit on the amount of these donations. Some Muslims have spent all they had for the cause of God. 'Take alms of their substance, that thou mayest cleanse and purify them thereby.'[28] A legal portion of war-booty and of whatever is drawn from land or sea belongs to the public depository of Muslims. 'And know ye, that when you have taken any booty, a fifth part belongeth to God and to the Apostle and to the near of kin and to orphans and to the poor and to the wayfarer.'[29] The needy are treated equally by the public depository (the treasury). They all receive their allowances according to their needs without discrimination or preference; or if any, it would be solely based on their piety alone. Omar Ibn al Khattāb has given the most exalted example, for he never took more than his allotted share, and was compelled due to his tallness to complete his shirt from the portion assigned to his son.

We find in the Koran, therefore, the basis of social justice or what we call today socialism. The socialism of Islam, however, is founded on justice, fairness and respect for human rights.

This is a brief survey of the message of Islam. Fourteen centuries ago, Islam, no less than contemporary thought or modern history, has thrown human values into prominence. It emphasizes the existence of the individual as a separate entity and frees him from the domination of his clan or tribe. It recognizes his rights and treats all men equally, regardless of their race or colour. It maintains a just balance between the individual and society. This is perhaps one of the most crucial problems of contemporary society. Islam certainly places the interests of society before the interests of the individual whenever necessary, provided that this would not dehumanize him or cause him lose his freedom and dignity.

In the light of these principles Islam has conceived the essence of man. Its concept originates from the Koran and the custom of the Prophet (*Sonna*). It was developed and elaborated by the various Islamic schools of jurisprudence, theology, philosophy, and Sufism.

[28] *Surah* 9, verse 103.

[29] *Surah* 8, verse 41.

3. THE ESSENCE OF MAN

The problem of the essence of man has occupied people's minds from time immemorial: man has tried to know himself. Sometimes he conceived that his life was a mere material existence based on organic and physiological phenomena. At other times he thought that there was a spiritual life beyond this material existence and that in this spiritual life lay his essence and real being. The belief in the existence of the soul is as old as man himself. Ancient oriental thought revolves almost entirely round the idea of the soul, its origin, its return, and its purgation and purification. The ancient Egyptians believed in life after death and the *Book of the Dead* explains the progress of the soul beyond the grave. The Hebrews believed that man is composed of a body and a soul, that the body returns to dust while the soul returns to God to be rewarded or punished. The Zoroastrians believed that the world is made up good and evil spirits and that they are in a state of continual strife which will end up with the ultimate victory of the good over evil. The wisdom of the Brahmans is based on the salvation of the soul and the renunciation of the body leading to the attainment of ultimate reality (Brahman). If this discarnate state is not achieved, the soul will wander endlessly from body to body.

Islam has come to awaken the souls from their slumber and to purge and purify them of their sins. In the Koran the soul is addressed clearly and is warned against its passions and appetites. 'Oh, thou soul which art at rest, return to thy Lord, pleased and pleasing Him.'[30] 'Yet I hold not my soul clear, for the soul is prone to evil.'[31] There are *Hadiths* which refer to the origin of the souls and their return as well as to the fact that their existence is previous to that of the body. 'The souls are mobilized ranks; those which get acquainted among them become intimate, and whose which are discordant differ.'[32] Indeed, divine services and prescribed duties require bodily exertion as in ritual prayer and fasting, but their fundamental aim is the purgation and purification of the soul which is man's essence. In order to grasp this fully, we have to discuss the Islamic view of the human soul as regards its essence, immortality and felicity. It may also be worth while to point out the extent to which Islam and the Muslims cherish freedom of

[30] *Surah* 89, verses 27–28. [31] *Surah* 12, verse 53.

[32] Ibn Qayyim al Jauziya: *Al Ruh*, pp. 9–62, Haiderabad 1906.

thought and independence of will, both being the pillars on which personality is established.

(i) *The Human Soul:*

Muslims have from the start tackled the question of the soul, although some of the verses of the Koran discourage them from doing so. 'And they will ask thee of the spirit, say: the spirit proceedeth at the Lord's command, but of knowledge only a little to you is given.'[33] Though the authorities of the early period avoided this subject, and Mālik (785), al Shāfi'ī (825) made it sacrosanct,[34] and though the predecessors did not examine it thoroughly, yet the various Islamic sects and schools, whether Sunnite or Shi'ite, thrashed it out. It may be sufficient here to refer to the views of the theologians [Motakallimun], the Sufis and the philosophers.

The controversies of the Arab theologians concerning the nature of the soul were not different from those of the Greek thinkers. Some of them were inclined to extreme materialism and some were inclined to extreme spirituality.[35] Some of the materialists completely denied the existence of the soul or claimed that it is the body or an accident of the body. Foremost among them were the protagonists of the 'atomistic' theory (*Gawhar Fard*) and their precursor was Abu Al Hodhail Al Allaf (848), one of the Mo'tazila-Shaikhs and the first advocate of this theory in Islam. He established that the soul is an accident of the body and that it is in a state of constant flux.[36] Abu Al Hassan Al Ash'ari (935) follows in his footsteps, for he adopted the idea of the 'indivisible part' (atom), though he rejected the Mo'tazila school in general. Al Ash'ari doubts the spirituality of the soul[37] and is followed by his disciple Al Bāqillānī (1013), who was regarded as the first partisan of the 'atom-theory' (*Gawhar Fard*) among the Ash'arites. In his opinion, the soul is an accident and means nothing but life.[38]

On the other hand, the spiritualists believe that the soul is neither body nor its accident; it is a spiritual power that stirs

[33] *Surah* 17, verse 85.
[34] Ibrahim Madkour: *Fi Al Falsafa Al Islamiya*, p. 154, Cairo 1947.
[35] Massignon: *Receuil des Textes inédits Concernant l'histoire de la Mystique en pays d'Islam*, p. 131, Paris 1929.
[36] Al Ash'ari: *Maqalat Al Islamiyin*, Vol. II, p. 337, Leipzig 1929.
[37] Ibn Qayyim Al Jauziya: *Al Ruh*, pp. 81, 178, and 282.
[38] *Op. cit.*

and directs the body. Mo'ammer (835) was one of the partisans of this theory. He asserts that the soul is pure knowledge and pure will.[39] Ibn Hazm Al Andalusī (1064) attacks the atomistic theory violently, and firmly believes that the soul is essentially different from the body. He demonstrates his opinion by reference to the fact that one can purify his mind and rectify his views by shaking himself free of his senses and the dross of the body.[40] Imām Al Haramain (1085) is in his own right the first of the Ash'arites to claim the spirituality of the soul. It is in his own opinion a spiritual substance of divine nature.[41] He is, therefore, the founder of the spiritual school to which his disciples, Al Ghazzālī (1111) and Al Rāzī (1209) adhered. Imām Al Haramain became one of the pillars of the Sunnite doctrine and his teachings are still considered to be valid.[42] The Imām (Muhammad 'Abduh, 1905) emphasizes the fact that the soul is different from the body and it lives after its separation from the body in another world.[43]

A Sufism that denies the existence of the soul has no foundation and is fruitless; for unless it admits the spirituality and immortality of the soul, it would be purposeless.[44] All the Sufis of Islam expressed very clearly the view that the soul is spiritual and different from the body. In their opinion, it is a spiritual substance derived from God. It is one of his created manifestations; an influx of His light with which we are endowed. It is the essence of man, that which makes him different from all other beings. As it is of heavenly origin, it always tends to return to the source from which it emanated. It is only the sins and dross of the body that prevent the soul from attaining its end.[45] The Sufis discussed some psychological phenomena such as love, passion, pleasure, and pain. They discussed these states at length and their studies can be regarded as an important chapter in the history of the psychology of emotions.[46] They resorted to 'introspection' and made use of it long before modern

[39] Al Razī: *Mohassal Afkar Al Motaqaddimin Wa Al Mota'akhirin*, p. 164, Cairo 1905.

[40] Ibn Hazm: *Al Fisal Fi Al Milal Wa Al Ahwa' Wa Al Nihal*, Vol. V, pp. 47–48, Cairo 1928.

[41] Ibn Qayyim Al Jauziya: *Al Ruh*, p. 81.

[42] Ibrahim Madkour: *Fi Al Falsafa Al Islamiya*, p. 157.

[43] Muhammad 'Abduh: *Risalat Al Tawhid*, p. 9, Cairo 1933.

[44] Massignon: *Receuil*, pp. 131–132.

[45] De Boer: *Encyclopaedia of Ethics and Religion*, Ts. 11, p. 746.

[46] Dr Abu Al'ila Afifi: *Al Tasawwof*, pp. 15–26, Cairo 1963.

psychologists started employing it on a large scale. In short, Sufism was a spiritual revolution in Islam, a revolution against worship which is reduced to mere bodily movements devoid of feeling or sentiment, and against dogmas which are based on abstract speculation divorced from experience or taste. Sufism, in fact, is a life of the soul and for the soul.

The Islamic philosophers' preoccupation with the subject of the soul can hardly be paralleled in ancient and medieval history. They investigated its problems, fathomed its depth and wrote extensively about it in poetry and prose. They unanimously agree on the existence of the soul and its difference from the body, though they disagree about its essence. Al Kindī (873) thinks that the soul is a simple substance of noble nature, emanating from God and that, on leaving the body, all truths are revealed to it.[47] Al Fārābī (950) asserts that the rational soul is the highest faculty, for it can apprehend the universal and communicate with the spiritual world.[48] Ibn Sina (Avicenna, 1037) does not equivocate about the existence of the soul and its essence; he tries to substantiate this in various ways. He concludes that there exists an essence not identical with the body and entirely different from it. Following Aristotle, he claims that it is a form and an essence at the same time. In his opinion, it is a spiritual substance, subsistent in itself and can exist when separated from the body, whereas the body cannot exist without it.[49]

The Andalusian philosophers in general held opinions similar to those of their eastern colleagues. Both Ibn Bāja (1138) and Ibn Tofail (1185) speak of the supremacy of the soul over the body and admit that it can communicate with the divine world.[50] But Ibn Roshd (Averroes, 1198) adopts the language and principles of Aristotle and insists that the soul, as the form of the body, cannot be a substance (*Gawhar*) and cannot be separated from its matter either, and adds that form is, at any rate, different from matter.[51]

The thinkers in Islam, therefore, unanimously agree about the existence of the soul, though they disagree about its nature.

[47] *Rasa'il Al Kindi*, p. 271, ed. by Dr Abu Rida, Cairo 1950.

[48] Madkour: *La Place d'Al Farabi dans l'École Philosophique Arabe*, pp. 122–128, Paris 1934.

[49] Madkour: *Fi Al Falsafa Al Islamiya*, pp. 200–202.

[50] *Ibid.*, pp. 55–57.

[51] *Ibid.*, p. 239.

Though some of them are inclined towards materialism, the majority maintains spirituality and holds the view that the soul is a non-material entity entirely different from the body. They describe it as the source of feeling and thinking and even of life and movement. This spiritual concept of the soul is basically similar indeed to that of St Augustine and St Thomas Aquinas among the scholastics and to that of Descartes among the moderns. The existence of the soul is a basic necessity for a future life and a fundamental concept for a moral order. Without it all talk about judgment, punishment, or reward becomes irrelevant. It is also a means to the ultimate happiness, to which sages aspire through contact with the world above. The supreme good and the supreme happiness which we strive to attain lead us to believe in the existence of a spiritual world and a second life beyond the grave.

(ii) *Immortality:*

Immortality is a cherished hope to which we cling so much that we cease to treat it as such and think of it as a reality. To us it is present, a comfort in privation and misfortune, a revenge for death, which spares neither the young nor the old. It is perhaps the love of life that first inspired man with the idea of its renewal. This renewal was conceived in various shapes and forms. Primitive people thought that man would be reborn in the shape of a great giant who would be able to revenge himself on his enemies. Some civilized people thought of it as a kind of reawakening in which man enjoys complete beatitude. For this reason they kept ready in their tombs ornaments and finery together with delicious food and drink. The advent of revealed religions made this hope a goal and an aim, and made religious duties dependent on it. They invested the second life with material, spiritual, sensual and intellectual attributes.

The teachings of Islam establish the idea of immortality very clearly in order to make religious duties and judgment meaningful. 'Every soul shall taste of death, and ye shall only receive the recompenses on the day of resurrection.'[52]

In Islam there is the interrogation by the two angels in the grave and there is resurrection 'when the hour comes', there shall be 'congregation and recall to life', interrogation and judgment,

[52] *Surah* 3, verse 185.

punishment or reward and eventually either paradise or hell-fire.

All these are revelations that form a part of the religious dogma. Muslims everywhere accept these dogmas, though they may differ about their details. Since early times there was disagreement about those who commit grave offences. Should they be considered believers or unbelievers or would they be in a state between the two? This led to another question: Would such offenders be committed to hell-fire for all eternity? Or would they spend a prescribed time there to expiate for their sins before they will be finally transferred to paradise? Are reward for the inhabitants of paradise and punishment for the inhabitants of hell eternal? Some people thought that both heaven and hell were a kind of eternal silence attended either by pleasure or pain.[53] Therefore, there is no equivocation about immortality among the Muslims in general. This belief has been supported by revealed evidence, but some people are not satisfied with it and like to add rational demonstration to it. They have made, in fact, various attempts in this direction, of which the greatest and the most far-reaching is that of Avicenna. In his diverse and profound explanation, he states that the soul, in spite of being an accident, a created thing, does not vanish or die with the body. This is due to the fact that the relation between them is not essential and integral; it is the relation of a superior and a subordinate, for the soul directs the body and arranges its affairs. The soul is undestructible since it is a simple indivisible substance. Avicenna finally declares that the soul belongs to the world of separate intellects and eternal astronomical souls and so whatever emanates from it is also immortal.[54]

This demonstration by Avicenna is similar indeed to Plato's Dialogue, *Phaidon*, in which he tries to prove the immortality of the soul. We do not intend to discuss Avicenna's demonstration or point out its shortcomings here. Al Ghazzali has partly done this in his work, *The Destruction of the Philosophers*.[55] And in spite of this, the demonstration was destined to survive in the East and the West. In the East, theologians and philosophers alike consider it valid still. In the West, it was well

[53] Zohdi Jar Allah: *Al Mo'tazila*, pp. 117–119, Cairo 1947.
[54] Madkour: *Fi Al Falsafa Al Islamiya*, pp. 231–234.
[55] Al Ghazzali: *Tahafot Al Falasifa*, pp. 333–343, Cairo 1903.

received by the Christian schools, and Gundissalinus (1190), who translated Avicenna into Latin, accepted it. Albert the Great (1280) as well as St Thomas Aquinas (1274) believed that the spirituality of the soul would logically lead to immortality. On the whole, we can say that Avicenna is one of the three who occur to the mind when the subject of immortality is mentioned: they are Plato in antiquity, Avicenna in the Middle Ages, and Kant in modern times.

There is no doubt that the idea of immortality enhances the value of man and reaffirms his responsibility. In spite of the fact that revealed evidence is sufficiently clear to convince the believer and fill his heart with certainty, researches in the field of philosophy and theology wanted to add rational demonstration to revelation. They used the nature and function of the soul as a means to demonstrate its immortality. Their task was not easy, for immortality is not susceptible of proof by logical reasoning. But if reason is unable to demonstrate immortality, it is equally unable to deny it. It is a mistake on the part of the materialists to claim that their experiments do not admit the existence of life beyond this one, for the field of human experiment is limited. To pass judgment about things that are beyond the reach of experiment and claim the sanction of science for the judgment is truly absurd.

(iii) *Felicity:*

Felicity is the goal and aim of man; he seeks it assiduously and spares no effort to attain it. Some people find it in wealth and prosperity, others are satisfied with position, reputation and everlasting memory. There are those, however, who think of happiness as a kind of spiritual contemplation or abstract meditation which purges the soul and makes it aspire for perfection. Happiness is, therefore, either material or spiritual, and is achieved either here or hereafter. It is fundamentally based on the satisfaction and contentment of the soul. It differs from one individual to another, and varies according to personal passions and inclinations. The happiness of the individual is closely allied to the happiness of the community; they are interdependent and complementary. Some philosophers did not hesitate to make happiness the ultimate goal of morals and behaviour as well as a touchstone by which to test good and evil. In short, they make happiness the greatest of virtues.

Ancient and modern philosophies discussed happiness and revealed religions explained its notions and designed the ways and means to lead to it. Islam encompasses religion as well as worldly affairs. It does not encourage anything like Christian monasticism or Indian asceticism. It does not deprive the Muslims of worldly pleasures, it rather encourages them to 'take their share of them'. It forbids them from abstaining from the good things of the world which have been allowed by God. It exhorts them to compete in work and production, and to excel in achieving honour and glory, provided they abide by the commandments of God and preserve the welfare of the people. If they follow this course, they are sure to attain happiness in this world and the next. But if they are deceived by the vanities of the world, they will miss real happiness.

Muslims have to strike a middle course and take both worlds into account. 'And neglect not thy part in this world but be bounteous to others as God has been bounteous to thee.'[56] 'Work for your worldly good as if you should live eternally and pray as if you should die tomorrow.' There are people who are attracted by the other world, and so they shun this one and prefer asceticism and mortification. Such people are known as the Sufis. The Sufis of Islam, like the Christian mystics, find happiness in refining their souls through spiritual exercise and self-purification, with the hope of perceiving hidden mysteries and of obtaining revelation and inspiration. Some of them go even a step further and admit incarnation (*holūl*) and hypostatic union (*ittihād*), binding the heavenly and the earthly, the human and the divine. In the Koran we find compassion as well as cordial intercourse for hearts and souls; we find, in short, the seeds of Sufism which soon flourished and became efficacious in the hands of the different Sufis. To them happiness implies nearness to God through constant meditation on Him; their sole object is to lead lives of unending joy and uninterrupted vision.

Islamic philosophers have explained happiness in almost the same way. In their opinion, happiness is achieved when the soul attains a state of purity and perfection enabling it to communicate with the spiritual world, to comprehend the unknown and to unveil the hidden, transcending the sense world to reach

[56] *Surah* 28, verse 77.

the world of vision and everlasting joy.[57] This is described as a state of passionate love and permanent longing; passionate love being nothing but the ecstasy of conceiving oneself in the presence of the Almighty, and longing being the unceasing desire to perfect this joy.[58]

In Islam, therefore, the only happiness is that which takes the future life into account. Beatitude can only be attained through a work, an utterance, or a thought that brings us nearer to God. Happiness in this world is insignificant compared with eternal beautitude. 'As for those who are happy, they are in the Garden therein to abide as long as the heavens and the earth remain.'[59] Real happiness, therefore, is spiritual and intellectual, everlasting and eternal. It is primarily based on just action and aims at the common good.

(iv) *Freedom of Thought:*

Islam called for freedom of thought, and emancipated man's reason from the shackles of the past, patriarchal domination, and the fetters of custom and tradition. It invited man to consider the wonders of the universe and cited examples in this connection to guide and direct him. 'Will they not look forth in the realms of heaven and on earth, and on all things which God hath made?'[60] 'Let man look at his food, and it was we who rained down the copious rains, then cleft the earth with clefts and caused the upgrowth of grain, and grapes and healing herbs, and the olive and the palm and enclosed gardens thick with trees.'[61] We have already pointed out that Muhammad gave wide scope to freedom of thought and opinion. He disliked the time-server who would say 'that people did well, when they did well; and that they did evil, when they did evil.' He encouraged his companions to indicate their opinions concerning certain questions, and asked them to try and solve whatever problems confronted them.

The Muslims proceeded along those lines; they applied their minds to the religious and secular problems that were not referred to in the Holy Book or in the tradition of the Prophet

[57] Al Farabi: *Ara'Ahl al madīna al fādila*, p. 47, Leiden 1895.
[58] Ibn Sina: *Al isharat wa al tanbihat*, p. 197, Leiden 1892.
[59] *Surah* 11, verse 108.
[60] *Surah* 7, verse 185.
[61] *Surah* 51, verses 20–21.

(*Sonna*). Sometimes they explained the text and interpreted it so as to suit their needs. Abu Bakr, for instance, fought those who refused to pay the legal alms, treating them by analogy as renegades. He distributed equally the war-booty also among the emigrants and the defenders (*ansar*). However, when the Caliphate was handed over to Omar, he treated them differently, distributing the booty among them according to the degree of their faith and contribution in the holy war. Muslims never disapproved this difference of opinion and were never opposed to it. This is precisely what we mean by freedom of thought. 'Whoever practises independent judgment [*ijtihād*] and is successful receives a double reward, and who practises it and commits an error receives the reward of his individual judgment [*ijtihād*].' Muslims did not only encourage individual opinion, but also invited the opinion of the community and consulted the leaders and the most prominent men. Abu Bakr and Omar used to summon the elder companions for an exchange of views whenever a dilemma presented itself. If an agreement on the point under discussion was reached, they decided the matter accordingly. In this way, two principles of Islamic legislation were laid down: analogy and consensus. They are based in fact on two kinds of decision: individual and collective.

Independent judgment had its supporters and protagonists in those who introduced legislation and gave formal counsel under its guidance. In so doing, they took into account the common welfare, the rationale of the law as well as the environment and the social circumstances. They deduced reason and causes, and pointed out differences and concordances or, in other words, pros and cons of every case. Furthermore, they studied the ramifications and detected correspondences and equivalences. To stimulate deep thinking and diligent investigation, they even discussed hypothetical cases. Independent judgment resorted to 'approval' and 'utility' or public welfare when they had to consider matters according to common advantage, and the general notion of the legislator. The legist soon acquired through practice and experience a 'juridical taste', which enabled him to pass independent judgment and to make deductions and inferences. Traditional studies have provided for research in the field of independent jurisprudence and laid down certain rules and stipulations.

We can safely say that all the great Islamic schools of jurisprudence accepted more or less individual judgment. Abū Hanīfa (767) prefers it to tradition and oral report, and Mālik (795), though the first compiler of *Hadith*, does not neglect it either. Al Shāfi'i tries to control it, regulate its methods, and define its limits. Ibn Hanbal (855), though he adheres to *Hadith* and the views of the predecessors, resorts to analogy when the need arises. Even Dāwod al Zāhīrī (883), who holds fast to traditional texts, accepts analogy that is supported by cause and reason.

Ages of decadence, however, rely usually on imitation and tradition and do not find their way to research and renewal. The Muslims lost their personality for five centuries (fourteenth-nineteenth) and denied themselves the freedom of thought. They erroneously believed that the way to individual judgment had been blocked. They have, in fact, deluded themselves into such a belief; for the way to individual judgment was open and still is. As soon as the Islamic nations reawakened, they embarked on this practice once more. Jamal al Din al Afghani (1898) and Muhammad 'Abduh (1904) set the example. Egypt in particular took the initiative. It has enacted towards the end of the last century laws dealing with family rights that are in line with the spirit of the age. It is still endeavouring to improve and develop these laws. Other Muslim countries are now trying to benefit by these experiences.

Freedom of thought in Islam was not only applicable to jurisprudence and legislation, it was extended to the doctrine and principles of the faith. The Muslims insisted on conceiving divinity as intellectual, abstract and free of all anthropomorphic elements. They paid particular attention to the question of the unicity of God, and rejected all anthropomorphism and polytheism. The Mo'tazila contributed to a great extent to the formation of these tenets. They are incontestably the founders of the theological science. They denied that God has attributes in addition to his essence, and reinterpreted the verses of the Koran and the passages of the *Hadith* if they seemed to imply anthropomorphism. They appealed to the authority of the human reason and its ability to distinguish between good and evil. Nothing can be good or evil simply because it is allowed or forbidden by the canonical law. It is good or evil because of certain qualities and characteristics inherent in it. If God allows or forbids something, He does so out of wisdom and because He sees its advantage and disadvantage. Human reason is capable of detecting the qualities and characteristics inherent in things and can thus distinguish between good and evil. Belief based on reason is, therefore, as imperative as belief based on revelation. This is similar, indeed, to the language of the eighteenth century partisans of natural religion, i.e., Rousseau and Voltaire.

These are two examples of the freedom of thought practised in Islam: we have cited them to indicate the degree of freedom carried out in two very important fields, viz., the field of dogma and worship, and that of unicity and jurisprudence. All religious teaching, in fact, revolves round these two. We hardly need to point out that the theological schools, and particularly that of the Mo'tazila, enjoyed a freedom unprecedented in the history of theological studies. We have also noticed that the freedom was in no way less than that enjoyed by the great intellectual schools, ancient or modern. A student could very well oppose his teacher, and a teacher could argue freely with his colleagues, all using arguments, demonstrations, logic and reason. The legists also were free in their deductions and analogies; and that is why they were split into schools and each school had its sub-divisions. We notice also the same sort of freedom practised in the philosophical and scientific schools. The Muslim scholars resorted to observation and experimentation and established laboratories where they could carry out experiements on metals and stones. They built observatories to study the courses of the various constellations, and to investigate the movement of stars. The growth of all the Islamic sciences was based on this freedom, whose influence was felt later on in the Latin world.

(v) *Freedom of the Will:*

Islam addresses man directly, not through a master or a tribal chief. He is answerable only for his own action. 'And the heavy laden shall not be laden with another's load.'[62] Islam strengthens man's will and gives him the choice to follow whichever path he selects. 'Let him then who will believe, and let who will, to be an infidel.'[63] Man is judged, rewarded or punished according to this free will. 'What he has gained stands to his credit, and what he has piled up stands against him.'[64] 'And whosoever shall have

[62] *Surah* 17, verse 15; *Surah* 35, verse 18; *Surah* 39, verse 7.
[63] *Surah* 18, verse 29.
[64] *Surah* 2, verse 286.

wrought an atom's weight of gold shall behold it, and whosoever shall have wrought an atom's weight of evil shall behold it.'[65]

To the theologians, the problems of man turn around his actions, and the freedom of his will. It was perhaps the latter that attracted the attention first. They started discussing it towards the end of the first century of the Hijra (seventh century A.D.). They began to wonder whether man is free to do what he likes or is predestined to do what he has to do. They continued to discuss this point for centuries; opinions differed and schools multiplied. It would be sufficient to refer here to the attitude of Mo'tazila and the Ash'arites, the two great Islamic schools of theology.

The Mo'tazila believe that man's will is free and that he acts according to his own choice. He is answerable only for the action he deliberately intends to do and in this way the distinction between the action that he wills and natural actions which are not subject to his will, become possible. Morals as well as punishment and reward are based on free will. Once we lose this freedom, religious obligation and responsibility become meaningless. It would be unjust to hold a man responsible for what he never intended to do. Divine justice requires man to have a will of his own, an independent will. The Mo'tazila scholars thought that free will was not enough, for they attributed 'power' also to man. A responsible person makes a choicc by his free will and carries it out by his power. In this way, his actions are created by him; they become his own work.[66]

Here the Ash'arites differ from the Mo'tazila for they ascribe all action to God. They fear that the attribution of power to man might imply his participation in running the universe, or even impair God's omnipotence.[67] Nevertheless, they admit that man has a free will by which he could make a choice. It is this free will that decides him one way or another. His decision is accompanied or followed by the action which is accomplished through God's will.

Both the Mo'tazilites and the Ash'arites agree, therefore, that man's will is free and independent, though they differ about the means of its realization. This freedom tallies with the spirit

[65] *Surah* 99 verse 88.
[66] Zohdi Jar Allah: *Al Mo'tazila*, pp. 92–112.
[67] Al Ash'ari: *Al Loma fi al radd 'ala ahl al Zaigh wa al bida*, pp. 39–41, Beirut 1955.

of Islam, the message of the Prophet and the enjoined obligations. Ibn Hazm goes a step further when he declares that it corresponds with feeling, expression, and language.[68] In this connection, Muhammad 'Abduh says: 'As a man of good sense and sound reason knows that he exists and needs neither proof nor teacher to indicate this to him, so does he realize that his actions proceed from his free will. By the help of his reason, he weighs the consequences of his actions, then carries them into effect by a certain inherent power. A denial of this process is a denial of one's existence, an offence against a self-evident truth.'[69]

Freedom of thought and freedom of the will helped the Muslims to investigate, analyse, observe, experiment, criticize, discuss and argue. They discussed man, nature and metaphysics, and this led to a scientific movement which was complex and many-sided. They engaged the partisans of other religions and philosophies, both Eastern and Western, in controversies which indicated the considerable freedom they enjoyed and the heights of rational thinking they reached. They rejected untenable hypotheses, criticized traditions that were not well-founded, and eliminated many superstitions. They began to practise criticism early in their history. Companions began to criticize one another, and the following generation criticized them all. The partisans of every school exchanged criticism, and their criticism often dealt with religious opinions and serious political attitudes. Omayyade and Abbaside Caliphs were subjected to criticism, and even the orthodox Caliphs did not escape censure. Abu Bakr as well as 'Omar appreciated every remark made to them. It should be remembered that some criticism is sincere and constructive, while some is biased and detrimental. However, some honest critics were molested and ill-used.

4. CONCLUSION

In the heyday of Islamic culture, man perfected his humanity, for he thought independently and investigated freely. His enquiries extended to religious as well as to worldly affairs. He applied his mind to whatever he tackled; and his freedom of

[68] Ibn Hazm: *Al fisl fi al Milal wa al ahwa'wa al nihal*, pp. 39–41, Cairo 1902.
[69] Muhammad 'Abduh: *Risalatal Tawhid*, p. 59, Cairo 1932.

will was stipulated for his punishment or reward. Without free will, all obligations and responsibilities, both religious and worldly, would be meaningless and insignificant.

The concept of man in Islam is ideal indeed; it is based on a message and aims at a definite goal. Man is not created in vain, and is not left to the whims of his passions and lusts. His rights are prescribed, his duties enjoined, and his relations with others regulated. He is given a wide scope for thinking and working, provided they are not to the detriment of his fellow-men. There are certain values which he must sanctify and maintain; otherwise, chaos, injustice, and violence would reign.

In this concept of man, we find also a clear spiritual aspect which depends on something nobler than the body. It appeals to the reason and to the heart and penetrates one's internal world. If this internal world is put on a sound footing, the outward self is rectified. True happiness can be found in the serenity and purity of the soul: then can each soul sympathize with other souls in their grief and misfortune, or enjoy brotherhood and true affection, experiencing in all this a deep sense of compassion and commiseration. The spiritual world throws open before us the gates of hope, mitigates our present suffering, and establishes our contact with the world of light and mercy.

Through spiritual endeavour man can cleanse his soul and ascend to higher states of being; in short, he can become a 'perfect man'. The concept of the 'perfect man' is basic to all the Sufi thinking in Islam and is definitely much more evident in Islam than in Judaism or Manichaeism. Briefly stated, it implies that man, the microcosm, mirrors the perfection of the macrocosm and deserves, therefore, to be the representative of God on earth. At its best, the human race embodies physical, intellectual, and spiritual perfection. Prophet Muhammad is considered by Muslims the most perfect human being, and every Muslim can emulate him, draw nearer to his person, and approximate to his perfection.

The conception of the 'perfect man' is an ideal worth striving for, an objective that should be aspired to. It is a call for ascension to a luminous and angelic world.

CHAPTER VIII

The Concept of Man in Marxist Thought

MARK MITIN

I. INTRODUCTION

MAN is an old and eternally philosophical problem. From times of old, man, his essence, his existence, aims and actions, his past and future have been a subject of philosophical research. In cognizing the world about him, man has meditated upon his place in this world. When changing the surrounding reality, he has pondered his role in the world, his strength and possibilities. 'Know thyself'—this principle became a categorical imperative of philosophy at the dawn of civilization.

Karl Marx noted that only man succeeded in leaving his impress on nature; he transferred various species of plants and animals from one place to another, radically changed the external appearance and climate of his dwelling place, even changed the plants and animals to such an extent that 'the consequences of his activity can disappear only with the general extinction of the terrestrial globe.'[1]

In our epoch, which is so replete with dynamic events that affect science, politics, philosophy, sociology, and moral values, in the epoch that has no equal in the preceding history of mankind for the strength of social antagonisms, for the tempestuous pace of life, for the unprecedented scientific discoveries and the great profound dangers that threaten all the achievements of culture and civilization, in the epoch when outer space is actively investigated and man has gone beyond the limits of the Earth, when his genius and reason have so deeply penetrated the secrets of matter, a correct solution of the problem of the philosophical, sociological analysis of man, his essence and existence acquires especially great significance. These problems,

[1] Karl Marx and F. Engels: *Collected Works*, Vol. 20, p. 357.

taken all together, without any exaggeration, concern the fundamental questions of life, culture and progress of mankind.

Evolution of Man and Nature's Metabolic Processes:

Despite the great diversity of trends in pre-Marxist and modern western sociology, despite the differences between them, they suffer from one common failing—their inability to provide a correct solution of these most important, vital problems.

A fundamental defect of bourgeois sociological concepts is their idealism. This defect makes itself felt when solving one of the basic problems of sociology, the problem of the interrelations of man and nature, existence and consciousness. The idealists regard the spirit, thinking, consciousness as a creative, active, mobile basis, and try to stress the primacy of consciousness over matter, the 'purification' from which is seemingly capable of providing scope for the independence of the spirit and bringing man real freedom. Nature is thus reduced to a certain force hostile to the spirit, to a sort of ballast that retards the flight of human thought.

Idealism does not always appear in a frank form. Some modern western thinkers, for instance, intensively stress the role of nature in the life of man; but they interpret the very concept of nature idealistically, objectively, preaching, on the one hand, the impotence of man over nature, his subordination to the blind, elemental forces of nature, and, on the other, proclaiming the contemplative activity of man's soul as his highest designation. Naturally, such an interpretation can offer nothing for an understanding of the mutual relations of man and nature.

Certain theories which, while stressing man's tie with nature, regard him, however, as a purely biological creature, have become widespread in modern western sociology, and all phenomena are evaluated through the prism of biological laws.

We can, therefore, affirm with all responsibility (and this affirmation will be proven by the entire trend of this exposition) that only Marxism is the doctrine that correctly explains the essence of man, and that, scientifically, deals thoroughly with the problem of the interrelations of man and nature.

The essence of man, as well as the relation man and nature, can be understood only on the basis of a materialistic solution of the basic issues of philosophy. Marxism interprets nature as meaning the universe, which is matter in all its diversity of manifestations. It is the objective reality that exists outside and independent of consciousness and that has existed before consciousness appeared in any form whatsoever.

Man is a product of nature, its highest manifestation and creation, the highest stage of living organisms on the Earth. Man appeared on the earth not because of some need of matter to be aware of itself, but in virtue of the self-development of nature, in virtue of the natural laws of evolution. In this sense we can say that in man and through man nature seems to arrive at its own self-knowledge. Man, in subduing nature, is adopting it to his goals; in subordinating it to his conscious activity on the basis of the knowledge of the laws of nature's development, he remains at the same time a profoundly natural creature, a part of nature itself. In the course of the development of society, man separates from nature more and more, becomes ever more independent of natural conditions, and at the same time attains ever closer ties and harmony with nature, 'harmonizes' it, improves the conditions of his life.

Man lives in a definite natural environment, and uses the products of nature in his life. He actively influences it, changes and transforms it. Man derives the means of his existence from nature and only from it. Therein lies the most profound meaning of the mutual relations of man and nature. These mutual relations are of the nature of metabolism between man and nature. Man's labour is, as a matter of fact, the process of metabolism between nature and man. In the process of this change, man appropriates to himself the matter of nature and uses it for his own aims and interests to support and reproduce himself, his life and its conditions.

Thus production becomes a connecting link between man and nature, the basic motive force of human progress. Marx wrote: '*Industry* is the *real* historical attitude of nature, and, subsequently, of natural science, towards man.'[2] Marxism sees the real essence of man in social labour, in a productive tie with nature, in social relations with others similar to him, and in the cognition of objective reality. And the deeper man penetrates the secrets of nature, the more successfully will he be able to regulate its processes according to a plan that has been thought

[2] K. Marx and F. Engels: *From Early Works*, p. 595, Moscow, 1956.

out in advance and, as Engels wrote, 'the more will men once more not only feel, but also know themselves to be with nature, and thus the more impossible will become the senseless and anti-natural idea of a contradiction between mind and matter, man and nature, soul and body, such as arose in Europe after the decline of the classic antiquity and which obtained its highest elaboration in Christianity.'[3]

Man, like animals and plants, uses the substances of nature. But there is a fundamental difference here: animals use only those products of nature that exist in ready form; man, however, when using the substances of nature, remakes them and adapts them to his aims and needs.

Work as the Differentia of Man from Animals:

Man distinguished himself from the world of animals and became a human being only through work. In this sense we can say that 'work created man himself'. It is only thanks to his labour, thanks to the working processes that man gradually became transformed into a human being in the real sense of the word. Labour developed his body, enriched his mind, and perfected his intellect. It is only thanks to his labour that man's hand, as though through magic, attained that perfection which brought to life the paintings of Raphael and Leonardo da Vinci, Rembrandt and Repin, the sculptures of Phidias and Michelangelo, the music of Paganini and Tchaikovsky.

Production is a permanent condition for the existence of man, an eternal, natural need. Without production, metabolism between man and nature would be impossible and so would be human life too.

Man as Part of Nature's History:

However, the interpretation of this metabolism as a one-sided process is a profoundly incorrect one. Some western philosophers and sociologists frequently depict this interaction by analogy with the relations of exploitation that exist in capitalist countries. By considering all the phenomena of nature from only the viewpoint of man's needs, interpreted in a limited way, and the history of man as the simple alternation of the needs that arise and those that are satisfied, they evaluate the changes

[3] F. Engels: *Dialectics of Nature*, p. 141, State Political Literature Publishing House, 1955.

produced by man as the constant exhausting of the sources of nature and even as a regress in its development.

Such views on the relation of man to nature as depict him as only an 'exploiter' of nature, lose sight of an important factor, namely, that the history of man 'is an *actual* part of the *history of nature*, of the formation of nature by man'.[4] This thesis refers to both man himself and his social organization, and also to the rest of nature; for man's productive activity imparts new motion to it. The creation of qualitatively new forms of bodies, new processes,—new not only for man, but also for nature—is evidence of the progress not only of man, but also of nature.

The character and degree of man's influence on nature are different in the different historical epochs, for in different epochs people are organized differently in the struggle against nature and their socio-economic relations are not the same. These relations, their forms and character are determined not by the strivings and wishes of people, but by the objective conditions and circumstances of their life, depending on the level of development of the productive forces in the given epoch and on the dominating method of production. The different socio-economic structures that have existed in the history of human society are characterized by not what was produced in the given historical epoch, but by the manner in which it was produced, by the means of production used and by the implements of labour.

There have been many technical revolutions in the history of human society, revolutions that were turning points, significant landmarks in the process of affirming the domination of man over nature. The transformation from the stone axe to implements of labour made of bronze was a technical revolution, one which afforded new opportunities for mankind's advance and for the development of his culture. The transition to agriculture, the invention of the steam engine, the discovery of electricity and the possibilities of its industrial use must also be regarded as great technical revolutions.

A tremendous technical revolution connected with the discovery of the possibility of using atomic energy is now taking place. It is a striking index of the mighty strength of the human mind and marks the beginning of a new age in the subjugation of the forces of nature by mankind.

[4] K. Marx and F. Engels: *From Early Works*, p. 596.

The process of subordinating nature to man has been going on for many centuries. On the other hand, in virtue of the historically established social relations of people in exploiting societies (the slave-holding system, feudalism, capitalism) man became dependent on the elemental forces of social development. Man, who became an ever stronger and all-powerful ruler of nature, as a result of the social conditions of his existence, proved to be the slave of blind necessity, the elements dominating in society. Those who, by their labour, created all material values did not enjoy equal rights and were subjected to exploitation. This fact reflects *the tragedy of men of labour, the greatest of all known in the history of mankind.*

Falsity of the Malthusian Doctrine:

The theories which assert that nature possesses limited resources, that it is not able to provide for the increasing rise in population, are refuted by indisputable facts. It is a known fact, for instance, that only seven per cent of the land surface of our planet is now occupied by useful vegetable trees, garden plants, and forests. The area of the used soil, together with forest plantations and gardens, is less than 2,500 million acres.

According to the calculations made by the Soviet scientist L. I. Prasalov (on the basis of a world soil map and a map of the world's agriculture), the area of all the land (including the Arctic and the Antarctic regions) is about 149 million square kilometers. Of this area, the best fertile soils of the plains amount to 12·5 per cent, the transitional belts of the soils of the plains to 36·4 per cent, mountain pastures and forests to 11·8 per cent, deserts and tundra where agricultural activity is possible to 8 per cent. Thus 70 per cent of the land surface, or 25,000 million acres, if feasible measures to improve the fertility of the soil are taken (such as irrigation of deserts, moving agricultural crops to the north, reclamation of swamps, etc.) can be used for agricultural purposes. We can easily imagine what a tremendous quantity of products for the inhabitants of the earth could be obtained from these additional 25,000 million acres of cultivated areas.

It has also been shown that even the present level of development of agricultire us sufficient to feed several times as many people as now inhabit our planet.

John Bernal was right when he noted that Malthusianism is an admission of one's own impotence; and an unlimited number of people could live an interesting life on earth. The English economist, Colin Clark, had calculated that, if the increase in the world population amounted to about 1 per cent per year, agricultural production per head of population could increase annually by 1·5 to 2 per cent just due to the use of agrotechny.

Further, an inexhaustible source for increasing the nourishing materials for man is the sea, one that is used most inadequately at present. The food resources contained in the seas and oceans are exceptionally great. Competent ichthyologists consider it fully possible to increase the catch of fish many times and to organize the artificial breeding of fish and crustacea in the seas and oceans on a tremendous scale. The water has valuable algae that are fit for feed, and it is possible to grow plants in water, which contain a large amount of mineral salts and vitamins. A new branch of science and practical work, the so-called marine agriculture, is already coming into being, one which has boundless prospects.

Man makes very little use of the tremendous supplies of mineral products. As to power resources, the discovery of atomic energy makes them practically inexhaustible.

Man and Nature in Capitalism and Socialism:

How can we explain the fact that the colossal forces of nature, those that have already been subjugated by man, are not used or are used to an absolutely insignificant degree to improve the well-being of people and constantly to better their life? How can we explain the fact that the huge, unlimited opportunities for increasing material benefits are not used in many countries of the world, and that the great achievements of science cannot be applied to practical activity and give us their results? The reason for this is to be sought in the archaic, unorganized nature of the social structure of capitalism.

History has clearly shown that wars are a constant companion of capitalism. In the past one hundred years there has not been a single decade without bloody conflicts, skirmishes, or wars.

During the First World War there were about 70 million people in the armies of the belligerent powers, and during the Second World War over 100 million people. During the First

World War 10 million people perished in the battlefields and over 20 million were crippled. According to incomplete data, over 22 million people were killed and more than 34 million were wounded and crippled during the Second World War. These figures do not include the losses in China and the people murdered in the fascist concentration camps.

As for the amount of material values spent on waging these two world wars and the destruction that took place during them—these cannot be calculated.

Economists have calculated that, if the money spent on the First World War had been used to improve the well-being of the people, it would have been sufficient to enable each of the 74 million mobilized soldiers to buy themselves a good home with a large plot of land. And the direct expenditures on the Second World War would constitute such a sum as would be sufficient to give all the children of the world a secondary school education, to build five-room houses for all families of our planet, and to equip a beautiful hospital for every 5000 people on Earth. It is easy to conceive what a gigantic rise in productive forces could have been attained if the millions of people who took part or perished in the wars had been employed in productive work, if the countless material resources spent on waging the wars had been used to subdue nature and to increase the production of articles to suffice people's need. New cities and health resorts would have sprung up, automobile highways would have been built; and there would be no more deserts on the earth, for they would have been transformed into blossoming gardens.

A scientific-technical revolution is now taking place, the greatest of all that ever occurred in history. It truly affords people boundless opportunities for conquering nature, for creating an abundance of material wealth which will satisfy all the needs of people to the maximum degree possible. This revolution is connected with the use of atomic energy, with the gigantic increase in velocities. Whereas some fifty to hundred years ago, it took months and even years to get to some distant parts of our world, to-day jet-propelled planes cover the distance in an little over ten hours. The exchange of cultural achievements also can now take place more effectively.

Some western sociologists assume that 'industrialization for the sake of industrialization' is a universal law of socialism. However, it is an erroneous idea about socialism.

Under socialism all social production is effected for the sake of man and in the interest of the whole society. It is exactly under socialism that production is effected not for the sake of production, but for the sake of man. The banner of socialist society bears the words: The highest goal is the welfare of the people. The truly humanist content of socialist social relations is most forcefully manifested in these words.

Those who think that public ownership of the means of production does not afford scope for the development of the creative activity of personality and for its initiative, are grossly mistaken. It is only in the collective and through the medium of the collective that personality attains real freedom. In a society where private ownership of the means of production dominates, there is scope for the activity of only the person that possesses the capital. In virtue of this, such a person is set off against society. In a society where social ownership of the means of production dominates, the interests of the collective are harmoniously combined with those of the individuals, and the conditions are created for the complete emancipation of personality, for the manifestation of the talents and abilities of millions of people.

Whereas in a society where private ownership of the means of production dominates, the technical revolution now getting under way acquires a one-sided character and is used almost exclusively for military purposes; under socialism it is directed towards the all-round improvement of the life of the people. It is now admitted that the Soviet Union is in the lead as regards the use of atomic energy for peaceful purposes. Soviet scientists were the first to send the sputniks of the Earth and the Sun into outer space, thereby opening new horizons for the development of science and for man's penetration of the as yet unexplored secrets of nature.

To-day there are all grounds for declaring: Man is interested in creating the most rational social structure for society, a society that best satisfies the aspirations of all mankind as well as the interests of each individual person, so that man may more successfully use nature's potentialities. In other words, the key to the maximum mastery of the riches of nature for the sake of a great humane goal—the welfare of man—is socialism, the social and political system that best meets his aim.

There is no need in this article to give a detailed description of society in which man and nature would attain ideal harmony. We need only point out some of the important principles of such a society.

Harmony between Man and Nature in Socialist Society:
Genuine harmony between man and nature presupposes the equality of conditions for all people in using the boons of nature and in the right to participate in the collective endeavour of all people to influence nature. This means that there should be no privileged social groups in society. It is understandable that, if individual people or social groups have the opportunity to appropriate the fruits of the labour of other people, it is only unjust; but it inevitably gives rise in them the desire to consolidate their privileges by political means. Under such conditions, it is of course difficult to speak of harmony between personality and society. The latter must be so organized that every individual gets the opportunity to take part in labour, to work in his speciality, revealing his abilities and talents. If all people take part in creative work, the life of each will be better, richer, and more joyful.

Science and technics give mankind great discoveries by means of which it would even now be possible, if social relations were wisely organized, to destroy such social calamities as wars, unemployment, poverty, hunger, disease, fear and uncertainty as to the morrow etc. The countries that are advancing along the socialist path of development have already successfully overcome such social vices as the contrast between poverty and riches, unemployment, uncertainty as to the morrow, national hostility etc. And they have rid themselves of the domination of militarism and so forth.

Mankind is faced with the task of advancing along the path of progress as quickly as possible. The creation of a truly harmonious society, such as the communist is, will affirm the domination of man over nature to a tremendous degree, and will most fully contribute to the use of all the boons of nature, everything that is valuable and necessary for the happiness and flourishing of people.

Socialism was built for the first time in the history of the world in the Soviet Union, and the Soviet Union has now entered the period of the comprehensive building up of a communist society. All the countries of the socialist camp are developing successfully along the socialist path; and together with the Soviet Union they will arrive at communism more or less simultaneously.

Such, in their most general aspects, are the basic principles of the communist concept of man. Further on we shall attempt to expound these problems in greater detail and to reveal the philosophical and sociological foundations for this concept.

2. THE CONCEPT OF MAN IN THE HISTORY OF PHILOSOPHY

From the Ancient Philosophers to Hegel:

Philosophical thought in all its aspects, in the gnosiological, ontological, ethical, anthropological and social, has, throughout its history, been engaged in studying man. The history of human thought in this sphere is, in a certain sense, the history of the discovery of man's problems and of a number of gains along the path to their solution.

Certain ancient Indian and Chinese philosophers who lived thousands of years before our era, when pondering the essence of man, subjected to doubt the naïve religious conceptions of man and began to preach that man originated from material substances such as water, air, fire etc. The problem of the body and soul and ethical questions to which the entire study of the problem of man was, in the main, devoted, occupied a considerable place in these doctrines.

The philosophical study of man occupied an even greater place in ancient Greek philosophy. Heraclitus raised the question of man's relation to the Logos, the universal law. Democritus attempted to substantiate an optimistic world outlook for man. Socrates, Plato, and Aristotle advanced the problem of consciousness and self-consciousness as the most important. Socrates contrasted self-knowledge and the cognition of nature. For him wisdom lay in the knowledge of man, in the cognition of truth and of what is moral. Characteristic of Socratic ethics is the affirmation of the identity of knowledge and virtue, and the reduction of various virtues (wisdom, courage, temperance, justice—these four basic virtues of Greek consciousness) to the basic virtue—wisdom. This reflected the general rationalistic character of the Greek thinkers, who valued reason in man more than anything else. According to Socrates, the greatest virtue becomes accessible to the sage, the philosopher. Apparently this is what prompted Plato to draw the conclusion that philosophers should be the rulers. Plato developed to the utmost the aristocratic tendency of Socrates' teaching, formulating the thesis that real knowledge (which means real virtue as well) cannot be attained in our earthly life, but must be brought to our earth by a soul of the kingdom of ideas. According to Plato, different people possess different souls, base or lofty, wise or such as are devoid of wisdom. Thus, back in the days of antiquity there were already attempts to give an anthropological substantiation for social inequality and elitism. Plato was also deeply interested in studying human society. He wanted to correct the untruths of the world and to avoid disasters. But it seemed beyond his ability to make a radical correction through the spiritual regeneration of human nature; he busied himself, therefore, with the problem of the transformation of social relations. He dedicated his doctrine of the state to this task. It was in the spirit of his elitism that Plato considered the 'ideal state', which was headed by the aristocratic nobility, as the highest embodiment of virtue and justice.

Aristotelian philosophy paid much attention to the study of man. Aristotle, who was the most outstanding mind in ancient Greek society, considered problems of ethics in connection with the social life of the people. This was a considerable step forward in the development of the philosophical study of man. Aristotle regarded ethics as the doctrine about the morals of man as a social creature, as a 'political animal'. He showed that it was only the social world that distinguished and raised man above the animal. This conclusion was, without doubt, a great achievement in philosophical thought.

Medieval thinkers, as a rule, ignored the human aspect of man, his living, sensuous, transient nature. They spoke of the immortal soul and its divine essence; but this one-sided posing of the question did not include love for man. In contrast to this, the philosophers of the Renaissance period revived the humanistic side in the understanding of man.

In modern times one of the first philosophers to study man was Francis Bacon, the founder of the empirical method in science. In contrast to the medieval scholastics, Bacon considered man a material, bodily creature. He created his doctrine about the material, 'feeling soul' of man, which was a sort of materialistic antipode of the 'eternal', immortal soul of man, which religion spoke about.

Descartes' *cogito* was a great achievement in the philosophical teaching about man. As G. Vico rightly noted, this thesis advanced the mind of man, the consciousness of an individual, transient, limited, yet thinking creature as the only criterion of truth. This was an important principle, even though its Cartesian interpretation and exposition in our time have become, of course, an anachronism.

The philosophy of Immanuel Kant, who created a special ethical system, devotes much attention to the problem of man. Kant's ethics was based on abstract, artificial principles, such as the categorical imperative, a universal moral law, freedom of the human soul, the immortality of the soul, the existence of a god etc. Kantian ethics was of an abstract, above-historical nature, and resembled ethics that was in opposition to man, torn away from living life. Kant's dry, rigourist morals grew out of the conditions of Germany's development of those days.

Marx and Engels revealed the essence of Kantian ethics when they pointed out that 'Kant contented himself with but "good will", even if it remained absolutely futile, and he transferred the *realization* of this good will and the harmony between it and the needs and interests of individuals, to *the world beyond*.'[5]

Yet we should not ignore the positive factors that are to be found in Kant's doctrine of man. Kant said that two great things amazed man's mind: the starry sky above us and the moral law within us. In our day of great cosmic achievements and magnificent social accomplishments, this striking idea of Kant's acquires even more profound meaning. Kant's categorical imperative, despite its formalism and anti-historical character, contained a remarkable idea: man must be a goal for man, and not a means. The significance of this idea and of the rational factors contained in it is especially obvious in our day when absolute moral relativism has unfortunately come to occupy a dominating position in many countries and in many philosophical doctrines.

We must especially note what Kant said about war and peace. In his work *Zum ewigen Frieden* (For Eternal Peace), he expressed a critical attitude towards the military adventures of

[5] K. Marx and F. Engels: *Works*, Vol. 8, p. 182.

the Prussian rulers of those days, and advanced the idea of the need to establish peace among peoples. Pointing out that war can lead to peace 'only in a gaigntic cemetery of mankind', Kant pleaded for the attainment of universal peace by means of agreement and set forth the conditions which, in his opinion, should be included in this agreement. He expressed the idea that 'permanent armies should completely vanish with time'.[6]

In Hegel's doctrine, man is regarded as a subjective spirit, and the anthropological side of human existence is considered its first, natural distinction. Further on, man is regarded as a phenomenological and psychological essence. In the final analysis, the subjective spirit develops into an objective one and finally into an Absolute spirit. A decisive condition for this is, first, labour, thanks to which man develops as self-consciousness, and secondly, the inspiration of human activity through the state, religion, art, philosophy, in a word—thanks to social relations and forms of social consciousness.

As Engels pointed out, Hegel's contribution to the study of man and society lay in the fact that 'for the first time, the whole world, natural, historical, intellectual, is represented as a process, i.e., as in constant motion, change, transformation, development; and the attempt is made to trace out the internal connection that makes a continuous whole of all this movement and development. From this point of view, the history of mankind no longer appeared as a wild whirl of senseless deeds of violence, all equally condemnable at the judgment of mature philosophical reason and best forgotten as quickly as possible, but as the process of the evolution of man himself. It was now the task of intellect to follow the gradual march of this process through all its devious ways, and to trace out the inner law running through all its apparently accidental phenomena.'[7]

This presentation of the problem, as the further development of philosophy showed, included very rich possibilities. However, Hegelian idealism, the reducing of human personality to a spirit that is devoid of individuality, the principle of the identification of being and thinking—all of this made it impossible for Hegel to provide a scientific-philosophical solution of the problem of man.

[6] I. Kant: *Zum ewigen Frieden*, p. 33, Leipzig, 1954.

[7] K. Marx and F. Engels: *Selected Works in Two Volumes*, Vol. II, p. 123.

Feuerbach and the Anthropological Viewpoint:

Feuerbach attempted to overcome the basic defect in Hegel's philosophical system. He declared that idealism is speculative theology, and that anthropology constitutes the secret of the latter. Feuerbach interpreted philosophical anthropologism as the summary of the entire previous development of philosophical thought.

Feuerbach was thus the father of the comprehensive system of anthropological philosophy. He regarded man as the starting point and the chief basis of philosophy. He made an appeal to 'contemplate nature, contemplate man: Here, before your very eyes, you have the mystery of philosophy!'[8]

Feuerbach's anthropological philosophy regarded the essence of man as something indivisible, in contrast to idealism, which either identified the essence of man with thought or divided it into a spiritual and physical part which were seemingly in conflict with each other. Feuerbach incessantly stressed the oneness and integrity of the nature of man. He considered that man is a corporeal, physical creature and that he has the ability to contemplate the surrounding world and to think.

The anthropological principle of Feuerbach's philosophy did away with the gap between the spiritual and physical sides of man.

Feuerbach taught that the real basis for the oneness of man is his body, which he regarded as part of the objective, real world. He considered man, as nature, a real and most important object of philosophy. 'The new philosophy', he wrote, 'transforms *man, including nature as the basis of man, into the only, universal and highest object* of philosophy, and, consequently, transforms *anthropology, including physiology, into a* universal science.'[9]

Feuerbach criticized religion, especially Christianity, from the position of his anthropological philosophy. His book, *The Essence of Christianity*, is universally known. Engels said, when writing about it, that it produced a truly 'liberating effect' on the minds of the progressive representatives of the German intellectuals of that epoch.

Feuerbach's ethics was based on his anthropology. He con-

[8] L. Feuerbach: *Selected Philosophical Works*, Vol. I, p. 129, Moscow, 1955.
[9] *Ibid.*, p. 202.

trasted to the sanctimonious and ascetic religious morals his ethical doctrine which stated that the striving for personal happiness for the satisfaction of one's needs underlay all of man's deeds and that man strives for good and avoids evil. Such morals are, Feuerbach admitted, egoistic, but they are 'healthy, simple, straightforward, and honest morals, human morals that penetrate the flesh and blood, and not fantastic, hypocritical morals that are only seemingly sacred.'[10] Proceeding from his anthropological principle, Feuerbach considered that morals are based on love of man for man. He pointed out, therefore, that truly human morals '... do not know any personal happiness without the happiness of the other person, they do not know and do not want any isolated happiness that is separate from and independent of the happiness of other people...they know only comradely, common happiness.'[11]

But despite Feuerbach's love for man, his ethics was of an abstract nature inasmuch as its starting point was 'man' in general, with his invariable 'nature', and not the concrete, historical, social man who belongs to a definite social class, as is really the case in life. Karl Marx and Friedrich Engels revealed this chief defect in Feuerbach's anthropologism and ethics. When evaluating Feuerbach's ethics, Engels pointed out that 'it is designed to suit all periods, all peoples and all conditions, and precisely for that reason it is never and nowhere applicable.'[12]

Feuerbach's man, Engels notes, remains always the same abstract man who occupied the field in the philosophy of religion. For this man is not born of woman; he issues, as from a chrysalis, from the god of monotheistic religions.'[13]

Thus philosophic thought gradually revealed the basic problems of man, one after another. However, neither idealistic anthropology nor pre-Marxistic materialism was able to create an integral, logical, and truly scientific doctrine about man. The further development of nineteenth-century bourgeois anthropologism proceeded along a descending line, arriving at the antihumanism of present-day bourgeois philosophical trends, which aggravated its weakest sides and gave rise to new ones.

[10] L. Feuerbach: *Selected Philosophical Works*, Vol. I, p. 624.
[11] *Ibid.*, p. 621.
[12] K. Marx and F. Engels: *Selected Works*, Vol. II, p. 365.
[13] K. Marx and F. Engels: *Works*, Vol XXI, p. 295.

3. PESSIMISTIC CONCEPTION OF MAN

From Schopenhauer to Existentialism:

Schopenhauer's doctrine about man was, in our opinion, profoundly pessimistic and irrational in character. He regarded society as a basically invariable crowd of individuals and scornfully called it a human herd. The human herd was the basis over which towered the 'genius' that lived at the expense of the herd, just as the head lives at the expense of the body.

Schopenhauer considered man as an 'evil animal', who possessed savage passions that were never satisfied and an insatiable thirst for existence for the sake of existence. In his opinion, man differed from other animals only in his greater malice and envy. According to Schopenhauer, the life of man is an existence full of suffering, torment and grief, and man himself was only an actor in the tragi-comedy that is called life.

Inasmuch as the world is ruled by the blind, rash, irrational will, man is unable to change anything. He must meekly drag out his existence that is full of suffering and grief, and must not think, must not strive for a better future, must bury himself in pure self-contemplation and not think of satisfying his urgent needs. Thus Schopenhauer's views of man and society were profoundly misanthropic. His philosophy is the philosophy of anti-humanism.

The philosophical doctrine of Friedrich Nietzsche, the spiritual forerunner of fascism, contained even greater hatred and contempt for man. Nietzsche proclaimed as the only motive force of nature, of society and human activity, 'the insatiable yearning for the manifestation of power or the application of power, the use of power as a creative instinct'.[14] Regarding the aspiration for power as 'cosmic conformity with law', as the basic law of any life, including the social, Nietzsche justified exploitation and oppression as phenomena ensuing from the very essence of life. And he built his ethics on this basis—the 'morality of the masters', which is permeated with racism and chauvinism. Nietzsche's 'ideal' is a barbarian of the Aryan origin, a representative of the class and race of the 'chosen', who should traverse the earth as devastators, inspiring terror in all peoples, especially in those who oppose and resist their will to power. These morals of the 'race of masters' were an

[14] F. Nietzsche: *Complete Works*, Vol. IX, p. 298, Moscow, 1910.

attempt at a 'theoretical substantiation' of the wars for world domination conducted by the German monopolistic capital.

Equally reactionary and anti-humanistic were the writings of Oswald Spengler in the 1920's. 'Man is a beast of prey. I shall say it again and again',[15] he prophesied.

Of the modern western philosophical trends, *the philosophy of existentialism studies the problem of personality of man* more than anything else.

'My philosophy begins where the problem of human existence begins, and it ends where this problem ends', Jaspers declared in his work, *Philosophy*. This is, without doubt, the statement of an adherent of the anthropological principle, for he admits that the problem of man is the basic problem of philosophy.

Thus, in existentialism, the principle that characterizes the general features of the anthropological approach to man is sustained more consistently, perhaps, than in any other philosophical trend. At the same time, existentialism is a striking index of the crisis, the impasse into which anthropologism falls generally.

Existentialism is, in essence, a criticism of the 'socialness' of human existence, as it is understood by modern western sociology. As conceived by modern western sociologists, the 'socialness' of the individual is the conformity of his behaviour to the values dominating in society. Man is considered to be a simple *aggregate* of roles (i.e., normatively, functions of the individual as established in society's opinion). Man is social to the extent that, in his activity, he satisfies the patterns that already exist in the official consciousness, the models of 'a family man', 'a fine chap', 'a conscientious worker' etc. It is through the performance of these roles, literally like an actor in a play, that the individual comes into 'social' contact with other people. By himself, he is only a point of intersection of many roles, many characters that he performs, well or ill.

The existentialists struggle against this 'sociological' definition of man with the same methods with which Feuerbach and Stirner in their day fought against the theological version of the 'social' nature of man. Man, they showed, is not an aggregate of 'roles' that he performs; he is something integral in himself. Man can sense this integrity in any act of self-consciousness,

[15] Oswald Spengler: 'The Return of the Caesars', *American Mercury*, Vol. 31, p. 137.

distinguishing himself in the capacity of simply 'being' from what he appears to be to himself and to another in the capacity of a 'social being'—from his role. Indeed, in reflection we can distinguish ourselves from ourselves as much as we desire. Even a glass, if it possessed self-consciousness, would be able to distinguish itself from a glass as a vessel for drinking inasmuch as this is only one of its possible definitions. But how, in actual fact, does a glass differ from a vessel for drinking, if it is used as a vessel for drinking?

Existentialism cannot supply a clear-cut reply to this question. According to all the rules of anthropologism, the reference to man 'as he is' in distinction from the way he appears in society should have signified the natural distinctness of man. But existentialism denies the natural distinctness of man. Perhaps it breaks away from anthropologism in general and goes over—in counterbalance to the concept of 'normative order'—to a consideration of man's existence in society as his material relation in production? By no means. That elementary fact that the material relations objectively distinguish man from his 'roles' in which he appears to the consciousness of bourgeois society merely as a social creature, the fact that man, who but yesterday was aware of himself in a social plane and who himself became aware of himself as a 'good member of the trade union', a 'punctual tax-payer', a 'member of a philanthropic society' etc., and who to-day, as a result of the economic depression, which upsets all models and all roles, all formations of a 'normative order', explains to himself his real existence as a wage worker—this fact always remains beyond the field of vision of the existentialists.

In distinction from the earlier forms of anthropologism which connected man's natural self-consciousness with the sense of the fullness of life (Feuerbach, Wagner, Nietzsche), existentialism, especially its German version, does not regard the human personality from the aspect of its all-round development, perfection, creative possibilities and its other positive sides and states; on the contrary, it concerns itself with the darkest, most negative sides and states of human personality and sees the true revelation of the natural existence of man in the intrusion of disease and death.

The theme of disease occupies an exceptional place in Jasper's philosophy. The healthy man is absolutely a 'social' man, one who is occupied, who has no leisure in order to come to know himself as he is, 'blind in relation to his own real self', and who wholly devotes himself to performing his 'roles'. According to Jaspers, the value of disease lies in the fact that it takes a person out of his usual, conformist ideas about life, transforms him into an asocial being (i.e., into an anthropological individual), and for the first time enables him to 'come to', to 'collect himself' and to see himself 'as he is' (as existence). In these ideas we see one of the continually repeated illusions of anthropologism: anti-normative (anti-theological, 'anti-social') consciousness is direct, real consciousness. In actual fact, disease does not give the individual new consciousness, it merely, in a definite way, intensifies some of his usual ideas, transfers them from the 'optimistic' modus to the 'tragic'.

Jaspers' supposition that disease and the approach of death make our concept of life clearer and more profound is thoroughly illusory. Nietzsche's superman with his brutality and cult of cruelty shows us what the real essence of such a concept of life is.

In principle, we could say the same about the problem of death, to which existentialism pays especial attention. In face of death, according to Jaspers, the 'wreck of all myths' takes place, man is cleaned of his socialness, of the ideas about himself, about the goals of lief and the nature of human society, which have been instilled in him.

No one knows what the dead thought immediately before their death. As regards the expressions of their consciousness and self-consciousness that have been observed, dying as a form of behaviour reveals no more and no less human possibilities than ordinary life. As yet no one has succeeded in ascertaining from a dying person socially non-verifiable emotional experiences.

The idea that the 'wreck of all myths' takes place at the threshold of death is absolutely fictive. Realistic literature has long reflected the fact that the method of awaiting death, the torments evoked by this waiting, the very concept of death is a psychologically preformed picture of the life that has been lived.

The existentialist doctrine of spiritual purification and perfection, about self-cognition in the critical moments of the life of man, and not in his active creative life, in his 'normal' state, is evidence of the profound inner spiritual crisis of capitalism, and characterizes existentialism as a philosophy of despair, a philosophy that is profoundly pessimistic in its essence. This philosophy not only belittles human personality, but actually denies the right to existence of a healthy, normal human being, denies the right to perfect oneself, to develop and to grow.

These ideas about disease, death, and fear are characteristic of the philosophical doctrine of Heidegger. According to him, man is somehow thrown into a world in which fear has become the main situation of existence. Fear, which keeps arising all the time, drives him from his daily, impersonal form to his extremely profound 'self'. Man, according to Heidegger, '. . . is a sinful creation, the ultimate, contained between birth and death, full of disease, fettered to death by god, to the fulfilment of the most human possibilities of his existence, whose existence is "existence for death". . .'.[16] Thus the existentialist 'I' is an 'abandoned creature', a creature in despair, a creature that grieves, that is within the grip of pessimism and hopelessness. Heidegger declares that the real essence of human personality is disclosed, and its freedom is revealed only in a state of fear. 'Only in fear', he wrote, 'is there the possibility of disclosing oneself because it estranges people.'[17]

By using, in his philosophical system, the special concept of 'Man', which expresses the impersonality of the human individual, the mediocrity of the consciousness of man according to social norms and standards, Heidegger characterizes the mutual relations of human beings in society in the following way: 'The joint stay in "Man" is by no means a reserved, indifferent existence of one near another, but the tense, ambiguous observation of one by another, secret mutual over-hearing. Under the guise of "one for the other" we have "one against the other".'[18]

And so in the opinion of the existentialist Heidegger, the basis of mutual relations of people in society is the fear that separates them, and this is manifested in their suspiciousness, in their shadowing one another, secretly over-hearing one another, and so forth.

Heidegger comes to the conclusion that a man becomes a personality and acquires individuality only through death.

[16] Hübscher: *A Thinker of Our Times*, Moscow, Foreign Literature P.H., 1962, pp. 204–205.

[17] M. Heidegger: *Sein und Zeit*, First Half, 1913, pp. 190–191.

[18] *Ibid.*, p. 175, 1931.

The French variety of existentialism, which is represented by Jean Paul Sartre and his followers, preserves in principle all the initial positions of existentialism: the subjective 'self' of personality, the concentration of attention on the inner, spiritual, emotional experiences of the subject, on the so-called 'freedom of choice' etc. But, whereas the German variety of existentialism in the philosophies of Jaspers, Heidegger, Bolnow and others arrives at politically reactionary, anti-humanistic conclusions, at the philosophical justification, in the end, of a thermo-nuclear catastrophe of mankind, the French variety of the 'philosophy of existence', in the person of Sartre, on the contrary leads to the humanistic denial of war, to the struggle for peace, to a high evaluation of Marxist philosophy and the admission that Marxism is good ideological 'climate' for the development of philosophical thought. In Sartre's opinion, Marxism correctly explains society, but it must be 'supplemented' with the philosophy of existence, which, seemingly, alone can provide an interpretation of the subject, personality, its existence and essence.

Existentialism as a whole, as a philosophical trend, in its initial point and in its conclusions is a profoundly pessimistic, irrational, nihilistic philosophy that leads to the denial of ideals, real scopes, possibilities, and results of man's activity.

We cannot but consider existentialism, a philosophy of despair, as evidence of the profound inner spiritual crisis in which present-day western society finds itself.

4. SOME RECENT ATTACKS ON THE MARXIAN CONCEPT

Gabriel Marcel:

At the XIII International Congress of Philosophy, existential views on the problem of man were presented in a report by Gabriel Marcel, one of the eminent representatives of theistic existentialism. Marcel's report, 'The Existentialist Aspect of Human Dignity', is a characteristic expression of the modern idealistic concept of man and society. Marcel proceeds from an abstract scheme of the historical development of human society. He considers as the initial stage of history that society in which the relations of its people were based on a feeling of the 'sacred'. Marcel actually idealizes the religious structure of the patriarchal-communal Middle Ages. He regards further historical development not as the history of real social relations that underlie the development of mankind, but as a process of the loss of the feeling of the 'sacred' and of the humiliation of, and insult to human dignity connected with 'desacralization' of human relations. In Marcel's opinion, the loss of a direct, pure attitude towards God is the reason for the loss by the people of a frank attitude towards one another.

Marcel considered the human personality worthy of respect only in virtue of the mystery of the sources and the goal—to communicate with the deity. The irrationalism of Marcel's views on the 'ontological' basis of man is clearly seen in his theory of the 'ontological' integrity of man, which is the only thing in which the 'sacred' can be manifested.[19] 'Ontological integrity' consists in man's helplessness, in his mortality, in his age-old weakness and defencelessness in the face of fate.

Marcel himself admits that the existentialist interpretation of the dignity of man as respect for his weakness and 'finiteness' cannot serve as a basis for vital activity. Marcel does not attempt to build up an optimistic theory of man. His man, separated from society, is only an object of compassion. The helplessness, the inefficacy of Marcel's humanism consistently develops into a rejection of life in which there 'is no manifestation of the sacred'. 'As I have already said', Marcel declares, referring to previous works of his, 'we can hope to attain a change in life and in the sacred only if we turn our glances away from the spectacle of a universal, inexplicable treachery; life as we observe it from without, was actively directed against something that, perhaps, underlies it, that is likely to be the very principle of life.'[20]

The anti-historical feature, the substitution of derived, interpersonal relations of 'respect', 'disrespect', 'tactfulness', and 'lack of tact' etc., for the real relations of people under the conditions of an antagonistic class society, in existentialism, acquires the form of belittling man and his historical achievements. Marcel reproaches modern man for considering people the equals of gods, and for their attempt to become the masters and conquerors of the universe.

[19] G. Marcel: 'L'aspect existentiel de la dignité humaine', *Memorias del XIII Congresso Internacional de Filosofia*, Vol. I, p. 11, Mexico, 1963.

[20] *Op. cit.*

We can clearly see from Marcel's report what the specifically modern form of idealism, in understanding society and man, consists of. In place of objective social relations (as private property and exploitation on the one hand, and co-operation and mutual aid on the other), abstract psychological definitions of direct ties among people are substituted ('belittling', 'insults', or on the contrary, 'respect', 'the recognition of human dignity' etc.).

In this connection, Marcel comes out, in his report, against what he calls 'practical anthropocentrism'. He writes: 'To-day we see that right before our very eyes is being established practical anthropocentrism, which is based on the absolute hegemony of technics.' 'It consists in the assertion of the irrefutable obviousness of the fact that only the human mind is capable of contributing significance to the world which, taken by itself, does not possess it, and must be interpreted only as a sort of primary matter on which genius leaves its imprint. This anthropocentrism, in its extreme form, risks becoming acosmism.'[21]

The first thing that must be said against this attack is that Marxist philosophy, as the most consistent form of materialism, proclaims a struggle against religion in all its forms and varieties. Marxism shows that religion is one of the chief ideological instruments for belittling man and insulting his dignity. But the Marxist thesis about the unlimitedness of man's practical and intellectual possibilities has nothing in common with the so-called 'idolization of man' with the simple attribution to him of those 'perfections' which theology discovers in God. Anyone who is in the least familiar with the polemics of Marx and Engels against Feuerbach's 'religion without God', cannot help but know this. The Marxist idea about the character of man's power over nature is free from any elements of pragmatic voluntarism whatsoever. There is nothing more alien to dialectical materialism than the view of nature as formless, structureless 'primary matter', to which the mind merely contributes its relations and laws. On the contrary, dialectical materialism considers that every successful step in the conquest of nature is evidence of the existence of objective laws that do not depend on the will and consciousness, and their existence becomes ever more obvious to man as his practical might rises. Man cognizes the laws governing the development of nature and society and

[21] *Op. cit.*

uses this knowledge for his own welfare and the welfare of mankind. In accusing dialectical materialism of 'acosmism', Gabriel Marcel actually ascribes to it the aims of pragmatic philosophy (a trend of thought typical of many representatives of clericalism).

Marxist philosophy never defended the absurd idealistic thesis of the 'hegemony of technics' in social development. Furthermore, Marxism was the first to criticize various forms of technical fetishism. Marxism interprets technics as a material system of the implements of labour, a system that is dead without man, the nature of using which is determined by the social relations dominating in the given stage of history. Marxism is far from regarding technics as a simple 'material expression' of some trend in the human consciousness, such as the embodiment of 'practical will to power' as Nietzsche said, or as the embodiment of 'atheistic vainglory' as modern Christian existentialism says. Such abstract psychological interpretations from the very outset bars the path to a scientific analysis of society. With such an approach, technics as such and the attitude towards it, the methods of using it, which is characteristic of a given social system, are merged into one united picture among these representatives of bourgeois philosophy, for instance, into the picture of 'practical anthropocentrism' (analogous to the ideas of the 'devil principle' in medieval theology).

From Gabriel Marcel's further arguments, we clearly see how abstract, after this, is the very idea of man and his individual dignity. As a matter of fact, Marcel comes to the conclusion that in modern society not a single deed, not a single real activity of man, can serve as an object of real respect. Respecting man for his deeds, we value only a certain 'functional role' that he performs, and not man himself. In this world man, as an individual who acts and attains definite goals, does not possess real dignity.

We cannot agree with Gabriel Marcel when, showing how the individual is belittled, he confines himself to describing only certain ways of affecting the consciousness, certain psychological methods with the help of which the feeling of respect for oneself is eradicated in individuals. This abstract, basically idealistic posing of the problem loses sight of the chief material means of belittling man: the poverty of the masses, exploitation, suppressing the national life of entire peoples under the conditions of colonialism.

The problem raised in Marcel's report is not a fictive one. The dignity of man is indeed one of the greatest moral values. But it would be naïve to think that it is possible to develop in man a feeling of self-respect without developing man himself as a social being, without creating real, material conditions of his education, cultural development, and the satisfaction of his numerous needs. The dignity of man is not something that belongs to the world beyond. Man exists on earth, and it is here, on earth, that the conditions must be created so that people can be aware of their real possibilities, develop their abilities and aptitudes. This is what communism strives for, it is this very task that socialist society is accomplishing, in ensuring the conditions for all-round social progress.

It must further be pointed out that the concept of 'dignity' should not be considered apart from time, apart from historical circumstances, apart from the concrete social environment. The nobleman's concept of honour, the bourgeois idea of prestige, and the working man's feeling of self-respect are entirely different things, forms of consciousness that cannot be equated to one another. An analysis of the concept of 'dignity' apart from the concrete conditions can contribute nothing new to the scientific understanding of the problem.

By ignoring these basic social relations, Gabriel Marcel is unable to correctly analyse even those examples of the belittling of man which he himself quotes in his report and which, judging from everything, evoke his sincere indignation (e.g., the segregation of the Negroes in U.S.A.). For the very same reason, Marcel is unable to give a scientific analysis of such a social phenomenon as fascism, even though he returns to this theme time and again. In the best of cases, Marcel succeeds in revealing only some superficial traits of the national-socialist ideology; but he does not show the real nature of fascism as a misanthopic system directed towards suppressing every democratic movement and towards destroying entire peoples. Gabriel Marcel does not see the connection between fascism and imperialism and the danger of the revival of fascism with which the present situation in the capitalist world is fraught.

A frank anti-social attitude has conditioned the vagueness, speculativeness, and wordy indefiniteness of the basic theses of

Marcel's report, which shows how far removed are his views from a genuine scientific approach to the problem of man. A number of these formulated by Marcel (defining the modern epoch as the completion of the process of 'desacralization', the attempt to present communist ideology as some sort of technocratic doctrine, his orientation of the 'ontological basis' of human consciousness) were repeated in almost all the speeches of the bourgeois philosophers on the problem of man.

F. J. von Rintelen:

The West German philosopher-Thomist, F. J. von Rintelen, tried to prove, in his report, that the source of our diseases of our epoch is the violation of the medieval harmony between the body and soul. Even in his earlier book, *Demonism of the Will*, which is a distinctive synthesis of Thomism and Nietzscheism, he declared that the way to the solution of modern problems is through the elaboration of the sort of mystic unity of carnal and spiritual forces, the unity of *Dionysus and Apollo*. Proceeding from these same premises, von Rintelen, in his report at the Congress, attempted to deal with the problem of the nature of values as the unity of the universal and the individual, which elevates man above the relativism of subjective evaluations.

A. M. Alonso and the Problem of Man's Freedom:

The problem of freedom, which is advanced by existentialism as a basic one, was most fully interpreted at the Congress by the Spanish philosopher, Adolfo Munoz Alonso in his report, 'Man Without Shelter'.

At first glance, Alonso's report appears as a passionate speech in defence of the freedom of personality. However, actually such was by no means the case. Here, as in the majority of existentialist works, we fail to find that inspiration with which the demand for freedom was advanced and defended by the ideologists of the bourgeoisie that had come to the fore. On the contrary, in Alonso's report freedom is analysed rather as a sort of onerous burden which is beyond the strength of modern man to bear and of which he is trying to free himself. The endless abstract discourses about freedom cannot conceal the ambiguity of the initial principle of the report: freedom elevates man above all creatures that inhabit the earth, but for man himself it is more of a torment than a blessing. 'Freedom', Alonso declares, 'strips man, frees him of the social garment that covers him and places him in a sphere of complete alienation, leaves him without shelter. To be without shelter in the power of the elements and in face of the bad weather, disputing with inclement weather or submitting to it—such is the terrible state of man.'[22]

The logic of the existentialist ideals of freedom leads to a fear of freedom, fear of the real liberation of man. Like the other existentialists, Alonso fully refuses to analyse freedom as a social category. He regards freedom as a sort of innate trait of man.[23] Strictly speaking, this generally does away with the question of the need to fight for freedom in the sphere of economics, politics, national relations etc. The countless etymological and psychological distinctions that, in existentialism, crowd out all other methods of analysis, further heighten the confusing effect of such investigations.

In those cases where Alonso succeeds, in spite of everything else, making his way to actual reality, he offers his audience pessimistic prophesies concerning a theme already familiar to us. 'Man', Alonso declares, 'will perish either from an electric charge or from collective rage, or from an incredible bomb, which will deprive him of his life and anchor And inasmuch as we are writing this in the year 1962, we can fully assert that if the ontological basis fails, man will have to yield to technics, and the sphere of personal freedom will prove dehumanized.' An appeal to the 'ontological' basis of man, that is, to certain abstract traits of the individual which are inherent in him even before his transformation into a social being, desparate fear of technics, hatred for social progress, slander of the masses—these are the things that permeate the report of this eminent Spanish philosopher.

M. Sciacca's View:

The close tie between the existentialist and the openly religious interpretation of freedom was clearly manifested in the report

[22] A. M. Alonso: 'El hombre a la intemperie' in *Memorias del XIII Congreso internacional de Filosofia*, Vol. I, pp. 55–56, Mexico, 1963.

[23] This was formulated most categorically in the address given at the Congress by L. Tarnoi, who declared: 'Mitin wanted to make us believe that freedom is a social problem, forgetting that man is an individual who carries freedom within himself.'

of the well-known Italian spirutualist, M. Sciacca, 'The Structure of Freedom in the Ontological "Constitution" of Man'. Sciacca sees the source of freedom in man's permanent relation to God, in a mystic orientation to the transcendental. In his report, freedom is regarded not as a property of man, but as a property of 'being', which is revealed to man when he has renounced his worldly goals and plans. 'Being' is free so far as it is indeterminate.

'In this sense, freedom does not manifest itself', Sciacca declares, 'it is affirmed, it *is*, it is the *act* from which all problems inherent in it are born. . . .'[24]

According to Sciacca, the human personality is somewhere between the world beyond and this world. Man, in his mundane experience, goes further and further from God and falls into the power of definite empirical social conditions, but the more this dependence develops, the more lasting does his inner 'free' connection with the transcendental, super-empirical existence of God become. As Sciacca puts it, God lives in the very depths of man, but people 'live in God', at least ever since history began. Thus in Sciacca, we have a sort of 'fundamental co-ordination' between man and God: it is senseless to raise the issue of God without relation to man, and just as senseless to raise the problem of man irrespective of God. The traditional ideas of subjective idealism about the relation of the subject and the object here, as we see, become filled with especiallye ractionary content.

From this there follows the virtual devastation of the idea of freedom by spiritualism, the rejection of real ideas about it and its transfer, with the help of pseudo-dialectical casuistry, from the field of real human relations to the sphere of 'intuition of the idea of being', to the field of religious feeling etc. 'Freedom of the ultimate creature', Sciacca declares, 'is formed by the mind of the creature, let into its entire, endless duration, in which the system to which all creatures belong, is its law.'[25] This system appears to man's mind as an 'Idea, an endless act which is actualized through its specification, never being realized to its end. . . .'[26]

[24] *Memorias del* XIII *Congreso Internacional de Filosofia*, Vol. 1, p. 22.
[25] *Ibid.*, p. 26.
[26] *Ibid.*, p. 25.

Carlo Giacon and Despair about Human Depravity:

Another well-known Italian philosopher, Carlo Giacon, in his report expressed with special force endless pessimism in the solution of the problems of man and the progress of society. For him it is not only man who is problematic, but even the very attempt to explain the problems connected with man. (Giacon's report was called interestingly enough 'The Problem of the Problem of Man'.) The crisis of bourgeois reality, the contradictions of the exploiting society are generalized by Giacon to the point of an ever present crisis of the 'total reality of man', which is profoundly irrational in its incomprehensibility. '... It seems', he says, 'that even before his birth man is destined to vegetate or to commit crimes, that a curse hangs over the innocent youth who amuse themselves in the power of mysterious, unattractive forces.... Thus has it always been, and nothing will convince us that it will not be thus for all time. Thus has it been despite all attempts to change the grievous fate of mankind. Such is the evidence of history, that very same history that man creates but which he is unable to change.'[27]

Everything in life—life itself, its meaning and contradictions—makes Giacon feel disheartened and at a loss. In his report he tried to prove that we may expect from future social development only changes of form, but that 'the content, the problematic, dramatic and tragic basis of human life, will remain unchanged.'[11] As a result, whereas the existentialists and spiritualists who addressed the Congress and whom we referred to above, voluntarily or involuntarily tried to discredit man and his ability to develop 'normally' and acquire freedom, the Thomist, Giacon, made a direct appeal to reconcile oneself, in some 'faith', with the path of trials along which man is doomed to go, to 'consciously perceive' the abnormality of one's life. 'Universal rationality is absurd, partial irrationality is a mystery that is incomprehensible to us, but which is a part of some higher wisdom. If such a view is faith, then let it be faith, but a faith that perceives. It is the enlightened "faith", which should arouse a desire to live, to perceive life consciously, even if it is abnormal life, but life....'[29]

[27] *Ibid.*, p. 152.
[11] *Ibid.*, p. 154.
[29] *Ibid.*, p. 156.

Central Ideas of Recent Trends:

Evaluating the above-mentioned addresses of some western philosophers as a whole, we can draw the following conclusions:

1. The problem concerning the being and essence of man are elaborated in the West primarily by the advocates of existentialism and neo-Thomism, who ever more resolutely place philosophy at the service of religion, actively criticize Marxist-Leninist ideology and frankly deny progress.

2. A characteristic feature of all the above-mentioned concepts of man is the militant anti-historical method, the idealization of the past, the striving to build abstract schemes of social development (such, for instance, is the definition of the modern epoch as an epoch of 'secularization' which, as a matter of fact, includes in one unbroken period all events and social processes that took place in the world since the time of the religious Reformation).

3. Characteristic of modern bourgeois interpretations of man and society are the deepening irrationalism and psychologism, the attempt to substitute for an analysis of objective social relations, the revealing of the subjective positions and emotions of individuals which function under the conditions of a society that develops spontaneously.

4. Characteristic of all these concepts are fear of a class analysis, the attempt to avoid the vitally important social problems of the present epoch. No matter how refined the terminology in which the western philosophers vest their ideas is, they are unable to conceal their inner emptiness, their isolation from life, from the actual content of the history of the past decades.

5. THE HUMANISM OF MARX AND ENGELS

One of the most widespread, most broadly used arguments against Marxism is the thesis that Marxism-Leninism, seemingly, does not pay any attention to man, does not recognize the importance of the individual, and reduces everything to the collective; that communism means the rejection of the interests of the individual for the benefit of the masses, the collective; that under communism the individual is dissolved in an amorphous mass; that communism negates individuality, personal needs and interests, the spiritual world of man, his struggles, aspirations, passions, moods, fears, emotional experiences etc.

The above criticism is such a widespread phenomenon that it is, perhaps, impossible to open a single book by modern western philosophers without coming upon such fantasies.

Representatives of various trends of modern bourgeois philosophy widely exploit this thesis in their speeches against communism and its Marxist ideology.

For instance, the neo-Thomist Bogliolo, in his article entitled 'The Anti-Humanism of Marxist Philosophy', declares that Marxism, seemingly, does not recognize anything higher than the material needs of man.[30]

The Thomist Sh. Buaill declares the communists' concern for the material welfare of the masses belittles the human personality. 'Communism, by being primarily concerned about material needs, belittles the noble activity of man, making it relative and unstable.'

The West German Catholic critic of Marxism, Bochenski, falsifies the Marxist doctrine about personality and declares that 'when Marxists speak of man, what they have in mind is society'.[31]

As a matter of fact, only Marxist philosophy has given a genuinely scientific interpretation of the problem of man. Human personality occupies the centre of attention in Marxist philosophy. In distinction from the old, classical anthropology of the Feuerbach type, the man in Marxist philosophy is not a man in general, but a man who is social, concrete, historical, and creative. In distinction from the anthropology of existentialism, he is not a man of death, plunged in fear and disease, isolated from social ties, theoretically 'free in his choice' inwardly, but actually a slave of natural and social necessity; he is a man of life, a man of labour, of transformation, a master of nature, a man who is free in relation to both natural and social laws to the extent in which he realizes their necessity.

Marxist philosophy has produced a genuine revolution in the views regarding man and human society. Marxism has advanced a fundamentally new point of view regarding man.

The basis for the scientific solution of the problem of man and

[30] See Collection, *The Philosophy of Communism*, p. 252, New York, 1952.
[31] I. Bochenski (G. Niemeyer): *Handbuch des Weltkommunismus*, Freiburg, München, 1958, p. 636.

society is the theory of historical materialism. According to this theory, society is a social organism that is based on material production and has its own laws that are specifically characteristic of it. Marxist philosophy with its logical materialistic gnosiology, with its social and historical analysis, is a genuinely scientific philosophical interpretation of man.

Marx and Engels show that the so-called natural and eternal needs of man, which, in any anthropological conception invariably become transformed into a measure for evaluating existing social relations, and also into a criterion of its subsequent social development, in actual fact are always a product of the existing level of development of production and the material relation that already exist. Marxism thus defined the rational content of earlier bourgeois concepts as the idea that the universality of man and his essence are not something super-human and of the world beyond. However, it decidedly opposed any attempt to depict the essence of man as a passive (passive 'feeling' as Feuerbach put it) principle, and explained the real definition of man by his *object-practical activity*.

The above definition does not, however, mean that man appears in the role of a petitioner, who presents to society a list of his 'eternal and natural needs', which in fact are always a reflection of his wretched state, his insignificance to which he has been brought by the existing social system. Man does not need philanthropy. He himself can be the master of his destiny and is capable of creating marvels, of setting gigantic forces into motion if his labour and creative energy are liberated. In place of the idea of existing society as a system of the usurpation of the natural inclinations of man, Marx and Engels advanced the scientific concept of the exploitation of labour; and they associated their humanism with the demand that this exploitation be done away with. They noted that to assume man's 'natural nature' as a prerequisite for an understanding of man is equivalent, willy-nilly, to transforming into a prerequisite that existence which the masses drag out in a society of exploiters. The prerequisite for an understanding of man and the initial point of real humanism must be an analysis of that objective process by means of which man, in actual fact, distinguishes himself from nature: an analysis of work and material production. And if Marxist philosophy, when speaking of the human personality, focusses its attention on the social and productive essence of that personality, it is not in order to forget about that individuality, about its inner world, about its spiritual potentials and moral qualities, but in order to reveal its real, and not illusory, essence.

Whereas, according to Marx, philosophy until now was occupied with explaining the world in order to change it, as applied to human personality we can say that until now previous philosophy was engaged only in explaining man, forgetting about the concrete conditions of his existence. However, what is most important is to change the conditions of man's existence, both the natural and the social, in order to create a paradise on earth and not in the sky, in order to create real possibilities for the all-round, harmonious development of human personality. The entire Marxist theory of the revolution, the entire Marxist programme for the transformation of social relations, the programme for the building up of communism, is directed towards exalting man, towards creating normal living conditions for him, for his existence, conditions under which his inimitable personal individuality, his essence will be genuinely revealed. In this sense, Marxist philosophy removes and resolves all the contradictions of the old and modern type of philosophical anthropology.

Marxism put an end to the sentimental conception of mankind as a passive, suffering mass. It penetrated the real paradoxes of the epoch much more profoundly than the other philosophies did. The source of all existing calamities lies in the fact that, although man is potentially omnipotent, his own energetic forces, the means and many-sided social ties of the process of labour, which he has brought to life, oppose him as alien forces. Behind the poverty and misery of the masses, which many thinkers had strikingly described even before Marx and Engels, Marxism discerned the tremendous latent force and the constructive principle of history.

The internal possibilities of the productive forces created by man greatly excel everything that can be recorded in the register of his personal, 'natural', needs. The tools and forms of the social combination of labour, which have been created for the production of one or another particular product, contain many more possibilities than the creation of just the given type of product. 'The plough is much more considerable than the grain that is produced with its aid', Hegel wrote. When summarizing

Hegel's *Science of Logic* Lenin characterized this idea as the embryo of historical materialism.

The liberation of all the internal possibilities of material production, the full development of man's creative, active forces—such is the only real basis on which the diversity of man's personality and the richness of his needs and tendencies can be developed.

The humanistic conception elaborated by Marx and Engels in the 1840's and which was called 'real humanism', was no longer an expression of abstract ideals of a passive, suffering mass, as was the case in the preceding socialist and some bourgeois-radical teachings. It focussed attention on man-the-creator, man-the-worker, and investigated, first of all, the question of the ways of liberating his active, creative, constructive potentialities. This conception did not regard the man of the future as something ready, given naturally, something that could simply be found within the limits of the existing society, isolated from that society and transformed into a criterion of the subsequent historical development. To reason in this manner, meant to make the misfortune and mutilation of the existing individual a measure of progress.

The transition from the present to the future is a process that is subordinated to objective laws. It is only within this process, only in an active struggle for the reorganization of the world, that this man can appear, the man whom anthropological philosophy rashly transformed into a natural prerequisite of history. Marx and Engels connected inseparably the understanding of the personality of man, his consciousness, the innate structure of his 'Ego', with the concrete socio-historical process of the decomposition of the old and the birth of a new social formation. Thus was the idea of the abstract, timeless, 'natural' essence of man overcome. The problem of the active historical action of the masses was the first discovered real basis which alone makes possible a correct understanding of the problem of personality and its freedom, the problem of the all-round development of man.

Marxism took as the starting point for its philosophy of man a live, concrete person living and working in a definite historical environment, and not an imaginary, abstract individual who is isolated from society and life. 'In direct contradistinction to German philosophy, which descended from heaven to earth',

Marx and Engels wrote, 'we here rise from earth to heaven, i.e., we start out not from what people say, imagine, picture to themselves; nor do we start out from imaginary people who exist only in words, in order to go from them to real people; for us the starting point is really active people, and from their real, vital process we also deduce the development of ideological reflections and the echoes of this vital process.'[32] We cannot deny the fact that it was Marxism that, for the time in the history of philosophy and sociology, provided a scientific explanation of nature and the essence of man, and revealed the real significance of the spiritual aspect of man's activity as that of a being who is consciously and purposefully transforming the world.

Marx and Engels taught that 'the human essence is no abstraction inherent in each single individual. In its reality it is the ensemble of the social relations.'[33]

6. CONCRETE MAN AS A SOCIAL CREATURE

Marxist philosophy proceeds from the thesis that the individual is a social creature. So any manifestation of his life, even if it does not appear in the direct form of a collective manifestation of life, accomplished jointly with others, is nevertheless a manifestation and affirmation of social life. Marx and Engels considered that the individual and the social life of a person are not different things, even though they have different forms of expression. They considered that both of these sides of man's life are interconnected, and each of them is manifested in the other in a higher or a lower degree.

Proceeding from this idea, the founders of Marxism came to the conclusion that the personality of man can achieve full development only in the collective. 'Only in the collective does the individual receive the means enabling him to develop his inclinations in every respect', they wrote, 'and, therefore, it is only in the collective that there is real freedom. In the substitutes for collectivity that existed until now—in the state etc. —personal freedom existed only for individuals who developed within the framework of the dominating class, only because they were individuals of this class. Sham collectivity in which individuals had united heretofore, always contrasted itself to

[32] K. Marx and F. Engels: *Works*, Vol. III, p. 25.

[33] *Ibid.*, p. 3.

them as something independent; and inasmuch as it was a union of one class against another, it represented, for the subordinated class, not only absolutely illusory collectivity, but new fetters. Under conditions of real collectivity, the individuals acquire freedom in their association and through it.'[34]

'Man can settle down only in society,' Marx wrote, 'only in society can his individuality be revealed in accordance with the social conditions.'[35]

A characteristic feature of all anti-Marxist theories is the assertion that there exists an insoluble contradiction between society and the individual.

The following ensues from the theory of the eternal antagonism between the individual and society: either society must repudiate all interests of the individual, or the individual must be independent of society. In this connection, diverse, 'age-old' biological and psychological properties and emotions, instincts and feelings are attributed to the human individual. Such is the basis of the countless sociological schools that compose 'psychological', 'bio-physical', 'anthropological', and other definitions of the person.

In his preparatory works for his book, *Critique of Political Economy*, Marx notes three stages in the mutual relations of society and the person, in which the historical change of these mutual relations during the course of the entire development of human society is unfolded: 'The relation of personal dependence (in the beginning absolutely primitive) are the first forms of society in which the productivity of people develops only in an inconsiderable volume and in certain places. Personal independence, which is based on eternal dependence, is the second large form under which there is created, for the first time, a system of the universal metabolism, of universal relations, of comprehensive needs and universal abilities. Free individuality, based on the universal development of individuals and on their subordination to the collective, social productivity as their social property—such is the third stage.'[36]

Marxism is opposed to the abstract and timeless interpretation of man both in idealistic doctrines and in pre-Marxist materialism. Thus, when revealing the narrow-mindedness and

[34] K. Marx and F. Engels: *Works*, Vol. III, p. 75.
[35] K. Marx and F. Engels: *From Early Works*, p. 558.
[36] *Archives of K. Marx and F. Engels*, Vol. IV, pp. 89–91.

inadequacy of the approach of the old materialism to the individual, Marx pointed out, in his *Thesis About Feuerbach,* that 'Feuerbach resolves the religious essence into the *human* essence. But the human essence is no abstraction inherent in each single individual. In its reality it is the ensemble of the social relations.'

Feuerbach, who does not enter upon a criticism of this real essence, is consequently compelled:

1. To abstract from the historical process and to fix the religious sentiment (*Gemüt*) as something by itself and to presuppose an abstract-*isolated*-human individual.

2. The human essence, therefore, can be comprehended only as 'genus, as an internal, dumb generality which merely *naturally* unites the many individuals.'[37]

Here Marx reveals the very profound bases of Feuerbach's anthropologism, the gnosiological and logical bases of his abstract-theoretical statement of the problem of the essence of man and he gives a basic, programmatic, initial Marxist description of the essence of man as the aggregate of social relations.

The idea of creating personal and social harmony can be clearly traced through all the doctrines of Marxism and Leninism. In the *Manifesto of the Communist Party,* Marx and Engels wrote that 'in place of the old bourgeois society, with its classes and class antagonisms, we shall have an association, in which the free development of each is the condition for the free development of all'.[38] Enlarging on this thought, F. Engels later on pointed out that society cannot free itself without having freed every individual person.

The idea of the creation of harmonious relations between society and the individual, which can be traced through all the basic works of the classics of Marxism-Leninism, figures in the new Programme of the C.P.S.U. as one of the basic ideas permeating all its content.

The harmonious union of the individual and collective, of the person and society, implies the flourishing of the spiritual side of the activity of the individual and society. This does not contradict, but, on the contrary, organically merges with the high level of development of the material productivity of man. It is, therefore, ill-intentioned and absurd to declare, as is done by

[37] K. Marx and F. Engels: *Works,* Vol. III, p. 3.

[38] K. Marx and F. Engels: *Works,* Vol. IV, p. 447.

some bourgeois philosophers who are hostile to Marxism or by people who know of it only from hearsay, that Marxism apparently rejects the spiritual world of the human 'Ego', dissolves man in the mass, in the collective, and does not recognize the human personality.

Anyone who wishes to become acquainted with the works of K. Marx, F. Engels, V. I. Lenin and their followers in an unprejudiced and objective way, will easily be convinced that Marxism recognizes the exceptionally great role of the consciousness, thought, ideas and spiritual life of man. Marxism pays especially great attention to explaining the significance of social consciousness in the development of human society. Marxism recognizes the inspiring role of progressive ideas in the life of man and human society, and in their development.

Spiritual Life in Marxism:

Marxism recognizes also the relative independence and inner logic of the development of various forms of social consciousness. At the same time, it is different from all forms and types of idealism by its recognition of the material principle, material existence as the basis of all mental processes. And Marxism differs from vulgar, metaphysical materialism by its dialectic, that is, its flexible, all-round approach to the problem of man's life. It categorically rejects the anti-scientific, vulgarly materialistic, metaphysical identification of the process of thinking, of the spiritual life of man, and matter. Marxists, unlike the vulgar materialists, do not reduce the mental to the physical or the physiological, they do not fuse the spiritual in the physical. Marxism recognizes the existence of a spiritual life, but when doing so, it points out that the basis of that spiritual life is objective, material existence. It says: first there is matter, existence, and then consciousness; consciousness is the other side of matter, its derivative.

While paying due credit to the ideas, thoughts and spiritual sphere, while admitting their exceptionally great significance in the accomplishment of this and that event, Marxism insists only on one thing—the earthly origin of ideas and thoughts of man's spiritual world. *We can say it was Marxist philosophy that, for the first time in the history of science, provided a logical, scientific solution of the problem of man and the human 'Ego'.*

Not a single one of the pre-Marxist and modern non-Marxist philosophical systems was able to raise to such a level the role and significance of man and his activity in the world, to understand so comprehensively and to shed light upon his transforming role in nature, his unlimited possibilities for cognizing and changing the world and the cosmos, as Marxist philosophy has been able to do.

Not a single pre-Marxist or present-day non-Marxist philosophical system has raised to such a level the spiritual world of man, his great spiritual potentials, his spiritual activity and, at the same time, has revealed the material, social bases of this activity, its meaning and significance, as Marxist philosophy has. There is not a single problem in man's spiritual world, whether it concerns his emotional experiences, his joys or sorrows, his creative successes, the flight of his fancy or petty everyday affairs, his consciousness of responsibility to the collective, and, at times, the feeling of solitude, sickness and fear of death etc., etc., which could not be and was not the subject of Marxist analysis—psychological, logical, social and moral. And it is only on the basis of Marxist methodology that the scientific foundations of such manifestations of man's spiritual world are revealed.

At the same time, whereas many modern philosophical trends dig into the so-called 'border situation', by which they mean fear of death, dependence on chance, suffering, fault etc., Marxist philosophy affords real prospects and positive conditions, forms and possibilities for the development of spiritual potentialities. Marxist philosophy stimulates and teaches man to think not about death, but about life, about its transformation, improvement and flourishing; not about solitariness, but about the collective, about social welfare, about mankind as a whole. Man who supports the positions of a Marxist world outlook does not and cannot feel lonely, cannot feel doomed, condemned to vegetate in life; for Marxist philosophy scientifically substantiates that he, man, is a member of society, of the collective, the master of nature, transforming it in accordance with the demands of the objective laws of the development of matter.

Bourgeois Individualism:

Thus Marxism does not deny individuality and its significance in the process of the formation and development of the human personality, but it denies bourgeois individualism.

The denial of bourgeois individualism, the material basis of which is private ownership, and the establishment of collectivism in a socialist society, collectivism that is based on social, socialist ownership, by no means signifies the denial of the individuality of each human personality, or the levelling of personalities. On the contrary, it is only under the conditions of socialism, when, for the first time, all the necessary real, material and spiritual prerequisites have been created for the all-round physical, mental, ethical and aesthetic development of the human personality, that the necessary conditions are created for the full development and flourishing of the inimitable individuality of each human being, freed from the oppression of exploitation, inequality, ignorance, crises, unemployment, poverty, hunger, disease, and other social evils. It is only in a socialist collective, in free creative labour for the benefit of society and the entire people, that the human personality can develop in all ways and manifest its individuality. In an article entitled 'About the Old and the New', Maxim Gorky wrote: 'In denying bourgeois zoological individualism, the new man excellently understands the lofty integrity of the individuality which is closely connected with the collective; he himself is such an individuality, freely drawing his energy and inspiration in the mass, in the process of his work.'[39]

Marx and Engels pointed out that only in a communist society, where real and not imaginary collectivism will reign, where the development of society will be limited only by the level of the development of the productive forces, and not by the egoistic interests of individual social groups, will there be unlimited scope for the development of the human personality, for the full manifestation of the originality of each individual, that is, for real, complete personal freedom. In their *German Ideology*, Marx and Engels wrote that 'within the limits of a communist society, the only society in which the distinctive and free development of the individual ceases to be a mere phrase—this development is conditioned by that very tie of the individual, a tie that is to be found partly in the economic prerequisites, partly in the necessary solidarity of the free development of all, and, finally, in the universal nature of the activity

[39] M. Gorky: *Collected Works*, Vol. XXVI, p. 290, 1953.

of the individuals on the basis of the existing productive forces. This, it follows, refers to individuals in a definite historical stage of development, and by no means to any accidental individuals, to say nothing of the inevitable communist revolution which, itself, is a general condition for their free development.'[40]

The contradictions between the individual and society, which have developed under the conditions of antagonistic formations, and the detrimental contradictory development of the indi vidual himself are eliminated only on the basis of socialism, which does away with private ownership. People of a socialist society, in which the domination of a social ownership conditions the spirit of collectivism, possess a high level of consciousness of their social duty, which has been instilled in them by the Communist Party. They learn to place social interests above their personal ones, learn to combine their personal interests with the social.

7. PRIVATE PROPERTY AND THE SELF-ALIENATION OF MAN

Marx and Engels pointed out that the real formation of the human personality begins only with the abolition of private property, which will come with communism; for the domination of private property fetters all the manifestations of the natural traits and inclinations of the human personality, and the domination of the exploiting systems does not permit the human personality to develop fully, but suppresses it.

The founders of Marxism pointed out that 'the abolition of private property means the complete emancipation of all human emotions and traits.'[41] So only 'communism, which removes private property, signifies the demand for a really human life as the inalienable property of man, signifies the formation of practical humanism.'[42]

In an exploiting society, the domination of private-ownership relations over people led to the suppressions of human individuality by all sorts of fortuities resulting from archaic market relations, capitalist competition, and other laws governing commodity production. Capitalism, especially its highest stage,

[40] K. Marx and F. Engels: *From Earlier Works*, p. 592.
[41] *Op. cit.*
[42] K. Marx and F. Engels: *From Earlier Works*, p. 637.

imperialism, brings this contradiction to its sharpest and most universal forms of expression. Only a socialist revolution and the replacement of domination of chance in social life by definite laws, a replacement conditioned by that revolution, will put an end to the contradictions in the life of society. Socialism establishes, in place of the domination of relations of fortuity over individuals, the domination of individuals organized in a socialist society over fortuity and its relations. Marx and Engels wrote that 'this task, which is prompted by modern relations, coincides with the task of organizing society on communist principles'.[43]

Thus communism appears as that very form of organization of society under which the self-alienation of man, born of private property, ends, and there begins real human existence for all members of society, for the many millions of working people, and not merely for a small handful of members of the dominating class. Marx characterizes the position of the person under communism as follows: 'Communism as the positive abolition of private property—that self-alienation of man—and in virtue of this, as the real acquisition of human essence by man and for man....'[44] In this sense, Marx wrote that communism carries the genuine solution of the contradiction between man and nature, between freedom and necessity, between the individual and the species, and thereby is the 'solution of the riddle of history'.[45]

It is only under the conditions of socialism that the personality receives, for the first time, the possibility of truly all-round development, for concern for man; and the all-round development of his personality constitutes the essence of socialism and communism. 'What is most important for us, for the builders of communism, is man', N. S. Krushchev says. 'The struggle for communism is a struggle for a better life for man, everything for the sake of man, everything for him.'[46]

In bourgeois society, which declaratively proclaims the universal equality of rights, democracy etc., the equality and freedom of the human personality, and its right to development remain, for the overwhelming majority of the members of society, mere formal possibilities, as they do not possess the

[43] K. Marx and F. Engels: *Works*, Vol. III, p. 440.

[44] K. Marx and F. Engels: *From Early Works*, p. 588.

[45] *Op. cit.*

[46] N. S. Krushchev: 'To Raise the Level of Management of Agriculture', *Pravda*, March 1, 1961.

necessary material conditions for the practical realization of these possibilities.

V. I. Lenin forecast that 'only with socialism does the rapid, real, truly mass advance movement begin in all spheres of social and personal life, with the participation of the *majority* of the population, and then of the entire population.'[47] The experience of the development of the world socialist system convincingly confirms this thesis.

Under socialism man lives in the collective: he studies in the collective, then works in it, spends his leisure in the collective etc. The collective exerts a decisive influence on the development of the personality of each of its participants, ensuring him the possibility of improving his knowledge, vocational qualifications, and the development and perfection of his abilities and natural gifts by giving him its support.

In order to become a personality, the individual must reveal in his work and actual practice his inner qualities with which he has been endowed by nature.

'It is one's calling in life, one's designation and the task of each person to develop all his abilities in all ways', Marx and Engels taught.[48]

In various idealistic philosophical trends we find also attempts to substantiate the need for self-perfection. Furthermore, many of them, inasmuch as they are unable to build an optimistic theory of the progress of society as a system of social and productive relations, wholly rely upon the perfection of the individual, which, seemingly, is capable of leading to the reorganization of society. Such are many Christian theories of the development of personality, of the building of a 'positive' French and Italian existentialism.

For instance, according to Sartre, the isolated personality, taken by itself, creates its own personal qualities and forms itself.

'Man is only what he himself makes of himself',[49] Sartre declares, and history is merely a multitude of individual destinies.

Of course, self-education plays a definite role in the formation

[47] Lenin: *Collected Works*, Vol. XXV, p. 443.

[48] K. Marx and F. Engels: *Works*, Vol. III, p. 282.

[49] J. P. Sartre: *Existentialism is Humanism*, Moscow, Foreign Literature, p. 9, 1953.

of the human personality. But this role is not the only one or the chief one. The conditions of social life, the environment in which the given individual lives, play a decisive role in the formation of the human personality. And these outer conditions exert a formative influence on the personality also not by themselves, but through the system of education and instruction that exists in society and through the process of work.

The erroneousness of the viewpoint of Sartre and thinkers like him, in our opinion, lies in the very fact that they ignore the role of that environment and those objective conditions that influence the formation of the human personality, and they concentrate all their attention on the individuality, which they interpret as the individualistic isolation of the personality from society, the alienation of the personalities from one another.

Concrete Freedom and Personality:

Not a single pre-Marxist or present-day non-Marxist philosophical system has been able to solve the problem of the freedom of man's will. Only Marxism has been able to give a scientific solution of this problem by showing, on the basis of materialism, that *freedom is a consciously realized necessity*. As Marxism understands it, freedom of will in man is the ability to rule over oneself, to subordinate the surrounding world to oneself, to transform it on the basis of the cognition and practical mastery of the objective laws.

Reared on Marxist philosophy, the man of socialist society is a striking example of a truly free personality, free to the maximum degree as compared with people of previous social formations.

The truly free person is a fighter, a creator, a citizen, and an active public figure. And such, in fact, is the person who is inspired by the ideas of Marxist philosophy. He is a new Man, a builder of the most humane, most harmonious social system in history—communism.

Speaking of the so-called 'freedom' in bourgeois society, Lenin very aptly expressed its essence as follows: 'Freedom in capitalist society always remains about the same as it was in the ancient Greek republics: freedom for the slave-owners.'[50]

[50] V. I. Lenin: *Works*, Vol. XXV, p. 432.

Exposing the formal, hypocritical, and false character of bourgeois democracy and the freedoms and rights of the personality that it declaims, Lenin wrote: 'There can be no real and effective "freedom" in a society based on the power of money, in a society in which the masses of working people live in poverty and the handful of rich live like parasites.'[51]

Lenin gave an exhaustive criticism of bourgeois democracy, its formal, false and hypocritical character, and in this connection he showed the entire illusiveness of the notorious freedoms and guarantees of the rights of personality, so solemnly and pompously proclaimed by the apologists of capitalism. Lenin wrote that 'under capitalism such conditions are usual, not as individual cases, but as typical phenomena, when it is impossible for the oppressed classes to "realize" their democratic rights.'[52]

Among a number of western ideologists, it is fashionable to call capitalist society a 'free society'. Contrary to the truth, the ideologists of imperialism assert that the human personality enjoys real freedom only under conditions of the domination of private property, private enterprise, i.e., capitalism.

But the essence of such 'freedom of the personality' was long exposed by Lenin, who showed that the bourgeoisie and its ideologists, when speaking of the freedom of personality, meant 'freedom' of enterprise and of the exploitation of man by man, freedom of the imperialist monopolies to plunder the working masses. Lenin, writing about the bourgeoisie and its ideologists, said that, when they speak of the freedom of personality, what they mean is 'freedom to make a profit, freedom for the few to enrich themselves, freedom of trade...,'[53] that 'freedom and equality' in a bourgeois system (i.e., so long as there is private ownership of the land and of the means of production) and in a bourgeois democracy remain merely formal concepts, signifying, in actual fact, the *hired slavery* of the workers (formally free, formally having equal rights) and the omnipotence of capital, the oppression of labour by capital.'[54]

Human personality is free when it has all the necessary material and spiritual prerequisites and conditions for the all-round disclosing and development of its natural gifts and

[51] V. I. Lenin, *Works*, Vol. X, p. 30.
[52] *Ibid.*, Vol. XXIII, p. 61.
[53] *Ibid.*, Vol. XXIX, p. 495.
[54] *Ibid.*, p. 350.

talents, when it is rid of the oppression of exploitation, works for the benefit of society and at the same time for itself, is a full and equal member of society which possesses the means of production, when it really, and not formally, takes part in the management of all affairs of society, when it is free from all social, political, and national oppression and lawlessness. 'The criterion of real freedom and happiness is a social system which frees man from the tyranny of exploitation,' says N. S. Krushchev, 'gives him broad democratic liberties and the opportunity to live in fitting conditions, a system that inspires him with confidence in the morrow, unfetters his individual abilities and talents and makes him feel that his labour is for the good of society. Socialism is such a social system.'[55]

Only socialism and communism give the personality real freedom, enable it genuinely, really to realize its rights which are not proclaimed in laws, but are materially guaranteed by the fact that equal opportunities for the realization of these rights are created for all members of society.

Genuine freedom of the personality in a socialist society is ensured first of all by the fact that in it such social calamities have been wiped out as exploitation and unemployment, poverty and ignorance of the toiling masses, whom the Communist Party has raised to a profound understanding of the tasks of communist construction and whom it continually draws in an ever greater degree into active political and social, productive and cultural-educational work.

Real freedom of the personality under socialism is ensured by materially guaranteed rights to work, to education, to rest, to social security in case of illness and in old age, to free instruction in all schools, to free medical aid etc. Real freedom of the personality under socialism proceeds from the fact that, for the first time in the history of civilized mankind, it is in a socialist society that equality in all spheres of social, state and economic life, equality between man and woman, between people of all nationalities and races, has been realized.

Revealing the essence of a truly scientific, Marxist-Leninist, communist understanding of the freedom of personality, N. S. Krushchev says: 'We regard freedom as the right of people to a

[55] N. S. Krushchev: 'An Account to the Party and the People', *Report of the Central Committee of the Communist Party of the Soviet Union to the 22nd Congress of the Party*, p. 102, F.L.P.H., Moscow, 1961.

worthy life without exploitation and exploiters, the right to real political equality, the right to enjoy all the achievements of science and culture. We understand freedom as the liberation of people from the horrors of unemployment and poverty, from racial, national and social oppressions.'[56]

The communist society which is now being built in the Soviet Union will bring to every personality even greater freedom and will raise it to an even higher level of development.

Under the conditions of socialism and the comprehensive building of communism, the human personality forms, develops, unfolds and perfects itself primarily in the process of work for the benefit of society.

Work and Freedom:

Work has always been a most important factor in the life of the individual personality and of all society as a whole. Some thinkers understood this even before Marx. For instance, the English economist J. Bellers wrote that 'labour being as proper for the body's health as eating is for its living...Labour adds oil to the lamp of life, when thinking inflames it....'[57]

But in an exploiting society, labour, as Marx expressed it in his *Economic-Philosophical Manuscripts of 1844*, is in a state of alienation as regards the subject of that labour—the worker. Labour does not belong to his essence in virtue of the fact that the worker labours through compulsion, and not of his own will, he labours not for himself but for someone else. That is why, in an exploiting society, '...Labour is, for the worker, something foreign to him, something that does not belong to his being; the worker does not assert himself in his work, but denies himself, does not feel happy, but unhappy, does not freely display his physical and spiritual energy, but exhausts his physical nature and destroys his spirit. That is why the worker feels he is really himself only when he is not at work, and feels isolated from himself in the process of work. He feels at home with himself when he does not work; and when he works he no longer feels at home with himself. In virtue of this, his work is not voluntary, but forced, it is *forced labour*. This is not the satisfaction of his need

[56] N. S. Krushchev: *For Victory in the Peaceful Competition with Capitalism*, p. 126, State Political Literature Publishing House, 1959.

[57] K. Marx and F. Engels: *Works*, Vol. XXIII, pp. 499–500.

for work, but only a *means* to satisfy other needs than the need for work. This alienation of work is clearly seen in the fact that, as soon as the physical or other compulsion for work ceases, the workers flee from work as from plague. Superficial work, work in the process of which man alienates himself, means sacrificing himself, it means self-torture. And, finally, the superficial nature of labour is manifested for the worker in the fact that this labour does not belong to him, but to someone else, and that in the process of the labour he himself does not belong to himself, but to someone else. Just as in religion the independent action of the human imagination, the human brain and the human heart influence the individual regardless of himself, i.e., as some alien activity, divine or satanic, so the activity of the worker is not his independent action. It belongs to someone else and is the loss by the worker of him himself.'[58]

It is only under conditions of the absence of private property, which enslaves people and the toiling masses first of all, only under conditions of socialism and communism does the alienation of labour vanish, does labour bring man satisfaction, and gradually begin to be transformed into one of the expressions of the human essence, the essence of the all-round developed human personality. Free labour for the benefit of human society becomes, under socialism, a matter of honour and glory, valour and heroism for most members of the society, and in the process of gradual transition from socialism to communism labour gradually becomes transformed into one of the main, vital needs of the all-round developed human personality, needs that bring it the joy of creative endeavour and the happiness of creation. Thereby work becomes a most important expression of the human essence, the essence of the all-round, harmoniously developed personality of the man of communist society.

'Man's beauty and his fame', says N. S. Krushchev, 'stem from his work, from what he does, from that which he has created or that which he has performed. The abilities and talents of people, the genius of man, are revealed in labour, the immortality of man is in his labour.

'The training of man for his life's work, the steeling of people through labour, the inculcation of love and respect for labour as

[58] K. Marx and F. Engels: *From Early Works*, p. 563, State Political Literature Publishing House, 1956.

a vital necessity, is the central feature of all work in the field of communist education.'[59]

Characteristic of our day and the period of the comprehensive building of communism in the U.S.S.R. is the undeviating rise in the conscious attitude of the masses of working people towards labour, which finds expression in the nation-wide communist work movement.

The patriotic understanding, by Soviet people, of state interests and of their duty to society, to their people, their country, to the Communist Party, is manifested most strikingly and concretely in their highly conscientious attitude towards their work. It is this profound understanding of state interests and their duty to society, and not merely concern for earnings, that prompts many members of Soviet society to work actively, creatively, inspiredly, even though they are in a position not to take part in work at all for plausible reasons, such as their age and so forth. Hero of Socialist Labour Nadezhda Grigoryevna Zaglada, who is a foremost Ukranian collective farmer, a team leader at Pervoye Maya (First of May) Collective Farm in Chernyakov District, Zhitomir Region, explains as follows the reasons prompting her to work selflessly at her collective farm: 'I am 69 years old, but I try not to lag behind the young people, I do not take things easy. And not because I lack anything at home. And I could live an easy life, rest, enjoy myself with my grandchildren. But the times are not such, comrades.

'All age-old agricultural workers, the creators of communist abundance, are deeply interested in having collective-farm Ukraine advance rapidly. . . .'[60]

Here is another example. A basic questionnaire was circulated among the workers of the First State Bearing Plant in Moscow. The answers received from 800 workers clearly characterize the spiritual world of Soviet workers (see Table No. 1, p. 526).[61]

As can be seen overleaf, most of the people selected answers that reflect the social significance of work. Only 2 per cent of the people did not object to doing any work only if it paid well; 1·5 per cent proved to be of the type whom work oppresses, and

[59] N. S. Krushchov: *Report of the Central Committee of the C.P.S.U. to the 22nd Congress of the Party*, p. 134, F.L.H.P., Moscow, 1961.

[60] *Pravda*, August 25, 1962.

[61] Magazine *Sovietsky Soyuz*, No. 1, 1964, p. 19.

relatively few—2·5 per cent—were indifferent to the question. Here is a characteristic detail: of those who replied that work oppresses them, some found it necessary to give a reason for the answer. The most widespread explanation was that they had to travel far from their homes to their plant.

Table No. 1

Basic Question	*Choice of Replies for Basic Question*	*Answers in Percentage of Number Questioned*
With which of these opinions do you agree?	We must not forget about earnings, but the chief thing is the meaning of work and its social value	42
	Any work is good if it pays well	2
	The earnings are the main thing, but we must think of the meaning of the work ..	12
	That work is good in which you bring greater value, in which you are needed	40
	Work oppresses me	1·5
	I do not know	2·5
	Total	100%

Work and Education:

For the foremost people of Soviet society work is not only the fulfilment of their duty to society. Work offers them much more than the simple realization of the honest fulfilment of their duty. This 'more' is the joy of creating material and spiritual values that people and society need, values that communist construction needs. Man begins to feel that he is not only a useful worker, but more than that—the creator of part of that new life the building of which constitutes the entire meaning of the activity of the Soviet people.

Expressing this joy of creation, creative labour, Deputy to the Supreme Soviet of the R.S.F.S.R. I. D. Leonov, who is a foremost Soviet worker—a milling machine operator at the S. M. Kirov Works in Leningrad—writes: 'How can one not be proud and rejoice that he is a worker! And everything that scientists contemplate, everything that engineers and architects outline in their projects, everything, thanks only to you and to your golden hands, clear mind and pure conscience, is transformed from a dream into the real wealth of the people.'[62]

For such people as Leonov, labour is something more than simply honest work for the benefit of society. For them, labour constitutes the meaning of life, it is inspired creative work without which man would consider his life empty, meaningless, and useless.

The above attitude towards work as towards creative endeavour arouses in many people the desire to broaden and deepen their knowledge, to improve their education in order to be able to rationalize their work. But once having begun to study and acquire knowledge, the man of creative labour does not, as a rule, stop, but continues to extend his horizon. His spiritual riches gradually increase more and more. He begins to be interested not only in narrowly special sciences, but also in many other subjects connected with them, begins to be concerned about raising the general level of his culture, begins to show an interest in literature, art, etc. His interests become ever more diverse, and frequently, when speaking with such a person, it is difficult to determine what he does, and what his speciality is, what social group he belongs to: whether he is a worker, a collective farmer, or an intellectual.

The level of development of the personality of a Soviet worker, his spiritual interests and needs, are very concretely illustrated by the literature the workers read.

The subscribers' cards of the libraries of the Palaces of Culture of the Urals Engineering Plant and the Verkh-Isetsk Iron and Steel workers in the Urals show how broad is the range of interests and spiritual needs of the readers, who are workers of these plants. Judging from the subscriber's card of V. N. Mikhailova we would find it hard to determine what education she has and what her speciality is, so diverse are the books she reads. She has read the works of many Soviet and foreign writers, such as M. Gorky, M. Saltikov-Shchedrin, D. Mamin-Sibiryask, A. Pisemsky, Emile Zola, Jack London, Henri Stendhal, John Steinbeck, Elsa Triolet, Mitchel Wilson, B. Polevoi, K. Fedin, V. Ketlinskaya, V. Kochetov, and others.[63]

[62] *Pravda*, September 5, 1962.

[63] See *Rise in the Cultural and Technical Level of the Soviet Working Class*, p. 431, Moscow, Sotsgiz, 1961.

This list reflects the many different spiritual needs of the reader. Yet her education is most modest—that of the primary school, and she works as an apprentice at the Verkh-Isetsk Iron and Steel Works. But this working woman continually extends her horizon, and there is no doubt whatever that she will not remain at her former level of development, but will develop into a person who is developed in all respects. Her eager interest in knowledge and life is an earnest of such a development.

S. T. Guryanov, a Soviet sociologist, studied the reading interests of 8000 workers of the First State Bearing Plant. In order to make his investigations, he studied one out of every eight subscribers' cards of the eight thousand subscribers, covering a period of six months. He thus selected 840 subscription cards which represented about 10 per cent of the workers. The following are some of the data obtained (see Table No. 2).

Table No. 2

BOOKS READ ACCORDING TO TYPES OF LITERATURE

Theme of Literature	*Total Number of Books read according to types of Literature in six months by 840 Workers*
Classical	301
Adventure Stories	164
Historical Novels	129
War Memoirs	98
Science Fiction	68
Modern Soviet	3525
Foreign	1973
Literary Magazines	473
Socio-political Magazines	62
Technical Magazines	30
Social Sciences	509
Technics	727
Art	197
Literary Criticism	221
History	329
Travel	119
Total	8925

Of the 8925 books read by 840 workers in half a year, 6928 were books of fiction. It was established that a worker reads about two books a month. These data, which are typical of

Soviet life, clearly reflect the diversity and breadth and range of the workers' reading interests according to themes, and their scientific cognitive interests.

The striving continually to perfect oneself, to develop oneself in every way is seen especially clearly in the affairs of the Soviet youth, who combine work in industry with study, who try to learn as much as possible, to do as many valuable things in life as possible, to solve the most difficult tasks that confront the people in the process of communist construction, while combining work and study with sport and recreation activities, traits organically inherent in youth. It is in this way that an all-round developed personality is formed, one that possesses the necessary physical and spiritual traits, moral purity and firm convictions. These character traits of Soviet youth were strikingly expressed in the replies to a questionaire circulated among the youth by a newspaper, *Komsomolskaya Pravda*, in 1 61. The main question was: 'Do you have a definite goal in life, and what is it?' Of the 17,446 people who filled the questionnaires, 16,674 or 96·5 per cent answered the first part affirmatively. The replies to the second part of the question varied, of course, reflecting the individuality of those who answered it. But despite their diversity, the overwhelming majority of the answers had one common feature: they were all permeated with the noble ideal of service to the people and their country. The personal goals of most of the participants were conditioned by the desire to serve the cause of communism and communist construction.

A 26-year-old worker of the city of Sevastopol, who replied to the questionnaire of the *Komsomolskaya Pravda*, a young man who is also a correspondence student, wrote about himself and his friends: 'We are governed by one idea—to be of value. We work a great deal, and sometimes each day we live is a real battle. But whenever we talk about this, we always come to the same conclusion: we could not live in a different way, more easily, simpler. I'm no longer a youngster. I've been working since 1949 and study in the evening. I've worked as a fitter, a painter and a stoker. At present I work as a heater in a forge shop. Difficult? Yes, it is. But how interesting!'[64]

A 24-year-old nurse of the city of Sverdlovsk writes about the

[64] B. Grushin, V. Chikin: *The Confession of a Generation*, p. 225, Molodaya Gvardiya (Young Guard) Publishing House, 1962.

same thing, although in different words: 'I want my modest work to serve the cause of the building of a communist society. I keep asking myself how can I do this. Work honestly and conscientiously? Of course. But this is not all. We have to put our soul into our work. I find daily happiness in my small, modest profession: after all, I work with people, and that is a great honour for me. I shall attain my goal because I am preparing to live in a communist society. In my thoughts I am already living there.'[65]

Another young Soviet person, G. Nikiforov, who lives in Karaganda region and whose speciality is that of a bricklayer, wrote: 'I am a bricklayer and build homes for miners, hospitals, and schools. My goal in life is to build a garden city.'[66]

These replies to the question about their goal in life show how, in the process of creative work for the benefit of society, people who are developed in all ways, people with rich inner content, with a rich spiritual world, grow up, people whose goal is communism, that is, the universal happiness of people.

Work and Service to Humanity:

It is obviously such people whom another participant in the above-mentioned questionnaire, Nikolai Cheboterev, a turner of the city of Rostov and a university student, had in mind when he wrote to the *Komsomolskaya Pravda:* 'One person brings a soft divan into his apartment: his aim is to create comfort in his home. Another seeks diamonds in the frozen Taiga mountain ranges: his aim is to create comfort in the whole world.'[67]

This concern of the foremost people of the Soviet society about 'comfort in the whole world' is one of the most convincing evidences of the diversity of their vital interests, the lofty, all-round development of their personality, the personality of the builders of a communist society.

There is nothing similar to it in the so-called 'average people' of capitalist society. The aspiration towards lofty ideals and service for the benefit of society is alien and incomprehensible to them. At times many of them do not even have a clear goal in life, and they have the most limited, egoistic, petty interests.

[65] B. Grushin, V. Chikin: *The Confession of a Generation*, p. 229.
[66] *Ibid.*, p. 125.
[67] *Komsomolskaya Pravda*, July 22, 1961.

This is especially true of the youth of the capitalist countries, whom capitalism cripples at the very outset of their path in life, demoralizing and devastating them ideologically, corrupting them physically, thereby transforming them into prematurely old people who have lost their interest in everything that is wholesome in life.

The following example is very significant in this connection. In the autumn of 1961 the French journalist, Michel Chevalier, spent several weeks travelling in West Germany for the purpose of becoming acquainted with the young people there. He questioned them about their past, their present and their thoughts about their future. As a result, he came to the following conclusion: 'The past is burdensome for the youth; their motto for the present is: money and amusement; and their future is a solid mist.'[68]

Continuing his account about the youth of present-day capitalist society, about the youth of the country of the 'economic marvel' as the imperialist propaganda calls West Germany, Michel Chevalier writes: 'We sought the new generation, but found bare statistics. Fifty per cent of the young people have no goal whatever, the others mention their parents, cinema stars or sportsmen as their ideals. Only 50 per cent read one book a month. There is no political platform, there is little faith, and no risk—only concern about preserving and increasing their property....'[69]

How can we help but recall the words of the great scientist of our day, Albert Einstein, to the effect that 'the crippling of human personality is the worst of evils brought by capitalism.''[70] Very aptly and correctly worded!

In contrast to this, the personality of the Soviet person, the builder of communism, is ever being enriched with new traits, ever being perfected, and is constantly developing in the process of the creation of a new society.

The builders of communism, when transforming social relations and perfecting them, at the same time transform the traits of their own character, their own personality, perfecting and enriching them.

What spiritual beauty, what crystal moral purity and perfec-

[68] B. Grushin, V. Chikin: *The Confessions of a Generation*, p. 138.
[69] *Ibid.*, p. 139.
[70] V. Lvov: *The Life of Albert Einstein*, p. 209, Moscow, 1958.

tion of the human personality are expressed in the simple sentence pronounced by a foremost Soviet person, the well-known builder and innovator, Hero of Socialist Labour Nikolai Musyka: 'It is more interesting to live for others!'

This sentence, which is so profound in its philosophical meaning and significance, which was pronounced by Nikolai Musyka in reply to a question about why, every time he organizes a strong collective of his brigade, he goes to work in some backward brigade, is evidence of the concern of its author and other similar foremost people of our day about the social welfare, about the happiness of the entire people, about the building of communism in our country.

This trait—concern about the welfare of society—is a *truly* communist trait of personality. It is about this quality of the human character that Lenin wrote in his *A Great Beginning* viz., that communism begins where people show concern not about what they and their 'close' kith and kin will get, but about what their 'distant' kith and kin, i.e., society as a whole will get.[70]

Concern for society as a whole, for its welfare, for the welfare of the entire people is one of the necessary conditions for the further growth and development of a communist attitude towards work.

Work and Creativity:

Creative work in the collective, a communist attitude towards work contributes to the all-round development of the human personality. If the attitude of a person towards work, even that which is purely physical, is one of love, of enthusiasm, then it necessarily develops the spiritual side of his personality as well. He is interested in the technology of his work, studies it, perfects his skill not haphazardly but systematically, regularly; for, otherwise, he will not be able to attain new success in his favourite occupation. Thanks to his favourite occupation, which is an organic need of his, the man of creative labour, whether he is a painter or driver, an actor, steelmelter, doctor or fitter, is constantly being enriched spiritually, constantly develops his personality, and rises to an ever higher level, forming, we may say, the *culture* of his personality. This trait, the culture of the personality, develops as a synthesis of a high level of culture in his favourite sphere of work and the general culture and educa-

[70] V. I. Lenin: *Works*, Vol. XXIX, p. 394.

tion of man. And it is not a matter of his possessing one or another diploma testifying to his education (although we cannot deny the importance of diplomas as documents), but of how deeply and permanently culture and education have become part of the consciousness of the given person, have become the content of his personality, his individuality, his 'Ego'.

The high level of development of the personality begins from high labour efficiency, but is not limited to it. A high level of efficiency in labour arouses in the person a thirst for knowledge, stimulates many-sided interests in him, gives rise to numerous spiritual needs, makes him continually raise his level of knowledge, his general cultural level, and inspires him to master the achievements of spiritual culture to an ever greater degree.

Marx and Engels, speaking of the development of the personality, pointed out that 'the real spiritual riches of an individual depend wholly on the riches of his real relations.'[71]

The epoch of comprehensive communist construction in the U.S.S.R. is richer in the diversity of social relations than any other epoch.

Hence the spiritual world of the personality in this epoch, in Soviet society, is richer than it has ever been in world history.

The many millions of working people participate not only in multifarious, diverse productive activity, but also take a most direct and active part in the political life of the country, in the administration of the state, in all aspects of the life and work of society. Such was never the case formerly, before the socialist revolution. By taking part in the work of the central and local Soviets of Working People's Deputies, and in the standing committees organized under them for various concrete problems, in the work of the Party organizations, trade unions, the Young Communist League, co-operatives, scientific and sports voluntary societies, and in other public organizations, and when participating actively in the preparations for, and the conducting of the election campaigns etc., the masses of the working people create and experience the genuine 'wealth of real relations' in social life.

The all-possible rise in the role of the public in the life of the country, and the broad development of the activity of public organizations of the working people, as provided for by the Programme of the C.P.S.U. and already being realized

[71] K. Marx and F. Engels: *Works*, Vol. III, p. 36.

in the U.S.S.R., even further develop the wealth of social relations in the period of comprehensive communist construction.

These factors immeasurably enrich the spiritual world of personality for the builder of communism, the 'average person' of Soviet society, and raise him to an unprecedented height as compared with the level of development of the personality not only of the 'average', but even of the outstanding person of past epochs.

Work and Spiritual Development:

The wealth of social relations, the many-sidedness of spiritual interests and the scope of the spiritual world of the personality in the period of comprehensive communist construction considerably increase both in virtue of the general high level of culture of the country as a whole and of each person individually.

From all this we get the many-sidedness of the spiritual world of the personality under communism, its all-round harmonious development, and a qualitatively new historical type of personality—the personality of the man of a communist society.

The motto of communism is: 'Everything for the sake of man, for the benefit of man!' Only in a communist society does man attain full, all-round, harmonious development, his personality, his spiritual 'Ego', his inimitable human individuality flourish to the maximum degree as compared with any previous period in world history. *The position of man in a communist society can, with every reason, be characterized as that of a free individuality based on the universal development of individuals and on subordination to the collective, social productivity as their social merit.*

It is only from these positions that we can understand the meaning of that colossal activity that is under way in the Soviet Union for man, for the creation of a material and technical base for communism, for the formation of new social relations, for the rearing of the man of communist society, the all-round and harmoniously developed personality.

8. CONCLUSION

And so, Marxism has never ignored the problem of man either in the period of the preparation and formation of Marxism, or in the period of the maturity of Marxist theory, or throughout its entire tremendous history; it has never lost sight of this problem, never dismissed it, never dissolved the personality in society, never reduced it to the collective, but has supplied the only scientific solution of this most intricate problem.

In various historical periods one or another aspect, one or another feature is advanced to the foreground in Marxism. Accordingly, in various periods of the development of Marxism, the correlation of personality and society was advanced to the foreground in greater or lesser degree, and sometimes it retreated to the background.

In the first period of the existence of Marxism, it was more necessary to stress the role and significance of society, the collective, the group, in opposition to all the bourgeois, petty bourgeois and reformist theories.

In the present period, the period of comprehensive communist construction in the Soviet Union, the problem of personality arises in all its scope and fullness.

And let the numerous philosophical schools and trends assert that evil is ineradicable in man, that man is a beast, that egoism is innate in his very nature and can be destroyed only with the destruction of man himself—life mocks such theories and will severely mock them when a communist society will have been built in the U.S.S.R. and in other countries.

CHAPTER IX

Epilogue

P. T. RAJU

ANYONE who has read all these chapters will have obtained a fair acquaintance with seven main philosophical traditions and with some comparative reflections. These traditions have many apparent and deep-reaching similarities and differences, which the reader will have noticed. He may have noticed also the relevance of all the ideas to the concept of man. Some of them confirm one another, some conform to one another, some are opposed to one another, some suggest one another, some are alien and new to one another, and the others appear to be compatible but indifferent to one another. If all of them are relevant to the concept of man and if there is any truth in them or in the lines of thought that led up to them, the reader may now be prepared to bring them all to a single focus and discover their underlying unity.

I once asked an American friend about his religion. He answered that he was seldom mindful what it was, but if anybody criticized Judaism, he was a Jew, implying that he would defend Judaism if it was attacked. Otherwise, he would live like the men of every other religion and live with them. It is time for us to realize that what matters most is having the ability and education to live together—call it co-existence, co-operation, or friendly give and take, as you will—but not whether we live in the name of a religion or ideology. Only if we are attacked for holding on to a particular religion or ideology, which we accept freely, should we fight in its defence and for ourselves. A religion or ideology that prevents one man from living in harmony with another is now out of date. Humanity ought to be not only wise, but also clever and shrewd enough to see that to attack in the name of religion or ideology is futile and dangerous in this atomic age. We have to be alive to attack and to recognize the fruit of the attack. For the days have come when all attacks recoil on the attacker and destroy him also. Not only the methods of war but also the human—international—situation is completely changed. For instance, now it is not the conqueror but the conquered that ask for reparations—a kind of a precedent introduced by America after the last World War in the name of helping the conquered to recover from the defeat. The guiding idea here is to make it possible for humanity to live in peace and harmony. The conditions for such an idea to work include mutual understanding and appreciation, the readiness to give and take, and the ability to rise above provincialism of all types. What is needed is insight into the true nature of man and into the unexpressed aspects of all religions, ideologies, and philosophies. And as philosophy covers the other two so far as understanding goes, we need a true philosophy of man even if it takes us beyond our provincialisms.

There are many nations that are surprised when told about their ideology; for the idea of ideology came to acquire significance in the hands of Marx and his followers and it is thought that all those who are not Marxists have no ideologies. But willy-nilly in distinction from Marxism, other nations also are putting together and integrating their basic, guiding ideas and developing their guiding philosophies without calling them ideologies, even though such developments have not taken definite shape. If ideology means the system of all the guiding ideas of our life here,[1] it will in the end be little different from philosophy. If, as maintained earlier, philosophy is philosophy of life and the question of the applicability to man's life arises for every philosophy, and as life here cannot exclude the empirical and mundane, philosophy will become ideology also, unless the latter is very severely restricted in its meaning. Then philosophies can and ought to be compared with ideologies, just as they are compared with theologies, with the aim of knowing the truth about man. We cannot base the plan of our life on false or incomplete philosophies and we should not be afraid of truth. Fear of self-reflection and self-examination amounts to fear of truth.

As there is no final chapter comparing all the traditions, a few guiding questions may be given here to help the student or

[1] The word was first used by Destutt de Tracy for a study of the empirical development of intelligence out of sensibility and the philosophers of France at the beginning of the nineteenth century were called ideologists. (W. Windelband: *A History of Philosophy*, Vol. II, p. 457, Eng. tr. Harper Bros., New York, 1958.)

reader to collect the relevant answers and compare them. These questions are not exhaustive; additional questions may be framed by the reader from the perspectives of his own philosophy and also from those of the others. For in some philosophies we find a greater importance given to some aspects of man and the problems relevant to them than in the others. Again, the reader should ask himself how his own philosophy solved the problems on which emphasis is laid by other philosophies. And in every case, he should ask himself whether the solutions are adequate and whether they are able to touch the deeper roots of the problem concerned. Some questions already mentioned in the Prologue are given here also for convenience.

1. What is the relation between man and nature? Is man a part of nature, is he different from it, or is he opposed to it?
2. Should man be understood as only a member of society? What are the advantages and disadvantages of understanding him thus? Can he be understood without reference to society? And what will be the advantages and disadvantages of such an understanding?
3. Does man's being contain anything that distinguishes him from nature and society? If it contains something, what is it and what are grounds for accepting its reality?
4. Should we accept the reality of God for an adequate understanding of man? What are the grounds for acceptance or rejection?
5. Is man a mere product of natural evolution? What are the reasons for giving a negative answer? Examine them.
6. What factors does the nature of man contain?
7. What is the aim of man's life?
8. What is the aim of the education of man?
9. How can man live a rational life, an ethical life, or a spiritual life? Can all the three kinds of life be lived together?
10. Examine the definitions or concepts of man you come across in this work and make a critical estimate of them. Try and develop a concept, comprehensive in its content.
11. How can ethics, religion, and social philosophy be related? Examine the attempts made by the different philosophies of man to relate them.
12. Is man really free? What are the foundations of his freedom?

13. What is the significance of the expression, 'the dignity of the human individual'? Collect the answers you may find in the different traditions and evaluate them.

14. How can philosophy relate the freedom of the individual with an ordered cosmos and the creativity of God?

15. What is meant by spirit and spirituality? Is the word spirit a substantive? What can be the reasons for taking it or not taking it to be a substantive?

16. What is the difference between man and the essence of man? If there is any difference, how are the two related?

The above sixteen are only leading questions meant to cover all the chapters. The student should first collect the answers from all the philosophies, reflect over them, estimate them, and may even frame an answer of his own. In this task, he may need the assistance of his teacher. He may then be able to have a deeper and more adequate idea of the nature of man and his destiny than before he started to learn about the other traditions. The questions are not and should not be intended merely to collect the answers given by the seven philosophies of man and to find out in an inductive way similarities and differences, but also to act as incentives for reflecting over the answers and to lead to more adequate formulations of the idea of man and his destiny. As said already, comparative philosophy becomes insignificant, if it is not purposive, whether or not the purpose is immediately realized.

INDEX

There are difficulties in preparing an index for subjects for a volume like the present one. Yet it is really important to have their index at least as a rough guide to what the different traditions have said about the ideas concerned. The difficulty is due to several reasons. *Firstly*, the problems do not arise in the same way in the same contexts and are not designated by the same names. *Secondly*, in many cases the problems or their solutions are presupposed or implied. Often some of the truths are taken for granted. For instance, freedom is taken for granted even by the early Mīmāmsā doctrine of *karma* in its most rigorous form, although rejecting the idea of *mokṣa*, which is translated as liberation, freeing, freedom. What the Mīmāmsā accepts is ethical freedom, the freedom of man to do good and evil, but not the liberation of spirit from the laws of nature and ethics. *Mokṣa* in Indian thought is a technical (*rūḍha*) term for the latter kind of freedom. But as there is no technical term in Sanskrit for the former kind of freedom, one may think that ethical freedom is not accepted by the Mīmāmsā—which will be wrong. For the Mīmāmsā says that man can increase his merit and demerit or decrease them by further good or evil deeds and has the power to make free choices. Then in any index the word *mokṣa* does not come in directly when the idea meant is freedom of man or will, but only indirectly through its relevance to the metaphysical foundations of all kinds of freedom. And *thirdly*, in some cases it is not even realized by some traditions that there are problems corresponding to the index words. The present Index is not supposed to be exhaustive; it is only a rough guide for the reader who wants to push his enquiries further. He is advised, in consulting this Index, to look up all the related concepts known to him, which may suggest still others and their inter-relationships. It should be noted that the chapters are not and could not be written with exact uniformity, because of the type of material presented. What should motivate the reader is to find out whether what is accepted in one tradition and is true, even if it is not openly discussed in other traditions, can find a place in the latter and whether the latter takes it for granted or can give a place for it. For instance, values, aims of life, and virtues are very closely related concepts. But a tradition may give preference to one expression or conceptual form rather than to another. And it will be more enlightening to look for values or aims of life accepted by a tradition than for its lists of virtues; for the number, nature, and derivation of virtues follow from the number and nature of values or aims of life.

Abbas, 458
Abdu, Muhammad, 471, 474
Abraham, 125, 142, 155
Activism, 219 fol., 447 fol.
Adler Felix, 367
Adṛṣṭa, 291
Afghani, Jamal al Din al, 471
Āgamas, 240, 243, 273 fol., 278, 281, 283, 294
Agents, The Five, 179, 195
Ages, The Three, 338
Aggregates, 261 (see *Skandhas*)
Albert the Great, 74, 106, 467
Alexander of Aphrodisias, 101
Alexander, S. S., 304
Alexander the Great, 18, 73, 86
A. Farabi, 464
Al Kindi, 464
Allaf, Abu Al Hassan Al, 462
Alonso, A. M., 502 fol.
al Shafi'i, 462
Andalusi, Ibn Hazm, Al, 463
Antahkaraṇa, 288 fol.
Anthropoligism, 494 fol.
Anthropology, Christian, 395 fol.
Anthropology, Philosophical, 10, 490 fol.
Antiphon, 100
Aquinas, Thomas, 106, 107, 136, 465, 467
Archelaus, 59
Aristotle, 9, Chap. I, 310, 315, 320, 323, 325 fol., 338, 350 fol., 358, 365, 464, 486
Arndt, Johann, 398, 399
Arnold, Gottfried, 434
Art in Judaism, 132
Art Medieval, 407 fol.
Asceticism, Christian, 445 fol.
Asceticism, Indian (see *Āśramas*)
A'sha, 457
Ash'ari, Abu Al Hassan Al, 462
Asharites, 473 (see Ash'ari)
Āśramas, 209 fol., 211 fol.
Athanasius, 437
Augustine, 398, 402, 444, 465
Avatar (Incarnation), Indian, 405 fol.
Averroes, 103–105
Avicenna (Ibn Sina), 103–106, 446 fol.
Avidyā, 257 (see Ignorance)
Āyatanas, 261, 356

Bach, 115
Bacon, Francis, 487 fol.
Bādarāyaṇa, 278
Bāja, Ibn, 464
Bakr, Abu, 459, 470, 474
Baquillāni, 462
Beginnings, The Four, 168, 323, 350
Behaviourism, 30, 31
Ben Azzai, 156
Bernal, John, 482
Bocheński, I. M., 507
Bodhisattva, 265 fol., 441
Body, Causal, 233, 269
Boehme, Jacob, 405, 417
Bogliolo, 507
Bolonow, 497
Bosanquet, B., 22, 356
Bradley, F. H., 36
Bṛhaspati, 279
Bridgman, P. W., 17
Buddha and Buddhism, 30, 32, 160, 240, 244 fol., 252 fol., 268, 273, 355, 401, 407 fol., 411 fol. 426, 441, 445, 450
Buddhism, Chinese, 160

Callicles, 51, 53
Capitalism, 37, 448, 482 fol., 517 fol.
Cārvaka, 218, 237, 250, 256, 279, 308, 354

Cassirer, E., 30, 31
Castes, 212 fol., 251, 253
Catholicism, 420
Chang Tsai (Chang Hung-ch'u), 178, 179 fol., 185 fol., 190
Chardin, Teilhard de, 417
Cheng Brothers, 180
Ch'eng Hao (Ch'eng Ming Tao), 180 fol., 185
Cheng Hsüan, 192
Ch'eng I (Ch'eng I-ch'uan), 186, 203 fol.
Ch'eng King, 162
Chevalier, M., 531
Chou, Duke of, 161
Chou, Tun-yi, 337
Christ, The Body of, 441 fol.
Christianity, Secularization of, 402 fol.
Christology, 405
Christophorus, 411
Chung Tze (Tzu, 191, 197 fol.
Chu Hsi, 179 fol., 195 fol., 203 fol.
Chu Hui, 187
Church, Early (Old), 404, 410, 440, 444
Church, Eastern, 412, 417, 430, 444, 448
Cicero, 30
Clement of Alexandria, 437 fol.
Clerk, Colin, 482
Communion, 326–28
Communism, 37, Chap, VIII, 450
Conant, J. B., 16, 19, 27
Confusianism, 32, Chap. III
Confucius, 17, 33, 253, 318, 321, 326, 337, 349 fol., 359, 365, 375, (see the whole of Chap. III)
Constantine the Great, 411
Cornford, F. M., 308, 325
Covenant, 122–3
Critias, 48, 57, 58

Dante, 30
Darśana, 308, 309
Debts, The Three, 246, 274
Del Vecchio, 360, 370
Democracy, 15 fol., 57, 457–59
Democritus, 49, 100, 301, 318
Demuth, 38, 128
Descartes, 26, 465, 488
Dewey, John, 15, 272
Dharma, 222 fol., 236 fol., 278, 296 fol., 298, 368, 369
Dharma, Arya, 245
Dharma, Vedic, 245
Divinity (Divine Spirit, Supreme Spirit, God, Absolute etc.), 47 fol., 59 fol., 61, 81 fol., 201 fol., 325, 436–38
Dostoevsky, 408 fol.
Durkheim, E., 134

East and West, 28 fol., 35, 376 fol.
Eckhart, Meister, 396, 403, 447
Eddington, A., 114
Education, 51 fol., 70 fol., 95 fol., 201 fol., 245 fol., 270 fol., 295, 273 fol., 526 fol.
Einstein, A., 531
Elijah, 134
Emotions, 194, 324, 374 (see also 429–435, 511–15, 530–34)
Engels, 479 fol., the whole of Chap. VIII
Epics, 249, 272 fol.
Epicurus, 100, 354
Evil, 145, 148 fol., 150 fol., 177 fol., 402 fol.
Evolution, 48, 60, 84 fol., 237 fol., 282 fol., 335 fol., 477 fol.
Existentialism, 492 fol.

Feuerbach, 490 fol., 494, 499, 508
Fludd, Robert, 417
Force, Psychic, 234
Forces, 179 fol., 195
Forms, 56, 64, 84
Francis of Assisi, 397
Francke, August Herman, 423
Freedom, 16, 64 fol., 82, 219 fol., 402–405, 455, 469 fol., 472 fol., 502 fol., 520 fol., 523 fol., 532 fol.
Fu Sju-niel, 164, 175
Fung Yu-lan, 312

Galloway, G., 27
Gandhi, M. K., 12, 31
Gazzāli, Al, 463, 466
Ghost, Holy, 439 (see Paraklete, Holy Spirit)
Giacon, Carlo, 505 fol.
Glaucon, 46, 57
Good Life, 95
Gorgias, 51–53
Government, Forms of, 58, 80
Gundissalimus, 467
Guryanov, S. T., 528

Haas, W. S., 35 fol.
Hanbal, Ibn, 471
Han Fei, 172
Hanīfa, Abu, 471
Han Yu, 170, 174, 175, 176, 184
Harmain, Imam Al, 463
Harītha, Zaid ibn, 456
Hasidism, 151 fol.
Hazm, Ibn, 474
Heaven, Mandate of, 161 fol., 349
Heaven, Way of, 164
Hedonism, 100
Hegel, G. W. F., 35, 228, 489, 509
Heidegger, M., 496 fol.
Heraclitus, 45
Herodotus, 12
Hīnayāna, 268
Hippias, 53, 56
Hippocrates, 52
Hobbes, Thomas, 47
Homer, 62
Hsieh Liang-tso, 174
Hsing, 163 fol., 349
Hsüan-tsang, 318, 349, 350
Hsün Yüeh, 174
Humanism, 18, 45–48, 158 fol., 183 fol., 219 fol., 506 fol.
Huxley, Julien, 15

'I', the, 227 fol., 232 fol., 237, 300
Idealism, 203, 300, 338, 489
Ideals, see Values
Ignorance, 259 (see *Avidyā*)
Illusion, 180
Image (Reflection, Copy) 56, 60, 126–145, 359, Chap. VI
Imago dei, 398 fol., 402 fol., 407 fol., 415 fol., 429 fol., 434 fol., 440 fol. (see also Image)
Imam Muhammad 'Abdu, 463
Immanence, 331, 346
Individualism, 59, 302, 322, 511 fol., 515 fol., 517 fol.
Industry (Labour, Work, Activity), 447–49, 508, 523 fol., 526 fol., 530 fol., 532 fol.
Inscription, Western, 185
Instrument, Inner, 288 (see *Antahkaraṇa*)
Inwardness, 241

Jaeger, Werner, 74
Jaimini, 267, 273, 278, 280
Jainism, 240, 244, 252 fol.
Jaspers, K., 495 fol.
Jen, 184 fol., 313, 369, 374
Jesus, 136, Chap. VI
Jina, 240, 257
Jiva, 232, 235
Joachim de Fiore, 437
Job, 142, 155
John of Damascus, 419
Justinian, Emperor, 101

Kanāda, 280
Kant, Immanuel, 110, 324, 353, 363, 467, 488
Kao Tzu, 167, 173
Kapila, 280
Karma, 218 fol., 257 fol., 260, 262, 277, 282, 297 (see Industry etc.)
Kavod, 130
Khādija, 456
Khansā, Al, 457
Kierkegaard, 431 (see Existentialism also)
Knot of the Heart, 236, 357
Knowledge, Two Kinds of, 248
Ko Hsi, k60
Ko Yi, 18
Kruschev, N. S., 518 fol., 522, 524
Kumārila, 270
Kung-sun Ni, 165
Kuo Hsiang, 192

Lao Tze, 315
Law, Mosaic, 419
Law, Roman, 428
Legalism, 419
Legalists, 172, 184
Leibniz, 10
Leonov, I. D., 526 fol.
Li Ao, 170, 176
Life, Good, 357
Life, Rational, 357
Li Ssu, 172
Logos, 232, 250, 298, 320, 333, 334, 357, 363, 406 (see Cosmic Person, Spirit, Soul)
Loka, 279
Lokāyata, 218, 279
Luther, M., 427

Macrocosmos, 230 fol., 241, 399 (see Spirit, Soul, Cosmic Person etc.)
Madhva, 310, 332
Mādhyamikas, 264
Mahābhārata, 9, 273

Mahāvīra, 244, 253 fol. (see Jina, Vardhamāna)
Mahāyāna, 261, 268, 441
Maimonides, 145
Malik, 462
Malthusianism, 482 fol.
Man as Creative, 9, 31 fol.
Man and Nature, 46 fol., 54 fol., 75 fol., 197 fol., 218 fol., 241, 255 fol., 304, 314 fol., 399 fol., 401 fol., 477 fol., 479 fol., 482 fol., 485 fol.
Man and Society, 56 fol., 79 fol., 191 fol., 319 fol., 441 fol., 450, 459 fol., 485 fol., 511 fol.
Man, Constitution of, 49 fol., 61 fol., 86 fol., 132 fol., 141 fol., 188 fol., 193 fol., 224, 237, 259 fol., 286 fol., 348 fol., 395 fol., 405 fol., 418 fol., 461 fol., 479, 485 fol., 492 fol., 511 fol.
Man, Definitions of, 10 fol.
Man, Eastern and Western, 28 fol., 375 fol.
Man, The Perfect (Ideal), 183 fol., 310 fol., 435 fol., 461–69, 520–34
Mandate of Heaven, 161 fol., 200
Manichaeism, 402, 445
Man-man, 436 fol.
Manu, 366, 369
Manumission, 429
Marcel, G., 497, fol., 500 fol.
Maritain, J., 15
Marx, Karl, 476 fol. (see the whole of Chap. VIII)
Materialism, 25, 100, 218, 449, Chap. VIII
Māyā, 268, 283
Mencius, Chap. III, 314–18, 321 fol., 342, 349, 350, 353
Mercier, G., 15
Michelangelo, 479
Microcosmos, 230 fol., 241, 399 (see Cosmic Person, etc.)
Midrash, 124
Mikhailova, V. N., 527
Mīmāmsā, 12 fol., 207 fol., 219 fol., 267, 277 fol., 253
Mind, Enlarging of, 181 fol.
Mitsvah, 138, 152, 155, 157
Mo'ammer, 463
Mo'tazila, 462, 471, 473
Mo Tzu, 167
Mohammed, 31, Chap. VII
Mohammadanism, 103 fol., Chap. III
Mohenjo-Daro, 211, 277
Mohism, 184
Moloch, 125
Montague, W. P., 373
Moses, 155
Musyka, N., 532
Mysticism, 149, 151 fol., 197, 327, 330, 357, 399, 402 fol.

Naturalism, 316 (see Man and Nature also)
Nature, 52, 164 fol., 180 fol., 198 fol., 349, 350, 361, 372 (see Man and Nature also)
Nature, Original, 316, 324
Neo-Confucianism, 169, 177, 178, 179 fol., 202 fol., 350, 372
Neo-Platonism, 101 fol., 402
Neo-Taoism, 192, 199
Niebhur, R., 155
Nietzsche, F., 429, 493 fol., 500
Nihilism, 51
Nikiforov, G., 530
Nirvāṇa, 261, 268, 331, 342, 355, 356, 361, 370, 372, 441
Noah, 277 fol.
Northrop, F. S. C., 34, 35
Nyāya, 277 fol.
Nyāya-Vaiśeṣika, 237, 281, 353

Occasionalism, 25
Ockham, 77
Oetinger, F. C., 417
Omar, Caliph, 459 fol., 470
One and Many, 189
Optimism, 49, 145, 163 see Pessimism
Orphism, 351, 352, 358
Otto, Max, 23

Pāñcarātra, 278, 283 fol., 304, 338, 360, 361
Pantheism, 101, 345
Paraklete, 416 fol. (see Holy Spirit)
Pāramitās, 265 fol.
Pascal, Blaise, 9
Pāsupata, 278, 283 fol., 304, 338
Patañjali, 277, 280
Peginini, 479
Pepper, S. C., 23
Pericles, 44, 57
Person, Cosmic, 363
Personality, 261 fol., 297 fol., 520 fol.
Pessimism, 145, 492 fol.

Phidias, 479
Philosophy, Aim and Nature of, 12 fol., 16, 307 fol.
Philosophy, Comparative, 17–36, Epilogue
Pietism, German, 423
Plato, Chap. [illegible] fol., 314, 319, [illegible] 336, 351, 352, 35[illegible] 377, 398, 426, 466 fol., 486
Plotinus, 53, see Neo-Platonism
Polus, 51
Prāṇa, 229 fol., 260, 288
Prasalov, L.I., 481
Pratītyasamutpāda, 258
Pretziger, 430
Proclus, 42
Prodicus, 53
Protagoras, 44 fol., 53, 63, 87, 98, 99, 314, 315
Pythagoras, 333, 351, 352, 358

Qelalah, 130

Rabbi Aba ben Ada, 123
Rabbi Akiba, 129
Rabbi Elimalech of Lizhensk, 152
Rabbi Hanina ben Dosa, 147
Rabbi Harish, 150
Rabbi Jacob, 147
Rabbi Joshua ben Levi, 139
Rabbi Levi ben Hama, 140
Rabbi Meir, 130
Rabbi Nahman of Kossov, 153
Rabbi Raphael of Bersht, 151
Rabbi Schneur Zalman of Ladū, 147
Rabbi Tahuma, 129
Radhakrishnan, S., 15, 18, 25
Rāmānuja, 228, 232, 310, 322 (see Chap. IV)
Raphael, 479
Rational Life, 298 fol., 352, 378
Rational Soul, 62, 359
Rāzī, Al, 463
Reason, 78, 79, 89, 283, 287, 289, 314 fol., 322, 324, 326, 333, 339, 340, 351, 352, 353, 360
Reason Cosmic, 64, 231 fol., 298 fol., 320, 333 foil, 353, 355, 357, 363, 371 (see Logos)
Reasonableness, Chinese, 163
Reductionism, 23
Relativism, 54
Religion, Naturalistic, 328
Religion and Morality, 329, 333, 343
Religion in the Vedas, 215 fol.
Religion of Tribal Origins, 328
Rembrandt, 479
Repin, 479
Reversal, The Principle of, 337
Rhys Davids, Mrs, 256
Righteousness, 151, 175, 321, 325
Rintelen, F. J. von, 502
Ritual, 361
Roshd, Ibn, 464
Roth, Leon, 38
Rousseau, J. J., 259, 316, 349, 472
Russell, Bertrand, 16, 308

Sagehood, 177
Śaivism, 240 fol., 273, 293, 294
Śaivism, Kasmir, 292
Śāktism, 240 fol., 278, 294
Salman the Persian, 458
Samurai, 255
Śaṅkara, 228, 245, 267, 270, 273, 281, 332, 345
Sāṅkhya, 277 fol., 284 fol., 338, 339, 340, 353, 354
Sāṅkhya-Yoga, 281
Saqifa, 459
Sartre, J. P., 15, 497 fol., 519 fol.
Schiller, F. C. S., 15
Schopenhauer, 492 fol.
Schweitzer, A., 37
Sciacca, M., 503 fol.
Self-control, 264
Sentiments, 324
Sextus Empiricus, 99
Shakespeare, W., 114
Shang-ti, 161
Shao, Duke, 162
Shun, 177, 178
Silesius, Angelus, 396, 404
Simmias, 62
Sin, 163, 402 fol., 415, 419, 425 fol.
Sina, Ibn, 646 (see Avicenna)
Skandhas, 261 (see Aggregates)
Smartism, 240 fol., 293
Socialism (Communism), 441 fol., 450, 459 fol., Chap. VIII (see Man and Society)
Socrates, Chap. I, 17, 298, 307, 309, 314,, 319, 323, 325, 336, 350, 351, 352, 358, 486
Solomon, 136
Sophists, Chap. I, 319, 325
Soul, 62, 64, 65, 87, 180, 462 fol., 465–72 (see Spirit)

Spengler, Oswald, 493
Spirit (*ātman*, Brahman, God, the Divine etc. ,) 201, 225 fol., 230 fol., 258 fol., 263, 282 fol., 346, 498, 426 (see Soul)
Spirit, Holy, 429 fol., 431 fol. (see Paraklete)
Stirner, 493
Stoics, 30, 316 (see Chap. I)
Subjectivism, 54
Sufism, 462 fol., 468 fol.
Sunna (*Sonna*), 366, 369, 460, 470
Śūnya, 261, 264, 269, 331, 335 fol.

Talib, Oquail ibn Abu, 458
Tao, 189, 316 fol., 326 fol., 331, 337, 342, 361, 372
Taoism, 32, 184, 197, 342, 365, 372
Tao-sheng, 178
Tathatā, 331
Taylor, A. E., 59
Tertullian, 446
Thales, 314
Thomas, St. (see Aquinas)
Thrasymachus, 51
Tofail, Ibn, 464
Torah, 123, 129, 131, 366, 367, 369
Totalitarianism, 59, 367
Transcendence, 83, 331, 346, 355, 371
Transmigration, 262
Trinity, 398
Tselem, 127, 138, 140
Tsou Yen, 337
Tzu-chieu, 165
Tzu Szu, 199

Übermensch, 417
ÚNESCO, 29
Unio mystica, 396
United Nations, 29
Universals (see Forms)

Vacuity, 179 fol., 182, 350
Vallabha, 290, 292
Values (Ideals, Aims of Life etc.), 18, 27, 50 fol., 65 fol., 91 fol., 113 fol., 141 fol., 183 fol., 201 fol., 245 fol., 263 fol., 291 fol., 309, 310 fol., 347, 353, 361 fol., 395 fol., 402 fol., 420–39, 448, 449 fol., 453 fol., 485 fol., 499 fol., 505 fol., 515, 516, 517 fol., 520 fol., 530 fol., 532 fol.
Vardhamāna, 240
Vedānta, Chap. IV, 208 fol., 242, 270, 277 fol.
Vedas, 208 fol., 210 fol., 249
Vico, G., 488
Vijñāna, 259, 262, 268 fol., 355
Virtue, 47, 67 fol., 93, 96, [illegible], 161, 186 fol., 265 fol., 291, 299, 308 fol., 324, 361, 374 (see Values)
Vital Principle (Life Principle), see *Prāṇa*
Void, see Vacuity and Śūnya
Voltaire, 472

Wagner, 494
Wang Ch'ung, 165, 175, 176
Wang Yang-ming, 186, 202 fol.
Wars, World, 448
Way of Action, 263, 273, 292, 303
Way of Devotion, 273, 292, 303
Way of Knowledge, 266, 273, 292, 299, 302
Way of The Great Harmony, 189 fol.
Wayfarer, 296
Weber, Max, 448
Wesley, John, 423
Whitehead, A. N., 34
Word, 250, see Logos

Xenophon, 53, 55, 56, 59, 325
Xerxes, 44

Yang (and Yin), 173 fol., 179 (see Forces)
Yang Hsiung, 173, 178
Yang Kwei-shan, 185
Yao, 177, 178
Yin (and Yang), 173 fol. (see Forces)
Yin-Yang, 197, 318, 337, 349, 350
Yoga, 231, 241 fol., 273 fol., 277 fol., 283
Yugas (Aeons), 338

Zaglada, N. G., 525
Zahiri, Dawood al, 471
Zen, 176
Zinzendorf, 423
Zoroastrianism, 403, 461